MUIRHEAD LIBRARY OF PHILOSOPHY

An admirable statement of the aims of the Library of Philosophy was provided by the first editor, the late Professor J. H. Muirhead, in his description of the original programme printed in Erdmann's *History of Philosophy* under the date 1890. This was slightly modified in subsequent volumes to take the form of the following statement:

'The Muirhead Library of Philosophy was designed as a contribution to the History of Modern Philosophy under the heads: first of Different Schools of Thought—Sensationalist, Realist, Idealist, Intuitivist; secondly of different Subjects—Psychology, Ethics, Aesthetics, Political Philosophy, Theology. While much had been done in England in tracing the course of evolution in nature, history, economics, morals and religion, little had been done in tracing the development of thought on these subjects. Yet "the evolution of opinion is part of the whole evolution".'

'By the co-operation of different writers in carrying out this plan it was hoped that a thoroughness and completeness of treatment, otherwise unattainable, might be secured. It was believed also that from writers mainly British and American fuller consideration of English Philosophy than it had hitherto received might be looked for. In the earlier series of books containing, among others, Bosanquet's *History of Aesthetic*, Pfleiderer's *Rational Theory since Kant*, Albee's *History of English Utilitarianism*, Bonar's *Philosophy and Political Economy*, Brett's *History of Psychology*, Ritchie's *Natural Rights*, these objects were to a large extent effected.'

'In the meantime original work of a high order was being produced both in England and America by such writers as Bradley, Stout, Bertrand Russell, Baldwin, Urban, Montague, and others, and a new interest in foreign works, German, French and Italian, which had either become classical or were attracting public attention, had developed. The scope of the Library thus became extended into something more international, and it is entering on the fifth decade of its existence in the hope that it may contribute to that mutual understanding between countries which is so pressing a need of the present time.'

The need which Professor Muirhead stressed is no less pressing to-day, and few will deny that philosophy has much to do with enabling us to meet it, although no one, least of all Muirhead himself, would regard that as the sole, or even the main, object of philosophy. As Professor Muirhead continues to lend the distinction of his name to the Library of Philosophy it seemed not inappropriate to allow him to recall us to these aims in his own words. The emphasis on the history of thought also seemed to me very timely; and the number of important works promised for the Library in the near future augur well for the continued fulfilment, in this and in other ways, of the expectations of the original editor.

H. D. LEWIS

MUIRHEAD LIBRARY OF PHILOSOPHY

General Editor: H. D. Lewis
Professor of History and Philosophy of Religion in the University of London

Know Thyself by BERNADINO VARISCO translated by GUGLIELMO SALVADORI

Language and Reality by WILBUR MARSHALL URBAN 3rd impression

Lectures on Philosophy by G. E. MOORE edited by C. LEWY

Matter and Memory by HENRI BERGSON translated by N. M. PAUL and W. S. PALMER 7th impression

Memory by BRIAN SMITH

The Modern Predicament by H. J. PATON 3rd impression

Natural Rights by D. G. RITCHIE 3rd edition 5th impression

Nature, Mind and Modern Science by E. HARRIS

The Nature of Thought by BRAND BLANSHARD 3rd impression

On Selfhood and Godhood by C. A. CAMPBELL

Our experience of God by H. D. LEWIS

The Phenomenology of Mind by G. W. F. HEGEL translated by SIR JAMES BAILLIE revised 2nd edition 5th impression

Philosophy in America by MAX BLACK

Philosophical Papers by G. E. MOORE 2nd impression

Philosophy and Religion by AXEL HAGERSTROM

Philosophy of Whitehead by W. MAYS

The Platonic Tradition in Anglo-Saxon Philosophy by J. H. MUIRHEAD

The Principal Upanisads by RADHAKRISHNAN

The Problems of Perception by R. J. HIRST

Reason and Goodness by BLAND BLANSHARD

The Relevance of Whitehead by IVOR LECLERC

The Science of Logic by G. W. F. HEGEL

Some Main Problems of Philosophy by G. E. MOORE 3rd impression

The Theological Frontier of Ethics by W. G. MACALGAN

Time and Free Will by HENRI BERGSON translated by F. G. POGSON 7th impression

The Ways of Knowing: or the Methods of Philosophy by W. P. MONTAGUE 6th impression

Values and Intentions by J. N. FINDLAY

The Muirhead Library of Philosophy

EDITED BY H. D. LEWIS

HISTORY OF ÆSTHETIC

A HISTORY OF ÆSTHETIC

BY

BERNARD BOSANQUET

M.A. (Oxon.) Hon. LL.D. (Glasgow)

Formerly fellow of
University College, Oxford

LONDON: GEORGE ALLEN & UNWIN LTD
NEW YORK: HUMANITIES PRESS INC

FIRST PUBLISHED IN 1892
SECOND EDITION 1904
REPRINTED 1910, 1917, 1922, 1934, 1949, 1956, 1966

© *George Allen & Unwin Ltd.*, 1966
Library of Congress Catalog Card No. 66 – 27376

PRINTED IN GREAT BRITAIN
BY UNWIN BROTHERS LTD
WOKING AND LONDON

PREFACE

———

ÆSTHETIC theory is a branch of philosophy, and exists for the sake of knowledge and not as a guide to practice. The present work is, therefore, primarily addressed to those who may find a philosophical interest in understanding the place and value of beauty in the system of human life, as conceived by leading thinkers in different periods of the world's history. It is important to insist that the æsthetic philosopher does not commit the impertinence of invading the artist's domain with an *apparatus belli* of critical principles and precepts. The opinion that this is so draws upon æsthetic much obloquy, which would be fully deserved if the opinion were true. Art, we are told, is useless ; in a kindred sense æsthetic may well submit to be useless also. The æsthetic theorist, in short, desires to understand the artist, not in order to interfere with the latter, but in order to satisfy an intellectual interest of his own.

But besides professed students of philosophy, there is a large and increasing public of readers who are genuinely attracted by a fairly clear and connected exposition of any philosophical science the subject-matter of which comes home to them, be it Logic or Ethic, Sociology, or the theory of Religion. Such readers are approaching philosophy through the subject-matter that already interests them, instead of approaching the particular subject-matter simply because it is an integral part of philosophy. I confess to cherishing a hope that in spite of the defects which deprive this book of the charm that a more skilful writer might have given to such a subject, many intelligent lovers of beauty will be glad to make acquaintance, through it, with the thoughts of great men upon this important element of the spiritual world.

I have regarded my task, however, as the history of æsthetic, and not as the history of æstheticians. I have not paid much attention to the claims of historical justice. While I feel sure that no writer of the first rank is omitted, I could not venture to say that all the writers included are more important than any that are excluded. I have thought first of the arrangement necessary or convenient in order to exhibit the affiliation of ideas, and their completest forms, and only in the second place of the individual rank and merit of the writers to be dealt with.

Moreover, as the first chapter will show, I have not been able to persuade myself to treat my subject as a mere account of speculative theory. No branch of the history of philosophy can be adequately treated in this way, and the history of æsthetic least of all. My aim has therefore been to exhibit philosophic opinion as only the clear and crystallized form of the æsthetic consciousness or sense of beauty, which is itself determined by conditions that lie deep in the life of successive ages. I have desired, in fact, so far as possible, to write the history of the æsthetic consciousness.

Many readers may complain of the almost total absence of direct reference to Oriental art, whether in the ancient world or in modern China and Japan. For this omission there were several connected reasons. I was hardly called upon, even if I had been competent for the task, to deal with an æsthetic consciousness which had not, to my knowledge, reached the point of being clarified into speculative theory. It was, moreover, necessary to limit my subject in some definite way; and it seemed natural to exclude everything that did not bear on the continuous development of the European art-consciousness. In so far as contact with Oriental art influenced the early Greek, and again the Byzantine development, a reference to it is implied in Hegel's and Morris' treatment of those periods. And finally, this omission is not without a positive ground, though here I really touch on a matter which is beyond my competence. The separation from the life of the progressive races, and the absence of a reflective theory of beauty, must surely have a fundamental connection with the non-architectural character pointed out by Mr. Morris in the art of China and Japan (p. 456). Without denying its beauty, therefore, I regarded it as something apart, and not well capable of being brought into the same connected story with the European feeling for the beautiful. A study of such art from a competent hand, in the light of æsthetic theory, would be a welcome aid to modern speculation.

With reference to my use of authorities, while there is often more egotism than modesty in calling the public to witness the course of an author's reading, I feel absolutely bound in this case to warn my readers that the reliability of the different parts of my work is unequal. For the mediæval period between Plotinus and Dante, and in a lesser degree for the Hellenistic period between Aristotle and Plotinus, my knowledge is not, for the most part, at first hand, and represents a voyage of discovery rather than a journey on ground familiar to me. I have not for these periods been able to follow the scholar's golden rule—never to quote from a book that he has not read from cover to cover. I have drawn my quotations from works of reference, and though I have, *as a rule*, carefully verified them and endeavoured to judge of the context, my estimate of the writer's position usually rests on the authority, in many cases Erdmann's *History of Philosophy* and the articles in the *Encyclopædia Britannica*, which I have consulted for information. In the case of Thomas Aquinas in particular, I profess no original knowledge at all. The very full quotations most courteously furnished me by Dr. Gildea appeared too significant to be left unused, and his authority warranted me in supposing that in these passages the principal materials for forming a judgment were before me. I do not desire it to be understood that he agrees with me in the estimate which I have formed of St. Thomas's æsthetic views.

It would have been foolish, I thought, to omit the more obvious points of the mediæval development, both in art and in opinion, the mere mention of which might be suggestive to my readers, simply because I had to take them from such writers as Prof. Adamson, Prof. Seth, Prof. Middleton, Mr. Morris and Mr. Pater, and not from original research. Some division of labour must be allowed, though the fact that it has been resorted to should always be made known.

Acknowledgments for assistance are due from me above all to Prof. A. C. Bradley, who not only furnished me with a list of books which has been of the utmost service, but lent me out of his own library many of those works, which I might otherwise have had a difficulty in procuring. I also owe the most cordial thanks to Mr. J. D. Rogers, for permitting me to embody in an Appendix his analyses of some instances of musical expression—models, as I think, of what such analyses should be—and to Dr. Gildea, for the information mentioned above. And, finally, it is only right to say, that it is on the Council of the Home Arts and Industries Association, and in contact with its workers, that I have learned to appreciate, as I hope, with some degree of justice the writings of Mr. Ruskin and Mr. Morris, which may easily remain a sealed book to those who have not observed in simple cases the relation of workmanship to life. Many readers, who are familiar with the average

work of the classes of that Association, may think that it reveals
no great mystery of beauty ; but I am convinced that the leaders of
the Association have sound insight, and that experience, to an increasing extent, is justifying their principles.

LONDON, *April*, 1892.

PREFACE TO SECOND EDITION

MY chief duty in preparing a second edition of this work has been to remove so far as possible, by corrections in the form of notes, the defects which arose from its being published previously to Professor Butcher's Treatise on *Aristotle's Theory of Poetry and Fine Art.* I have made no pretence of re-writing, as it was impossible for me seriously to attempt the task. I have therefore let the text stand, except in case of obvious misprints, and have admitted errors or made observations on criticisms in notes appended to the chapters which they concern. These notes are indicated by letters of the alphabet, and will, I hope, be readily distinguished from the footnotes indicated by numbers. On meeting with a reference " *a*," the reader has only to turn to the last page of the chapter before him, where he will find the note referred to.

I do not think that my general view of the relation between ancient and modern Æsthetic is seriously modified by Professor Butcher's treatment of Aristotle, while my æsthetic theory on the whole is corroborated by it. As a worshipper of the Greeks, I am only too glad to follow him towards ascribing on the whole a deeper suggestiveness to their views than I had previously permitted myself to find there. In my anxiety not to go too far, I may hardly have gone far enough. At any rate, I wish to say that my references to his work cannot possibly discharge a reader who cares for the subject from the duty and pleasure of studying it for himself.

I have not attempted to modify my interpretation of Aristotle's definition of Tragedy, which is simply that of Bernays. Professor Butcher has developed a modification of this view, which the student should learn from Professor Butcher's work.

I hope that the fact of a second edition of a work like this being called for may indicate that with all its defects it has a point of view which is felt to be valuable. And I hope that this point of view may soon come to be more effectively presented by more capable critics and more attractive writers than the author.

ST. ANDREWS, *March* 1904.

CONTENTS

xv

CHAPTER IV.

SIGNS OF PROGRESS IN GREEK THEORY CONCERNING THE BEAUTIFUL.

A*

CHAPTER VII.

A COMPARISON OF DANTE AND SHAKESPEARE IN RESPECT OF SOME FORMAL CHARACTERISTICS.

CHAPTER VIII.

THE PROBLEM OF MODERN ÆSTHETIC PHILOSOPHY.

CHAPTER IX.

PAGE

THE DATA OF MODERN ÆSTHETIC PHILOSOPHY.

Limits of the Subject 188
1. Classical Philology 188
   i. Joseph Scaliger 188
   ii. F. A. Wolff 189
2. Archæology 190
   i. Early Discoveries on Italian Soil 191
   ii. Early Travels in Greece 192
   iii. Herculaneum and Pompeii 192
   iv. Greece proper 193
3. Art-criticism 197
   i. Pierre Corneille 197
   ii. Fontenelle and Voltaire 201
   iii. The British Writers 202
     a. Burke and Lord Kaimes 203
      a. Burke's Purgation Theory . . . 203
      b. The Sublime akin to Ugliness . . . 203
      c. Painful Reality not Disagreeable . . 204
      d. Anticipations of Later Ideas . . . 205
     β. Hogarth 206
     γ. Reynolds 209
   iv. Germans before Lessing 210
     a. Gottsched 211
     β. The "Swiss" 214
   v. Lessing 216
     a. His Conception of Criticism 217
     β. Aim of the Laocoon 220
     γ. Demarcation of "Painting" and Poetry . 223
     δ. Lessing's Attitude towards the Problem of Ugliness 225
     ε. A point in which his Classicism was justified . 229
     ζ. His Theory of the Drama 230
   vi. Winckelmann. His Characteristics . . 239
     a. Feeling for Art as Human Production . . 240
     β. True sense of a History of Art . . . 242
     γ. Recognition of Phases in Beauty . . 244
     δ. Conflict between Beauty and Expression . . 248
   vii. Data not utilized by the Critics 251
   viii. Indications of a Transition 252

CHAPTER X.

CHAPTER XI.

CHAPTER XII.

CHAPTER XV.

APPENDIX I.

APPENDIX II.

HISTORY OF ÆSTHETIC

CHAPTER I.

PROPOSED TREATMENT, AND ITS CONNECTION WITH THE DEFINITION OF BEAUTY.

The History of Æsthetic, and the History of Fine Art. 1. It was not before the latter half of the eighteenth century that the term "Æsthetic" was adopted with the meaning now recognised, in order to designate the philosophy of the beautiful as a distinct province of theoretical inquiry. But the thing existed before the name ; for reflection upon beauty and upon fine art begins among Hellenic thinkers at least as early as the time of Socrates, if not, in a certain sense, with still earlier philosophers.

If, then, "Æsthetic" means the Philosophy of the Beautiful, the History of Æsthetic must mean the History of the Philosophy of the Beautiful ; and it must accept as its immediate subject-matter the succession of systematic theories by which philosophers have attempted to explain or connect together the facts that relate to beauty.

But this is not all. It is found necessary in a historical treatment, even of logic or of general philosophy, to bring them into continuous relation with the concrete life that underlies the formal conceptions which are being passed in review. The speculation of every age issues on the one hand from the formal teaching of the past, but on the other from the actual world as it urges itself upon consciousness in the present. As the history of logic or of general philosophy cannot be wholly dissociated from the history of science or of civilization, so the history of ethical or of æsthetic ideas is necessarily treated in some connection with the history of morals or of fine art. But within this analogy there is a notable distinction.

B

When we read, for example, the history of the Inductive
Sciences in connection with the growth of logical theory, we
can take little interest in the bygone phases of particular
branches of knowledge, except in as far as they help us to
understand that development of the human mind which is at
the moment the subject of our study. Antiquated chemistry
or astronomy have for us an interest of curiosity no greater
than that which a pile-dwelling or a flint hatchet has for the
anthropological student. The same is true of many other
elements of civilization, such as the details of political form or
of social custom, the niceties of language, the minutiæ of religious dogma. In all these aspects of life, although it is true
that to have deciphered the past greatly aids us in understanding the present, yet on the whole, excepting with a view
to scientific research or historical realization, we are accustomed to let bygones be bygones. Moral and religious ideas,
indeed, such as have been all-powerful in a remote past, generally retain a capacity of arousing our present interest ; so deep
is the identity of man's moral nature throughout all its manifestations. But nothing is in this respect on a level with the
greater creations of fine art, including noble literature. They
alone have an importance which rather increases than diminishes as the ages go by. And thus when we attempt the
task of tracing the æsthetic consciousness through the stages
of its development, we have before us a concrete material not
of mere antiquarian interest, but constituting a large proportion of what is valued for its own sake in the surroundings of
our present life. The History of Fine Art is the history of
the actual æsthetic consciousness, as a concrete phenomenon ;
æsthetic theory is the philosophic analysis of this consciousness, for which the knowledge of its history is an essential
condition. The history of æsthetic theory, again, is a narrative which traces the æsthetic consciousness in its intellectual
form of æsthetic theory, but never forgets that the central
matter to be elucidated is the value of beauty for human life,
no less as implied in practice than as explicitly recognised in
reflection. In spite of the natural repugnance which may be
felt against analytic intermeddling with the most beautiful
things which we enjoy, it must be counted an advantage of
this branch of the history of philosophy that it promises us
not merely a theoretical interpretation of what is past and
gone, but some aid at least in our appreciation of realities

which appear to be the least perishable inheritance that the world possesses.

2. I have assumed in the last section that Fine Art may be accepted, for theoretical purposes, as the chief, if not the sole representative of the world of beauty. It is necessary to explain the point of view from which this assumption appears justifiable.

The Relation of Natural Beauty to the Beauty of Fine Art.

All beauty is in perception or imagination. When we distinguish Nature from Art as a province of the beautiful, we do not mean to suggest that things have beauty independently of human perception, as for example in reactions upon one another such as those of gravitation or solidity. We must therefore be taken to include tacitly in our conception of natural beauty some normal or average capacity of æsthetic appreciation. But if so, it is plain that " nature " in this relation differs from "art" principally in degree, both being in the medium of human perception or imagination, but the one consisting in the transient and ordinary presentation or idea of the average mind, the other in the fixed and heightened intuitions of the genius which can record and interpret.

Now in studying any department of physical causation, we should not think it possible to restrict ourselves to considering the so-called facts which daily meet the eye of the untrained observer. It is from science that we must learn how to perceive ; and it is upon science that we rely, both in our own observations as far as we are qualified observers, and also in the organized and recorded perceptions of others, from which almost the whole of our natural knowledge is practically derived.

Nature in the sphere of æsthetic is analogous to the perception of the ordinary observer in matters of physical science. In the first place, it is limited for each percipient to the range of his own eyes and ears as exercised on the external world, for it does not exist in the form of recorded or communicable contents ; and in the second place, it passes into the province of art, not by a sudden transition, but by continuous modification, as the insight and power of enjoyment to which the beauty of nature is relative are disciplined and intensified by æsthetic training and general culture. Therefore, just as in speaking generally of the real world we practically mean the world as known to science, so in speaking generally of the beautiful in the world we practically mean the beautiful as revealed by art. In both cases we rely upon the recorded perceptions of those who perceive best, both because they are the best perceptions and because they are recorded. This habit does not exclude the necessity of interpreting, appreciating, and, so far as may be, correcting the recorded perceptions by help of our own. Nor does the beauty of art, thus understood, exclude the beauty of nature. The fact that a completed " work of art " is a definite thing or action, which in some cases does not even represent any natural object, must indeed be duly considered, and the creative spirit must be recognised as a factor in artistic production. Nevertheless, it is a blunder to imagine that there is no art where there is no "work of art," or that whenever the painter is not at work on a picture he sees the same nature as we see and no more. For this reason it is justifiable in theory, as it is necessary in practice, to accept fine art as the main representative of the beautiful for the purpose of philosophical study. Even such an analysis of natural beauty in the light of physical fact as has been attempted by Ruskin in the *Modern Painters* is chiefly directed to showing how great artists have extended the boundaries of so-called natural beauty, by their superior insight into the expressive capabilities of natural scenes and objects. The standard by which the critic measures the achievement of the artist, when he says that he is measuring it by nature, is of course in the last resort his own artistic feeling and more or less trained perception. Nature for æsthetic theory means that province of beauty in which every man is his own artist.

The Definition of Beauty and its Relation to the History of Æsthetic.   3. There is no definition of beauty that can be said to have met with universal acceptance. It appears, however, to be convenient that an explanation should now be given of the sense in which the term will be employed in the present work. And if in such an explanation the fundamental theory of the ancients can be presented as the foundation for the most pregnant conception of the moderns, the resulting definition will at least lend itself readily to the purposes of a history of æsthetic.

Among the ancients the fundamental theory of the beautiful was connected with the notions of rhythm, symmetry, harmony of parts ; in short, with the general formula of unity in variety. Among the moderns we find that more emphasis

is laid on the idea of significance, expressiveness, the utterance of all that life contains ; in general, that is to say, on the
conception of the characteristic. If these two elements are
reduced to a common denomination, there suggests itself as a
comprehensive definition of the beautiful, " That which has
characteristic or individual expressiveness for sense-perception
or imagination, subject to the conditions of general or abstract
expressiveness in the same medium."

The quality which is thus defined is of wider range than
the predicate "beautiful " as commonly understood. It will
be for the subsequent historical treatment to show that
neither fine art nor average æsthetic perception can in the
long run be confined within narrower limits than these. A
few words may be added here by way of anticipatory explanation.

The commonplace view is not wholly at fault which sees in
the great art of the ancient Hellenes chiefly the qualities of
harmony, regularity, and repose. Although the whole theory
of modern æsthetic may well find application and support in
the real variety and significance of Hellenic decoration, sculpture, and poetry, yet, as science begins with what is most
obvious, it is not surprising that æsthetic reflection should
have called attention in the first instance to their pervading
harmony and regularity. Qualities of this type, because they
symbolize, in a mode that appeals to sense-perception, the most
abstract relations of systematic and orderly action or existence,
may fairly be set down under the head of general or abstract
expressiveness. The recognition of these relations as constituent elements of the beautiful was the main contribution
of ancient philosophy to æsthetic analysis.

But when with the birth of the modern world the romantic
sense of beauty was awakened, accompanied by the craving
for free and passionate expression, it became impossible that
impartial theory should continue to consider that the beautiful
was adequately explained as the regular and harmonious, or
as the simple expression of unity in variety. The theory of
the sublime now makes its appearance, at first indeed outside
the theory of the beautiful ; but it is followed by the analysis
of the ugly, which develops into a recognised branch of
æsthetic inquiry, with the result of finally establishing both
the ugly and the sublime within the general frontier of beauty.
The instrument by which this conciliation is effected is the

conception of the characteristic or the significant; and the conflict between the harsher elements thus recognised and the common-sense requirement that all beauty should give pleasure, is mitigated, on the one hand by a *de facto* enlargement of average æsthetic appreciation, and on the other hand by the acceptance of such primary relations as harmony, regularity, or unity, in the light of essential elements organically determining all imaginable contents, and demanding, in their degree, characteristic expression for sense.

Thus in the definition of beauty above suggested, the pregnant conception contributed by the moderns is merely a re-application in more concrete matter of the formal principle enunciated by the ancients. In the widest sense, then, and omitting to insist upon the narrower and commoner usage in which the characteristic—in the sense of individually characteristic—is opposed to the formal or symmetrical, it would be sufficient to define beauty as " the characteristic in as far as expressed for sense-perception or for imagination."

If, indeed, we were attempting a psychological determination of the feeling that attends or constitutes the peculiar enjoyment known as the enjoyment of beauty, we should probably have to deal with a term not mentioned in the definition above proposed—the term pleasure. But in attempting to analyse the content which distinguishes perceptions or imaginations productive of this enjoyment from others which are not so productive, it appears to me that we should commit a serious error of method if we were to limit " expressiveness " or "characterization" either by beauty, which is the term to be defined, or by pleasantness, which is a quality not naturally coextensive with the term to be defined. The former error is not, in my judgment, wholly avoided by Goethe, when he insists that the characteristic, although essential to art, is yet a principle limited and conditioned by beauty in the strict sense, which is needed to soften the rigidity or abstraction of the characteristic. Thus the definition is made self-destructive, beauty being at once the term to be defined, and an unanalysed limiting condition in the defining predicates. The latter error is committed in any such definition as that suggested by Schlegel, " the pleasant expression of the good." Things give pleasure sometimes because they are beautiful, and sometimes for other reasons. They are not beautiful simply because they give pleasure, but only in so far as they give æsthetic pleasure ; and the nature of the presentation that gives æsthetic pleasure is the matter to be ascertained.

It will be seen that the part played in Goethe's account by the term beauty or grace, as a formal condition of artistic treatment, and in Schlegel's account by the differentia pleasant, intended to guard against caricature or defect of harmony, is transferred in the definition which I have ventured to suggest to the formal or general element of characteristic expression, the element of unity or totality as symbolised by harmonious, symmetrical, or coherent dispositions of lines, surfaces, colours, or sounds. It would be tautology to superadd the condition of pleasantness to this formal element of the characteristic, if the two terms mean the same thing, as I believe that in æsthetic experience they do ; while if pleasantness were taken in the normal range of its psychological meaning, and not as thus both limited and extended by identification with *æsthetic* pleasantness, the definition would become indisputably too narrow, even supposing that its other elements prevented it from being also too wide. The highest beauty, whether of nature or of art, is not in every case pleasant to the normal sensibility even of civilized mankind, and is judged by the *consensus*, not of average feeling as such, but rather of the tendency of human feeling in proportion as it is developed by education and experience. And what is pleasant at first to the untrained sense—a psychological fact more universal than the educated sensibility—is not as a rule, though it is in some cases, genuinely beautiful.

The definition, then, should be either purely analytic of contents accepted as beautiful—purely metaphysical, if we like to call it so—or purely psychological. To introduce a psychological differentia into a metaphysical definition obtained by comparing the actual data of beauty, is to introduce a factor which we cannot control, because the differentia so introduced is itself in need of analysis and limitation on purely psychological ground before it will coincide with the data to be investigated. Some attempts at psychological analysis will be recorded and criticised in the course of this history ; I will at present simply suggest as an approximate psychological definition of æsthetic enjoyment " Pleasure in the nature[a] of a feeling or presentation, as distinct from pleasure in its momentary or expected stimulation of the organism." Such pleasure would always, it is my belief, be connected in fact with the

significance of the content of feeling, but the meeting-point
of the psychological and metaphysical definitions would not
fall within the scope of psychology.

In hope of dispelling any prejudice that may be raised
against this conception on account of its apparent tendency to
intellectualism, I will show in a few words how it is generated
by consideration of extreme cases in the domain even of non-
æsthetic feeling. *If* anything in the region of taste, smell,
touch, heat or cold, has a value akin to that of beauty, it is
not, surely, either the strongest or the most delightful sensation, but rather the most suggestive sensation, or that which
is most highly charged with associated ideas, so normal that
we do not take them to be accidental. Not the scent of
Eau-de-Cologne, but the smell of peat smoke or of the sea,
not the comfortable warmth of the house, but the freshness of
the morning air, are sensations of a kind in which we may
feel a certain disinterested delight not wholly dissimilar to
æsthetic enjoyment. The merest germ of the sense of beauty
seems to imply a distinction between stimulus and signifi-
rance.

I have thus, I hope, justified in three respects the procedure
which I intend to adopt.

First, I have given my reasons for treating the history of
Æsthetic as an account, not merely of æsthetic systems, but,
so far as may be in my power, of the æsthetic consciousness
which has furnished material for these systems, and has formed
the atmosphere in which they arose.

Secondly, I have explained the necessity which compels
æsthetic theory to accept fine art as the main representative
of the beautiful, and I have attempted to show that this
necessity does not force us to neglect any important element of
the facts with which we are to deal.

Thirdly, I have propounded, in a few words, a definition of
the beautiful which lends itself to the development of modern
out of ancient æsthetic by a natural progression from the
abstract to the concrete, analogous to the equally natural advance from the classical to the Christian world of artistic production and insight into nature. And I have attempted to
lay down a thorough distinction between the analytic and
comparative treatment of beautiful presentations with reference
to their common properties *qua* beautiful as progressively
recognised in the development of culture, and the psychological

inquiry into the nature and differentia of that enjoyment which these presentations produce. It is plain that these two investigations have a common frontier in the connection between elements of presentation and elements of enjoyment ; but in order that they may effectually co-operate, it is essential that they should not at the outset be confused.

In the next chapter I propose to begin the examination of the æsthetic feeling and theory prevalent among the ancient Hellenes.

a. This definition has been condemned as obscure. Yet I have seen no other, professing to be more distinct, which does not rest simply on a part or consequence of the characteristic here laid down. The point is one which cannot be grasped without some attention, because it involves the distinction of two aspects of sense-perception, which probably coexist in all perceptive experience, but appear as if at a certain level the one took the place of the other. I refer to what might roughly be called the mental and the bodily aspect of a sense-perception. There is its peculiar character, by which it addresses us differently from any other sensational content ; warm, blue, high or low (of sound), and so on. There is also the disturbance or excitement which it causes, whether pleasurable or painful, merely, I suppose, in virtue of the physical reaction to stimulus which it involves, in common with every physical reaction which enters into consciousness at all, say, for instance, organic sensation. I have expressed this distinction by the words "nature" and "stimulation." I would willingly replace "nature" by "form," if it were clearly understood that this had nothing to do with space or time in particular, and might include, for example, a significant intensity ; or by "relation," if it were understood that this did not exclude the special sensation-quality of a colour or sound, in so far as this speaks to us differently from the content of any other sensation of the same or of another sense.

Take, for example, our pleasant feeling of the warmth of the fire on a cold day, and that of a simply pleasant colour, without pattern, say, in curtains or wallpaper. It seems to me quite plain that in the enjoyment of the colour there are two distinguishable elements. One which it has in common with higher perceptions of beauty in art and nature is an interest in the peculiar utterance of the colour as if a word in the great language of the sensuous world. It is different for every colour and spatial arrangement of colour, and different for colour from what it is for any other sensation. It is not an abstract intellectual meaning, but it is to the colour what meaning is to a word. The other element may be described by contrast as "physical." It is the bare fact that in the sensation we are pleasurably excited, soothed, or gently stimulated. The supposed perception of colour has it in common with the feeling of warmth, and with many cases of the organic feelings. I do not doubt that some causal connexion exists between the two elements. But it seems to me incontrovertible that the relation is not directly proportional. The enjoyment of warmth or of health feels in one way exactly like the simple enjoyment of the colour. But it seems to be in want of something. Its "mental" element, or "nature," is hardly traceable ; its pleasant stimulation is almost, though not quite, a blank fact *per se*.

Now I do not doubt that these two sides are really present in all sensation and sense-perception, from organic feeling to the highest regions of æsthetic enjoyment. But they are not proportional, and in complex cases may be discrepant, as when a "sensation" mars the unity of what would be a good work of art, and thereby increases the enjoyment of the weaker spectator. The reasons for admitting the presence of the "nature" throughout are first that it seems a truism that every state of consciousness has a nature, if we were skilful enough to detect it ; secondly, that great writers sometimes show us, through their unusually delicate analysis, the presence of a significant nature where we should fail ourselves to detect it (cf. Dr. Middleton's praises of wine in the *Egoist*) ; and thirdly, that thus by this distinction we remove the difficulty arising from the early stages of almost physical attractiveness on the part of sensation, as when a child turns towards a bright light.

CHAPTER II.

THE CREATION OF A POETIC WORLD, AND ITS FIRST ENCOUNTER WITH REFLECTION.

Early Reflection Hostile to Art. 1. IF we approach the earlier Greek philosophers, or even Plato, the prophet of beauty, expecting to find in them a simple reflex and appreciation of the plastic and poetic fancy of their countrymen, we shall be seriously disappointed. The thought of Hellas passed through all the phases which were natural to profound and ardent intelligence at first freely turned upon the world ; and the partial truths which it successively attained were uttered with a definiteness and audacity which conveys a first impression of something like perversity.

When a modern reader finds that the fair humanities of old religion aroused among the wisest of early philosophers either unsparing condemnation or allegorical misconception, he is forced to summon up all his historical sympathy if he would not conclude that Heracleitus and Xenophanes and Plato, and the allegorising interpreters of whom Plato tells us, were incapable of rational criticism. But in reality this moral and metaphysical analysis, directed against the substance of a poetic fancy which was thus beginning to be distinguished from prosaic history, was the natural sequel of artistic creation, and the natural forerunner of more appreciative theory.

Creation of the World of Beauty. 2. The creation of Hellenic poetry and formative art may be regarded as an intermediate stage between popular practical religion and critical or philosophical reflection. The legendary content of this art was not the work of the poet or the formative artist, but of the national mind in its long development out of savagery. Its imaginative form, on the other hand, was due indeed to the national mind, but to this mind chiefly as it acted through the individuality of poetic genius, investing the national thought and emotion with progressive significance and refinement. For although it may be doubted whether the word corresponding to beauty or the beautiful was ever used in the whole range of Hellenic antiquity in a meaning perfectly free from confusion with truth or goodness, yet it is certain that art is more than nature, and that the definite presentation of ideas in beautiful shape cannot but prepare the way for an explicit æsthetic judgment by developing a distinct type of sentiment and enjoyment.

Thus in Hellenic art and poetry, as it existed in the middle of the 5th century B.C., we find embodied a consciousness in relation to beauty, which, if much less than theoretically explicit, is much more than practical and natural. There is a naive apprehension of a profound truth in the familiar saying of Herodotus,[1] that Homer and Hesiod made the Hellenic theogony, and determined the forms and attributes of the gods for Hellenic belief. The full force of this reflection is measured by the interval between the early wooden image and the Phidian statue, or between the superstition of a savage and Antigone's conception of duty. It was in the world of fine art that Hellenic genius had mainly recorded, and, in recording, had created, this transformation.

Reason for the Attitude of Reflection.

3. When therefore the first recognition of the existence and significance of art takes the shape of hostility to the anthropomorphic content which it retains, we see not only that the reflective idea of beauty is still conspicuous by its absence, but that theory in advancing beyond the popular faith fails to recognise the actual refinement of that faith by which poetic fancy has paved the way for the speculative criticism which condemns it.

On the other hand, we must observe that the criteria now actually applied—the wholly unæsthetic criteria of reality and of morality—spring from a principle from which we shall only in part escape within the limits of Hellenic antiquity.

This principle is, as we shall see, that an artistic representation cannot be treated as different in kind or in aim from a reality of ordinary life. To make distinction between them is always a hard lesson for immature reflection ; but for a Hellenic thinker there were reasons which made it all but impossible. The Greek world of ideas, before or outside the philosophic schools, was wholly free from dualism. Its parts were homogeneous. The god, for example, was not conceived as an

[1] Hdt. 2. 53.

unseen being merely capable of an incarnation, such as could
not express or exhaust his full spiritual nature ; rather his real
shape was human, though to reveal it to mortal eye might be
a rare favour, and he lived in a particular hill or in a particular temple.   The representation of a divine being was to
the Greek not a mere symbol, but a likeness ; not a symbol
which might faintly suggest Him who could be known only in
the spirit, but a likeness of one who dwelt on earth, and whose
nature was to be visible, and not to be invisible.   Thus, in
speaking of a question about the supernatural in Homer,
Schelling has said that in Homer there is no supernatural,
because the Greek god is a part of nature.   And therefore,
although a work of creative idealization unparalleled in the
history of the world had been performed by the plastic fancy
of Greece in the age that culminated with the highest art of
Athens, yet in the absence of any mystic sense of an invisible
order of realities the prevalent impression produced by this
world of beauty was rather that of imitative representation
than of interpretative origination.

4. Even the idea of imitation, indeed, contains
Neglected
Suggestion in the germ of a fuller æsthetic truth than was ever
Idea of Imitation. attained by Hellenic thought ; for the translation
of an object into a plastic medium involves a double and not
merely a single element,—not merely a consideration of the
object to be represented, but a consideration of the act of
imaginative production by which it is born again under the
new conditions imposed by another medium.   Natural common sense expressed this truth in one of the earliest æsthetic
judgments that Western literature contains, when on the shield
of Achilles, the Homeric poet says,[1] " the earth looked dark
behind the plough, and like to ground that had been ploughed,
*although it was made of gold; that was a marvellous piece of
work.*"

The "marvel" is that the mind can confer *on a medium of
its own choosing* the characteristic semblance of what it desires
to represent.   But of all that depends upon this side of imitation
—the spiritual second birth of beauty—we hear but little explicitly in Hellenic science, although, within defective formulæ,
some glimpses of it forced themselves upon Aristotle.   For
the reasons which have been indicated—the tendency of all

[1] *Il.* 17. 548.

immature reflection to judge by reality and utility, and the absence of a belief in anything which could not be visibly imitated—the poetic or creative side of artistic representation did not wholly come to its rights in antiquity. Perhaps it was even less regarded by the philosophers than it was, in the consciousness of poetic inspiration, by the epic and lyric poets, or by Plato himself outside his formal treatment of the metaphysic of imitative art.

Wide Use of term "Imitation" in Ancient Philosophy. 5. It is however the case that the term imitation in ancient æsthetic theory is opposed rather to industrial production than to artistic origination, and is compatible with a considerable variation and expansion of import, which I shall endeavour to trace in a separate chapter. It is natural that the earliest formula adopted by reflection should be strained to breaking point before it is abandoned.

Further Explanation how Greek Art could be called "Imitative." 6. It may still appear extraordinary to us, after all is said, that the art which we contrast with our own as in a peculiar sense ideal, and as equally remote from the vicious attempt at illusion, and from the justifiable delight in detail, should have been characterized by enlightened opinion in its own day as a mode of imitation or mere representation.

If this is our feeling, we may profitably consider in two respects the nature of the art which we are discussing.

Facility of Imitative Art makes it Ideal. i. In the first place, just because the Hellenic artist or poet was free from the overwhelming sense of spiritual significance which is the essence of mystic symbolism, he was able to delineate in large and "ideal" outlines the general impressions which he gathered from life by a scrutiny not too microscopic. It is not unnatural that the art which sets itself to portray what attracts it in a complete and actual world should be more full of repose and less tormented with the subtleties of expression than an art to which every minutest human or natural feature may be of unutterable symbolic significance.

Hellenic Art not so Abstractly Ideal as has been thought. ii. And if we thus see how an imitative art, unburdened with a "mission" or revelation, may be ideal simply because it is at ease; on the other hand we must to some extent correct our traditional conception of the degree in which Hellenic beauty was devoid of strangeness, and humour, and animated expression. The

critics from whom we have derived our current notions of the
"classical" and the "antique" have of course performed a
necessary task, and have revealed a distinction as deep as
life between the ancient and the modern world. Yet, after
all, the ancient world also was alive, and possessed a range of
sympathetic expressiveness which was but inadequately rendered in the first impression made upon modern theorists by
fragments of its monumental sculpture. The identification
of the ancient ideal with the general or abstract, which a due
regard to Greek literature might at once have proved to be a
very partial truth, has been further modified by the labour of
more than a century in piecing together the plastic surroundings of this ancient life, and appreciating the descriptions
which assist us to realize them. "The task before me," [1]
writes one whose work in this direction must be a revelation
to all who are not specialists in archæology, "The task before
me is touched with inevitable sadness. The record we have
to read is the record of what we have lost. That loss, but for
Pausanias, we should never have realized. He, and he only,
gives us the real live picture of what the art of ancient Athens
was. Even the well-furnished classical scholar pictures the
Acropolis as a stately hill approached by the Propylæa,
crowned by the austere beauty of the Parthenon, and adds to
his picture perhaps the remembrance of some manner of
Erechtheion, a vision of colourless marble, of awe, restraint,
severe selection. Only Pausanias tells him of the colour and
life, the realism, the quaintness, the forest of votive statues,
the gold, the ivory, the bronze, the paintings on the walls,
the golden lamps, the brazen palm-trees, the strange old
Hermes hidden in myrtle leaves, the ancient stone on which
Silenus sat, the smoke-grimed images of Athene, Diitrephes all
pierced with arrows, Kleoitas with his silver nails, the heroes
peeping from the Trojan horse, Anacreon singing in his cups ;
all these, if we would picture the truth and not our own
imagination, we must learn of, and learn of from Pausanias.
"But if the record of our loss is a sad one, it has its meed of
sober joy ; it is the record also of what—if it be ever so little
—in these latter days we have refound."
It is not a false opinion that harmony, severity, and repose

---

[1] *Mythology and Monuments of Anct. Athens*, by Miss J. E. Harrison, xi.,
xii.

are fundamental characters of Hellenic craft and fancy ; the history of a single decorative form, such as the acanthus foliage, is enough to illustrate the profoundness of the contrast thus indicated between the antique and the modern. But we must master and adhere to the principle that although the given boundaries of Greek æsthetic theory can be in some degree justified by the comparative limitations of the art which was its material, yet this justification is only relative, and means not that Greek æsthetic was an adequate account of Greek art, but only that it was a natural and obvious one.

Thus we shall find that true æsthetic analysis among the Greeks extended only to the most formal element that enters into Hellenic beauty ; while its passion and its human signifi- cance and its touches of common things attracted the censure of an unæsthetic criticism and supported the classification of the whole range of artistic utterance under the superficial title of " imitation." Had the realism of the antique been less modest and refined, it would have challenged an analysis which would have replaced censure by explanation. But the time for this was not yet ; and it will be seen that in spite of the protests of the philosopher and the satirical comedian, theory was forced in the long run to become more subtly appieciative as art became less severely noble.

The Ground Prepared for Æsthetic Theory. 7. We have now arrived at the point where the strictly philosophical consideration of æsthetic phenomena may be expected to begin. A world of beautiful shapes and fancies has been brought into being, which must of necessity have trained the perception to re- cognise beauty as displayed in the corresponding province of nature, that is, mainly in the human form, and must have developed some partly conscious sentiment of the beautiful as distinguishable from the good and the true. This imaginary world has been recognised as a new creation both negatively by the claims of the metaphysician and the moralist, and positively by the naive appreciation of the historian and the allegorising construction of the mystic. The mystic is the forerunner of a later age ; but the historian and the philo- sopher agree, by their acquiescence and their censure respec- tively, in treating it as claiming to pass for a simple reproduction of natural reality. And thus the immense panorama depicted by Hellenic imagination enters the range of philosophic vision under the title of mimetic or representative art.

CHAPTER III.

THE FUNDAMENTAL OUTLINES OF GREEK THEORY CONCERNING THE BEAUTIFUL.

The Principles and their Connexion. THE present chapter will be devoted to stating in logical connexion, regardless of any historical development within the limits of antiquity, the general principles which determine all Hellenic thinkers in their inquiries concerning the beautiful. The task of tracing historically the pressure which progressive insight and experience brought to bear upon these conceptions, with the consequent straining of the formulæ until breaking point was reached, will be attempted in the following chapter so far as space and ability permit.

The cumbrous expression, "theory concerning the beautiful," has been intentionally adopted. For of the three connected principles which constitute the framework of Hellenic speculation upon the nature and value of beauty, there is one only that can claim the more convenient title of "æsthetic theory."

The two other principles in question might be respectively described as moralistic and as metaphysical, although the common root of both is itself a metaphysical assumption which is also responsible for the limitation of true æsthetic analysis in the third principle to the abstract conditions of expression.

This metaphysical assumption, natural to incipient speculation, is to the effect that artistic representation is no more than a kind of common-place reality—of reality, that is, as presented to normal sense-perception and feeling—and that it is related precisely as the ordinary objects of perception are related, to man and his purposes, subject only to a reservation on account of its mode of existence being less solid and complete than that of the objects from which it is drawn.

This belief is intimately bound up with the conception of a homogeneous or thoroughly natural world, which makes it

necessary to assume that the essence of art and beauty does
not lie in a symbolic relation to an unseen reality behind the
objects of common sense-perception, but in mere imitative
relation to those common objects themselves.   It was this
prevalent idea that dictated the philosophical treatment to be
accorded to the newly recognised phenomena of an art which
produced only images of things, and not the useful realities
known and handled in every-day life.   It was not as yet observed that the ultimate import of these phenomena, involving
the total separation of æsthetic semblance from practical
reality, was incompatible with the idea which throughout
antiquity controlled their interpretation.

A sufficient verification of the predominance of this principle
is to be found in the current generalisation by which both
Plato and Aristotle gathered up the arts which we call the
fine arts under the name "imitative" or "image-making" as
contrasted in the first instance with those which are "productive" or "thing-making."[1]   Even in Plotinus imitation is the
general term which describes the attempt to create beautiful
forms or fancies for the purpose of æsthetic enjoyment.   It
may be well also to point out a passage in Aristotle's Politics[2]
which may fairly be paraphrased, as asserting that man is, as a
matter of course, affected by the reality of a fact in the same
way as by its representation, so that what we learn to like or
dislike in the semblance for its mere form, we shall similarly
like or dislike in the reality.   This is a doctrine which Aristotle in part knew how to qualify, as will be seen in the next
chapter ; but Plato followed it uncompromisingly through his
entire theoretical treatment of the imagination.

From this metaphysical assumption there arise in close
connection the two principles concerning beauty, which I have
called metaphysical and moralistic respectively ; and also the
restriction of æsthetic theory proper, to what is contained in
the third principle.   I arrange these principles in an ascending order according to their æsthetic value.

Moralistic Principle.   1. If artistic representation is related to man
only as common-place reality, then to represent an
immoral content is only to double the examples of immorality,
and to strengthen, by suggestion, the incitements to it.   In
other words, it follows that *morally* the representations of art

[1] Plato, *Sophist*, 266 D.   Ar., *Phys.*, 199 a. 15.[a]
[2] *Ar., Pol.*, 1340 a. 26 ; *De Part. Anim.* 645 a. 4 (see Butcher, 155).

C

must be judged, in respect of their content, by the same moral
criteria as real life.

Metaphysical Principle.   2. If artistic representation differs from the
nature which it represents, whether human or other,
only in the degree and completeness of its existence, then
it differs only for the worse, and is a purposeless reduplication
of what already was in the world.   In other words, it follows
that, *metaphysically*, art is a second nature, only in the sense
of being an incomplete reproduction of nature.

Æsthetic Principle.   3. If artistic presentation can never have a
deeper content than the normal or common-place
object of perception which it represents, then there can be no
explanation of beauty involving any deeper attributes than
those which normal perception is able to apprehend in common-place reality.   In other words, it follows that, *æsthetically*,
beauty is purely formal, consisting in certain very abstract
conditions which are satisfied, for example, in elementary geometrical figures as truly as in the creations of fine art.

I will discuss these principles in order, with reference to
their general predominance in Hellenic theory, and to their
æsthetic significance.

Moralistic Principle.   1. It would be idle to deny that both Plato and
Aristotle are encumbered with moralistic consider-
ations throughout the whole of their inquiry into the nature
of fine art.   How far either of them approached the accepted
modern doctrine that æsthetic interest in the beauty of a presentation is distinct from the real or selfish interest in its
actual existence for the satisfaction of desire, is, according to
the plan which I have adopted, a question for the next chapter.
It is enough at present to establish the general point of view
before us as actual in Hellenic theory by the following consideration.

How it shows itself.   *a.* The moral and practical judgment is the first
intellectual outcome of organized social life, and is
inevitably turned upon the world of beauty so long as this is
undistinguished from the objects which constitute the means
and purposes of real action.   Not only Heracleitus and Xenophanes, with their condemnation of Homer, but Aristophanes,
with his praise of him as a teacher of good life, and with his
corresponding censure of Euripides, are examples of this
mode of opinion, which, in fact, persists strongly in unpractised
minds even in the modern world.

The two great philosophers betray in this respect, though in somewhat different degrees, a naïve directness of judgment extremely trying to any modern reader who is not thoroughly trained in the habit of historical appreciation. They appear to abandon themselves almost unsuspectingly to the above-mentioned principle, that the resemblance has the same effects as the normal reality. The distinction between image and object, which was destined in the long run to grow into a recognition that beauty and practical reality affect the mind in quite different ways, has for Plato mainly the effect of intensi-fying his moralistic suspicion of the unreal simulacrum which fancy supplies. For the imagination, he believes,[1] is psycho-logically connected with the emotions ; and therefore the imaginary world of art, while sharing the power of the real world to form habit by example, possesses that of creating emotional disturbance in a far greater degree.

And it cannot be maintained that Aristotle breaks the net of this assumption, which we saw that he expressly formulates, however much he may have done to strain it. The student of modern æsthetic will find himself, when he reads the Poetics, in a region almost wholly strange to his ideas of criticism. It is plain, for example, that Aristotle shrinks from a true tragic collision,[2] in which passion or character determine the indi-vidual's destiny, and this in spite of the abundance in which such individualities as those of Prometheus, Clytæmnestra, Œdipus, Aias, Antigone and Medea, were presented to his view by ancient tragedy. And the reason plainly lies in his subjec-tion of all criticism to his division of character into good, bad, and indifferent,[3] excluding, *ipso facto*, all that conflict of a great passion or purpose with the surrounding world, in which tragic interest properly consists, and which make the character a symbol of forces that lie behind the phenomena of life as named by current morality. The conclusion that the hero of tragedy must be neither very good nor very bad,[4] and that his fate must be determined by error[b] and not by wickedness, is unintelligible to modern judgment. We think that the hero may be both very good and very bad, that is to say, that he must above all things be great, and comprehend in himself the

---

[1] *Republic*, p. 606.
[2] *Poet.*, xiii. 3 and 4. See Susemihl's notes, which represent Aristotle's idea in the most modern colours possible.
[3] *Ibid.*   [4] *Ibid.*

differences which make possible the highest discord, and therefore the highest harmony.   All these ideas are excluded *ab
initio* by the moralistic categories under which Aristotle sub-
sumes his species of tragic plots.

Then again, as we should expect, it is his preference[1] that
the fatal action in which a tragedy culminates should be done
in ignorance, and its nature only discovered afterwards ; for
the discovery, if made in time, would have, he thinks, the
effect of preventing the terrible action from taking place.   The
plot of the Medea, which he mentions in this context, is
therefore naturally censured by implication as shocking.

So, too, with the classification of artists.   Here the natural
pre-eminence of the moralistic point of view is very trenchantly
laid down.   It is simplest to quote the passage (the point
being to distinguish species of imitation, according to the
objects which they imitate):—[2]

" Now all artistic representation is of persons acting, and
these must necessarily be either noble or inferior (for all moral
temperament [ēthos] conforms to this distinction ; for it is
goodness and badness of moral temperament by which all
men are distinguished from each other)—that is, either better
in comparison with us, or worse, or just like ourselves.   So
we may see with the painters : Polygnotus painted people
better, Pauson worse, Dionysius just like ourselves.   From
all this it is clear, that each of the kinds of representation which
has been mentioned will include these differences, and will
have different species according as the objects which it represents differ in this way.   For these dissimilarities may occur
even in dancing or in performances on the flute or the lyre,
and so too poetry may display them whether it be with or
without verse ; for instance, Homer represents nobler characters, Kleophon average ones, Hegemon of Thasos, the
first to make parodies, and Nicochares, who wrote the Deliad,
below the average.   .   .   .   And this is the difference that
distinguishes tragedy from comedy, for the latter aims at
representing worse people, and the former better, than those
of present reality."

Here again the student, not only of Shakespeare and
Goethe, but of Homer and of the Attic drama, entirely loses
his bearings.   It seems to him that the poetic world is stronger

---

[1] *Poet.*, xiv. 6, 8, 9.   [2] *Poet.*, ii.

and more emphatic in its attributes, alike in the good as in the evil, than the world of every-day life, as presented to every-day observation. What about Thersites? as Mr. Mahaffy asks. The poet who should represent individuals as only better than common men, or again as only worse, would be to us simply a monster, except in so far as the art of Aristophanic comedy is concerned ; and even here the adjective "worse," with its moralistic associations, does not at all express the true bearing of the representation, which it seems probable that Aristotle was unable to appreciate.

Many subtleties might be urged against this interpretation of Aristotle, and to some of them it will be attempted to do justice when we speak of modifications within Hellenic theory. But it does not appear to me that we should be justified in hampering ourselves by such refinements, to the extent of denying that Plato and Aristotle had their feet firmly planted within the compass of naive practical moralism, however much they may have looked away to other and more fertile regions.

Æsthetic Value. β. It must be remembered, however, that granting the almost total absence of a distinctively æsthetic standpoint, there is no form in which a healthy sense of relative values could assert itself with respect to art, except the form of moralistic criticism. The content of such a criticism is the determination that the central core of life shall have justice done to it in the representation of life, and this determination is characteristic of the temper in which not only genuine speculation, but the greatest works of art, have always originated.

The development of moral reflection by Plato into apparent hostility to nearly the whole world of classical beauty must be regarded historically speaking as a reduction *ad absurdum*, not of the human content, but of the non-æsthetic form of the principle which he professed to be advocating. And it is hard to believe that in this and other respects he was wholly unaware of some such ironical import in his own speculations. The technical defect thus revealed consists in substituting a direct connection of subordination for an indirect connection of co-ordination between the spheres of beauty and of the moral order. By this subordination beauty is required to represent the moral order as moral, and nothing more ; whereas it is really an expression, co-ordinate with the moral order as a whole and not bound under its rules, of that larger complication and unity of things which reflects itself in the sense of beauty on the one hand, and on the other hand in the social will.

But not only is the substance of early moral criticism sound; in one definite relation even its form is justifiable.

Beauty, indeed, within its own territory of expression for expression's sake, is secure from praise or censure upon purely moral grounds. But wherever expression is not for expression's sake, but is determined by alien motives such as the promotion of virtue or knowledge, or again the stimulation of sensuous desire, then it is outside the æsthetic frontier, and moral criticism upon it is justified not only in substance but also in form. It is doubtful, indeed, whether ancient philosophy ever thoroughly applied the distinction between æsthetic and practical interest ; but it is plain that this very failure to distinguish between them in theory is largely owing to the constant confusion between them in practice, and that the censure which pronounced much of fine art to be immoral involved a consciousness that true æsthetic interest must be pure, and was only mistaken in admitting that which it condemned to be fine art at all.

Then the estimation of beauty by the practical standard of right and wrong, although unæsthetic in form, contains two elements of æsthetic value. It bears witness to the instinctive demand for depth and completeness in art as representing the powers that reveal themselves in that order of the world of which the moral order is one among other significant reflections ; and it embodies the conviction that there is a spurious art and beauty, which being not free but subservient to a practical or sensuous end, cease to be objects of æsthetic judgment and become the legitimate prey of moral censure or commendation. And censure of these must indeed always be one degree truer than commendation ; for a fraud, however pious, can never be wholly satisfying to morality. Now the pretence of beauty, in a presentation the true interest of which is other than æsthetic, must always be in some degree a fraud.

A difficulty presents itself at this point which cannot be treated in full till we come to deal with the niceties of modern analysis. At present we can only observe that this distinction between free and servile or spurious beauty depends not on the description, necessarily abstract as all language is, which the artist or percipient may give of his own purpose or ground of enjoyment, but on the degree in which, as a matter of fact, an abstraction due to an alien purpose of any kind whatever is apparent as distorting the presentation.

The Metaphysical Principle. 2. The formative and poetic art of Hellas at the close of the 5th century B.C. had attained a completeness in itself which was emphasized by a pause in its development and an indication of new tendencies. It was natural that at such a moment its significance should challenge the attention of the great contemporary philosopher, and also that his treatment of it should consist in an explicit formulation of the current Hellenic conception, such as on the one hand to lay by its help the foundation-stone of all sound æsthetic theory, while on the other hand to exhibit by a *reductio ad absurdum* the onesidedness of the conception itself. In estimating the achievement of such a philosophy, it is not necessary to consider how far it was intentional. We have to accept its doctrines in their actual significance, and not to inquire whether Plato may ever have entertained any other view of art and imagination than that which he found it necessary to analyse.

How it shows itself. a. I quote a passage which summarises the doctrine of Plato's well-known polemic against all representative art.[1]

"And there is another artist [besides the workman who makes useful real things]. I should like to know what you would say of him.

Who is he?

One who is the maker of all the works of all other workmen. . . . This is he who makes not only vessels of every kind, but plants and animals, himself and all other things—the earth and heaven, and the things which are in heaven or under the earth; he makes the gods also. . . . Do you not see that there is a way in which you could make them yourself?—there are many ways in which the feat might be accomplished, none quicker than that of turning a mirror round and round—you would soon make the sun and the heaven and the earth and yourself, and other animals and plants, and all the other creatures of art as well as of nature in the mirror.

---

[1] *Republic*, bk. x. Jowett,

" Yes, he said ; but that is an appearance only.

" Very good, I said, you are coming to the point now ; and the painter, as I conceive, is just a creator of this sort, is he not ?

" Of course.

" But then I suppose you will say that what he creates is untrue. And yet there is a sense in which the painter also creates a bed ?

" Yes, he said, but not a real bed.

" And what of the manufacturer of the bed ? did you not say that he does not make the idea which, according to our view, is the essence of the bed, but only a particular bed ?

" Yes, I did.

" Then if he does not make that which exists he cannot make true existence but only some semblance of existence ; and if any one were to say that the work of the manufacturer of the bed, or of any other workman, has real existence, he could hardly be supposed to be speaking the truth.—No wonder then that his work too is an indistinct expression of truth.—Well then here are three beds, one existing in nature which as I think that we may say, is made by God—there is another which is the work of the carpenter ? And the work of the painter is a third ? Beds then are of three kinds, and there are three artists who superintend them : God, the manufacturer of the bed, and the painter ?—God, whether from choice or necessity, created one bed in nature and one only ; two or more such ideal beds neither ever have been nor ever will be made by God. . . . Shall we then speak of Him as the natural author or maker of the bed ?

" Yes, he replied, inasmuch as by the natural power of creation He is the author of this and of all other things.

" And what shall we say of the carpenter ; is not he also the maker of the bed ?

" Yes.

" But would you call the painter a creator and maker ?

" Certainly not.

" Yet if he is not the maker, what is he in relation to the bed ?

" I think, he said, that we may fairly designate him as the imitator of that which the others make.

" Good, I said ; then you call him who is third in the descent from nature an imitator ; and the tragic poet is an imitator, and therefore like all other imitators he is thrice removed from the king[1] and from truth?

" That appears to be the case.   Then about the imitator we are agreed   And now about the painter ; I would like to know whether he imitates that which originally exists in nature, or only the creations of artists [artificers] ?

" The latter.

" As they are, or as they appear ? you have still to determine this.—I mean, that you may look at a bed from different points of view, obliquely or directly or from any other point of view, and the bed will appear different, but there is no difference in reality.   Which is the art of painting —an imitation of things as they are, or as they appear—of appearance or of reality ?

" Of appearance.

" Then the imitator, I said, is a long way off the truth and can do all things because he only lightly touches on a small part of them, and that part an image.   For example : a painter will paint a cobbler, carpenter, or any other artificer, though he knows nothing of their arts ; and if he is a good artist, he may deceive children or simple persons when he shows them his picture of a carpenter from a distance, and they will fancy that they are looking at a real carpenter. And whenever any one informs us that he has found a man who knows all the arts, and all things else that everybody knows, and every single thing, with a higher degree of accuracy than any other man—whoever tells us this, I think that we can only imagine him to be a simple creature who is likely to have been deceived by some wizard or actor whom he met, and whom he thought all-knowing, because he himself was unable to analyse the nature of knowledge and ignorance and imitation.   And so when we hear persons saying that the tragedians and Homer, who is at their head, know all the arts and all things human, virtue as well as vice, and divine things too, for that the good poet must know what he is talking about, and that he who has not this knowledge can never be a poet, we ought to consider whether here also there is not a similar illusion.   Perhaps they may have been deceived by imitators, and may never have remembered when they saw their works that these were but imitations thrice

---

[1] The allusion is to bk. ix. p. 586 ff.

removed from the truth, and could easily be made without any knowledge of the truth, because they are appearances only, and not real substances ?   Or perhaps after all they may be in the right, and poets do really know the things about which they seem to the many to speak well ?—Now do you suppose that if a person were able to make the original as well as the image, he would devote himself to the image-making branch ?   Would he allow imitation to be the ruling principle of his life, as though he could do nothing better ? —The real artist who knew what he was imitating, would be interested in realities and not in imitations ; and would desire to leave as memorials of himself works many and fair ; and instead of being the author of encomiums, he would prefer to be the theme of them."

Here we see the theory of imitation laid down in a definite metaphysical form, ostensibly as an annihilating criticism on the value and reality of art, though consisting in a simple formulation of the current conception regarding it.   Three decisive points in the passage call for our notice.

Æsthetic Semblance.   i. Art works with images only and not with realities such as can act or be acted upon in the world of ordinary life.

Relation to Common Reality.   ii. These images are not *symbolic* of the ultimate reality as created by God ; that is, in our language, of the relations and conditions which to a perfect knowledge would be present as determining or constituting any real object in the order of nature.   The appearances in which fine art consists are superficially *imitative* of the second or common-place reality which is relative to every-day purpose and sense-perception.

Inferiority by this Standard.   iii. The images of art must be judged—and therefore condemned—by their capacity of representing common reality either with sensuous completeness or with intellectual thoroughness ; the reality is in every way preferable to the imitation,[1] and, it is added lower down, even beauty depends on a correct representation of use.

Of these three characteristic assertions the first must be reserved for treatment under the head of æsthetic value. Here we need only observe that it is fundamentally and absolutely true.

---

[1] Plato, *Rep.*, p. 601.

The second and third constitute the differentia of the non-æsthetic account of art natural to Hellas ; and till their contentions are fairly challenged and repudiated, we are safe in saying that no true æsthetic of representative or concrete art has been attained or is possible. For, so long as they are admitted, the standard of judgment lies *ex hypothesi* in the appearance and purposes of reality as accepted by every-day action and experience.

Whether Plato is serious or consistent with himself in insisting that the relation of art is to the " second," and not to the " first " reality, does not concern us here. It is sufficient to note that the essence of a mimetic theory could not be more trenchantly formulated than by this classification of realities, on the assumption which I believe to be indisputable, that Plato's first and highest reality has for us an intelligible meaning as practically corresponding to the completest conception in which the order of nature can be presented to a human mind.

It may occur to the reader that Aristotle, not holding to the metaphysical dualism so sharply expressed by Plato in the passage which has been quoted, was not under the necessity of repudiating the relation of art to common reality there laid down, so definitely as Plotinus afterwards repudiated it. Common perceptible reality, it would then be alleged, contained for Aristotle the true real and universal, and therefore the dependence of art upon the former was not for him definitely separable from its dependence upon the latter. And hence, it might be urged, the refinements which we shall find in his theory and his criticism, are not mere practical qualifications of the old conception, forced upon him by increasing critical experience and closer observation of the healthy love of beauty, but are satisfactory evidence of a fundamental change of standpoint in the direction away from the mimetic and towards the symbolic art-consciousness. I believe, however, that such a view would be erroneous. In the first place, the difference between Plato and Aristotle in regard to philosophical dualism is not at all such as is commonly supposed, or such as the above passage from the Republic might lead a reader to imagine, who is unacquainted with the varying and subtle gradations in which the so-called "doctrine of ideas" presents itself throughout Plato's writings. The appearance of dualism is produced by efforts to apprehend the principle that the object is relative to the subject, and bearing this principle in mind we shall not find more than a difference in degree between the metaphysical position of the two great philosophers. The distinction between reality for perception and reality for thought is essentially the same to both of them.

And in the second place, if we add to the evidence above referred to regarding Aristotle's moralistic position that which has also been adduced with respect to his view on the effect of resemblance in comparison with that of reality, and if we observe the weak psychological qualification by which alone he limits this latter principle,[1] we cannot doubt that as a matter of fact Aristotle thoroughly adhered in metaphysical as in moral criticism to the conception of art as a mimetic representation of the world in the shape which it takes for normal action and perception.

Its Æsthetic Value.   β. This metaphysical estimate of image-making fine art, closely associated at least in Plato with an analogous psychological estimate of the imagination, although in form non-æsthetic, and profoundly hostile to the value of the poetic world, is in substance an important foundation-stone of æsthetic theory.

Æsthetic Semblance.   i. It is not sufficiently recognised that in the Polemic of Republic, Book X., taken in conjunction with other well-known passages in Plato, there is laid down the essential doctrine of æsthetic semblance as plainly as in Schiller or in Hegel. The imputation of inferiority—that the appearance is superficial compared to the sensuous reality— is of merely transient importance in itself, but is of the highest significance as a phase of estimation through which the æsthetic appearance must naturally pass on its way to complete recognition as distinct from common-place fact. The double-edged nature of the phenomena of imitation now necessarily begins to reveal itself. "To imitate," means no doubt to produce a likeness of; but what is a likeness? In what medium does it exist? Of what relations to practice and to reality is it capable? To all these questions the criticism of naive metaphysic has its answers. A likeness is a projection or superficial reproduction of a real thing, in a medium incapable of exhausting the content of the original reality, or of fulfilling the purposes or satisfying the interests which

---

[1] See ch. iv.

attach to it.   And art is constituted entirely of likenesses, and
its mental medium is the imagination or image-receiving
faculty   The censure of inutility which follows upon this
trenchant distinction, by denying the naive conception of an
adequate relation to reality, leads us to the recognition of an
æsthetic interest which is not that of utility, nor of relation to
any satisfaction connected with the sensuous impulses.   Moreover, when Plato insists that the appearances employed by the
artist are in relation not with the unseen world of thought and
law, but with a lower reality which is itself only an image of
that unseen world, it is impossible not to observe in this a
strong though negative suggestion of the function of beauty
as a symbol for spiritual things.   And indeed as regards
beauty, though not as regards art, this suggestion even takes
a positive form, when it is laid down[1] that the Creator in
making the world beautiful necessarily modelled it on the
ultimate underlying order ; whereas anything modelled upon
the created world itself, and therefore especially such presentations as those of art, must inevitably be devoid of beauty.

There could not be a more definite challenge to subsequent
reflection, which could hardly fail to ask, whether to reveal the
beautiful in the deeper significance thus accorded to created
things might not be the purpose and essence of art.

ii. Besides enforcing the truth implied in the
Semblance In- mimetic theory, Plato reduces to an absurdity its
adequate to   element of falsehood.   This element, it must be
Reality.
remembered, he found expressed in the reflective opinion
of his time,[2] just as he found an element of non-æsthetic interest in its artistic practice.   All that he has to do, is to formulate the received opinion with perfect self-consistency, and
draw the inference which immediately presents itself.   Whether
in his own mind he sympathized with that inference, I believe that we can never know.   If it were possible to conjecture, on the basis of his general and less strictly scientific
utterances, I should venture to think it possible that the problem pressed upon him as one of fundamental importance ;
that the current Hellenic theory, within which he found himself,
agreed only too well with some phenomena of existing art,
and was profoundly unsatisfactory to the great thinker ; and
that he therefore examined this theory seriously, with the re-

---

[1] *Timæus*, 28 B.   [2] l.c. above, p. 25

sult, " If, *and in as far as*, this is the true explanation of art, art has not the value which popular judgment assigns to it." The further suggestion, " There must be more in it than this," must no doubt have presented itself to him, as we can partly see, in various forms, with various degrees of explicitness and urgency. But his final utterance as a metaphysical theorist on representative art considered as imitation of reality, is in brief : "*so far as* the value of æsthetic appearance depends either upon its sensuous or upon its intellectual adequacy to natural and human reality so far it is a failure and does not merit the attention of serious men." That is to say, either artistic representation is worthless, or, out of the conditions imposed and possibilities revealed by reproduction in the medium of appearance, there must be developed an aim and interest, other than the aim and interest presented by the reality which is represented. It should be added that although the conclusion as here stated and motived is absolutely just, yet there is also a minor question of true æsthetic involved in discussing the degree of the artist's actual knowledge. Though his object is not to rival reality, but to seize its suggestions, he depends profoundly and increasingly on his knowledge of it, which Plato seems to us to under-estimate.

The above negative result, together with the former and positive result that " Art has its being in appearance," not yet extended to the generalization " that beauty has its being in appearance," form the elements of permanent æsthetic value contained in the metaphysical principle upon which Hellenic theory concerning fine art is founded.

Æsthetic Principle.   3. We now approach the consideration of the one true æsthetic principle recognised by Hellenic antiquity in general. This may be described as the principle that beauty consists in the imaginative or sensuous expression of unity in variety.

I call this an æsthetic principle in contradistinction to the moralistic and metaphysical principles which we have hitherto been examining, because it raises no question of other attributes or relations in the beautiful object, such as conduciveness to virtue, or degree of reality, nor does it involve the assumption which underlies such questions, that art is a mere reflection of nature ; but it does, directly and in general form, attempt a solution of the problem, " What is the nature of beauty as a characteristic of experienced presentations ? "

The Hellenic answer to such a question was necessarily formal. The reasons for which art appeared at first to be the mere reproduction of reality are also the reasons which prohibited æsthetic analysis from insisting on the concrete significance of what is beautiful in man and in nature.

So long as common reality—the object of average perception—is regarded as the standard of art, there is an insurmountable barrier against the identification of beauty with the spiritual expressiveness which only a higher perception can apprehend. Or, in other words, to accept the imitation of nature[d] in the widest sense as the function of art, is simply to *state* the problem of concrete beauty in the rudest manner possible, admitting a total inability to solve it. For to say that the material of beautiful presentation is in some way drawn from the objects of sense-perception does not touch the question, " *What* can art do *more than nature ?* " But when we ask *in what respects*, that is, in virtue of what general character or conditions, a reality, whether presented or represented, is *beautiful*, then we have raised the specific question of æsthetic science. And to this a mimetic theory, for which one reality is, in strictness, as good a model as another, has *ex hypothesi* no answer.

But there are simple cases and traits of beauty which either have nothing to do with the direct representation of life and nature, or are to be found in such representations merely as limiting conditions imposed by the same principles which constitute the entire content of the former and simpler cases of beauty. The analysis of these cases and characteristics is not barred by the mimetic theory, which has only a remote and metaphorical application to them. And although we asserted that for ordinary Greek life there was no unseen or spiritual world to which a sensuous presentation could be related as a mere symbol, yet the most general principles of action and knowledge soon became familiar to the intelligence of so gifted a race, and were naturally applied by its thinkers as spiritual principles to the analysis of such formal and abstract beauty as obviously did not consist in the reproduction of natural reality.

In dealing with a true æsthetic conception we need not, as before, separate the account of its application from the estimate of its æsthetic value. A review of the cases in which it is applied, beginning with the most general statements of its range, forms the best criticism of the principle, which may be further elucidated at the close of this chapter by comparison with some modern researches.

General Statements in Ancient Writers. *a.* The synthesis of the one and the many was, as we all know, the central problem and the central achievement of Greek philosophy. The conception of unity in variety is the indispensable basis of that idea of system or totality of interdependent parts, which was destined to be the structure erected by modern speculation upon the definite foundation laid by the Greek thinkers. The relation of whole to part—a slightly more concrete expression for unity in variety—has never been more perfectly elucidated and more justly appreciated than by Plato and Aristotle, and it is in recognising the satisfaction afforded to the mind by the sensuous or imaginative embodiment of this relation that they make a first step in genuine æsthetic analysis.

When we say with approval of a poem or of a musical composition, that it has a beginning, middle and end, we are probably not aware that we are repeating a principle which Aristotle, in dealing with the drama, after the precedent of a less explicit passage in Plato,[1] has defined with naive profoundness. "A tragedy[2] is a representation of a whole action —a whole is what has beginning, middle, and end. A beginning is what does not necessarily come after something else, but is so constituted as to have something else come after it ; an end, on the contrary, is what is so constituted as to come after something else but to have nothing after it ; and a middle is what is so constituted as to come after something else and also to have something else after it—for beauty depends upon size [so that the relation of the parts may be appreciable] and order."

So, again, we may often hear about any beautiful object, "it would be impossible to add or take away the smallest part without spoiling it." This is genuine Greek æsthetic. "Just as," Aristotle says,[3] "in all other representative arts a single representation is of a single object, so the story [of a drama] being the representation of an action, must be of a single one, which is a whole ; and the parts of the scheme of incidents must be so arranged that if any part is transposed or removed

[1] *Phædrus,* 268 D. See ch. iv.   [2] Ar., *Poet.,* vii. 1-4.   [3] *Poet.,* viii. 4.

the whole will be disordered and shattered ; for that of which the presence or absence makes no appreciable difference is no part of the whole."

Moreover, the relation of the one to the many or of the part to the whole is represented in comparative purity by geometrical figures, or again by rhythms or spatial intervals that bear numerical relation to one another. And for this reason Greek philosophy is inclined to select mathematical form, ratio, or proportion, as the pure and typical embodiment of beauty.

"Now since the good and the beautiful are different (for the former is always a property of action, but the latter extends to objects free from motion), those are mistaken who affirm that the mathematical sciences say nothing of beauty or goodness. For they most especially discern and demonstrate the facts and definitions relating to them ; for if they demonstrate the facts and definitions relating to them, though without naming the qualities in question, that is not keeping silence about them. The main species [elements ? εἴδη] of beauty are order, symmetry, definite limitation, and these are the chief properties that the mathematical sciences draw attention to."[1]

I subjoin a passage from Plato, to which reference will have to be made again. It is worth while to observe that almost all the actual material of Aristotle's thought, as distinct from the method of his treatment, may, as in this case, be discovered in Plato. "The principle of goodness has reduced itself to the law of beauty. For measure and proportion always pass into beauty and excellence."[2]

"I do not mean by the beauty of form such beauty as that of animals or pictures, which the many would suppose to be my meaning ; but, says the argument, understand me to mean straight lines and circles, and the plane and solid figures which are formed out of them by turning-lathes and rulers and measurers of angles ; for these I affirm to be not only relatively beautiful, like other things, but they are eternally and absolutely beautiful, and they have peculiar pleasures, quite unlike the pleasures of irritating an itching place (which has been taken above as the type of pleasure mixed with pain). And there are colours which are of the same character, and have similar pleasures. . . . When sounds are smooth and

---

[1] Ar., *Metaph.*, 1078 *a*.   [2] *Philebus*, marg., p. 64.

clear, and utter a single pure tone, then I mean to say they
are not relatively but absolutely beautiful, and have a natural
pleasure associated with them." [1] The exclusion of life and
pictures of life, in this passage, from the realm of absolute beauty,
to which regularity and unity are essential, is a striking case
of the limitation which we have seen to be inherent in Greek
æsthetics. The concrete individual unity which underlies the
apparent disorder of the beauty of life was not likely to be
appreciated until after the same principle had been recognised
in the more abstract or formal cases and conditions of its
embodiment.

And it is plain that formal beauty, as recognised in such
passages as these, of which all Greek philosophy is full, is
constituted by a symbolic relation—a presentation to sense of
a principle which is not sensuous. Such "presentation," in
default of a more precise term, may sometimes be called an
"imitation"; [2] but it is impossible to "imitate" a non-
sensuous principle in a sensuous medium.

Particular   β. Of such symbolism or presentation we find
Cases.   the following principal cases to have attracted the
attention of Plato or Aristotle.

Colour and   i. There is no more obvious type of unity appeal-
Tone.   ing to sense than is to be found in the self-identical
quality of a colour extended in space or of a tone extended
in time. These, as was shown in the passage quoted above
from the Philebus, Plato recognised as beautiful, [3] and, according to the whole context of the passage and the expressions
employed in describing the sounds in question, for the reason
here suggested, namely as sensuous presentations of unity.
Not, of course, that this is the *reason* apprehended by the
subject whose enjoyment is being analysed. That would at
once transfer beauty from perception to reflection. It is only
suggested as the *cause*, observed and assigned by the theorist
who is conducting the analysis *ab extra*.

The same observation upon the beauty of pure colours and
sounds as types of unity in diversity is made by Kant, and
will have to be considered as a question of modern æsthetic.
It is obvious that not only the facts of artistic perception, but
the physical analysis furnished by science, throw a certain
difficulty in the way of the explanation. For if "pure" means

---

[1] *Philebus*, marg., p. 51.   [2] *Republ.*, iii. 400 A.   [3] Cf., *Timæus*, 80 B.

unmixed, as Kant defines it to mean, are such pure sounds or colours, even if they can be said to exist at all, the most beautiful? It will be found however that the explanation will maintain itself, though in a more subtle form than that suggested by Plato, or even by Kant. Mr. Ruskin's account of "Purity as the type of divine energy,"[1] while solving the difficulties referred to, presents a wonderful analogy with the idea as it first dawned on Plato.

Elementary Geometrical Forms. ii. Elementary geometrical forms, even the straight line, and more particularly certain triangles, are set down as absolutely beautiful.[2] We have interpreted this to mean that they are among the purest examples of unity in the form of simple regular or symmetrical shape.

Strange as this assertion may appear to our æsthetic perception, which demands a more varied and concrete revelation of order or unity, I do not think that it can justly be denied. There is a degree of beauty belonging to every shape or structure which in any way affects perception with a sense of regularity or symmetry, that is, of the unity of parts in a whole as it displays itself where the whole is lacking in highly concrete differentiation.

And if we bear in mind that architecture and decorative ornament, of the severe though refined type congenial to Greek civilisation, fell outside the frontier of imitative reproduction, we may better understand how a Greek theorist might be content with a plain curve as a type of beauty, and how such a type might really involve a degree of delightful refinement which later ages have not again attained by such simple means. Plato indeed is apparently contemplating such examples as the straight line and the circle ; whereas, if our experts may be trusted, these most abstract of shapes are replaced in Hellenic architecture and decoration by delicate curves due to the skilled eye and hand of the artist-workman. But this contrast would only show, what the whole history of æsthetic must illustrate that theory follows but tardily after practice.

In such cases as the above, although the principle of unity is presented under very different sensuous embodiments, yet they all agree in being highly abstract, and the principle

---

[1] *Mod. Painters*, vol. ii.   [2] *Philebus*, l.c., *Timæus*, l.c., Ar., *Metaph.*, l.c.

therefore appears rather as their substance than as their limiting form.   In any case we have here solid observations of
æsthetic fact.   If the explanation which Greek theory offers
should appear inadequate, still it has done good service in
drawing attention to these simple instances of beauty, which
would in that case have to be dealt with on one or other of
the two extreme views known respectively as Formal Æsthetic, and as the Æsthetic of Feeling.

We now turn to those cases in which the abstract principle
of unity is plainly inadequate to the concrete significance of
the content, and yet is the only æsthetic explanation of it
which Greek theory could furnish.   Here, then, organic
unity though alleged to be the substance is in fact nothing
more than the condition of beauty.

Simple Song-   iii. Plato's restriction of permissible music to
music.   very simple song-tunes of a severe type, although
it has a moralistic aspect, is also a result and example of
his genuine but inadequate æsthetic.   The long discussion of
music and metre in the third book of the *Republic*, in which
the conception of unity that permeates the ideal common-
wealth is repeatedly contrasted with the multiplicity and
variety inherent in imitative or dramatic music, makes it plain
that the simple song-tune is acceptable to Plato partly because
he is able to formulate to himself its symbolic function as
expressive of a principle which has profound import for the
soul.   The music which he rejects is partly indeed for him
expressive of evil—and so far his rejection of it is moralistic
and not æsthetic—but to a far greater extent its defect in his
eyes consists in being concretely reproductive of natural
reality, and therefore not expressive of ideas nor related to
life in any way that he is able to comprehend.   And his
refusal on this ground to recognise such music as healthy art
is a proof of genuine æsthetic insight.   What has no expressiveness is not beautiful.   As a matter of fact very simple
tunes [1] have an unrivalled capacity of symbolising elementary
moods and ideas.   Aristotle, following Plato, observes upon
this phenomenon with results to which we shall have to
return in the next chapter.

Ethical and   iv. The extreme generality of the principle which
Logical Wholes. we are tracing in its applications produced a dan-

---

[1] Mr. L. Nettleship in Abbott's *Hellenica*, p. 118.

ger of confusion which Greek philosophy did not entirely escape. But we must not overrate the extent of this evil.

It is true that we constantly find in Plato fine arts or their productions compared, in respect of systematic reasonableness,[1] both with moral or political relations and with industrial or non-representative crafts. But we must bear in mind that this is an absolutely just comparison, so long as it only serves to insist upon the common character of organic unity by help of the pre-eminent examples which fine art affords. The comparison of a member in a political whole to a feature in a statue,[2] with regard to the subordination which is essential in the one case as in the other, is perfectly adequate for the purpose for which Plato employs it. And no one is entitled to accuse him of a confusion between morality and æsthetic because he compares right and beauty in a point in which they are fairly comparable.

But although it is an error to charge Plato on this ground with introducing æsthetic ideas into ethical or logical reasonings, yet there was one direction in which, owing to the generality of its principle, Greek æsthetic unquestionably cast its net too wide.

Beauty, as we understand it, is only for sense and for sensuous imagination. The "beautiful soul" of modern romance appears to derive its appellation from a metaphor which indicates a certain directness of delight afforded by the contemplation of its spiritual qualities, analogous to the directness of delight which attends the perception of sensuous beauty.

Beauty of soul, or beauty in the supra-sensuous world, as recognised by Greek philosophy,[3] depends upon a somewhat similar metaphor, enforced by a degree of failure in differentiating the unreflective traditional use of the term "beautiful" and therefore partaking of the nature of a confusion, although an expressive confusion. More especially the notion of an intellectual conception or archetype of beauty such as itself to be beautiful, is a very serious mistake in æsthetic. We should have hoped to find that beauty was regarded as essentially the sensuous expression—not of the beautiful, nor even of the good—but simply of the real.

---

[1] *Republic*, i. 349 D.   [2] *Republic*, iv., *init.*
[3] Plato, *Phædrus, passim*, and Ar., *Rhet.*, 1366 A.

This idea is plainly close at hand in the distinction between the beautiful and the good, but is destroyed by the co-ordination of the two as equally archetypes in a supra-sensuous world.

We must not however make the matter worse than it is. It is not the case that the principle of beauty, though in metaphorical passages spoken of as beautiful, was alleged to be the sole genuine beauty to the exclusion of the things of sense. Plato does not regard it as a mistake to believe in the beauty apparent to educated sense-perception; on the contrary, both he and Aristotle make the acquisition of such perceptive capacity a main purpose of education. What he censures is not the belief in many beautiful things, but in many conflicting "beauties";[1] that is, conflicting principles or standards of beauty.

The Lesser Arts and Formative Art.   v. Granting however that the generality of the relation of whole and part misled the Greeks into making their æsthetic theory too wide in one direction, it at least encouraged them not to make it too narrow in another. If they erred by including moral and mental qualities in beauty, they did not err, as modern philosophy has been apt to, by neglecting to notice the lesser arts and handicrafts as within the region of the beautiful. Although, as we have seen, the distinction between representative and directly productive art was forcing itself into prominence in the fifth century B.C., yet no such contrast as that between art and industry had as yet entered into ordinary language; and the profession, the trade, the craft, and the fine art, were all designated by the same term, and regarded alike as examples of reasonable systematic activity. And wherever such activity took form in objects that appealed to sense-perception, there, for the Greek philosopher, the æsthetic sphere was entered.

But with regard to the content to be expressed in their varied concrete shapes, from the works of architecture and decoration and the accompanying lesser crafts of life to the great independent formative arts of painting and sculpture, theory in Hellenic antiquity takes us no deeper than the analysis which seemed adequate for the beauty of a simple

---

[1] *Republic*, v. 479 D, "Τὰ τῶν πολλῶν πολλὰ νόμιμα καλοῦ τε περὶ καὶ τῶν ἄλλων."

curve, say, of a plain moulding, or of a single colour or tone.
"And [1] all life is full of them," we read in the *Republic*, at
the close of the discussion on music and metre before referred to, "as well as every constructive and creative art—
painting, weaving, embroidery, the art of building, the manu-
facture of utensils, as well as the frames of animals and of
plants; in all of them there is grace[2] or the absence of grace."
It is worth noticing that the beauty of animals and of plants
is here mentioned in the same line with the beauty of various
arts, showing how impossible it is to distinguish in any
theoretical treatment between the direct perception or beauty
of nature and the artistic perception or beauty of art. The
limitation is remarkable as well as the inclusion. We find
nothing about the mountains, or the sea, or the sky, and might
have risked the suggestion that the forms of inanimate nature
had not caught the eye of the Greek artist and critic, were
it not for the magnificent sense of cloud movement, revealed
without warning or sequel by Aristophanes.[3] Certainly however the Greek expression for "painter" in the sense of artist
—a painter of living things—is full of strange suggestiveness.

In all this region of expressive workmanship, which we
must judge not merely by its relics but by written records,
æsthetic theory had nothing to point out but propriety of
form ("grace"), rhythm, symmetry or balance. But in
presence of concrete significance and expression all these
ideas sink into postulates, that the relation of the unity to the
diversity or of the whole to the part shall be right and just;
shall be, that is to say, whatever the individual import of the
presentation may demand, subject to a general regard for the
principle of systematic reasonableness as one that can never
be neglected without loss in any sensuous or imaginative
expression. Much as these postulates signified to the Greeks—
whose splendid composition, we are told, distinguishes their
commonest work [4] from that of all other beauty-loving men—
they are in themselves, for æsthetic theory, mere abstract
formulæ or conditions, embodying only the fundamental fact
that system is the first law of expression.

Poetry and the Drama. vi. And even in reflecting upon the most
profoundly human of all arts, upon poetry and

---

[1] *Republic*, Jowett's trans., marg., p. 401.   [2] Εὐσχημοσύνη.
[3] *Clouds*, 323 ff.   [4] *Lectures on Art*, Poynter, p. 69.

the tragic drama, Aristotle has little to say within æsthetic limits that does not flow from the postulated relation of part to whole.[1]   We have seen how pregnantly he succeeds in treating this formal condition of art, and it would be wrong to depreciate the conception of dramatic unity and consistency which modern criticism inherited from him, and was long unable to appreciate in the full depth of its author's meaning.

We have thus seen exemplified within the limits of Greek theory that relation between formal and individual expression which was embodied in our definition of the beautiful, and which also determines the direction of progress from ancient to modern æsthetic.

In music and poetry, indeed, the relation did not lend itself to a simple demarcation between two regions of each of these arts, although it expressed itself in the difficulty of appreciating their more complex forms.   But within the limits of formative art the distinction is tolerably plain.   Individual expressiveness emerges along with what the Greek calls "imitation," beginning above architecture and the non-representative lesser arts, with naturalistic as opposed to geometrical decoration, and becoming more and more concrete throughout the higher kinds of plastic art and painting in which the abstract conditions of reasonable expressiveness only continue to assert themselves as the principle of unity and composition. But Greek theory was necessarily unable to enrich its æsthetic analysis by the deeper spiritual content which a complete explanation of concrete beauty would have demanded, and therefore the Greek mind merely accepted the problem as one of "imitation," of somehow or other getting at reality, and supplemented its abstract æsthetic principle which it was unable to deepen by the immature ethical and metaphysical reflections which we have considered.   And these, as we saw, have at least the merit of bearing witness to the perception of certain essential relations both positive and negative between life and art, but do not contribute anything to strictly æsthetic investigation.

Relation of Formal to Concrete Beauty. Fechner.   4. I will conclude this chapter with an illustration, drawn from modern research, of the mode and degree in which the abstract conditions of expression are in themselves symbolic of ideal content, and

---

[1] Cf. *Phædrus*, 268 D.

are at the same time, in virtue of the abstract and universal nature of this content, related to more concrete utterance as form to substance.

Assuming for the sake of argument that observation, as Fechner thinks,[1] bears out the idea that a certain type of rectangle is simply as a figure in space, and apart from any other known relations, more universally pleasant to the eye than any other rectangle, we seem compelled to suppose that it owes this property to some peculiar adequacy with which it embodies the general relation of part to whole—that is, to some unique symmetry or balance of its form. If it were possible to trace the alleged preference for the "golden-section" rectangle, which is the type in question, to some association with utility, this would make no difference to the present argument. An association which is sufficiently universal to generate a preference that no one can discover to be biassed, is such as must be grounded in the nature of the object. In such a figure then we have an example of mathematically formal beauty.

But further, many of the instances which have been examined by Fechner are rectangular picture-frames. Now here we at once come upon a possible conflict of principles. The preference for a golden-section rectangle, which depends upon its form alone, is plainly not of sufficient weight in determining the shape of a picture to counter-balance any requirements that may arise from the nature of the subject. It is not found that the same shape is thought appropriate to all easel pictures even when the shape is freely chosen; while we know that almost any form of surface prescribed by an architect can be utilised with success by a master of pictorial composition.

But yet it must suggest itself, as a matter of pure theory, that in a rectangular picture, a striking deviation from the rectangle which has most beauty on its own merits must entail a loss of expressiveness, which is no doubt readily compensated by the gain of higher elements of content, but, if quite wantonly incurred, would in its degree be a defect.

[1] Fechner, *Vorschule der Æsthetik*, 190 ff.
[2] A rectangle formed according to the golden section is a figure determined by a ratio of its sides such that the less is to the greater as the greater to the sum of the two. This ratio is roughly satisfied by 8 : 13, or 21 : 34.

I do not now propose to discuss the more subtle manifestation of the same principle of unity in the composition of the picture itself.   My purpose was only to give a perfectly plain example of the relation in which the most formal element of beauty, having in itself a real though scanty substantive import, stands to the concrete revelation of spiritual insight which is clothed in natural shapes.   In Stothard's picture of the Canterbury Pilgrims, for example, the shape of the canvas draws its justification from the necessities of the subject, and very obviously sacrifices the slight superficial beauty of the golden-section rectangle.   Whether such a sacrifice can be compensated so as not after all to be a sacrifice is a question which will return upon us in modern æsthetic.   The point which we are now endeavouring to make clear is that formal symmetry and concrete significance are not two heterogeneous elements of beauty, but are related purely as abstract and concrete.   The next chapter will be devoted to tracing the advance towards a more thorough theory made by the Greek mind, at first within the outlines which have now been described, and ultimately passing beyond them.

a (17 note 1). Professor Butcher has convinced me that this passage from the *Physics* is not here in point.   But the general meaning of μιμητικαὶ τέχναι (Butcher, *Aristotle's Theory of Art*, p. 121) bears out my statement.

b (p. 19). See, however, Butcher, *op. cit.*, viii., for the moral meaning of ἁμαρτία.   I cannot quite admit that even so interpreted "Aristotle's phrase will include the most significant of" tragic conflicts.   I need only point to Professor Butcher's observations on the Antigone.   It will be enough, perhaps, for my point to beg the reader to note that Aristotle's ideal play was the *Oedipus Tyrannus*, while Hegel's, for instance, was the *Antigone*.

c (p. 28). This phrase perhaps too nearly suggests the modern conception of representative art.   See Butcher, *op. cit.*, pp. 122-3, on the object of æsthetic imitation according to Aristotle ; "men in action" ; or ἤθη, πάθη, πράξεις.

d (p. 31). Imitation of nature in the modern sense, roughly equivalent to Plato's account of art in *Rep. X.*   It has nothing to do with the meaning of Aristotle's identical phrase, which does not apply to fine art more than to industrial art.

CHAPTER IV.

SIGNS OF PROGRESS IN GREEK THEORY CONCERNING THE BEAUTIFUL.

The three Antitheses. 1. WE saw in the last chapter but one that poetic art in Hellas was encountered by the earliest reflective criticism with a decided hostility, which was only the most primitive form of a misapprehension essentially involved in Hellenic thought. It is clear that Plato was alive to the existence of this critical antagonism, which his own views reproduced with a deeper significance. The object of the present chapter is to point out in their actual succession the most important changes by which the naive standpoint of Hellenic speculation upon beauty is at first modified ; paving the way for those by which, in the dawn of a later period, it is altogether transformed.

The cardinal points which determined Greek theory must now be considered with reference to three antitheses, which correspond to the content of the three principles discussed in the last chapter. The antithesis of imitation and symbolism corresponds to the metaphysical principle, the antithesis of real interest and æsthetic interest to the moralistic principle, and the antithesis of abstract and concrete analysis to the æsthetic principle.

Each of these antitheses expresses a contrast between the Hellenic point of view and that of later times, and therefore indicate a direction in which modification became apparent even within the classical mode of thought. By keeping in view these leading contrasts it may be possible to preserve a degree of unity in tracing the process of modification through the speculation of successive thinkers.

The pre-Socratics. 2. The later pre-Socratic philosophers may be mentioned with reference to the first antithesis only. We observed among them a hostility to imaginative art arising from a naive conception of its relation to reality ; but they also show traces of the opposite and equally one-

sided conception of art as allegory.   The interpretation of
Homer by the ascription of hidden meanings (ὑπόνοια) was a
familiar phenomenon to Plato, and is ascribed by later tradition to the school of Anaxagoras.   At any rate the mythological phraseology of Heraclitus and Empedocles obviously
leads up to such a conception, although it would be unhistorical to suppose that the Erinyes,[1] or Hephaistos, or Strife,
or Friendship were for these philosophers as they would be
in similar speculation to-day, names consciously drawn from
the mere analogy of a different sphere, for agencies known to
be purely physical.   It is plain that in the allegorical interpretation of the time just preceding Plato, and in writings kindred with allegory, such as the fable, the artificial myth, and
the scientific epos, the crude idea of imitation was supplemented by a reaction which itself fell into the opposite and
hardly less crude extreme.   For in allegory the reflective
meaning and the sensuous embodiment are not fused into
one, but are clearly distinguished, running in separate though
parallel lines.   Thus the allegorical expositions of Homer
seem to have been directed to break the force of moralistic
criticism, by reducing the content of the poems to a bald
scheme of abstract truths.

Allegory, therefore, is in its essence defective symbolism—
symbolism in which form and content are at bottom indifferent
to one another—and its presence whether in criticism or in
production at this early period reveals a discontent with the
limits of " imitation " together with an incapacity to grasp
the nature of concrete symbolism.

Can the   3. Assuming that the Socrates of the *Memora-*
Invisible be   *bilia* may be treated, comparatively speaking, as
Imitated ?   the historical Socrates, I notice two points of
interest in his recorded ideas.

a. It is exceedingly remarkable with reference to the first
antithesis that he directly raises [2] the question " Whether the
invisible can be imitated."   The invisible to which he refers
consists of mental moods, such as good and bad temper, and
these, he is reported to have argued in discussion with Parrha-
sinus, can be rendered by means of the expression of the face,

---

[1] " If the sun leaves his path, the Erinyes, allies of justice, will find him
out."—HERACLITUS, Ritter and Pr. no. 37.

[2] Xen., *Memor.*, iii. 10.

and more particularly through the look of the eyes. It is also remarkable that he lays stress on the artistic expression of vitality.[1] Although these suggestions do not profoundly modify the idea of imitative representation—for common usage would quite allow that anger is through its effects an object of sense-perception, yet the formulation " Is the unseen imitable ? " is at least suggestive ; and the demand for " expression " in pictorial art is an important anticipation of later theory. The view of Socrates as to the capacity of painting is not quite in agreement with that of Aristotle, which it appears to have suggested by opposition.

It may be added that the necessity for something more than sheer imitation is recognised by him through the crude conception of gathering together, from different originals, elements of beauty which nowhere exist in combination. In so early a period this idea is interesting, because it shows the consciousness that art needs in some way to bring a deeper insight to bear upon reality than untrained perception can supply. As a formal theory in later times it is simply tedious, being obviously no more than the first uncriticised shape of a very simple postulate.

Æsthetic and Real Interest. β. The attitude of Socrates to the question, " Has a beautiful thing as such a real interest ? " that is, an interest relative to a practical or to an appetitive purpose, is so far as we know uncritical, although the course of his thought may remind us of a feature in that of Kant. He refused, so we are told, to contemplate the possibility that beauty could exist except as relative to a purpose. To us, such relativity appears to destroy the æsthetic point of view, and the conception of beauty. It is well however to remember how naturally the postulate of reasonable system, which is the fundamental æsthetic requirement, takes shape in the conception of teleological relativity. The addition suggested by Kant when he describes beauty as the character of adaptation to a purpose *without relation to an actual purpose* is probably a very fair gloss on the immature idea of relative beauty. Both Plato and Aristotle are in advance of the Socratic standpoint in this respect.

---

[1] The way in which these qualities are led up to in Xen., l.c., as something beyond συμμετρία and χρῶμα leaves no doubt in my mind that Plotinus, in whom the sequence of terms is exactly the same, was much indebted to this passage in the *Memorabilia*.

Fythagoreanism. 4. It is hard to elicit much of definite historical fact from the traditions that refer to early Pythagoreanism. It seems certain, however, on the authority of Aristotle that philosophers known as Pythagoreans had pursued mathematical investigations with success, but had interpreted some of their results after the manner of mysticism. It is also definitely asserted that the numerical relations of the musical scale were discovered by them.

Symbolism. α. With reference to the antithesis between imitation and symbolism, the habit of a mystical interpretation of numerical relations and also the habit of referring musical effects to mathematical relations, opened a wide pathway of escape from the idea of common sensuous reality as ultimate standard and original.[1] More especially, such investigations no doubt influenced the view on which Plato and Aristotle, we shall find, were substantially agreed as to the pre-eminent moral import of music.

According to Aristotle[2] the Pythagoreans actually treated number as the original of which things were " imitations," an expression which Plato superseded, so Aristotle continues, by the phrase " participation " ; meaning that they exist by participation in abstractions and not as representations of them. This shows us how boldly the term " imitation " was capable of being applied, but also that Plato was inclined on the whole to introduce a somewhat greater strictness into the usage.

Passing over the second antithesis β, which does not concern us here, we may notice that—

Concrete Analysis. γ. The genesis of æsthetic criticism, through a real hope and conviction that the principle of unity could be applied in the analysis of shape, rhythm, melodies, organic existences, was due in great measure to the prospect opened up by the progress of geometrical science and of elementary mathematical acoustics. The idea that a musical effect or symmetrical figure could be shown to owe its charm to a mathematical relation, having itself, probably, a further significance more or less justifiably imputed to it, plainly animated the scientific imagination much as the physical theory of light and sound has animated it in the present day.

Plato's[3] account of the science of " harmony," analogous, I

---

[1] See *Timæus*, p. 80.   [2] *Metaph.*, A. 5 and 6.   [3] *Republ.*, vii. 530 ff.

presume, rather to acoustics than to counterpoint, and of the different classes of students who pursue it, some of them experimentalists and some mathematicians, shows that the attempt at detailed analysis of musical effect was no new thing, and his own suggestions were obviously encouraged by the consciousness of a scientific movement in the direction. However mystic might be its accessory ideas, still the enthusiastic conviction that form and number underlie the structure of the universe imparted a comprehensiveness and audacity to critical analysis such as, on a very different plane of actual knowledge, characterises modern speculation. It must be borne in mind that the 5th and 4th centuries B.C. were a period of genuine advance in mathematical theory. The life of Euclid falls about the close of the 4th century, and the knowledge embodied in his *Elements of Geometry* was growing up, partly by the researches of the " Pythagoreans," through the previous two hundred years. We may mention in this context the tradition that a canon, or rule of abstract proportions, was embodied by Polycleites in his statue of the Doryphoros.[1] Enquiry into proportional relations is one thing, the substitution of an abstract rule for creative perception in art is another. It is not at all impossible however that the two were confused, as is constantly the case in the theory of practical men, and that thus the analysis of an abstraction was made to do duty for the analytic criticism of concrete expressiveness.

Plato.   5. In Plato we see both the completed system of Greek theory concerning art, and, side by side with this, the conceptions that were destined to break it down.

Symbolism.   *a.* When we found that the idea of symbolism, that is, of the embodiment of invisible realities in sensuous form, is conspicuous by its absence from Plato's explicit theory of representative art, our conclusion ought to have excited some surprise. For, in the growing rebellion against a natural monism, fostered by abstract science on the one hand, and by abstract mysticism on the other, Plato appeared as the prophet of a dualism between nature and intelligence, or sense or spirit, which might be said to have had the effect of turning the whole perceptible universe into a symbol of ideas. It is difficult not to suppose that later European

---

[1] Overbeck, *Schriftquellen*, 953 ff.

theology, to which fine art became so profoundly related, has its ultimate source in the great simile of the *Republic* by which the Sun and its light are conceived as the offspring and symbol of the absolute good and its manifestation or utterance. And in a somewhat different arrangement of the same scheme, the only-begotten universe of the *Timæus*, the god perceptible to sense, who is the image of the ultimate reason, also suggests ideas which were destined to become for centuries the principal content of symbolic imagination.

But by Plato himself this connection was not established. Images and imagination, for him, rank below nature and science. What he cares about, as every sympathetic student must feel, is reality at first-hand; and the generalization that representative art is reality at second-hand is still fresh and serious in his mind.

Thus the conceptions from which a new symbolic art was one day to spring do not coalesce with his theory of the rank and aim of artistic creation.

This need not be less true even if the Platonic myths are genuine works of poetic imagination. No one doubts that the great art of Hellas in fact contained a symbolic element; but our inquiry deals mainly with the conscious theory of it, and on this the artistic creations of the theorist himself throw little more light than any other works which might be known to him. But although the myths are by no means pure allegories, they are rather allegorical than symbolic. They are not exactly fables like those of Æsop, nor apologues like Prodicus' Choice of Herakles, but they resemble these stories in being subservient to conveying abstract ideas, the pictorial embodiment of which is expressly admitted to be indifferent. "A man of sense ought not to say,' the Platonic Socrates concludes the great myth of the Phædo, "nor will I be too confident, that the description which I have given of the soul and her mansions is exactly true." Poetry, in the strict sense, cannot distinguish so coolly between the content and the form.

Thus we can hardly admit that the myths are genuine examples of symbolic art; we should rather look for such art as this in the simple human drama of the dialogues, in their pathos, humour, and portraiture. But this, as has been implied, throws no real light on Plato's theory of beauty.

It is important however to note that Plato was familiar

with the idea of allegorical interpretation.[1]   But this, as his good sense rejected such a method of arriving at the meaning of great poets, seems rather to have indisposed him towards a spiritual interpretation of art than to have recommended such a conception to his mind.

On the other hand we may observe in Plato a few distinct theoretical deviations from the doctrine which restricts representative art to the imitation of commonplace reality.

Formal Beauty.   i. Enough was said, in the last chapter, of the general analysis of formal beauty as embodying the principle of unity.   This analysis was applicable, in Plato's mind, to all arts and crafts as well as to natural objects, and he actually employs the word "imitation" to express their embodiment of spiritual ideas in sensuous form.[2]

Musical Symbolism.   ii. In the case of music this is especially remarkable to a modern reader, and when we are told[3] that certain rhythms, and, apparently, certain melodies, are "imitations" of certain types of life or temper, we feel that the limit between the image and the symbol is overstepped.   No doubt it was only very simple music which had for him this distinct expressive capacity, and it is not difficult to trace in his discussion a transition from the idea of reproducing in narrative such tunes or songs as a man of a certain character would willingly use, *i.e.* an imitation *in pari materia*, of sound by sound, to the consideration of the tune or rhythm reproduced in its direct relation to the mood of the man whose feelings it expresses.

We shall see that Aristotle goes still further in the same direction.

Beauty which is more than formal.   iii. It is also worth remembering that outside Plato's definite theory of art the beautiful is principally spoken of as the manifestation of intelligence,[4] and the idea of poetic inspiration which earlier literature had possessed, and which the criticism of imitation had perhaps unduly thrust aside, is adopted by him with varying degrees of irony,[5] but always, probably, with a sound psychological insight that the creative and critical genius are distinct, and that the apprehension of truth which belong to creative imagination is other than that which proceeds by methodic reason.

---

[1] *Republic*, 378 D.   [2] *Republic*, iii. 401.   [3] *Republic*, iii. 400 B and D.
[4] *Cratylus*, 416.   [5] *Phædrus*, 245 A; *Laws*, 719 C; *Meno*, 99 D.

E

But these suggestions were not reconciled with the general explanation of representative art, and the poet and artist rank in Plato's eyes many degrees[1] below the true lover of beauty, who is on a level with the philosopher.   Thus it has even been maintained that for Plato fine art falls outside the province of the beautiful.[2]   We have already seen under what limitations this assertion is true.   He recognised that in fact the expression of ideal contents was especially noticeable in the works of man, but his theory of representation prevented him from founding upon this observation any definite notion of the beautiful as revealed more especially in art.

Æsthetic Interest.   β. Estimation of beauty according to a practical interest is as we saw equally unæsthetic, whether the interest is moral or sensuous.   Not that pleasure, in the ordinary sense of the term, as descriptive of pleasant feeling, indicates an unæsthetic interest ; for in saying that we mean a thing to afford pleasure we only say that we mean it to please ; and the question now raised is more concrete than this, and the answer depends upon whether the pleasure is expected to arise from the sheer expressive effect of the æsthetic appearance, or from purposes or associations connected with the existence of the real objects of which that appearance reminds us.

Therefore we must not look for Plato's attitude towards true æsthetic interest in the contrast which he too frequently draws between art which has for its object to give pleasure, and art which might have for its object to produce moral improvement.   Although, as we saw in the last chapter,[3] the demand of early criticism for moral elevation in art implies a sound judgment on the substantive relation of beauty to life, yet when we are estimating the progress of æsthetic theory proper, we must not recognise moral improvement as an æsthetic interest any more than the pleasures of vice.   It is rather within the region of pleasurable presentation, as conceived by Plato, and in the contrast between pure and impure modes and conditions of such presentation, that we must look for something corresponding to the antithesis which we have in mind.

But this contrast again is apt to be presented in a way which does not directly answer our question.   Pure pleasures,

---

[1] *Phædrus*, 248 E.   [2] Schasler, i. 89.   [3] Cf. also Nettleship in *Hellenica*.

such as according to Plato arise from true beauty, are free, no doubt, from selfish interest in the bad sense of the words; thus much is clear; but whether they are distinct from the pleasurable side of the nobler real affections and volitions is often by no means clear. Impure pleasures, again, are full of sensuous, and even of painful or uneasy interest; but whether they are separated from the pleasures of true beauty because they are relative to real desires (as morality also is), or because *qua* pleasures they are disfigured by uneasiness, or only in so far as they are conceived to be of an immoral type—this is by no means plain.

We may take as extreme examples of Plato's leanings in these two directions, first the above-quoted passage from the *Philebus*[1] relating to the beauty of form or unity; and secondly that in the *Gorgias* dealing with musical and tragic art, through an ironical comparison of them with the routine—denied to be an art—of cookery.[2] For instance, " and to what does their solemn sister [sister of choric and dithyrambic poetry, musical execution has also been mentioned], the wondrous muse of tragedy, devote herself? Is all her aim and desire only to give pleasure to the spectators, or does she fight against and refuse to speak of their pleasant vices, and willingly proclaim in word and song truths welcome and unwelcome? Which is her character?

" There can be no doubt that Tragedy has her face turned towards pleasure and gratification.

" And is not that the sort of thing which we were just now describing as flattery?"

In the *Philebus* it is assumed, and in the *Gorgias* implicitly denied, that pleasure is at least an essential element of the characteristic impression for which beauty ought to be valued. But in the passage in which this is assumed, the pleasure in question is strictly limited with reference: i. To the kind of sense-perception which can give rise to it—the perceptions of eye and ear only, with a doubtful inclusion, on a lower level, of the sense of smell; and, ii. To the cases in which these sense-perceptions can give rise to the characteristic pleasures of formal beauty; cases that are free from the uneasiness of desire, and, as above explained, are distinguished by their symbolic character.

---

[1] See p. 33, *supra.*   [2] *Gorgias*, pp. 501, 502.

The demarcation between the æsthetic and non-æsthetic senses, strongly insisted on in the *Hippias Major*[1] which, if spurious, is interesting as showing a growth of definite ideas on this point, is a fair indication that the boundary between æsthetic and non-æsthetic interest is coming into view. Negatively, the "theoretic senses" are not connected with material consumption of the thing perceived, and positively, they and no others, with the doubtful exception of touch and muscular sense, have the capacity for the recognition of structural totality, the first condition, as we have seen, of the expressiveness in which beauty consists. The doubtful inclusion of smell most emphatically illustrates the genesis of the distinction in Plato's mind. If we judge by "purity" in Plato's peculiar meaning, viz. as freedom from the intermittent uneasiness of desire, the pleasures of smell are pure ; if we judge by purity in the sense of significant unity or concentrated energy as revealed in the expressive character of a presentation,[2] the pleasures of smell are not pure, but are as a rule mere occurrences in the way of pleasurable sensation.

If then, in the passage from the *Gorgias* referred to, the fault ascribed to art were nothing more than that what it aims at and generates is pleasure, we should find a discrepancy between the two passages. But the aim ascribed and condemned in the *Gorgias* is pleasure *as such*, which means, as Plato seems rightly to insist with all his force, pleasure at any price and in anything.[3] "Cookery," he says (it is cookery with which poetry and music are being ironically compared, as equally forms of "flattery," *i.e.* mere provision of the pleasant) "in attending upon pleasure *never regards either the nature or reason of that pleasure to which she devotes herself* nor ever considers nor calculates anything." This comparison shows that the satisfaction of real desire is not far from Plato's mind as the ground to be alleged against the nobleness *of the concrete arts*. It is exceedingly suggestive that in order to carry out this comparison he proposes to divest poetry of its poetic form, and consider simply its matter, that is, to change it from art into something else. But he does not name this ground, and passes on to the old

---

[1] *Hipp. Major*, 297–8.
[2] See Ruskin's *Modern Painters*, vol. ii., on Purity.
[3] *Gorgias*, 501 A., Jowett.

antithesis of pleasure-giving as an aim, contrasted with moral improvement, so that he himself actually approves as the purpose of art not an æsthetic but a real, *i.e.* a moral interest.

The conclusion must be that Plato has a clear view of æsthetic as distinct from real interest only in so far as he recognises a peculiar satisfaction attending the very abstract manifestations of purely formal beauty. In those concrete forms of representation which we think the higher arts, he was unable to distinguish the pleasure of expressiveness from the practical interest of morality, which he desired to see predominant, and from the pleasure of realistic suggestion which he utterly condemned.

This view of Plato's meaning is not, in my judgment, to be very seriously impugned on the ground of the noble account, several times repeated in the dialogues, of beauty as the object of educated love.[1] The question is whether the feeling for beauty so described is to be understood as a real enthusiasm for an idea, or even for a person sublimed into an idea,—an enthusiasm such as demands the reality or realization of its object—or as an ideal delight in a perfectly concrete sensuous appearance which charms as an appearance only. A pure affection for a good and attractive friend, or an enthusiasm for the cause of order or of knowledge, is likely to be attended by refined perceptions, but it is not in itself the same thing as a feeling for beauty. Again, a delight in the expressive force of perfectly concrete fancies or appearances independent of the real practical existence of the objects corresponding to them, can hardly indeed exist except in a mind of large and noble purposes, but is not in itself an affection for any actual person, or enthusiasm for any actual cause. If Plato's "beauty" is an abstract purpose or principle, his "love of beauty" is a refined enthusiasm for real purposes or principles ; if his "beauty" is a value or import felt in the world of sense-perception when taken simply as expressive and not as a means to any end, then, and then only, his love of beauty is an æsthetic delight not concerned with the real existence of its objects.

It is plain that both these elements enter into the Platonic love-philosophy, and that they are not as a rule distinguished. The former belongs to abstract and the latter to concrete

---

[1] *Symposium; Rep.*, iii. ; Phædrus.

idealism ; for if beauty is out of the sensuous world, it is undistinguishable from the object of will and knowledge ; while
if it is in the sensuous world, it belongs to a perfectly definite
sphere of appreciative perception.   Plato's thought undoubtedly alternated between these two extremes.   What we have
to bear in mind is that moral purity in the purpose of art or
beauty does not constitute æsthetic purity, though moral
impurity in the purpose of art or beauty does constitute
æsthetic impurity.

It is further worth remarking that Plato had observed
the special connection between imagination and emotion,[1] and
was not wholly unaware that free utterance of passion[2] might
bring relief and calm, and again that the representative arts
might be contrasted with the practical arts as play[3] with
earnest.   This latter conception, invested with profound
import in modern times by the genius of Schiller, is in Plato
a natural accompaniment of the view which makes the representation an inferior species of the reality, as when we say
contemptuously of a dilettante that he is only playing at work.
Yet this, like so much of the groundplan of Plato's thought,
was full of possibilities which only needed a larger experience
of spiritual needs and achievements to become realities.

Concrete   γ. The last observation calls upon us to notice
Criticisms.   the immense substantive contribution made by
Plato to the material for a true concrete criticism.   For real
advance in the theory of a great subject it is less important
that a thinker's verdicts should be unimpeachable than that
he should have gathered into a connected whole the right
kind of experience and treated it in a way that suggests the
most important issues.

Plato has sketched the fabric of æsthetic experience on a
coherent plan, which subsequent history has proved to be in
accordance with the nature of the phenomena.   He left to
those who came after him the definite conception that there
is a group of representative or imaginative arts consisting in
chief of sculpture, painting, music, and poetry, with the
addition of architecture and its auxiliary handicrafts, which
are united with one another at least by a common difference
from the merely useful productive trades, and the value of
which presents a problem to those who care for the highest

---

[1] *Rep.*, x., 606 D.   [2] *Laws*, 790.   [3] *Laws*, 889.

concerns of life. The chief points of view under which Plato attempted to penetrate the significance of these phenomena have already been set forth. It only remains to state that in spite of the abstract limitations within which he worked the mass of experience to which he called attention was such as to lay a sound foundation for a more concrete criticism than his own. He gave a *raison d'être* to the distinction of epic, lyric, and dramatic poetry, not in itself new, by analysis[1] turning on their respective degrees of dramatic personification ; he pointed out that a tragedy is an organic whole,[2] and not a string of speeches expressive of various morals ; he made an attempt of which the import is largely lost to us, but the suggestion is still valuable, to determine the ethical and symbolic affinities of metres melodies and other features[3] of the vocal and instrumental music of his day ; he pointed out, though primarily as a proof of remoteness from reality, that the painter's third dimension[4] is ideal and not actual ; he insisted, as we have seen, on a symbolic value, though only of a very abstract and simple kind, as shared by all the formative handicrafts including architecture, with the more elaborate representative arts, and explained it more especially in the case of geometrical figures and simple tones and colours. The mere distinction, which was mentioned just above, of the æsthetic from the non-æsthetic senses, bequeathed to later philosophy a problem of extreme interest and difficulty, while the place assigned to beauty in education bears witness to the philosopher's practical feeling for it as the sensuous representative of reason, and has recently revived as one of the profoundest guiding ideas of modern life.

Thus Plato's philosophic instinct enabled him to gather and organize an experience which suggested far more than was included in his abstract æsthetic theory, and to set the problems which only a more concrete criticism could solve.

6. It is needless to enter at length into the twice-told tale of the general relation in which Aristotle stood to Hellenic life and thought. If there never was a greater intelligence, certainly no intelligence had ever a nobler opportunity. In the sphere of realized beauty with which we are here concerned, not only had the greatest works already

Aristotle.

---

[1] *Rep.*, i–iii. 3. [2] *Phædrus*, 268.
[3] *Rep.*, i–iii. ; *Timæus*, 80 B. [4] *Rep.*, x.

been produced, and attained complete recognition,[1] but an after-prime had subsequently set in, the nature of which could not fail to stimulate theoretical reflection. And for this reflection the material was not only complete, but had been in great part organized by the thought of Plato. Thus to the greatest of originators there succeeded the greatest of investigators.

Symbolism.   *a.* First, then, in conformity with our previous method, we are to inquire how far Aristotle may have modified the essential Hellenic idea that only such reality as pleases in ordinary experience is that by the reproduction of which fine art hopes to please ; how far, in other words, the differentia "imitative," which he does not discard from the definition of art, retains for him its natural meaning of copying something which is such that it can be copied. Does "imitation" in Aristotle lean at all to "symbolism" ?

Selection of Phenomena.   i. It is important that we should notice what æsthetic phenomena chiefly attracted his attention. In Æsthetic, as in other branches of philosophy, Aristotle is the earliest writer to leave us a separate treatise. But its title of *Poetic* confines its immediate subject matter to literature, and within literature to the art of invention or composition, usually though not necessarily in verse, of which three principal kinds, Epic, Tragedy, and Comedy, formed the heads of the discussion. Music is alluded to only as an incident of poetry. The arts of acting and of the rhapsode are referred to as essentially outside the arts of drama and epic respectively ; so that although these classes of poetry are considered throughout with reference to the feelings of an audience or of spectators, yet we are not wrong in saying that they are essentially treated as literature. Lyrical poetry has as yet no single name, and is not recognised as a species. Formative art, including Architecture and the lesser decorative crafts, fall outside the scope of the treatise, although painting is alluded to more than once by way of illustration. Observations upon music and painting occur in other writings ; but there is no systematic inquiry into the pleasure arising from these arts. Aristotle's treatment of the subject is therefore not co-extensive

---

[1] As in the law of Lycurgus providing that statues of the three great tragedians should be erected, and that correct MSS. of their dramas should be prepared and preserved.

with the philosophy of Fine Art.   How far such a philosophy
can be gathered from him will appear as we proceed.

But if his selection of phenomena is baulking to our
curiosity, which would have welcomed his criticism of the
Parthenon pediment-sculpture or of the Phigaleian frieze, it is
eminently favourable to advance in æsthetic science.   For it
is most particularly the poetry of Hellas that we cannot
possibly reconcile with the formal æsthetic theory natural to
Greek thought, which finds some justification in its monumental sculpture and its temple architecture.   In technical
language, an inquiry into Greek epic, tragedy, and comedy,
must at least include elements belonging to the æsthetic
theory of the sublime and the ugly ; and it would be impossible to penetrate far into these distinctively modern provinces
of æsthetic without throwing off the subjection of art to that
which pleases in everyday perception.   The treatment of
comedy in the *Poetic*, of which the details are unhappily lost,
was therefore in principle a most important extension of Plato's
reference to the drama.

The Ugly.   ii. In conformity with the choice of subject matter is the remark [1] that the laughable is a subdivision of the ugly—the laughable being the subject of comedy,
and therefore falling within fine art and its essential quality
the beautiful, though I do not affirm that Aristotle was aware
of this implied paradox.   And more consciously suggestive, in
the same direction, is the observation, frequently and emphatically repeated, and extended to the whole sphere of " imitative " art, that an imitation is often agreeable though the
thing imitated or copied is disagreeable.   I quote a characteristic passage in this sense, with the attempt at explanation
which the phenomenon elicits.[2]

" It seems that the origin of poetry is entirely due to two
causes, both of them consisting in natural tendencies.   First,
imitation is innate in human beings, as we see from childhood
upward, and man differs from other animals in being so given
to imitation, and his earliest acquisition of knowledge is by
means of imitation ; and pleasure in imitation too is innate in
all men.   There is evidence of this in the facts ; for we take
pleasure in looking at the most carefully executed pictures of
things which in themselves we dislike to look at, such as

---

[1] *Poetic*, 5, 1.   [2] *Poetic*, 4.

the forms of the most ignoble animals, or of corpses.   And
secondly,[a] there is this cause, that not only men of science
enjoy the exercise of apprehension, but the rest of mankind
enjoy it too ; only their capacity for it is limited.   So this is
why they enjoy seeing the likenesses of things, because it is
an incident of seeing them that they apprehend and infer what
each thing is, as for instance ' This is he ; ' for if the
spectator has never seen the thing before it will not be the
likeness [lit. ' imitation '] which will cause the pleasure, but
the execution or the colour or some such reason."   The second
" cause " is meant to be an explanation of the first, as the
following passage shows.[1]   " Since the use of the intelligence,
and the feeling of wonder, are both of them pleasant, it
necessarily follows that things are pleasant which are of the
class of mimetic art, such as painting and statuary and poetry
[it is most remarkable in connection with what will be said
below, that music is here omitted] and everything which is
well imitated, even when the object itself is not pleasant.
For it is not the object which gives the pleasure, but inference takes place that ' This is that,' so that an exercise of
the intelligence is brought about."

The phenomenon thus insisted on opens up vistas that lead
to romantic art and modern theory.   How far did Aristotle
appreciate its significance ?   We are here face to face with
the recurring problem set by the apparent simplicity of
Aristotle's thought.   We shall see below that a rough and
ready interpretation of his terms, by merely converting them
into their current equivalents, will certainly at times lead us
astray.   Yet where the text gives no hint of subtlety, it can
hardly be right to import it.   Literally understood, the above
passages account for the pleasure which we take in representations of the unpleasant, by our enjoyment of the intellectual
act and achievement involved in simply recognising the object
portrayed.   And of the existence of such a pleasure there is no
doubt whatever.[2]   But it is plain that by merely pressing upon
the meaning of the term μανθάνειν, " to apprehend," and συλλογί-
ζεσθαι, " to infer," we might introduce such a conception as that
of entering with full appreciation into the idea, perhaps even into

---

[1] *Rhet.*, 1371 b, 4.
[2] See Fra Lippo Lippi : " The monks closed in a circle and praised loud,"
etc.

the mood, embodied in the artistic representation. In this case we should have reached an explanation to which modern theory has little to add. Aristotle's omission to refer to mood or emotion makes in my judgment strongly for the former alternative ; and it is almost impossible, so it seems at least to the modern reader, to over-estimate the naiveté of Greek criticism. But though in the present case I believe the less pregnant interpretation to be nearer the truth, we shall see below that we are skating on thin ice when we prefer the more superficial explanation of Aristotle. It should be needless to remind the reader that no Greek term with all its content and associations can by any possibility find a precise equivalent in any English term ; and we are not entitled to argue strictly from any single rendering, but we must consider how much ground a simple term may have covered before the necessity for more subtle phrases was perceived.

However this may be, it is clear that the fascination of ugliness in representative art was a newly observed phenomenon in contradiction with the simple assumption that the representation affects us as does the corresponding reality. Not the content of the likeness, but something, whatever it might be, involved in the fact of its being a likeness at all, was thus suggested to be the secret of its attraction.

Poetry Philosophic. iii. When we read in the *Poetics*[1] that "poetry[b] is more philosophical (or scientific) and more serious than history" we are apt to imagine ourselves in a modern atmosphere ; and certainly the remark shows a recognition of the ideal in art quite foreign to Plato. Yet when we observe that this principle is introduced as an inference from the postulate of *unity* in the plot or action of a drama, that this single and self-complete action is more or less contrasted with the portrayal of human individuality, and that the "scientific" element of poetry lies in its typical generality, we are obliged to doubt whether the idealisation thus acknowledged is more akin to the formal limitations or to the positive greatness of Greek drama. If Aristotle, as the sequel of the above passage appears to indicate, really preferred on this ground the enfeebled later comedy of types and manners[2] to the pregnant Aristophanic comedy of humour and portrait-satire, his ideas are far less kindred to ours than his language.

---

[1] *Poet.*, 9, 3.   [2] See *Poet.*, 5, 3, with reference to Crates.

It will be necessary to recur to this point when we come to consider his attitude towards concrete characterisation ; at present it is enough to note how clearly he enunciates the principle that representation is not to be wholly fettered by given reality.

Musical Symbolism.   iv. It will be remembered that the Xenophontic Socrates discussed the possibility of a presentation of the unseen by formative art, and instanced the indication of mental moods by look and feature.   In Plato all art is regarded as capable of being thus significant, but attention is drawn more especially to the expressive capacities of music and rhythm.[1]   In Aristotle we find that the presentation of mental or moral moods is in the strict sense ascribed only to music and poetry, to the explicit exclusion of the relation between formative art[2] and mental emotions. For these, according to Aristotle, are in pictorial art only *indicated* through external symptoms, such as gesture and complexion, which do not constitute *in themselves* any resemblance to the mental feelings. But musical tunes, and words accompanied by music, "contain *in themselves* likenesses [lit. 'imitations'] of moral moods." Such expressions certainly seem to convey an intentional exclusion of the view which Socrates suggested, and an intentional restriction of that adopted by Plato. " Imitation " is thus not merely extended over but confined to the expressive relation, of whatever kind, by which feeling passes directly into rhythm and melody.

Compare with this the very significant suggestion in his jottings of problems for inquiry, " Why does what is heard alone of the objects of sense possess emotional import ?[3] for even a tune without words has it ; but colour [as such,[4] apart from indirect portrayal by its means], and smell and taste have none."

Then is imitation at last freed from " likeness " to a sensuous reality, and have we here, in essence, the romantic conception of music as a direct embodiment of spiritual emotion ? I hardly think so.   Aristotle's central proof that music directly

---

[1] *Rep.*, ii. 400 B.   [2] *Pol.*, 1340 ; cf. *Laws*, 654–5.

[3] *Probl.*, 919 b, 26. διὰ τί τὸ ἀκουστὸν μόνον ἔχει ἦθος τῶν αἰσθητῶν.   The simple phrase ἔχει ἦθος is a good example of Aristotle's curtness.   Our rendering of this phrase determines our whole ideas of his æsthetic.

[4] The strictness of this reference to colour has an affinity with Kant. The truth of the opinion expressed in the text is at least doubtful.

contains the essence of emotion is that in practice it produces
emotion, particular tunes giving rise, it would seem, to particular forms of excitement,[1] just as the music of the dance
or the march or the hymn reproduces certain elementary
feelings and active tendencies almost with the certain operation
of a drug.   The movement of the music, I suspect he meant,
when contrasting it with the *indirect* expression of painting, *is*
the actual movement[2] of the mind or impulses which arises
when the music is heard.   So far then from "imitation" being
here refined into the æsthetic idea of symbolism, it might even
be doubted whether what it describes is an æsthetic effect at
all, if, by an æsthetic effect, we mean not merely response to a
stimulus but pleasure in an expression.   But Aristotle loves
to work upwards from physical fact to its ideal import ; and
we shall probably be near the truth if we say that, starting
from the fact of involuntary response to musical stimulus, he
accepted an analogical kinship between moral emotion and
musical expression such as Plato had already insisted on, and
that therefore he did, as we should certainly judge at first
sight, admit a symbolic element into his idea of "imitative"
representation, while excluding from it the simple case of
copying by formative art.

Art corrective
of Nature.
v. Finally it may be observed that there is at
first sight a striking resemblance in the analogy
which Aristotle saw between Art and Nature,[3] to some post-
Kantian speculations.   But for our present purpose it must
be borne in mind that though Nature is in both schemes
likened to an inferior art, yet in Aristotle the art which
makes good the imperfections of Nature is *industrial,*[d] as
opposed to the copyist art which reproduces her creations.
There is *here* no hint whatever that the art which represents
is entitled, in modern phrase, "to liberate the real import of
appearances"[4] from the falsities of commonplace reality.

Our conclusion then must be that Aristotle was driven to
stretch the idea of imitation, but that he did not reject it in
favour of the idea of symbolism.   Given reality was still for
him the standard, but he saw the difference which treatment
produced in it—he saw that it must be idealised.   This is a
position fairly in accordance with the apparent actual process

---

[1] *Pol.*, l.c. cont.   [2] *Probl.*, l.c.   [3] Φυσ., 198.
[4] See Introd. to Hegel's *Æsthetic*, Eng. Trans., p. 15.

of art, but ultimately inconsistent with itself, and unstable.
For, if given reality is the standard, what is to indicate the
direction in which it is to be idealised ?   The true answer, "a
deeper reality," is excluded *ex hypothesi* so long as given reality
is the standard.   The unæsthetic answer, "morality is the
guide," is terribly obvious, and I cannot think that Aristotle
wholly escaped its influence.[1]   The answer of abstract æsthetic,
"Unity and symmetry are the rules," is the confusion of fundamental abstract conditions of art with its concrete content, and
suggests to us ideal trees that are no trees in particular, and
ideal dramas whose chief concern is to observe the unities.
How far in detail Aristotle escaped this confusion, towards
which the limitations of his æsthetic tended to force him, we
shall endeavour to determine below.   In the meantime it
seems that his conception of fine art in its relation to nature'
may be fairly summed up as the idealising imitation of
given reality.

Aesthetic   β. We are now to ask how far Aristotle escapes
Interest.   from the moralistic limitation natural to Hellenic theory, by recognising the demarcation of the peculiar
pleasure afforded by beauty from all satisfaction attaching to
practical relations with reality, whether moral, non-moral, or
immoral.

Beauty, Virtue   i. When we turn to his general utterances on
and Pleasure. the subject of beauty, we find distinctions obviously
of the nature in question ; but, after Aristotle's manner, each
element of the distinction is only insisted on for the purpose
of the moment, so that what is clear in one passage seems
obscured in another.

Where it is maintained that mathematics[2] can treat of
attributes that belong to beauty, the beautiful is distinguished
from the good ; where the mean life[3] is contrasted with the
noble life, beauty is distinguished from expediency, but is
identified with a form of the good ; where sexual preference[4]
is being contrasted with æsthetic selection, real beauty is distinguished from beauty which only has reference to desire.
Thus the boundary between the beautiful and the merely
pleasant is more firmly maintained than that between the beautiful and the moral ; and we are disappointed to find in the
context of the most attractive definition of beauty given by

---

[1] See ch. iii. above.   [2] *Metaph.*, 1078.   [3] *Rhet.*, 1390.   [4] *Probl.*, 896 b.

Aristotle—" the beautiful [1] is that good which is pleasant because it is good "—that virtue is explicitly included under the
head of the beautiful. Nevertheless it is probably thus classi-
fied not on moralizing grounds, but as possessing a certain
immediate splendour analogous to the beauty of sense.[2] We
see, however, that the differentia which should confine the
beautiful to the province of sense and imagination is conspicuous by its absence, except in as far as it is implied in the
amount of attention devoted to " imitative " art.

There can be little doubt that Aristotle, if led to define
beauty in all its relations at once, would have traced its frontier satisfactorily. But he has not, in fact, left us a systematic
treatment of the general subject, and does not seem to have
conceived such a treatment in his own mind.

Educational Interest.   ii. It has been suggested [3] that Aristotle's interest in beauty was mainly educational. It is true
that the chief account which he gives of music and drawing
occurs in the educational sections of the *Politics*. But we
must remember that to introduce æsthetic interest into education is not the same as to introduce educational interest into
æsthetic. The former Aristotle certainly did at least in one
instance ; how far he did the latter may be best discussed in
connection with his celebrated definition of tragedy.

The noble saying which is Aristotle's criticism upon the
received estimate of drawing as an element in education, is a
proof that he regarded education as incomplete without an
attempt to develop true æsthetic perception. Drawing is to
be taught, he suggests,[4] not merely to impart skill in estimating the commercial value of articles, but because it makes the
pupils good observers of the beauty of objects. How far a
similar æsthetic interest is indicated in the discussion of the
aims with which music is to be taught depends largely on our
interpretation of the definition of tragedy, which is echoed in
part of the educational inquiry. It is plain, indeed, that Aristotle values both music and drama, not only as an educationist
for their effect on character, but as a man of the world for
their recreative and social function. The question is as to
the precise nature of the higher recreation as understood by
him.

[1] *Rhet.*, 1366.   [2] See above on *Beautiful Soul*, p. 37.
[3] *Ulrici, in Müller*, 2, 181   [4] *Pol.*, 1338.

The Function of Tragedy. iii. It will be well now to consider the question before us in connection with the only account of a form of this higher recreation which has been preserved to us at all completely as it came from Aristotle's hand.

Materials from Aristotle. *a.* The celebrated definition of Tragedy in the *Poetics* may, I believe, be fairly paraphrased as follows. " Tragedy is a representation [lit. imitation] of an action noble and complete in itself, and of appreciable magnitude, in language of special fascination, using different kinds of utterance in the different parts, given through performers and not by means of narration, and producing, by (the stimulation of) pity and fear, the alleviating discharge of emotions of that nature." Of these defining terms, "noble" distinguishes the subject-matter which tragedy shares with epic from that, viz. forms of the inferior or ugly, which comedy shares with satire. " Complete in itself " refers to the demand for organic unity of structure, having beginning, middle and end, which is the only form of unity strictly demanded by Aristotle. Unity of time is alluded to only in the remark that the action of tragedy is confined as a rule to one day or little more ; unity of place is not mentioned. " Of appreciable magnitude " refers to the necessity that a beautiful thing should be readily apprehended in its parts and also as a whole. " Language of special fascination " refers to the employment of rhythm and melody ; " with different kinds of utterance " to the difference between iambic declamation and choric song ; " given through performers " distinguishes drama from epic ; it is noticeable, however, that Aristotle admits that a drama can be judged of by reading. The remaining portion of the definition has been the subject of much controversy, which will never perhaps be finally laid to rest. Space forbids me to defend at length the rendering which I have adopted with full conviction.[1] I merely mention, on account of its surpassing historical interest, the fact that Lessing, in harmony with the spirit " of his century, not yet set free by Goethe,"[2] rendered the term κάθαρσις, which I have paraphrased as " alleviating discharge," by the equivalent " purification," and held it to indicate a conversion of passion or emotion *in general* into

---

[1] Resting on Bernays' *Zwei Abhandlungen über d. Aristotelische Theorie d. Drama*, Berlin, 1880 (first published 1857), which cannot be too strongly recommended for its suggestiveness and lucidity.

[2] Bernays, l.c.

virtuous dispositions ; that Goethe rightly protested on general grounds against such an interpretation, but proposed in its place one quite incompatible with Aristotle's Greek ; and that Hegel,[1] while not directly challenging the authenticity of the current expression, "purification of the passions," interprets it and restricts it in a way that makes it a vehicle for the most pregnant meaning that could possibly be ascribed to Aristotle.

The definite explanation of the term κάθαρσις, which Aristotle had given in the *Poetics*, has not been preserved. The rendering here adopted is chiefly though not solely founded on a passage in the *Politics*,[2] treating of certain effects of music, from which it appears that "purification" (or rather "purgation") does not fall within the educational province, and that it is a special term indicating an action upon persons predisposed to pity and terror (which all are in some degree) analogous to that by which orgiastic strains produce first excitement and then restoration to tranquillity in persons of ecstatic temperament. It is by a similar operation of music (theatrical music is explicitly mentioned) that all persons, in so far as they are predisposed to pity and fear, may be brought to undergo "a kind of purgation and relief accompanied by pleasure." The analogy is medical, and indicates a relief from the passions rather than a purification of them.

It may be added to this necessarily slight account of our materials for estimating the aim of tragedy as conceived by Aristotle, that he regarded the laws of the beautiful as necessarily applicable to the tragic treatment of action ;[3] that the psychological connection of pity and fear as laid down in the *Rhetoric* suggests to us the conception of an idealised terror, acting through human sympathy, as the essence of the tragic emotion referred to ; that its aim, or at least an element in its aim, was pleasure, not however all pleasure, but the pleasure[4] arising from pity and fear by means of artistic presentation (lit. by means of imitation), but that the "purgative" function of good music—and, we may presume, of good poetry—though plainly separate from education or edification on the one hand, does also appear to be distinguished on the other hand from the sheer entertainment or recreation (ἀνάπαυσις) to be provided by inferior music for the more vulgar kind of audience.[5]

---

[1] *Æsth.*, 3, 531.   [2] *Pol.*, 1340 a, 1342 a.   [3] *Poetic*, 7, 4.
[4] *Poetic*, 14, 3.   [5] *Politics*, 1341.

F

Estimate of his　　*β.* In contrasting Plato and Aristotle with refer-
Meaning.　　ence to their estimates of the secondary effects of
tragedy, we are apt to forget how closely they agree with
regard to its primary psychical operation.　The spectator
at a play [1] indulges his emotions, chiefly those of pity, or
fear, without the restraints of practical life, and finds a pleasure in such indulgence, and this pleasure, Plato at least
maintains, the tragedian is ready to purchase at any price,
shrinking from no source of emotional excitement.　The
difference begins after this point.　Plato thinks only how
emotion is intensified by habit and contagion ; Aristotle
applies another principle, not wholly alien to Plato, but in this
context a practically new departure.

The principle is in general, that emotion may be relieved,
discharged or mitigated by mere indulgence.　This is not
the same as to say with both Plato and Aristotle in their
educational theory that emotion may be disciplined by being
excited under moralising influences.　But whether Aristotle
meant the full opposite of this conception, that is, to accept
as the basis of art the fact of psychical excitement pure and
simple, without considering the relation to life of the content
active in the excitement, is the question which we now have
to approach.

The problem is complementary to that of Aristotle's
psychological explanation of enjoyment in the portrayal of
the unpleasant.　There the question was, " Does he refer
to the pleasure of bare recognition, or to the satisfaction of
profound appreciation ? "　Here the question is, " Does he
refer to the pleasure of any thrilling emotion ending in an
agreeable languor, or to the delight of pregnant conflicts of
feeling issuing in a calm which is reasonable as well as pathological ?　Does he, in short, take account of ideal content as
well as of psychical sensibility ? "　It is the same question in
another form when we ask whether for him as for Plato the
pleasure which is the aim of tragedy is pleasure at any price.

It appears to me that we have here a case of the heterogeneous definition which we saw [2] to be so tempting and so
fallacious.　It is clear that the pleasurable thrill of the commonest passion—anger,[3] for example—was a fact observed

---

[1] *Rep.*, x. 606. cf. *Phædrus*, 268.
[2] Chap. i.　　[3] *Rhetoric*, 1370 b, 10.

by Aristotle, and influencing him in his æsthetic theory. It is clear that the pathological phenomena which furnished the analogy for his conception of alleviating discharge are akin as well to the narcotic languor which succeeds the morbid excitement aroused by a thoroughly vicious play or novel, as to the tranquillity of assuaged emotion which is brought about by reading the *Antigone* or the *Œdipus at Colonus.*

But it is no less clear that he did not mean to identify the vulgar or morbid affections with the operation of tragic art. The object of tragedy is pleasure, but only the pleasure of tragedy, and the pleasure of tragedy is a form of enjoyment strictly limited by the conditions which were explained in its definition. Now if we ask, how this limitation, this picking and choosing within given reality, can be justified, we shall find no real answer short of the complete liberation of art, not only from the standard of common reality, but from the kindred aim of thrilling the common sensibility. " Idealisation " would be then a simple consequence of the demand for the most pregnant expression, and the mere discharge of feeling would be recognised as an extreme no more proper to art than the opposite extreme of moral purification. Aristotle, not being prepared to break away in principle from the presentation of common reality, could not reconcile these aims, all of which he saw to be essential. They are therefore simply thrown together to limit each other as best they may. Pleasure and emotion are necessary, but not at the expense of nobleness ; nobleness is necessary, but not at the expense of the power to stimulate emotion.

The emphasis which he rightly laid on utterance and intelligence did not lead him to the idea that the delight of these factors of art was no mere psychical accident, but was the manifestation of joy in self-expression, the ultimate root and ground of æsthetic pleasure ; and therefore when we are asked whether Aristotle recognised æsthetic as apart from real interest (either moral or hedonistic) we are thrown into perplexity. Emotional utterance, rational content, a free dealing with reality, all these he recognises as elements of art. But instead of combining them as " the emotional utterance of rational content in forms freely drawn from reality," he inclines to separate them as " the pleasure of utterance," " the formal beauty of ideal content," " the moral emendation of reality," so that perhaps we ought to reply that he recognises

all the elements of æsthetic interest, but that he tends to
speak of them in terms that indicate their origin in common
reality rather than their transfiguration in artistic enjoyment.
But at any rate the stress laid on the enjoyment of expression
and self-utterance, although in contents and emotions which
as such are painful, is a step substantially incompatible with
the relation of allegiance to given reality, and has kinship
with the modern idea of sport or simulated action as the discharge of superfluous vitality, as well as with the conception
of expression for expression's sake.

Concrete   γ We have seen that with Aristotle the stan-
Criticism.   dard of commonplace reality began to yield before
the observed necessities of idealisation, and that fine art in
its highest form was pronounced by him to centre in emotional
self-utterance. We are now to ask, in terms of our third
antithesis, how far in detail his critical insight broke down
the formal abstractness of Greek æsthetic, and took the
shape of analytic inquiry into concrete expressiveness and
characterisation.

History and   i. Aristotle even loses, as compared with Plato,
Elements   something of that kind of concreteness which arises
of Drama.   from a various object matter. He left, it would
appear, no æsthetic recognition of architecture and the minor
crafts, while even sculpture and painting, though referred to in
the discussion of particular problems, are held to be on a lower
level of expressive capacity than music and poetry. It is only
in virtue of such references, and of his retention of the common name "mimetic" for fine art in general, that we are
entitled to draw conclusions from his treatment of music and
poetry to anything like a general æsthetic theory.

But yet the first attempt to analyse the structure and evolution of a form of art, and to deduce its origin from fundamental tendencies in human nature, marks an epoch in æsthetic
reflection, which has always been most vital when most historical. For history cannot but involve some recognition that what
men do expresses what they are, and the most elementary
analysis of structure pioneers a way by which reflection can
gain access to its object.

That "imitation"[1] or representation is an innate tendency
in man ; that from the first it has taken in poetry two co-

---

[1] *Poetic*, 4.

ordinate forms, so that the *Iliad* or *Odyssey* is a forerunner of tragedy just as the *Margites* of comedy ; that both species of drama developed through many changes out of performances in which poet and actor were one, but that comedy was later than tragedy in arriving at completion, and that the iambic metre was adopted in the course of this development from the very nature of the case, being nearest of all metres to common speech ; this, - with the well-known details as to the number of the actors, and with the opinion that tragedy had at length reached a final because adequate form, is the substance of Aristotle's brief history of the drama.

Nature, he says, was its cause, through the mimetic impulse ; and the diverging tendencies of man's disposition, towards the noble and the ignoble respectively, have been its guides.

Even from this imperfect summary the reader will feel that the great naturalist breathes vitality into his subject, and has grasped the unity of human nature in its most splendid self-manifestations.

The importance of the function which he assigned to artistic imagination, though he acknowledged no such faculty by name, may be illustrated by the technical terms employed by him in the analysis of tragedy. It is not necessary to suppose that they were all originated by himself.

Omitting the quantitative division of tragedy into Prologue, Parodos, etc., although even these show the sense of a necessary order in the work of art, we should notice the six [1] qualitative elements, three forming the object represented, *viz.* fable or plot, character or moral temperament, intellectual reflection ; two constituting the means of representation, *viz.* linguistic expression and music ; and one being the mode of representation, *viz.* the *mise-en-scène,* including to a Greek the masks of the performers.

Not all of these elements need special remark. The "Fable," or "Composition of the incidents," is the life of the play, and the great test of the poet.[2] All the above-mentioned postulates of *unity* refer to it. It may be "simple" or "complex," and in every case contains a transition from happiness to misfortune, or the reverse, and, if "complex," will contain, as the instruments of this transition, "surprising reversals" or "recognitions." The fable will also contain

---

[1] *Poet.*, 6, 7.   [2] Cf. *Phædo*, 61 B ; *ap.* Bernays, p. 186.

the "Pathos," which is "a disastrous or painful incident."
The external reference of "pathos" as here first mentioned
is worth noticing.

The construction of the fable and its parts is further
analysed with a view to securing its conformity to the conditions of tragic emotion. The nature and content assigned
to such emotion in Aristotle's theory has already been discussed. Human life was to be the interest ; but what human
life we find a more difficult question.

Every tragedy, finally, may be divided into a "knot" or
entanglement (which might also be called the plot, if that
term is not appropriated to the "fable" or argument), and
a *dénoûment* or solution.

It will at once be seen how many ideal requirements are
imposed by this analysis on the art which "imitates" reality
—how it is directed to the task of concentrating the confused
panorama of life into a single, coherent, striking, and natural
picture. It is worth observing, as a touch of distinctness in
advance of Plato, that the *mise-en-scène* is dismissed as not
belonging to the poet's art, though fascinating in itself.

It is further worth pointing out that Aristotle is disposed
in several ways to defend poetic licence against a too literal
criticism, observing that interpretation must recognise a certain
play of language,[1] that what is an error judged by a special
science is not, unless wanton, necessarily an error judged by
poetic purpose, and that an action in a play must be criticised
according to fitness as well as according to merit.

Plot and Char-
acter-drawing. ii. I have reserved for discussion by itself a
very important relation between two of the six
"elements" of tragedy. What place does character-drawing,
or characterisation, hold with reference to plot ?

I start, as in other cases, with the rough and ready notion
of Aristotle's meaning, which we obtain by simply accepting
current renderings as literal. In the present case I may state
it by a quotation from Mr. Mahaffy :[2]

"Of these various elements [the six above-mentioned],
Aristotle justly considers the plot as by far the most important, observing that recent tragedians had succeeded, by
paying attention to this point, without any character-drawing"
[ēthos]. The term "ēthos," which I have rendered above

[1] *Poet.*, 25. [2] *History of Greek Literature*, vol. ii. p. 409.

by "moral temperament," is here translated "character" in the sense apparently in which character is understood to-day to be the object of artistic portraiture in Shakespeare or Thackeray.

The view thus ascribed to Aristotle is in startling antagonism with our ideas. Pure plot-interest without character is for us on a level with the interest of a puzzle and its answer, and therefore in art, with the interest of a story whose characters are mere ciphers manœuvred through strange and intricate combinations. True, we demand a well-constructed plot ; but we think no art worthy of the name in which the action fails to issue necessarily from human character. Yet Aristotle's language sounds strong in the opposite sense. I reproduce the whole passage on which our judgment must mainly depend, retaining the actual word "ēthos" in place of any rendering. I believe that I am right in saying that the normal *application* of ēthos in Plato and Aristotle is to types of character *as described by a single term with a moral connotation*, such as "courage," "temperance," "gentleness," and their opposites.

After enumerating the six qualitative elements of tragedy, Aristotle continues : [1]

" The most important of these elements is the composition of the incidents [the plot or fable]. For tragedy is a representation [imitation] not of men and women, but of action and life. Now good and ill fortune attend upon action, and man's purpose is always some kind of activity, not a quality ; but what ēthos determines are the qualities of persons, while action makes them happy or unfortunate. And so poets do not represent persons acting in order to display their ēthos, but they take it in as an accessory to action. Thus the incidents and the fable are the purpose of tragedy ; and in everything the purpose is the most important. Moreover there cannot be a tragedy without action, but there can be without ēthos ; most of the later tragedies are without it, and among poets in general it is rare. For they are like Zeuxis compared with Polygnotus among painters : Polygnotus is a good painter of ēthos, while the art of Zeuxis indicates nothing of the kind. [Could Aristotle mean that Zeuxis was unable to paint characteristic likenesses ?] Again, if you string together speeches

that have ēthos,[1] and are excellent in expression and reflections, yet you will not attain the aim of tragedy nearly so well
as with a play inferior in these respects, but having a fable (or
plot) and composition of incidents.   It is just as in painting ;
to put on the most beautiful colours at random would not produce as much pleasure as to draw a portrait in chalk.   Nay,
more ; the most fascinating elements of tragedy, the surprises
and recognitions, belong to the fable.   And it is a further proof
of our view, that beginners in poetry attain completeness in
expression and ēthē [plural of ēthos], before they are capable
of composing the march of incidents ; almost all the earliest
poets are instances of this.   So the fable is the mainspring
and, so to say, the life of the tragedy, and the ēthē are
secondary; for the tragedy is a representation of an action and
of agents only for the sake of the action."   With this should
be compared the passage translated in chapter iii.[2]

It will be observed that if the term ēthos here corresponds
to character or character-drawing in the modern sense, it results that in the comparison with painting characterisation is
contrasted with portraiture and assimilated to non-pictorial
colour effect; which latter, however, must rather be an extreme
simile to show how far removed this ēthos is from what we
call character.   For according to the *Problemata* mere colour as
such has no expressive capacity, not even for mood or temper
(ēthos), much less, therefore, I presume for individual
character.

Further, " ēthos " determines " of what sort "[3] a person is ;
and this " sort " means primarily whether he is good or bad.[4]
Speeches which have no ēthos are such as display no relation
positive or negative to a purpose ;[5] it is the kind of purpose,
i.e. primarily, whether it is good or bad, that marks the ēthos
of the speaker.   Again, the idea of stringing together " ethical "
speeches is clearly I think a reminiscence of Plato's distinction
between emotional harangues, which are beginners' work,[6]
and composition, which is the test of the master.   The fact
that " intellectual reflections " are an element distinct from
ēthos testifies to the same thing, for in every true character-
portrait the vein of intellect is included.

Therefore it appears to me that ēthos in Aristotle's æsthetic

---

[1] Cf. *Phædrus*, 268.   [2] p. 20, sup.   [3] *Poet.*, ib.
[4] Quot. above, chap. iii. p. 20.   [5] *Poet.* ib.   [6] *Phædrus*, 268.

meant not individual character, the concrete living creation at once mysterious and intelligible, that we look for in modern art, but something more typical and generic, not without a moral reference, as we say "good" or "bad" character. And so if we look at what is demanded of ēthos in tragedy,[1] we find four requirements : *first*, it must be good ; then appropriate to the person ; then natural ; then even or consistent ; and if the person is to be of inconsistent temper, then consistently inconsistent. No doubt these latter requirements show some awakening to the importance of characterisation ; but it is to be noted that they are all secondary to goodness. The possibility that this demand for goodness may be a confused attempt to require that tolerableness or beauty which splendid characterisation can bestow on the worst character, does not entitle us to interpret Aristotle's postulate in a way which he nowhere suggests.

Thus it occurs to us that the antithesis which seems indicated by a literal rendering of Aristotle, may not be that which he had in mind. He may not have been contrasting the plot, as a mere puzzle and solution, with the portrayal of individual human character, but he may rather have intended to oppose the man as revealed in action, or in speech which contributes to advance the march of incident, to monologue or conversation simply intended to emphasize this or that type of disposition in the interlocutors. The illustration from painting confirms this suggestion. The plot seems to be compared to a portrait, not indeed of persons as such, but, we must suppose, of action and life ; that is, we may venture to suggest, of persons in action according to the necessities of their character. A mere plot-puzzle is not a portrait of life. And yet the stress laid by Aristotle upon the incidents of good and ill fortune ought perhaps to make us feel that the child-like interest in the mere event, the triumph or failure of a human being, not because he has great character, but because our attention is drawn to him, may have been more natural to the Greek than to us.

If, however, we were to press home the suggestion which has forced itself upon us, we should find that instead of the most infantile of all views of the drama we were attributing to Aristotle the most profound. We should no longer imagine

---

[1] *Poetic*, 15.

that Aristotle rated ingenious plot-construction first (for apart from character it could not be more than ingenious), and held the revelation of the mind and heart to be secondary and superfluous ; we should understand him to be contrasting the revelation of human lives in their necessary movement and collision, produced by character in action, with moralising argument or with the mere display of sentiment.

The tragedians after Euripides are to us mere names ; and whether Euripides himself, who died before Sophocles, was to Aristotle an instance of ancient or modern style, is hard to conjecture. I do not think it possible to elucidate the problem before us by reference to literary history. It could hardly be suggested that the tendency to characterisation diminished in the later tragedians, although some among the creations of Æschylus have in this respect never been surpassed. But it may well have been the case that such a play as the *Prometheus Bound*, depending for its attraction wholly on a picture of superhuman courage and endurance, and hardly possessing any element of a plot, did not seem to the æsthetic philosopher to be in the strictest sense a drama. I suggest this as an example of a play that has ēthos, and has not dramatic composition. It has been doubted whether our great modern dramatic analyst has displayed genuine capacity to construct a play that will march. If this doubt is justified, Browning may be cited as an illustration of the antithesis between stringing together monologues that display the good and bad in character, and composing a dramatic action.

I believe, however, that neither of the conceptions which I have thus contrasted would express Aristotle's exact position, which lies somewhere between them. He must, we are driven to conclude, have accepted that element of character which is the moving spring of plot as a part of the human situation and conditions to be portrayed. But his failing to insist upon this element in its subjective aspect shows that his point of view was still on the whole Hellenic, and was more simple and more external than that which takes the human mind to be the essence in all drama. And we still are at one with him in holding the mere exhibition of temperament in its moral aspects, when not genuinely elicited by the necessities of the story, to be dramatically superfluous.

Thus we cannot allege that Aristotle explicitly breaks the fetters of Greek æsthetic, by throwing his interest into the free

representation of spiritual powers as embodied in great characters and their collision. His chief care is for organic unity
and dramatic composition. Only as he presses this unity into
detail after detail, it becomes more and more concrete and
pregnant ; and we almost incline to believe that in substance,
though certainly not in form, he identifies the object of artistic
representation not with the common shows of life, but with
spiritual forces in their deepest reality.

It has been maintained that throughout his æsthetic
discussion Aristotle is covertly criticising Plato.[1] This
is a needlessly disagreeable way of observing that the
later writer's mind is wholly permeated with ideas drawn
from the earlier. It is by no single origination that the
advance was made which I have endeavoured to depict.
It consisted, first, in Aristotle's unhesitating recognition of a
supreme value in the whole sphere of beauty—an attitude
natural to the successor who inherits at one blow the conceptions which their author elaborated gradually and without
realising their entire significance—and secondly, in the definite
ascription of important functions and properties to representative art all along the boundary-line where it faces commonplace reality. Thus throughout the three antitheses by which
I have attempted to gauge the flowing tide of Greek æsthetic
speculation, the reality of common experience shows in Aristotle a tendency to lose its controlling position ; for, metaphysically, art, and we must suppose all formal beauty in its
degree, is credited with the power to represent what is unseen,
and the deeper truth ; ethically, the interest of beauty is at
least not wholly identified either with moral or again with
sensuous aims ; and æsthetically there is revealed in the beautiful, under pressure of an appreciative analysis, an ideal unity
of structure such as to display the events of life in their essential connection, which is in some degree acknowledged to
have its roots in human character.

But, on the other hand, not only does Aristotle retain the
technical term " imitative," as the differentia of the art that
realises beauty, qualifying it by no scientific expression that
recognises the idealisation which in practice he admits, but,
what is more important, he has no distinct answer to the question what principle prescribes the direction which this idealisa-

[1] Schasler, i. 149–153.

tion is to take. To say "the direction of beauty" is tautology; to say "the direction of symmetry and unity" is
dangerously formal and empty; to say "the direction of
morality" is simply false. All these directions are hinted at
by him, and no deeper theory is suggested? Therefore we
cannot pronounce that he abandoned the essential limitations
of Hellenic theory concerning the beautiful.

a (p. 58). The rendering in the text is erroneous; it should run "the cause of this again
is, that not only"——. The second cause of poetry is not the love of learning but the
instinct for rhythm, mentioned by Aristotle in a later paragraph. My observations on the
significance of this love of learning must now be held to refer to the deeper meaning which
Aristotle sees in man's enjoyment of imitations.

b (p. 59). On this paragraph cf. Butcher, *Aristotle's Theory of Art*, 149–50.

c (p. 61). A reader might be puzzled by this discussion compared with Butcher, *op. cit.*,
p. 124, where symbolism is sharply denied to Aristotle. The discrepancy is only verbal.
Professor Butcher is speaking in Aristotle's language, while I am following modern usage.
And the two, as Professor Butcher in part explains on pp. 128–9, are almost exactly
opposed; see p. 60 of this work. For Aristotle, the symbol is less than a "likeness"; for
the modern it is more.

d (p. 61). I hope that, as is pretty certain, Professor Butcher is right and I am wrong on
this point. Aristotle's *Theory of Art*, p. 152: "The artist in his mimic world carries forward this movement (of organic nature toward, 'the better')" to a more perfect completion."

e (p. 62). See chap. iii. notes *c* and *d* (p. 42).

f (p. 74). See Butcher, *op. cit.*, 330 ff. with the reff. to Mr. R. P. Hardie's article in *Mind*,
vol. iv. no. 15. I think I may say that Professor Butcher and Mr. Hardie endorse my
conclusion on the whole matter of plot in relation to character, though both of them are
against me on the point of regarding ἦθος as "typical and generic." My term was perhaps
ill chosen. But, following Mr. Hardie's view that ἦθος has to mean expression of character
in speech, as well as character, I do still think that Aristotle lays a double requirement on
ἦθος, and not merely the natural one that it shall be human and correlative to πρᾶξις. I
think he wants it to be emphasized as "good." All naïve criticism does this, and Aristotle
is partly naïve. ἦθος to him oscillates mainly between the poles of good and bad. It does
not equally accent the whole capacity of human nature.

g (p. 76). See note *d* above and Butcher's chapter on "Imitation as an Æsthetic Term."
The question is what sort of idealization or expression of the universal is suggested by
Aristotle's theory. I adhere on the whole to the view of the text, while admitting that
Aristotle starts along a road where it is difficult precisely to measure his advance.

CHAPTER V.

ALEXANDRIAN AND GRECO-ROMAN CULTURE TO THE REIGN OF CONSTANTINE THE GREAT.

Character of the Period. IN the hundred and fifty years that ended with the death of Aristotle there had lived and worked in the city of Athens, containing a population about equal to that of Glasgow, three of the greatest philosophers, four of the greatest poets, and more than one of the greatest formative artists, that the world has ever seen. If we further represent to ourselves the speculative, poetic, and plastic activity of Hellas in general throughout or before the same period, taking as a background to the whole picture the *Iliad* and *Odyssey*, which imply at least two poets of the very highest rank, we shall be in some degree prepared to estimate the change that came over the civilized world during the fourth century before Christ. It is only the simple truth if we say that no speculative thinker of at all the same calibre as Aristotle existed again before the time of Descartes, no formative artist *singly* [1] on a level with Praxiteles before the time of Giotto, no poet having the strictly poetic greatness of the Athenian dramatists before the time of Dante. And if we were resolved to take account of nothing but the supreme moments of the æsthetic consciousness, and the clearest crystallizations of the thought that reflects upon it, we should at this point be forced to the *salto mortale* of 1,600 years to Dante, or 2,000 to Burke or Lessing. But such a procedure could only be justified if it were the fact, or if it were conceivable that after this immense interval, which would then be inexplicable, the thread of reflection and production had been taken up again from the point at which it was dropped.

Now the fact is, on the contrary, that in this interval the æsthetic consciousness had traversed an enormous distance

---

[1] The emphasis to be laid below on mediæval architecture will explain this reservation.

from its Hellenic origin, partly as latent in the general movement of mind and history, but partly also in its own shape as
art and literature and critical or speculative reflection upon
beauty.

We must therefore attempt in this and the following chapter
to set up landmarks, however few and distant from each other,
by which the appreciation of the beautiful may be followed
through the complex movement which carried the old world
forward into the new.

For six centuries at least after the death of Alexander the
civilization which had its roots in Hellas was the civilization of
the world. If we ask at what date it ceased to be so, a
definite reply cannot be given. New principles emerge in
history and obtain supremacy, gradually, and not at one blow.
Before Justinian closed the schools of Athens in 529 A.D., the
art of the new world had been growing for at least two hundred years, and had already attained its first climax in the
Church of the Heavenly Wisdom at Constantinople. Nor did
Proclus in the fifth century carry the philosophic tradition of
a thousand years far beyond the point to which Plotinus had
brought it in the third.

I shall therefore limit myself in the present chapter to the
period between the death of Alexander in 323 B.C. and the
inauguration of Constantinople as the seat of government for
the Roman empire in 330 A.D. It has been well observed
that the earliest known building which displays the principle
of modern architecture undisguised by traditional Hellenic
forms—the palace of Diocletian at Spalato—was erected [1]
within a few years of the latter all-important change. And
the historian of philosophy may add, that Plotinus, who died
in the latter half of the third century A.D., had, as the last great
Hellenic thinker, broken the bonds of ancient theory concerning the beautiful, while the later writer Augustine, at the
close of the fourth, was to announce the distinctively modern
principle of a certainty implied in intellectual doubt. [2] And
although the Greek poetry of the Anthology revealed a last
after-prime of classical genius in the reign of Justinian, and

---

[1] In 313 A.D. See William Morris, *Lecture on the History of Pattern-
Designing*, in a volume of lectures by himself, Mr. Poynter and others
Published by Macmillan, 1882.
[2] Augustine, *de Trinitate*, x. 14. See Rigg, *Pico d. Mirandola*, Introd.

lived, or at least existed until the dawn of the Renaissance, yet the true prime of this minor poetic art had passed away with Meleager before the Christian era.

We are accustomed to regard the Alexandrian and Greco-Roman ages as a time of decadence in culture. They form about one-half of that mysterious transition during which the whole of Europe produced no work of individual genius that could compare with those which had been common things throughout the creative period in Athens and in Ionia. Our judgment to this effect has acquired peculiar associations from the portrayal of a world lying in wickedness and impotent for intellectual or moral good, which Christian advocates have impressed upon the popular mind. But in the first place, those who take a natural view of history must assume that every apparent decadence has operative within it the causes which lead to the subsequent advance—in so far as that advance is not due to nations outside the range of the decadence. And in the second place, as soon as we consider with impartial attention the phenomena of Alexandrian and Greco-Roman art and letters, we see that we have before us a movement of extraordinary width and variety, which at every turn reveals new elements of feeling and a new spirit akin to modern humanism.

To define the tendencies of this period, in contrast, for instance, with those of the Periclean age of Athens, is a task which strongly impresses us with the defects of abstract language. We had a foretaste of the same difficulty in attempting to explain what Aristotle meant by ēthos in poetic art as indicating a quality in which the more recent writers were deficient. The antithesis between Ethos and Pathos, which is currently read into these observations of Aristotle, is hardly justified by his language. But assuming that it fairly represents what is implied in his expressions, it still remains very hard to interpret. The portrayal of "character" belongs in one sense more to Æschylus than to Menander, in another sense to Menander more than to Æschylus; and if "Pathos" is equivalent to "a sensation" in the modern literary meaning of the term, and it is much nearer to this than to what we call pathos—it is hard to imagine that the later drama had more of it than the Agamemnon or the Œdipus King.

And thus again if we try to lay down that culture in the

period now before us is rather "subjective," and in the earlier time of a more "objective" cast, we are met by the apparent contradiction that in the later time philosophy becomes in great part less speculative and more inclined to physical conceptions, poetry is more devoted to natural beauty and to the presentation of daily life, formative art takes among other directions that of landscape, of portraiture, of anatomical study, while literary criticism develops a sense of history and an elaborate discrimination of individual styles.

Or if we attempt to apply the antithesis of social and individual interest, and to treat the peculiarities of the later period as depending upon the self-concentration of the individual's powers in his own life instead of their devotion to a community, we are again face to face with the paradox that in the world of art and letters we meet with no such commanding individualities in the later age as in the earlier, while we everywhere find evidences in it of a growing sensitiveness, unknown before, to the idea of humanity as a whole.

Thus it might seem that the application of the above antitheses might just as well be reversed. Is it possible, then, at all to describe in general language that distinction between the two periods which we can very readily feel?

The fact is that we are here dealing on a small scale with the contrast between the antique and the modern spirit. And the reason why no simple antithesis appears to meet the case is that whereas the antique spirit is single, the modern is divided. Tested, therefore, by the extreme of any abstract tendency, the modern spirit overpasses the antique; only the completeness and thoroughness, whether intellectual and imaginative or political and social, that marks the highest perfection of genius as of life, is for this very reason difficult of attainment in a "modern" period, and was not in fact attained during the six centuries of transition which we are now preparing to consider. Thus we can understand how the culture of the "decadence" was at once more "objective" and more "subjective," more individualistic yet more alive to humanity as a whole, more ascetic and yet more romantic, than that of the preceding age.

It will be worth while to adduce in a brief summary the principal aspects of this many-sided movement, rather in order to recall to the reader what he already knows, with a view to a certain interpretation, than with the idea of adequately describing a huge complex of phenomena which the meanest of text-books would not attempt to deal with in the space at my command.

We will speak first of the tone and temper of life evinced by the philosophies of the time, which must be treated for this purpose as mere data in moral and intellectual history, and of the actual sense of beauty revealed in the art and letters of the so-called decadence. And, secondly, we will bring down the history of æsthetic criticism and speculation, if our fragmentary treatment of this period deserves the name of history, to the close of origin il Greek speculation in Plotinus.

General Philo- 1. The extreme tendencies which have been sophy and Art. alluded to sometimes displayed themselves—as extremes will meet—within a single group of productions or of opinions; but as a rule were dispersed among different schools of thought or different modes of art.

Philosophy. *a.* It would be unfair to say of Plato and Aristotle, and notoriously untrue to say of Socrates, that their philosophy was not essentially concerned with practice. Yet even for Socrates, and still more for his great successors, practice was bound up with social devotion, with civic solidarity, and with a positive faith in reason. But when Hellenic city-politics had lost their importance, and the organic philosophy of Hellas had broken up like the empire of Alexander, a new temper supervened in which, it may be observed in passing, some clues of thought were picked up again which had been thrust aside for the moment by the centralized[1] speculation of Imperial Athens. The Heraclitean and the Cynic found a new development in the Stoic, the Atomist and the Cyrenaic in the follower of Epicurus, the Eleatic, and the Megarian, and in some degree Socrates himself, in the negative speculation and practical interest of the earlier Scepticism.

In the new political conditions all correspondence between the outer and the inner reason, between social organization and the social will, was for the time destroyed. And thus the individual man was thrown back upon himself; upon his private needs and interests on the one hand, and, on the

[1] Cf. Mr. Mackail's remarks. *Greek Anthology*, p. 289, on the interruption of epigrammatic production during the bloom of Periclean Athens. See below, p. 86.

G

other hand, upon his non-political relations with friends or
with humanity.   The new recognition of these latter forms
of fraternity is a typical example of the modern breadth and
audacity with which sentiments and ideas were now pushed
to their extremes.

But such general sentiments of community were not then,
and probably never can be, enough to absorb and direct a
life's energies.   Therefore the problem of practice emerged
in a new perspective and proportion.   The question is no
longer " What great end can be attained in a world which
corresponds to the needs of the rational will?" but, " How can
the individual live decently and not unhappily in a world
which is indifferent and may be hostile ? "   In moments of
despair Plato [1] himself anticipates this inquiry, the theoretical
relations of which are at once evident when we observe that
the founders of Scepticism, of Stoicism, and of Epicureanism
were all living at the same time towards the close of the
fourth century before Christ, and that in popularity and influence, the two latter distinctively ethical schools completely
dwarfed the critical and positivist successors of Plato and
Aristotle, and assumed the magnitude and importance of
religious persuasions not co-extensive with any political or
tribal group—the first considerable phenomena of the kind
known to the Western world.

By the side of this new personal ethic, which the Stoic
based on the feeling of reasonableness, and the Epicurean on
reasonableness of feeling, there was both in these and other
schools a positive and naturalistic tendency of reflection.
Theophrastus in the chair of Aristotle treated largely
of plants and metals ; and, also, following a descriptive tendency already apparent in the Nicomachean Ethics, wrote
on morals in such a way that his account of "character" was
extracted and preserved for its own sake.   Strato, again, the
successor of Theophrastus, substituted the conception of a
blind nature for that of God, and he all but anticipated [2] the
famous phrase of Laplace : " Je n'avais pas besoin de cette
hypothèse-la."

The same is true of Epicurus, and notably of his great

---

[1] E.g. *Republic*, 426.
[2] Cic. Acad. pr. ii. 38.   *Negat (Strato) opera Deorum se uti ad fabricandum
mundum.*

follower Lucretius. Besides their persistent effort to reduce everything to matter and motion, the Epicureans seem to have made "the first attempt to write the natural history of civilisation,"[1] and especially with reference to the origin of language they introduced conceptions which are of considerable interest to-day. Yet while thus helping to render the world intelligible, they rejected the notion which the Stoics accepted of an immanent plan or design ; and we shall have to return below to their reflection on art and beauty, which for this reason, though by no means valueless, necessarily ignored the æsthetic problem as we conceive it. A physical theory traceable to Heraclitus was developed by the Stoics, as that traceable to the Atomist was by Epicurus.

But once more, in the conflict of positivist and of ethical abstractions with the scepticism that was their counter-part, we meet with a growth of technical terms and distinctions that bear a modern aspect, and have in fact descended through later writers to modern times, in which they have hitherto been far more familiar than the less formal expressions of the older classical philosophy.[2] This growth of technical terms is characteristic of the time, and extended, as we shall find, to æsthetic science.

Thus the actual names "Sceptic,"[3] "Dogmatist,"[3] and " Empiric," begin in this period to be bandied about, as they are to-day. The Stoics desire to establish a "criterion"[3] of truth ; an attempt which is an unfailing sign of logic deteriorating into formalism. The term occurs indeed in Plato,[4] but in a passing expression which alludes not to a test or touchstone of truth, but simply to the faculty or faculties, not restricted to either sense or reason, by which it is apprehended.

And because of this same growing sense of division between the mind and the world, we now find germs of the Conceptualist terminology which has descended through Latin writers to our own mental science. Terms which indicate a

---

[1] Prof. Wallace's *Epicureanism*, p. 117 note. Of course there is much in Plato and Aristotle to suggest problems of this nature.

[2] We inherit many terms of great importance from Plato and Aristotle, but those which are here referred to are a larger and later crop of peculiarly modern import.

[3] Σκεπτικός, Δογματικός, ἐμπειρικός, κριτήριον.

[4] *Rep.*, 582 A.

complete or anticipatory seizing[1] or comprehension by the
mind, or again an inward thought or notion[1] defined as a
mental presentation and nothing more, take the place of the
" form "[2] or " racial group,"[2] which were the first simple
designations for facts understood in their order and essence,
and not yet distinctly contrasted as thoughts with things.
The famous comparison of the mind at birth to a sheet of
paper prepared for writing on comes to us through the
Stoics;[3] and the whole simile from which such current
phrases as "mental impression" are derived, although
originating in a carefully worded illustration employed by
Aristotle,[4] received the rough mechanical form which it now
bears from the Stoics as interpreted by Cicero. The
Latinised terms, which may be closely rendered as " Impulsion
brought to bear from outside," "assent," "comprehensible,"
"comprehension," " impressing notions in the mind," "a
plain judgment (*declaratio*, Greek ἐνάργεια) as to the things
which are seen " (contrasted with a visual sensation attended
by no such judgment)—all these modern-sounding phrases
occur in a single passage in which Cicero is explaining the
Stoic theory of sense-perception.[5] A similar relation of
impact between mind and objects was assumed by the
Epicureans, whose technical terms in mental science were
in part the same as those of the Stoics.

It may be added that many of the traditional names for
grammatical cases and forms of verbs descend to us from Stoic
investigations.

And by the side of these philosophies, which might be
called rationalistic as opposed to mysticism, though not as
opposed to sensationalism, the Pythagorean vein of speculation maintained itself, and was reinforced after the Christian
era by Gnosticism and Neo-Platonism, which almost suc-

---

[1] πρόληψις, κατάληψις, ἔννοια, ἐννόημα, φάντασμα διανοίας, *Diog. L.* in R. and
Pr., 403.

[2] ἰδέα, εἶδος, γένος.

[3] χαρτίον ἐνεργὸν εἰς ἀπογραφήν. *Plut. de Plac. Ph.*, 4, 11, R. and Pr., 339.
If, as I suppose, the phrase " tabula rasa " represents this expression, then the
qualification " rasa " does not lay stress so much on the blankness of the
paper, as on its state of preparedness to receive impressions—a *nuance* which
has some speculative importance.

[4] *De Anima*, 424 a, 18.

[5] Cic. Acad. Post., i. 11. R. and Pr., 398.

ceeded in grasping the fundamental idea of evolution ; *viz.* that the derivative is not necessarily the inferior.

If now we return to our former attempts at definition, and repeat what is certainly true in a philosophical sense, that the culture of this age is distinguished from that which preceded it by subjectivity and individualism, we must understand that we are speaking of a complex modern subjectivity, and a relative modern individualism. It is a subjectivity which in its sceptical divorce from metaphysic throws itself into materialistic science as one complement, if it falls into mystical intuitionism as another ; it is an individualism which separates itself from the narrow selfishness of the tribe or city no less than from its limited self-sacrifice, and in busying itself with the problems of reasonable pleasure is never far from the aspirations of religious asceticism.

In the necessary progress of such a culture, one feature is most remarkable and most important for our present purpose. This is the extraordinary combination of subtlety and pedantry, of a technical language extended by widening experience and an unspeculative petrifaction of the technical terms themselves, which first delights us at the advance of analysis, and then jars us by its superficiality. Ideas drawn from the great masters of philosophy become the catchwords of sectarian dogma or of rhetorical criticism ; but in this very loss of speculative fluidity they form a centre for the attachment of growing experience and deepening sentiment. Such an idea, for example, is the Stoics' " Nature," which had for them actually less ordered metaphysical content than for Aristotle ; but yet as the banner of a creed and the symbol of a juristic ideal became a rallying point for the new aspirations evoked by the extension of the civilised world. We shall find this curious contrast throughout the time we are dealing with. Observation, expressiveness, sentiment, and even partial theory, advance by the inertia of motion ; in an active and cultured society every writer refines somewhat upon the suggestions of his predecessors, and brings his own insight and conviction to bear upon the material laid before him. Obvious criticisms are propounded, meet their obvious refutation, and are re-asserted less crudely than before ; so that without leaps and bounds the literary world moves gradually onwards ; and even in the absence of that profounder criticism which belongs only to ages of organic

speculation, reason slowly perfects its language, becomes
familiar with important distinctions, and encounters life with
a more many-sided appreciation.

Poetry.   β. How much was achieved in the period of
which we speak rather by the dispersive pressure
of humane culture than by depth of inspiration is especially
apparent in poetic art.

New and Latin   i. The New Comedy of Athens, whose chief
Comedy.   representative Menander is said to have been in
youth a friend of Epicurus, must have presented a very striking embodiment of the complex changes which have been
indicated. Bringing it together, as for our very general purpose we fairly may, with the comedy of Plautus and Terence
a century later, from which alone we substantially know its
nature, we cannot but recognise in it a kinship to our modern
feeling which is wanting in Aristophanes, and even, perhaps,
in the great Attic tragedians.

The removal of the chorus which had unquestionably been
a hindrance to realistic dramatisation, and the division into
Acts and Scenes [1] which formed an unobtrusive framework to
the play, and greatly facilitated the comprehension of an intricate plot, agreed well with the new matter and tone of
comedy as an unpretending but ingenious representation of
common life.

In spite of the conventionality of their characters, the plays
of Plautus and Terence speak to us with the same simple
human voice as *Tom Jones* or *Vanity Fair* while the splendid
genius of Aristophanes has left us hardly a touch of family
incident or of homely pathos, except where, in a literary
satire, he drops a word of regret for a good poet mourned
by his friends. A family drama of every-day events—and
such, however incomplete in its portraiture, the new comedy
certainly was—touched a chord which no Greek poet had
sounded, except the authors of the *Iliad* and *Odyssey* before
the peculiar development of Athenian genius, and Euripides
as it drew to a close. The absolute distinction between comic
and tragic interest begins to fade when we have in comedy a
story of actual suffering seriously faced, in which the facile
reconciliations that seem incompatible with earnestness are

---

[1] Due, it seems to be believed, to the Latin poets.

not completely carried out.[1] It is not merely that the love
intrigue or love romance (not always irregular), and the human
nature of common men and women are subjects akin to those
of modern literature, but that in the tone and treatment we no
longer feel that hardness of naive egoism with which the Greek
of the Ajax or Ion, the " Knights " or the " Clouds," grasped
at his own advantage and repelled every interloper as an
enemy, excepting when one of two or three great interests
demanded the devotion which he reserved for them alone.
Mere unmotived kindness has become a greater force. The
loyalty of the adventurous slave to his master is not wholly
selfish, and sometimes amounts to nobility. And though this is
a motive known to classical tragedy—hardly to Aristophanic
comedy—yet its central place in art belongs to a time in which
the servile virtues were beginning to receive the recognition
which Christianity finally awarded them, and in which Terence,
a Carthaginian slave, could be a leading man of letters at
Rome, as Zeno, a Phœnician stranger, had founded the influential Stoic school at Athens.

Thus, without any great creative impulse, the dramatic
" imitation of life " in the new comedy brings into the light a
fresh region of experience, and, as it happens, one of undying
interest for civilized men. And in so doing art enriches itself with a larger insight into the beauty and goodness of
common things, and with more subtle capacities of imitative
presentation, thus gradually paving the way both for a wider
range of beauty and for a profounder theory of artistic utterance. It was a great thing for Terence to speak the word,
that to a human being nothing human can be indifferent.

The Idyll. ii. And besides the beginning of humane comedy,
the generation of Epicurus witnessed the birth of
pastoral poetry. Nothing could be more profoundly suggestive
than this of the change which was coming over the world. That
conscious self-assertion of individual feeling which has been
called sentimental or romantic finds expression, still simple
and healthy, in the Theocritean Idyll. When poetic fancy is
coloured at once by the yearning of passion, the charms of the
country, the sense of a beauty in art and song, and the humours

---

[1] So the Captivi, which is quite a serious drama of life. Aristotle's " No
one kills any one " (in comedy) is clearly contemptuous. Cf. close of *Much
Ado*, " Think not on him till to-morrow "

of a busy and splendid town, we shall not be far wrong in in-
ferring that man is seeking nature because he already feels
that he is parted from it. A contrast of this kind is implied
in all distinctions between the ancient and the modern spirit.
Theocritus, indeed, is but at the starting-point of the long and
eventful course which romanticism had before it. In him
there is no sense of unattainable depths and inexpressible
meanings ; there is merely the trace of a new sensitiveness[1]
in the imagination which indicates the germ of a new longing
in the heart. And so the fancy of Theocritus is not wholly
remote from life, and the songs which he ascribes to his
Sicilian peasants are such as they still sing. The romantic
Faust did not yet exist ; but the classical Helena was beginning to have strange dreams. Within a hundred years
after Theocritus the first true love romance of known literature was written in the *Argonautica* of Apollonius Rhodius.

The Anthology.   iii. And finally, beside the poetry of love, of art,
and of rustic nature, we find in the Greek culture of
this period the poetry of poetry. In the Garland or Anthology
(" flower-gathering ") of epigrams collected by Meleager just
before the Christian era, we have not only to note the beauty
of his own love verses, but to consider the significance of the
fact that such a gathering should be made at all, and prefaced
with the beautiful dedicatory poem in which the verses selected
are compared to various flowers. A subtle feeling for poetic
style, and more than that, something like a sense of historical
continuity, are implied in this first garland of the poets, the
earliest portion of that huge Greek Anthology which did not
receive its last addition till after the *Divina Commedia* had been
written.

Roman Poets.   iv. To treat the classical Italian poets, from
Lucretius to Juvenal, as merely the greatest
writers of a decadence is a course that can only be justified
by very carefully bearing in mind the peculiar purpose of our
treatment. We are less concerned with the magnitude than
with the specific quality of artistic achievement ; and while no
sane man will deny that Vergil and Lucretius were great poets,
yet most careful critics will admit that their strictly poetical
genius, although indispensable to their greatness, did not

---

[1] For a necessary warning against exaggerating the love and observation of
nature implied in pastoral poetry, see Mackail, *Anthology*, p. 57*a*

constitute its central core in the same sense as with Homer
or with Sophocles. Catullus, on the other hand, though a poet
through and through, may fairly be ranked as a minor poet,
not merely in the quantity of his work but in the limits of his
inspiration.

But considered as great men, endowed with poetic genius
and conscious of representing the very heart and system of
the civilised world, Vergil and Lucretius are examples of the
art of a decadence all the more startling because in their
powerful hands this art itself has greatness thrust upon it.

All the peculiarities which we have observed in the fading
genius of Greece are here revealed in their most emphatic
form.

First among these ranks a further phase of the influence
which we observed in the New Comedy, a prevailing moral
earnestness and sense of duty and of humanity. Strange
attributes, it will be said, by which to characterise a decadence
of culture! But as we have seen the reflective sentiment of
morality was especially characteristic of this age, in which the
individual was lonely in a crowd, and had to shape his life by
his own common sense. And the atmosphere of serious
purpose and goodwill which belongs to the Roman poets is a
strong instance of the power which the natural progress of
mankind possesses to place the lesser and later genius ethically in advance of the greater and earlier; while, in so far as
didactic moralising or critical theology intrude into art, we
have here exemplified that division of the mind against itself
which marks the comparatively modern spirit of the time
under discussion. Roman "urbanity"—the very word is significant—and Roman moralising satire, are not the natural
geniality of Homer or the semi-political orthodoxy of Aristophanes. They are, on the contrary, the product of reflection
and of a partly theoretical idea, and are thus analogous in
some degree to the ethical protest and sentiment of Euripides. But they are more tinged, than his, with worldly
wisdom, and arise not only out of a prolonged education
through popular philosophies, but out of a mature experience
of government and toleration among many creeds and civilisations.

And in this more humane atmosphere we are not surprised
to find that the beauty of domestic love and life was at last
fully revealed to poetic apprehension. Nothing, I believe,

had before been written like the "Torquatus, volo, par-
vulus,"[1] or the "Carmen Nuptiale"[2] of Catullus, since the
parting of Hector from Andromache and his child was described in the *Iliad*. And Ovid's *Heroidum Epistolæ*, though
no very forcible works of genius, breathe an atmosphere of
simple affection in which our modern sentiment at once feels
at home.

And although only Catullus, and not Horace or Ovid, can
be compared to Theocritus for freshness and reality of love-
romance, yet the immensely increased range and subtlety of
poetic expression in that province is a fact of the first importance for the history of art. Love, for the poet, is now in
some cases a matter of sentiment rather than passion, a
delicate and even playful feeling; sometimes, again, a pure
and elevated affection. What touch[6] of human interest the
Æneid can claim, it gains from the romance of Dido; while
the variations of mood in the Lesbia poems of Catullus, with
his description of Ariadne, taken together with the odes of
Horace, form a gamut of emotional expression almost comparable with that of Elizabethan song. From the lament
over Lesbia's sparrow—a lyric which goes, I should imagine,
directly to the heart of every nineteenth century reader—to
the praise of the lover without fear and without reproach,[3]
whom a pure affection preserves even from bodily peril, all
shades of romantic playfulness, irony, and seriousness are
now commanded by poetic art. And if the playfulness of
Horace appears to us, as indeed it is, a feeble thing contrasted
with the passion of Sappho, yet we must not forget that there
is something noble and civilised—something worthy of Shakespeare—in being able now and again to smile at the terrible
love-god. Art, as we know from Goethe, and have since
ascertained that we ought to have known from Aristotle, is
the great liberator.

---

[1] The whole verse runs :—

> "Torquatus, volo, parvulus
> Matris e gremio suæ
> Porrigens teneras manus
> Dulce rideat ad patrem
> Semihiante labello."

[2] Containing the well known passage, beginning, "Ut flos in septis secre-
tus nascitur hortis."
[3] The " Integer Vitæ " of Horace.

And at the extreme border of the art of passion, we find in the *Atys* what, as far as I know, is the first poetical study of the counter-frenzy. This partly "dramatic" lyric, for its horror and pathos, and its sense of correspondence between the moods of man and of nature, might be the work of the very boldest among romantic writers. If, after reaching this point in the growth of art, we turn back to Aristotle's explanation of the pleasure produced by representations of what is unpleasant, we shall feel that it needs much stretching to include our charmed self-abandonment to the impetuous rush of Catullus' lyric, charged with the passion and desolation of a ruined life.

Once more, this sympathy between man and external nature is seen to be gaining depth and substance. It is idle to deny that the Athenian and Ionic poets have felt the spell of the outer world ; but in the Roman writers the increasing subtlety and detail of descriptive expression, though still immensely short of modern landscape poetry, bear witness to a refinement of conscious delight in natural beauty for its own sake which is different in principle from the reference to it, as in Homer, by allusive epithet or illustrative simile. It is most significant that Horace should have thought it necessary to protest against descriptive insertions.[1] The principle which I am endeavouring to elucidate, that so long as art is alive its range of appreciation and expression extends itself by a natural process, in which the "apperception" of later artists is prepared by the recorded perceptions of their forerunners, could not be better illustrated than by a criticism which I will venture to quote at length, from one who writes of what he well understands :—

"Everything,[2] then, in Vergil's history, shows him a genuine poet of the country, and at the same time no one who really knows his poems can deny that they fully bear out the evidence of his life. It is true that he drew very largely on other poets, and could not disengage himself from the antecedents of his art. From Homer, Hesiod, Aratus, or Theocritus, for example, come nearly all the passages in his works in which birds are mentioned. But though they

[1] *Ars P.*, 16. "They describe the grove and altar of Diana, or a river's course through pleasant fields, or the rainbow."
[2] *A Year with the Birds*, by an Oxford Tutor, p. 110.

descend from these poets, and bear the features of their
ancestors, they are yet a new and living generation, not
lifeless copies modelled by a mere imitator ; and their beauty
and their truth is not that of Greek but of Italian poetry.
Let any one compare the translations of Aratus by other
Roman hands, by Cicero, Festus, and Germanicus, with
Vergil's first Georgic, and he will not fail to mark the difference between the mere translator, and the poet who breathes
into the work of his predecessors a new life and an immortal
one.   There is hardly to be found, in the whole of Virgil's
poems, a single allusion to the habits of birds or any other
animals, which is untrue to fact as we know it from Italian
naturalists."   I do not doubt that the passages on which
Vergil thus improves had served as guides and starting points
for his own observation.

And with the love of Nature we must compare its complement and condition—the feeling of city-life.   The intensification of pastoral sentiment by contrast with the busy splendour
of Rome, lending an extraordinary stateliness to the verse
which this combined emotion animates, is distinctly mirrored
both in Virgil and in Horace.   The nineteenth-century
dweller in a huge city, whether London or Paris, Berlin or
New York, is quite at home in this subtle sense of complementary pleasures, in which the simple charm of country life
is really to some extent a foil to the recognition of supreme
powers and interests—" res Romanæ perituraque regna "—
centred in the city.

These two extremes therefore, the love of the country
and the sympathy with town life—are there nobler lines in
Vergil than the " Si non ingentem foribus domus alta
superbis ? "—unite in a new and dominating form of feeling,
not possible to the world in any great degree before the
Roman age.   The " praises of Italy " express something
more than an affection for Italian scenery.   They are deeply
coloured with historical sentiment, the sentiment of national
duty belonging to the head of civilisation—an emotion of a
nature to heighten and be heightened by the appreciation of
the picturesqueness in life and manners produced by the
relations of Rome with all quarters of the known world.   The
feeling of the picturesque is essentially historical, and though
I do not think that we find its advanced form, such as the

admiration for ruined buildings, in any ancient writer,[1] yet this is only an outgrowth of the relation to humanity which is really at the root of all delight in external nature.[2]

In any case, the feeling of a national " mission " by which Vergil was clearly inspired when he wrote of Rome, adds a new dignity and significance to all the external aspects of life, and communicates a fresh acuteness to feeling, and a peculiar majesty to expression.

But we may notice in the constellation of Roman writers one sure sign of a decadence. The minor poets are the more complete artists. Lucretius and Vergil were, it might be said, too great as men to be complete as poets in an age whose mind was on the strain, and divided against itself. Much of Lucretius is pure science. Much of Vergil, though not artificial in the most vulgar sense, as opposed to genuine or sincere, is yet dictated by practical or purely historical interest characteristic of the age, but incompatible with the simple-mindedness which belongs to art.

Formative Art and Architecture. γ. We are not writing the history of fine art, but only noting some salient points at which, by definite influences, the working idea of beauty was deepened and enlarged. It is needless, therefore, to say much of formative art and architecture, the tendencies of which fall for the most part within the lines of those which have just been traced in literature. But it seems necessary to mention a few definite phenomena of extreme significance.

One of these phenomena is the prevalence of " allegorical " treatment in the painting and sculpture of the fourth century and later. Allegory, as I understand it, is opposed both to natural symbolism, such as that by which the lines of a flower-bud indicate growth and vitality, and to a deeply rooted tradi-

---

[1] There is an approach to the feeling in question in the famous letter of Sulpic. Ruf. Cic. *Ad Fam.*, 4, 5, and in many epigrams of the first and second centuries B.C. See Mackail, *Anthology*, p. 62.

[2] The degree in which this definite historical sentiment may fairly make a difference in the charm of landscape as such is a very difficult question. Compare Vergil's "Praises of Italy" (*Georgic* ii., 136 ff, esp. lines 167 ff.) with the following passage from Ruskin, *Seven Lamps of Architecture*, p. 163: "Those ever-springing flowers and ever-flowing streams had been dyed by the deep colours of human endurance, valour, and virtue; and the crests of the sable hills that rose against the evening sky received a deeper worship, because their far shadows fell eastward over the iron wall of Joux, and the four-square keep of Granson."

tional symbolism, such as that by which the goddess Athena was connected with ideas of courage and of wisdom. As a rule, therefore, an imaginative presentation which is named after an abstract idea has an allegorical character. Of course there are degrees of this relation. Eros, the love-god, for example, is primarily an imagined person with attributes fixed by tradition. No one would call him an allegory of love, because he is more than a mere sign with content limited to a definite intellectual idea. The question whether the statue of " Kairos" (Opportunity) by Lysippus was[1] or was not strictly allegorical turns partly on the degree in which the conception was traditional—following for example, as is now alleged, the treatment of Hermes—and partly on the issue of fact whether it did or did not bear a knife, *merely* to recall the popular Greek phrase for a critical moment, "on the razor's edge." At any rate, the Calumnia of Apelles, Lucian's description of which is embodied by Botticelli in the well-known picture of the Uffizi, must be considered as wholly allegorical, and it seems that allegorical figures representing such ideas as Virtue, Concord, Justice, and the like, formed a regular branch of sculpture in Greco-Roman times.

Again, the ideal personification of towns, countries, and peoples, not unknown to the great time of Athenian art, takes a prominent place in the period before us. Such is the figure of "the Fortune of Antioch," by Eutychides, a pupil of Lysippus.[2] This further connects itself with the peculiarly Roman art of triumphal relief, in which historical interest is substituted for artistic value. And the full antithesis to abstract allegory seems to be finally supplied by the great Greco-Roman art of *genre* and portrait sculpture ; which, however, through the ideal or deified portrait, such as that of Alexander as Zeus or of Antinous, almost returns again into the allegorical region.

In other directions an analogous variety displays itself In the Rhodian school of sculpture we find a special tendency to situations of horror, cruel rather than tragic ;[3] at the court of Attalus in Pergamus the hostile contact with the Gauls re-

---

[1] Carriere, ii. 396, treats it as an allegory. Overbeck, ii. 107, doubts this, on the grounds that, a, the treatment was traditional ; β, the presence of the alleged attributes is uncertain.

[2] Overbeck, ii. 134.

[3] A tendency showed by painting in this epoch, from Parrhasius downward. *Plut. de Aud. Poetis*, 3.

sulted in a new pathetic and characteristic interest, of which the statue of a dying Gaul, known as the "dying Gladiator," is a famous example. In Rome, again, towards the end of the Republic, the school of Pasiteles strangely combines the tendencies of refined sentimentalism, affected archaism, and anatomical observation from the living model.

A certain development of landscape painting, to which the mural decorations in Pompeii bear witness, does not sustain the hypothesis of a direct appreciation of the beauty of scenery, which it might naturally suggest. It is a curious observation that "on all the walls of Pompeii and Herculaneum there is perhaps not one subject which can be positively identified as local."[1] This indicates that the sources of inspiration were chiefly traditional, although the capacity of these painters for naturalistic execution—as, for example, in painting fruit—is spoken of by modern experts in the highest terms.[2]

With reference to the position of architecture and the minor arts, after simply noting that such crafts as that of gem-cutting and gold and silver work, with the minute skill and subtlety which they imply, laid hold more and more on the interest of the wealthy Roman world, superseding the comparatively severe beauty of the painted earthenware vase, I may venture to indulge the reader and myself in a somewhat long quotation from an author,[3] who best of all men is qualified to judge. I have found myself unable to express the essence of this passage in my own words either more shortly or more suitably for my purpose.

"Now this question of the transmission of the forms of Greek architecture leads us at once to thinking of that of Rome, since it was by this road that all of it went which was consciously accepted as a gift of the classical times. The subject of the origin of all that is characteristic in Roman art is obscure enough, much too obscure for my little knowledge even to attempt to see with it; nay, even in speaking of it, I had better call it the art of the peoples collected under the Roman name; so that I may be understood to include all the influences that went to its creation.

---

[1] Art. 'Archæology," *Encycl. Brit.*, A. S. Murray.
[2] *Encycl. Brit.*, " Archæology " and " Mural Decoration," Prof. Middleton. Cf. Poynter, in *Lectures on Art*, Macmillan, 1882.
[3] Wm. Morris, in *Lectures on Art*, Macmillan, 1882, p. 151 ff

"Now if we are asked what impression the gathered art of these peoples made upon modern art, I see nothing for it but to say that it invented architecture—no less. Before their time, indeed, temples took such and such forms among divers nations, and such and such ornament grew on them ; but what else was done with these styles we really do not know ; a frivolous pleasure-town built in a late period and situate ın Italy,—which destruction, so to say, has preserved for us—being the only token left to show what a Greek house might perhaps have been like. For the rest, in spite of all the wonders of Greek sculpture, we must needs think that the Greeks had done little to fix the future architecture of the world ; there was no elasticity or power of growth about the style ; right in its own country, used for the worship and aspirations which first gave it birth, it could not be used for anything else. But with the architecture of the men of the Roman name it was quite different. In the first place they seized on the great invention of the arch, the most important invention to home-needing men that has been or can be made. They did not invent it themselves, of course, since it was known in ancient Egypt, and apparently not uncommon in brick-building Babylonia ; but they were the first who used it otherwise than as an ugly necessity, and in so using it, they settled what the architecture of civilisation must henceforward be. Nor was their architecture, stately as it was, any longer fit for nothing but a temple—a holy railing for the shrine or symbol of the god ; it was fit for one purpose as for another—church, house, aqueduct, market-place, or castle ; nor was it the style of one country or climate ; it would fit itself to north or south, snow-storm or sand-storm alike. Though pedants might make inflexible rules for its practice when it was dead or dying, when it was alive it did not bind itself too strictly to rule, but followed, in its constructive part at least, the law of nature ; in short, it was a new art, the great art of civilisation.

"True it is that what we have been saying of it applies to it as a style of building chiefly ; in matters of ornament the arts of the conquered did completely take the conqueror captive, and not till the glory of Rome was waning, and its dominion became a tax-gathering machine, did it even begin to strive to shake off the fetters of Greece ; and still, through all those centuries, the Roman lords of the world thought the little timber god's house a holy form, and necessary to be impressed on all stately architecture. It is a matter of course that the part of the architectural ornament of the Romans, which may be definitely called pattern-design, shared fully in this slavery; it was altered and somewhat spoiled Greek work, less refined, and less forbearing. Great swinging scrolls mostly formed of the Acanthus foliage, not very various or delicate in their growth, mingled with heavy rolling flowers, form the main part of the Roman pattern design that clove to the arts. There is no mystery in them, and little interest in their growth, though they are rich and handsome; indeed, they scarcely do grow at all, they are rather stuck together; for the real connected pattern, where one member grows naturally and necessarily out of another—where the whole thing is alive as a real tree or flower is—all this is an invention of what followed Roman art, and is unknown both to the classical and the ancient world. Nevertheless, this invention, when it came, clothed its soul in a body which was chiefly formed of the Greco-Roman ornament, so that this splendid Roman scroll-work, though not very beautiful in itself, is the parent of very beautiful things. It is, perhaps, in the noble craft of mosaic—which is a special craft of the Roman name—that the foreshadowing of the new art is best seen. In the remains of this art you may note the growing formation of more mysterious and more connected, as well as freer and more naturalistic design; their colour, in spite often of the limitation forced on the workman by simple materials, is skilfully arrayed and beautiful; and in short there is a sign in them of the coming of the wave of that great change which was to turn late Roman art, the last of the old, into Byzantine art, the first of the new.

" It lingered long. For long there was still some show of life in the sick art of the older world; that art had been so powerful, so systematized, that it was not easy to get rid even of its dead body. The first stirrings of change were felt in the master-art of architecture, or, once more, in the art of building. As I said before in speaking of the earliest building that shows this movement, the palace at Spalato, the ornamental side of the art lagged long behind the constructional. In that building you see for the first time the arch acting freely, and without the sham support of the Greek beam-architecture; henceforth. the five orders are but pieces of history, until the time when they were used by the pedants of the Renaissance to enslave the world again."

It has been necessary in the foregoing review of the Hellenistic and Greco-Roman decadence to lay stress on its positive achievements, from which the reflective æsthetic consciousness of the time had to draw its material. I am aware that I run the risk of being asked whether I mean to deny that there really was a decadence, whether I have forgotten the vulgar and brutal features of Greco-Roman civilisation, and whether I imagine that the intellectual darkness, extending to the great individual forms of art, which followed upon the Christian era, was a historical accident unconnected with a moral and intellectual bankruptcy in ancient life.

A thorough treatment of this question can only be attempted in connection with the philosophical side of our subject.[1] It must suffice at present to suggest that the features which indicate a decay in the civilisation of the old world are themselves one great term in the set of contrasts which I have been attempting to represent. The spirit which was ultimately destined to burst the bonds of classical tradition began by to some extent reanimating it ; but that in the old life which could not be inspired with new meaning naturally fell into greater and greater corruption. And it was natural that the process of forging sensuous forms adequate to a new impulse should be tedious and gradual in proportion to the greatness of that impulse, and that during a long transition the spirit should be for the most part hostile to sense or the flesh, although the continuity underneath the transition was never really broken. Through all the surface conflicts of intellect and feeling and faith, the unconscious art of architecture, in which necessity blossoms into expression, continued to develop, so that the problem of reconciliation was solved by going on, and spiritual religion had found a sensuous manifestation before it knew that it needed one. The degree in which, before the revival of letters, the tradition of the old world, whether in art or in speculation, continuously affected the new, is a most difficult and interesting question. But it must be remembered that we are only now adjusting our historical consciousness to the conception that the Christian era marked

---

[1] For a statement of it see Prof. Harnack, Art. "Neo-Platonism," *Encycl. Brit.*

no miraculous new birth of the world, and it is probable that the continuity of progress has hitherto been under-estimated rather than the reverse.

Reflective Æsthetic. In turning to the reflective æsthetic of the Alexandrian and Greco-Roman age, we must at once admit that we have to deal, not with complete systems in continuous succession, but with tendencies fragmentarily indicated. Numbers of post-Aristotelian treatises on art are lost to us ; but it is also clear that true æsthetic speculation was not, and could not be, a matter of central interest to the predominant philosophies before Neo-Platonism. The theory of beauty can only be fertile for the thought which grasps life as a whole ; in half-systems such as Stoicism, Epicureanism, or Scepticism, there is no place for the belief that reality may find utterance in human feeling or fancy. And although Neo-Platonism was also a half-system, being fundamentally mystical, that is to say, having lost faith in life and science, and being compelled for that reason to yield the sceptre to Christianity, yet just as Christianity, although a concrete principle of life, constantly fell into repellent onesidedness, so Neo-Platonism, though not a concrete principle of life, was profound enough to inspire a great mind for a time with a comprehensive faith in the reasonableness of reality.

But partial philosophies are often definitely suggestive just because they make the most of the little which they acknowledge, and here Stoicism and Epicureanism are no exceptions. After saying something of these philosophies in their æsthetic aspect, it will be necessary to comment shortly upon the more literary and rhetorical criticism, before closing the present chapter with a reference to Neo-Platonic theory in the third century A.D.

Stoic. i. The Stoic Pantheism led Chrysippus in the third century B.C. to the conception that " many animals have been produced by nature with a view to beauty, in which she takes delight, enjoying their colouring " ;[1] and, for example, that the peacock was produced for the sake of his tail, because of its beauty. Rash as such a suggestion must appear to us, who cannot find room in nature for any purpose, but only for causation, it has the merit of unmistakably signalising the fact and problem of natural beauty, which is,

---

[1] χαίρουσα τῇ ποικιλίᾳ. Plut. de Stoic. Rep., 21.

however it may have come to be so, analogous to man's creations, and harmonious with man's emotions.

"The universe alone is perfect," says Cicero,[1] quoting Chrysippus; "man is not, though he has in him some particle of the perfect, and he is born to contemplate and imitate the universe." The mere laxity of the language seems to bring these ideas near to us; we hear sentiments that ring like them from Christian divines and from nineteenth-century art-critics. To "contemplate and imitate" might surely at least include to reproduce in plastic and poetic form; and some Stoics were not wholly without such a liberal conception. Poseidonius, two centuries after Chrysippus, described poetry, almost on the lines of Aristotle, as "comprising an imitation of human and divine things."

But this was not the ordinary Stoic meaning, and it became less and less so. They took the imitation of the universe rather in the sense familiar to us from George Herbert :—

> "Entice the trusty sun, if that thou can,
> From his ecliptic line, beckon the sky.
> Who lives by rule then, keeps good company."

The mechanical view of imagination, the negative or intellectualist view of emotion, the complete subordination of "theoretical" to "practical" interest characteristic of an age for which practice had become chiefly an affair of theory, all these influences hindered the Stoic from completing his view of man's place in nature by an adequate theory of æsthetic expression. And at last, in Seneca, by a disordered reminiscence of Plato which we shall trace among the Epicureans as well, the formative arts are reckoned as mere ministers to sense, like the art of cookery. The only true liberal art, for him, is philosophy—the art which aims at virtue—and poetry in so far as it is capable of being made a vehicle for philosophic ideas. For speculative purposes such a conception means a complete obliteration of all fruitful distinctions.

Epicurean. ii. The Epicurean school were opposed to the Stoic belief in Providence and in a reasonable kinship between man and nature, and therefore, for the opposite reason to the Stoics, but like them in the result, they disbelieved in the objective value of art as expressing a reasonable content. "Music," writes Philodemus, a contemporary of

Cicero, is "irrational and cannot affect the soul or the emotions, and is no more an expressive art [lit. imitative] than cookery."[1] This censure is aimed straight at the principal line of advance towards a profound analysis of expression which we observed in Plato and more especially in Aristotle.

The æsthetic of mere feeling, resting as it does on the acceptance of simple facts as to what gives certain pleasures, joins hands with the opposite extreme, the æsthetic of pure form.   I cannot assent to Schasler's contemptuous treatment[2] of the powerful lines in which Lucretius refers the harsh scream of the saw and the musical sound of a skilfully played instrument to the respective angularity and smoothness of the physical elements operative in each case, and proceeds to apply a similar explanation to colours and to smells.   Of course this assertion was for him but a guess, and it may be that in the two latter cases it will never be justified.   But the difference between harshness and harmony in musical sound is a difference in impact on the organ, which is at least conveniently symbolised by difference of shape[3] in the graphical representation of the impinging movement, and although a difference in sensuous agreeableness does not explain or coincide with every difference in artistic beauty, yet it is an essential element of æsthetic to understand the former, if only in order to show the limits of its connection with the latter.

The historical hypotheses thrown out by the same poet in another passage[4]—that men learnt song from birds, and instrumental music from the wind in the reeds—are notably inferior to the æsthetic anthropology of Aristotle.   Yet a pervading idea of human progress and a resolute adherence to physical explanations conjoined with a large sense of natural beauty, to which as in Virgil the movement of the verse is magically responsive, confer upon Lucretius something of the splendour and mystery which belong to our own feeling for a beauty founded in necessity.

---

[1] I quote from Müller, 2, 193 : οὐδὲ γὰρ μιμητικὸν ἡ μουσικὴ μᾶλλον ἤπερ ἡ μαγειρική.
[2] *Krit. Geschichte der Aesth.*, i. 210.   Lucret., ii. 408.
[3] Cf. Helmholtz, *Popular Scientific Lectures*, Series I., p. 68 (E. Tr.). "Tuning forks, with their rounded forms of wave, have an extraordinarily soft quality ; and the qualities of tone generated by the zither and violin resemble in harshness the angularity of their wave-forms."
[4] Lucr., 5, 1378.

Aristarchus and   iii. The Alexandrian literary criticism of Aris-
Zoilus.   tarchus and Zoilus in the third century B.C., must
just be mentioned as contributing to the formation of a historical sense, if only in the inferior form of a canon or class-
list of great writers, which repeats itself in later Roman
criticism.[1]   It would seem indeed that Zoilus must have
worked rather to enslave interpretation by a captiously literal
reading, than, like Aristotle, to liberate it by an intelligent
allowance for figures of speech.   The habit of recognising
a "canon" of writers, with a parallelism, usually groundless,
between Greek and Roman authors, was connected with the
custom of classifying styles under three categories, or tacking
on a single distinctive epithet to every writer—a tendency
of which the more appreciative side is exemplified by the
poetical introduction to Meleager's *Garland of Poets.*

It is very curious that the distinction of the three styles
was not merely applied to Homer's speakers, but ascribed to
Homer as having been remarked by him ;[2] an idea which, in
respect of the two extremes of a copious and a neat style, is
really not without foundation in Antenor's remarks on the
speaking of Ulysses and Menelaus.   The formation of a
medium beside the two extremes would readily suggest itself.

All this aspect of literary and rhetorical criticism is apt to
appear to us to be idle and tedious.   But it helped to condition more important movements.

Later Greco-   iv. The rhetorical interest of the later Roman
Roman critics.   critics produced a substantially liberal appreciation
of the aims of art, though it was for the most part not
couched in æsthetic form.   After all, oratory, like art, is a mode
of self-expression ; and the comparison or confusion of poetry
with oratory—formative art being by a stock simile connected
with poetry—emphasizes the expressive purposes and organs
of art.   Some of the criticism suggested by the analogy thus
obtained between oratory and formative art shows a high
degree of historical sympathy.   Thus Dionysius of Hali-
carnassus [3] in the first century B.C. writes : "There are ancient
pictures, simple in colouring and without variety in the mixtures of pigments, but true (ἀκριβεῖς, severe ?) in outline and

---

[1] Prof. H. Nettleship, in *Journal of Philology*, xviii. 230 ff.
[2] Cf. Prof. H. Nettleship l.c. w. quotation from Gellius. See *Iliad*, 3, 200.
[3] See Prof. Nettleship, l.c.

possessing a great charm in this respect; while the later ones are less good in outline but are more elaborately finished with varying effects of chiaroscuro, and have their strong point in the variety of mixtures." We have not the pictures in question; but the description seems to correspond to the well-known difference between art in its youth and in its decay. When Aristotle said that all the work of the ancient artists was bad, let us hope that he was referring to a different period![1]

But yet criticism was stereotyping itself and losing its vitality. Even in Cicero we find a tendency to brief and formal characterisation of the great painters and sculptors, though the writer is still animated by a real love for their art; in Quintilian the originality appears to be less, and the school-book tendency greater,[2] while, to make a long story short, Fronto, in the third century, A.D., writes as if he had been taught a single epithet for each artist or poet.

In Cicero however, in the work on the Sublime which passes under the name of Longinus, in Plutarch, in Dio Chrysostom, and in Philostratus there is something more that calls for notice.

Cicero was an eclectic in philosophy, and we are not to expect original speculation from him. Yet he was earnest, candid, and thoroughly well read, while retaining the power of direct perception that marks a man versed in practical life. Thus, when he presupposes the Greek view of beauty as constituted by an apt relation of the parts to the whole,[3] we see that this view had become a commonplace of reflection; when he travesties[4] the Platonic doctrine of abstract forms by identifying the form of beauty with a mental picture from which the artist copies, which is apparently the same for a Zeus and for an Athena, and which in "our" minds is always capable of a higher beauty than that of the greatest work of Pheidias, we understand that he takes art so seriously as to identify the artist's mental image with that supreme objective order which Plato precisely denied that the artist could ever apprehend or represent. We must not lose sight of the practical reversal of Plato's position for the better which this identification involves, while condemning the outrageous abstraction by

---

[1] *Problemata*, 895 a 35.
[2] For this judgment I rely chiefly on Prof. Nettleship, l.c.
[3] *De Officiis*, i, 27.   [4] *Orator.*, cc. 2 and 3.

which the mental ideal is treated as though it were an innate idea, not dependent on genius, labour, and experience.

And along with this seriousness in Cicero's estimate of art we find, as in the Roman poets, an increasing sensitiveness to the beauty of natural scenery, combined as in Chrysippus and constantly in modern times with a sentimental form of the argument from design.[1] There is perhaps a lack of distinction between beauty and use, but on the other hand there is something approaching to a feeling for the picturesque and the sublime.

And the absurd reference to a single abstract and apparently innate form of beauty is more than atoned for by the really important suggestion, " Seeing that there are two kinds of beauty, one of which consists in grace, the other in dignity ; we must consider grace as feminine, and dignity as masculine beauty."[2]

The subdivision of beauty (apart from so-called moral and intellectual beauty) into *kinds* is a step which I do not know to have been explicitly taken before this date. Aristotle can only be said to do it inferentially, as a consequence of the distinction between forms of art. It is a step incompatible with adherence to the mere formal æsthetic of Hellas, and is an essential condition of a more appreciative analysis.

The work on the Sublime, bearing the name of Longinus, a man of letters of the third century A.D., and secretary to Zenobia, is now on the whole believed by the best authorities[3] to belong to a date soon after the time of Augustus. The mere existence of the word ὕψος "sublimity," lit. "height," as a technical term in æsthetic or rhetorical criticism,—one of a vast number of such technical terms current in the Greco-Roman age,[4]—is a notable fact. The philosophical importance of the treatise is rather in its evidence that consciousness has become sensitive in this direction than in any systematic insight into the nature of the sublime. Nevertheless the writer has

---

[1] *De Natura Deorum*, xxxviii., xxxix. "Let us dismiss refinements of dispute, and look with our own eyes at the beauty of those things which we allege to be formed by divine providence." Rough rocks, caves, and mountains are named in this list of beauties.

[2] *De Officiis*, 1, 36. Had Schiller this passage before him in *Anmuth u. Würde?*

[3] See A. Lang's Introd. to Havell's *Longinus*.

[4] Prof. H. Nettleship, *Journal of Philology*, xviii. 236.

elements of such insight. " Sublimity is, so to say, the image of greatness of soul."[1] " It was not in nature's plan for us, her chosen children, to be base and ignoble—no, she brought us into life and into the whole universe, as into some great field of contest, that we should be at once spectators and ambitious rivals of her mighty deeds, and from the first implanted in our souls an invincible yearning for all that is great, all that is diviner than ourselves. Therefore even the whole world is not wide enough for the soaring range of human thought, but man's mind often overleaps the very bounds of space. When we survey the whole circle of life, and see it abounding everywhere in what is elegant, grand and beautiful, we learn at once what is the true end of man's being. And this is why nature prompts us to admire, not the clearness and usefulness of a little stream, but the Nile, the Danube, the Rhine, and far beyond all the Ocean."[2] " When a writer uses any other resource, he shows himself to be a man ; but the Sublime lifts him near to the great spirit of the Deity."[3] Whereas then in statuary we look for close resemblance to humanity, in literature we require something which transcends humanity—a remark bearing closely on the place[4] of sculpture in ancient, and poetry in modern art. On the other hand, as showing that there is not really a definite grasp of any distinctive notion of the Sublime, we may note such a description as this, " when a passage is pregnant in suggestion, when it is hard, nay impossible, to distract the attention from it, and when it takes a strong and lasting hold on the memory, then we may be sure that we have lighted on the true Sublime." [5]

We may say, perhaps, that the writer was fairly on the track of some such conception as that of the Sublime depending on an effort or reaction on the part of the mind, occasioned by some form of contest with the suggestion of magnitude or force, in which effort or reaction the subject becomes assured of a deeper spiritual strength in himself than he commonly experiences. The absence of any persistent attempt to drag out the essence of the matter by definition is exceedingly remarkable, and the writer's real strength is in his literary judgment and the selection of examples.

In the discussion of style he betrays a consciousness that

---

[1] Havell's *Longinus*, p. 15 (c. ix.). [2] Havell's *Longinus*, cxxxv. p. 68.
[3] *Ib.*, c. xxxvi. p. 69. [4] *Ib.*, p. 70. [5] *Ib.*, cvii. p. 12.

sublimity has some connection with incompleteness, but this idea, which forms rightly or wrongly an important factor in the theory of Kant, he does not pursue to any speculative result.   He is very much alive to the false sublime—frigidity or bombast—as proceeding mainly from over-elaboration of conceits, and is thus well aware that reserve and suggestiveness are connected with the Sublime.

And it is a notable sign of the times that Hebrew poetry here first appears within the field of Greek æsthetic.   "And thus also the law-giver of the Jews, no ordinary man, having formed an adequate conception of the Supreme Being, gave it adequate expression in the opening words of his 'Laws': God said—what?—'Let there be light,' and there was; 'let there be land,' and there was." [1]

However philosophically incomplete, this work adds one to the distinctions which experience was revealing within the sphere of beauty, and is probably responsible for the exceedingly important part played by the theory of the Sublime in modern speculation. [2]

Plutarch of Chæronea, 50–100 A.D., attacks both Stoics and Epicureans, and does not, so far as I know, profess himself an adherent of any school of philosophy.   For our present purpose the most significant of his works is a discussion of the question, how, in view of the base and immoral matter treated of by poets, young men are to read them ["hear" them] without sustaining moral injury.   In spite of his moralistic attitude, the imbecility of some of his advice and interpretations, and the want of intelligence in his constant references to the arguments and poetical quotations of Plato's *Republic*, he has the merit of stating in plainer terms than Aristotle—owing to the accumulation of æsthetic experience during the long interval between them—the strictly æsthetic question : "Can what is really ugly become beautiful in art?"   No doubt he perpetually confuses this with the question : "Do we commend an act morally because we admire it in a work of art?" which he rightly answers in the negative, but which is not a problem of æsthetic, but only of the distinction between æsthetic and ethics.

---

[1] *Ib.*, c. ix. p. 18.
[2] It was first edited in modern Europe in 1544, and often since, notably by Boileau in 1674.   See Lang's Introduction to Havell's *Longinus.*

But he also raises the real problem in distinct terms—the terms of ugliness and beauty, asking in effect, "Can what is ugly in itself be beautiful in art? If Yes, can the art-representation be suitable to and consistent with its original? If No, how does it happen that we admire such art-representations?" I have framed the above question out of Plutarch's answer,[1] which runs thus: "In essence the ugly cannot become beautiful; but the imitation is admired if it is a likeness. The picture of an ugly thing cannot be a beautiful picture; if it were, it could not be suitable to or consistent with its original. . . . Beauty, and to imitate beautifully [which cannot mean to make a beautiful picture, but only to imitate *successfully*] are quite different things." And "the reason[2] why we admire such representations in art, both poetic and pictorial,[3] is because the artist's cunning has an affinity for our intelligence, as may be observed in the fondness of children for toy animals, and in such cases as that of the audience who preferred Parmeno's imitation of a squeaking pig to the real pig.

The mere looseness of Plutarch's language in this explanation seems to give his view a generality which places it in advance of the precisely limited analysis furnished by Aristotle, through a reference to the enjoyment of inference. But Plutarch is still essentially on the same ground as Aristotle. He, like Aristotle, is speaking of the response of our intelligence to the artist's skill, not of the affinity between the artist's intelligence and the significance of the things which he portrays. The natural sense-perception[4] is the same, he expressly says, with that which the artist gives us; that is, the latter owes nothing of its content to the passage through a human mind. The only difference between the two is in our concomitant knowledge whether the presentation is natural or artificial. This is for him the moral of the story about Parmeno, and excludes the interpretation that the audience preferred the ventriloquist's imitation because it was exaggerated with humorous intention, which would be the natural explanation from a modern point of view. This example is

---

[1] *De Audiendis Poetis* iii.   [2] Συμποσ. προβλ., v. 1.

[3] Plutarch insists on this stock comparison to show that poetry being imitative, like painting, is not wholly responsible for the nature of its subjects.

[4] Συμπ. προβλ., v. 1, τὸ αὐτὸ τῆς αἰσθήσεως πάθος οὐχ ὁμοίως διατίθησι τὴν ψύχην, ὅταν μὴ προσῇ δόξα τοῦ λονικῶς ἢ φιλοτιμίᾳ περαίνεσθαι τὸ γιγνόμενον.

a strange counterpart to Kant's case of the nightingale
imitated by the human voice, which, he says, becomes tedious
the moment the deception is discovered.   The common
ground must be that we expect more from a man than from
an animal, only in the one case we think we get it, and in
the other we do not.

Though, therefore, Plutarch does not help us to understand
how art appeals to our intelligence, except in the mere fact
of its power to copy, yet it is very remarkable that he thinks
himself a champion of the intellect as concerned in the artistic
pleasure of painful subjects, against the Epicureans,[1] who
ascribed it to mere sensation without the countervailing pain
of knowing the suffering to be real.   But his only genuine
advance upon Aristotle lies in the urgency which the problem
of ugliness in art had acquired for him, as evinced by the
very numerous examples which he gives of it (though not
adequately distinguishing it from the painful and the immoral),
and by the definiteness with which he states the strictly æsthetic problem, "Can the ugly, if represented in a way
appropriate to it [in short, without falsification], be beautiful
in art?"   In estimating the value of Plutarch's answer, "It
remains ugly, but we rightly take pleasure in it by reason
of the intelligence involved in obtaining the likeness," we
must not forget that the power to copy is a phase, though
elementary, of the power to re-create by intelligence.   And
therefore to recognise a legitimate pleasure in the skill that
copies what is ugly, is the germ of a recognition that what is
apparently ugly, but admirable in art, has something in it
which the trained perception can appreciate as beautiful.

Dio Chrysostom, a Bithynian (A.D. 50-117), a writer of
popular lectures on philosophical subjects, makes in two respects a distinct advance on what we know of his predecessors.

First, he[2] recognises the ideal for art, quite in the opposite
sense to that of Cicero, as a concrete form in which the
artist gives adequate reality to conceptions which before and
apart from such realisation are not definite ; so that the result
is *not* that after seeing the Pheidian statue of Zeus every one

---

[1] Συμποσ. προβλ., l.c.   The Epicureans, it seems, pointed out that the actor
can represent suffering better than the sufferer can.   This is the point which
Plutarch, if a true art-theorist, ought himself to have made, but does not
make.

[2] Dion. Chrys. *de Dei Cognitione Orat.*, 12, p. 402, Reiske.

can imagine something more beautiful; *but* that after seeing it, no one can imagine the god in any other way.

Obviously we are here on the track which Herodotus, with his naive profoundness, had entered 500 years before. A particular case of this conception is the treatment of the human form[1] as the most adequate visible symbol of the invisible quality of intelligence—a striking anticipation of modern ideas, in some degree itself anticipated by the Xenophontic Socrates.

And secondly, Dio Chrysostom examines the commonplace comparison between poetry and formative art with a view, not merely to the resemblances, but also to the differences between them; drawing attention to the larger field open to language both in the kind of ideas represented, as it has words alike for the sensuous and the non-sensuous, and in the time and action[2] included in its descriptions contrasted with the single moment and attitude into which the formative artist must compress all that he desires to convey.

The above views are expounded in a criticism,[3] or rather panegyric of the Olympian Zeus of Pheidias, which reads almost as if the demands of Christianity were already stimulating the adherents of older creeds to demonstrate a spiritual and human significance in their own conception of deity.

In Philostratus (first half of third century A.D.), author of the life of Apollonius of Tyana, and of the description of a real or imaginary collection of paintings at Naples, there is much matter of æsthetic interest. Two points are all to which attention can here be drawn.

First, in the biography of Apollonius, the antithesis of

---

[1] *Id. ib.*, Reiske, 404. I translate this remarkable passage, "No sculptor or painter can portray reason and wisdom as they are in themselves. For having no perception or experience of such things, but knowing for certain *in what* they come to pass, we make it our resource, investing the god with the human body, the vessel of wisdom and reason—seeking to manifest the imageless and unseen in the visible, which can be portrayed—better than the way in which some of the barbarians make likenesses of their gods as animals."

[2] *Id. ib.*, 410. "We (sculptors) have to make each likeness in a single attitude; which must be stable and permanent, and comprise in it the whole nature and quality of the god. But the poets may include many forms in their poetry, and ascribe movement and rest and actions and words to their personages."

[3] Dion. Chrysost. *de Dei Cognitione Orat.*, 12.

imitation and imagination as two co-ordinate principles of art is stated with the full consciousness of its novelty and impor- tance.   Apollonius [1] is attacking the Egyptian representations of gods in animal forms.   The Egyptian interlocutor retorts in effect, " How do you know your Greek representations are any truer ?   Did your Pheidiases go up to heaven and take the gods' likenesses, or did something else guide them in their work ?"   "Something else guided them—a thing full of wisdom."   "What was that ?   You cannot mention any such thing, except imitation."   " It was *imagination* that wrought these forms, a more cunning artist than imitation. Imitation will make what it has seen, but imagination will make what it has not seen."   [This does not necessarily mean "the invisible," but may include it].

But secondly, it is more remarkable still that this opposition, which in its unmitigated form is thoroughly vicious—that is to say, when imagination is treated not as directing but as supplanting the presentation of reality—at once begins to shade off into the more modern idea of a mental (or, as we should say, imaginative) imitation.   It is this inward imitative power, we are told for example, that makes us see the forms of animals in the clouds,[2] which are not really there, or see a negro face drawn in white chalk as the portrait of a black man.

But though the opposition is thus mitigated, it is not destroyed.   Inward or mental imitation does not for Philo- stratus amount to imagination.   For us, however, in view of his instances, it is not easy to distinguish them.   He keeps very far indeed from confounding the fantastic with the imaginative.   Rather, it would appear, he finds true imagination in the invention and suitability, the higher degree of significance and expression, which he esteems in a picture above truth to nature on the one hand, and formal beauty on the other.   " Any one," he says, "professing to describe a picture of Ariadne in Naxos, could paint a beautiful Theseus and a beautiful Ariadne, but the Dionysus is painted simply

---

[1] Philostr., *Vita Apoll. Tyan.*, vi. 19. I quote from Overbeck, *Schrift- quellen zur Geschichte d. Bildenden Künste*, 801, compared with Müller, ii. 317.

[2] Quoted in Müller, ii. 319, ἀλλὰ μὴ τοῦτο βούλει λέγειν τοσαῦτα μὲν ἄσημά τε καὶ ὡς ἔτυχε διὰ τοῦ οὐρανοῦ φέρεσθαι, τόγε ἐπὶ τῷ θεῷ, ἡμᾶς δὲ φύσει τὸ μιμητικὸν ἔχοντας ἀναρρυθμίζειν τε αὐτὰ καὶ ποιεῖν.

as dictated by his love."[1] How invention and expression are brought together in his conception may be illustrated by a curious piece of sentiment which he praises in a landscape, where a male palm tree leans across a stream so as to touch a female palm with its branches, forming a kind of bridge. The recognition of sentiment in landscape is an important datum in the history of art ; whether in this instance the sentiment is of the best kind is a different question.

This recognition of imagination as the power of creating an adequate expression for intelligence and sentiment, places the conception of Philostratus on a higher level than the idealising imitation of Aristotle, in which the difficulty in what direction to idealise is not coped with as a matter of principle.

Plotinus.   v. Plotinus, born in Egypt, 205 A.D., a pupil of Ammonius Saccas of Alexandria, taught in Rome from 245 A.D. till his death in 270 A.D. The tradition that Ammonius was an apostate [2] from Christianity on account of its hostility to the arts and sciences may serve to remind us of the varied influences under which Neo-Platonism arose, although it does not appear [3] to be ascertainable how far in fact Ammonius and Plotinus were acquainted with earlier Alexandrian speculations, or with Judaic or Christian theology.

It is natural to regard a non-Christian philosopher who writes in Greek in the century before Constantine as belonging to late antiquity ; but Plotinus has also been treated as belonging to the early middle age.[4] The doubt indicates his position better than any decision. Neo-Platonism is a counter-part of Christianity, but in a disguise of half-Hellenic theory which curbs its freedom. It is, as we said before, a half-system, of the kind known as mystical ; which does not mean that it is too spiritual, but that, intending to be wholly spiritual, it is really not spiritual enough ; for, like Christian monasticism, it interprets the spiritual renunciation of the world in a material fashion. It shares however with Christianity the reaction against the still more partial systems

---

[1] Philostr., *Imagines*, i. 15, Müller, ii. 324, ἀλλ'οὗτός γε ὁ Διόνυσος ἐκ μόνου τοῦ ἐρᾶν γέγραπται.

[2] Erdmann, E. Tr. i. 237.

[3] Harnack, art. "Neo-Platonism," *Encycl. Brit.*

[4] Erdmann, l.c.

that immediately preceded it ; it rejects all compromise with sensual self-seeking, and has faith in a reality deeper than phenomenal nature, deeper than civic or national relations, deeper even than mind.   Like Plato's Form of the Good, to which it corresponds in being above existence,[1] this Unity or Primal God is above reason, and above the life of the world, which two latter principles are identified by historians with the Aristotelian " intelligence," and the Stoic "universal life."[2]   As derivative, these two elements are necessarily inferior, and the adherence to this axiom of subordination, that the derived is necessarily below the original, distinguishes Neo-Platonism from a true evolutionary doctrine, such as was latent though not at first obvious in Christianity.

But much as Plotinus renounces, in the way of knowledge and practical life, he refuses to renounce material beauty.   In the directness with which it is perceived beauty has an analogy to mystical intuition which often makes it find favour with those who think methodic science too circuitous for an available avenue to truth.

It is worth while to recall, in treating of Plotinus, those three antitheses by which we attempted to gauge the anticipations of a larger æsthetic that were to be found in Plato and Aristotle.   It will be remembered that each of these antitheses corresponded to a characteristic feature not indeed of Greek æsthetic theory, for as regards two out of the three Greek theory fell short of an æsthetic standpoint, but of Greek conceptions relating to the beautiful.   We arranged them as—

i. The antithesis of imitation and symbolism, corresponding to the metaphysical problem : " What kind of reality does art represent ? "

ii. The antithesis of æsthetic and practical interest, corresponding to the moralistic problem : " Is the content of beauty related to the will in the same way as the motives of practical life ? "

iii. The antithesis of abstract and concrete criticism, corresponding to the true æsthetic problem : " Is the nature of beauty exhausted by the formal definition which identifies it with the sensuous presentation of unity in variety, or is a wider and deeper content traceable in it by observation and analysis ? "

We saw that the limitations of purely Greek theory in these

---

[1] ἐπέκεινα τῆς οὐσίας, *ep.* vi., p. 509.   [2] Erdmann, l.c.

several respects were intimately connected together, and it follows that no substantive advance could be made in one of the three problems without tending to stimulate an advance in respect of the other two.   But the third being more directly dependent on experience and observation was capable of gaining considerably in depth and breadth of treatment during an interval in which speculation was unequal to readjusting the other two doctrines in conformity with this new analysis. And such an interval had elapsed, in spite of occasional gleams of philosophic intelligence, between Aristotle and Plotinus. Little of theoretical value either on the distinction between imitation and symbolism, or on the distinction between æsthetic and practical interest, has been adduced in our review of æsthetic reflection current during this period.   And there is no reason to suppose that of the numerous writings which are lost any rose considerably above the philosophical level of those which have come down to us.   Only in the later writers, such as the author of the treatise " on the Sublime," Dio Chrysostom, Philostratus, we find a tendency to recognise in so many words that art is not a mirror of common perception, but an expression of something great or reasonable in a sensuous form. Even this recognition, however, is so little elaborated in theory that it belongs rather to the deepest recognition of an expressiveness beyond mere formal symmetry than to a doctrine of the relation between art and reality.

Symbolism.   *a.* Such a doctrine we do find in Plotinus. The realisation, he is explaining,[1] is indeed always less than the idea, and the created less than the creator—this is the point on which he is still Platonic, and which makes his theory one of emanation and not of evolution—" but still," he continues, " if any one condemns the arts, because they create by way of imitation of nature, first we must observe that natural things themselves are an imitation of something further [viz. of underlying reasons or ideas], and next we must bear in mind that the arts do not simply imitate the visible, but go back to the reasons[2] from which nature comes ; and further, that they create much out of themselves, and add to that which is defective, as being themselves in possession of beauty ; since Pheidias did not create his Zeus after any perceived pattern, but made him such as he would be if Zeus deigned to

---

[1] Creuzer's ed., p. 1002   [2] λόγους.

appear to mortal eyes." This passage leaves no doubt of the writer's intention to take up the gauntlet thrown down by Plato in his "three removes from truth." [1] It seems natural, too, with Dio and Philostratus in our minds, to suppose that the truth claimed for the Pheidian statue is that of adequate symbolism for a god whose nature is spiritual, and not that of imaginative representation of a god who is material, though as a rule unseen by man.

It is needless to enlarge here on the philosophical significance of this passage, which the discussion of Plato's position has fully prepared us to appreciate. It is true that Plotinus retains the self-contradictory conception of spiritual or immaterial beauty by the side of the idea of natural beauty ; but as the latter is not defined, or not merely defined, by its relation to the former, but is explained in terms of other attributes, the value of the theory as dealing with material is not seriously impaired. "A beautiful material thing [2] is produced by participation in reason issuing from the divine." This sentence sums up the conception.

Plato's whole terminology is modified and re-applied by Plotinus in this sense. Material beauty is still an image or a shadow, but it is an image or shadow issuing from reason, and appealing to the soul through the same power by which reason brings order into matter. A portrait,[3] indeed, *if* it give the mere features and no more, is, as Plato would have called it, an image of an image, and thus Plotinus evokes from the Platonic view that deep æsthetic significance which we saw that it might really claim.

Therefore the whole metaphysical assumption that art is limited by ordinary perception, which assumption is one with the imitative theory of fine art, is now broken through. It is henceforth understood that art is not imitative but symbolic.

Æsthetic Interest.   β. What, then, is the nature of æsthetic interest or the love of beauty, and is it distinct from practical interest or desire ?

The answer is unambiguous and complete. *In the material beautiful,* and not merely in the cunning of the artist's imitation as Aristotle[e] and Plutarch suggested, the soul recognises

----

[1] *Rep.,* x.   [2] Creuzer, p. 102.
[3] Porphyry's *Life of Plotinus.*

an affinity to itself. This affinity consists [1] in the participation
in reason and form, and is co-extensive with the beautiful.
For the ugly is either that which being capable of rational form
has not received it ; or that which is incapable of rational form
and refuses to be moulded by it.   Hence beauty is only in
the form, not in the material, and this must be so *as it is the
form alone* [2] *that can enter our apprehension.*   The exclusion
of desire for the sensuous reality from the interest in the
beautiful is effected by this view of æsthetic semblance as
thoroughly as by that of Schiller.

Thus, in strict theory, the moralistic limitation of beauty is
thrown aside, as we foresaw, together with its metaphysical
limitation.   Beauty comes to be regarded as a direct expression of reason in sense by way of æsthetic semblance only
and is therefore co-ordinate with morality and not subordinate
to it.   I do not say that Plotinus would necessarily interpret
his own principle in its full breadth ; that would depend on
the limits which he might assign to reasonableness of form.
In this interpretation he might be influenced by his ascetic
tendency ; but there is no room for doubt as to the bearing of
his philosophical theory.   All that symbolises in sensuous or
material form the laws or reasons eternally active in the
world has a right, by this theory, to rank as beautiful.

On the other hand, his conception of ugliness is defective, *if*
we regard it as a defect to assert that nothing is ugly.   For
interpreted by modern views of nature, it would come to this.
We know of nothing that does not in one way or another
symbolise reason.   We speak about " higher " and " lower "
laws, but we know of nothing in which law is not revealed.
If therefore we mean to maintain that real ugliness—ugliness
which is not beautiful—can exist, we must set some limit
to the idea that all is beautiful which symbolises reason.
Whether such a limitation can be maintained, and with it the
existence of real ugliness, is a great problem of modern
æsthetic.   It was at any rate a merit in Plotinus that he
stated the question so broadly and clearly.   By doing so
he vastly extended the recognised province of beauty, in
agreement with the need for such an extension which we saw
to have been practically making itself felt in art and criticism.
In all probability, however, he would have classed as formless,

---

[1] Creuzer, pp. 100–1.   [2] Creuzer, p. 1003.

in accordance with the enlightened popular feeling even of our own day, which his theory fairly represents, much that trained perception ought to recognise as full of form and beauty, and much again, which may be really ugly, but cannot be strictly called formless. For in reality nothing is formless. Logically speaking, he has confused the bare negative which is in fact a nonentity, with the positive opposite or contrary. It is not absence of form, but false form—confusion of the forms appropriate to different things and meanings—in which, if anywhere, we must look for real ugliness.

Yet all these considerations are refinements, only rendered possible by the broad comparison of beauty and ugliness as representing the rational and irrational, in which for the first time Plotinus brought the whole subject under one comprehensive point of view, capable of including the diverse forms and deeper sentiments of beauty which the age of transition had been developing.

Concrete Criticism. γ. As we should anticipate, the identification of beauty with mere symmetry, or unity in variety, —the limitation which makes æsthetic purely formal — is broken down when the beauty of art ceases to be subordinated to the standards of ordinary reality. Plotinus repeatedly protests against the identification of beauty with symmetry; and although the arguments by which he sustains his protest do not always appear to be sound, nor does he display a very consistent apprehension of any mode beyond that of mere symmetry or harmony in which reason can exhibit itself to sense, yet it is plain that he understood the growing need for a modification of æsthetic theory in this direction. I quote a passage which shows his main argument from feeling and observation.[1]

" Beauty is rather a light that plays over the symmetry of things than the symmetry itself, and in this consists its charm. For why is the light of beauty rather on the living face, and only a trace of it on that of the dead, though the countenance be not yet disfigured in the symmetry of its substance ; and why are the more life-like [2] statues the more beautiful, though the others be more symmetrical ? and why is an uglier living man more beautiful than a statue of a beautiful one, except

---

[1] *Ennead.*, iv. 7, 22. See Müller, p. 313.
[2] See above ch. iv., p. 45, on Socrates in Xenophon.

that this (living beauty) is more desirable, and is so because it is more of the nature of the good ? " And he even seems to have taken up the thought of the Xenophontic Socrates, and insisted that "the portrait painter must aim especially at catching the look of the eye, as the mind reveals itself in it more than in the conformation of the body." [1] This would certainly indicate a peculiar sensitiveness to the effects of painting, which, as Schasler points out, is significant with reference to the new relation which painting and sculpture were destined to assume in the later middle age.

Of course "vitality" or "expression" must be embodied in some kind of symmetry, but as symmetry is a much wider and less definite attribute than vitality and expression, it is plain that we have here a great advance towards concrete æsthetic theory.

When however Plotinus supports his denial that beauty can consist in mere symmetry, by the argument that if so, the simple parts of a beautiful whole, such as colour, lightning, the stars, could not be beautiful in themselves, whereas in reality a beautiful whole must have parts which are beautiful separately as well as in combination, he arouses a whole swarm of æsthetic questions—to do which is in itself a great merit—but does not escape serious confusion. To begin with, it is clear that a beautiful whole does not necessarily consist of parts which are beautiful in isolation. Again, although, as he alleges, some things which are relatively simple appear to be beautiful even taken by themselves, it is not certain that their beauty falls outside the explanation suggested by Plato for "pure" sounds and colours, which, of course, however simple, have parts in which their simplicity is manifested. And further, it is not easy to estimate Plotinus' own explanation of the peculiar beauty which he finds in light. "The beauty of colour, which is simple, consists in its overcoming darkness by a principle which is immaterial, and is reason and form." Whether colour, considered as beautiful, is really simple, and is not rather, *qua* simple, merely pleasant, but *qua* beautiful, suggestive of harmonies and relations ; whether Plotinus the spiritualist is not, like so many spiritualists, fascinated by the idea that an imponderable agent is somehow more akin to mind than heavy matter can be ; and whether, if

---

[1] See Schasler, i. 246

light does conquer obscurity by producing lucidity, this implies any element of beauty deeper than those involved in
order and symmetry, are questions which present themselves
at once in dealing with this conception.   Leaving these difficulties, which it is enough to point out, it must be observed
that Plotinus' devotion to light is connected with the immense
importance which Plato's comparison between the Sun and the
Good had in Neo-Platonism, and that from a purely æsthetic
point of view he falls behind Aristotle by the comparatively
slight attention which he pays to music as a medium of
spiritual expression.   It was this, we remember, that so
strangely and suggestively perverted the mimetic terminology
of Aristotle ; music, he observed, had a higher expressive or
imitative capacity than the formative arts.   And in this conception, if freely interpreted, we saw a foreshadowing of the
profoundest modern romanticism.   For Plotinus, music is of
course an audible symbol of inaudible harmonies, but it is
beautiful only in a secondary degree as compared with painting, whereas we should have expected that a thinker of his
tendency would have developed the suggestion of Aristotle,
and recognised music as a pre-eminently spiritual art.   If, as
seems probable, some superstition about the immaterial
affinities of light was the cause of this non-recognition, we
have here an example of the law that quasi-poetic imagination,
when admitted into philosophy, blinds the intelligence to what
is truly of poetic value.

The creative impulse of Hellenic philosophy ended with
Plotinus.   For more than two centuries after his death in
270 A.D. the schools of Athens remained open, but it does not
appear that Proclus, who died about forty years before their
closing in 529, and was the last considerable Greek philosopher, added anything of serious importance to the ideas of
Plotinus, which he systematised.

We have now traced the history of the Hellenic formulæ
relating to beauty, and have endeavoured to indicate not only
the conditions of their formation and the degrees by which
they were stretched and ultimately broken, but also the
actual force that was at work in the concrete perception of the
beautiful as it first strained and then snapped them.   The
definite antagonism of the sensuous and the spiritual world—
the latter being regarded as something more and other than an
intelligible system or better understanding of phenomena—

meant the disintegration of ancient thought, and the genesis of what on the great scale of world-history may fairly be called the modern mind.

It may be indeed that what we thus distinguish as "modern" will one day be called "mediæval," and that we shall learn to date perhaps from Shakespeare or from Goethe the inception of an æsthetic mood which is symbolic like that of the middle age, but without its arbitrary mysticism, and unartificial, like that of classical Greece, but free from its imitative naturalism. For the present however it is enough to note the original growth of that deeper and subtler consciousness, which however its antagonisms may be reconciled, can never, having once appeared, be substantially lost to the world, and which must for ever form the ultimate distinction between classical antiquity and all that in the most pregnant sense can be called modern.

a (p. 57, note 1). Observe however in Metrodorus (answer to Posidippus, who wrote in 3rd cent. B.C.) the first definite allusion to "the charm of nature." I owe this reference to the kindness of Mr. Mackail.

b (p. 90). This judgment seems quite wrong. I need hardly refer the reader to Mr. Mackail's *History of Latin Literature* for a true estimate.

c (p. 91). On the contrary, the subject, as I learn from Mr. Mackail's *History*, was often treated in the Alexandrine period. I still think my mention of it not wholly irrelevant.

d (p. 97). "god's house." If this implies that, e.g., the Parthenon or Propylaea produce *an effect* of smallness, it is surely quite wrong. They are, *in effect*, among the "biggest" buildings of the world.

e (p. 114). Aristotle's suggestions went further. See Butcher, *op. cit.*, 155 note, and *Ar. de Part. Anim.* 645 a. 4.

CHAPTER VI.

IT is natural, especially for the Protestant peoples of Europe,
to regard the Renaissance as the beginning of modern life.
The long struggle for intellectual and political freedom which
still gives the tone to our aspirations, appears to us to have
had its starting point in the revival of Greek learning, and the
awakening of physical science. And we have therefore been
too apt to think even of the Renaissance in poetry and formative art as a new departure, stimulated from without, and
forming portion of a homogeneous development rather into the
times that followed, than out of the times that went before.

But any such view is coming to be less and less approved
by the deepest and most sympathetic criticism ; and thus it
will be worth while (1) to put together some indications of a
growing tendency in modern thought to pursue the roots of
the Renaissance further and further back into the earlier
middle age, before (2) attempting a very slight sketch of the
intellectual attitude assumed by the mediæval Church and its
greatest thinkers towards formative art and the sense of beauty.

Tendency to extend Renais-sance back towards Christian Era. 1. As the movement of the Renaissance in
poetry and fine art passed from the productive to
the critical stage, it was natural that criticism
should first turn its attention to the later phases of
production, which were in many senses nearer to itself. Just
as scholarship travelled back to the Hellenic world by way of
the Greco-Roman, and was long before it distinguished Zeus
and Athene from Jupiter and Minerva, so it would seem as if
æsthetic interest was first attracted by the full-blown and later
Renaissance, both in letters, in painting, and in architecture,
and only worked backward by degrees to " Gothic " buildings
and early Tuscan painters. We all know the beautiful passage
in Goethe's autobiography,[1] in which he supports the noble

---

[1] *Wahrheit u. Dichtung*, Werke, 17, 347–8.

paradox, " What youth desires, old age abounds in," by his having lived to enjoy the awakened interest of others in Gothic architecture, the study of which had fascinated him in his youth.   The art lectures of our own Academicians show the need of a similar retrogression.[1]   We find in them, indeed, some slight references to Cimabue, because of Vasari's conspicuous mention of him, but hardly a word of Giotto, and not a word of Botticelli or Fra Angelico.   The Caracci's, on the other hand, are continually in the writers' minds, just as Lessing's criticism was first directed to the Gallicising poets of his own day.   The brilliancy of the first years of the sixteenth century seems to have marked that period as the true point of departure, and attention was given by preference rather to what came after it than to what went before.   The fall of Constantinople in 1453 furnished a conveniently definite reason, and in some degree a real cause, to which this great effect could be attributed ; and so the term Renaissance in its narrowest acceptation indicates the influence of Greek studies and antiquities on art and letters, an influence which had, however, in fact begun before the latter half of the fifteenth century, to which it is usually ascribed.   Because of this usage, the word has often to-day a disparaging connotation with reference to the history of art and architecture, which is apt to perplex the student who interprets it more generally.

Pre-Raphaelite   i. The present century has seen this tendency
Painting.   reversed, at least in England, by the æsthetic movement, of which the pre-Raphaelite brotherhood was a symbol, but which acted in conjunction with many fundamental impulses of the age, and, in short, with the whole principle of evolutionary science and history.   It is quite plain that this general movement, which includes a strong bias against the assumption of purely extraneous causes for any development within a society, has shifted the centre of our interest in Italian formative art to a point rather before than after the close of the fifteenth century, and has pushed back its further limit to the first signs of change in the practice of painters, that is to say to the middle of the thirteenth century. As for architecture, we shall see directly that in it the later Renaissance may now be said to form the nearer frontier of our interest, while the remoter boundary has gone back to the

---

[1] Barry, Opie, Fuseli, between 1790 and 1810.

very threshold of the earliest middle age. But when this more comprehensive scope is given to our care for the Renaissance, the term itself has lost its narrow reference to the revival of Greek letters in the fifteenth century, and has been extended in conformity with its literal import to the whole movement and aspiration revealed in Dante and Giotto and their successors.

Thirteenth Century French Literature. ii. This being so, however, the principle is conceded that the European movement known as the Renaissance was not purely dependent on stimulation from without, and we are driven to trace its genesis yet further back than the time of Dante. We cannot refuse to see in the early French stories written as we have them during the thirteenth century, but older no doubt in their origin and circulation, a Renaissance within the middle age,[1] on which the signs of the new spirit are distinctly impressed.

Mr. Pater's quotation from *The Friendship of Amis and Amile* should be read in the beautiful setting he has furnished for it[2] by those who desire to realise the many sidedness of the romantic sentiment embodied in these matin songs of modern Europe. We notice in them on the one hand the tenderness and sensitiveness of romanticism, and more especially its delight in beautiful workmanship, the carved wooden cups of Amis and Amile playing the part almost of persons in the story ; and on the other hand we are struck by the outburst of passionate rebellion against a dogma, once spiritual, but now grossly material, and hostile to human feeling. Nothing is more extraordinary in view of our common notions about the Dark Ages, than the audacity alike of sentiment and of speculation that we meet with inside their bounds.

One famous outburst of such audacity I think it well to reproduce from the story of *Aucassin et Nicolette.* It is the passage to which Mr. Pater refers as sounding a note of rebellion too strident for his pages. Aucassin is threatened with exclusion from heaven, if he makes Nicolette his mistress. "You will never," the adviser concludes, "enter into Paradise."

---

[1] I am following, of course, *non passibus æquis*, the delightful study in Mr. Pater's *Renaissance* called "Two Early French Stories."

[2] *Renaissance*, Essay I.

" In Paradise what have I to do?" is Aucassin's answer.
" I do not seek to enter there, but only to have Nicolette, my
sweet love, whom I love so. None go to Paradise but those
whom I will tell you. There go the old priest and the halt
and the maimed, who all day and all night crouch before the
altars and in the old crypts, and those that are clothed in old
shabby cloaks and old rags naked and barefoot and *sansculotte,*
who die of hunger and poverty and cold and misery. These
go to Paradise ; with these I have nought to do. But to hell
I will go ; for to hell go the fair scholar, and the fair knight
who dies in tournays and noble wars, and the good squire and
the free man. With them I will go. There too go the beautiful courteous ladies, who have two or three lovers, with their
husbands, and there go the gold and silver and the precious
furs, and there go the harper and the minstrel, and the kings
of this world. With these I will go, only I must have with
me my sweet love, Nicolette."

When we recall that these words were probably written
in the lifetime of Thomas Aquinas, who was Dante's guide
in theology, we begin to understand how deep rooted in the
life of the age were the contrasts of dogma and romance which
amaze us in the *Inferno.* " *Le bel clerc* "—these words
sound like an echo of the too famous personal history which
so tragically embodied this antagonism.

Abelard. iii. For a little further back, in the first half of
the twelth century, lies the troubled career of Abelard, whom
we are here to consider, not as a philosopher, but as the actor
in a real tragedy, which must have deeply affected the feeling
of the age, and as the writer of the letters to Heloise, and of
songs in the vernacular which the Paris students sang. In
the actual incidents of his fate, as in the mediæval legend of
Tannhäuser,[1] we see no mere vulgar aberration, but a rebellion,
relatively justifiable, against conditions and ideas which mankind was not destined permanently to endure. The claim
upon the sympathy of the age, which is embodied in the
divine forgiveness as represented in the Tannhäuser legend,
must also, one would think, have been recognised in Abelard.
It has been well observed[2] that Dante, by omitting so familiar
a name from the *Divina Commedia,* almost seems to refuse to
judge him.

---

[1] The comparison is drawn from Mr Pater's *Renaissance.*   [2] Mr. Pater, l.c.

iv. We have now traced back the signs of the "Renaissance" spirit to the beginning of the twelfth century, before the sculptures of Poitiers or of Chartres, which are perhaps the earliest indications of a revival in the higher formative crafts, as contrasted with mere architectural decoration. In these higher crafts of sculpture and painting, as also in the highest of all arts, the art of poetry, it appears that a long period of barrenness or rigidity preceded the development of the twelfth and later centuries. For this we shall in part be able to account when we discuss the attitude of the Church. But the roots of the Renaissance must be pursued further still.

For we must again insist on what was alluded to in the last chapter, that the age of beautiful architecture, while it includes the centuries of which we have just been speaking, extends upwards in an unbroken continuity from them to the time of Justinian. In the later Renaissance, on the other hand, the tradition is severed, and whatever the merits or defects of the architecture that followed, it no longer springs organically from that which went before.

It is quite natural that the great artistic craft which is rooted in necessity and does not intentionally represent imaginative ideas, should be the one to maintain itself through the inrush of uncultured peoples into Christendom and through the disputes and misunderstandings of a creed, prone to the heresy that the spirit is essentially hostile to the flesh. Including those crafts of decoration which do not necessarily deal with the human figure, and therefore escape questionings aroused by anthropomorphism, architecture was well able to represent and carry forward the impulse of freedom and individuality, which was one day to find a fuller expression in the achievements of painting, music and poetry. I have at this point no alternative but to supplement the quotation which I made in the last chapter, with reference to the architecture and decoration of the Roman decadence, by others from the same author,[1] dealing with the early days of that "modern," or mediæval architecture which sprang from it.

"Spalato was built about 323 A.D., St. Sophia in 530. More than 200 years are between them, by no means fertile

---

[1] Mr. Wm. Morris, in *Lectures on Art*, Macmillan, 1882. Cf. Prof. Middleton, *Encycl. Brit.*, art. "Sculpture."

of beautiful or remarkable buildings, but St. Sophia once
built, the earth began to blossom with beautiful buildings, and
the thousand years that lie between the date of St. Sophia
and the date of St. Peter's at Rome may well be called the
building age of the world. But when those years were over,
in Italy at least, the change was fully come ; and as a symbol
of that change there stood on the site of the great mass of
history and art, which was once called the Basilica of St.
Peter, that new Church of St. Peter which still curses the
mightiest city of the world—the very type, it seems to me, of
pride and tyranny, of all that crushes out the love of art in
simple people, and makes art a toy of little estimation for the
idle hours of the rich and cultivated." [1] " But, one thing came
of it [of freedom in the realm of art at least] in those earlier
days—an architecture pure in its principles, reasonable in its
practice, and beautiful to the eyes of all men, even the
simplest."—" It was a matter of course that the art of pattern
designing should fully share in the exaltation of the master
art. Now at last, and only now,[2] it began to be really delightful in itself ; good reason why, since now at last the mind of a
man, happy in his work, did more or less guide all hands that
wrought it. No beauty in the art has ever surpassed the
beauty of those, its first days of joy and freedom, the days of
gain without loss—the time of boundless hope. I say of gain
without loss; the qualities of all the past styles which had built
it up are there, with all that it has gained of new. The great
rolling curves of the Roman Acanthus have not been forgotten,
but they have had life, growth, variety, and refinement infused
into them; the clean-cut accuracy and justness of line of one side
of Greek ornament have not been forgotten, nor the straying
wreath-like naturalism of the other side of it ; but the first has
gained a crisp sparkling richness and freedom and suggestion
of nature which it had lacked before ; and the second, which
was apt to be feeble and languid, has gained a knitting-up of
its lines into strength, and an interest in every curve, which
make it like the choice parts of the very growths of nature.
Other gain it has of richness and mystery, the most necessary
of all the qualities of pattern work, that without which, indeed,

---

[1] *Lectures on Art*, p. 131.
[2] I understand the writer to be referring, in the first instance, to the decoration of St. Sophia. See Prof. Middleton, l.c.

it must be kept in the strictly subordinate place which the scientific good taste of Greece allotted to it." The writer goes on to point out that Byzantine art rather made the character of what we call Eastern art, than derived its own character from what Eastern art then was, although the East had much to do with the new life of this which he calls the "true Renaissance." "But surely," he continues, "when we have sought our utmost for the origins of all the forms of that great body of the expression of men's thoughts which I have called modern art (you may call it Gothic art if you will, little as the Goths dealt with it), when we have sought and found much, we shall still have to confess that there is no visible origin for the thing that gave life to those forms. All we can say is, that when the Roman tyranny grew sick, when that recurring curse of the world, a dominant race, began for a time to be shaken from its hold, men began to long for the freedom of art ; and that even amid the confusion and rudeness of a time when one civilisation was breaking up that another might be born of it, the mighty impulse which this longing gave to the expression of thought created a glorious art, full of growth and hope, in the only form which at such a time art could take—architecture to wit—which of all the forms of art is that which springs direct from popular impulse, from the partnership of all men, great and little, in worthy and exalting aspirations. So was modern or Gothic art created, and never till the time of that death or cataleptic sleep of the so-called Renaissance, did it forget its origin."

Here, we are to observe, the art of the sixth century A.D. is referred to as the sign of " the true Renaissance," which does not mean a rebirth of "classical" forms, but rather a rebirth of the human spirit in a vesture entirely new, though woven out of the robes it had laid aside. We must bear in mind, however, that great works of individual origination in the expressive arts are not to be found during the six centuries which we have just traversed so lightly ; and although it is not hard to explain this phenomenon, yet it cannot be explained away.

Christian Art and Song of the earliest centuries. v. But we may go at least one step further. "As if in anticipation of the sixteenth century, the Church was becoming humanistic, in a best and earliest Renaissance." This saying of the same writer [1] who

----

[1] Mr. Pater, *Marius the Epicurean*, vol. ii. 141.

pointed us to the French or Provençal Renaissance of early romance, refers to the second century of our era—the minor 'peace of the Church" under the Antonines. At this time, it is suggested, before those conflicts of body and soul which preceded or characterised the later "peace of the Church" under Constantine, she was "truer than perhaps she ever would be again to that element of profound serenity in the soul of her founder, which reflected the eternal goodwill of God to man, 'in whom,' according to the oldest version of the angelic message, ' He is well pleased !'"

The signs which indicate some such frame of mind in the Church before Constantine appear to be :—

a. The allusions from which an early development of liturgical music, analogous to that described by Augustine as recently introduced at Milan, may be inferred to reach back, though in less ceremonial forms,[1] to New Testament times.

b. The remains of early Christian painting in the catacombs, of which some part may belong to very early years, though the more complete frescoes probably come down to the fourth century. What is remarkable in these oldest relics of Christian art is in the first place the complete adoption of a simple symbolism, resting partly on Scripture and partly on natural allegory, in which the cross, the lamb, the fish,[2] the stag (after the Psalm, "As the hart panteth"), and the phœnix or peacock, all stand directly for ideas belonging to the faith, symbols such as these having for unlettered minds an extraordinary power of comfort and fascination, when they have become the vehicles of a common experience and a common hope. And in the second place, as pictorial capacity increases among the Christians, there arises the habit of representing scenes from the life of Jesus, never in childhood nor in suffering, but always as a godlike man in some happy or triumphant activity, as the Good Shepherd (with an echo of Hermes), or in the entrance into Jerusalem, or even before Pilate ; or again, as the teacher among His disciples, or under the form of Orpheus, who also overcame death, and tamed the

---

[1] The Council of Laodicea, 367 A.D., restricted singing in church to the trained choir. Carriere, iii. 94 ff.

[2] The first letters of the Greek words for Jesus Christ, Son of God, Saviour, form the Greek word for fish.

fiercest creatures, in a Phrygian cap, playing the lyre among wild beasts.[1]

c. The hymns and sacred poetry of the early Church do not appear to have attained independent poetical rank,[2] but, beginning with some verses quoted or written by Clement of Alexandria in the end of the second century, and going on through Nazianzen in the fourth century and Synesius in the fifth, they evince[3] a completely new force and freedom in, so to speak, taking possession of the universe with all its strength and majesty, as something that shares, in its degree, man's relation to the Creator. This relation does not appear to be either argumentatively or fantastically conceived ; it is rather directly and simply felt, as the content of a faith and a ground for prayer. The Hebrew Scriptures, especially the Psalms, no doubt had a profound influence on this mood and its expression ; but the doctrine of the incarnation, which seems generally to be near at hand in these hymns, immensely strengthens what I have ventured to call the sense of possession or proprietorship which replaces for the Christian the Judaic sense of inaccessibility or remoteness in the Creator. In this feeling, which is very strongly marked in the Synoptic Gospels, we unquestionably have one and that the most fundamental note of the Christian attitude towards beauty. But yet Christian art had far to go and much to suffer before it could realise this aspiration of its early days.

It is worth while to adduce two quotations from the prose literature of the fourth century, which show first the profound sense of unity with the world that survived down to that time among Christians ; and secondly, this same unity just beginning to rend itself in the long struggle which was probably unavoidable if its full depth was ever to be realised.

Gregory of Nyssa writes : "When I see every hilltop, every valley, every plain covered with fresh sprung grass, and then the various array of the trees, and at my feet the lilies, doubly furnished by nature, both with pleasant scent and with beauty

---

[1] See an elaborate treatment of early Christianity in all its æsthetic aspects in Carriere, iii., 77–138, and cf. for the catacombs, Prof. Middleton, in *Encycl. Brit.*, " Mural Decoration."

[2] It is now thought that Gregory of Nazianzus was not the author of the Euripidean tragedy on " the suffering Christ," which used to be ascribed to him. See his life, *Encycl. Brit.*

[3] I judge from the translations in Carriere, l.c.

of colour ; when in the distance I behold the sea, to which the wandering cloud leads the way, my mind is seized by a melancholy which is not without happiness ; and when in autumn the fruits [corn ?] disappear, the leaves fall and the boughs are left bare, we are absorbed in the thought of the eternal and continuously recurring change in the accord of the marvellous forces of nature. Whoever apprehends this with the intelligent eye of the soul, feels the littleness of man compared with the greatness of the universe." And Chrysostom : " When you look at gleaming buildings, and the aspect of colonnades allures your eye, then turn at once to the vault of heaven and to the free plains in which herds graze at the water's brink. Who does not despise all the creations of art when at dawn in the stillness of his heart he admires the rising sun, as it sheds its golden light over the earth ; or, when resting by a spring in the deep grass or under the dark shade of thick-leaved trees, he feasts his eye on the far distance vanishing in the haze ?"

I do not think that we can be mistaken in saying that these passages show a sympathy with nature which is quite of a modern type. But in both of them this feeling is beginning to turn against the sense of worth in man and his productions, and so doing to cut at its own root. Nothing could be more pregnant than this opposition, more especially in the second passage, where it is specifically directed against architecture, the non-imitative art. On the one hand it emphasises unmistakably a new attitude of æsthetic perception to external nature, the like of which we have not found in any Hellenic or Greco-Roman writer, but on the other hand it betrays a faint shadow of that hostility to artificial beauty which maimed the higher imaginative arts in the middle age, and in doing so, deadened in the end man's sensibility even to natural loveliness.

There is ground, then, for the suggestion which finds the earliest Renaissance in the earliest age of peace experienced by the Christian Church after it became a completed organism ;[1] and it is not to be denied that the Founder of Christianity[2] looked out upon the external world with free and

---

[1] See *Marius the Epicurean*, ii. 135.

[2] I doubt whether such disinterested apprehension of floral beauty—so free from moralising or allegory—as that of the text, "Consider the lilies of the field," can be found outside, or prior to, the Christian intelligence.

K

friendly eyes, or that the ultimate tendency of this religion is
to make man feel that the world and he himself are parallel
expressions of one and the same Divinity.

Necessity of an.
Interval of
Austerity.
    vi. But yet there seems to be another side to
this question. The half-Hellenic cheerfulness, in
subjects and treatment, of the catacomb-paintings,
the abounding grace and force of some early Christian sculptures,[1] and the naive devotion of the early hymns and sacred
odes, could scarcely perhaps have led by direct development
to so great a range and depth of characterisation, as that
which reveals itself in the twelfth century and after. The
later dogmatic and ascetic tendency may no doubt be said to
have laid fetters on the highest uses of art; but was it not
necessary that the opposition between the spirit and the flesh
should be pushed to the furthest point, both within the realm
of art, and between art and dogma, in order that the entire
gamut of expression might be mastered, and that the arduous-
ness of the task, to represent all that there is in man, might not
be understated? If the God-like or heroic Christ had never
passed into the man of sorrows, if crucifixions and martyr-
doms and the forms of emaciated ascetics had never been
brought within the range of representation, would not an
element have been wanting to the complex expressiveness of
Botticelli and Leonardo, and to the modern feeling, which is
our peculiar pride, for a beauty as wide as life? And if no
party in the Church had maintained, and no Council had
decided, that "Christ in His glorified humanity was . . . too
exalted to be figured by human art in an earthly material,
after the analogy of any other human body,"[2] would there
have existed, when imagination at length came to its rights,
the full sense of mystery which Raphael, for example, embodied in the Divine child of the Sistine Madonna? It is
said that the Christian painters attained a mastery over the
expression of the face long before they could deal adequately
with the figure, whereas with Greek sculptors the order was
the reverse of this. Such a contrast, which is certainly characteristic, only applies to the Christian art of a later age, and
not to that of the first four centuries.

    But none the less it is true that the re-birth of humanity

---

[1] Carriere, iii. 114. Prof. Middleton in *Encycl. Brit.*, art. "Sculpture."
[2] Council of 754, not œcumenical. *Encycl. Brit.*, art. "Image-worship."

began with the Christian era, or rather, as we said in the last chapter, long before it ; and the apparent aberrations of the later middle age were but necessary grades in the process which vindicated the full breadth and intensity of the human ideal.

Intellectual Continuity of Æsthetic from Plotinus. 2. The profound conception of Plotinus, which finally destroyed the theoretical restriction of beauty to formal symmetry and of art to imitation, was essentially maintained—whether or no in direct inheritance from its author—by the intellectual consciousness of Christendom. It was, as we have seen, only an application of the thought of Plato, for which everything visible or material was a sign or counterpart of something invisible or immaterial. In a dialogue[1] of Scotus Erigena, who might be called the last Neo-Platonist and the first Scholastic,[2] the "teacher" says, "Consider whether these local and temporal recurrences of the parts of this visible universe are devoid of a certain mystery or not," to which the "disciple" replies, " I could not readily affirm that they are devoid of mystery ; for there is nothing, as I think, of visible and corporeal objects which does not signify somewhat incorporeal and [purely] intelligible." Scholastic disputes about the logical or metaphysical existence of universals do not touch this fundamental conviction, which, formulated by Plato after the great age of Hellenic art, sank deep into the European intellect under the influence of the so-called decadence, including the birth of Christianity, and governed the modern perception of beauty till rationalised by the later Renaissance. For the time, therefore, the consciousness of Christendom was dualistic, as opposed to the naturalistic monism of the ordinary Hellenic creed before Plato. But the Christian dualism was only the outward sign of an arduous struggle to realise a higher or spiritual monism. From the first and throughout history a sense of reconciliation was active in the Christian faith, however militant.

Thus the slight indications of the mediæval attitude towards beauty, which are all that can be dealt with here, appear to indicate a remarkable circuit of theory, beginning with a special sympathy for nature as opposed to the works of

---

[1] *De Divisione Mundi*, § 3, ninth century.
[2] Art. " Scholasticism," *Encycl. Brit.*

man in the Christian successors of Plotinus (in the same age
which adopted evolutionary monism as the root of orthodox
theology), passing through a phase of hostility to the higher
and more human arts in the destruction of Paganism and the
iconoclastic controversy, and ending with a complete recognition of a more significant beauty as the manifestation of the
Divine both through art and nature in the age of St. Francis,
St. Thomas, Dante, and Giotto.

This whole circuit is determined, as constantly happens
with dualistic theories, by a shifting location in empirical
reality of the two factors which constitute the dualism.   The
underlying conception is that nature and art, belonging to
the visible [1] universe, are beautiful if and in as far as they
worthily symbolise the Divine power and goodness, and consequently do not appeal to sensuous interest or desire.   But
their respective fitness for this purpose is differently judged
at different times, and the course of this judgment reminds us
in some degree of Plato's speculation, especially when nature
is reckoned as nearer to the creative original than art, when
art is condemned as unable to portray divinity, or when all
beauty, whether of nature or of art, is rejected as a mere
stimulus to sense.   There seems always, however, to be in
the background, more positively than in Plato, at least the
conditional admission that material beauty is divine, if rightly
and purely seen.

From Emanation   i. We should note, to begin with, that in the
to Evolution. fourth century, some two generations after the
death of Plotinus, the great step from emanation to evolution was irrevocably made by Christian dogma in the settle-
ment of the Homoousian dispute.   Whether this idea is or
is not in the sense of the Synoptic Gospels, it certainly marks
the final and essential abandonment of heathenism, and the
climax to which Platonism and Neo-Platonism had gradually
been approximating.   There can be developed, it affirms, out
of the one supreme principle of the world, a progressive and
active content, which does not lose anything, nor become

---

[1] The extraordinary prominence given to the sense of sight in this antithesis from Plato downwards necessarily governs our terminology, and theory
has sometimes, as we shall see in St. Thomas, suffered from this prominence,
which arises both from obvious reasons in the nature of the sense, and probably also from the metaphysical convenience of analogies founded on it as
well as from historical causes.

secondary, by the fact of this development. However verbal or pedantic this may appear to us to-day, it is, if contrasted with the ideas of the greatest Greeks, excepting perhaps Aristotle, a necessary protest against a pessimistic limitation. It denies the rule of progress to be that the first is best, the second a little less perfect, and the third more imperfect still.

Dualism and Love of Nature. ii. And thus we saw how in this fourth century both Chrysostom and Gregory of Nyssa, like the early Christian hymn-writers, fully recognised the beauty of material nature as the direct work and symbol of Divinity, and even accented this recognition by a tendency to disparage, in comparison, the works of man. As early, indeed, as the year 306 A.D. a Spanish Synod[1] had decided that "pictures ought not to be in a church, lest that which is worshipped and adored be painted on walls," and the genesis of iconoclasm goes back in part to the Decalogue and the Judaic element in Christianity. In the language of philosophy this tendency of the fourth century A.D. means that the dualism between sense and spirit is first asserting itself in antagonism to what is most plainly of human origin, as in the modern sentiment that " God made the country and man made the town." Audaciously as this antithesis inverts the true relation of things, it performs a temporary service to culture by forcing into prominence the charm of external nature. But such an effect, if isolated, must be transient ; a dualism which condemns the beauty fixed in art must soon threaten the sense of a beauty perceivable in nature. Before this comes to pass, however, the momentary situation leaves a permanent result in Augustine's account of beauty, dealing, as is natural from his theological position, rather with the world than with fine art, which he, like others of his time, was beginning to distrust.[2]

Augustine on "Beauty of Universe." iii. In his early life, he tells us,[3] he had written books on the Beautiful and Fit, about which writings he now no longer cared, nor knew whether

---

[1] Synod of Elvira. Art. " Image-worship," *Encycl. Brit.*

[2] Augustine lived 354–430 A.D. He expressed disapproval of looking for Christ on painted walls rather than in the written word. There is a letter ascribed to Eusebius of Cæsarea, early fourth century, addressed to the sister of Constantine, refusing a request for a picture of Christ as unlawful, and saying that he had taken away from a lady friend pictures of Paul and Christ which she possessed. *Encycl. Brit*, art. " Image-worship." [3] *Conf.*, iv. 13.

they existed or not. His former interest, however, sufficed
to furnish him with a formal doctrine of beauty, which is indicated by the above-mentioned title, and does not in general
go beyond the conception of symmetrical relations between
parts as belonging to a whole. What is peculiar to him and
constitutes an advance that merits more attention than it receives, is the application of this view, specially supported by
the analogy of fine art, to the universe as a whole considered
as containing evil or ugliness (deformitas). By reason of
this application, due of course to a theological motive, his
view receives a deeper content than the easygoing providential creed of Cicero, which in general expression it very
greatly resembles.

The variety correlative to unity in ancient formal æsthetic
is deepened by Augustine into the opposition of contraries.
This he considers to be essentially included within the symmetry of the universe, as in a beautiful song,[1] or in the antitheses of rhetoric, or in the shadows of a picture, which do
not make it ugly if rightly placed. Poisons, dangerous
animals, and the like, all have their due place in the world,
and so far are elements in its beauty. We have here nothing
to do with the question whether this bold treatment of sin
and suffering can be justified theologically ; but its æsthetic
bearing, which in Augustine's hands is very decidedly emphasised, brings us at once up to the level of modern popular
theory with reference to ugliness, such as we find implied in
poetical or orthodox sentiment to-day. The essence of this
theory is to recognise the ugly as a subordinate element in
the beautiful, to which it serves as a foil,[2] contributing however on the whole to an effect which is harmonious or symmetrical quite or almost in the traditional sense. And it has the
merit of attacking the problem of ugliness more directly than

---

[1] *De. Civ. Dei*, xi. 18, 23 ; xxii. 19.   I quote the title of xi. 18.   " De
pulchritudine universitatis, quæ per ordinationem Dei etiam ex contrariorum
fit oppositione luculentior."   I do not know of what kind the " antitheta " in
a song would be ; I suspect it of simply meaning the responses as sung by
the two sides of the choir under Ambrose at Milan.   In that case, the comparison from music has not the modernism of a reference to discord.   Augustine's modernism in one doctrine, that of the certainty implied in doubt, " Si
dubitat, cogitat," etc., has been mentioned above, p. 78.
[2] " Why rushed the discord in, but that harmony should be prized."—
Browning's " Abt Vogler."

any Greek could attempt, more directly than Plutarch, who excluded the ugly from art except as an evidence of artistic skill, and than Plotinus, unless we interpret his view of the formless so as to give it a positive and not merely a negative bearing. It belongs to an intermediate stage between the abstract and the concrete perception of beauty. Symmetry, it admits, may be enriched by contrast, but symmetry and not characteristic expressiveness is still the ruling principle. It is a note of this popular view to insist on the small quantitative proportion in which it alleges the ugly to exist relatively to the beautiful, and this popular note we find in Augustine as in modern sentiment. But this is not really a consideration of any speculative importance, and tends to confuse the subordination of ugliness to beauty as a factor, with the overpowering of our sense of ugliness by the greater mass of the beautiful—which, if that were all, would be a mere inaccuracy in our perceptions.

There is historical interest in the stress laid by Augustine on the element of colour as a part of beauty in addition to symmetry. We saw that when Socrates conversed about beauty with Parrhasius, the painter was familiar with colour and symmetry as features in the beautiful, although Socrates' account of expression was new to him.[1] The same two terms are adduced by Plotinus in the forefront of his discussion as representing the æsthetic tradition which he censures as inadequate ; but the strange thing is, that in spite of this, they descended *as an adequate account* of the beautiful to Thomas Aquinas through the pseudo-Dionysius,[2] who has very much in common with Plotinus. Here, too, in Augustine, about the contemporary of the pseudo-Dionysius, we find them occupying the same unquestioned place,[3] as though the conspicuous reference of Plotinus to these terms had had more permanent effect than his criticism of them. I transcribe a passage from Augustine which illustrates this point, and also has an interest from containing a thought which reappears in Dante's *Paradiso*.[4] " The beauty of any material object is

---

[1] Xen. *Memor.*, 3, 10.

[2] Thomas Aquinas, *Summa Theologiæ*, secunda pars secundæ partis Sect. 145, which quotes Dionysius by name.

[3] *De. Civ. Dei*, xi. 22, " moles " mass, in contrast to symmetry, and Augustine's view that size is indifferent in beauty, also remind us of Plotinus.

[4] *De. Civ. Dei*, xxii. 19.

congruence of parts together with a certain sweetness[1] of
colour. . . . But how great will be the sweetness of
colour when the righteous shall shine forth like the sun in the
kingdom of their Father."

Suppression of Paganism and Increasing austerity. iv. Augustine, as we saw just now, allowed to
perish as trivial his early writings on the Beau-
tiful and the Fit, which we should have valued so
highly. Yet his whole view of the universe had a strongly
æsthetic tinge, and we must be careful how we interpret as a
datum of the history of æsthetic, the violent suppression of
Paganism which took place in his lifetime by the edicts of
Theodosius, "with the loud and unanimous applause of the
Christian world."[2] The widespread destruction of temples
with their decorations, and their abandonment to decay, tells
of religious hostility combined with brutal indifference to art;
but we must remember that the Parthenon, though disfigured
in the fifth century by its conversion into a church, was hopelessly ruined only by a siege twelve hundred years later; and
the Pantheon, having been preserved at first, we must suppose, by peculiar favour of the authorities, owed its subsequent immunity to consecration in the sixth century.[3] There
is a certain pathos attaching to the fact that the roll of Olympic
victors closes in 393 A.D. with the name of an Armenian, after
a reputed continuance of more than eleven centuries, while
the Pheidian statue of Zeus was carried off to Constantinople
—a step which shows some sense of its value on the part of
the Christians, though we lament that it perished by fire in
476 A.D.

The suppression of Paganism, then, was in the first place
not universally carried out with equal rigour; and in the
second place, though indicating the deepest ignorance, and
indifference to the value of art, did not mainly arise from the
same fanatical repugnance to artistic representation which
subsequently revealed itself in the iconoclastic controversy.
There was indeed in the fourth century already a rising tide of
opposition even to Christian art, but, for the time, the censures
recorded only serve to measure the still increasing employ-

[1] "Suavitas." In the clause following those which I quote "suavitas" is
replaced by "claritas," the term used 800 years later by Thomas Aquinas.
[2] Gibbon's *Decline and Fall*, ch. xxviii. See Gibbon's and Milman's notes
on the attitude of St. Augustine, from whom conflicting passages are quoted.
[3] Gibbon, l.c.

ment of painting and mosaic on the walls of churches.   And
it is plain that the austerity of the later peace of the church [1]
was now beginning to assert itself positively within the sphere
of art as well as negatively against it ; for stories of martyr-
doms were painted on the walls of basilicas,[2] and somewhat
later even the passion and death of Christ were depicted,[3]
contrary to earlier custom.

Along with this change in subjects there grew up, it would
seem, the Byzantine manner of representation, gloomy and
rigid in itself, but powerful by forcing a new element upon
art, which was one day to be assimilated as a new element in
beauty.

Significance of   v. But the same restless dualism—restless be-
Iconoclasm.   cause in principle a monism—which in the visible world preferred nature to art, and in art itself preferred
the absence of what had hitherto been felt as beauty—
in both these aspects repeating the thought of Plato—was
destined to go still further in Plato's track, and turn its distrust
of the visible both against the whole of pictorial art, and
against the whole beauty of the visible world.   In the time
of Gregory the Great (sixth century), the bishop of Marseilles [4]
ordered the removal and destruction of all sacred images
within his diocese, in consequence of which violent action
Gregory laid down the distinction that it is one thing to worship
a picture, and another to learn from the language of a picture
what that is which ought to be worshipped.   What those who
can read learn by means of writing, the uneducated learn by
means of looking at a picture—that, therefore, ought not to
have been destroyed which had been placed in the churches,
not for worship, but solely for instructing the minds of the
ignorant.   The same moderate line which Gregory adopted
was afterwards taken by Charlemagne, and became the rule
of the Western Church, which however, we are told, was by
no means free from iconoclastic opinion.   The didactic value
and mission of art has partly been discussed in connection
with Plato and Aristotle, and though in strict form it falls out-

---

[1] See p. 127 above.
[2] Arts. "Image-worship," and "Mural Decoration," *Encycl. Brit.*   Paulinus
of Nola (d. 431 A.D.) had subjects from Christian history painted as a means
of instruction.
[3] As in the church of San Clemente, at Rome.
[4] Art. "Image-worship," *Encycl. Brit.*

side æsthetic, yet in substance it affects important issues regarding the comparative position of art in literary and in illiterate ages, and if only for this reason will have to be dealt with below.

The actual iconoclastic controversy arose and ran its course within the Eastern Church, covering, with intervals, a period of about 120 years, from 726 to after 842, and it is worth while to note from an æsthetic point of view, the probability that the emperor Leo the Isaurian, whose edict against images began it, had been influenced by intercourse with Jews and Arabs.[1] The high-water mark of the agitation was the Council of Constantinople in 754, attended by 338 bishops, but never recognised as œcumenical, which determined that " Christ in His glorified humanity, though not incorporeal, was yet exalted above all the limits and defects of a sensuous nature, too exalted therefore to be figured by human art in an earthly material after the analogy of any other human body," and pronounced anathema on all who attempted to express by visible colours the form of the Logos in His incarnation, and on all who delineate dumb and lifeless figures of the saints, which could never serve any profitable end.[2] And although the Eastern Church after 842 returned to a theoretical position much like that of Gregory and Charlemagne, yet the Byzantine manner of painting maintained itself in Italy till the twelfth century, and survives in Athos till the present day, under the influence, it would seem, of a distinctly ascetic theory and code of rules.[3]

In this dispute we see yet another phase of the shifting dualism between the spirit and the flesh. Reinforced by the extra-mundane monotheism of Jews and Mahometans, the faith in a spiritual order now turns decisively, as in Plato, against all sensuous presentations as essentially inadequate to that order ; and attains the result of recording a protest, like that of Plato, that in so far as to represent means to copy something that can be copied, so far the spiritual, as such,

---

[1] Gibbon, ch. 49.
[2] Art. "Image-worship," *Encycl. Brit.*
[3] Cf. the alleged remark of a Greek monk on some pictures of Titian, which he had ordered and refused to accept : "Your scandalous pictures stand quite out from the canvas ; they are as bad as statues."—Gibbon, ch. 49 note. "Images," it seems, down to the ninth century, mean pictures and mosaics. Sculptures are only mentioned in the ninth century and later.

cannot be represented in a sensuous form.   The difference is
that now the conception of symbolism is in the air, and the
whole problem is therefore on the level to which Plato raised
it, and not on that from which he started.   The "other" or
spiritual world of which he was concerned to demonstrate the
reality, is now (however crudely apprehended) the one object
of faith to the popular mind ; and the deceitfulness of sensuous
forms is no longer the conclusion of the solitary thinker, but
the premiss fanatically urged by a section of the common
crowd.   Therefore the weight of the problem is thrown in a
new direction ; not towards exalting the value of the "other"
world, but towards re-establishing or maintaining its cohesion
with this.   And though Gregory the Great was indifferent to
learning, and Charlemagne could hardly write, yet the logic
of facts and the experience of ages drove them into a solution
which Plato, just because he helped to make it possible, only
recognised when at his very best.   For the position of these
authorities, who could not be expected to talk the language of
philosophy, and who were conditioned in their policy by all
sorts of passions and necessities affecting the Church of their
respective times—which after all were necessities of human
life—may fairly be paraphrased thus : "We know that
pictures cannot be copies of an essence which is inaccessible
to sensuous perception, and therefore they are not to be
worshipped ;[1] but they can teach, because visible things can
have a meaning ; and therefore pictures are not to be rejected,
but are to be retained as means of instruction and as aids to
memory."   In æsthetic philosophy such a view is incorrect, or
incorrectly formulated.   But the effect of art is not limited by
the grounds which the powers that be allege for permitting it
to exist, and in the widest historical sense, though not in the
strict language of philosophy, there is no doubt whatever that
art is the instructress of peoples.

The System of   vi.   It was in the ninth century, just about the
Scotus Erigena. time at which the controversy regarding pictorial
art in sacred buildings was decided both in the East and the
West, that a really considerable thinker formulated mediæval
ideas in a complete system, and, as a part of it, laid down the
place and nature of material beauty.   The position of this

---

[1] "Es hilft nichts, unsere Knie beugen wir doch nicht mehr." Hegel, *Aesth.* i.
132, describing the inevitable modern distinction between art and religion.

philosopher, Scotus Erigena, from whom I have already[1] quoted
a typical statement of mediæval symbolism, is one of the circumstances that make it hard to know precisely where we are
to look for the Dark Ages.   We are apt to think of them as
a prolonged period, ending with the Renaissance, in which
disputants, ignorant alike of science and of real philosophy,
wrangled about logical forms that were in truth subordinate
to theological doctrines.   But we saw above that our conception of the Renaissance is leading us to trace it ever further
back ; and on the other hand the modern estimate of Erigena
tends to throw the origin of Scholasticism proper somewhat
later than his lifetime.   Scholasticism proper, then, is in fact
the beginning of the end, and coincides with the two or three
centuries of definite intellectual advance that preceded the life
of Dante, assuming that we refuse to attach importance to it
after his day.   But if Scholasticism—the conscious adjustment
of relations between philosophy and theology—marked the
close of the Dark Ages, the speculation of Erigena, continuous
with that of Greek as well as Latin writers, apparently was
before their beginning, in which case the long tract of obscurity,
that represents them to the popular imagination, had really no
existence, and the attributes of the middle age must be stated
with greater care and sympathy.

To begin with, Erigena was a Greek scholar ; the last, I
suppose, in the West before the time of Roger Bacon (twelfth
century).   He writes much in the sense of St. Augustine, but
he also translated from the Greek the writings of the pseudo-
Dionysius, and uses long quotations, rendered into Latin from
Maximus (seventh century).   Dionysius, thus Latinised, affected the opinions of Aquinas ; and so the ideas of Plotinus,
with which Dionysius was saturated, form a continuous strand
throughout the thought of the greatest mediæval teachers.

And again, Erigena was a philosopher ; true philosophy
and true theology were for him coincident, not in the sense of
subordinating either to the other, but in the sense that truth
agrees with truth.   His general views do not strictly concern
us here ; but to show that a writer in the age of faith, whose
use of fact and of analogy is absolutely childish, may yet be
very rational in his leading thoughts upon central questions,
it is worth while to mention that he maintained the Eucharist

---

[1] Page 131 above.

to be merely a symbolical and commemorative rite ; treated the Mosaic account of the creation as purely allegorical, and ascribed to hell no local existence, but regarded it as an inner state of the will.[1]

This is not the opportunity, and I have not the ability, to treat the vast problem involved in the mixture of reason and folly presented to us by the age of faith ; but I may be allowed to point out that in the division of labour, which the course of history enforces, it fell upon the middle age to make the first sketch-plan of a new life, and teach its use to illiterate peoples ; and it is natural that attention could not be given to accuracy of details till after the main bearings had been roughly set down. Neither the philosophy of the great Greek classics nor the wide survey of methodic natural science would have met fairly and squarely the problems which pressed upon Augustine, Erigena, or Dante ; and therefore it seems as if all had happened in its due order, and as if the instruments which did accomplish the task were the only ones which could have done so.

In æsthetic, Erigena does not seem to make any definite advance of detail upon Augustine, and even falls back in comparison with him by a less vivid appreciation of the problem of ugliness. His strength, as is natural for a systematic philosopher, is rather in discriminating the relations which respectively constitute the true and false beauty of the visible world, as depending upon the position which the human mind may assign it with reference to the invisible world. He discusses this question in connection with the story of the Fall, following Maximus in his interpretation of the "tree of knowledge of good and evil." This, the exposition says,[2] stands for the nature of visible things, which, if apprehended in their "reasons"[3] or significance gives the knowledge of good, if taken as the object of desire gives the knowledge of evil that brings death. The "woman" stands for sense, the "man" for reason. God[4] made the visible creation in order that through it, as through the invisible, His praise might be multiplied, and He might be known,—not *what* He is, but that He is the single author of all creation both visible and in-

[1] Prof. Adamson, art. "Erigena," in *Encycl. Brit.*
[2] Erigena, Works, Floss' ed., p. 842.
[3] Rationes, cf. Plotinus' λόγοι.
[4] *Ib.*, 843 B.

visible.   And therefore [in the story of the Fall] God forbade
human nature to take delight in the visible creation before it
(human nature) arrived at the perfection of wisdom in which
being made one with God (deificata), it might be able to converse with God about the significance of visible things.   Nor
would the woman, that is the fleshly perception, be able to attract
the man, that is the intellect,[1] to take delight in the material
creation externally considered (*i.e. not* in its significance), if
he purposed to have the knowledge of the Creator before the
knowledge of the created.   Therefore it was the order laid
down by the divine law, *first* to learn of the Creator and His
unspeakable beauty, and then to regard the creation in a
significant or spiritual sense, conforming to the inclinations
of the intelligence, and to interpret the whole of its beauty,
whether it exist inwardly in significance or outwardly in
sensible forms, as showing forth the praise of the Creator.
" It[2] is not therefore the creation that is bad, nor the knowledge of it, but the perverse impulse of the reasonable mind,
which abandons the contemplation of its author and turns with
lustful and illicit appetite to the love of sensible matter."
And following Gregory[3] of Nyssa, he identifies the ugly with
matter that has no form or the wrong form ; that is, once
more, that is not apprehended or desired in its true relation
to the will of God.   From the point of view of the universe,
I imagine, there is according to Erigena's conception no real
ugliness.
    We find in him no special philosophy of fine art ; the dis-
tinction between the theoretical and the non-theoretical senses
is indeed touched upon,[4] but is rather minimised than accented ;
and the general doctrine of beauty is exceedingly defective on
the side of the distinction between beauty and knowledge.
    Nevertheless we have here a two-edged idea of great im-
portance in the history of the æsthetic consciousness.   In
the first place, Erigena crowns the ascetic movement which
had shown itself in iconoclastic opinion, by a sweeping condemnation of the whole charm of the visible world, including
both art and nature, except on a certain definite condition.
Thus on the one side the antagonism of sense and spirit
finds a thoroughgoing representative in him.
    But in the second place, the condition which he lays down,

---

[1] Animum.   [2] *Ib.*, 844 D.   [3] *Ib.*, 789-90.   [4] *Ib.*, 854.

as essential to real beauty, that the visible creation shall be apprehended as a revelation of the glory of God, and therefore apart from the relation of sensuous desire, appears to me to have more than a rhetorical value. It implies no doubt a *disinterested* sense of the real teleology in man and nature, and therefore approximates technically to Kant's definition, " teleology without an end." And moreover it applies this sense of rationality to the whole world through and through, not merely to art nor to the choicer parts of nature ; thus manifesting that conviction of universal significance which lies at the root both of modern science and of modern art. If we look back to Plato and Aristotle, we shall see that the mediæval " pulchritudo," taken as something co-extensive with the visible universe considered as the work of God which He has pronounced to be good, has become a far more familiar working conception and factor in opinion than was their καλὸν in this particular application to the beauty of material things. And the transition from imitation to symbolism immensely facilitated this generalisation. Imitation is only a rule of art, and *prima facie* can make nothing beautiful which is not given as beautiful. Symbolism is a mode of interpretation ; and with all its enormous risks of arbitrariness, has the one advantage of absolute universality. If all that has a meaning may be beautiful, then there is nothing in which we may not chance to detect an element of beauty. It is easy to see how hopeful is such an idea, and how rich a prospect it opens, in comparison with the notion of the beautiful as finally and unalterably given to perception.

Anticipation of End of World in 1000 A.D. vii. The antagonism between "this" world and the "other" takes its sharpest form for Christians in anticipations of the second coming ; and it is said[1] that in the tenth century these assumed so definite a reference to the year 1000 A.D. (1000 years from the Incarnation) as to give a decided check to the erection of great buildings. Such a revival of the belief in the short-livedness of the whole visible frame of things forms an appropriate climax to the movement which began with a distrust of formative art, and ended with a condemnation, conditional in theory, but probably unconditional in practice, of material beauty as a whole.

[1] *Encycl. Brit.* arts. "Architecture." "Millennium." "Illumination."

After the year 1000, whether owing to relief from the expectation of the end, or to the incipient organisation and
national life of Europe, the practice of building was resumed
with greater zeal than ever, and, as if a crisis had been passed,
even the art of sculpture—though especially hateful to the
ascetic spirit—began to make headway in conjunction with
architecture.

It does not seem, however, that either beauty in general
or fine art in particular received theoretical consideration from
the earlier scholastics.   We find in Abelard's hymns[1] the
familiar sentiment that nature is above art, and he sums up
the discussion, whether the heathen poets should be read by
Christians, unfavourably to the poets,[2] relying in part on the
example of Plato.   His life, and the vernacular love-songs
he wrote, must have had an influence greatly opposed to his
teaching, which was probably determined by a revulsion of
feeling almost analogous to that of St. Augustine on his conversion.

The
Modern Mind
in St. Francis.
viii. St. Francis of Assisi (1182–1226) must be
mentioned here, not only as the earliest Italian
poet, in virtue of the Cantico delle Creature, but
on account of the peculiar qualities exhibited in his life and
character.   No more striking representation of the modern
mind in contrast with the antique, no more felicitous union of
the complementary and contrasted attributes which imply each
other in the logic of evolution, could be invented by the his-

---

[1] Abelard lived 1079–1142.   For the hymns see Cousin's edition of the
Works, 1. 300.   Some verses from a hymn on the Creation are worth quoting.
The beginning of rhyme is noteworthy, and so is the mixture of Horatian
and Christian sentiment.

> Impensis, dives, nimiis
> Domum casuram construis ;
> Falso sole pingis testudinem
> Falsis stellis in cœli speciem.
>
> In veri cœli camera
> Pauper jacit pulcherrima ;
> Vero sole, veris sideribus
> Istam illi depinxit Dominus.
>
> Opus magis eximium
> Est naturæ quam hominum ;
> Quod nec labor nec sumptus præparat
> Nec vetustas solvendo dissipat.

[2] Works, 2. 442.

torian of philosophy to illustrate his argument. We said, in entering upon the post-classical time of decadence, that the modern mind in comparison with the ancient is a divided mind. It is not distinguished by inclusion within one side of an antithesis as against the other, but by presenting both sides of the antithesis, whether reconciled or not, in a form which is at first sight that of the most trenchant antagonism.

First, then, we observe in St. Francis the very height of mystical asceticism, that is, technically speaking, the approach to God by irrational contemplation in withdrawal from the actual world. The story of the stigmata clearly points to habitual self-concentration of this kind.

But, secondly, there is ascribed to him by common consent an extraordinary sympathy with nature, both animate and inanimate. The address to " Brother Sun " is strictly and logically Christian in spirit. The self-concentrated modern mind turns hungrily to nature, as æsthetic theory has pointed out in various formulæ, just because it finds in itself so deep a need.

And thirdly, in the mind of this mystical ascetic and sympathetic lover of nature there was an innate capacity for one great form of reasonable work — for organisation and the management of men. It is needless to enlarge on this characteristic in the founder of the Franciscan order.

Even in so great a character as that of St. Francis these varied tendencies impress us with a sense of mystery and contradiction. They do not display themselves in the same action, and have an external appearance of being rather vicissitudes of life than revelations of a single purpose. They are much less easily explicable than the attributes of the poet who is a citizen poet, or the hero who is a citizen hero, or the philosopher who is a citizen philosopher. And in the lesser moderns they do in fact to some degree fall apart, as they did in the sects and men of the decadence,—the Stoic, the Epicurean, the Neo-Platonist, the amatory or pastoral poet. But yet they have an underlying connection, and in all their rich and apparently lawless profusion are essential attributes of the modern mind. Thus, for example, the self-concentration of St. Francis in his devotional raptures[1] cannot have indicated a mind abstracted or detached from organic reason and

---

[1] It will be remembered that Socrates is said to have been subject to trances of some kind.

reality, but only an element of abstraction and detachment
which is the outward aspect of possession by profound and
complex ideas. Especially this is the case, when, in the intervals of action, ideas fall into shapes of feeling prescribed
by tradition. The depth of the intelligence is correlative and
not antagonistic to its breadth, and the reason which grapples
most energetically and sympathetically with things outside,
both needs, and for that very reason possesses, the profoundest self-concentration within. The meditations of the mere
recluse are generally shallow meditations.

The Æsthetic Ideas of St. Thomas Aquinas. ix. Not much less active and brilliant in his
day, though less known to posterity by other than
literary achievements, was the greatest of Schoolmen, the Dominican Thomas of Aquino. Born in 1227, the
year after the death of St. Francis, he lived on the public
stage as an ardent controversialist in the interest of his order
and of liberty of teaching, as a lecturer in Paris, Rome, and
Bologna, and as the adviser of king and pope on questions of
ecclesiastical management; and closed his amazingly laborious
career at the age of forty-seven, as St. Francis at the age of forty-
four. I insist upon these biographical details because it appears
to me that only by realising the energy of such brief and
versatile lives are we enabled, as also in the history of Abelard,
to place our finger on the quickening pulse of the time. It
might be worth while even to raise the question whether the
weakness of mediæval science and philosophy was not connected rather with excess of practice than with excess of
theory. What we justly stigmatise as the subordination of
philosophy to theology is, in other words, a subordination of
science to a formulated conception of human welfare, with a
strictly mundane if also with a transcendental side. The
question is not unimportant, for it indicates that the essence
of scholasticism is present, not wherever there is metaphysic,
but wherever the spirit of truth is subordinated to any pre-
conceived practical intent, whether mundane or extra-mundane. Some such considerations as these force themselves
upon us, however much we allow for the dissociation of men's
practice from their opinions, when we contrast the busy
public lives of Abelard in his greatness, or of Anselm, of
St. Francis or St. Thomas, with the cloistered industry of
Newton or Locke or Spinoza.[1]

---

[1] I do not think that a comparison even with Descartes and Leibnitz, how-

The *Summa Theologica*, which was to bring to a focus, as we should say, the bearings of all knowledge upon man's highest interests, was the antitype in science of St. Thomas' ideas of political and ecclesiastical unity. In this *Summa* the nature of beauty is more than once referred to.[1] The following points may be noted in accordance with the scheme previously adopted.

Symbolism.   1. The substantive account of beauty is drawn through the pseudo-Dionysius (translated, it will be remembered, by Scotus Erigena) from the tradition which was already a tradition in the time of Plotinus, and was criticised by him as inadequate. The precise correspondence of terms between St. Thomas, in a passage[2] where he cites chapter and verse from Dionysius for his view, and Augustine, Plotinus, and Xenophon[3]—the terms are " Claritas et debita proportio " (brightness of colour and symmetry)=$\chi\rho\hat{\omega}\mu\alpha$ κ. $\sigma\nu\mu\mu\epsilon\tau\rho\iota\alpha$—leaves no reasonable doubt that this is so. In another place[4] " Integritas sive perfectio " is added as a third element of beauty to " Debita proportio sive consonantia" and " Claritas—*i.e.*, color nitidus." But this addition makes no difference of principle, only insisting from the side of the whole on the same condition which " debita proportio " imposes upon all the parts. As in Plotinus, the ultimate ground of attraction in beauty is the affinity, revealed in symmetry, between the percipient and the perceived. Although St. Thomas makes the senses the direct bearers of this affinity— " The senses are charmed with things duly proportioned, as analogous to themselves ('Sicut in sibi similibus'[5])"—yet he clearly adopts the derivation of all beauty from God,[6] and gives, like Plotinus, the first rank to the sense of sight[7] because of its affinity to the intellect.

---

ever prominent in the world these great men were, really invalidates this suggestion. Leibnitz was led by his practical interests to write a *Systema Theologicum* in the interest of Catholic-Protestant reunion. Even Francis Bacon has the scholastic attribute that his logic is moulded rather by a final cause in a human need than by real conditions in the nature of the subject matter.

[1] See Preface.
[2] *Summa Theol.*, 2 pars 2 partis, q. 145, art. 2.
[3] See pp. 45, 117 *supra*.
[4] *Summa*, 1 pars, q. 39, art. 8.
[5] *Ib.*, 1 pars, q. 5, art. 4.
[6] l.c. note 2 above.
[7] *Summa contra gentes*, bk. 3, ch. 53.

Thus we may conclude that symmetry is beautiful, for him as for his predecessors, because symbolic of reason and divinity ; but he does not, any more than they, follow Plotinus in the demand for life and expression as something more than symmetry.

Æsthetic Interest.   2. St. Thomas lays it down that in beauty desire is quiet, or is quieted. The meaning of this, which is *per se* ambiguous, for desire may be quieted by being satiated, seems to be made plain by the inference drawn from it, that the beautiful is the concern of the specially "cognitive" senses of sight and hearing ;[1] and more generally, that beauty has to do with the cognitive power.[2] I think that this does not indicate a confusion between beauty and knowledge, but only a distinction between perception and appetite.

Concrete Criticism.   3. The distinction between the æsthetic and unæsthetic senses—" we do not speak of beautiful tastes or smells,"—is taken on the ground that sight and hearing are more the instruments of reason and more perceptive in their character than taste or smell. This seems to mean, first, that the semblance is in them more separable from the reality which arouses desire ; and, secondly, that they are capable of apprehending a structural whole. That there is no confusion between beauty and knowledge is shown by the clear contrast laid down between material and spiritual beauty, the latter being explained as something named by analogy from the characteristics of sensible beauty.

The primacy assigned to sight as nearer to intellect rests no doubt on the same general grounds which have been analysed above.[3] In estimating it we must bear in mind that the great romantic art of music, as we know it, had not then arisen, while we all the more respect the prophetic insight of Plato and Aristotle, who in great measure understood the extraordinary power of sound.

Thus it appears that the Neo-Platonic tradition was the principal element in the intellectual æsthetic of the middle age. Though a part of Plotinus' concrete application was lost, yet the general scheme of his view was in conformity with the Christian consciousness, which, partly by inheritance and partly by origination, made an analogous conviction its

---

[1] I pars 2 partis, q. 27, art. 1.   [2] I pars, q. 5, art. 4.   [3] p. 117.

own peculiar attribute. That beauty is the revelation of reason in sensuous shape, that its fascination consists in its affinity with mind, and that consequently the entire sensible universe, as a symbol of the Divine reason, must be beautiful to the eye that can see it in relation to its Creator, all this had sunk deep into Christian sentiment, and is familiar to us both in profound and in shallow readings of the argument from design. Unquestionably, the middle age, throughout its long development, was inspired by this conviction, unconscious in its art which was an achievement, but conscious in its theory which was a postulate.

Only there remained, and remains, a certain half-heartedness in theoretical dealing with the phenomena of apparent unreason, for æsthetic as for theology. From the place of the grotesque and the ascetic, the mysterious and the sublime, in Gothic architecture and Byzantine painting, we should infer the boldest and most concrete practical monism, or acceptance of all that is as at least a part of beauty. But, on the other hand, from the total absence, so far as we have seen, of theoretical study directed to the concrete analysis of austere or recondite beauty in nature or in art, we should infer that for mediæval theory the beauty of the universe was rather an abstraction, to be justified in detail by a later age, than an indication of genuine sympathy with the romantic consciousness.

For all that, however, the conception of universal beauty was there in name at least, and by St. Augustine was felt to be capable of including real or apparent contradiction in some degree.

Thus, by the side of a comprehensive and concrete artistic practice there had come down and been accepted a theory more comprehensive still, as including external nature, but bare of detailed application; and when the æsthetic consciousness of the middle age had passed, not indeed from death to a second birth, but from birth and infancy to maturity and articulate utterance, then æsthetic theory was absorbed into artistic practice, which filled it at last with adequate content, destined one day to become in turn the material of more fruitful theory.

Dante was born in the lifetime of St. Thomas, and speaks with his voice, both in the formal theory of beauty, and in the meaning which he ascribes to the universe. Whether he

would himself have said that his great poem was beautiful
according to his own definition of beauty can hardly be
judged ; but if not, it would none the less be true that he
was actively inspired by that conception of universal beauty
which for the mere thinker had probably been little more
than a phrase or a dream.   This wide conception, explicit in
mediæval faith, as implicit in mediæval workmanship, was
represented in the higher imaginative forms by Dante and
his fellow artists, and in being realized was carried far beyond
all previous intellectual ideas of beauty, and very probably
beyond theoretical recognition on the part of those who
realized it.

CHAPTER VII.

A COMPARISON OF DANTE AND SHAKESPEARE IN RESPECT OF SOME FORMAL CHARACTERISTICS.

Limits of the Subjects. The very strict limitations under which the present chapter must be written may seem likely to annihilate its interest, but will really, I hope, preserve it from intolerable tediousness; for any writer would be tedious, I imagine, who, not being qualified by a life-long study of fine art, and being guided only by ordinary cultivated opinion, should wander over the immense field of the Renaissance in search of an æsthetic moral.

I propose, therefore, in the first place, to confine my consideration, except in mere passing remarks, to the two great poets who appear respectively to open and to close the age of the new birth, when we consider it not as a fresh departure in letters and science, but as the flowering time of a beauty that had long been in the making. It will be possible to point out in these two typical cases some important features of the great movement in its course and issue.

And in the second place it would, I should suppose, be unendurable that any ordinary writer should throw out, so to speak, in passing, his general appreciations of these two suns of literature, upon whose splendours the greatest critics and philosophers of the modern world have expended their most industrious study. But under the strict limitations which I propose to adopt there is something definite to be said which is not wholly without value. I may illustrate my meaning by reference to the exploded idea that great artists are guided in production by æsthetic recipes or prescriptions. If it were so, what could be of greater historical interest than to disentangle from their works and to compare with one another the abstract schemes according to which these works were created? And although no such formulæ exist, yet undoubtedly there is in every work of art an element of distinct intention, subject moreover, like all our conscious purposes, to limits perfectly obvious to an onlooker though hidden from the author him-

self, with regard to the species of art to which it is to belong
the sort of subject about which it is to treat, and the sort of point
or significance which it is to possess. Such an element of formal
purpose is especially inevitable in the case of modern artists
who live in an atmosphere of reflection, and among them more
particularly in the case of poets, whose imagination is forced
to be conversant with explicit language and articulate ideas.
It is to this element of formal intention, with its most obvious
limits as regards subject and treatment, that I intend to restrict myself in comparing Dante and Shakespeare.   In itself,
it is in each case a fact no less positive than that Turner
painted landscapes, and Reynolds portraits, or that Goethe
drew from Marlowe the connection of Helena with Faustus.
It is therefore the legitimate prey of the historian, who is
attempting to trace the extent and position of the spheres
successively occupied by the beautiful in the intellectual system.   For the sense and modesty of his interpretation he, of
course, remains responsible.

The Selection of Artistic Form by the two Poets.   First, then, there is a notable contrast in the
selection of artistic form by Dante and by Shake-
speare.   I say "in the selection of artistic form "
and not "in the artistic form selected."   For it might be replied,
" Shakespeare was a dramatist, and Dante was not ; what
then " ?   But this is not quite the point.   The remarkable point
is that Dante, though a worshipper of Vergil, and apparently
well acquainted with Latin poetry in general, and charged,
moreover, in every fibre of his being with respect for intellectual authority, nevertheless devised a totally new species
of poetic art, coming under no possible category in the accepted classification with which he was perfectly familiar.[1]
He himself called his great work a Comedy first because it
begins grimly and ends pleasantly ; and secondly, because it
is written in the vernacular, in which even women converse,
and therefore must be regarded as, in a humble style, contrasted with that of tragedy.[2]

But we need not say that it is not a comedy ; for it is not
even a drama, having neither dramatic form nor dramatic
unity.   Nor can it seriously be taken as an epic,[2] for the in-

---

[1] Letter to Can Grande.   Dante's Works, ed Fraticelli. 3. 508 ff.
[2] As Mr. O. Browning seems to class it, *Encycl. Brit.*, art. " Dante."   Cf.
for the whole of this question Schelling's brilliant essay " Ueber Dante in
Philosophischer Beziehung," *Werke,* 5, 153.

cidents are not in any normal sense parts within a single action ; there is in fact no action, and thus once more, the poem cannot be called a romance. To compare it to a didactic poem would plainly be futile ; and although it contains lyrical elements, yet nothing so heavily burdened with plastic and historical content could conceivably be called a lyrical poem.

And yet it is anything but formless. From the scheme of the versification to the order of the argument, all is symmetrically planned ; and so symmetrically that we should certainly call it pedantic were not its definiteness simply an attribute of perhaps the most vivid imagination that ever expressed itself in poetry.

The *Divine Comedy*, then, is absolutely unique in form. By setting the traditional classification at defiance it raised, at the outset of modern art, the fundamental æsthetic problem whether art-species are permanent. All this significance is lost if we go about in a half-hearted way to effect an approximation between it and an epic or a tragedy. And being unique, it is a very type of individuality. It is, says Fraticelli, "a political, historical, and ethical picture of the thirteenth century."[1] Although it is such a picture, it yet has its central interest in the fate of souls, and more particularly in that of the poet's soul. Nothing could be more universal, and nothing could be more individual, nothing even more personal. It is the climax of the long movement which we have attempted to trace, in which the individual spirit has deepened into a universe within, because it has widened into oneness with the universe without.

When we turn to Shakespeare, we find that in the form of art this unique and personal individuality is to some extent toned down. The comparatively slow development of English genius, together with the local remoteness which was in part its cause, had apparently enabled our great poet to take suggestions from the later or pseudo-classical Renaissance, without, however, being subdued by it into the formalism which elsewhere was rapidly setting in during his lifetime. He is aware of the classical tradition, and takes from it that which he needs The sixteenth century in England had been full of critical dispute and poetical experiments. The "dramatic unities" of time and even of place were maintained by one

---

[1] Fraticelli's edition, Introduction.

party with an absoluteness which we think unreasonable, and
know to be un-Aristotelian   But for this there may have been
a comparative justification if, as Sidney alleges, the common
romantic dramas of his day were even more careless of the
contradictions which they forced upon the audience than the
play of *Ferrex and Porrex* (1561), in which incidents that
would occupy several hours begin and end while a single
speech is being delivered on the stage.[1]   Sidney however
evidently thought that not merely reason, but tradition and
the custom of the ancients, followed, as he tells us, by the
modern Italians, were decisive arguments on behalf of stricter
form.[2]   The " mungrell Tragy-comedie " vexes him greatly;

---

[1] See Sidney's *Apologie for Poetrie*, circ. 1580. Shuckburgh's ed. p. 51 ff.
and notes.   *Ferrex and Porrex* is the play known as *Gorboduc*, in the style of
Seneca.   Sidney only refers to Aristotle as enjoining the restriction of time to
one day, which is correct except for the absoluteness he lends to the "precept."   The unity of " place " he lays down, but does not ascribe to Aristotle.

[2] The whole passage is so picturesque, and so exactly illustrates the scene
on which Shakespeare was just about to appear, that I venture to quote it *in
extenso*.   Shuckburgh's ed. pp. 51–54.

"Our Tragedies, and Comedies (not without cause cried out against) observing rules neyther of honest civilitie nor of skilfull Poetrie, excepting *Gorboduck* (againe, I say, of those that I have seene), which notwithstanding, as it
is full of stately speeches and well-sounding Phrases, clyming to the height of
Seneca his stile, and as full of notable moralitie, which it doth most delight-
fully teach, and so obtayne the very end of Poesie; yet in troth it is very
defectious in the circumstances: which greeveth me, because it might not
remaine as an exact model of all Tragedies.   For it is faulty both in place
and time, the two necessary companions of all corporall actions.   For where
the stage should alwaies represent but one place, and the uttermost time presupposed in it should be, both by *Aristotle's* precept and common reason, but
one day: there is both many dayes, and many places, inartificially imagined.
But if it be so in *Gorboduck*, how much more in al the rest? where you shal
have *Asia* of the one side, and *Affrick* of the other, and so many other under-
kingdoms; that the Player, when he commeth in, must ever begin with telling
where he is ; or els, the tale wil not be conceived.   Now ye shall have three
Ladies walke to gather flowers, and then we must beleeve the stage to be a
Garden.   By and by, we heare newes of shipwracke in the same place, and
then wee are to blame, if we accept it not for a Rock.   Upon the backe of
that, comes out a hidious Monster, with fire and smoke, and then the miserable beholders are bounde to take it for a Cave.   While in the mean-time,
two Armies flye in, represented with foure swords and bucklers, and then
what harde heart will not receive it for a pitched fielde?

"Now, of time they are much more liberall.   For ordinary it is that two
young Princes fall in love : after many traverces, she is got with childe, delivered of a faire boy ; he is lost, groweth a man, falls in love, and is ready to
get another child, and all this in two hours' space : which how absurd it is in
sense, even sense may imagine, and Arte hath taught, and all auncient

but we can hardly be sure whether his censure would have applied to Shakespeare's humour in tragedies, for Shakespeare himself objected in terms not unlike Sidney's, to the officious interference of the clowns in serious passages. Translations from Seneca and an adaptation of the *Phœnissæ* of Euripides were succeeded on the stage by the wild imaginations of Marlowe ; and to Ben Jonson and Shakespeare the whole conflict of forms and tendencies was full of instruction and suggestion.[3]

Coming upon the arena thus prepared for him, Shakespeare adopts a distinctly traditional dramatic form. He accepts the

---

examples justified : and at this day, the ordinary Players in Italie wil not erre in. Yet wil some bring in an example of *Eunuchus* in *Terence*, that containeth matter of two dayes, yet far short of twenty yeeres. True it is, and so was it to be played in two daies, and so fitted to the time it set forth. And though *Plautus* hath in one place done amisse, let us hit with him, and not misse with him.

" But they wil say, how then shall we set forth a story, which containeth both many places and many times ? And doe they not knowe, that a Tragedie is tied to the lawes of Poesie, and not of Historie ? not bound to follow the storie, but having liberty, either to faine a quite newe matter, or to frame the history to the most tragicall conveniencie. Againe, many things may be told which cannot be shewed, if they knowe the difference betwixt reporting and representing. As for example, I may speake (though I am heere) of *Peru*, and in speech digresse from that to the description of *Calicut :* but in action, I cannot represent it without *Pacolets* horse : and so was the manner the Aunciencts tooke, by some *Nuncius* to recount thinges done in former time, or other place.

" But beside these grosse absurdities, how all theyr Playes be neither right Tragedies, nor right Comedies : mingling Kings and Clownes, not because the matter so carrieth it : but thrust in Clownes by head and shoulders, to play a part in maiesticall matters, with neither decencie nor discretion. So as neither the admiration and commiseration, nor the right sportfulness, is by their mungrell Tragy-comedie obtained. I know *Apuleius* did some-what so, but that is a thing recounted with space of time, not represented in one moment : and I knowe, the Auncients have one or two examples of Tragy-comedies, as *Plautus* hath *Amphitrio*. But if we marke them well, we shall find that they never, or very daintily, match Horn-pypes and Funeralls. So falleth it out, that, having indeed no right Comedy, in that comicall part of our Tragedy we have nothing but scurrility, unwoorthy of any chast eares : or some extreame shew of doltishness, indeed fit to lift up a loude laughter and nothing els : where the whole tract of a Comedy shoulde be full of delight, as the Tragedy shoulde be still maintained in a well raised admiration."

[3] Cf. Ben Jonson, Prologue to *Every Man out of his Humour,* 1599, where a reasonable inference is drawn from the fact that dramatic form has had a historical development, to the conclusion that all precepts concerning it are subject to modification in accordance with felt needs that may emerge. Cf. also Polonius in *Hamlet,* " The best actors in the world," etc.

complicated organic structure of Latin comedy, with its five
acts and separate scenes.   He is more careful than his rude
predecessors to motive or excuse his violation of the unities.
He observes, except in the histories, with hardly any deviation, the sharp distinction between tragedy and comedy which
Dante applied so strangely.[1]   That is to say, in the plays of
which the catastrophe is not tragic, the happy ending or
reconciliation is absolutely complete, and no irrevocable misfortune befalls any character in the play.   Cloten in *Cymoe-
line*, and Antigonus in the *Winter's Tale*, are the only exceptions to this rule outside the historical dramas, which are the
continuance of a pre-Shakespearian and romantic form of play.
By the great place he gives to histories, therefore, he so far
defies the traditional classification of dramatic form.   Moreover he refuses to employ the choruses, to observe the unities,
or to push the distinction between tragedy and comedy so far
as to dissociate the former from the humour that belongs to
every complete representation of life.

And in thus accepting a dramatic form he has accepted
its freedom from personal reference.   Perhaps in one well-
known passage there is some playful malice against an old
enemy.   Otherwise, as is only too clear to us, there is no
self-betrayal in Shakespeare.   Even the story of the sonnets
has practically to be accepted in its universal meaning.   Its
personal reference, whether ascertainable or not, is not
woven into the texture of the poems.   What a contrast with
Dante!

Thus in Shakespeare's poetic form the later or classical
Renaissance is modifying the earlier creative or romantic
Renaissance.   And in this he differs from Dante, whose form
is unique, individual, even personal.

The Kind of Sig-   3. With regard to subject-matter and kind of
nificance aimed   significance a parallel contrast may be noted.
at by each.
              Dante's subject-matter is nominally the other
world.   However profoundly he may conceive the unity of the
soul's fate after death with its terrestrial action and character,
this primary peculiarity colours his whole artistic scheme.
Unity and symmetry of parts in the whole, which to him, as

---

[1] "A tragic beginning and a comic ending" seems to have been a stock
mediæval phrase for "a good beginning and a happy ending."   See Dante to
Can Grande, sect. 10.

to the earlier mediæval writers, constituted beauty,[1] is no doubt the ultimate burden of his thought, but the vehicle of its expression is a dualism. In this it represents the mediæval or early modern mind whose utterance it was. The same fate had befallen the kingdom of heaven that befel Plato's ideas. The very principle of unity itself was hardened into something material, at all events into something sensuous, and was set in opposition over against that of which it was meant to be the unity, as "another" world against "this." Such a course of thought was inevitable. Reality, for early ages, must mean material reality, and the spiritual world could not become an object of popular belief except as a non-terrestrial abiding-place. This first dualism between our world of images and the other world of images, forms the content of Dante; but beside and behind it there is also another, the dualism of the entire universe of sense-images over against its spiritual or moral meaning. This dualism within a dualism is never wholly absent from views to which heaven and hell are the necessary complement of earth.

And thus the visions of Dante's art were in the first place fantastic, being dislocated from their human context, and thrown into a shape in accordance with the imagination of a world beyond the grave; and secondly they were consciously and intentionally allegorical or symbolical. He accepted the four concurrent senses acknowledged by mediæval canons of interpretation,[2] as illustrated by himself in the following paragraph from his letter to Can Grande, (c.7.). " In order to a clear understanding of what I am about to say, you must know that the sense of this work [The *Commedia*] is not simple; rather the work might be called 'of many senses.' For there is one sense which is got from the letter, and another which is got from the things signified by the letter; and the former is called literal, the latter allegorical or mysti-cal. This mode of treatment, for the better understanding of it, may be considered in the case of these verses : ' When Israel came out of Egypt, and the house of Jacob from among

---

[1] *Convito*, ii. 5 ; cf. *Paradiso*, i. 103 :
  " Le cose tutte quante
  Hann' ordine tra loro ; e questo è forma,
  Che l' universo a Dio fa somigliante."
[2] " Litera *gesta* docet : quid *credas* allegoria,
  Moralis quid *agas* ; quid *speres* anagogia."—*Fraticelli.*

a strange people, Judah was His sanctification [Vulgate] and
Israel His dominion.[1]   For if we look at the letter alone,
there is signified to us the exodus of the children of Israel
from Egypt in the time of Moses; if at the allegory, our
redemption by Christ ; if at the moral sense, the conversion
of the soul from the grief and misery of sin to a state of grace;
if at the anagogic [elevating sense], the exodus of the holy soul
from the bondage of corruption to the liberty of eternal glory.
And although these mystic senses are called by different
names, yet generally they may all be called allegorical, seeing
that they are different from the literal or historical.   For
'allegoria' is called so from the Greek ἀλλοῖος, which means
in Latin ' alienum' or 'diversum.'"

Are these two elements, then, the fantastic element resting
upon the subordination of this world to the next, and the allegorical and abstract element resting on the subordination of
all perceptible forms to a whole hierarchy of spiritual or ethical
interpretations,—are these what is demanded by a theory which
gives the weight we have persistently claimed to creative
imagination and spiritual symbolism in the analysis of beauty ?
Certainly they do not impress us in this way, when thus set
out in abstract language, for, to mention no other objection, it
would seem that thus taken anything could be made to mean
anything, so that all reality and definiteness in the perception
of beauty would be destroyed.   If beauty indeed lies in symbolic meaning, and if symbolic meaning is utterly arbitrary,
then we ask with Fra Lippo Lippi :

> " Why for this
> What need of art at all ? A skull and bones,
> Two bits of wood nailed crosswise, or, what's best,
> A bell to chime the hours with, does as well."

I hope that the distinction which solves this paradox will
become clear of itself, through the very contrast which we are
now engaged in considering.   But with reference to Dante
and mysticism in general, I must recall the principle which I
have insisted on more than once before,[2] namely that the
æsthetic value of mysticism, like the scientific value of alchemy,
lies not in its precepts but in its practice.   A man is not a
great artist because he is prepared to see in everything, in a
beautiful woman, in a classical poet, in a wood or a mountain,

---

Quoted in *Purgatorio*, ii. 46.   [2] Ch. 2 and ch. 6 *supra*.

or in the extraordinary attitudes or sufferings of human beings, types of theology and science, of ignorance, aspiration, and various kinds of sin ; this general tendency of mind Dante merely shared with the whole middle age from Plotinus downward. But yet, the faith in a meaning is a great assistance to looking for one ; and as a general rule the more a man looks for, the more he will see. Beauty, in short, thus ceases to be a datum, and becomes a problem ; and in pursuing a fanciful interpretation, the mind will often extract the expressive essence of sensuous forms, with incomparable subtlety. Dante is not a great poet because in speaking of a she-wolf he signifies by it at once the temporal power of the Pope and the sin of avarice ; but because in his intentness upon the issue and the meaning, nothing that has a natural significance escapes his eye and ear. The place of *sound* in the *Commedia*, though suggested by Vergil,[1] is so developed into importance as to be something new to art ; much of the horror of the *Inferno* consists in it, while the beauty of its introduction in the *Paradiso* gives that part of the poem almost a lyrical character.[2] Remarkable as is Dante's love and perception of light,[3] in which he follows the mediæval tradition, and probably the superstition inherited from Plotinus, yet the modern theorist cannot complain that he has inadequately recognised the power of sound. And the same is true of human speech and gesture. No Hellene, however skilled a spectator in the theatre of this life, has portrayed the beauty and terror of visible and audible things with so true and piercing a touch as this mystic hierophant of another world.

In the art of Shakespeare, as distinguished from his private life and opinions, with which we are not here concerned, we find neither this kind of subject matter nor this kind of significance.

In the first place, the balance of forces in the machine of humanity is for him not seriously affected by what lies beyond the grave. We could disregard "the life to come" ; what affects our action is that "we still have judgment here"—an antithesis with Dante, which is really profound, but appears even profounder than it is if we fail to realise how for Dante

---

[1] *Æn.* 6. 426. " Continuo auditæ voces," etc.
[2] Schelling, l.c.
[3] See Church's *Essay on Dante* for a collection of passages.

too, heaven and hell lay ultimately in character. Yet when all this is allowed for, the difference remains immense. The first of the two dualisms which we found in the middle age, has in Shakespeare almost ceased to exist, and with it disappears the fantastic side of imagination, the dislocation of the visible world. Just here and there the presentation of real con- nexions is bordered or interwoven with a playful or mysterious supernatural, which does no more than furnish a decorative heightening to the true line of causal construction So far then, in sheer form of imagination, Shakespeare reverts to- wards the Greeks ; for their world also was one, and their divine was not supernatural. But the one world of Shake- speare included all that was not fantastic, all that was not mere machinery in the two worlds of the middle age ; and his naturalism therefore was on a different plane from that of the Greeks. It was in the very widest sense a romantic as con- trasted with a classical naturalism.

And the second dualism, which we found in Dante, also ceased to exist, as a dualism affecting the form of imagin- ation, in Shakespeare. Conscious allegory or symbolism, in which a thing and its meaning are two, like a riddle and its answer, was to Shakespeare a form of mediæval pedantry, just as the dramatic unities were a form of classical pedantry. Nothing does more to bring him near to us as a modern of the moderns than his easy superiority and cultured experience in face of the pseudo-classical and romantic oddities that had come down to his age. The allegory or arbitrary symbol is dis- cussed between Pistol and Fluellen ; the "elegancy and facility and golden cadence of poetry," insisted on by Holofernes ;[1] the figure in rhetoric is given over to Touchstone, and the syllogism and law of identity to the clown in *Twelfth Night*. Indeed, without pressing dramatic expression into doctrine, it is fair to take note of Hamlet's sentences, "for anything so overdone is from the purpose of playing, whose end, both at the first and now, was, and is, to hold as t'were the mirror up to nature ; to show virtue her own feature, scorn her own image, and the very age, and body of the time, his form and pressure." Whether by chance or by some freak of tradition,

---

[1] It is Holofernes who says "*Imitari* is nothing, so doth the ape his keeper " ; and seems to prefer "the flowers of fancy, the jerks of invention." Is this a chance satire on some rebellion against the Greek theory of art ?

these words accept for the drama (I do not think that "play-ing" need here be sharply distinguished from the play) the very comparison by which Plato believes himself to represent the utter worthlessness of poetry, of the unreal making of things. It may be worth while to re-quote his words, which are cited in chap. II. of this work. "There are many ways in which this feat (of 'making' everything) might be accomplished, none quicker than that of turning a mirror round and round—you would soon make the sun and the heaven and the earth, and yourself, and the animals, and plants, and all the other creations of art as well as of nature, in the mirror." Thus once more, in comparison with Dante, we are back among the Greeks. Something indeed in the phrase which Shakespeare throws out even thus by the way, "the body of the time," "his form and pressure," indicates the representation of life as a whole, of a tendency, and a spirit, and so far modifies the simile of the mirror. But the artificial symbol, the reality, not merely wrenched apart into separate worlds, but cut and thinned down to fit its abstract meaning, has disappeared along with the hierarchy of separate interpretations; and, if we are to consider only the great world-epochs of the æsthetic consciousness, is gone for ever.

But though the machinery of spiritual interpretation is thrown aside, the essence of it survives as a permanent gain. The value of human souls and the significance of their destiny[1] are no longer operative as abstract principles to be clothed in allegorical fantasy, but as an added force and tenderness in the penetrative imagination. It is worth while even to point out that as nature repeats herself with a difference in the phases of evolution, a relation justly perceived in one part, will as a rule bear a genuine analogy to many relations on other planes of experience ; and therefore even

---

[1] " Is it true that we are now, and shall be hereafter
But what or where depends on life's minute?
Hails heavenly cheer, or infernal laughter
Our first step out of the gulf, or in it?
Shall man, such step within his endeavour,
Man's face, have no more play and action
Than joy that is crystallised for ever,
Or grief, an eternal petrifaction ? "
BROWNING, *Old Pictures in Florence.*

M

the hierarchy of allegorical meanings, if its fantastic or arbitrary
element were withdrawn, might turn out something more real
than was known by those who formulated it.   At any rate,
the "reasons," laws or powers which work in man and in nature
are now represented in their operation as character and expression, not outside it as Deity, or theological principle or
reward and punishment.   Thus the definition of Plotinus,
identifying beauty with the expression of the rational, was for
the first time fulfilled without abstraction or divorce of the
elements involved in it, and the mediæval aspiration to see
the universe as beautiful in spite of all its contradictions, was
accomplished with even a more perfect unity than that revealed by Dante.

The true Relations   4. In concluding the comparison which forms
of the later
Renaissance,   the subject of this chapter, we must recall the two
conceptions of the Renaissance which we spoke of as linking
it respectively with what came after and with what went before.

We are accustomed in accordance with the former habit
of thought to regard Shakespeare mainly as the creator of
our present poetic world, and the inaugurator of our national
greatness in the field of literature.   Now in one sense this
is all very true.   He forms the most brilliant starting point
of our literary art, just as Newton does of our science and
Locke of our philosophy.   But if we think that our art and
its conditions are continuous with his art and its conditions,
and that the perception of beauty as a living and active
force was awakened in his time and has had a continuous
development from then till now, in that case I imagine
we are deceived.   Within the history of the concrete feeling
for beauty, to which poetry, and especially the drama belongs on one side, though it also borders closely upon the
province of intellect, Shakespeare in every way marks not
the opening but the close of a period.   Since him there has
been no national drama.   To-day in England the drama, in
the sense of stage-plays which are poetic literature, does not
exist.   And I imagine that what of this kind exists elsewhere,
and has existed since the middle of the seventeenth century, is
only enough to show clearly that some conditions, whatever
they may be, have during all that time been hostile to dramatic
art.   By the year 1600 the genuine productive impulse of the
earlier Renaissance—the only productive impulse which the

Renaissance contained—had already exhausted itself every-where but in England, where it was later felt. Our two most competent critics agree in substance though probably not in feeling about the import of that painting by Raphael in the Vatican, which seems to set heathen poetry under Apollo on an equality with Christian doctrine under Christ. [1] And this room in the Vatican had been painted about 1508. Since then, although new movements of an isolated kind were preparing, the rich and simple beauty which was rooted in the middle age had become a thing of the past. Mannerism and the classical Renaissance on one side, science and philosophy (Descartes was born in 1596), the reformation, the English revolution, industrial changes, and the spread of printed liter-ature on the other, were rapidly making an end of the great artistic and architectural age of the modern world. Nothing is more striking than the present revulsion of feeling on the part of the most competent judges, against the architecture of St. Peter's at Rome.[2]

To condemn a revolution of this kind is like condemning the course of nature. After the flower, the fruit ; no plant flowers for ever and all the year round. Shakespeare had, as we saw, the good fortune to come at the very close of the great creative time, bringing his pregnant and plastic genius to meet the growing influence of free thought and classic tradition, so that by wonderful good fortune he was able to deal with the whole mass of romantic material in a spirit of natural freedom that was almost classical. It was perhaps as well that he was not conversant with the Athenian dramatists. A single simile of Euripides, it is said, is all that can be proved to have filtered through, by translation and retranslation, from the great Greek tragedians to Shakespeare. It comes through " the Jocasta of George Gascoigne and Francis Kinwelmersh " (1566), a motley and incongruous piece built on the model of

---

[1] Ruskin, *Lectures on Painting and Architecture*, p. 213, says this was the Mene, Tekel, Upharsin, of the arts of Christianity. Mr. Pater, *Renaissance*, p. 186, says, "it is the classical tradition, the orthodoxy of taste, that Raffaelle commemorates." Irenæus (end of second century, A.D.) says that Gnostics set up images of Christ along with those of Plato and Aristotle. The same point was passed twice, first with faces set to leave paganism, and next with faces set to return to it.

[2] See Mr. Wm. Morris, quoted above, p. 125.

the *Phœnissæ*,[1] really translated from the Italian without any
trace of an appeal to the original, and it suggested the
splendid passage in Hotspur's speech: "By heaven, methinks
it were an easy leap ——" It is impossible to suppose that
even Shakespeare's genius, lightly as it dealt with Plutarch
and Ovid, and with Plautus and Seneca, would have stood
up quite unshrinkingly before Æschylus and Sophocles.   It
appears to us that in his case the true equilibrium of form and
matter was attained, and that any further reinforcement of
the influence of antiquity might have impaired that singleness
of vision which makes him not only the last artist of the age of
mediæval romance, but the first of that age which we rather
hope for than have arrived at, the age of romantic classicism
or modern classical naturalism.

For the pseudo-classical tradition, which, seconded by the
peculiar fulness and force of the time, was for the moment a
purifying factor in art, had many transformations to undergo
before it again became anything but a noxious influence in the
concrete æsthetic consciousness.   Ultimately, indeed, through
centuries of theory and criticism, it led back to a knowledge
of genuine Hellenic life and art and ideas.   And the best
perhaps that this knowledge in the hands of Lessing, Winckelmann, and Goethe did for art was to set it free from the
fetters which a shallower knowledge had imposed.   But in
the purely intellectual region very great things sprang from
this deeper and more genuine knowledge, and among these
great things there arose, as the course of general speculation
on its side demanded, a vital and profound æsthetic philosophy, which in its turn contributed a factor of very great
value to the general speculation of the early nineteenth century.

Æsthetic theory, then, as true philosophy develops, loses,
and rightly loses, its practical relation as a guide to art ; and
the work of the best æsthetic theorists has been in a great
measure to protest against that very misapplication of abstract
precept to art which was a survival, in the wrong place, of
the same critical tradition that had been the forerunner
of true æsthetic theory.   If, besides this negative function,

---

[1] Mahaffy's *Hist. of Greek Literature*, i. 366.   The original in Euripides
runs (*Phœnissæ*, 504, Eteocles)—

ἄστρων ἂν ἔλθοιμ' αἰθέρος πρὸς ἀντολὰς
καὶ γῆς ἔνερθε, δυνατὸς ὢν δρᾶσαι τάδε,
τὴν θεῶν μεγίστην ὥστ' ἔχειν τυραννίδα.

æsthetic philosophy can ever have a positive value for artistic creation, it can only be in the very secondary sense in which first through technical philosophy, and then through popular culture, it may insist on the relation of beauty to life, and explain that, for example, to " imitate " the Hellenes in the true sense is not to copy their sculpture, but to be, *mutatis mutandis*, such men as they were. The greatest of all new departures since the time of Shakespeare—the art of music and that of landscape painting—have been wholly independent both of æsthetic theory and of Hellenic example ; and although the widening of our world by the recovery of antique master-pieces cannot but be helpful when their effect has, so to speak, passed into the blood of our æsthetic organism, yet I imagine that Greek literature has done little directly for our greater poets, and that study from the Elgin marbles has been an influence not without its danger for our painters.

True æsthetic speculation, on the other hand, has been throughout in the profoundest sympathy with the new departures and growing freedom of that sense of beauty, from which its material is drawn. So far indeed as in passing it may permit itself to judge rather than to understand, which latter is its only true function, it laments the difficulty and interruption which has been experienced by the European mind since Shakespeare's time, in carrying forward the large and free expression of life in art which he inaugurated. Whether the future will show more continuity, and less that seems to be distraction and reaction belonging to a level which Shakespeare has transcended, it is not for us to predict. Our immediate task is go forward, through the awaking of free speculation and the deepening of current criticism, to the development of æsthetic theory as an integral element in modern philosophy.

a (p. 163). Mr. Churton Collins has shown that there is a good deal more to be said about Shakespeare's knowledge of the ancients. The question as between echoes and coincidences is most puzzling and interesting.

CHAPTER VIII.

THE PROBLEM OF MODERN ÆSTHETIC PHILOSOPHY.

The Process of Preparation. 1. THE beautiful is of interest to metaphysic as the tangible meeting point of reason and feeling, and to criticism as the expression of human life in its changing phases and conditions. The combination ot these two interests, after a protracted separate development, is the true genesis of modern æsthetic. Under the term criticism I understand for this purpose the whole detailed work of reflective thought in the exploration and appreciation of particular beautiful things, including therefore the services of classical scholarship in making accessible the great writers of Hellas, the labour of archæologists both in disinterring and interpreting the treasures of Herculaneum and the other remains of the antique world, and finally the activity ot art criticism in the narrower sense, as the literary judgment passed upon works that claim to be beautiful, with reference to their beauty.

In a general sense it might therefore be said that criticism from Sidney and Scaliger to Lessing and Winckelmann furnished æsthetic philosophy with its data, while metaphysic from Descartes to Kant supplied it with postulates or a problem. In each of these streams of thought further combinations of tributaries may be traced, and between them are all kinds of cross-connections. But the main distinction will, I believe, approve itself as just.

The Prolonged Interruption of Æsthetic. 2. In these preparatory processes, each of them extending over a period to be measured by centuries, we may find the key to a difficulty which necessarily confronts the student at the point we have now reached.

This difficulty, in its widest extent,[1] arises from the inter-

---

[1] The view referred to in the following pages is that of Schasler, *Aesthetik*, Buch II., Einleitung. I have attempted to indicate his conception, and my deviations from it, without the extreme lengthiness which a formal discussion of it would involve.

mission of æsthetic philosophy, considered as a theoretical study of fine art, from the time of Plotinus to the eighteenth century of our era.

But we may at once deduct from the period during which the absence of such theory is remarkable by far the larger part of the interval in question ; that is to say, the whole of the middle age down to the fourteenth century. The reason how-ever for which we may so deduct it is not that which an obsolete conception of the Renaissance is ready to assign. It is not that in the middle age there was no practical æsthetic consciousness, and therefore no object-matter to which a theoretical study of art could have been directed.[1] There was no æsthetic consciousness, it is said, because art was purely the handmaid to theology, and was not yet alive to its true purpose of creating the beautiful. Such an explanation combines a historical blunder with a philosophical fallacy. The actual æsthetic consciousness of the middle age was as a historical fact the most continuous and creative that the world has ever seen. And although for long centuries it was inarticulate in the more intellectually imaginative regions, and accepted theology, perhaps, as the expression of its essential instincts, yet to set this fact down as precluding its claim to rank as an æsthetic consciousness at all is to commit the serious philosophical confusion of identifying the concrete ex-pressive impulse with the reflective æsthetic intention. So far from its being true that there is no genuine art-conscious-ness where there is no intentional aim at beauty for beauty's sake, it is probable that such intentional aim is at least a grave danger to art, if not a sure symptom of decadence. It is not the case, then, that the absence of detailed æsthetic research during the middle age was owing to the absence of any object-matter for such research. It was owing not to the lack of an art-consciousness, but to the very directness of the art-impulse, combined with the pressure of those other needs and problems which belong to the youth of a new civilization, and which invariably hinder the mind of such an age from reflecting systematically upon its own productions. The elements of theoretical asceticism on the one hand, and of theoretical recognition of beauty in the universe on the other, which we traced throughout this period, only show that

---

[1] Schasler, l.c.

it was not the first but the second youth of the world—a second youth dealing according to its wants in naive and uncritical fashion with ideas handed down from a first maturity. A self-criticising theory could no more be expected of such an age, in spite of its not small intellectual equipment, than of Athens before the time of Socrates.

But there still remains to be considered the period after the culmination of religious art in the fifteenth century, when *primâ facie* it would appear that the object-matter of æsthetic existed in abundance ; and with regard to this period the question has been urged, " Why did not the full growth of modern æsthetic follow in two generations upon the art of Raphael, as that of ancient æsthetic did upon the art of Pheidias ?" The answer given appears to me to be a false application of a simple truth. Ancient art, it is said, was practically complete when its religious inspiration had attained full expression ; but the modern mind is reflective or divided, and modern art—the object-matter necessary as a condition precedent of æsthetic theory—was not complete till the cycle of secular as well as of religious interest had been traversed by it in a continuous advance lasting till the eighteenth century. Now of course in the largest sense the cycle of modern art is not complete even to-day, and we hope that it never will be. But relatively speaking, the great art-age of the world did begin to draw to its close in Raphael, although by special causes it was prolonged in other countries so as just to cover our Shakespearian drama. Therefore the question is wrongly put, for the completion of the same single and continuous period to which religious art belonged, falls after Shakespeare and not after Raphael ; and the answer is erroneous, inasmuch as it assumes a natural progress even in pictorial art from the sixteenth century onwards ; whereas really there was then setting in the close of a period, only somewhat disguised by various forms and rates of disintegration in different European countries.

The reflectiveness, range and versatility of the modern mind is rightly appreciated in the question and answer which we have examined ; but they fail to give weight to the distinction between such secularisation of art as that of Raphael's successors, which marks the end of the great period, and is itself a decadence not because it is non-religious, but because it is no longer an expression of vigorous life; and

such secularisation as that of the Elizabethan drama, which
belongs by its colour, strength and profoundness to the
middle age, though touched and liberated by more modern
influences.

After the Elizabethan drama in England, and earlier still
in Italy, the impulse of the middle age was exhausted, and
art had entered upon its chequered modern career, which did
not attain any special completion in the eighteenth century
such as would account by itself for the rise at that time of
æsthetic speculation. The proof of this statement with regard
to the close of a great continuous artistic age throughout the
cultured countries of Europe in the fifteenth and sixteenth
centuries could only be given by a complete survey of the
history of all those minor forms of beautiful workmanship
which are an absolutely infallible test of the extent and solidity
with which practical æsthetic consciousness is engrained in
the mind of any age. There has not been in any country of
Europe since the beginning of the seventeenth century a
generation really fertile in beautiful production, whether in
architecture, sculpture, metal-work or wood-carving. It is on
this ground, combined with the peculiar changes that passed
over painting and poetry themselves at the time referred to,
that we may safely affirm the position of art in Europe since
the sixteenth century, however occasionally brilliant, to have
been quite different from that which it occupied before.

Our question then is, not, why did æsthetic fail to arise
directly after the time of Raphael, but rather, why did it fail
to arise directly after the time of Shakespeare? And the
answer is, not that art retained continuous vitality till the
eighteenth century, so that before that time the material of
æsthetic was incomplete ; but that the peculiar nature of this
material in modern times, consisting largely of a tradition alien
to modern life, demanded a long process of critical appreciation before its content could fairly reach the mind. It is quite
true that the modern consciousness, in comparison with the
ancient, is divided and not single. The mere territorial extension and national subdivision of the area of European culture
in the seventeenth century is enough to bring this sharply
before us when we compare it with the Athenian period, or
even with that of Hellenism or Greco-Roman civilisation,
though this had great territorial extension and some tinge of
local colour. The architecture, painting, language and litera-

ture of France, Italy, and England alone, down to the seventeenth century, form a material which could not be organised
by reflection in one or two generations.   And yet this was
only, relatively speaking, one factor in the problem presented
to theory.   Each of the two great streams of intellectual
activity, that of philosophy and that of criticism, had not only
to absorb a present, that is, a recent past, of immense complication, but had also to adjust itself to antitheses bequeathed by
the remoter past called antiquity, both in its own content, and
in its relation to the present.   Till these two processes were
completed, and their results were ready to combine, there
could be no fertile æsthetic.

3. The philosophical preparation of the æsthetic
Preparation of problem, like the critical preparation of the
the Problem.
Descartes æsthetic data, includes more than one tendency.
to Baumgarten.
As ultimately stated in Kant's *Critique of the
Power of Judgment*, that problem was the outcome of those
two tendencies of modern thought, which determined his entire
philosophy—itself a statement of this same problem in all the
principal shapes which it was capable of assuming.

i. As a first approximation to indicating the
The two nature of these two tendencies, we may mention
Tendencies,
"Universal" and them under the technical names "universal" and
"Individual."
"individual" respectively ; the Cartesian school
with its descendant, the Leibnitz-Wolffian philosophy, being
marked, on the whole, by insistence on the aspect of rational
system and necessary connection in the universe (a tendency to
which the peculiar monadic theory of Leibnitz forms no real
exception) ; while the British empirical school, from Bacon to
David Hume, started rather from individual feeling or sense-
perception, and required that the theory of reality should be
derivative from what this was supposed to announce.   In the
eighteenth century this latter mood was backed by all the
forces of the time, especially by the passionate sentimentalism
of Rousseau and the less philosophical scepticism of Voltaire.

But the logical terms "universal" and "individual" do not
give us much help in appreciating the real nature of the tendencies thus described.   In all conceptions that have ever
approved themselves to reason, whether in ancient or modern
times, the factors thus designated necessarily find a place.
We must therefore, if we wish to get nearer our subject than
this general approximation, distinguish the particular shape in

which the universal and the individual tendency reveal themselves in modern philosophy before Kant, first from the shape
which they took in classical antiquity, and secondly from the
shape which each one of them takes within the current of
thought in which the other is predominant. If we can make
this clear, we shall have done all that is needed to explain
Kant's philosophical attitude towards æsthetic questions, and
happily we are not called upon to undertake the gigantic task
of narrating the whole development of pre-Kantian speculation. For philosophy proper, by which I mean the
speculations of men who are known as thinkers on other
grounds than their contributions to æsthetic criticism, reveals
its extraordinarily abstract character during this period by an
almost entire omission to deal with æsthetic questions, under
this or any other name. What little demands remark in Shaftesbury, Leibnitz and Baumgarten—Lord Kaimes, Lessing, and
Burke being counted among the critics, and not among
the philosophers—we shall find occasion to notice in explaining the tendencies to which they severally belong.

Distinguished from Ancient Philosophy. ii. First then, we are to distinguish the "universal" and "individual" tendencies of such
thinkers as Descartes and Locke respectively
from the corresponding tendencies in any philosophers of
antiquity ; let us say, of the Stoics on the one hand and of
Epicureans on the other,

We should begin by noting the difficulty of finding adequate contrasted examples of such tendencies in classical
philosophy. In Plato and Aristotle, for instance, the two
factors of thought are fairly in equilibrium, and we could hardly
find, to set against either of these thinkers, a school of real
importance in whom the balance was notably different.
While if we compare the Eleatics with the Atomists or with
Heraclitus, we feel that the antithesis with which we are dealing has no depth of application, such as the modern antagonism between free-will and necessity, or between passion and
reason. This difficulty of finding a good example shows
how little, comparatively speaking, the ancient mind was torn
and dragged asunder by the conflicting claims of partial elements in human nature each striving to pass for the whole.

But further, if we look at such a contrast as that between
Stoics and Epicureans, in which the mind of the old world is
beginning to pursue divergent ideals after a more modern

fashion, we see that the antagonism is far less internecine than its modern representative. On the one hand, neither of these aspects of life is irreconcilably differentiated from the other which is its complement; on the other hand, neither makes so jealous and exclusive a claim to be all that there is, and to annihilate its opposite out of the reasonable world. Stoicism is the outcome of one mood, Epicureanism of another. They are no doubt controversial in so far as they consist in rival theories, but each of them was to a great extent a way of life, and its adherents chose a path which suited their own tastes and did not bring them into conflict with the others. But, as we have amply seen, the characteristic of the Christian mind is to lay claim to the universe as belonging to the individual soul. Nothing is indifferent to this mind ; God is everywhere, and wherever He is there is something for man to know, to do, or to enjoy. During the long centuries of the middle age this faith had been formulated in positive doctrine, and had embodied itself unconsciously in the widening range of sensuous perception and pleasurable production, so that when the flower of formative art had passed away, and the free intellect of Christendom began to re-construct its world in terms of self-conscious reason, both " universal " and "individual" points of view asserted themselves only as deeper complications within a frame of mind which to begin with was pre-eminently individual. The infinite value of a soul was a lesson too deeply bought to be readily forgotten.

Thus the two tendencies of modern thought are distinguished from their ancient correlatives by their common point of departure in the thinking, feeling and perceiving subject. Scepticism, which marked the close of ancient philosophy, characterised the beginning of modern speculation. Augustine, as we saw, very nearly anticipated the principle that my thought involves my existence, or rather, in Augustine's words, that my doubt implies my thought ; [1] and on some such basis, the basis of existence as a separate but thinking being, the thinking, feeling and percipient subject in modern times deliberately invades the system of things, with the conviction that it will certainly find therein what it demands ; either a reasonable framework according to causal laws, or general truths in harmony with observed phenomena, or a life that

---

[1] Page 134 above.

will respond to its moral or hedonistic requirements. All that it finds is expected or required to be in conformity with the organ or faculty of the subject, so that starting from itself as centre it can critically verify and reconstruct the world, from which it began by ideally isolating itself. There is nothing in antiquity at all comparable to the combined feeling of externality and of assured dominion with which Bacon and Descartes look out upon phenomena.

And from each other. iii. This being the general type of modern as contrasted with ancient speculation, for which the history of the post-classical decadence and of the middle age has I hope prepared the reader, we have further to ask how, within this individual or modern mood, the ineradicable impulses known as "universal" and "individual" again assert themselves in philosophy. The history of philosophy appears to answer the question in the most straightforward way. In Descartes, Spinoza, Leibnitz, Wolff, Baumgarten we find a continuous march of thought which is abstractly rational and intellectual; in Bacon, Locke, Shaftesbury, Berkeley, Hume, Rousseau, we recognise an empirical or sensationalist tendency no less abstract. The two streams meet in Kant, and it is their convergence in his system that sets the problem to later modern speculation as a whole, and more especially and distinctively, owing to the peculiar conditions of this problem, to modern æsthetic speculation. "How can the sensuous and the ideal world be reconciled?" is the general problem; "how can a pleasurable feeling partake of the character of reason?" is the same problem in its special æsthetic form.

But we have further to note, as a characteristic of the modern temper, that inasmuch as each of the philosophical tendencies is theoretical and controversial, claiming absolute and exclusive universality, the logical force of facts compels each of them to be represented within the line of progression mainly dominated by the other; and it is therefore only by comparison, and in virtue of their respective bases and assumed points of departure, that the one chief course of thought is distinguished from the other. Bacon, who championed the cause of "particulars" as if they were an oppressed population, held himself to be the very prophet of exact science—the abstract universal ;—and Hume, whose point of departure is the isolated sensuous impression, not only admits the universal under the name of a fiction, but in his entire scope and method of reasoning is guided by a spirit of abstract analysis which makes him, though the extremest of sensationalists in metaphysic, a utilitarian rationalist wherever he touches on æsthetic.[1]

In the Cartesian school, on the other hand, the starting point is the abstract universal or the systematic intelligence, in terms of which feeling and sensation are taken into account only as obscure or confused ideas. Although in Leibnitz there is a concession to individualism, as against the monotonous abstraction of Spinoza, yet the system retains its purely intellectual form, and the estimation of sensation and feeling as inferior species of intellectual idea was adopted by Wolff, and in Baumgarten's hands determined the point of view under which æsthetic was for the first time enrolled among the accepted branches of modern philosophy.

Connection with Mediæval Dualism.

iv. We saw that the doctrinal dualism of early Christianity and of the middle age was only a materialised expression for a conviction which never exactly coincided with it. It would be ridiculous to say that such men as Dante, or Francis of Assisi believed the world of spiritual realities to lie far away beyond the grave. But it is true that they were unable to satisfy the whole strenuousness of their own and still more, probably, of the popular conviction, without insisting on the antagonism between flesh and spirit under the image of a temporal and spatial separation. And again the image had a double tendency. It addressed itself then, as always, not merely to the aspiration after a region of divine reasonableness, but to that after a complete satisfaction to individual romantic sentiment.

When therefore free thought set about the task of re-conquering the universe for feeling and intellect, this material separation, which had never represented the actual dividing line between reason and sense, nor determined which of these factors belong to "this" world and which to the "other," bequeathed to philosophy rather the habit or form of such an absolute antithesis as that between a "here" and a "beyond," than any particular distribution of content between the two sides of such an antithesis. It is true that the ideas of Freedom, God and Immortality continued to stand over

---

[1] *Treatise of Human Nature*, vol. ii. (Green and Grose), p. 151. See below, p. 179.

against such notions as those of necessity, nature, and the dependence of mind on body. But it would not be possible to identify the intellectualist school of thought as the heir of the former or supernatural point of view, and the sensationalist or "empirical" as the heir of the latter or merely natural point of view ; for in fact the antagonism of freedom and necessity, purpose and mechanism, mind and body, is represented with startling distinctness within the philosophic movement from Descartes, through Spinoza and Leibnitz, to Wolff and his successors; while the English and later French thinkers, who start from the "here" and "now" of sensation and desire, begin by transmuting it into a system of scientific and therefore ideal necessity, against which individual feeling, having learned its own importance from being treated as a primary datum and standard, asserts itself for example in Rousseau with a claim for freedom and satisfaction both here and hereafter.

Thus either reason or feeling may seize upon the place of the supernatural, and either of them, again, may be interpreted into a purely natural system. Either of these, so long as they remain purely abstract opposites, may be regarded as freedom when identified with the willing self, and must turn out to be mere necessity when found to exclude an element that the self seems in concrete experience to contain. It is not easy to decide whether one would rather be a being without affections, as Spinoza, it appears, would represent man at his best, or the defenceless prey of successive solicitations of appetite according to the strictest interpretation of Hume. What is really gained by the pre-Kantian treatment of these antagonisms is a gradually growing demonstration, owing to the manner in which they dissolve into one another, that their cause must be somewhere in the nature of mind.

Æsthetic Ideas in pre-Kantian Philosophy. v. The observations upon beauty thrown out by philosophers whether in England, France, or Germany, before Kant, do not possess the note of progressive modern æsthetic, and are not the true progenitors of that study. For, as we have partly seen, and shall further see when we come to deal with Kant, it draws its peculiar import from the fact that it constitutes an essential and almost primary element in the treatment by which Kant attempted to reconcile the conflicting philosophical movements that converged upon him ; and it would be false history to represent as springing from certain external symptoms of these move-

ments the problem which really sprang from the whole
system of forces to which they belonged.   Kant no doubt
borrowed from his predecessors in philosophy both the name
of æsthetic and certain features of its treatment ; but the need
of it lay deeper in his thought than any suggestions of theirs,
and the material which was destined after Kant's time to meet
this need more fully was being stored up elsewhere than in
abstract metaphysic.

We must therefore regard pre-Kantian æsthetic, so far as
it exists at all in the great philosophers, not as the generating
cause of its later development, but only as an external attribute of the movement which was really such a cause.   It is
not necessary to treat it in great detail.

The pioneers of free thought do not give much attention
to the phenomena of the beautiful.   Descartes and Spinoza,
Bacon, Hobbes and Locke, throw themselves at once into
what seem the most urgent and central issues of man's
position in the world—into questions relating to human freedom, the nature of God, the extension of knowledge, the
nature of the mind and of society.   And in some degree the
severe rationalism of these philosophers, whether its root be
intellectualist or sensationalist, implies an attitude towards
fine art that reminds us not a little of Plato.   But yet in
substance their ideas are far more favourable to its importance
than are those of antiquity, for they stand on the firm foundation slowly laid by the Christian consciousness in all the
popular developments of the argument from design ; which
is equivalent to saying, that even if they doubt the teleology
of the world, they do not doubt its being rational and accessible to intelligence through and through.   Now on the basis
of this conviction, upon which the modern mind is firmly
established, the due consideration of beauty and knowledge
is a mere question of time ; it is only natural that reason
should first consciously appreciate itself in its more plainly
and directly intellectual expression.

It is noticeable from this point of view that Descartes
(1596–1650) wrote a " Compendium Musicæ "—music, it
must be remembered, formed part of the educational " quadri-
vium " of the middle age along with arithmetic, geometry and
astronomy, under the name of a science—and though Spinoza
(1632–1677) seems to have recognised no meaning at all in

the term beauty,[1] which for him could only designate a confused form of intelligence, yet we find in—

Leibnitz.   (a) Leibnitz (1646–1716), an expression echoing
mediæval associations, while containing the germ
of many later researches into the power of sound ;[2] " Musica
est arithmetica nescientis se numerare animi,"[3] " music is
counting performed by the mind without knowing that it is
counting," or, translating negative into positive terms in conformity with Leibnitz's system, " music is a *felt* relation of
number." This, however in need of further explanation, is
a plain case of "reason in the form of feeling," and so more
generally Leibnitz falls back on the æsthetic point of view
of Augustine by comparing the permission of evil in the
universe to the introduction of ugly colour or discordant
sound by an artist, enhancing the beauty of his work as a
whole. This, of course, involves the assumption that what
is beautiful to feeling is ultimately an expression of harmony,
though capable of including apparent contradiction.

The above is enough to indicate in general the starting-
point of modern philosophy, so far as it affects the place of
beauty in the system of things ; it is separated from classical
antiquity by that whole interval of a new faith which separates
Augustine or Erigena from Plato, but it is also inspired with
its own freely analytic and progressive impulse.

(b) Shaftesbury (1670–1713) stands, so far as æsthetic is
concerned, on the same metaphysical ground of the Christian
intelligence, believing beauty to be an expression of the
divine life of the world, which he contrasts with dead matter
in a way too much akin to Plotinus, and is therefore unable
to find an explanation for ugliness or evil. He sees, however,
that the true purpose of art is to bring before the mind ideas
and sentiments in shapes drawn from sense-perception, the
trained eye and ear being ultimate judges of what is beautiful
or not. His extension of the terms " beauty " and " sense "
to the goodness of morality and the faculty by which we
judge of it, is fatal of course to a distinct demarcation of the
æsthetic region. But yet, by insisting on the education of

---

[1] Erdmann, E. Tr., ii. 85.
[2] We shall notice later the effect on æsthetic of the rise of musical art.
Between Descartes' birth and Leibnitz's death, Opera sprang up in Paris,
Italy, Germany and England.
[3] See Lotze, *G. d. A.*, 275.

the art-sense, and by his detailed attention to the phenomena
of art, he marks a stage in the growing tendency to appreciate beautiful production as in its own right an important
activity of human life, and an important element in history.
His criticisms on the limits of time over which an action,
represented in painting, may extend, anticipates some of the
discussions in Lessing's *Laocoön.*

So far as we can judge, the content of reason which beauty
embodies for sense did not signify for Shaftesbury anything
more than the formal principle of antiquity—the principle of
unity in multiplicity.   The advance lies in the complete and
confident identification of beauty with the aspect presented
by art and nature to trained perception.   It is easy to speak
of Shaftesbury as a Platonist ; but we must remember that in
place of a fierce anti-sensuous dualism, only indicating at times
the identification of fact and reason, and for the most part
hostile to art, we have now an easy-going pantheistic monism,
almost identifying God, reason, and ordinary material Nature,
and taking the charm of visible things as an obvious outcome
of the divine principle.   It is the world that has moved
on, and that has verified the highest of Plato's suggestions ;
Shaftesbury is far from being a great philosopher, and does
little but reproduce, in terms of the individual's sensibility,
the current ideas of his age.

Hume.   (*c*) It is worth while, before leaving the
British philosophers, to notice the observations
upon beauty made in passing by David Hume (1711–1776)
in the *Treatise of Human Nature*, published in 1738.   I
should hardly have thought it fair to lay stress upon them,
being fragmentary, and contained in a youthful work, were it
not that they are in fact of considerable value.

" If [1] we consider all the hypotheses which have been formed
either by philosophy or common reason, to explain the difference betwixt beauty and deformity, we shall find that all of
them resolve into this, that beauty is such an order and construction of parts, as either by the primary constitution of our
nature, by custom, or by caprice, is fitted to give a pleasure
and satisfaction to the soul.   This is the distinguishing character of beauty, and forms all the difference betwixt it and
deformity, whose natural tendency is to produce uneasiness.

Pain and pleasure, therefore, are not only necessary attendants of beauty and deformity, but constitute their very essence." "—Beauty, like wit, cannot be defined, but is discerned only by a taste or sensation." The greater part of the pleasure of beauty arises, however, from the idea of convenience or utility. Now the point which seems deserving of attention, is the precise mode of connection between this idea of utility and the sensation of beauty. For Hume lays down with absolute clearness that beauty, as a rule, arises from a utility which does not at all concern the spectator whose sense of beauty is awakened, but only the owner or person immediately affected by the real properties of the object. It is therefore only by sympathy that the feeling of beauty can exist for the spectator. A curious example is as follows :[1] — "I know not but a plain, overgrown with furze and broom, may be, in itself, as beautiful as a hill covered with vines or olive-trees ; though it will never appear so to one who is acquainted with the value of each. But this is a beauty merely of imagination, and has no foundation in what appears to the senses."

This example seems to indicate a concession to what might be called the vulgar doctrine of utility, because monetary value does not imply high structural organisation. But we must not fail to notice in it the pregnant distinction between beauty of imagination—what would now be called beauty of relation—and beauty for the sense, or beauty of form. If we ask for the nature and grounds of the latter, I think we must suppose that Hume resolves it into a more obvious case of the relation of utility—a case in which utility is plainly expressed in the physical form of the object. And here again, the pleasure or pain upon which beauty or deformity depend, as in the uneasiness produced by an ill-balanced figure in a painting, gains its "vivacity" through sympathy alone.[2] I suppose that his reason for not distinguishing, in the case of a work of art, between the spectator and the person really affected, is simply that in this case there can be no such person, and therefore our sympathy can only be with each other's ideas, and not with any person's actual advantage or injury.

Whatever we may think of the mechanism of impressions and ideas as described by Hume, it is plain that his doctrine of

---

[1] *Ib.*, p. 151.   [2] *Ib.*, p. 152.

utility in beauty does not involve a selfish interest on the part
of the spectator, and that it practically implies a distinction in
natural beauty as well as in art between æsthetic semblance
and real effect; and further, that his idea of an æsthetic
generalisation of pleasure and pain through sympathy is strikingly parallel to Aristotle's idea of an artistic generalisation
of fear through pity.　We thus get an approximate anticipation of Kant's "form of teleology without the idea of an end,"
and also of his "disinterested pleasure."　It is so easy to be
unjust to any one who mentions the term utility in connection
with beauty, as Socrates too did, that these observations
seemed to me to be necessary.　And moreover, we have in
Hume more distinctly than in Shaftesbury, and far more
plainly than in Hutcheson, the important conception of a taste
or sensation which though a mere feeling is affected with
pleasure and pain by structural forms and relations of a definite character, analysable by reflection, though not analysed
by the appreciating sensibility itself.　Such an attempt to
trace the content of beauty is not to be set down as the mere
abstract identification of it with pleasure-producing quality.

Nature of the
Advance.　　(d) It is of course a twice-told tale that the
individualistic thinkers of Britain from Bacon to
Hume, in the sphere of metaphysic or general philosophy,
drove a destructive analysis deeper and deeper into knowledge until with Hume the last word of sensational empiricism
was spoken.　But it is a total misconception to apply the
principle of this progression to the province of positive æsthetic research, which did not at that time form a central issue in
metaphysical philosophy.　And thus when we are told[1] that
British æsthetic passed from Platonism (in Shaftesbury) to
Aristotelianism (in Lord Kaimes) and subsequently ran into
materialistic empiricism of the shallowest kind in Burke and
Hogarth—Reynolds being omitted—we feel that the great
formulæ of historical philosophy have in this case hardly been
grasped with the thoroughness which is needed for their concrete application.　The age in question was an age of reflection, of antagonistic abstractions, of the meeting of extremes;
all this is quite true.　But if we are going to interpret history
by such a conception, we must not pick out a thinker here
and a critic there, and throw them into a succession according

---

[1] Schasler, i. 313.

to their intellectual characters, quite apart from their special forms of preoccupation with the problems of the age. We must realise that the reflective character of the time, like all such dominant tendencies, was no mere intellectual instinct of certain writers in philosophy and literature, but was dictated by the whole existing situation of facts and forces, which placed the individual subject in presence of a set of completed systems, antiquity, mediæval art, theology, political authority, by overcoming which and reasserting itself in spite of them it had to win a new positive freedom and positive content. Now if we compare one of these forms of conquest with another—even though the same thinker is engaged in both, as may well happen—we construct a transition and imagine a tendency which is altogether unreal. As the English passed, in æsthetic, from Platonism to Aristotelianism, so the French passed, we are told,[1] from Aristotelianism (in Batteux) to Platonism (in Cousin), and thus the necessity by which one-sided abstractions work out their opposites is supposed to be exemplified.

All this is utterly unhistorical. Sidney, Corneille, Shaftesbury as an art critic, Lord Kaimes, Batteux, Lessing, were all interested not in the issues of metaphysic, but in the adjustment of modern æsthetic feeling, always comparatively speaking somewhat romantic, to the classical tradition, represented at first by conventional conceptions of Aristotle and of Greek beauty, and then, as criticism deepened, by something nearer the real Aristotle and real Greek art and poetry. Within this domain of criticism the work of reflection took the form, prescribed for it by circumstances, of struggling with the given antithesis which was the primary fact of the situation, and as reflection gradually broke through the rind of tradition, its results became more and more empirical in the sense of being more vital, more concrete, more akin to the true philosophical speculation which was to arise from its endeavours. It is a wild confusion to identify the appeal to æsthetic fact in Hogarth, Burke and Reynolds, under the ambiguous name empiricism, with the increasingly severe and abstract analysis of general experience which culminated in the metaphysic of David Hume. The one made content richer, as we have seen in the æsthetic suggestions of Hume himself; the other

---

[1] Schasler, l.c.

made it poorer for the moment, and only richer in a constructive sense, by helping to prepare the place which a fuller content would one day occupy. The two movements together
were therefore, as we have urged throughout, pioneering the
junction which followed in and after Kant.

I may add that in order to gain probability for the perverse
view which has been indicated, Schasler omits Sidney at
the beginning of the English development, and adds on
Cousin, who belongs to a wholly different age, at the end
of the French. The "critical" movement, in the sense defined at the beginning of the present chapter, is in England
from Sidney to Burke and Hogarth, in France from Corneille
to Rousseau and Diderot, in Germany from Gottsched and
Ramler to Schiller and Goethe. If the true nature of this
movement had been understood, the attempt would not have
been made to display an antithetical progression by simply
passing in the account of English thought from a metaphysical
to a critical writer, and in that of French thought from a
critical to a metaphysical one.

The movement of eighteenth-century metaphysic in France
needs no separate treatment. The operative forces that
framed the problem for Kant are adequately represented
within the region of philosophy, by the British school on the
one hand, and the Wolffian, containing in it many elements
of French (Cartesian) origin, on the other.

Baumgarten. (*e*) If the British school, starting from what is
most individual in the individual, worked upwards
to æsthetic ideas from observing the trained artistic sense, or
from analysing the conditions of disinterested pleasure, the
Cartesian school, continuous for our purposes with the Leib-
nitzian, worked downward to æsthetic ideas by ultimately
attempting to extend its intellectualist theory, which dealt
primarily with knowledge, to the phenomena of feeling and
perception. And the extension thus initiated by Baumgarten
(1714–1762) under the name "Æsthetica," was so far characteristically concerned about the theory of beauty as to hand
down the term Æsthetic as the accepted title for the philosophy of the beautiful.

The genesis of his conception appears to have been as
follows. Descartes, Spinoza, Leibnitz, and Wolff, form as
intellectualist philosophers an unbroken sequence, in spite of
Leibnitz's revolt against the abstract unity of Spinoza's "sub-

stance." Throughout this whole succession the passions and sense-perceptions are described in terms of the abstract intelligence, and therefore negatively, that is to say, by the attribute in which they differ from an abstract idea Both sense-perception and passion are, according to Spinoza, "confused acts of thought,"[1] and in Wolff's psychology there is a complete set of faculties belonging to the "obscure" portion of knowledge, and corresponding to the faculties of the distinct intellect. Now clear thinking was treated by Wolff in the science or method of Logic, both theoretical and practical, as an introduction to theoretical philosophy or metaphysic with its four parts, Ontology, Cosmology, Ethics, and Psychology. It occurs then to Baumgarten, who in every way continues to push the survey of science into detail—he wrote a *Sketch of Philosophical Encyclopædia* a term inherited by German philosophy from late Greek and mediæval education—to prefix to the Wolffian logic, or method of clear knowledge, a still prior science or method of sensible or obscure knowledge, to be called Æsthetic. Such a preliminary science might, it has been observed,[2] have taken the form of inductive logic, or it might be added, as in Kant, of an enquiry into the nature of the forms of sense. But Baumgarten is thoroughly consistent. Inductive logic and the theory of space and time both belong to the doctrine of clear knowledge—such a doctrine as that of modern logical textbooks where they deal with "the extraction of general propositions from sense-perception." But the subject of the Æsthetica is "obscure conception" *qua* obscure, that is knowledge in the form of feeling and remaining in that form. To us, no doubt, sense-perception is apt to seem the clearest of data, and we hardly see the force of a distinction which ranks it as "confused."

I imagine that what is meant by clear and confused through this whole succession of philosophies may be illustrated by the possibility of adequately expressing this or that matter in words.[3] I suppose that a clear idea is one which is so cut down and defined as to be communicable by a conventional sign with a tolerable degree of adequacy, while a confused

---

[1] Erdmann, E. Tr., ii. 85.
[2] Zimmermann, i. 169.
[3] See, *e.g.*, Erdmann on Leibnitz and Descartes, ii. 182.

idea is one which remains of a kind and complexity—such as a harmony of colour—which language cannot reproduce. That the "confused idea" can have an *order* of its own, which is appreciable to feeling, seems to be presupposed in the idea of beauty, and insisted on by Baumgarten in his discussion.

The sphere of æsthetic, then, is a whole complex of faculties, those which represent any connection in a confused form,[1] and which, taken together form the "analogon rationis," the parallel or parody of reason in the province of confused knowledge. Thus it is clearly more akin to the subject of psychology than to that of logic or elementary metaphysic, and appears to me to be a conception to which modern psychology, constantly finding parallels to logical processes in unconscious or subconscious mental movements, is bringing us back. But again it was not quite from this point of view, not as a parallel in the form of feeling to logical processes, that the region of obscure ideas pressed itself on Baumgarten's attention. Such a treatment would still make the excellence of sensuous perception consist in a form of *truth*—which can only exist in so far as the perception is after all interpreted into a judgment, a feeling *that* "something is so or so." Baumgarten maintained his distinction more thoroughly than this, and with a coherence for which he hardly receives due commendation. He gives to the perfection of sensuous knowledge, *i.e.*, of feeling or sensation, the name of beauty, as the manifestation in feeling—so I understand the accounts of him— *of that attribute which when manifested in intellectual knowledge is called truth*. Only it is difficult to see how he could call æsthetic thus construed the art of beautiful *thinking* (pulchre cogitandi),[2] for thinking always conveys to us the idea of an intellectual process.

His analysis of the content of this perfection is not adequate to his conviction as to the source from which it is to be drawn. In the former he does not advance beyond the theories of antiquity ; in the latter he shares the consciousness of his age, though hidden under a phraseology that recalls the old attitude of Plato. In every way therefore he is on the threshold of a new movement.

The idea of perfection had played a great part in the

[1] Zimmermann, *A.*, i. 165.   [2] Erdmann, ii. 240.

speculation of Descartes, Spinoza, and Leibnitz, and was directly transmitted from Wolff to Baumgarten. It might be generally defined as the character of a whole in so far as this whole is affirmed by its parts without counter-action, and thus perfection became a postulate of everything real, because reality depended upon power to harmonise with the greatest number of conditions. In Wolff, therefore, it naturally comes to mean the mere logical relation of the whole to part, or unity in variety, and this is the sense in which Baumgarten also employs it. The content of beauty for him is therefore nothing more than our old friend the formal principle of unity in variety which may, of course, at any moment take the form of teleology. Whatever is opposed to the perfection of sensuous knowledge, that is to the unity of parts in the whole of the sense-perception, is ugly.

But from the same tradition which gave him the abstract idea of perfection, he derives a peculiar conviction as to the source from which alone such perfection can enter the region of feeling. It must be observed that in speaking of perfection of sensation, when we might speak of sensitive appreciation of perfection, he is perfectly in his right. The character of the perceptive content as such and in itself is what concerns æsthetic, just as the character of knowledge as such and in itself is what concerns logic. The distinction of subject and object concerns metaphysics, but not logic nor æsthetic.

The greatest degree of perfection was to be found, according to Leibnitz, in the existing universe, every other possible system being as a whole less perfect. Baumgarten, inheriting this view, which is really a translation into philosophy of the Christian teleological consciousness, makes nature, the world accessible to sense-perception, the standard and pattern of art. This raises in a quaint form the whole problem of the fantastic imagination. The poetical world of fable and mythology possesses only " heterocosmic "[1] truth, and therefore has a less degree of perfection and of beauty than the actual world of experience. The introduction of the heathen deities in modern poetry appears to him therefore thoroughly erroneous. Imitation of nature is the law of art.

The fundamental connection of his views, in spite of their verbal coincidence with the doctrine of antiquity, is altogether

---

[1] " Belonging to another world."

modern.   The nature which is to be imitated is for him the
revelation of perfection, not as in Plato a secondary and
inferior world ; and to reproduce it is a high but possible task,
not an idle indulgence and a vain endeavour.   The hiatus
is between the formal principle of perfection, *i.e.* unity in
variety, and the immense and individual splendour of the
world, which ʰhat abstract principle is wholly inadequate to
comprehend.   A deeper analysis was needed to exhibit this
concrete content as a development of that abstract principle.

In many respects the attitude of later German philosophy
towards æsthetic was anticipated, perhaps influenced, by Baumgarten. The feeling that art was a sort of preparatory discipline
to speculative knowledge, and the doubt whether the two could
thoroughly co-exist, seems to reproduce itself in Schiller and
in Hegel, although they rejected the still more decided intellectualist prejudice which makes Baumgarten apologise for
his subject as something below the dignity of philosophy, but
after all interesting to the philosopher as a man among men.[1]
Again, the idea of beauty as *felt* perfection lends itself of
course readily to Kant's conception of teleology without the
distinct notion of an end, although the other important
Kantian distinction between the beautiful and the object of
desire, does not appear to have been made by Baumgarten
otherwise than through the general leaning to knowledge
more than pleasure as the central characteristic of beauty.
But all perfection gives pleasure and causes desire, and
beauty is a kind of perfection.   The desire for the real object
suggested in art, and the interest in the beautiful as beautiful, are perhaps not distinguished by him, as they are not
with absolute clearness by Kant.   Apart from this one point
of obscurity the definite demarcation of æsthetic from logic
and ethics was in itself a considerable service to philosophy ;
and the bias which its author showed against the " unnatural "
or " fictitious " started the enquiry into the ideal on the whole
in a right direction ;[2] only a certain weakness which Baumgarten had for allegory, as fiction in the service of truth,
perhaps affected Winckelmann or at least was shared by him.

It seems needless to discuss the views of other philosophers
between Baumgarten and Kant, such as Mendelssohn.   What

---

[1] Zimmermann, i., 159.   Hegel, *Æsth.*, Introd. E. Tr., p. 8.
[2] See for the solution *Modern Painters*, iii. 131.

is essential in the culture of the later eighteenth century belongs rather to the critical than to the speculative movement, and will be indicated in the next chapter. Kant took up the problem of general philosophy on its German side directly from Baumgarten, from whose compendia he was at first in the habit of lecturing.[1] When Hume and Baumgarten had written the array of strictly philosophical forces was complete. The suggestions made on points of æsthetic by them and other writers, although no doubt they furnished Kant with the technical term Æsthetic, and perhaps with some of his detailed ideas, were not the principal factors in the question that urged itself upon him. The question was, I repeat, in its general form, "How can the sensuous and the ideal world be reconciled?" and in its special æsthetic form, "How can a pleasurable feeling partake of the character of reason?"

It was the former question which gave, for Kant, its full import to the latter; and it was the concrete solution of the latter, following upon Kant's statement which was in itself half an answer, that paved the way for a new and more fertile treatment of the former.

---

[1] Erdmann, ii. 238.

CHAPTER IX.

THE DATA OF MODERN ÆSTHETIC PHILOSOPHY.

In the beginning of the last chapter we distinguished the processes which paved the way for modern æsthetic speculation into the formulation of the problem by philosophy, and the preparation of the data by criticism. This latter process forms the subject of the present chapter.

Criticism in the widest sense includes, as we saw, the work of classical scholarship or philology, of archæology, and of art-criticism or the appreciation of beautiful things as beautiful. Each of these movements represents in its own form that antithesis which is inherent in the position of the modern world as coming after the ancient, and which distinguishes its whole basis of thought and feeling, as historical and reflective, from the direct naturalism of antiquity. It is not necessary for our purpose to write a complete account of classical philology or of archæology from the Renaissance to the eighteenth century. Such an account of either as the late Mr. Mark Pattison might have written would be of the utmost value for the comprehension of modern philosophy, but would demand a knowledge such as few but he have possessed, and would considerably exceed in compass the whole of the present work.

Classical Philology. 1. I will simply recall two great moments in the history of philology which have been indicated by the writer to whom I have just referred.

Joseph Scaliger. i. In the year 1583 Joseph Scaliger[1] published his *De Emendatione Temporum*, the first attempt to apply modern astronomical knowledge "to get a scientific basis for historical chronology." This attempt led up to the *Thesaurus Temporum* (1606), "in which[2] every chronological relic extant in Greek or Latin was reproduced, placed in order, restored, and made intelligible."

---

[1] Mark Pattison's *Essays*, I. 162.   [2] *Ib.*, 162.

This great work involved nothing less than the conception of Universal History, breaking down the barrier, then considered absolute, between the classical and the biblical world, and including in the problem of historical research the extra-classical world also. The importance of this achievement for us is not so much in the active effect of its great idea—for, it appears, this idea remained unfertile through the seventeenth and eighteenth centuries—as in the proof which it affords that by the beginning of the seventeenth century the remains of antiquity were in the possession of the learned world in a degree which could suggest the conception of understanding the ancient civilisations as a whole.

F. A. Wolf.   ii. Just about two hundred years later,[1] in 1786, F. A. Wolf "prevailed on the Chancellor of the University (at Halle) to erect a philological seminarium for the special training of classical teachers." In the conduct of this seminarium[2] Wolf developed his conception of "philology," as a student of which—"Studiosus philologiæ"—he had insisted upon being set down twenty years before in the matriculation-book at Göttingen, where, as at other universities, no such faculty was then recognised.

Philology, he conceived, was now capable of becoming a study in its own right; the ancient[3] languages were no longer the mere introduction to law or theology, nor could they any longer be held as the storehouse of all knowledge. The purpose of philology was more and less than these. It was nothing short of the knowledge of human nature as exhibited in antiquity. That is to say, the inheritance of classical learning, which had so long appeared as a foreign element, mysterious alike in its value and in its worthlessness, within the romantic life of modern Europe, had now been mastered, and had become transparent, and was seen to deal with utterances of human nature belonging to a development of which we also, with our utterances and self-expressions, form a part. The Prolegomena to Homer, published in 1795, further and most profoundly stimulated thought in this direction, by show-

[1] *Id. ib.*, 363.
[2] A system of classes in which the intending teacher teaches under the eye of the inspector—in this case Wolf. For the origin and antiquity of this system see Hatch's Hibbert Lectures. He refers to it our term "*Prælector.*"
[3] *Id. ib.*

ing that " Homer [1] was no single poet, writing according to
art and rule, but a name which stood for a golden age of the
true spontaneous poetry of genius and nature." The fixed
ideas of the eighteenth century had been breaking up before
this time, and breaking up in this direction. An interest had
arisen in popular poetry. Ossian and Percy's Reliques had
stirred the sympathy of German poets and men of letters.
The whole critical movement, in the narrower sense of art-
criticism, which we shall consider below, had, from Gottsched
to Goethe, a tendency of the same kind. More especially,
British writings translated into German [2] had pointed out the
" naturalness " of Homer, and the probability that he composed without the help of writing. Thus when Wolf inaugurated his profound conception of philology and made clear
the difference between the natural and the artificial epic, the
time was obviously ripe for an appreciation of the classical
writings in their deepest relation to definite phases of life, and
as objects of such appreciation the works of ancient art and
poetry became materials for æsthetic philosophy. It is remarkable that the dates of Wolf's great achievements fall within or close upon the fateful decade (1790–1800) in which by
an unparalleled concentration of influences the future form of
modern æsthetic, and with it of modern objective idealism,
was in its essence determined.

Archæology.   2. The higher spirit of archæology is the same
with that of philology as Wolf defined it, and
indeed he included in the latter science the study and interpretation of ancient works of formative art. While, on the
other hand, that part of the work of such a student as Winckelmann, which bears most directly upon our subject, is of a
semi-philosophical nature, and must be treated under the
head of art-criticism rather than under that of archæology.
In the present section my purpose is only to point out one or
two tangible facts which appear to me to be significant, concerning the dates at which important relics of antiquity became
known to modern inquirers. I have not met with any conspectus of information on this head such as a historian of
ancient formative art could put together in a few lines, which
would be, as I imagine, of the utmost interest and value for
the history of culture. My own knowledge on the subject is

---

[1] D. B. Monro, art. " Homer," *Encycl. Brit.*   [2] See *id. ib.*

far too meagre; but I give some facts as better than none at all.

Early Discoveries on Italian Soil. i. It is a curious external illustration of the nature which we have ascribed to that classical tradition which the Renaissance handed down, that its earlier days were occupied with the later works of art. The Apollo Belvedere, probably a Roman copy of a fine statue of the third century B.C., was discovered about the end of the fifteenth century at Antium. The Laocoön, probably an original of the Rhodian school of about the second century B.C., was found at Rome in 1506, and was known to Michael Angelo, who attempted to restore the father's right arm. The Belvedere torso of Heracles, by Apollonius in the first century B.C., was found at Rome about the same time, and was enthusiastically admired both by Michael Angelo and by Winckelmann. The group of Dirce, an original of the same school as the Laocoön, was found in the Baths of Caracalla in 1525. The figures of the Florentine Niobe group, a Roman copy of a very fine original of the second period of Greek sculpture (of which better partial copies exist than the Florentine), were found at Rome in 1583. I do not know that before the middle of the seventeenth century any modern had seen a work of Greek sculpture executed between 500 and 400 B.C. Winckelmann,[1] one hundred years later, mentions that Montfaucon believed no works of Greek sculpture to be in existence more ancient than the Roman period.

This order of discovery is not accidental. It arises from the Latin character of the Renaissance, and from the consequent fact that its direct contact with antiquity was on Italian soil, where the greatest works of Hellas, even if some had been transported there by purchasers or plunderers, were infinitely out-numbered by productions of a later age, and by copies freely multiplied,[2] both from earlier and from later originals. The diversion of interest towards Greek soil was subsequent to this time, and parallel with the deeper interpretation of the classical tradition.

Just as we saw to be the case with classical form in litera-

---

[1] *Gesch. d. Kunst des Alterthums*, viii. 1. 26.

[2] If we compare a Greco-Roman Caryatid with the British Museum Caryatid from the temple of Athene Polias, we shall see the immensity of the gulf between different renderings of the same type.

ture, so too the ancient sculptures were regarded in the fifteenth and sixteenth centuries chiefly as models for artists.[1] After the sixteenth century a beginning of disinterested study was made under the influence of the conception that ancient poetry and ancient formative art were especially fitted to illustrate one another ; a conception which Lessing is really disputing in that part of the " Laocoön " which refers to the works of Spence and Caylus.[2]

Early Travels in Greece. ii. It was in the latter half of the seventeenth century, shortly before the fatal bombardment of the Acropolis by Morosini in 1687,[3] that Spon and Wheler published the narratives of their tour in Greece, and that Carrey, a French artist, commissioned by the French ambassador to the Porte, made those sketches of the Parthenon sculptures which are the earliest indications of their state. Morosini himself had, it seems, some of the collector's enthusiasm, or at least knew the value of the marbles ; and his desire of possession was no less ruinous than his warlike operations ; for not only did a shell dropping into the Turkish powder store within the Parthenon blow down the middle part of the building, but after the Venetians had occupied the city the workmen employed by Morosini to remove the horses of Athene from the western pediment let them fall on the rocks of the Acropolis, where they were dashed to pieces. Many fragments of statues were carried off by officers of Morosini's force, some of which have since been recovered.[4] Carrey's drawings do not seem to have been known to Winckelmann, and in fact they would be of little use before the sculptures themselves were accessible.

Herculaneum and Pompeii. iii. A remarkable stimulus to archæological research was given by the accidental discovery of antiquities at Herculaneum in 1709, leading to the commencement of excavations in 1738, and by similar discoveries leading to researches at Pompeii from 1755 onwards. Winckelmann arrived at Rome in this year, and from time to time

---

[1] *Encycl. Brit.*, art. " Archæology."
[2] The titles of their works are suggestive : Spence's *Polymetis, or, An Enquiry concerning the Agreement between the Works of the Roman Poets and the Remains of the Ancient Artists*, 1755, and Caylus' *Tableaux tirés de l'Iliade.*
[3] Murray's *Hist. of Greek Sculpture*, ii. 21.
[4] Overbeck, i. 291.

wrote reports of the Herculanean discoveries, on which part of his discussion upon the painting of the ancients is based.[1]

It does not indeed appear that any works of the best time were added to the data of æsthetic by the discovery of Herculaneum and Pompeii; what was gained, in addition to very considerable archæological knowledge, and a large mass of characteristic though late Greek art, was rather the sense of vitality and completeness in this new contact with antiquity. The concentration of æsthetic and partly æsthetic activity in England, France, and Germany round the year 1750, in which, as we saw, Baumgarten first gave the science its name, is exceedingly remarkable, and the Herculanean discoveries must take their place among its causes.[2] This interest was not confined to the Continent. Among Winckelmann's grumblings[3] at the destruction and improper restoration of many works of art in recent times, we find the complaint that lately and during his stay in Rome many noteworthy objects had been carried off to England, "where, as Pliny says, they are banished to remote country-houses." In Winckelmann's own opinion there was nothing at Rome in his day belonging to the high or grand style of Greek sculpture except the (Florentine) Niobe group then in the Villa Medicis at Rome, and a Pallas "nine palms high"[4] in the Villa Albani.

Greece proper. iv. From 1751 onwards the activity of Englishmen was directed to making known the monuments of Greece proper; and the labours and publications of many explorers[5] between that date and the early years of the present century no doubt marked and swelled the rising tide of interest which made it possible for Lord Elgin to conceive and carry out (in 1812) the idea of securing the Parthenon marbles for this country. It was not till about the same time that the pediment sculptures from Ægina, and the frieze from Phigaleia,

---

[1] *Gesch. d. Kunst*, Bk. 7, i. 3.

[2] *Gesch. d. Kunst, Einleitung*, xiv.

[3] It is fair to point out how the interest helped to create its own material. The fact that a prince, seeking crushed marble to make plaster for his new villa, was told by some peasants that they knew where there was plenty (Prince Elbeuf at Portici in 1709) would not in every period have led to the scientific excavation of the buried city.

[4] *G. d. K.*, 8, ii. 4, and see p. 245 below.

[5] Stuart and Revell, and the explorers sent out by the Society of Dilettanti (founded 1734), continued to publish drawings and descriptions at intervals throughout this period.

became known and were brought to Germany and England
respectively. The later labours of the nineteenth century, with
their magnificent result, do not concern us as yet.   It is of interest, however, to notice an aspiration of Winckelmann, which
his countrymen have in late years splendidly fulfilled.   " I cannot refrain," he writes,[1] "in concluding this chapter, from making
known a desire which concerns the extension of our knowledge in Greek art, as well as in scholarship and the history
of that nation.   This wish of mine is for a journey to Greece,
not to places which many have visited, but to Elis, to which
no scholar nor person skilled in art has yet penetrated. . . .
What, as regards works of art, is the whole Lacedæmonian
territory compared with the one town of Pisa in Elis, where
the Olympic games were celebrated ?   I am certain that in
this place the results would be inconceivably great, and that
by careful exploration of this soil a great light would dawn
upon art."

Hegel, in his æsthetic lectures, which continued down to
1828, profited by some at least of the discoveries of the early
nineteenth century.   He makes good use[2] of a description of
the Æginetan pediment sculptures, which was published, with
notes by Schelling, in 1817.   He was acquainted, at least by
hearsay, with the Elgin marbles, and probably learnt much
from the works of Hirt[3] and Meyer,[4] both contemporaries of
Goethe and historians of art.

Hirt describes in his preface how he had kept pace with
the advance of archæological knowledge from the time of his
paper in " Horen" (1797), and how great the harvest of
material had been during his lifetime, together with the effect
which in his judgment the extended study of the actual monuments must necessarily have on æsthetic theory.   As the
passage illustrates the natural development which the idea of
beauty passed through by the mere deepening and widening
of experience and appreciation, it will be well to quote it at
length.

" No age[5] has ever been more energetic and more fortunate
than ours in the last fifty years [written 1833] in the discovery

[1] *G. d. K.*, 8, iii. 20.
[2] Hegel's *Æsth.*, ii. 382 and 458.
[3] *Geschichte d. Bildenden Künste bei den Alten*, 1833.
[4] Same title, 1824–36.
   Hirt., *Gesch.*, etc., Preface.

and increase of materials and in the establishment of great collections for the benefit of students.

Egypt, with the neighbouring countries and the Upper Nile, have been opened up; so have Babylonia, Persia, Syria, and Asia Minor. Greece has been repeatedly explored, and its most important sculptures have passed into European museums. Zeal for the discovery of Italian antiquities has been augmented on all hands. Not merely the tombs of Sicily and Magna Græcia have surrendered their spoil, but so has the long mysterious Etruria. Then think of the metopes of Selinus, and of the most recent excavations of rare sculptures at Olympia [by the French expedition]. The excavations of the buried cities at Vesuvius continue to be fertile, together with the inexhaustible mines of Rome and the vicinity. Even more distant regions, such as the coasts of the Black Sea, France, Spain and Germany, have contributed to the mass of material . . . So [owing to Hirt's studies in Rome] I came into conflict with my predecessors Winckelmann and Lessing, as with my contemporaries Herder and Goethe. Objective beauty was assumed to be the principle of ancient art. I, on the contrary, pointed to the monuments, and showed by ocular demonstration that these monuments displayed all forms, the commonest and even the ugliest, as also the most beautiful, while the representation of the expression always corresponded to the character and the motives. Consequently, I maintained that the principle of ancient art was not the objectively beautiful and the softening (Milderung) of expression, but simply and solely the individually significant, or characteristic,[1] whether it dealt with the ideal representation of gods and heroes, or any mean or common object."

Hirt considered the characterisation of the centaurs in the Parthenon metopes very weak compared with that in later representations of the same subject. On the other hand, he would not believe that the Parthenon pediment sculptures were of the fifth century; he placed them, owing to their great tenderness ("Weichheit") of treatment, in the fourth century, which appeared to him to be the time of highest achievement in Greek sculpture. This curious perversity of judgment, as

---

[1] Hirt is supposed to have been the "Characteristiker" of Goethe's *Sammler u. die Seinigen*.

it appears to us, arose very naturally from Hirt's intermediate theoretical position, which was in itself untenable, although an advance on his predecessors.   For, accepting with Winck-elmann and others the antithesis between beauty and ex-pression, Hirt found the essence of art not in beauty, but in expression, which, by this antithesis, is narrowed down to mean the manifestation of something quite definite in the way of individuality or action or emotion.   Expressiveness of this kind is of course to be found in the later art much more decidedly than in that of the Periclean age ; and as it did not occur to Hirt to analyse "objective beauty" in terms of ex-pressiveness, he was obliged by his theory to prefer, as art, the monuments which really show a beginning of decadence, and to separate from their true context and refer to this later time those productions of the greatest age, in which the expressive force latent within their "objective beauty" partly breaks through its severe self-restraint.   As suggesting a con-trast to the idea of beauty, however, and forcing it out of its abstraction, his theories and observations were of the very greatest value, and like the romantic rebellion of the Schlegels and others between 1780 and 1800, really represented in the world of ideas that actual growth of material which I have been attempting to describe.

It should be observed that previously to this more extended knowledge of ancient sculpture and building a very great part had been played in archæology by coins and gems, which are more readily brought together in collections than larger plastic works.   Such a collection was that of Baron v. Stosch at Florence, which Winckelmann spent nine months in cata-loguing.   The evidence discussed in Lessing's beautiful little treatise, *How the Ancients Portrayed Death,* consisted largely of gems.   It is well known that gem-cutting (by a curious analogy with epigram-writing[1]) was not very active during the great fifth century at Athens, so that here again we see a reason why archæological interest began with the later time of art, and worked back to the earlier.

Enough has been said, I hope, to indicate the sort of pro-gress made in the collection of archæological material between the Renaissance and the time of Kant, and the sort of stimu-lus which increased knowledge imparted to the theory of art.

---

[1] See above, p. 86.

We have now to say something about the course of literary art-criticism in the same period.

Art-criticism. 3. Art-criticism must for this purpose include on the one hand the appreciative history of art, and on the other those reflections upon questions concerning beauty, which are not guided by a general speculative interest. Practically, as was observed above, we can only draw the line between this abstract criticism and philosophy proper by excluding from the present section the views of writers who are known in philosophy otherwise than by their reflections on beauty.

Pierre Corneille. i. We saw that Sidney's criticism and the structure of Shakespeare's plays bears witness to an influence derived ultimately from classical tradition, reacting against the formlessness of the earlier drama inherited from the middle age. In the reaction of the French seventeenth-century theatre against Spanish influence we see a parallel phenomenon, but with less happy issues. This reaction, initiated by Malherbe, reached its first culmination in the later plays, and in the dramatic theory, of Pierre Corneille (1606–1684). It is chiefly with his theories that we are concerned.

Towards the close of his life, after fifty years of work for the stage,[1] he wrote three essays on the drama: *De l'utilité et des parties du poème dramatique, De la Tragédie* and *Des trois unités*, the purpose of which may be fairly stated in the words of the latter, "accorder les règles anciennes avec les agréments modernes," an expression closely analogous to that in which Lessing's biographer states the purpose of the *Dramaturgie*[2] "to reconcile the idea of romantic poetry with the classical conception of beauty." To Corneille, however, the rules came as a prescription of indubitable authority, and he scarcely knew that the modifications which he made in applying them were really the first steps to reasoning on their merits. "Il faut, s'il se peut, nous accommoder avec elles (les règles) et les amener jusqu'à nous."[3] The interpreters of Aristotle and Horace have been, he goes on to say, scholars without experience of the theatre, and have

---

[1] *Discours de l'utilité*, etc.
[2] Lessing's *Leben*, Danzel, ii. 193.
[3] *Discours de l'utilité*, etc.

therefore thrown little light on their real meaning. He intends to interpret according to his experience of the stage.

The similarity between the atmosphere of Corneille's thought and that of Lessing's reflections, which are so often directed against him, can escape no one who has read the *Discours* and the *Dramaturgie*. Both are intent on building up a national drama from the foundations. Both were convinced that a just understanding of Aristotle's rules was the way to set about it. Thoughts and expressions from Corneille recur in Lessing. Lessing's scholarship indeed is to Corneille's as an Armstrong gun to a bow and arrow; and in place of the latter's complacent reference almost exclusively to his own plays, Lessing has at command the whole range of ancient and modern drama. Corneille accepts what he takes for Aristotelian *dicta* as a basis on which, out of his own experience, he tries to enlarge. Lessing contends that his adherence to the supposed *dicta* is at least valueless, while the supposed enlargements show a real failure to appreciate the depth of Aristotle's conceptions.

And, no doubt, when Corneille explains the famous " purification " passage in the *Poetics* to mean that by the pity and fear which tragedy excites we are led to avoid the passions which led to the misfortunes of the characters represented,[1] or when he denies that Aristotle conceived of pity and fear as necessarily interwoven in the same cause of emotion, suggesting that it would do quite well to have the fear without the pity, he falls an easy victim to Lessing's triumphant criticism.[2] But after all, they were two of a trade ; and in some respects a reader of to-day cannot but feel that Corneille's difficulties were too summarily disposed of by Lessing, who would never admit that a case could have been omitted by Aristotle.

We saw,[3] for example, in treating of the *Poetics*, that Aristotle refuses to face the full shock of a tragic collision ; he will not allow that a thoroughly good man's ruin can be a fitting subject for tragedy. Corneille attacks this limitation, as also that which excludes a thoroughly bad man from being the object of tragic interest. And I think that his instinct is right, though his argument is inconclusive. Lessing, who exerts[4] himself to condemn Weisse's Richard III. on ground

---

[1] *De la Tragédie.*   [2] *Dramaturgie*, ii., lxxxi.
[3] Supra, p. 19.   [4] *Dramaturgie*, ii., lxxxii.

of the one limitation—he has not, so far as I know, applied
his view in detail to Shakespeare's play on the same subject—
defends the other limitation also, saying,[1] it is a thoroughly
horrible conception that there can be persons who are unhappy
without any fault of their own.   The heathen put this horrible
thought as far from them as possible, and are we to cherish
it and to enjoy dramas which confirm it, we whom religion
and reason should have convinced that it is no less blas-
phemous than untrue ?   In all this Lessing was the child of
his century " not yet liberated by Goethe ";[2] I am only pointing out how close is the succession, not absolutely in all
respects an advance, from Corneille to him.   I cannot but
think again that Corneille has the best of it in his criticism
of Aristotle's remark, that morals in tragedy ought to be
good.[3]

And the dramatic writings show the same connection ; the
same abstract characterisation, typical rather than individual ;
the same submission to the rule of " one day "[4] and to the
comparative unity of place, interpreted much as Corneille
interprets it ; the same ingenious refinements of emotion,
which have caused a comparison between Lessing and Lope
de Vega,[5] but seem rather to indicate the direct connection
with Corneille.   The reformer is usually deep-dyed with that
which he feels the need of reforming, and it is remarkable
how powerfully the French seventeenth century worked upon
the age of Lessing.

Corneille, as we have seen, was not incapable of reasoning
upon the supposed rules of classical form.   His attitude to the
unity of the day is worth noticing, because he defends it, not
on the score of formal symmetry, but on the score of imitative
realism.   " Beaucoup déclament contre cette règle qu'ils nom-
ment tyrannique, et auraient raison, si elle n'était fondée que sur
l'autorité d'Aristote ; mais ce qui la doit faire accepter, c'est la
raison naturelle qui lui sert d'appui."[6]   Corneille states his

---

[1] *Dramaturgie*, l.c.
[2] Bernays.
[3] See *Dramaturgie*, ii., lxxxiii.
[4] I cannot think it accidental that both *Minna v. Barnhelm* and *Emilia
Galotti* begin by marking the hour as early morning, so as to give time for
all that has to pass before night.
[5] Lessing's *Leben*, Danzel., ii. 113.
[6] " Des trois unités."   It is worth noting, as we pass, that a striking sentence of Lessing, which introduces the long discussion on Aristotle and

" natural reason " as follows : the drama is an imitation or
portrait of nature, and is more perfect the more it resembles
it ; now " la representation dure deux heures, et resembleroit
parfaitement si l'action qu'elle represente ne demanderoit pas
davantage pour sa réalité." In the *Cid* therefore, we remember, the unhappy hero, having fought a duel one evening, and having been occupied the whole of the ensuing night
in repelling a night attack of the enemy, is sent off to fight
another duel first thing in the morning, in spite of the reasonable remonstrance of the king, who wants it put off till the
morrow ; but, owing, I imagine, to the imminent end of the
theatrical " day," can only obtain for the hero one or two hours'
breathing space.

Here, no doubt, Corneille mistakes his ground altogether.
The law of imitation or portrayal was understood, as we see,
far more profoundly than this by Aristotle ; and experience
does not show that the stage can possibly present an unre-
duced reproduction of two hours taken clean out of ordinary
life. Even conversation in a novel is epitomised and reduced
to its essence ; a stage letter is written in a few seconds ; a
stage ball may occupy perhaps an hour from the arrival to
the departure of the guests ; a stage banquet is merely a
sample or suggestion of the reality. I imagine that a reduction of scale in the parts is as essential to the drama as to
a picture ; but no doubt there is the further difficulty, as
Corneille implies, that large lapses of time at any point in
the drama make the reduction altogether disproportioned.
The ultimate principle must surely be to avoid shocking the
imagination of the spectators ; and to this he refers, advising,
e.g., that considerable lapses of time shall be between the acts,
and that notes of time shall be avoided.

I do not think there can be any doubt that however mis-
chievous the influence of Corneille's practice and theory may
have been on the French and German theatre, their effect in
drawing attention, and especially Lessing's attention, to the
antithesis of ancient rules and modern romance was a real
step towards a vital co-ordination of the two. At any rate,

Corneille, seems suggested by this passage, which Lessing must then have
had before him. His words are : " Mit dem Ansehen des Aristoteles
werde ich bald fertig werden, wenn ich es nur auch mit seinen Gründen zu
werden wüsste."

they show us one great element of the æsthetic atmosphere into which Lessing was born.

Fontenelle and Voltaire.   ii. To realise more completely the force and complacency of the tradition thus initiated, we may glance for a moment at the life of Corneille by Fontenelle [1] (1657–1757). A short quotation will suffice : " On recommenca alors à étudier le théâtre des anciens, et a soupçonner qu'il pouvait y avoir des règles." " Les règles du poème dramatique, inconnues d'abord et méprisées, quelque temps après combattues, ensuite reçues à demi et sous des conditions, demeurent enfin maîtresses du théâtre. Mais l'époque de l'établissement de leur empire n'est proprement qu'au temps de Cinna" (1640). We may add to this from Corneille's *Discours de l'utilité*, etc. : " Il faut observer l'unité de l'action, de lieu, et de jour, personne n'en doute," with Voltaire's note, " On en doutaient tellement du temps de Corneille que ni les Anglais ni les Espagnols ne connurent cette règle. Les Italiens seuls l'observaient. La Sophonisbe de Mairest (1604–1688) fut la première piéce en France où ces trois unités parurent. La Motte, homme de beaucoup d'esprit et de talent, mais homme à paradoxes, a écrit de nos jours contre ces trois unités ; mais cette hérésie en littérature n'a pas fait fortune."

These quotations from Fontenelle and Voltaire exhibit the continuity of French dramatic tradition from the seventeenth century through the eighteenth. I especially took the opportunity of introducing the name of Voltaire, because in his critical and dramatic activity, the influence of which was brought into the heart of Germany by his relations with Frederick the Great, Lessing found precisely what he wanted in the way of an object to attack. I conclude this very slight reference to the immense field of French criticism, the activity of which can be seen from Corneille's saying [2] that there were twelve current interpretations of Aristotle's " purification " doctrine, with Lessing's racy verdict on the whole dramatic and critical movement of which we have been speaking.

" Just the same thing [3] happened to the French as to Gottsched [Lessing's forerunner in Germany ; the comparison is of interest as bringing together the movements which

---

[1] *Oeuvres de Pierre Corneille*, vol. i.   [2] *De la Tragédie, init.*
[3] *Dramaturgie*, ii. lxxxi.

Lessing inherited]. Hardly had Corneille raised their theatre a little above barbarism, when they thought it all but absolutely perfect. Racine seemed to them to have put the last touch to it ; and so there was no question raised whether a tragic poet might not be yet more pathetic and more touching than Corneille and Racine ; but this was assumed to be impossible, and the aspirations of subsequent poets had to limit themselves to becoming as like one of these two as possible. For a hundred years they have deluded themselves, and to some degree their neighbours ; but let any one tell them so, and see what they will say!

"Of the two it was Corneille who did most harm, and had the most disastrous influence on their tragic poets. For Racine misled them only by example; Corneille both by example and by precept."

The British Writers. iii. Another set of materials which entered into the data of æsthetic, were furnished by the British writers on beauty and art. The chief of these, as distinguished from the philosophers in the strict sense, were Burke, Lord Kaimes, Hogarth, and Reynolds, of whom the first three exercised a traceable influence on the German movement, while the latter is of interest as championing the idea of the characteristic in a peculiar sense, intermediate between beauty and expression, and forming to some extent a point of departure for the author of the *Modern Painters*.

The works of these four writers fall almost within the decade following Baumgarten's first publication of part of the Æsthetic (1750). Hogarth's *Analysis of Beauty* was published in England in 1753, and a year or two later was translated into German by Mylius, with a preface by Lessing. Burke's *Essay on the Sublime and Beautiful* was first published in 1756—the complete second edition was brought out in 1757—and Lessing was long occupied with the project of translating it. Reynolds' papers in the *Idler* appeared 1758–9, and so far as I am aware were not known in Germany. Lord Kaimes' (Henry Home) *Elements of Criticism*, appeared in 1761, and was translated into German by Meinhardt, meeting with Lessing's warm approval.[1]

---

[1] My authority as regards these German translations is in every case Lessing's *Leben* (Danzel). The precise references are shown in the Index to that work under the several authors' names.

To all these works we might apply with much truth the
criticism made by Lessing on Burke in a letter of the year
1758 : " Although the writer's principles are not worth much,
still his book is uncommonly useful as a collection of all the
occurrences and perceptions which the philosophers must
assume as indisputable in inquiries of this kind.   He has
collected all the materials for a good system, which no one is
better qualified to make use of than you " (*i.e.* Mendelssohn).[1]

We may take Burke and Lord Kaimes together, as they
have much in common, and then the two artists, whose views
are related to each other as complementary opposites.

Burke and Lord   *a.* The fundamental point of agreement between
Kaimes.   Burke and Lord Kaimes, marking a decided tendency towards a new departure, is the contention carried out
by Burke with perverse ingenuity, that the natural exercise of
any emotion, even if painful in kind, such as an emotion of
terror or of sympathetic distress, is in itself delightful,[2] or as
Lord Kaimes most vehemently states it, a painful emotion, if
not abnormally violent, is agreeable upon reflection.

This view leads up to important results.

Burke's Purga-   *a.* In Burke, it is worked out in a doctrine of
tion Theory.   " Exercise necessary for the finer organs :"[3] according to which as these emotions (pain and terror) " clear the
parts, whether fine or gross, of a dangerous and troublesome
encumbrance, they are capable of producing delight."   The
resemblance of this conception to the later interpretations of
Aristotle's καθαρσίς is evident, and it makes possible,

The Sublime akin   *b.* An exceedingly free treatment of the sublime
to Ugliness.   as something beside and outside the beautiful.   Its
connection with beauty, indeed, is, by Burke, far too completely
dissolved.   It is referred to ideas of pain and danger,[4] as those
which produce the strongest of emotions, being connected as
Burke strangely says, with the principle of self-preservation ;
while beauty is referred to ideas of pleasure, which are connected with man's social nature.   It is well, however, in

---

[1] Lessing's *Leben*, i. 350.
[2] Burke distinguishes delight from pleasure.   See for the doctrine referred
to in the text, *Sublime and Beautiful*, sect. xiv., and Lord Kaimes' *Elements
of Criticism*, i. 97.
[3] *Sublime and Beautiful*, sect. vii.
[4] *Sublime and Beautiful*, part 1, sect. vi.

bringing up new matter for theory, not to be backward in
affirming its independence of the old; and although both
Burke and Lord Kaimes followed Longinus and the moderns
who had discussed his views,[1] yet the recognition of the sublime as co-ordinate with the beautiful indicates the beginning
of a great enlargement in æsthetic appreciation. Reconciliation of the two opposites comes later, Burke, for instance, is
prepared to accept ugliness, although the exact opposite of
beauty,[2] as partly coinciding with the sublime. This is a most
important admission. Many of the qualities in which he finds
the sublime, *e.g.*, formlessness, strength, magnitude, are taken
up into Kant's treatment of the subject.

Painful Reality   *c.* From the principle of the agreeableness of
not Disagreeable. even painful emotion, Burke obtains an ingenious
reversal[3] of the time-honoured problem, "Why do we take
pleasure in the representation of what is painful to see in
reality." The fact is not so, he replies; real distress and
disaster do not cause pure pain to the spectator, but, as experience proves, fascinate and attract him. For, considered as
emotions, they are "delightful," though painful (as we might
say) in content, and a theatre where the best tragedy in the
world was being acted in the best way would be emptied at
once by an announcement that a state criminal of high rank
was about to be executed in the next square.

We seem here to have the reality regarded as a representation, *i.e.* in abstraction from its real bearings and interest;
for, as Burke insists, no normal person *wishes* for such a real
catastrophe as he will run to see when it takes place. So
that, by a reverse movement compared with that of Plato, by
elevating reality to the rank of an æsthetic semblance, instead
of lowering art to the rank of useful reality, we seem to
have started the suggestion that reality can be looked at
æsthetically if looked at without practical interest, and therefore that the æsthetic temper consists, in part at least, in the
absence of such interest. Only, so far as art and fact remain on
one level, there is no room for identifying beauty with a deeper
reading of fact; and Burke, accordingly, is quite clear that

[1] Lord Kaimes alludes to a controversy between Boileau and Huet on the
sublimity of the text, " Let there be light," which is referred to by Longinus.
[2] *Sublime and Beautiful*, sect. xxi. " On Ugliness."
[3] Sectt. xiv. and xv.

art has no advantage over nature except that which arises from our pleasure in imitation.

Anticipations of later ideas.   *d.* Other details in these writers are of historical interest. The quality of grace is contrasted with that of dignity by Lord Kaimes, probably on a hint from Burke,[1] and is described as connected more particularly with motion, and also as peculiar to man. These ideas are fertile in later German thought, into which they passed partly through Lessing, who probably derived them from Lord Kaimes.[2]

These two writers, again, do much to suggest the distinction between poetry and painting. Burke quotes the passage of the *Iliad*, in which Helen's beauty is indicated by the effect of her appearance among the Trojan elders, contrasting [3] it, just in the manner of the *Laocoon*, which insists on this same passage, with a detailed description of a beautiful woman from Spenser. Poetry, he points out in the following section, is not strictly an imitative art ; and Lord Kaimes further insists that a picture is confined to a moment of time, and cannot take in a succession of incidents.

Many other details of importance might be noticed in Burke, who has been called materialist in æsthetic, but is rather perhaps in reality a formalist, in the sense that he simply notes as irreducible elements of beauty, certain "properties that operate by nature, and are less liable to be altered by caprice than any others."[4] He rebels,[5] as Plotinus did, against the identification of beauty with proportion and fitness,[6] point-

---

[1] Kaimes, i. 326 ; cf. *Sublime and Beautiful*, sect. on " Grace."

[2] Lessing's *Leben*, ii. 43. Schiller's *Anmuth u. Würde* is also definitely influenced by a passage in Winckelmann, in which "Grace" is compared to the girdle of Aphrodite. *Gesch. d. K.*, 8. 2. 16. I should assume them to be independent, though the thought is fundamentally the same as in Kaimes and Lessing.

[3] *Sublime and Beautiful*; sect. "On effect of words." Cf. Kaimes, 87 and *Laocoon*, S. 22.

[4] *Sublime and Beautiful*, sect. 18. The most materialistic suggestion in Burke is reproduced, though not as a fundamental principle of æsthetic, by Lessing, when he advises the actor to study the physical effects of passion on the ground that these effects, being well imitated, will tend to arouse the passion in question. Cf. *Sublime and Beautiful, Cause of Pain and Fear* with *Hamburg. Dramat.*, 1. iii. I imagine that modern psychology tends to support this suggestion.

[5] *Sublime and Beautiful*. Part III. ii.–vi.

[6] " In beauty, the effect is previous to any knowledge of the use." III. vii. Cf. Kant's definition of "Zweckmässigkeit ohne Vorstellung eines Zweckes."

ing out quite justly that proportion *per se* is simply a relation of quantity, and thus "wholly indifferent to the mind" (as judging of beauty). This argument is valuable as urging that not every proportion, and therefore not proportion as such, constitutes beauty ; but in pushing it to the limit of maintaining that in beauty there is no specially subtle orderliness, he seems to be denying what he ought to be investigating, and to be turning his back on his own important suggestions of the value of gradation or variation, and of variation of variation.[1]

Lastly, it is important to note that Lord Kaimes anticipates Lessing in pointing out the connection[2] between the unities of time and place, and the continuity of representation and uninterrupted presence of the chorus in Greek drama, and makes this an argument for greater freedom on the modern stage, while always demanding a certain economy of the spectator's imagination.

I do not wish it to be inferred from the space which I have devoted to these two critical writers, that I consider them to be æsthetic thinkers of a high rank, or that I desire to pull down Lessing from his eminence by the perpetual indication of his debt to them. The enumeration of details—and I have enumerated but a fraction of what well deserve to be mentioned—necessarily occupies more space than the statement of a single philosophical doctrine of the very first importance. But in history we must have details ; and to me at least the concentration of influences from all quarters in the microcosm of a great intellect is one of the most fascinating problems that can be put before a historian of philosophy. Lessing himself knew well what his genius owed to his learning ; especially he sympathised with the English mind, and to be well acquainted with the English literature was to win his warm commendation.[3]

β. Hogarth's *Analysis of Beauty* was published, as we saw, three years before Burke's *Enquiry*, and Hogarth is mentioned, with an approving reference to his "line of beauty," in Part III., sect. xiv. of the latter work. The *Analysis* was enthusiastically welcomed

Hogarth.

---

[1] *Sublime and Beautiful.* "Variation, why beautiful"?
[2] *Elements of Criticism*, 2. ch. 23. "The Three Unities."
[3] Lessing's *Leben*, ii. 5.

by Lessing in the *Vossische Zeitung* in 1754.[1] We may conveniently attach our account of Hogarth to Lessing's appreciation of him. In the review of 1754 (written when Lessing was only 25), he greets Hogarth's ideas as a new light on the whole material of art, as a system calculated to reduce to certainty men's conflicting ideas as to what is pleasing, and to abolish the wretched proverb that there is no disputing about tastes, "and as likely to make the term beauty suggest as much in the way of thought as it has hitherto suggested in the way of feeling." Later, however, in the preface to the German translation of Hogarth's work, Lessing lays his finger on the point of difficulty in its conception, viz. the question of determining, on general grounds, the degree and kind of curvature that constitutes beauty of line. For Hogarth "represents[2] in his first plate a number of undulating lines, of which he only takes one to merit the name of beautiful, namely that which is curved neither too much nor too little." Lessing had an idea that a mathematical investigation might solve the difficulty, which finds no answer beyond an appeal to unanalysed examples in Hogarth himself, whose idea was suggested to him by a remark ascribed to Michael Angelo. It is worth while to distinguish, according to the view which I have adopted throughout, the two elements of the problem, which Hogarth himself industriously confuses. If the question is, whether, as a simple geometrical form, one line is more beautiful than other lines, this is a legitimate problem, and can be answered, within certain limits, so long as the effects of suggestive representation are excluded. And from this point of view it is of the greatest interest to contrast Hogarth's idea of the undulating and spiral line with Plato's conception of the most beautiful form as the straight line or the circle.[3] For here we have the antithesis of ancient and modern reduced to terms of the ancient or formal theory. So far as Hogarth has any general conception it is still the " one in the many " that he believes to be beauty ; but with him it is the "intricacy," the " continuity

---

[1] Lessing's *Leben*, ii. 22. Schasler must have been misled by some misprint into supposing Hogarth's work to have been published in 1763, and so after the *Enquiry*. Why he put Burke's *Enquiry* after Lord Kaimes' *Elements*, in opposition to his own dates, I cannot imagine.

[2] Lessing, in the *Leben*, 223, note.

[3] See p. 33 above.

of variety" rather than the element of unity, which is the more important side. He even appeals to pure decorative design in support of this idea, describing in striking language the pleasure afforded him by the "stick and ribbon" ornament, which he compares with that of watching a country dance.

This pure decoration, without very complex representative suggestion, is the true sphere of pure formal or geometrical beauty ; and had he sought to apply his theory within this more abstract region, he might have laid a firm analytic foundation for æsthetic inquiry. As it is, he stands alone, I think, among eighteenth century writers in even alluding to this great branch of art, which presents the problems of beauty in their simplest and most general form.

But going at once to the most complex of all æsthetic problems, that of the beauty of the human figure, in which suggestions of character, intellect, passion, are inextricably intermingled, he loses his way, or rather, makes no progress at all in the attempt to reduce its wealth of meaning to any one formal type or principle, and does not even attempt to show within what limits his serpentine line—the line made by twisting a wire evenly round a cone—has that degree of continuity in variety which constitutes the beautiful. The fact is, that these lower or more abstract grades of expressive form are liable to have their significance overridden by the more complex suggestions connected with life and character, and it is not an axiom that a beautiful human figure can be constructed out of forms all of which have independently the highest geometrical beauty.

Thus Hogarth's analysis of beauty, drawn from formative art only, represents the abstract principle of unity in variety on its highest level, so as to form a point of transition to the analysis of the present century, which finds a *characteristic* significance in curves, for example, which vary progressively. It is against him that Burke is arguing when he disputes the importance of proportion and fitness in accounting for beauty. It is a fact both of interest and of importance that Hogarth's undulating line supplied Goethe with a name for the tendency which he ranks as the polar opposite of the characteristic, when representing in a scheme [1] the extreme inclinations of artists,

---

[1] *Der Sammler u. die Seinigen.*

and the central combination in which alone they produce true art. It is remarkable that in his artistic practice Hogarth himself pursues the characteristic beyond the border of ugliness.

Reynolds.

γ. Reynolds' three papers in the *Idler* for 1759, which form the point of departure for the chapter in *Modern Painters*, "Touching the Grand Style," [1] seem to be in more ways than one determined by opposition to Hogarth. "The flowing line, which constitutes grace and beauty," and the "pyramidal principle" [2] are satirised in the first pages. And though the satire is not serious in tone, being directed against silly connoisseurship and not against any genuine theory, yet the reference in this paper to a Vandyck portrait of Charles I., which the self-styled connoisseur refuses to admire, as a "perfect representation of the character as well as the figure of the man," prepares the way for Reynolds' own account of beauty. This, although fairly open to Ruskin's criticism in as far as it derives our pleasure in beauty from mere custom, suggests an actual ground for the force of custom in this province, which Ruskin does not notice. "Every species of the animal as well as the vegetable creation may be said to have a fixed or determinate form towards which Nature is continually inclining, like various lines terminating in the centre ; or it may be compared to pendulums vibrating in different directions over one central point; and as they all cross the centre though only one passes through any other point, so it will be found that perfect beauty is oftener produced by nature, than deformity." [3] It is true that Reynolds doubts whether *one species* is (as we should say) objectively more beautiful than another ; but he is clear that "in creatures *of the same species*, beauty is the medium or centre of all various forms."

Here then we have an intermediate position. Specific characterisation is set against geometrical formalism on the one

[1] Vol. iii. ch. i.

[2] More clearly aimed at Hogarth are the words in No. 82 : "but if he pretends to defend the preference he gives to one or the other (swan or dove) by endeavouring to prove that this more beautiful form proceeds from a particular gradation of magnitude, undulation of a curve, or direction of a line. . . he will find at last that the great Mother of Nature will not be subjected to such narrow rules."

[3] *Idler*, No. 82.

P

hand, and individual characterisation on the other, and constitutes, historically speaking, a point of transition between the
two.   We shall see that even for Goethe the "characteristic"
has some affinity with the specific type, and is opposed, in a
way which strikes us as strange, to the intensified rendering
of individual attributes.   Plainly, the movement of natural
science has played a part in the transformation of this conception.   Reynolds evidently thinks that a central or average
form in each species represents the purpose of nature.   I
suppose that if we to-day could attach any meaning to a purpose or inclination of nature, we should interpret it dynamically,
and should regard it as likely to be ahead of any existing individual forms, or at any rate as various, and incapable of exhaustion within a single typical or central figure.   This influence
must obviously force forward our conception of central or
essential reality from the species to the individual, and from
the "invariable" to the law of variation, which is itself a kind
of invariable.

Finally it is a curious anticipation of the German "period
of genius" that Reynolds contends for the rights of genius
against the tendency, exemplified in Hogarth, to attach practical importance to critical rules.   In all these—in Hogarth's
development of antique formalism, in Burke's acceptance of
the sublime as a complement to the beautiful, and in his revolt
against the worship of mere proportion, in Lord Kaimes' admission of the painful within the sphere of the agreeable, and
his desire to emancipate the modern drama from the rigid
unities of space and time, and in Reynolds' effort to dissociate
the grand style from decorative formalism, and explain it with
reference to a normal or central "inclination of nature" expressed by specific characterisation—in all this we find
embodied the antithesis of abstract and concrete expressiveness,
forced upon the modern world by the mere fact of its contrast
with the ancient, and especially with the very abstract tradition
by which that ancient world was represented to it.

Germans before   iv. We have now very briefly to trace the con-
   Lessing.   flicting elements in which this same contrast of
ancient rule and modern expressiveness existed in Germany,
before it was resolved into a vital and progressive æsthetic by
Lessing and his contemporaries.

The time—the early eighteenth century—was in Germany
one of immense and varied activity, in which foreign

material, both French and English, was being eagerly appropriated, and was producing strangely diverse effects on the
inexperienced genius of the nation. The few observations
by which I shall try to focus this animated scene as a background for the representation of Lessing's and Winckelmann's
æsthetic achievements will be, even more than the rest of this
work, devoid of all claims to full historical adequacy, and will
merely select those leading and causal tendencies which bear
directly on the growth of æsthetic perception.

The two great critical problems which Lessing inherited
from the generation immediately before him were, α, The
relation of a German national drama to the pseudo-classical
French theatre, and consequently to the true mind of antiquity which this latter parodied ; this was the essential subject
of his *Dramaturgie ;* and β, The value of strictly descriptive
or pictorial poetry, a species of art which marked both the
classical decadence and the first flush of the modern sentimental interest in nature, and which seemed to be justified
by the voice of antiquity, and by a misunderstanding of the
tradition that art lay in the imitation of natural objects.
The relation between poetic and pictorial beauty is the subject
of the Laocoon.

The former question is chiefly connected at this epoch with
the name of Gottsched ; the latter with the poetry and
theories of Bodmer and Breitinger, the " Swiss " or the
Zurich critics. I will speak of these two sects, as in fact they
were, very shortly, with reference to these problems.

Gottsched.   α. Gottsched (1700-1766) was lecturing at Leip-
sic in 1746, when Lessing matriculated there, both
on the History of Philosophy, using as a text-book his
own *Elements*, which is said to have been a Wolffian
compendium, and on " Poetik, ad critices sanioris normam,"
" the art of poetry in conformity with a sounder criticism." [1] He represented in Germany a similar reaction
against utter formlessness in the drama, to that which we
have observed to take place both in England and in France.
He set himself the task of creating a German literature, and
more especially a German drama, worthy to rank with that
of other nations. In attempting this, with the whole weight
of his position at Leipzig, then a leading literary centre, of

----

[1] Lessing's *Leben*, i. 51.

extreme industry, both on his own part and on that of his
circle, in original writing, in translation, and in journalism, and
of his friendship with an important society of actors (Neuber's),
who accepted the new plays in French taste which he prescribed, and were imitated in their submission by the ordinary
travelling companies, he succeeded for good or evil in banish-
ing the coarse and wild popular dramas of the later seventeenth century with the clown and the Faust, and replacing
them by plays of French origin, or on French models, representing the ideas of classical taste and correctness then current
in the literary world.   The *Deutsche Schaubühne* (1740–
1745) was the collection of plays, both original and translated,
which he issued as an instrument of his enterprise.[1]

Lessing, who relied on the Greeks and on Shakespeare as
his guides in dramatic questions, appears to have condemned
this interruption of German development by French influence
as a wholly false departure.   " No one will deny," a contemporary periodical had alleged,[2] " that the German stage owes
a great part of its earlier improvements to Professor Gottsched."   " I am that no one," rejoins Lessing ; " I deny it
altogether.   It were to be wished that Gottsched had never
meddled with the theatre.   His supposed improvements
either concern the most utter trifles, or are actually changes
for the worst.   He did not," Lessing continues, " aim at
improving the ancient German theatre, but at creating a new
one.   And what sort of a new one ?   Why, a Frenchified
one ; without considering whether this Frenchified drama was
suitable to the German mind."

Lessing's biographers, exceedingly careful students of the
German eighteenth century, do not assent to this extreme
view.   Admitting that there was a natural kinship between
the great English dramatists and the popular German drama
of the seventeenth century, they yet deny that the latter could
of itself have developed into a true national dramatic literature
cognate with that of England,   On the contrary, they maintain with great show of reason that Lessing's conception of
his problem, to establish a national theatre on the principles
of Aristotle and Shakespeare, only became possible after, and
because of, the work of Gottsched in bringing the German
drama into some kind of literary form.[3]

---

[1] *Encyl. Brit.*, art. "Gottsched."   [2] Lessing's *Leben*, i. 439.
[3] Lessing's *Leben*, i. 103, 438–7.

It must further be remarked that Gottsched, in his anxiety to prove that there was, and therefore could be, a German drama, and to bring all influences to bear upon remodelling it, called attention to the older plays, of whose form he entirely disapproved, by his historical notices of them in the "Nöthiger Vorrath zur Geschichte der Deutschen drama- tischen Dichtkunst" (materials for a history of German dra- matic poetry), and both himself, and through his wife, an indefatigable authoress and translator, brought much of real value to the knowledge of the German public. Thus Ma- dame Gottsched translated Molière's *Misanthrope*, the whole of the English *Spectator*, and Pope's *Rape of the Lock*.

Of Gottsched's dramatic theorising I give a single speci- men, from his rules for the construction of a tragic plot.[1] "The poet selects a moral doctrine, which he desires to im- press upon his readers in a sensuous form. For this pur- pose he devises the general framework of a story, such as to exhibit the truth of the doctrine. Then he searches in history for famous persons to whom incidents occurred somewhat similar to those of his story, and borrows their names for the personages of his plot in order to give them distinction." Lessing remarks on this that if the Hercules Furens contains any such doctrine, it must either be that virtue and heroism are an increased provocation to an angry Deity, or that one should avoid being a natural son of Zeus if one wants to escape the persecution of Hera. Lessing seems always just a little too clever. Even the English reader, if he knows Browning's translation of the Heracles, especially the chorus "Even a dirge," will be inclined to demur to the substance of Lessing's criticism no less than to the form of Gottsched's prescription. Yet Lessing himself retained throughout, and in some degree bequeathed even to Goethe, the pseudo-clas- sical and moralistic traditions of Corneille and Gottsched. And it is necessary to express a very serious doubt whether the enterprise in which not only Gottsched, but Lessing, Schiller and Goethe spent the best of their strength, the establishment of a German national drama, can be held to have thoroughly succeeded. Whether Faust is a sufficient reward to the world for the labours of several great men through two-thirds of a century, might well be questioned, if

---

[1] Gottsched, *Kritische Dichtkunst*, quoted in Lessing's *Leben*, i. 184.

it were worth while to quarrel with the course of history. The outcome of their labours, it may be held, was great indeed, but was not what they sought. The real German national art, the art of music, grew up of itself behind their backs while they were arguing about painting and poetry. What they did create by their deep and energetic study of the best utterances of mind and the best thoughts about those utterances, was not German art, but German philosophy.

The "Swiss."   β The "Swiss" critics and poets Bodmer and Breitinger, almost exactly Gottsched's contemporaries, with their friends and partisans, represent an influence on the whole opposed to that of Gottsched. In them the meeting of extremes, the sense of a unity between ancient and modern life, which was the sign of a deeper criticism and truer sense of beauty, began to show itself, though in a weak and superficial form, which gives a faint augury of the age of Goethe.

Wieland, 1733-1813, who in his youth was a friend of the Swiss,[1] and who lived to be satirized by Goethe, may be taken as a measure of the difference between the culture of the two periods. The Swiss critics stood up for Homer, Milton, Ariosto,[2] against Gottsched's pseudo-classicism, which allied itself, as a mechanical system of rules, with a narrow rationalism, attacking, for example, the use of the marvellous in Homer and Milton.

The openness of interest which gave them this power of sympathy with really great art, attracted them also to a modern type of poetry which though great things came of it afterwards, at first declared itself with a good deal of confusion in its aims. Sentimentalism, such as that of Klopstock,[3] whom the Zurich critics had influenced, and in whom they at first believed, and the interest in peasant life and romantic scenery, came together in their minds. Pictorial poetry was stimulated by Thomson's *Seasons*, which Bröcker[4] was translating between 1740 and 1750, and was commended by them in theory,[5] and produced, after Haller, by Kleist (Frühling, 1749) and Gessner (Idylls, 1756) who was a painter as well as poet.

---

[1] Scherer, ii. 41.
[2] Scherer, ii. 24 ; Lessing's *Leben*, ii. 18.
[3] Scherer, ii. 31.
[4] Scherer, ii. 38.
[5] In Breitinger's *Dichtkunst*, Lessing's *Leben*, ii. 18.

In speaking of Archæology I referred to the works of Spence and Caylus, which betray the idea that the difference of medium between painting and poetry makes no serious difference in the scope of those two arts, and this conception appears to have been generally current in the age before Lessing, although it found special expression in the criticism and poetry of the Zurich circle. The *Laocoon*, it is said, was aimed primarily at the Swiss,[1] as the *Dramaturgie* at Gottsched, Corneille, Voltaire; we have only to modify this by remembering that Winckelmann himself was at first a disciple of the Swiss, and that in his early work " on the imitation of Greek painting and sculpture " (1755) he actually says "that the limits of painting may be as wide as those of poetry, and that it is possible for the painter to follow the poet, just as it is for the musician.[2] Certainly, as Lessing's biographer observes, it sounds very much as if this sentence had suggested the second title of the Laocoon, " Of the limits of poetry and painting."

Before passing on, however, we must note that the Swiss genius, and the impulse of Thomson's poetry, were not exhausted in the crude thought and fancy that helped to elicit the Laocoon. Rousseau (1712–1778) and De Saussure (1740–1799) inherited the same genius in more powerful forms. The antagonism of Rousseau and Voltaire reproduces on a higher level that of Breitinger and Gottsched ; and Rousseau is the true inaugurator of modern romantic naturalism. It seems worth while to illustrate the many-sided influence of Rousseau outside revolutionary politics by a quotation from Amiel, himself too a native of Geneva. " J. J. Rousseau is an ancestor in all things. It was he who founded travelling on foot before Töpffer, reverie before René, literary botany before George Sand, the worship of nature before Bernardin de St. Pierre, the democratic theory before the revolution of 1789, political discussion and theological discussion before Mirabeau and Renan, the science of teaching before Pestalozzi, and Alpine description before De Saussure." . . . " Nobody, again, has had more influence than he upon the nineteenth century, for Byron, Châteaubriand, Madame de Staël and George Sand all descend from him.[3]

---

[1] Lessing's *Leben*.   [2] Quoted Lessing's *Leben*, ii. 20.
[3] Amiel, *Journal Intime*, E. Tr., i. 202.

If Rousseau was the first nature-sentimentalist, De Saussure, also a native of Geneva, was the first student-mountaineer. We can hardly realise to-day the void of knowledge and feeling in the time before 1787, when Mont Blanc was ascended by De Saussure, and also by another traveller, having never, it appears, been ascended before. In De Saussure, as all readers of the *Modern Painters*[1] are aware, we have an influence that has operated powerfully in impressing on the modern sense of Alpine beauty its peculiar character of loving and penetrating study, which involves the reconciliation of the scientific and artistic spirit, and is the root of our singular delight in observant sympathy with the characteristic law and essence of mountain conformation.

Lessing. v. I am convinced that Lessing ought to be treated in the history of æsthetic before Winckelmann, and not in the reverse order, which Schasler adopts. The mere dates of their lives and writings are not decisive. Winckelmann was indeed born twelve years before Lessing, and his assassination took place thirteen years before Lessing's death. It is also true that Lessing's Laocoon takes its text from an early work of Winckelmann, and mentions before its close his greater and later work, the history of ancient plastic art. But yet Lessing, as we have seen, springs from what went before him, from literary and dramatic criticism, and the conflict of the quasi-classical with the romantic drama which had been observed in the sixteenth century by Sidney, and throughout the seventeenth had been a subject of European interest. Lessing uses Winckelmann, it is true, but not as a younger man uses his predecessors ; rather as a recognised authority defines his position with reference to the ideas of a contemporary whose starting-point is other than his own. The historical side of Winckelmann's work, the recognition of variety and relativity in the beautiful of formative art, is as good as unknown to Lessing, whose capacity, and consequently his appreciation, lay entirely in the region of literature.

Now Winckelmann, on the other hand, made a new departure, which connects itself rather with what came after him than with what went before. It is true that he could not have seen any of Lessing's more important works before his own

---

[1] See especially *Modern Painters*, iv. 402.

were written. But his interest was pre-occupied with study in a different sphere, and Lessing's influence could not greatly have helped, though it might have hindered him. Practically, he possesses in the field of plastic art all that Lessing could in that region, have suggested to him, and he adds more to it.

Lessing, in short, represented an earlier tradition, and profited little by Winckelmann's great work, which came to him when his views were completed. Winckelmann represented a new departure on parallel, but different lines, and so far as we can judge, would not have written otherwise than he did if he had lived ten or twenty years later, and been well acquainted with the Laocoon.

Therefore continuity of subject is better preserved by dealing with Lessing first and Winckelmann second; and the chronological relations of the two writers do not amount to a contradiction of this arrangement, which is further justified by the superior concreteness of Winckelmann's analysis as compared with that of Lessing.

It must be understood that I can only speak of Lessing's contributions to the material of æsthetic. His theological and semi-philosophical writings do not concern us here, except in as far as they may have strengthened some particular elements of his critical influence.

His Conception of Criticism. *a.* Lessing (1729–1781) holds an intermediate position between the practical and the philosophical critic; between the legislator for art, and the investigator of beauty. No one man in modern times has done more than he to show the futility of art-formulæ uncritically accepted from tradition, and to substitute for them that living insight which reveals the common root of human nature in the classical as in the romantic world. And yet he believed in rules. He believed that the critic was the poet's guide. He thought that the true laws of poetry were embodied in Homer and Sophocles, and explained in Aristotle; and in withstanding the formlessness of the "age of genius," he did not appear to distinguish obedience to critical rules from practical training in artistic forms. Thus he strikes us throughout as attached to the older views by the purpose of his thought, if he belongs to modern criticism by its content. It is worth while to set this essential point in a clear light at starting, by quoting the famous self-estimate from the closing chapter of his dramatic

criticism, the *Hamburgische Dramaturgie* (1767–8), almost
his latest strictly æsthetic production.

"I am[1] neither actor nor poet. My friends often do me
the honour of acknowledging me to be the latter. But only
because they mistake me. So indulgent a conclusion should
not be drawn from some dramatic attempts on which I have
ventured. Not every one is a painter who takes a brush in
his hand, and daubs with colours. The earliest of those
attempts were written at an age when one so readily takes
enjoyment and facility for genius ; all that is tolerable in the
later pieces I am well aware that I owe simply and solely to
criticism. I do not feel in myself the living spring which
rises by its own power in pure and abundant jets ; I have to
press everything out of myself by force-pumps. I should be
so poor, so cold, so shortsighted, if I had not learned in some
degree to borrow others' wealth, to warm myself at others' fire,
and to strengthen my eyes with the lenses of art. Therefore
I have always been vexed or ashamed when I have heard
anything in disparagement of criticism. They say it chokes
genius ; I flattered myself that it had given me something
that comes very near genius. I am a cripple, who cannot
possibly be edified by a satire against crutches.

"But, no doubt, though crutches help a cripple to move
from place to place, yet they do not make him a runner : and
it is just so with criticism." . . . [After repeating that
he has been a student of dramatic form], "but one may study
oneself deeper into error. What assures me that I have
not done so, and that I do not mistake the essence of dramatic art, is the fact that I understand it precisely as Aristotle
has abstracted it from the innumerable masterpieces of the
Greek stage. . . . I do not hesitate to confess (even if in
these enlightened times I am to be laughed out of countenance
for it) that I hold the Poetics to be as infallible as the elements
of Euclid. Its principles are just as true and as certain, only
not so simple, and therefore more exposed to misrepresenta-
tion. Especially I believe that I can prove with reference to
tragedy, the account of which is preserved to us pretty complete, that it cannot move a step from Aristotle's direction
without departing from its own perfection in the same
measure." French tragedy, he goes on to say, had long

---

[1] *Hamburgische Dramaturgie,* ii. 101–104.

passed for the embodiment of the ancient rules; and then, genuine feeling being awakened by some English pieces which obviously broke the French rules, the German public went to the other extreme, and thought these rules were needless and perhaps injurious. "And even this might have passed—but they began to confuse *all* rules with *these* rules, and to set it down as pedantry to prescribe to genius at all what it may do and what it may not. In short, we were on the point of presumptuously forfeiting all the experience of the past, and of demanding that every poet should invent the art anew for himself.

"I should be vain enough to think that I had deserved well of our theatre if I could suppose that I had hit upon the only means of arresting this fermentation of our taste. At least I may flatter myself that I have worked to this end, for I have studied nothing so much as to attack the illusion of the regularity of the French stage. No nation has misunderstood the rules of the ancient drama more than the French. Some incidental remarks which they found in Aristotle about the most convenient arrangement of the drama, they have assumed to be essential; and on the other hand have so emasculated what really was essential by all kinds of limitations and interpretations, that such views could, inevitably, give rise only to works that must remain far below the highest effect which the philosopher had reckoned on in his rules.

"I venture at this point to make an assertion which you may take as you please. Show me the piece of the great Corneille, which I would not improve upon.[1] What will you bet?

"Yet no; I should not like this assertion to pass for braggadocio. So note carefully what I add to it. I certainly should improve upon the play—and yet be a long way from being a Corneille—and be a long way from having achieved a masterpiece. I certainly should improve upon it, and ought not to think much of myself for doing so. I should have done nothing but what anyone could do whose faith in Aristotle is as firm as mine."

Now we have to bear in mind that it is at least open to doubt whether the form of art about which Lessing's practical interest was thus pre-occupied had not already, at the time

---

[1] "Besser machen." I think it means not "amend," but write a better play on the same story.

when he was writing, become a matter of merely historical concern.   Granting that Shakespearian tragedy falls within it, as Lessing vehemently contended, it must still be held, as I suggested above, that there was not in Lessing's lifetime, and never has been since in any country of Europe, a continuous and considerable development of serious drama, which, while capable of maintaining itself on the stage, has also entered into the greater literature of the world.   It may be that the spirit of the Poetic applies to the novel, and to serious comedy, and to Wagnerian opera, and to the mixed realistic drama of our own day, in short to all imaginative narration and portrayal of life.   I am not at present discussing this substantive problem, but merely pointing out that neither in its Hellenic nor in its Shakespearian shape was the precise species of art which to Lessing is so present and vital an interest, apparently destined to revive.   His tone would have been entirely different, and his judgment of Corneille probably much more lenient, had he realised that the problem before him was one of history, involving gradation and at least external variation, and not of the practical resuscitation of a definite kind of play.

This difference between Lessing's actual position and that in which he believed himself to be placed, explains to us at once the nature and limits of his achievement.   He never understood his own function to be primarily that of unveiling the true connection between the modern and the antique in literature.   Everywhere the thought of the drama, especially of tragedy, as a species of art that has unique value, and is about to come to its rights, is in the background of his treatment.   This is the case even in the Laocoon ; so much so, that it was his intention[1] to have closed the treatise with a discussion that should have established the drama to be the highest form of poetry, and his definition of poetry as having action for its object-matter is contributory to this view (Action = " Handlung "=δράμα), although action at its widest may include for him anything that goes on in time.

Aim of the
Laocoon.   β. If now we recall that " the Swiss " with their friends, following Thomson, were introducing pictorial description into poetry, while Winckelmann in the early work which furnishes Lessing's text had declared for allegory as the highest purpose of formative art, we can very

---

[1] Scherer, E. Trans., ii. 68.

easily appreciate the main contention of the treatise which has for its title " Laocoon, or, of the limits of painting and poetry." Its aim was in short to expel pictorial description from poetry, and to deny to formative art any direct concern with action, and therefore with expression or significance. The writer's aim was no doubt impartial, and the limits of poetry were to be straitened in accordance with the same principle which was to cut off large provinces from the dominion of " painting " (formative art). And yet it is the case that Lessing, from the mere tendency of his genius, on the whole took the side of poetry, as Winckelmann did that of painting and sculpture, while Lessing left the idea of the latter arts in undeveloped abstraction, and Winckelmann did nothing for the theory of the former. The achievement of each, in his sphere, was nothing less than passing from the abstract to the concrete, recognising that beauty is an utterance which has many grades and forms, and facing the question of the relation between them and the possibility of their combination.

The *occasion* of the Laocoon was such as to show with a force amounting to irony, the superior importance of ideas as compared with particular facts. Winckelmann had said, in his treatise *On the Imitation of Greek Works of Painting and Sculpture*, that the expression in Greek statues always revealed a great and composed soul, and that this was illustrated by the famous Laocoon group, in which Laocoon's features expressed no such extremity of suffering as would be realistically in accordance with the situation, and more particularly, did not indicate him to be crying out, as Virgil describes him. Lessing, aroused, as he admits,[1] by the implied censure on Virgil, maintains that the absence of agonised expression in Laocoon's features, and of all sign of outcry —which he completely accepts as a fact[2]—is to be accounted for not by the demands of Greek character, but by the laws of Greek sculpture; in other words, that portrayal of extreme suffering and its expression, legitimate in poetry, was prohibited by the law and aim of beauty, which he alleged to be supreme in formative art.

[1] Laocoon, i.
[2] Lessing had of course never seen the original of the Laocoon, when this was written. I do not know that he had ever seen a cast; probably his judgment was formed from engravings.

Now the tendency of skilled criticism ever since Lessing's day has been to deny the alleged fact that Laocoon is represented in the marble group as silent or nearly so, and with an expression far removed from that of extreme bodily suffering.[1] The truth appears to be that the group is a work of the Rhodian school, which retained little of the great Greek style, and was chiefly distinguished by technical skill and forcible presentation of ideas.[2] The expression of pain is violent, and the abstinence from crying out is exceedingly doubtful. It is remarkable that the observation with reference to which such influential theories were propounded, should be of questionable accuracy. We have to bear in mind both that the real basis of a tolerable theory is always wider than the case selected for exposition, and also that a statue which seems almost un-Hellenic when compared with the marbles of the Parthenon, might appear full of Greek dignity when compared with works by the degenerate successors of Michael Angelo.

Passing from the occasion, which has an interest chiefly for curiosity, to the substance of Lessing's criticism, we find it to be introduced as follows. Winckelmann had treated the comparative calmness which he saw in the features of Laocoon as the *expression* of a great and composed soul which, in conformity with the Greek spirit, was above giving way to suffering. Lessing replied, appealing triumphantly to the example of Philoctetes, which Winckelmann had unwarily adduced, that it was not the fact that a great soul was held, among the Greeks, to be incapable of violent expressions of emotion; and that therefore the reason for the dignity or self-control apparent in the Laocoon must be other than that alleged by Winckelmann. And this reason, he continued, lay not in any form or law of expression relative to character, but simply in the demands of [formal] beauty, which he asserted to be sovereign in the province of formative art. Now between him and Winckelmann there was so far no very grave matter at issue. For Winckelmann's "expression" is always relative to that which it expresses; and the expression of "a great and tranquil soul," which he divines to belong to the greatest period of Greek art, is for him almost or quite within the lines of formal beauty. But for

---

[1] Overbeck, ii. 281.   [2] Murray, ii. 369.

Lessing this is a matter of principle. It is not any particular degree of expression, but the acceptance of expression as a principle of formative art, against which he feels bound to make war. Beauty and expression are for him incompatible, and the one can only exist at the expense of the other. Some feeling of the same kind will be found also in Winckelmann, who does not avoid inconsistency in explaining it away.

Demarcation of "Painting" and Poetry: γ. Lessing, however, does not rest in a pre-conception of this kind. He deduces the distinction between poetry and " painting " from the nature of their respective media, and in doing so, undoubtedly, as Mr. Sully observes,[1] he pioneers the true road of modern æsthetic. And he makes an advance, it must once for all be noted, as much by his style and method as by his results. He has been called, indeed, a man of the understanding, in the technical sense ascribed to the latter term by idealist philosophy, that is to say, a man of sharp antitheses, the sides of which are not explained in terms of one another, but are simply left as ultimate contrasts. In the first place, however, we must bear in mind that we are speaking of the *data* of æsthetic, and a clear statement of positive empirical contrasts is no bad thing in a collection of data. And in the second place the true distinction of understanding and of reason is of course one of degree rather than of kind ; antitheses, as we have seen throughout, were laid upon the men of this age ; but the attempt to reduce things to a principle is always the beginning of reconciliation and unity, and this attempt was characteristic of Lessing. His style, then, shows the man of the understanding at his very best. His positive knowledge in the field of literature is immense ; his skill in disputation is extraordinary, and this skill is in fact his great temptation, for he cannot resist proving the contradictory of every pro-position which an opponent sets up, with a precision which is too good to be true. But with all this his style has a conversational simplicity and directness, which produces an indescribably invigorating effect on the mind, and has some-thing of the touch of modern science at its best. He seems to say to the reader, " Is it thus or thus ? Here are the examples ; come and look at them ; how do they strike you ? Is it not thus rather than thus ?" Of course, when such a

[1] *Encycl. Brit.*, art. " Æsthetic."

writer does force a distinction, the impression is proportion-
ately painful. But these cases are rare, though they unquestionably occur.

His peculiar style loses terribly by translation ; but I feel
bound to reproduce the passage which is the core of the
Laocoon, both as an example of his reasoning, and as containing, in a page of print, his whole essential contribution to the
classification of the arts.

"I should like to attempt to deduce the matter from its
primary ground.[1]

"I infer thus. If it is true that painting employs in its imitations quite different media or signs from poetry, the former
employing shapes and colours in space, the latter articulate
tones in time ; if it is unquestionable that the signs must have
a convenient relation to the thing signified, then co-existing
signs can only express objects which co-exist or whose parts
co-exist, and successive signs can only express objects which
are successive, or whose parts are successive.

"Objects which co-exist or whose parts co-exist are called
bodies. Consequently bodies with their visible qualities are
the proper objects of painting.

"Objects which are in succession or whose parts are in
succession are called actions. Consequently actions are the
proper objects of poetry.

"But bodies exist not only in space, but also in time. They
continue, and in every moment of their continuance may
appear different, and be in different combinations. Each of
these momentary appearances and combinations is the effect
of a preceding one, and is capable of being the cause of a
succeeding one, and thus, so to speak, the centre of an action.
Consequently, painting is able also to imitate actions, but only
by suggestion conveyed through bodies.

"On the other hand, actions cannot exist apart, but must be
attached to beings. In as far as these beings are bodies, or
are regarded as bodies, poetry can depict bodies too, but only
by suggestion conveyed through actions.

"Painting, in its co-existing compositions, can only use a
single moment of the action, and must therefore choose the
most pregnant one, from which the preceding and subsequent
ones become most intelligible.

---

[1] Laocoon, sect. xvi.

"Just so poetry in its successive imitations can only use a single property of bodies, and must therefore select that which awakens the most sensuous image of the object in the aspect required.

"Hence flows the rule of the singleness of pictorial epithets, and of reserve in description of bodily objects."

The elements which enter into this brief and pregnant argument are collected from very various sources. The "convenient relation of signs to the thing signified" is probably suggested by Baumgarten.[1] The remark that poetry is not adapted for the complete description of visible bodies is due to Burke.[2] The observation that painting can represent only a moment of time is found in Lord Kaimes.[3] The underlying idea that poetry deals essentially with action is drawn no doubt from Aristotle's account of the drama as the central species of poetry, and is negatively suggested by "the Swiss." The corresponding idea that material or bodily beauty consists of pure unity in variety of form is a reminiscence of Hogarth and of classical æsthetic, and is negatively suggested by Winckelmann's treatment of allegory. But no one of Lessing's predecessors had united all these ideas in a single page of luminous deduction.

The value to be ascribed to the abstract distinction thus laid down will be evident, I hope, as our history progresses. It is enough to say for the present that however it may be related to any complete philosophy of the beautiful, the distinction by succession and co-existence occupied a place of very great importance in our present subject matter "the data of modern æsthetic." We now proceed to consider some consequences attached by Lessing to this principle.

Lessing's Attitude towards the Problem of Ugliness. δ. The term "beauty" is confined by Lessing to material beauty, and is not treated as the essential quality of poetry considered as art. Lord Kaimes, it may be noticed, confined the term beauty to objects of sight ;[4] and we have found the same tendency, far narrower than that of Plato or Aristotle, in mediæval writers[5] from Plotinus downward. Thus when we find Lessing discussing the place of "beauty" in poetry he is only asking how far *material* beauty can effectively be depicted in language, to

---

[1] See Schasler, i. 351.   [2] See p. 205 above.   [3] *Ib.*
[4] *Elements of Criticism*, i. 177.   [5] *e.g.* Aquinas, see p. 146 above.

which he answers, in accordance with his principle, that it can
only be either suggested by its effects, or represented as
charm (Reiz [1]), which following Burke's account of grace, he
defines as beauty in motion.   I do not know that Lessing has
framed a general conception of any essential quality shared by
poetry with the fine arts as a class.   He habitually employs
" Poetry " and " Art " as antithetical terms, a usage common
to-day, and always indicative of a failure or omission to co-
ordinate them in theory.   Even for his conception of the
poetical quality common to all species of poetry as such, I
believe that we should find nothing more explicit than his
account of the drama, which he with Aristotle regards as
poetry in its highest concentration.   He thus by omission
rather than of set purpose partially anticipates the questionings of the age of genius as to whether the essential quality
of modern art *is* really beauty, and not rather something else—
the interesting or the significant.   And this omission to force
poetry and formative art into the same theoretical scheme
enables him to deal freely with the former in spite of his
abstract conception of the latter.

Thus he admits the ugly [2] into poetry as a means to the
comic and the terrible, though the reason for which he does
so—that the effect of ugliness is weakened by presentation in
language—destroys in part the significance of his doing so.

Formative art, on the other hand, he very decidedly limits
to dealing with those visible objects which produce pleasant
sensations.   Although " as [3] an imitative craft it can express
ugliness, yet as a fine art it refuses to do so," even as a means
to the comic and the terrible.   The reason assigned for this
refusal is the persistent force of ugly forms in pictorial presentation, which causes their disagreeable effect, like that of dis-
gust (Ekel), to outlast the feeling of comedy or terror to
which they may have been a means.   Thus he rejects, so far
as concerns the ugly, even Aristotle's plea for the pleasant
effect of imitations of unpleasant reality, pointing out that the
ugly in form produces its disagreeable effect quite apart from
any reference to its real existence, and therefore in representation quite as much as in reality.   This is the point correlative to that to which Burke drew attention when he said that
a tragic reality, regarded apart from real interests, had the

---

[1] Laocoon, xxi.   [2] Laocoon, xxiii.   [3] Laocoon, xxiv.

same pleasures as its representation. Thus by distinguishing between qualities which are the same in representation as in reality, and qualities which are not, Lessing really suggests the distinction between æsthetic and practical interest.

If we now pursue our point by asking how far this exclusion of ugliness betrays an abstract and unindividualised tendency in Lessing's conception of material beauty, we are met by the difficulty of knowing precisely what he included under ugliness. We cannot quarrel with a critic for excluding the ugly from fine art, i.e. from the beautiful, unless we are sure that in doing so he is unaware how wide is the range of the concretely beautiful, and how narrow, even if we admit it to exist, is that of the insuperably ugly. We can only form a judgment of Lessing's position in this respect by examining the degree in which he recognises any beauty other than that of mere form—ultimately and strictly geometrical beauty as analysed by Hogarth.

In the first part of the Laocoon, before Winckelmann's History of Art had appeared, Lessing undoubtedly regards *expression* and *truth* as falling outside beauty. Not only does he regard beauty, thus abstracted, as the law of ancient formative art, but he stumbles into the terrible pitfall of treating it as the exclusive *aim* of such art. As ancient statues are plainly charged with meaning and special feeling, which takes shape in tangible "attributes," i.e objects denoting an individual deity or relation of a deity, Lessing is driven to defend his view by distinguishing between the works in which religious or conventional tradition fettered the artist,[1] and those in which he freely aimed at beauty for beauty's sake. But the demand for individual expressiveness in great and serious art is not confined to identification of a personage by tangible attributes ; and history shows that hazardous to art as the didactic spirit is, the mood of great masters in great art-periods is nearer to the didactic spirit than to the conscious quest for abstract beauty. All beauty, as we have seen, is ultimately expressiveness, and its substance and foundation falls away if the artist is not mastered by some burden or import for which he desires to find utterance. Probably it was as correcting this distinction of Lessing, that Goethe laid down the view that " The highest *principle* of the ancients

---

[1] Laocoon, ix.

was the significant, but the highest *result* of *successful treat-ment*, the beautiful." [1]   Beauty *comes*, that is to say, when a significant content is duly handled, but is not a conscious and abstract purpose.   We shall have to return to this view at a later stage.

Expression, then, and the significant, were *prima facie* ex-cluded by Lessing from the materially beautiful.   It is worth noting that he regarded the beauty of *drapery* as something very inferior; the idea of his generation was that Greek statues were characteristically nude, and the expressive force of the treatment of drapery, as we now know it in the works of the great time, was unthought of.   " Beauty was the pur-pose of art," he exclaims ; "necessity invented clothes ; and what has art to do with necessity ?" [2]   " I greatly fear that the most perfect master in drapery shows by this very skill where his weakness lies." [3]   When Lessing makes a mistake, he makes it thoroughly.

In the notes for the second part of the Laocoon, written after Winckelmann's History of Art had appeared, there is a change of phrase as compared with the first part ; but it is not a substantive modification.   He now admits into beauty an element of expression, viz. the " permanent expression," which is " not violent," and which " is not only compatible with beauty, but introduces more variety into beauty itself." [4] This view obviously follows Winckelmann's conception of the high or grand style of beauty which is united with an expres-sion of repose and tranquillity.   Winckelmann, as we shall see, goes further afield in expression, but Lessing does not follow him.

This is the extreme boundary of the variously expressive, significant, or characteristic, not to speak of the ugly, in Les-sing's idea of formative art.   Historical painting, for instance, he holds to be only justifiable as an excuse for a composition of various beautiful forms ; to paint a scene for the sake of its import is, he thinks, to make the means into the end.

Landscape painting is the mere work of eye and hand (had Lessing been reading Reynolds' criticism on the Dutch

---

[1] Hegel, *Introd. to Æsth.*, E. Tr., p. 36.

[2] Laocoon, v.

[3] We must remember that English portrait painters of that day used to employ an assistant to paint their draperies.

[4] Laoc., 2, iii.

painters?¹), genius has no share in it; for the inorganic and
vegetable world *are incapable of an ideal.* This seems to be
a further borrowing from the History of Art. The ideal, according to it,² is that perfection which is suggested by a comparison of natural examples; and we must suppose that in the
inorganic world and the world of plants he sees no such law
of types and tendencies as to make it possible for a more perfect form to be suggested for them by the exercise of the
intelligence on their given structure. " The highest bodily
beauty exists only in man, and in him only because of the
ideal," ³ *i.e.* I presume, because of his marked unity and coherence as a organism, which enables a partial defect to be
corrected by a suggestion drawn from another example,
whereas, of two mountain shapes, who can say which is the
right one? " There is no ideal of that in which Nature has
proposed to herself nothing definite." ⁴

We may conclude this part of the examination of Lessing's
views with his amazing question, " Would it not have been
better if oil painting had never been invented?" ⁵

After this we need ask no further questions about Lessing's
general attitude towards ugliness in formative art. His notion
of material beauty was fundamentally that of formal, geometrical, or decorative beauty, and even his selection of the
human form as the type of the beautiful is scarcely to be justified out of his æsthetic theory; for what is the human form
if it expresses no human qualities?

ε. In one point, however, modern feeling has
A point in which his classicism was justified. sympathised with Lessing's classicism, although
it will never cease to feel a certain attraction in
the quaint horrors of mediæval art. The Greeks, Lessing
had maintained in the Laocoon,⁶ and even their poets, had
never portrayed death under the image of a skeleton, in the
manner of mediæval and contemporary artists, but rather, in
agreement with Homer, as the twin brother of sleep. This
assertion drew upon him an attack to which he replied in
1769 with the short treatise, *How the Ancients Represented*

¹ *Idler*, No. 79.   See Ruskin, *Modern Painters*, "On the Grand Style."
² Winckelmann, *Gesch. d. bildenden Kunst d. Alten*, iv. 2. 35.
³ Laoc., 2. ii.
⁴ Laoc., 2. iv.
⁵ Lessing's *Leben*, ii. 57.
⁶ Laoc., xi. note.

Death. In this he identified the common monumental figure, resembling an Amor but leaning on a reversed torch, as the normal image of death among the Greeks, and found another explanation of the antique skeleton figures, whose existence had been alleged as an argument against him.   The sane though sympathetic manner in which he treats the whole subject—one of those in which romantic sentiment compares least favourably with the cheerful calm of the ancients—was perhaps the first simple and popular *rapprochement* between genuine Greek feeling and the profound convictions of modern life ; and in this respect anticipated the dawn of a new era in which Greek art and intelligence were felt to possess a real message for humanity.   It was this work, no doubt, that stirred Schiller to sing in the "Götter Griechenlands :"

> " Damals [1] trat kein grässliches Gerippe
> Vor das Bett des Sterbenden.   Ein Kuss
> Nahm das letzte Leben von der Lippe,
> Seine Fackel senkt' ein Genius."

Lessing's Theory of the Drama.   ζ. We have sufficiently seen that from the time of Corneille to that of Gottsched theories of poetry appealing to the authority of Aristotle were common both in France and Germany.   Lessing stands within this tradition which is modified in his case by peculiar circumstances.

To begin with, the pseudo-classical tradition itself had at this time reached a critical point.   By invading Germany, it had suggested, even in Gottsched's hands, the idea of a national drama.   And while making this suggestion, it had revealed that its own work was done.   Voltaire,[2] its most decided partisan, spoke with curious candour of the languor and rigidity of the French drama.   The form generated by classicism had become fixed, and had no fecundity.   The German genius, when awakened by its means, could not long be content with it.   Still less was this possible when, being essentially an appeal to Cæsar, the classical tradition was at length brought before his judgment-seat ; when the "ancients" whose supposed authority had warranted such strange things were produced in broad daylight as the touchstone of poetry,

---

[1] In those days no gruesome skeleton approached the bed of the dying. A kiss received the last life from the lips, and a Genius reversed his torch."
[2] Quoted in *Hamburgische Dramaturgie,* ii. 194.

by a genuine scholar with real poetical sympathy. For Lessing is the first popular writer among the moderns who knew and loved Homer and Sophocles as a cultivated man of letters knows and loves them to-day. The germs of the comparison in question lay in the whole history and tendency of the Renaissance and the subsequent age. It was impossible that the world should go on for ever talking about the ancients without caring to know what the greatest of them was like ; and Lessing happened to be the first man who had the critical genius necessary to make this plain. The first Renaissance was Latin ; the second was Greek ; and Lessing in one craft, like Winckelmann in another, opened the way from the first to the second.

But, in the next place, the French classical tradition was confronted in Germany not only by the true spirit of antiquity which it had aroused, because it was "classical," but by the spirit of intellectual kinship between England and Germany, which it aroused because it was French. The Germans were beginning to feel their affinity with the English mind and speech, and working backwards from the nearer to the more remote, according to the principle which we have so often observed, they first laid hold on writers contemporary or nearly so[1]—thus Gottsched on the *Spectator* and Addison's *Cato*, the Swiss on Thomson, Young and Milton, and then, in Lessing's generation, they traced the same affinity back to Shakespeare. It would be a crude account of Lessing's theory, but not wholly a false one, to say that his heart was set on proving Shakespeare, and not Racine, to be correct according to Sophocles and Aristotle. His synthesis of the true classical and the romantic drama owed much to the collision of the French and German mind, which expressed itself in his almost personal hostility to Gottsched and Voltaire.

And thirdly we have to observe that Lessing lived at a time[2] when the dramatic forms were being modified, and the novel of family life was beginning to exert an entirely new influence. As regards this modification of dramatic species, it is simplest to quote Lessing's own words.[3] " I desire to

---

[1] Lessing's *Leben*, i. 279.
[2] Lessing's *Leben*, i. 294, **ff.**
[3] Lessing's *Leben*, i. 294.

speak of the changes which in our time have been made in dramatic poetry. Neither comedy nor tragedy has been spared. The former has been raised several degrees, and the latter lowered in the same measure. In the former case it was thought that the world had had enough of laughing at the comic play and hissing ridiculous vices ; and so the fancy suggested itself, to let the world at last have its turn at weeping even in comedy, and find a noble entertainment in tranquil virtues. In tragedy again it was held unreasonable that no one but sovereigns and persons of rank should be capable of awaking our pity and terror ; so middle-class heroes were sought out, and the tragic buskin buckled on them, whereas before the only object had been to make them laughable. The former change created what its partisans call the pathetic, and its antagonists the crying comedy. From the second there arose bourgeois (middle class) tragedy." " The former change was made by the French,[1] the latter by the English. I should almost venture to say that both of them arose from the peculiar disposition of these peoples. The Frenchman is a creature that always desires to appear greater than he is. The Englishman is one who likes to pull down everything great to his own level. The former disliked to see himself always represented on the comic side ; a secret ambition drove him to show persons like himself in a noble light. The latter found it vexatious to give so much precedence to crowned heads ; he thought he could feel that violent passions and sublime thoughts belonged no more to them than to one of his own rank."

Lessing's early tragedy, *Miss Sara Sampson*, which was warmly welcomed in the *Journal étranger* for 1761, probably by Diderot,[2] was the first German "middle-class tragedy," and reveals the influence under which it was composed by the fact[3] that its motives are drawn from *The Merchant of London*—the first English middle-class tragedy,—and from *Clarissa Harlowe*, the first novel of family life, which introduced the poetry of the family to modern Europe. In one way or another, though in the case of comedy not in identical descent from the "Comédie larmoyante," the serious non-tragic

---

[1] *e.g.* Nivelle de la Chaussée, about 1740. For an account of the movement see Lessing's *Leben*, i. 291.

[2] Lessing's *Leben*, i. 467.

[3] Cf. i. 305.

drama and the middle-class tragedy were continued by Lessing himself and by Diderot. Lessing calls his *Emilia Galotti* a "middle-class Virginia,"[1]—"middle-class," not in contrast to Livy's story, but in contrast to the habitual treatment of the same subject on the French stage. And these two forms insensibly shade off into the novel-like mixed drama of real life with which we are familiar to-day. Whether any good can come of this movement in the future from the standpoint of serious dramatic art, appears problematic; but this appearance arises from the general difficulties attaching to dramatic art as such, and not from the abandonment of a forced distinction between tragedy and comedy. For the approximation between the two, not formally recognised before the time of which we are writing, was really a matter of older date. Goethe called Molière's *Misanthrope* a tragedy,[2] and this play is taken as the earliest modern example of serious comedy by the first theoretical writer on the subject, about 1740. And we all know what Shakespearian comedy is at its most serious points; we can hardly say whether *Measure for Measure*, and *Much Ado about Nothing*, are serious comedies or tragedies with happy endings.

Thus it was quite clear that if the theory of tragedy was to have a real bearing for romantic poetry it must in some degree be widened, and shown not to depend on the absolute distinction of the two sides of life which appeared to be presupposed both in practice of the ancients, and in Aristotle's history of the drama and theory of tragedy.

The problem through which more particularly the above influences—the serious study of antiquity, the national or racial spirit opposed to a foreign tradition, and the modification of the distinction between dramatic species—acted on Lessing's formal æsthetic criticism is that of the interpretation to be placed on Aristotle's account of the tragic emotions, and the estimate, consequent on this interpretation, of his ideas concerning the character of the true tragic hero.

---

[1] He took the plot from the story of Virginia, omitting the political background, intending thereby to isolate and purify the tragic motive. I imagine most readers will feel that the story is thus altogether spoilt, that outlook into a larger life which we get even in Romeo and Juliet, through the healing of the feud, being here entirely closed. Lessing's *Leben*, ii. 309 ff.

[2] Lessing's *Leben*, i. 294–5.

For as to the fundamental condition of the drama, its unity, the artificial demands of the pseudo-classical school fall into their places at once when Lessing points out that the only unity which is either fundamental in itself or essentially demanded by Aristotle, is the unity of action, and that the others, so far as necessary, are mere corollaries from this, made more important in the ancient world by the presence of the Chorus.[1]   This latter remark, it will be remembered, had already been made by Lord Kaimes.   This view of the unities is in itself the simplest case of the reconciliation between ancient theory and modern romantic practice.

Aristotle's account of the tragic emotions, of their effect on the mind, and of the character therefore required for a hero of tragedy, have been briefly explained in dealing with Aristotle's views at first hand.

But this appears to be the right place to point out their relation to the development of æsthetic criticism in modern times.

The paradox of Lessing's position is this : he contends that Aristotle's analysis of tragedy essentially justifies the romantic drama.   But his first duty as an interpreter of Aristotle is to convict Corneille and similar writers of having understood him *not* too narrowly, *but* too loosely.   It is not, therefore, through what what we might call the surface extension assigned to Aristotle's ideas, but by tracing them down to their root in human nature, that first Lessing, and then Bernays—who is to Lessing as the latter to Corneille—was able to maintain their essential value for poetry as we understand it.

For us, then, the question of Aristotle's meaning in selecting pity and fear as the special emotions of tragedy, is one of the same class which was described in general terms when we spoke of his views.   Throwing aside all minutiæ, we may state it thus on its merits.   Tragedy, we find in his definition, affects the mind in a certain way, "by means of pity and fear." Are these terms employed *currente calamo*, to indicate the first samples that come to hand, and, of course, as the first, the chief and most striking samples, of the various emotions which are aroused by the spectacle of any serious and complete piece of human history ; or is there a precise systematic

---

[1] Lessing's *Leben*, ii. 168.

intention in the exclusiveness with which these two and no
others are adduced, and an essential connection between the
one and the other ? How far are we dealing with a naive
though acute observation, and how far with a systematic
analysis conjoined with a general theory of serious poetry ?
Corneille, to judge from his comments, must have adopted
the former view, and thus he easily widens the definition by
laxity and on the surface. For we saw[1] that his aim in his
theoretical writing was the same as that of Lessing in the
Dramaturgie, to reconcile modern beauties with ancient rules.
Pity and fear, he says in effect, are not to be taken as essentially connected ; they are feelings either of which by itself
may form the interest of a tragedy, and there may be others
besides which Aristotle did not happen to notice, such as
admiration, so that his account of the tragic emotions is casual
and partial, and his exclusion of perfect and monstrous characters depended merely on his not having noticed that pity
could be successfully aroused by the one, and fear by the other.
His definition, in short, is taken as empirically descriptive ;
and so with a little good-will it can be extended to include
even the saints and monsters of Corneille's plays.

Now Lessing, to whom Bernays, intent upon the "purification" controversy, does less than justice as regards the
whole matter, brings to bear on the subject, and, as he claims,
almost for the first time, the reciprocal definitions of pity and
fear from the Rhetoric. His earlier view,[2] however, rejects
the exclusive interdependence of pity and fear as erroneous,
and is thus markedly more in harmony with Corneille than
that of the *Dramaturgie*. But he then makes, I feel bound to
contend, the great step on which the later and more subtle
theory both of Lessing himself and also of Bernays, is
founded. For he substitutes Burke's "sympathy," the German "Mitleid," on which Lessing even plays by calling it
"Mitleiden" (which merely means sharing the feeling or suffering of another, and does not necessarily indicate a specific
emotion attached to so doing), for the perfectly definite Greek
term ἔλεος, "compassion" or "pity." Thus there is dragged
in the whole modern or romantic conception, so powerfully
developed by Bernays, of the widening of the individual self
into the great self of humanity.

---

[1] Page 197, above.   [2] Lessing's *Leben*, i. 363, a letter to Nicolai before 1758.

In the *Dramaturgie*,[1] written some ten years later,[2] when Lessing, as critic to the Hamburg theatre, was doing his best to aid the creation of a "national drama" for Germany, he accepts the exclusive and essential connection of pity and fear as instruments of tragic effect, and does not attempt to extend the import of these expressions so as to include analogous emotion, except in as far as they describe the object-matter of the tragic purification as opposed to its instruments. Therefore his view comes to be essentially that of Bernays, that Aristotle intends to insist on the essential interconnection of sympathy and fear, in the sense that our feeling of a common nature and possibilities shared by ourself and the person in the drama awakens in us the thought of our own participation in that human destiny which can do such things as we see.

It is plain that in this exposition width of application is not obtained by a laxity like that of Corneille, but by confining the definition more strictly to the emotions which Aristotle named, and then interpreting these emotions with a larger and deeper reference to human nature.

And so in Bernays himself, who in his turn condemns Lessing for laxity, we find the tragic emotions traced so deep into the roots of human nature that no serious art whatever need fall outside their province. I quote a characteristic sentence :[3] "It is only when the actual [material, external] fear operates indirectly through sympathy with a person, that the process of purgation can take place in the spectator's mind, by the individual self being enlarged into the self of all humanity, and so coming face to face with the terribly sublime laws of the universe and their incomprehensible power, which envelops mankind, and being penetrated by that sort of fear which as an ecstatic shudder in presence of the universe ["dem All"] is pleasurable in the highest way and without disturbance." It is clear that while professing to remain within the Aristotelian theory of tragedy, we have here arrived at a generalised conception of tragic motive which is applicable to any serious portrayal of life however romantic, however formless, however free from external collision or catastrophe. Not only Shakespeare's tragedy and serious comedy, but the *Cenci* and *Vanity Fair* (although it is called

---

[1] II. Sect. 65.   [2] 1767–8.
[3] Bernays, *Zwei Abhandlungen*, etc., Berlin, 1880, p. 74.

"a novel without a hero") and *La Cousine Bette* are easily
and naturally included within such a doctrine. It may indeed
be admitted to be a development inherent in Aristotle's theory,
to which the strict interdependence of pity and fear, known
from the Rhetoric, undoubtedly gives a systematic value not
evident from the words preserved in the Poetic. Yet if we
are asked how far it represents Aristotle's meaning, I think
we can but answer, as we have answered in analogous cases,[1]
that his actual meaning lies somewhere between these two
extremes of naive observation and idealistic world-theory.
Of the two, I confess that I believe it to have approximated
more nearly to the former. It is a far cry from ἔλεος to
"Mitleid," and from "Mitleid" to "Mit-leiden"; and so it is
from φόβος to the overwhelming sense of law in the universe.

The characters demanded by Aristotle for the persons of a
tragedy strengthen this opinion. To an unbiassed reader his
treatment of this point must seem thoroughly naive. It is not
that he demands for the hero mere human nature, so that
our own human nature may feel itself implicated in his misfortunes; his idea of the qualities which have power to evoke
our sympathy and our fear is narrowly confined to unmerited
suffering and to an average moral disposition, The conception of greatness, whether in evil or in good, does not present
itself to his mind. Lessing has not, I think, treated Shake-
peare's Richard III. in connection with his Aristotelian
theorem; and I cannot imagine that in this instance he
could have made good his usual thesis. But if Aristotle had
construed his own theory as freely as Bernays or even Lessing
construes it for him, the deeper manifestations of individual
character and its collisions with necessity would have been
more prominent in his analysis of a tragic plot.

On the question of "purification" or rather "purgation,"
which has been treated in the chapter on Aristotle, there
seems to be no doubt whatever that Bernays is strictly in the
right, and that he is thoroughly justified in his ridicule of the
notion that tragedy was to transform the passions into "virtuous capacities," [2] and of the consequent application to them
of the misapprehended doctrine of the mean. Here we see
how Lessing stands between the earlier and the later moderns,

[1] See above, p. 73.
[2] "Tugendhafte Fertigkeiten," *Dramaturgie*, l.c.

and we feel that his presupposition of the moral aim of poetry,[1]
though most perfectly guarded against the suggestion of an
abstract didactic purpose, is painful to our consciousness
to-day.

The idea which lies at the root of the *Laocoon* and of the
Dramaturgie, that poetry deals only with action, seemed to
Herder to involve a massacre among poets which none but
Homer and the dramatists could survive. For lyrical poetry
Lessing had certainly little feeling ; yet " action," taken in
the widest sense, according to the definition which forms the
core of the *Laocoon*, might include the movement of emo-
tion in a human heart.

But however this might be, it was worth while to run the
hazard of a temporary onesidedness of appreciation, for the
sake of wholly freeing poetic art from such narrow laws as
those which Lessing understood to be the laws of material
beauty, and assigning to it the wide subject-matter of human
life in all its variations from the comic to the terrible. This
conception, culminating in the importance assigned to the
drama, and supported by a profound enthusiasm for Shakespeare and for the Greeks, stamped itself unmistakably upon
the poetry [2] and also upon the philosophy of the next generation in Germany.

---

[1] *Dramaturgie*, ii. 77.

[2] As in the conception of death, so in the estimate of dramatic value,
Schiller's poetry follows Lessing's criticism. The lines addressed by Schiller
to Goethe on the occasion of Voltaire's Mahomet being put on the stage at
Weimar are of great significance in this respect. I quote two stanzas :

> Einheim'scher Kunst ist dieser Schauplatz eigen,
> Hier wird nicht fremden Götzen mehr gedient ;
> Wir können muthig einen Lorbeer zeigen,
> Der auf dem deutschen Pindus selbst gegrünt.
> Selbst in der Künste Heiligthum zu steigen,
> Hat sich der deutsche Genius erkühnt,
> Und auf der Spur des Griechen und des Britten
> Ist er dem bessern Ruhme nachgeschritten.

> Nicht Muster zwar darf uns der Franke werden !
> Aus seiner Kunst spricht kein lebend'ger Geist ;
> Des falschen Anstands prunkende Geberden
> Verschmäht der Sinn, der nur das Wahre preist !
> Ein Führer nur zum Bessern soll er werden,
> Er komme, wie ein abgeschiedner Geist,
> Zu reinigen die oft entweihte Scene
> Zum würd'gen Sitz der alten Melpomene.

And if its actual outcome in the drama of Lessing himself and of Schiller and his contemporaries is of smaller permanent value for the stage than appeared probable at first, and if we even find a certain unreality in the supremacy which æsthetic, after Lessing's example, still assigns to dramatic form in an age when its vitality seems doubtful, yet in the preparation of data for modern æsthetic science there has been no much more potent influence than this co-ordination of the more comparable poetic forms of the antique and the modern world. For it involves *ipso facto* a combination of the more reserved and more exuberant, the more abstract and more individual kinds of utterance as alike expressions of human life and passion.

What Lessing was thus doing for poetry it was the task of Winckelmann to do for formative art, in which Lessing had not even taken the trouble to distinguish painting from sculpture.[1]

Winckelmann.   vi. Winckelmann (1717–1768) is now a mere name to most English students and to many of his own countrymen. This is the inevitable result of the peculiar nature of his services to æsthetic. Just because his work was fertile in its principles, it has grown in the hands of his successors, and there is nothing which we can now learn from him about the Greek spirit and history, and extant sculptures, so well as from Hegel and Goethe, Grote and Curtius, Overbeck and Murray. His style, though clear and striking, cannot compensate the modern reader for the tedium of lengthy discussions upon particular statues and parts of statues, in which the great works that mould our judgment are not taken account of. Yet Mr. Pater's delightful essay[2] may, it is to be hoped, sustain among English writers a certain permanent interest in the man whose ideas struck root in the minds of Schiller and Goethe, Hegel and Schelling, and have in an incalculable degree contributed to the human and sympathetic spirit which marks the historical and archæological researches of to-day.

The characteristics by which he produced the effect which

---

[1] The influence of casual circumstances is such that I hardly think it too audacious to suggest that Lessing's carelessness in taking his first title from a *group in marble* for a work whose second title mentions *painting* as its subject, was connected with the fact, that he had to judge of sculpture chiefly or solely from drawings and engravings.

[2] In *The Renaissance*, by Walter Pater : Macmillan & Co.

I have thus ascribed to him may be summed up under four
heads.

a. The sense of real contact with the human mind in the
study of workmanship.

β. The extension of this sense into an appreciation of
organic development in art correlative to that in social and
political conditions.

γ. The consequent recognition of various phases of expressiveness within the beauty of plastic art.

δ. The open admission of conflicting claims on behalf of
formal beauty and of expression, and their partial reconciliation.

a. It may seem a strange comparison to set the
name of Winckelmann beside that of Bacon. But
no one can read the constant diatribes of the
former against mere "book-learning,"[1] or against the work
of "Scribes,"[2] in comparison with the knowledge of the
educated eye, without feeling their motive to be fundamentally the same as that of Bacon, the eagerness for contact with
reality at first hand.[3] Thus "research and insight into art
we look for in vain in the great costly works descriptive of
ancient statues, which have as yet been published. The
description of a statue ought to demonstrate the cause of its
beauty, and point out the individuality in the style of its art;
. . . but where is it taught in what the beauty of a statue
consists, and what scribe has looked at it with an artist's eye?"
He contends that it is hopeless to judge adequately of statues
from drawings and engravings, and concludes that it is not
feasible to write anything of value upon ancient art except at
Rome, then the great storehouse of antiquities. Rome was to
him what external nature was to Bacon. You cannot qualify
as a judge of art by spending a mere month at Rome, he is
always repeating, in allusion to some countrymen of his who
had made no longer stay. Or again :

" How has it happened,[4] whereas profound treatises have
appeared in all other sciences, that the rationale of art and of
beauty has been so little enquired into? Reader! the fault

Feeling for Art
as Human
Production.

---

[1] " Belesenheit "—a curiously expressive term of disparagement.
[2] "Scribenten."
[3] *Gesch. d. Bildenden Kunst*, Introd. ii.
[4] *Geschichte*, iv. 2. 5.

lies in our innate indolence as regards thinking for ourselves, and in the wisdom of the schools. For on the one hand the ancient works of art have been regarded as beauties to the enjoyment of which we cannot hope to attain, and which therefore readily warm the imagination of a few, but do not penetrate the soul, and antiquities have only given occasion for shooting the rubbish of book-learning, but have afforded no nourishment or hardly any to the reason. On the other hand again, since philosophy[1] has chiefly been practised and taught by such as, through reading their dryasdust predecessors therein, are forced to leave little room for feeling, and cover it up, so to speak, with a hard skin, we have been led through a labyrinth of metaphysical subtleties and circumlocutions which after all have chiefly served to excogitate huge books and sicken the understanding."

The appeal to reason, feeling and understanding within the same page is characteristic of Winckelmann, whose apparent laxity of terminology, often amounting to absolute self-contradiction, indicates not merely a neglect of theoretical refinement, but also a genuine concreteness of thought.

Plainly we have in such passages as the above, which might be endlessly multiplied, the same craving of which Bacon is so eloquent an exponent, the craving for an escape from the world of books and reflection into that of direct sensuous observation, involving probably a consciousness that human faculties demand other nutrition and exercise than that which a mere literary medium can supply: " Hardly any scribe can penetrate the inmost essence of art."[2]

The difference between the two revivals is that the observation of which Winckelmann speaks is directed not to natural nature, except in human beings, to whose beauty he is exceedingly sensitive, but to artificial nature, which though material is yet the work and utterance of the mind. Inevitably therefore this later return to nature besides educating the perception of the beautiful, formed a bridge from physical and mathematical science to the anthropological and philosophical sciences. How deeply Winckelmann realised this aspect of his researches as grasping a new province of life, in the direct significance of which, however trivial its data may appear, mind answers to mind across the ages, may be indicated by

---

[1] Weltweisheit.   [2] *Geschichte*, Introd. ii.

R

one more quotation.[1]   " Even in this study (of Greek coins)
we shall not lose ourselves in trivialities, if antiquities are
regarded as the works of men whose minds were higher and
more masculine than ours ; and this recognition has power, in
conducting such a research, to exalt us above ourselves and
above our age.   A thinking soul cannot busy itself with low
ideas on the shore of the broad sea ; the immeasurable prospect widens the limits of the mind, which at first appears to
lose itself, but then returns to us greater than before."

I do not know that the self-assertive reaction of the mind
which constitutes the feeling of the Sublime had been thus
concisely described before these words were written[a] (1766),
although many suggestions of the idea are to be found in
Burke.   However this may be, it is certain that the fullest
theory of art is approached in proportion as we recognise that
the work is the expression of the workman's life.

True sense of a **History of Art.** β. Consequent upon this recognition is the
conception of art as something that has a history
and phases of its own—a growth and a decline—corresponding to and rooted in the history and conditions of peoples.
This organic standpoint in relation to art Goethe emphatically
ascribes to Winckelmann,[2] and although the ideas of concrete
history were in the air, and should not be hastily credited to
any one man, yet undoubtedly we find in him more than one
of the suggestions which have helped to make the greatness
of later students of antiquity.   Let us take for example
his conception of history[3] as a ἱστορία, a research and a
system, not a chronicle.   " The history of Art aims at
expounding its origin, growth, change, and fall, together
with the diverse styles of peoples, ages, and artists, and at
demonstrating this, as far as possible, from the extant works
of antiquity."   This attempt to trace a development extending through long ages in its essential causes and connection
was, he affirmed, a new thing in the literature of art.   I am
very much inclined to think, that, but for the great conception
of Scaliger,[4] it was a new thing in the science of history.

---

[1] *Gesch.*, Introd. xxiii.
[2] *Winckelmann u. sein Jahrh.*
[3] *Gesch.*, Einleitung i. ii.
[4] See p. 189 above.   For suggestions of it in ancient writers see Goethe,
Winckelmann u. sein Jahrhundert.

Among special points of historical significance which he treats in conformity with this idea I may mention four.

First, he observes that works of art are in their first beginnings all formless and all alike, just as are the seeds of different plants.[1]

Secondly, this acute observation enabled him to understand, in spite of appearances to the contrary, that Greek art was an independent development, not borrowed from oriental nations. This view maintains itself on the whole, through many vicissitudes, at the present day. It is admitted that in early times many technical processes, many modes of decorative ornamentation, and even certain detached phases of style such as that shown in the lions of Mycenæ, were introduced by aliens or imitated from their work. But as regards the archaic sculptures which belong to the Greek development proper, it appears to be agreed that their "Egyptian" appearance indicates no foreign connection, but is simply a result of a superficial similarity of treatment in the early art of different countries.

The two further points may be introduced in Winckelmann's own words. "The cause[2] and reason of the eminence which art attained among the Greeks is in part to be ascribed to the influence of the climate, in part to their polity and government, and the mode of thought formed by it."

Thirdly, then, in speaking of the *climate*[3] he follows up the idea which is referred to both by Plato and Aristotle, probably borrowing from Herodotus,[4] that Greece occupies a medium position between Europe and Asia in climate as in other respects, and that therefore the nature of the Greeks is the finest possible ; and their bodily formation, Winckelmann subjoins, corresponded to their fortunate natural conditions. He is also well aware of the historical importance of the subdivision of Greek territory by physical obstacles, and ascribes to this cause the later development of art in Greece as contrasted with Egypt.[5] Those who are familiar with the treatment of the climate, position, and physical conformation of Greece by modern writers, as for example by Curtius, will

[1] *Gesch.* i. 1. 1.
[2] *Ib.* iv. 1. 4.
[3] *Ib.* iv. 1. 6.
[4] Hdt. 3. 106. Plato. *Republ.* 435 E. Ar., *Pol.* 7. 7.
[5] *Ib.* i. 1. 7

feel the importance of these observations in a writer of the eighteenth century.

And, fourthly, if in speaking of the Greek political system he seems blind to its ignoble side, we must yet give him credit for the penetration and enthusiasm which enabled him, more than a century ego, to appreciate the splendid attributes of Hellenic freedom ; and we must remember that owing in great measure to him this larger sympathy for Greek life has been current in Germany ever since his day, while in England we owe it, as a general influence, to a comparatively recent interest awakened by our own political development. " In respect of the constitution and government of Greece," he says,[1] " freedom is the principal cause of the pre-eminence of their art. . . . It was freedom,[2] the mother of great events, of political changes, and of rivalry among the Greeks, that implanted as if at birth the germs of noble and lofty dispositions ; and just as the prospect of the immeasurable surface of the sea, and the beating of the proud waves on the cliffs of the shore, enlarges our gaze, and raises the mind above mean issues, so, in presence of such great things and persons, it was impossible to think ignobly."

Recognition of Phases in Beauty.

γ. I am convinced that Winckelmann's theory of beauty can only be understood in relation to his history of art. He always uses abstract terms in a relative sense, with reference to the character which he desires to emphasise in one period as contrasted with another ; and thus there arise constant verbal contradictions, which do not cause the smallest perplexity to any one who reads the history continuously, but which resist every attempt to interpret the terms as indicating a system of mutually exclusive qualities.

He divides Greek art into four periods,[3] suggested by Scaliger's periods of Greek poetry.

In the earliest or "older" style, taken to begin after the formless first attempts of art, and lasting to the generation before Pheidias, the drawing was emphatic but hard, powerful but without grace ; and the strong expression diminished the beauty.[4] This latter clause we might demur to so far as concerns the face, in which expression had hardly been attained. It might have more truth of the figure. Winckelmann remarks the strange minuteness of detail with which the

---

[1] *Gesch.*, iv. 1. 13.   [2] *Ib.*, iv. 1. 19.   [3] *Ib.*, viii. 1. 4.   [4] *Ib.*, viii. 1. 17.

robes are sometimes elaborated in the art of this "older" period.

The second, the "lofty" or "grand" style [1] arose "when the time of complete enlightenment and freedom in Greece appeared." This style, of which Winckelmann divined rather than knew the characteristics, he treated as beginning with Pheidias and including the work of Scopas, to whom he attributed the Niobe group. This group, and a statue of Athene then in the Villa Albani, and probably identical with one still preserved there,[2] were the only works in Rome, which means the only works known to Winckelmann in the marble, that he assigned to the period of this style. It is surprising to us that he should separate Scopas from Praxiteles, by including the former in this period and the latter in the next; but of course there is a strong tendency when examples are scarce, to extend the limits of a division so that it may not be empty. In this high or grand style, called "grand" because the artists made grandeur and not merely beauty their principal aim,[3] Winckelmann expected to find a certain hardness and angularity, though remarking that good drawing often seems hard to common critics both ancient and modern.[4] He constantly compares the art of this period with that of Raphael. Its characteristic is a lofty simplicity and unity, like that of an idea arising without help of the senses and without the labour of construction.[5] These expressions do not contain any theory of abstract idealism independent of sense-perception; they are simply intended to reproduce the author's strong feeling of the unity and spontaneity of great art. He illustrates them by Raphael's alleged power of drawing the outline of a head for his most sacred subjects with a single stroke of the pen, that needed no subsequent correction.

It is however idle to deny that Winckelmann, being, as we may say, never on his guard, did sometimes lean to the fatal

---

[1] "Hohe," or "grosse Stil," *Gesch.*, viii. 2. 1.

[2] Professor Brunn has kindly informed me that he is of opinion that the statue referred to must be No. 1012 now in the Villa Albani, and recognisable by having a lion-skin instead of a helmet on the head. "Sie ist in der That," he adds, "ein Muster des hohen Stils." I regret that I have never seen this statue.

[3] *Gesch.*, viii. 2. 1.

[4] *Ib.*, viii. 2. 3.

[5] *Ib.*, viii. 2. 4, "Die gleichsam unerschaffene Begriff d. Schönheit," cf. " d. Unbezeichnung," a quality of beauty, iv. 2. 23.

inference that true beauty, such as that of the high style, being one in conception, must also be capable of but one expression. This is established to demonstration by the fact that he assigns their participation in the highest beauty *as a reason for the likeness between Niobe and her daughters.*[1]

The next or "beautiful" style, also treated as the style of *grace,* began with Praxiteles and lasted till the first successors of Alexander. It is to the preceding style as the painting of Guido to that of Raphael. We shall see directly that the grace thus spoken of is only a relative and not an absolute distinction between this and other periods of art.

Last came the manner of the imitators, due to the fact that the idea of beauty—if he meant the *ancient* idea of beauty, the reason was a good one—was exhausted and could be pushed no farther. "Therefore, art, in which as in all the operations of nature, there can be no condition of immobility, was forced to go back as it did not go forward." It is noteworthy to find the author whose principle for modern art is supposed to be "the imitation of the Greeks," laying down as an axiom that he who follows must always be behind.[2] Art, like philosophy, became eclectic, and fastened upon trifles which had been thought detrimental to style in its prime.

Winckelmann's want of sympathy for modern painting has been greatly exaggerated. It is wild to say with Schasler that he recognised no art but that of the ancient Greeks.[3] On the contrary, he recognised the principles of history as of general application, and drew the parallel, which though obvious is none the less profound, between the four periods of Greek and four of Italian art. It is true that he does not show appreciation of the Dutch school, but how hard that was, and to many minds still is! Whereas the severity of his judgment upon later Italian painting and sculpture is only an approximation to the views accepted to-day, and his superiority in this respect to his age is shown by the dismay of his editors, Meyer and Schulze, at his round assertion that bad taste set in after Raphael and Michael Angelo, and that sculpture came to an end with Michael Angelo and Sansovino.[4] He even observes that Leonardo and Andrea del

---

[1] *Ib.,* viii. 2. 10.
[2] "Der Nachahmer ist allezeit unter dem Nachgeahmten geblieben," viii. 3. 1. Schasler, i. 209.   [4] *G. d. a. K.,* iii. 3. 18, with editor's note, 1023.

Sarto, who had had little opportunity for seeing the works of the ancients, thought and worked as we must suppose the Greek painters to have done.[1]

Whatever isolated expressions we may find in Winckelmann about simple and noble beauty, which seem to confine the beautiful to the abstract and the formal, it is plain that a writer for whom the beautiful comprehended so many phases and types of expressiveness, some of them though different yet treated as co-ordinate, cannot conceivably be reckoned as narrowing the range of beauty to a single abstract type. Before proceeding to discuss his antithesis of beauty and expression, I will give other instances of the contradictions which are partly reconciled by the re-adaptation of conceptions in his mind, as he discovers their relativity.

The " high " or " grand " style is, as we have seen, not the same as the " beautiful " style *par excellence*, but is distinguished from it much as the " sublime," a term frequently applied to the beauty of the grand style, is usually distinguished from the " beautiful." Yet the *high* style is expressly said to be the style which aims at " true " beauty. [2] Thus the grand or sublime is co-ordinated with the beautiful.

Again it is the principle of the grand style to express no sensibility ; [3] but yet there is not in human nature any state free from sensibility or passion,[4] and beauty without expression would be without significance.[5] In fact then, the grand style is " the expression of a significant and eloquent silence of the soul," and is, as Plato said, the most difficult form of expression possible ; anything violent is far more easily represented.[6] Thus the absence of expression and the highest form of expression are really identified, and how natural this meeting of extremes is to Winckelmann may be shown by contrasting with the reference to Plato just mentioned, a passage in which he suggests that, as free from passion, " the idea of the highest beauty may seem to be the simplest and easiest thing, demanding no inquiry into the passions and their expression." [7]

The conception of grace is first introduced as distinctive of the " beautiful " style,[8] but after a short discussion it breaks up into species, of which that originally mentioned, the char-

---

[1] *G. d. a. K.* v. 3. 28.   [2] viii. 2. 10.   [3] viii. 2. 11.   [4] iv. 2. 24.
[5] v. 3. 4.   [6] viii. 2. 11.   [7] iv. 2. 23.   [8] viii. 2. 9.

acteristic of the "beautiful" style, is to the first as the zone of
Aphrodite to the beauty of Hera [1]—a comparison developed
by Schiller in *Anmuth and Würde*. A section [2] that shortly
indicates this expansion of the idea of grace is worth quoting
at length :—

"Of the second or more amiable grace [the distinction
taken is that it is less self-contained, and appeals more consciously to the spectator, than the first] one may form a conception from the head of Leucothea in the Capitoline
Museum, and for a further insight into that wherein the ancient
artists held grace to consist, one should compare with these
and similar heads the pictures of Correggio, the painter of
grace. And then one will be convinced that from this modern
grace, not seldom affected and frequently exaggerated, to the
amiable grace of the ancient artists of the beautiful style, is no
smaller leap than true judges of art will have seen that it is
from the latter to the sublime grace of the "high" style."
Here we note again how simple contrast is replaced by
co-ordination. The author even applies to three types of
grace the terms tragic, epic, and comic grace. [3] The third of
these hardly coincides with the grace of Correggio, but rather
applies to children, Fauns, Bacchantes, and such subjects, in
which beauty is not completely attained. Thus we see how
wide Winckelmann is prepared to throw his net.

Conflict between Beauty and Expression. δ. We are partly prepared for Winckelman's
idea of the relation between beauty and expression,
both by the general form of the co-ordinations
just mentioned, and by the apparent contradiction of his views
on the place of expressiveness in the highest beauty. Here,
just as in the other cases, he starts with a direct antithesis.
Expression is detrimental to beauty. [4] The two are opposing
qualities. Beauty is in the first instance the beauty of pure
form, which appears to mean the beauty of shape as exhibiting unity in variety, emphasis being laid on the variety, as in
Hogarth. "The forms of a beautiful body are determined
by lines which are constantly changing their centre, and consequently never form part of a circle, but are always elliptical
in character and share this quality with the contour of Greek
vases." [5] Expression in art, on the other hand, is the imita-

---

[1] *G. d. a. K.*, viii. 2. 16.   [2] viii. 2. 18.   [3] *Ib.*, sect. 20.   [4] v. 3. 3 and 4.
[5] iv. 2. 29, see p. 208 above.

tion of the acting and suffering [1] condition of our soul and
body, of passions as well as of actions ; in the widest sense it
includes our action itself, in a narrower sense, merely the play
of feature and gesture which accompanies the action. It is
hostile to beauty, because it changes the bodily form in which
beauty resides, and the greater this change is, the more detrimental is expression to beauty. It does not occur to him as
possible that expression may modify habitual forms for the
better even by the standard of mere shape. The first distinction as it presents itself to his mind, to be subsequently
modified, is plainly that of repose as contrasted with motion.
In the more theoretical books [2] of the History, which deal
separately with the elements of art, Beauty is treated first, and
Expression separately, afterwards.

But in spite of this abrupt antagonism between the two, we
find, when we turn to the analysis of actual artistic portrayal,
and to the history proper, that within the limits of beauty even
in the strictest sense—divine beauty—there falls a great variety
of types [3] each appropriate to the character and functions of
the deity represented ; that the style which is called the
" beautiful " *par excellence* is compatible with more expression
than the earlier or grand style,[4] and that the grand style itself
has not the beauty of a mere vase-outline or geometrical
pattern, but is beautiful as the expression of a tranquil soul.[5]
And thus, though according to the strict theory of formal
beauty it would seem to be like pure water, best when most
flavourless, and so to be an easy and simple matter, needing
in the artist who is to represent it no knowledge of man nor
experience of passion,[6] yet really " beauty without expression
would be characterless, expression without beauty unpleasant,"[7]
and for the ancient artists beauty " was the tongue on the
balance of expression " [8] which was thus weighed out with
extreme nicety, being—for this is plainly the sum of the
whole—*an element at once essential to beauty, and tending to
destroy it.*

There can be no doubt that as a matter of general theory

---

[1] We must not translate " leidenden " by " passive," for the point is that
signs of being acted on are shown. It more nearly = " in passion." The connection between " passion " and " passive " is one of the most curious points
in word-history.

[2] Books iv. and v.   [3] Books iv., v., viii.   [4] viii. 2. 19.
      [5] viii. 2. 11.   [6] iv. 2. 23.   [7] v. 3. 4   [8] *Ib.*

Winckelmann leaves us in this intolerable contradiction, which Goethe himself rather acquiesced in than resolved. But Winckelmann's distinctive work was that of a historian, and it is not hard to see how in the concrete the matter forced itself upon his mind.

He unquestionably started from the antique or abstract notion of beauty, as unity and variety manifested in the form, that is, the shape, of works belonging to the lesser arts, and of the human figure. This theory of beauty does not really account for anything more complex than our pleasure in a geometrical pattern or the shape of a vase or moulding. It is, strictly speaking, inadequate even to the simplest appreciation of the human face and figure, and lends itself to the confusion, into which Winckelmann in one passage quite unquestionably fell,[1] by which there is supposed to be only one beautiful form, single and invariable—all reference to individuality being excluded—and this is consequently identified with the *conception* of beauty, which, like every intellectual conception, is single and self-identical. We are not, however, to connect this passing delusion with the constant reference to ideal beauty, as though the ideal for him essentially consisted in this abstract conception mistakenly identified with a single invariable shape. On the contrary, the term " ideal " always implies in Winckelmann the exercise of educated perception upon experience, his doctrine being based on the ancient notion that supreme beauty could only be attained by combining the partial beauties of nature.[2] He knows that " ideal " forms, *i.e.* forms modified by the observer's mental activity, need not be beautiful ; and he thinks[3] that Guido's " ideal " archangel, portrayed, according to the artist's account, after a mental image superior to experience, is much less beautiful than persons whom he has seen in reality, and betrays defective observation of nature. Thus the conception of ideal beauty does not to tend to narrow his doctrine, but to widen it.

Now his primary tendency was no doubt to identify this mere beauty of shape, which implies repose simply because motion would involve change of outline, with the beauty or sublimity of the grand style, and we see him arguing with himself in the famous comparison with pure water[4] whether

---

[1] See p. 246 above.   [2] iv. 2. 35.   [3] *Ib.*   [4] See p. 249 above.

this can really be the case. But looking at the concrete, and arguing back from the phases of more pronounced expression, he sees that this is impossible, and that the grand style is expressive of one state of the soul, if the beautiful style is expressive of others. And indeed, if the grand style is cognate with formal beauty through its simplicity, the beautiful style is so no less through its variety and charm of curvature, so that we get the contradictory but intelligible result which has been mentioned, viz., that true beauty—the beauty of the grand style—falls outside the distinctively beautiful style, while the factor hostile to beauty reaches its maximum in the style of which beauty is the distinctive attribute. Thus he breaks away from the view which would have been the natural conclusion from his premisses. He does not find that beauty is in inverse ratio to expression ; and he shows conclusively that in the concrete the two are never divorced, and that beauty breaks up into kinds and types in accordance with the mental content from which it issues. Though he fails to reduce the two elements to a common denomination, and they remain antagonistic in theory, he has done all that is necessary, in the realm of plastic art, to exhibit that correspondence between phases of the beautiful and the development of its content which holds a chief place among the data of modern æsthetic. It was thus that Winckelmann succeeded " in furnishing the mind with a new organ and new methods of study in the field of art."[1] This judgment of Hegel appears to be based upon that of Goethe, who speaks of his *Gewahrwerden der Griechischen Kunst* (his *Finding of Greek Art*[2]); and it is happy for the English reader that for him too, as I have already mentioned, the memory of Winckelmann is enshrined in a work[3] that belongs to our finest critical literature.

Data not utilised by the Critics. vii. Our account of the data of modern æsthetic may fitly close at this point. We have not attempted to take into our view those phenomena of art which had not been drawn into the focus of critical theory. We have said little or nothing about painting and music. Except through the suggestive paradoxes of Diderot the former of

---

[1] Hegel, *Aesth. Introd.*, E. Tr. p. 120.

[2] Cf. Goethe, *Winckelmann u. sein Jahrhundert*, and Pater, *Renaissance, Essay on Winckelmann*.

[3] Pater's *Renaissance*.

these distinctively modern arts was thus far hardly recognised
by criticism as having a separate existence, nor does anything
in the æsthetic reflection of the eighteenth century before
Goethe suggest to us that Bach and Händel lived in the first
half, and Glück, Haydn, and Mozart in the second half of that
period.   Before theory could deal with what was native and
familiar, it had to follow the toilsome clue afforded by the
inheritance of the past, because it had been brought up to
believe that there alone lay the treasure house of beauty.   But
the treasure was found to be hidden at our own door, and in
following the clue we have passed from abstract to concrete
antitheses.   Before Lessing and Winckelmann we were in a
dim half-light of tradition and empty formula, but after their
labours we are in the bright and populous thoroughfare of
human life, which binds the ages together.   This idea finds
general expression in Lessing's treatise, *On the Education
of the Human Race* (1780).   And an antithesis concretely
conceived is ripe for solution ; and the solution of a predominant antithesis carries with it the due organisation of a
hundred other issues, which could not find their places till
the main framework was fitted together.   Thus music, and
landscape painting, and Gothic architecture, and lyric poetry,
all of which were little noted by those who laid ready the
materials for the building of æsthetic philosophy, soon fell
into their places when the great master-thinkers came to draw
the ground plan.

Indications   viii. A few facts may be added, by way of con-
    of a   clusion, to point out how, historically speaking, the
Transition.   data were brought face to face with the problem and
passed into the concrete theory.

The year 1764, which saw the publication of Winckelmann's
History of Ancient Formative Art, saw also the publication
of Kant's *Observations upon the feeling of the Sublime and
Beautiful.*   In 1768, the year which Winckelmann did not
survive, Herder, a youth of twenty-four, dissatisfied with
Lessing's *Literaturbriefe* which were before him, gave voice [1]
to the need for another Winckelmann, who should apply in
the sphere of Greek poetry and philosophy the new conception of organic and scientific history which had been inaugurated in the field of plastic art ; in 1773, Goethe produced

---

[1] Herder, *Fragmente zur Deutschen Literatur*, Sammlung, 2, c. iv.

Götz von Berlichingen, the issue, monstrous in Lessing's eyes, of Lessing's own Shakespearian revolt, and also, more important still, the incomparable little essay on the architecture of Strasburg Cathedral, which fairly raised the banner at once of " Gothic " art and characteristic expression. [1] About 1775 Diderot's *Essay on Painting* [2] was written, marking almost the end of his long activity as a critic of contemporary painting, and beginning with the famous aphorism, *Nature is never incorrect.* Diderot might be called a preacher of romantic naturalism, as indeed throughout the time of these earlier antitheses, the two elements of romance and naturalism, which later sprang into polar opposition, formed a single extreme in the contrast with classical and mannered formalism ; and it is probable that the essential inter-dependence of romance and naturalism, or symbolism and imitation, the reason for which has been explained in an earlier chapter,[3] has never permitted, and will never permit, their opposition to have the fundamental character which is sometimes ascribed to it. I imagine, therefore, that Diderot's contention that all in Nature is " correct " because it is necessary in the economy of the whole, has a profounder bearing upon art than Goethe is disposed to allow. The issue whether beauty is hostile to necessity in principle, or only for our imperfect vision of the reasonable, belongs to the æsthetic of ugliness, and can only be dealt with in that connection. That up to a limit which appears to be capable of *practically* indefinite expansion, the works of natural necessity have been and are being transferred from the category of the ugly to that of the beautiful is a mere matter of every-day experience. Whether this practically indefinite expansion is theoretically without an end we cannot discuss just now.

In 1781 there occurred three events of the greatest significance in the history of æsthetic. The death of Lessing severed the last link between the old and new, the Latin and the Greek Renaissance ; the publication of Schiller's *Räuber* continued the inauguration of the genius-period—a reaction which was to Lessing almost as Lessing had been to Gottsched ; and the appearance of the *Critique of Pure Reason*

---

[1] Werke, xxv. I. First published with Herder and Möser in *Deutschen Art u. Kunst.*

[2] Translated by Goethe in 1805 rather as a contribution to æsthetic history, and as a basis for his own comments, than as retaining substantive value.

[3] See p. 158, and reff.

began the philosophical revolution which the problem and the data of æsthetic were destined to complete by their fusion. And when the *Kritik der Urtheilskraft* was produced in 1790, the philosophical problem was solved in the abstract, as we shall endeavour to make clear in the following chapter; and this abstract solution only needed a concrete development to become both a genuine philosophy of art, and an important influence upon future speculation in general.

Thus Goethe and Schiller, who are of course in one aspect immediate descendants of Lessing and Winckelmann, may most conveniently be treated after and not before the Kantian æsthetic has been considered. Both of them were to some extent—Schiller very profoundly—affected by Kant's ideas; and moreover the full weight of æsthetic knowledge and expression inherited by them and their contemporaries from the movement which I have been attempting to describe, was brought to bear on philosophy not before but after Kant had, almost independently, formulated the issues of æsthetic. We shall therefore be following the true *nexus* of events by treating first of Kant, then of Schiller, Goethe, and others with reference to the eventful decade between 1790 and 1800, and after that we shall be able without further interruption to follow the stream of æsthetic speculation which springs from the union of Kant's abstract æsthetic with the appreciation of art and workmanship as an utterance of the human spirit and as sharing its evolution.

a (p 242). The point is clearly made by David Hume in the *Treatise of Human Nature* (1739), Book II. Part iii. Sect. 8. This is prior to Burke or Lord Kaimes.

CHAPTER X.

KANT—THE PROBLEM BROUGHT TO A FOCUS.

His Relation to the Problem and the Data. 1. The data of modern æsthetic, described in the preceding chapter, produced no considerable effect upon Kant's philosophy. His work lay wholly in the path of metaphysical speculation, and before its point of junction with the concrete evolutionary idea. The history of thought can show no more dramatic spectacle than that of this great intellectual pioneer beating out his track for forty years in the wilderness of technical philosophy, and bringing his people at last to the entrance upon a new world of free and humanizing culture, which, so far as we can tell, he never thoroughly made his own.

We must remember that although Kant published his most famous works after the death of Lessing, and therefore long after the death of Winckelmann, yet he was born (1724) five years earlier than the former and only seven years after the latter. The title of his first work on æsthetic, *Observations on the feeling of the Sublime and Beautiful*, seems to show that Burke's Essay (1756) had been instrumental in drawing his attention to the subject ; and its date (1764) being earlier than that of Winckelmann's " History," and earlier than that of the Laocoon. indicates that his æsthetic interest had taken its bent before the new renaissance had well begun. His great æsthetic treatise of 1790, *The Critique of the Power of Judgment*, follows this same division into the Sublime and the Beautiful, and while explicitly referring to Burke's Essay indicates no interest whatever in the contemporary movement of archæology and art-criticism. We trace in it indeed here and there an idea drawn from Rousseau, or find an observation of De Saussure ; but these are exceptions that prove the rule, for, wide as his reading was, Kant preferred to rely on facts of nature and humanity freshly observed, whether by himself or others, rather than on secondary theory dealing with books and art.

His inquiries into the beautiful may thus have assumed their immediate form owing to suggestions in Burke and similar writers, and could not but show traces of the ideas fermenting around him. But the conditions that invested these inquiries with supreme importance at this particular crisis were not derived from preceding or contemporary art-theory, but from that movement of general philosophy which I have endeavoured to depict as determining the " problem of modern æsthetic." It was after Kant had brought into suggestive order the factors of this movement, using as a chief instrument in the work the ideas of the beautiful and the sublime, that an extraordinarily rapid and fortunate succession of great minds re-organised the data of art and learning by the help of his conceptions, and thus founded in one of its forms the concrete idealism which really governs alike the æsthetic and the metaphysic of the nineteenth century. The resolution of the given antithesis between the mediæval and the antique—the marriage of Faust and Helena—from which there sprang the completed modern spirit, was performed in great part independently of philosophy proper, and was taken into the sweep of metaphysical speculation at a point subsequent to the completion of Kant's system, by which the same antithesis had been resolved in other and more abstract forms.

Place of the Æsthetic Problem in his System.
2. In his lifelong labour for the re-organisation of philosophy, Kant may be said to have aimed at three cardinal points, dictated to him by the converging movements of thought in the focus of which he placed himself. First, he desired to justify the conception of a natural order ; secondly, the conception of a moral order ; and thirdly, the conception of compatibility between the natural and the moral order. The first of these problems was imposed upon him by Hume, and formed the substance of the *Critique of Pure Reason;* the second was a legacy from the Wolffian school, and was treated in the *Critique of Practical Reason;* the third necessarily arose out of the relation between the other two, emphasised by the distinctively modern recognition, which eighteenth century enlightenment exaggerated, that the sentient and intelligent individual has indefeasible claims both of sense and of rational freedom And although the formal compatibility of nature and reason had been established by Kant, as he believed, in the negative demarcation between them which the two first Critiques expounded, it was inevitable

that he should subsequently be led on to suggest some more positive conciliation. This attempt was made in the *Critique of the Power of Judgment*, published in 1790, a date to be remembered in connection with the remarkable literary history of the following decade.

The import of the two earlier Critiques may be indicated in popular language, simply and solely in order to explain Kant's relation to æsthetic theory, somewhat as follows.

When we examine the system of the physical sciences with reference to its logical texture, we at once become aware that in spite of its immense variety of object-matter it is permeated by certain common characteristics which appear inseparable from its intellectual existence. Such are, in modern phrase, the law of the uniformity of nature in its most formal rendering, and the law of Sufficient Reason with its sub-form the law of Causation, not to speak of the more sensuous abstractions of space and time. The use of these principles, by whatever name we call them, is found to be merely another name for the use of our own intelligence and perception, and, apart from the theory of mind, we are not in the habit of asking questions as to where we get them or by what right we apply them. If challenged on the subject to-day we should probably attempt to show, resting our demonstration upon the analysis of knowledge, that we cannot do the work of science without some such principles, and that we find no warrant in experience for the notion, which is implied in questioning their validity, that some alternative is open to us by which, discarding them, we might arrive at less artificial elements of knowledge.

Now this mode of argument, which expresses the result on our minds of such an attempt as that made by Mill to demonstrate the postulates of experience, seems to correspond with the substance of the *Critique of Pure Reason*, when stripped of the technical details and qualifications which arose out of the peculiar speculative conditions of the time.

Taken quite strictly, however, such an argument carries us but a short way. The vital relation in which it places intelligence to the matter of perception is very narrowly circumscribed. It leaves us in an intolerable perplexity as regards the element of experience over which we have no control—the element in physical reality which is undetermined and unexplained by the formal postulates of intelli-

S

gence. We see that natural knowledge, in as far as it comes
to us at all, forms itself by necessary processes into a conception of parts dependent upon one another in endless succession
and co-existence. What we do not see is any ground whatever
for supposing that the natural reality thus brought before our
minds, a reality which is taken to include our own sentient
and emotional nature, is in any way bound to continue in
accord with our intelligence, or in the smallest degree to take
account of our moral or eudæmonistic requirements.

In knowledge thus limited to the necessary interconnection
of parts, within a system not known and not justifiably to be
divined as a whole, we have the operation of what Kant chose
to call the Understanding, which we may interpret to ourselves by comparing it with the " eye of science," for which
no catastrophe either moral or material is disorder, so long as
its factors are taken to be connected according to the law of
Causation.[1] The *Critique of Pure Reason* is a demonstration
that theoretical knowledge is limited to this " Understanding"
as operative within the sphere of possible perception. The
whole can be known only in its parts and not as a whole.
Therefore the Reason, or that aspect of thought in which it
implies, for every part, a whole to which it must be related
and in which its import must lie, has no strictly theoretical
function, and cannot be the source of any theoretical propositions. It has no place within perceptive experience,[2] for the
whole as a whole cannot appear there ; nor outside perceptive
experience, for how could definite knowledge of the whole
come into being in a region where there is *ex hypothesi* no
perception of the parts ? Ideas of the Reason, therefore,
that is ideas concerning the nature of the universe as a
whole, such as those of God and Freedom, are incapable of
theoretical verification, whether within perceptive experience
or beyond it. For pure theory gives us a world of natural

---

[1] See Prof. Huxley (*Contemp. Review*, February, 1887) quoted and criticised in the author's *Logic*, ii. 214.

[2] I omit at this point the "regulative" application of Ideas of Reason to
knowledge, by which the inquirer is led to look for so much material order in
the objects of knowledge as may make science possible, though he must not
assert theoretically that there is such order. This principle is in fact a
material postulate of knowledge, parallel to Mill's "Uniformity" if interpreted to mean not merely "A is A" but "knowledge is possible," and
being inserted in the *Critique of Pure Reason* is a modification of Kant's
dualism *ab initio*

necessity, and outside it nothing can be with theoretical definiteness affirmed or denied.

The abstract distinction between the whole and the part in thinking being once assumed, this conclusion is inevitable. If we ask why the Understanding apart from the Reason did not show itself as empty a fiction as the Reason apart from the Understanding, the answer is that in approaching any system through a study of its parts we insensibly subordinate them to a makeshift or imperfect whole, such, for example, as the universe taken to be a physical reality endless in space and time. Thus we are able to order our experiences provisionally, and leave out of sight the difficulties which attach to their aspect of totality. Hence it has been said by Hegel with practical truth, "Understanding without Reason is something, Reason without Understanding is nothing." We need not plume ourselves to-day on seeing through the impossibility of Kant's abstraction, until we are quite sure that we have ourselves understood how all necessary connection must be founded in the relation of part to part within some given reality.

So far then, except for the regulative use of the ideas of Reason within experience, we have a purely negative demarcation between the world of natural necessity and the world of rational freedom. Plainly, Reason is at work in the conception of both worlds, but in forms at first sight incompatible.

In the *Critique of the Practical Reason* we find the complementary side of the demarcation. We all know that in order to live at all we must assume, whether we profess them or not, certain simple articles of faith, say, that food will nourish, that language will retain its meaning, that men will not turn to tigers without cause or warning, and in short that the acts necessary to be done are also possible. From some such elementary standpoint we may take a fairly appreciative view of Kant's *Practical Reason*, which has been so ridiculously parodied. As a being with a will, man cannot avoid putting before him certain aims and principles of conduct. Now conduct issues out into the world of physical reality, and is in fact, as we now recognise, through the human organism, in the closest correspondence with that world and its necessities. But according to the principles of the former *Critique* we can make no theoretical propositions whatever about the

possibility or impossibility of realising man's will within the
world of physical reality, nor, therefore, about the existence
of God, nor the truth of Freedom and Immortality. Nevertheless these unaffirmed ideas of the Reason, under which it
envisages the nature of the universe as a whole having a
unity beyond perceptive experience, are capable of guiding
the human being in his practical attitude to life. He is not
to say *how*, though he may say *that* their objects are real ; but
he is to make it his aim to realise life in accordance with them.
Thus, if we translate the essence of the matter into modern
terms, we find that the appeal is simply to the moral order
as found to be practically realisable in the moral life. This
alone—the moral life as a meeting-point of reason and nature
which displays their compatibility in act—is what we should
call a reality. Such a view should not be unintelligible to-
day, for in spite of its self-contradictions it is very widely
held. Those who, believing in a universe that as a whole is
in no way relevant to any rational end, nevertheless think it
practically certain that morality is possible and life, with its
implied reference to a nobler earthly future, is worth living,
are in a position to appreciate Kant's doctrine of the Practical
Reason.

The separate worlds of Nature and of Freedom were thus
established on the strength of two distinguishable orders of
facts—the facts of science and those of the moral life—and all
proof of their incompatibility was supposed to be rendered
impossible by the strict negative demarcation between them,
that is, by a necessity of ignorance.

It was not likely that such a position would be acquiesced
in without an attempt to complete it by a reconciliation between the two worlds. The need could not be more strikingly stated than in the following passage from the introduction to the *Critique of the Power of Judgment.*

" There[1] is thus a gulf which we cannot see across between
the territory of the conception of Nature, that is, the sensuous,
and the territory of the conception of Freedom, that is, the
supra-sensuous, so that from the former to the latter (by
means, that is to say, of the theoretical use of Reason) there
is no passage possible, just as if they were two different
worlds of which the former can have no influence on the

---

[1] *Kritik d. Urtheilskraft*, Werke, 4. 14.

latter. Nevertheless the latter *ought* to have an influence on the former, that is to say, the conception of Freedom *ought* to realise within the world of sense the aim imposed by its laws; and consequently, Nature must be thought of in such a way that the law-abidingness of its form may be compatible at least with the possibility of the ends, imposed by laws of freedom, which are to be effected within it. Therefore there must after all be a ground of the unity of the supra-sensuous which lies at the root of Nature with that which the conception of Freedom practically contains—a ground the conception of which, although unable to attain cognition of it (the ground) either in theory or in practice, and therefore possessing no peculiar territory, nevertheless makes possible a transition from the mode of thinking dictated by the principles of the one world to that dictated by the principles of the other world."

To be the meeting point of these two worlds, the representative of reason in the world of sense, and of sense in the world of reason, is the high position which Kant is here preparing to assign to the content of the æsthetic and teleological judgment. This content coincides, as we shall see, with the sublime and beautiful in reality and in art, and the products of organic nature. The pre-eminent importance thus assigned to real objects in which an idea seems indissolubly embodied, was the germ from which concrete idealism was to spring.

3. The reasons for finding the required meeting-point in the exercise of the power of judgment sound very strange in Kant's technical language.

Why the Æsthetic Judgment is the Answer to the Problem.

The power of Judgment, he says, is the connecting link between the Understanding and the Reason, as the feeling of pleasure and pain is between the faculties of knowledge and of desire (will). The power of judgment is reflective, not determinant, and prescribes *to itself* the conception of purposiveness in nature, *as if* nature in all its variety had had a unity imposed upon it by an Intelligence, such as to conform to our cognition. This conformity to our cognition or power of apprehension produces when perceived a feeling of pleasure wholly distinct from that which belongs to conformity with our desires. This feeling of pleasure is the predicate in the æsthetic judgment, and being pleasure in the presentation of an object by reason of its form only, is universal though sub-

jective. When the predicate is not a feeling of pleasure but
a relation to the idea of an end, then we have the teleological and not the æsthetic judgment.

Omitting the question of teleological judgment, we may
paraphrase this technical exposition as follows. Every judgment may be regarded as placing parts in relation to a whole.
Although, if we separate the Understanding and the Reason,
there cannot but be Judgment in each of them ; yet, in fact, as
we have seen, this separation except as a matter of degree, is
pure fiction. What is meant therefore by the intermediacy of
the power of Judgment between Understanding and Reason
is merely that all judgment is synthesis, and therefore judgment *par excellence*, in its most central types, always has a
tendency to gather up the relations of parts, which are supposed to be the sphere of the Understanding, in subordination
to a unity or totality, which is supposed to correspond to the
point of view emphasised by " Reason." And such a unity of
parts undoubtedly shades off by degrees into a working conception of purposiveness, as is sufficiently shown by considering the great predominance of the idea of purpose in the
determination of the significant names applied to what we call
" things." It is doubtful if the conception of an individual
" thing " would exist apart from organic and artificial products.
It is natural therefore to give the title of Judgment emphatically to the perception of characteristic form in objects, as at
least a notable case of the synthesis of parts into a whole.
It is thus that the power of Judgment is taken to be intermediate between Understanding and Reason, and to assume
the idea of purposiveness for the inseparable or *a priori*
principle that guides its reflections.

The feeling of pleasure and pain, again, is regarded as a
connecting link between the faculty of cognition and that of
will or desire, apparently because it is a characteristic which
is commonly associated with action or practical interest, and
when found as mere pleasure and pain, *i.e.*, as free from
such interest or satisfaction, is regarded as a half-way house
between action and theory. The discussion at some points[1]
reminds us of Aristotle's reference to the pleasure which we
feel in the sheer activity of recognition. But Kant means
more than this. He means that a conformity is brought to

---

[1] *Einleitung*, Sect. vi.

light between the perception of the object and the faculties of the subject, such that the subject is harmoniously affected in respect of the relation between fancy and understanding. We must assume this to mean that the image presented to fancy or pictorial perception in some way meets the needs, or accommodates itself to the rules of the understanding. Our difficulty is here and will be throughout to see how the individualities of different beautiful objects are allowed for by these formulæ. Are different harmonies of fancy and understanding correlative to different types of beauty?

Thus æsthetic pleasure combines the characteristics of desire and knowledge, as the nature of judgment combines in the idea of purposiveness those of the reason (unity) and the understanding (diversity or dissociation). This seems to be why the "æsthetic judgment" is selected as the guide to the required meeting-point of Nature and Freedom, Understanding and Reason, the sensuous and the intelligible.

The intermediate position of the æsthetic judgment is strikingly exhibited in the four paradoxes, corresponding to the four heads of categories employed in the *Critique of Pure Reason*, by which Kant determines its essence. We will place these paradoxes side by side.

In Quality, the Judgment of Taste is æsthetic; that is to say, the pleasure which forms its predicate, is apart from all interest. Interest is defined to be pleasure in the idea *of the existence* of an object. It is contrasted with pleasure in the mere presentation or sensuous idea of the object. Thus the beautiful is at once sharply distinguished from the pleasant and the good, which correspond to the lower and higher forms of the appetitive faculty. For in both its forms the appetitive faculty involves an "interest."

In the Quantity and Modality of the judgment of taste the beautiful is considered as the object of a pleasure which is *universal* and *necessary*, but without the intervention of a reflective idea. For this reason the universality and necessity are both of them subjective and not objective. I have ranked these two points together, though Kant does not, because according to modern logic we hardly care to distinguish between Quantity and Modality or between Universality and Necessity.

In the Quantity of the judgment beauty is distinguished from the pleasant and the good; from the pleasant by its

universality—for we demand agreement in the judgment of
beauty, though there is no disputing about tastes in food or
drink—and from the good by the absence of a reflective idea.
These distinctions are not repeated under the head of Modality.   The result would plainly be the same.

In respect of the Relation which the judgment of taste
implies, the beautiful is the form of purposiveness in an
object, in as far as this can be perceived *without the idea of
an end*.   Once more then, the beautiful is separated from the
pleasant, which involves a distinct subjective purpose ; and
from the good, because this involves the idea of an end,
whether external to the object as in the case of utility, or
immanent in the object as in the case of perfection.   Perfection, therefore, even when confusedly thought, is not as the
Wolffian school supposed, the same as the beautiful, but is
different in kind.   We cannot ascribe perfection to an object,
however confusedly, without applying to it, as the standard
of judgment, some idea of an end.

The "form of purposiveness" lies primarily, for Kant,
in a harmonious relation to our faculties of imagination and
understanding, so that we are not sure at first sight whether
to take it to be purely accidental or to depend on that appearance of organic unity in an object which is suggested to us by
such a phrase as "purposiveness without a purpose."   It seems
worth while to reproduce the note which shows how Kant
himself understood his paradox.

"It[1] might be adduced as an example that tells against this
explanation (of beauty), that there are things in which we see
a purposive form without recognising a purpose in them—for
instance, the stone instruments found in ancient tumuli, with
a hole in them as if for a handle, whose shape clearly shows
a purposiveness the actual purpose of which we do not know
—which nevertheless are not called beautiful.   But the fact
that we regard them as productions of art [*sic*, we must take
it to mean industrial art] is enough to force us to admit that
we refer their shape to some purpose and to a definite end.
So there is absolutely no immediate pleasure in the perception
of them.   But a flower, for instance a tulip, is considered
beautiful, because a certain purposiveness is found in the
perception of it, which is not, within our act of judging, re-

---

[1] *Krit. d. Urtheilskraft*, p. 87 footnote.

ferred to any end." It appears then, that the harmony of perception depends on a perception of harmony, although no explicit proposition can be made about the objective nature of the latter.

The place and nature of the æsthetic consciousness is finally determined for philosophy by these four paradoxes. Only they set down the judgment of taste as "subjective," a limitation which it remained for Kant's successors explicitly to remove.

Demarcation of Æsthetic Consciousness. i. The æsthetic consciousness has now received its final negative definition. It is plainly marked off from the region of abstract intelligence on the one hand, and from that of sensuous gratification and moral satisfaction on the other. If the latter pair of contrasts, those between æsthetic interest and the two forms of practical interest, depend on a common-sense distinction (between existence and appearance) which is not easily translated into exact psychical terms, it will be found that Kant himself furnishes the indication by which the antithesis can be made good. The peculiarity of æsthetic interest, which presented such difficulties to the greatest of the ancients, has never been mistaken by serious thinkers since thus trenchantly formulated by Kant. We may fairly assent to Hegel's verdict, when he finds in the introduction to the *Critique of the Power of Judgment* "the first rational word concerning beauty."[1]

Positive Essence of Æsthetic Consciousness. ii. Moreover, the æsthetic consciousness is now recognised in its positive essence as the meeting-point of sense and reason. All that we have thus far learnt about it has pointed to this conclusion, but Kant, with his usual calm audacity, was the first to lay down the principles which felicitously describe our everyday experience of the beautiful, while in the light of abstract metaphysic they appear to be the flattest self-contradictions. A feeling of pleasure which has no relation to practical interest, which depends on the purposiveness of a perceived content, and lays claim to universality and necessity, though

---

[1] *Hist. of Philosophy*, iii. 543. He has just quoted the sentence, "An object is beautiful, the form of which (not the material element, *i.e.*, sensation-stimulus, of its perception) is judged to be the ground of the pleasure taken in the image of such an object."

remaining all the time a pure feeling, wholly free from explicit conceptions of purpose or class or antecedent and consequent,[1] —such a feeling is a sheer impossibility alike to a sensationalist and to an intellectualist philosophy. It is not a clarified form of sense-gratification ; it is not a confused idea of perfection ; these are merely efforts to explain it upon wholly inadequate bases. It is *bonâ fide* feeling, and *bonâ fide* reasonable. Such is the paradox which Kant propounds. It involves a hopeless "no thoroughfare," unless there is a unity, not accidental but inherent, between feeling, sense, or nature on the one hand, and reason, intelligence, or freedom on the other.

Its "Subjectivity." iii. But upon all these other contradictions he superimposes a limitation which ostensibly withdraws the sense of beauty from the central position which at first sight he is supposed to claim for it. We are to bear in mind throughout that the judgment of taste is "subjective." The very phrase "judgment of taste" points to the partly British ancestry of Kant's doctrine, and to the sensationalist and empirical prejudices out of which he had to raise the whole question. The "judgment of taste" contributes in no way to cognition. It simply expresses a felt harmony in the play of our own powers on occasion of a certain perception. I have already touched on the issue how far the felt harmony in us implies a harmony in the object. At first sight however, and in his general language, Kant guards himself most anxiously against any such inference. We constantly meet with such expressions as "the universal subjective validity of the pleasure which we attach to the idea of an object which we call beautiful." How can a feeling that has universal validity remain subjective *in the sense which excludes objective?* Is not the whole idea a pure self-contradiction ? Yet there was no going back. Kant was right to be tenacious of his point. Beauty *is* subjective ; it exists in and for a percipient and not otherwise. But its subjectivity is no bar to its being objective as well. Kant says this in effect, but not in set terms. When it was said, the limitation of abstract subjectivity was removed, and the two worlds of dualistic tradition had their frontiers broken down.

Thus far we see the Judgment of Taste recognised as a

---

[1] Necessity is the relation of antecedent and consequent in judgment, " If A, *then* B."

mental phenomenon carrying a number of contradictory attributes, only to be conciliated by assumptions which we may
suggest, but cannot affirm, much less demonstrate. We
have now to observe the development of this recognition, first
in the hands of Kant himself and then in those of his successors, into the conception of a concrete unity, demonstrated
by æsthetic science in the appreciative and productive sense
of beauty, and by other philosophic methods in the history
of nature and man. The immanence of the idea in reality is
the root of objective idealism, and of this immanence the
æsthetic perception furnishes the simplest and most striking
example.

Conflict of Ab-
stract and Con-
crete in Kant's
Æsthetic.
4. Kant's starting-point in æsthetic theory was,
as we have seen, the judgment of taste, which
depends upon a *de facto* conformity between the
percipient and that which is perceived. Here we have the
common germ of an æsthetic of feeling and an æsthetic of
pure form, two abstract extremes which are really inseparable.
The unanalysed datum of disinterested pleasure in certain
perceptions is an aspect of the unanalysed datum that certain
perceptions give disinterested pleasure. These views, by
their common opposition to discursive rationalism in æsthetic
judgment, have the merit of vindicating the immediateness of
æsthetic perception ; but by confusing this concrete immediateness with the absence of any significance that can be analysed
by theory, they condemn the beautiful to absolute bareness
of character and import.

So long as Kant is absolutely true to his principle that
without abstract conceptions there can be no objective judgment, and that beauty can involve no abstract conceptions, it
follows that the pleasure of beauty, though possessing the
formal attributes of reason—disinterestedness, universality,
necessity—is yet *ex hypothesi* destitute of content, that is to
say, destitute of any definite implication as to the positive import of those forms, on the contemplation of which æsthetic
pleasure arises.

Now Kant never brings himself to admit that the judgment
of taste can be objective, but he tampers to some extent with
both of the principles which prevent him from admitting it.
Without asserting that there can be objective judgment in the
absence of definite abstract ideas, he admits a pregnant import into the form of beauty, through its relation to indefinite

ideas ;[1] without admitting that taste can involve intellectual conceptions, he both qualifies it as an organ of communicable feeling, and distinguishes its higher forms by close association with objective and abstract ideas.   It is only for the sake of his thesis that he sets down the judgment of taste, when thus associated, as "impure."

Isolated tones and colours raise the difficulty at once. Have they æsthetic form ? If they have, in what can it be said to consist ?   If they have not, their claim to beauty, as distinct from sensuous pleasantness, is annihilated.   And in this latter case an exceedingly hazardous Sorites is received into the theory.   If there are isolated sensations, such as enter into the beautiful, which have only pleasantness and no beauty, where does beauty begin to arise out of pleasantness ?

Kant is prepared in some degree to assign pregnant form to simple tones and colours.   This is the first lodgment effected by concrete import within his abstract judgment of taste.   They are beautiful, he says, only because and in so far as they are *pure*, which he explains as meaning free from perturbation by mixture.   Mixed colours and tones, he actually ventures to say, are not (in this sense) beautiful.   This explanation, which reminds us of Plato, would not bear interpretation either by physical analysis or by direct perception. The eye and ear do not necessarily tell us which colours and sounds have the most uniform physical causes ; nor, if either sense or science detects a mixture of tones or spectrum colours, do we necessarily judge that mixture to be devoid of æsthetic purity, much less of æsthetic beauty.   Would any unbiassed perception select a primary colour (red, green, or violet) or the tone of a tuning-fork (one of the few sounds that are fairly free from harmonics) as a type of purity ?

It is perhaps some consciousness of this difficulty that drives Kant to a further suggestion, which in a modified shape has still a tendency to revive.   Perhaps, he suggests, the rhythmical pulsations, which are the exciting cause[2] of tones and colours, may not merely have their effect on the organ of sense, but be actually perceived by the mind (which Kant " still greatly doubts ").   In that case colour and tone

---

[1] See *Antinomie d. Geschmacks*, and its solution, *K. d. U.*, 213 ff.

[2] Kant refers to Euler for the physical theory.

have formal quality as unities of a manifold, and thus are beautiful in their own right.

It can hardly be doubted that the unity, or unity in diversity, in which Kant thus endeavours to find the form of simple perceptions, has in his mind a reference to the conception of totality, which is an idea of the reason going beyond experience, and therefore indefinite for knowledge, though regulative for practice. We shall see that æsthetic ideas are in his view pendants to ideas of Reason.

But he is not quite sure whether this doctrine of significant form will work, and is partly inclined to abandon the beauty of colour as such, and to treat it as merely an ocular stimulus that enhances the visibility and value of line. Here we pass into a confusion between metaphysical "form" as the relation of parts in a significant whole, and "form" as the shape of visible bodies. It is plain that form in the metaphysical and æsthetic sense includes the harmonies of colour-composition, no less than those of linear or solid contour.

If we grant, what is very doubtful, that single tones or colours can ever be considered in their isolation, their æsthetic quality as thus isolated depends upon a great variety of subtle suggestions,[1] among which the idea of purity is only one, being a species of unity in variety, and not arising from the mere fact of such unity. Ruskin's account of purity[2] shows how much definite significance this idea contains. The above is a typical case of Kant's vacillation between safe adherence to the abstract datum of æsthetic pleasure, and the sense that if he cannot find a content for it, his doctrine of form becomes inane.

The case which in Plato ranks along with single tones and colours, that of very elementary geometrical figures, is rejected from the sphere of beauty by Kant. The abstract conception is too nearly implied in them, he thinks, to harmonise with the unreflective character of beauty. Here again he shows a needless dread of a specific content. The abstract conception behind them, so to speak, cannot prevent them from affording a slight degree of æsthetic pleasure to direct perception, in virtue of their presentation of certain qualities.

[1] See Baldwin Brown, *The Fine Arts*, Sect. 98. Kant himself develops the moral meaning which we find in colours and tones, "Courage, joyfulness," etc.

[2] *Mod. Painters*, vol. ii. p. 73 ff.

Further, the doctrine[1] of free and dependent beauty, *the latter including the ideal*, exhibits in a striking light the difficulty which pressed upon Kant when he tried to associate a positive import with the judgment of taste.

"Free" beauty rests on no definite conception, and the judgment of taste that appreciates it is pure. "Dependent" beauty is conditioned by the definite conception of an end, and therefore so far violates the principle of purposiveness without a purpose, and the judgment of taste that appreciates it falls short of purity.

Not only the lowest beauty, which subsequent philosophy would agree in calling subservient, but also the highest is ranked as dependent in virtue of this distinction. Architecture is plainly subordinate to use, and we are not surprised to find the beauty of buildings set down as dependent beauty. Rather it surprises us to be told that decorative art such as pattern-designing is "free" because it is not bound to represent any object conditioned by a positive idea. We should naturally set down decoration as attached on the whole to architecture and governed by human use, and therefore, like architecture, dependent. But even architecture, Kant will insist, as having a very wide range of possible purposes, is although strictly dependent, yet free in comparison with ideal beauty.

Natural beauty, except in those objects which are chiefly considered *qua* useful to man—such as the horse, or the [fruit] tree—is free. We must note the reason of this, which is simply that we cannot impose upon it any idea of a purpose. The beauty of a flower is free, for "no one but the botanist knows what a flower is meant to be ("Was eine Blume für ein Ding sein soll"), and in judging of its beauty even he takes no account of this." I imagine that we should distinguish between knowledge of the purpose as enabling us to pronounce upon utility or perfection, which we should admit to be of no æsthetic value, and knowledge of the purpose as enabling us to appreciate organic unity, which we should take to be an enrichment of æsthetic insight No one but a botanist, I should certainly maintain, can really feel the beauty of flowers. If their beauty is "free" then, in comparison with that of a house or church, it is not because we are ignorant of their purpose, nor

---

[1] *Kr. d. U.*, Sectt. 16 and 17.

again, as in great works of art, because their purpose is expression for expression's sake, but because what we must call their purpose is one with their own existence, and though usually conditioned by other lives [1] is not at any point cut in two by its relation to them. *For us*, therefore, the flower is harmoniously expressive throughout, in virtue of being a reasonable unity. All objects, even works of art, are conditioned by external agencies ; it is not the fact of a relation to condition or purpose, but the marked conflict of purposes within the system which man's will has power to introduce, that stamps the mark of subserviency on the decorated instruments of human life.

Most dependent and least free of all, according to Kant, is the beauty which is capable of an ideal.   There can be no ideal either of the lower dependent beauty, or of the intermediate free beauty. *An ideal* can only be fixed *by objective purposiveness*, and objective purposiveness is *ex hypothesi* outside beauty, and can never be judged of by a pure judgment of taste, but only by one which is partly intellectualised. Ideal means the presentation or imagination of a particular being as adequate to an idea of the reason.

The ideal then has two elements.   First, there is the unknown type, or intention of nature, in every race of men or animals.   Such a type is represented through the automatic work of the imagination, which strikes an average of shapes out of the thousands of individuals that have been seen.   This process is illustrated by a comparison to optical images thrown upon one another, which suggests Mr. Galton's method of generalised photographs.   Every breed of animals will present, and every race of men will present and possess, a " normal idea" thus constituted ; and this will form the foundation or *conditio sine qua non* of beautiful presentation in and for that race.   Both this idea of an average as the key to the intention of nature, and the allusion to the taste of negroes and Chinese as probably conditioned by the type familiar to them, remind us of Reynolds in the *Idler*, and point forward to Hegel, who depreciates mere "taste" on this very ground.

And in Kant's treatment what we have to note is his attitude to the "normal idea."   His language suggests that he thought at first, as Reynolds did, that this "idea" *was* the

---

[1] Those of insects.

ideal of beauty ; for it appears that he called it so in the earlier
editions of this Critique, and the phrase " Normal idea of
beauty " still occurs in the discussion.   But he subsequently
saw how little import this average type possessed, and the
Critique now expressly says that it can contain nothing characteristic [1] of a person, is not beautiful but merely correct,[2] and
that the average regularity of feature, which it brings out in
man, usually indicates mediocrity of mind.   The normal proportions which it exhibits are however the limit or condition
sine qua non upon which true beauty is founded.

The ideal of Beauty in the strict sense is something beyond
this, and has meaning only in the human race.   It consists in
the revelation of moral import through bodily manifestation in
the human form.   Without this the object cannot give universal and positive pleasure as distinct from the mere customary
and negative pleasantness of the " correct."   It is the highest
problem of the artist, and requires pure ideas of reason, and
great powers of imagination.   But as the standard thus set
involves a definite conception of man as an end, it follows
that "judgment by such a standard can never be purely
æsthetic, and judgment according to an ideal of beauty is no
mere judgment of taste."   Beauty judged according to an
ideal is therefore not free but dependent beauty.   And thus it
only just misses being admitted as objective ; for, though not
objective *qua* beauty, it is objective in virtue of that conception which makes it dependent.

Now if beauty is regarded as subservient to morality, or is
judged by the standard of specifically moral ideas, it is beyond
a doubt unfree or dependent.   But if the content of life and
reason is taken into beauty and perceived not as the expression of morality, but as the utterance in another form of that
reasonableness which is also to be found in morality, then we
first destroy the restriction of ideal beauty to man—for there
is reasonableness in all nature—and we secondly break down
the extraordinary paradox that the highest beauty is the least
free.   That beauty which is the largest and deepest revelation
of spiritual power is not the most dependent but the freest
beauty, because it implies no purpose whatever excepting that

---

[1] The " characteristic," the central idea of modern æsthetic, had been emphasised in Goethe's *Deutsche Baukunst,* 1780 ; but its appearance in Kant is
noteworthy.

[2] *Schulgerecht.*

which constitutes its own inmost nature, the expression of reason in sensuous form. It is plain that Kant felt this and practically recognised the true rank of such beauty, but was baffled in attempting to include it in his formal datum, the judgment of taste.

Yet with his strange persistence, approaching his subject like a beleaguered city by sapping up to it on different sides, he has still a great deal in reserve that affects this unacknowledged objectivity of the judgment of taste. He is clear, for example, that taste involves a " common sense," *not* the understanding which employs abstract ideas, but some kind of common feeling. And this, he thinks, may perhaps in the last resort represent a demand of the reason that sense is to be made harmonious or congruous in its utterances.[1] At least the communicability which is distinctive of æsthetic feeling gives it a high social interest from the most primitive times, although this is not an interest in beauty as such. In this discussion we find at once an anticipation and a criticism of an important modern view, that which lays stress on the social and festal origin of art.[2]

Moreover, when he comes to consider what must be added to taste in order to make up productive capacity in fine art, he decides that this is "genius," a conception in which he analyses, without any historical reference whatever, the watchword of the "period of genius" then hardly gone by. The essence of genius he finds in the power to portray æsthetic ideas ; and æsthetic ideas are imaginative presentations such that no conception is able to exhaust their significance. In this they are the counterpart of ideas of the reason,[3] to which no presentation can be adequate.

If we ask how the æsthetic idea is the counterpart of the idea or postulate of reason, we find that the relation is explained by a definite doctrine of symbolism.[4] A symbol is for him a perception or presentation which represents a conception neither conventionally as a mere sign, nor directly but in the abstract as a " scheme," but indirectly though appropriately through a similarity between the rules which govern our reflection in the "symbol" and in the thing (or idea) symbolised. Thus when we think of a monarchical state as an

---

[1] *Kr. d. U.*, p. 92.   [2] Prof. Brown, *The Fine Arts*, Bk. i.
[3] Pp. 185-6.   [4] P. 231

T

organism if the system is constitutional, and as a machine if it is despotic, organism and machine are symbols, the resemblance to the monarchical state depending in each case on the principle of cohesion which we impute to the things compared.

In this sense of symbolism *Beauty is a symbol of the moral order*,[1] and this order is the intelligible or supra-sensuous reality to which the judgment of taste ultimately points. It is this relation which expresses itself in the semi-rational nature ascribed to beauty in the four paradoxes. On this ground, again, interest in the beauty of nature is the sign of a good mind, because the reason is concerned that its ideas or demands shall not only have validity but find objective reality within the world of sense. And the traces of conformity in nature to a disinterested judgment in us, which constitute natural beauty and testify to an underlying unity between nature and the moral order, are therefore of interest to human thought. We should now extend this idea to the beauty of Art ; but it is remarkable that Kant, probably under Rousseau's influence, explicitly refuses to do so, thinking of art not as a revelation of existing beauty, but as made to conform to our ends and too often to flatter our egoism.

In all this account of beauty, which accords to it the highest significance, the term objective is still lacking ; but it is obvious that nothing of objectivity is lacking except the name. And with the objectivity thus practically conceded, there come in significance, and the characteristic, and natural as opposed to conventional symbolism. All these were the watchwords of the time just beginning, as taste and beauty had been the watchwords of that which had gone by. In general, including both nature and art, beauty is for Kant the expression of æsthetic ideas,[2] which means, as we have seen, the suggestion in sensuous form, of demands or aspirations or principles of reason which no such perception can completely and adequately contain.

5. We have seen that in his general theory Kant is forced to admit a concrete import into what was at first an unanalysable deliverance of feeling. How far, we must now enquire, does he

Range and Subdivision of Æsthetic Perception.

---

[1] " Sittlichkeit," p. 232. Even in Kant this word has not quite the isolated personal reference of our English term " morality."   [2] P. 192.

himself contribute to determining the actual field of æsthetic perception, and the relation between its content and the sensuous media in which it can be clothed ? The answer to this enquiry is in the doctrine of the sublime and the classification of the arts.

i. Kant's account of the sublime is interposed between two parts of his account of the beautiful, and appears to have had the effect of forcing upon his mind the deeper symbolic character in beauty which at first he was disposed to find only in sublimity. Historically speaking, his theory was probably occasioned by that of Burke, and on its spiritual side might very well have been suggested by a single remark of Winckelmann, whose name, however, so far as I am aware, does not occur in Kant. Its subsequent effect may be traced in Hegel's conception both of symbolic and of romantic art, and more generally, it was the true forerunner of all æsthetic theory which brings apparent ugliness within the frontier of beauty. For Kant's allusion in another context to the ugly as capable of being beautifully portrayed in art is a weak survival of Lessing's ideas, and has little to do with the growing modern sympathy for what is undisguisedly sombre, wild, or terrible.

Theory of Sublime.

The firm and plain basis of Burke's distinction between the beautiful and the sublime was, it will be remembered, the difference between the pleasantness of pleasure and the pleasantness of pain. It is undoubtedly upon this foundation that Kant erects his theory, in which fear, corresponding to Burke's " passions relating to self-preservation, which turn mostly on pain or danger," suggests a principal case of sublimity. Winckelmann's remark that in looking upon the sea the mind is at first depressed and then recovers itself more strongly, might very well have suggested Kant's idea of the spiritual reinvigoration occasioned by perceptions which in some way do violence[1] to our sensuous fancy.

For Kant, as for Burke, there is no acknowledged synthesis of the sublime with the beautiful, although the final conception of beauty as attained by Kant in the latter part of his discussion would admit of such a synthesis. We cannot say, therefore, that he makes the sublime a species of the beautiful. Both, rather, are species of the æsthetic judgment, but only

---

[1] " Gewaltthätig für d. Einbildungskraft," *Kr. d. U.*, p. 99.

beauty belongs to the judgment of taste, while the sublime is rooted in an emotion of the intelligence (Geistesgefühl). The two modes of feeling share indeed the semi-rational character, subjective yet universal, which marks the æsthetic judgment as such, but they differ widely in the nature of their object-matter and in their consequent relation to it.

Beauty always has to do with form ; sublimity may depend on form or on " Unform," a useful idiom which may cover both formlessness and deformity.[1] The object of sublime feeling (we may not in strictness speak of a sublime object) is always one that resists our power of judgment, and so far from being harmonious, is rather incongruous with it. For this reason the sublime is one degree more subjective than the beautiful, and in every way is more difficult, making higher demands upon the mind. Its essence is to throw us back on ourselves, to depend upon our acquired culture and ideas, of which it demands much more than the sense of beauty, to give an austere or negative pleasure akin to awe and admiration, to communicate a serious and stirring, not a playful and tranquil movement to the imagination, and as incapable of residing in any sensuous form to stimulate only the ideas of the reason and not those of the understanding. For the former, which can be represented in no sense-perception, are evoked in us by the very conflict or incongruousness which exhibits to us the inadequacy of sense. This special relation to reason was probably intended to be a radical difference between the sublime and the beautiful, but is obliterated as a distinction by the concluding account in the Dialectic which places the latter also in essential relation to ideas of reason or of the moral order.

In spite of this inward and ideal character, however, Kant tries to restrict the sublime, like the beautiful, to mere abstract feeling. We must not appeal in our perception of it to distinct conceptions drawn from our knowledge. We must accept the feeling as it follows from what we directly see. We must not think of the stars as suns with their systems, nor of the sea as the reservoir of the clouds or the highway of the nations. We must judge them æsthetically only as a crowd of luminous points in an immeasurable vault, and as

---

[1] Kant never, I think, uses "hässlich" of the object of sublime feeling. He does use "grässlich."

a shining surface or menacing abyss.   To our minds to-day this dualism seems unreasonable.   We cannot understand why feeling should be void of content, especially as the sublime exists in the reaction of our ideas, and is explicitly characterised, in language that anticipates Ruskin, as dependent on relations.   But the result is that this peculiar stimulation is chiefly to be looked for in unwrought [1] and inorganic Nature, a striking testimony to the widening of the æsthetic sense.   It is also said to be suggested, strictly in accordance with the theory, by the extreme of formlessness in the Jewish prohibition, "Thou shalt not make to thyself any graven image."   Longinus, it will be remembered, had drawn an example from the books of Moses.   In the instance adduced by Kant, an idea taken from a consciousness hostile to expression through sense, becomes, by a very curious meeting of extremes, the content of poetry at the point where it tends to pass out of the sphere of art.   Thus the extremes of consciousness below and above the region of beautiful expression, appear in this case to join hands.

The idea which underlies Kant's theory is thus quite clear. It is closely analogous to his view of the moral law, which is in his mind throughout.   The sublime in its two species— mathematical, *i.e.* excited by objects which reveal the impotence of sense to satisfy the idea of totality, and dynamical, *i.e.* evoked by objects or occurrences which reveal our powerlessness as natural beings to overcome the forces of Nature, though our moral freedom is superior to their omnipotence,— depends on the stimulation of our moral ideas, which nothing in sensuous nature can either represent or overcome, by a primary non-conformity between an external object and our power of judgment.

I do not know whether any stray echoes of Kantian speculation penetrated to the poet Thomas Campbell (d. 1844); but the mental reaction in which Kant finds the sublime is fairly represented by the closing stanzas of his lyric, "The Last Man." [2]   Kant would, however, remind us that God and Immortality are postulates, not facts.

---

[1] " Roh."
[2] " Go, Sun, while Mercy holds me up
        On Nature's awful waste,
    To drink this last and bitter cup
        Of grief that man shall taste ;—

It is a conception which bears noble testimony to the inspiration which sea[1] and mountain[1] were beginning to impart. But in its true place, as a theory of apparent ugliness in relation to beauty, it has a fatal defect of principle. This defect was signalised above as the absence of any synthesis of the sublime with the beautiful, and is rooted in the subjectivity ascribed by Kant to beauty, and the double subjectivity imputed to the sublime. In beauty the "form" has a content which can be analysed, although its purposive import must not be definitely affirmed, but the essence of the sublime falls *wholly* within the mind, so that absolutely no conformity is assumed between stimulus and reaction, and therefore no attempt can possibly be made to attach expressive significance to the objects which by purely negative behaviour serve as such stimuli. And so the link of expressive or characteristic structure, which stands ready to guide us step by step from facile and orderly beauty to the more sombre and intricate aspects of life and nature, is absolutely cut asunder; and we are never taught to look for the form of the beautiful in those very perceptions which startle us at first sight by superhuman force or magnitude. And therefore the ideas of reason thus negatively evoked can have only a bare moral victory, and are not recognised as prevailing, in an intricate orderliness and significance, throughout all the terror and immensity of the external world. With Turner and Ruskin before us, we do not comprehend the æsthetic perception to which, as to Kant, the stormy sea was simply horrible, and the elements of splendid beauty in the lines and masses which express its resistlessness made no positive appeal to the imagination. The sublime with all it implies could not be rightly valued until it came to be appreciated as an *extension* of beauty, indeed, but still an extension *of beauty*.

Go tell the Night that hides thy face,
Thou saw'st the last of Adam's race
On earth's sepulchral clod,
The darkening Universe defy
To quench his immortality,
Or shake his trust in God."

[1] The references to De Saussure, combined with the restriction of the sublime proper to wild inorganic nature, prove, I think, that the Alps were largely in Kant's mind. His phrase, "rohe Natur," is erroneously referred to beauty and organic beings by von Hartmann, *Æsthetik*, i., 15. Kant often mentions the sea.

But for a view which shut up both attributes within a subjective mental reaction, no positive meeting-point in the significant form of perceptions was open to them. Without a concrete analysis no synthesis was possible.

So much for the range of beauty, which, if we follow for the moment our general sense of the term as equivalent to "æsthetic quality," Kant has immensely amplified in accordance with modern feeling, by his theory of the sublime.

Classification of Arts. ii. In dealing with the sensuous vehicles of beauty,[1] as they constitute the different arts, Kant is very brief and unsystematic, though in many places he anticipates later contentions. The theory of a developing art-consciousness, and an appreciation of the antithesis between the ancient and modern world are conspicuous by their absence,[2] a lacuna plainly connected with his dread of objective teleology. For the same reason, there are but few traces of a desire to regard the material media of the arts as forming an orderly system in which all necessary kinds of expression might find a place. In distinguishing fine art from science however, with the claims of the "period of genius" before his mind, he makes a striking suggestion, which Hegel adopts, and which in Kant leads up to important results. It is true, he says, that genius though not independent of training or reflection, is a gift rooted in nature, of which it shows the *unconscious* creative power, and is the peculiar organ of fine art, which may even be defined as the art of genius. This natural gift is not in the same sense needed for exact science, which is pursued purely through conscious intellectual operations. Anyone, (having *enough* intellect, we must suppose) could learn all that Newton taught ; but he could not, by taking thought, even begin to learn how to make a poem. Here we have at once an immense advance on Lessing and eighteenth-century ideas,[3] though Kant is above the wildness of the youthful Goethe and Schiller.

---

[1] Kant drops out the sublime almost entirely from his theory of art. The product of art comes too near implying an objective conception to be connected with a feeling which, even more than beauty, demands absolute purity. For a combination of beauty and sublimity Kant once refers us to "rhymed tragedy," a strange proof how little he approached a synthesis.

[2] The conclusion of *Observations on the feeling of the Sublime and Beautiful* shows how Kant stood on the old lines about the Renaissance and Gothic art.

[3] Dr. Johnson took the opposite line. "Newton could have written a great epic if he had chosen."

Fine art, then, is closely akin to nature. The paradoxes of beauty explain how this must be. All beauty, and therefore nature *qua* beautiful, has the form of purposiveness. All beauty, and therefore the beauty of art, is free from definable purpose. Art, therefore, is beautiful, when, although known to be art, it apears as free—unconscious of rule or set purpose—as nature. Nature is beautiful when it appears to possess the purposiveness of art. These ideas, thrown out in a few sentences, have their consequences in the views of Schiller and Hartmann.

Kant's actual classification of the fine arts,[1] on which the author himself lays no great stress, rests on a fantastic deduction from the true principle, that beauty whether of art or of nature is expression. Expression *par excellence* is speech, and this as communicating at once thought, perception and feeling, has the three elements, word, gesture, and modulation or accent. On this analogy he divides the fine or expressive arts into arts of speech, of form, and of play of sensation. Judging from an earlier passage, in which he has said that the form of all objects of sense is either " shape " or " play," the distinction between simultaneity and succession would seem to be also in his mind.

We find in his table two crafts which ought not to be included among fine arts, the art of oratory and the art of landscape gardening. The former is plainly dominated by practical intent ; the latter does not deal with a true expressive material. The former he ranks with the arts of speech, the latter with those of form.

I mentioned the origin of this unfortunate classification, because the distinction between speaking and formative art has been erected into a principle, and oratory being necessarily omitted, has led to the species of poetry being set out in an imaginary parallelism to the non-poetical arts, as by Schelling, the former being called the Ideal and the latter the Real series, and this notion of two parallel series, under these or other headings, has continued to operate in later German philosophy with the most unnatural results, grave difficulty being found, in particular, as to the place which music ought to hold.

Kant's nearest approach to a linear classification is given in

---

[1] P. 73.

his comparison of the æsthetic value of the fine arts. In this, poetry is assigned the first place, and some words of this estimate set the keynote for Schiller's doctrine of "semblance" and "play." "Poetry *plays* with the semblance,[1] without deceiving; for it declares its occupation to be mere play." Painting, it should be noted, has already been called the art of sensuous *semblance*, and plastic, including architecture and sculpture, that of sensuous *truth*. Of course for the complete doctrine of æsthetic semblance, which Kant only offends against in expression and not for a moment in thought, the form of sculpture is a "Schein" as much as that of painting, only less adaptable and so less ideal. Painting therefore ranks above it. This gradation prepares us for the series of the arts according to ideality in Hegel. About the rank of music there is a curious variety of suggestions. For us they have the interest that a later theory of the original import of music as depending on its relation to the emotional modulations of the voice, is here suggested and accepted as a fact, but put aside as not bearing on æsthetic value, but on associations which are only of interest to private feeling. The æsthetic value of music is referred to the mathematical interrelation by which the complex of sounds is made into a whole attended with an abundance of thoughts too full for verbal expression. But these thoughts depend on purely mechanical associations; and the essential content of music is therefore so bare, and the culture it implies so slight, that apart from its mere pleasantness, in which it ranks first of all arts, and its charm and emotional power (due to voice associations), in which it ranks second, it ought to be placed lowest of the whole list. This remark, like almost the entire content of Kant's æsthetic, reappears in a much modified form in Hegel. And the analysis of musical beauty as depending on the mathematical relations which bind its parts into a coherent whole recurs in conjunction with a less humble estimate of its æsthetic value, in the deepest modern appreciation of musical significance, that which regards it as representing the spirit or idealised form of occurrence or existence.[2] In noting Kant's perplexities about music, we may remember that he made little use of the ancients who knew something of its true value, which we have seen to be greatly neglected through the middle age and in eighteenth

---

[1] "Schein," *K. d. U.*, 201.   [2] "Hanslick," in Lotze, *G. d. A.*, 486 ff.

century criticism. And we should be grateful to Kant for at least striving to recognise the greatest art of his time.

Kant gives no account of the comic within the limits of fine art. He inclines to regard the jest[1] as belonging rather to the arts of pleasure. Nevertheless his famous definition of laughter as an affection arising from an expectation suddenly brought to nothing,[2] probably had to do with Hegel's definition of comedy. His direct connection of the mental shock thus experienced with the muscular convulsion of laughter has a materialistic sound, recalling Burke ; but modern psychology has much to say of the bond between mental and muscular tension, and the simplicity and abruptness of Kant's identification should count in his favour, if, as seems probable, it contains an important truth. When we hold our breath in expectation, and then undergo a violent change of tension through the expectation coming to nothing, we certainly go through a process like that which Kant describes. And although expectation and tension have many causes, it might be maintained that there is a peculiar suddenness and completeness of contrast in the relaxation that accompanies amusement, which is well described by Kant's phrase " brought to nothing." In the case of serious disappointment for instance, the expectation changes to something positive though opposite.

Kant, we must insist, was a good observer. His shrewd and decisive criticisms of society, literature, and national character have an Aristotelian quality. A translation of well-chosen extracts from the *Critique of the Power of Judgment*, and still more from the earlier work—in itself a mere note-book—*Observations on the Feeling of the Sublime and Beautiful*, would throw quite a new light on the popular idea of the great metaphysician. The habit of taking up into his theory great numbers of everyday terms which he explains in passing by terse and pregnant definitions, is characteristic of Kant and Lessing, as of Aristotle. It was adopted by Schiller and Hegel, and has much to do with the grasp and solidity of objective idealism.

Conclusion.   6. If we now recall, for the last time, in order to measure the difference between the starting-points of ancient and modern æsthetic, the three principles and anti-

---

theses by which we judged the theories of the Greeks, we shall find ourselves in a different world.

i. The metaphysical criticism of fine art which treated it as an inferior species of common reality and therefore as subordinate to that reality in import and beneath it in utility, has yielded to a view which ranks it as the superior co-ordinate of natural products, both having beauty only as freely symbolic or expressive of supra-sensuous meaning. Imitation is replaced by symbolism, and even if art is held to be in one sense bound by external reality, it is understood that in as far as it deals with mere form or with imaginative ideas it has the advantage of nature and not *vice versâ*. The metaphysical criticism is replaced by theories of the metaphysical import of beauty.

ii. The moralistic criticism with its confusion between æsthetic and practical interest, is almost wholly swept away. With the frank acceptance of what Plato treated as its inferiority, the restriction to imaginative form or semblance, now opposed alike to sensuous solicitation and to definitely conceived purpose, the beautiful is finally freed from the suspicion of sensuality and from the claims of moral proselytism. Only in Kant a trace of moralism remains in as far as the permanent value of the beautiful is referred by him exclusively to its representation of moral ideas and the moral order, in consequence of the subjectivism which hinders him from plainly asserting the existence of any more general system which might express itself not only through morality in the world of conduct, but otherwise in other spheres. In pointing however to a supra-sensuous unity common to the world of nature and of freedom, he really transcends this false subordination ; and we might say that beauty is for him a symbol of morality only because and in as far as he understands morality to symbolise the order of the universe.

iii. The formal principle of unity and variety, which stood in the way of a concrete analysis of beauty, is being transformed into the principle of expressiveness, characterisation, significance. In Kant's discussion of colours and tones we saw the meeting-point of the two. A positive or concrete structure of æsthetic science is as yet, indeed, only in the making. The outlines are firmly traced and the materials are lying about in heaps, but the building is hardly begun. The idea of beauty is still, if I may use the expression, a con-

crete conceived in the abstract, a meeting point of polar extremes not yet exhibited in the kinds and phases determined
by their varying relations.

Thus we may henceforward confine ourselves to the æsthetic problem proper, and its import, if any, for general philosophy. A distinct and reflective æsthetic consciousness has
been created both for philosophy and for art. It is only since
Goethe, it has been truly said, that the artist has been conscious of his "mission." Whether, as Kant seems to assume,[1]
this consciousness is a fortunate condition for creative genius,
must be very seriously doubted. But for philosophy reflecting upon beauty it is indispensable.

The æsthetic problem[2] as inherited by Kant consisted in
the question "How can a pleasurable feeling partake of the
character of reason?" To this we have seen his answer in
the four paradoxes and their corollaries. Its expansion we
shall have to trace in later thought. The problem of general
philosophy which gave urgency to the æsthetic issue consisted in the question, "How can the sensuous and the ideal
world be reconciled?" The answer to this we have seen in
the relation between the three portions of Kant's critical
problem. The order of nature and the moral order must, he
contends, have a common root, which is manifested most
strikingly in the spontaneous harmony of natural necessity
and ideal purpose exhibited to the perceptive and creative
sense of beauty. The unconsciousness and freedom which
fine art shares with nature indicates that this purposiveness
is really immanent in material things, and is not forced from
without upon the sensuous or natural elements. If so, they
too are inherently rational, and the compatibility, nay more,
the ultimate unity of the natural and moral order is established.

Kant, as we know, wrote the reservation "subjective" over
the entire outcome of his æsthetic and teleological researches.
Even when he anticipated later theory by a suggestion for a
Universal History which should establish a purpose of nature
in the life of the human race, evolving moral civilisation through
the conflicts of pain and desire, and when he combated, on
this ground, the difficulty that earlier generations are sacrificed

---

[1] *Observations*, etc., "Conclusion."
[2] See ch. viii. end.

to an end they will never know,[1] all this is to him simply a point of view, a way in which the aggregate of facts may be reduced to a system.

It is clear that either the idea or the reservation is untenable. What experience compels us to assume, is objective for us. What is not essential to explain our experience, we have no right to dwell upon in serious thought. It was rather the nature of objectivity than the reality of the immanent idea that was called in question by Kant's reservation.

A new spirit would be brought to the consideration of this issue, when the concrete idea, as Kant had obtained it by the resolution of the inherited antithesis of nature and freedom, should be accepted as the nature of the real, and further enriched by the same antithesis in its historical form as between the ancient and the modern mind. For the immanent reason would then reveal itself to be not merely a statical but a dynamical unity, not merely an equilibrium but an evolution.

---

[1] "Build a house they will never live in." This essay, *Werke*, vol. 7, was written in 1784, but its views are practically reaffirmed in the *Critique of Judgment*.

CHAPTER XI.

THE FIRST STEPS OF A CONCRETE SYNTHESIS—SCHILLER AND GOETHE.

The Position of Schiller. I. "The above may be taken as the leading results of the Kantian critical philosophy, so far as they interest us in æsthetic   It forms the point of departure for the true comprehension of the beauty of art.   Yet such a comprehension could only be realised by an overcoming of the Kantian defects through a higher appreciation of the true unity of necessity and freedom, of particular and universal, of sensuous and rational.

"And so it must be admitted that the art-sense of a profound mind—which was philosophic as well as artistic—demanded and proclaimed the principle of totality and reconciliation before the time at which it was recognised by technical philosophy.   In so doing it opposed itself to (Kant's) abstract infinity of thought, his duty for duty's sake, and his formless 'understanding' which takes account of nature and reality, sense and feeling, only as a limit, as something absolutely hostile, and therefore antagonistic to itself.   It is *Schiller* then to whom we must give credit for the great service of having broken through the Kantian subjectivity and abstraction of thought, and ventured upon going quite beyond it by intellectually apprehending the unity and reconciliation as the truth, and by making them real through the power of art. . . .   Now this unity of the universal and particular, of freedom and necessity, of the spiritual and the natural, which Schiller scientifically apprehended as principle and essence of art, and unweariedly strove to call to life by art and æsthetic culture, was in the next place erected into the principle of knowledge and existence as itself the Idea, the Idea being recognised as the sole truth and reality.   It was by this recognition that science attained in Schelling its absolute standpoint." [1]

---

[1] Hegel, *Æsth.*, i. 78, 80.   (E. Tr. p. 116.)

It is thus that Hegel in his maturer years recalls the history of the time, when, as we shall see in the following chapter, his youthful friendship with Schelling was still unbroken, and when the two friends, in close correspondence, were forming their views under the twofold influence of Kant and Fichte on the one hand, and of Schiller and Goethe on the other.

It is strange that historians of æsthetic take no notice of this remarkable testimony. Hegel was not the man lightly to give credit to an amateur thinker at the expense of philosophy proper. I shall therefore attempt simply to illustrate his statement in dealing with Schiller's conceptions, which definitely initiated the fusion of Kant's abstract synthesis with the historical data of æsthetic.

Schiller was on one side of his mind a Kantian, while on the other he was both a classicist by study and sympathy, and a romanticist by his period and his genius. Thus he formed a link between Kant and Goethe. For Goethe shared these factors of Schiller's mind in inverse proportion. Though as a rule barely tolerant of metaphysic, he was not untouched by Kant, while the marriage of Faust and Helena is a symbol of his lifelong devotion to the reconciliation of Hellenism with what is best in the romantic spirit. Hegel, with obvious justice, connects the deeper interpretation of the beautiful, which now began, with the growth of romantic feeling in art.[1] Thus the relations between Schiller and Goethe were preeminently favourable to the investiture of Kantian abstractions with living reality.

The achievement which Hegel ascribed to Schiller is in its essence, 1, the abandonment of the reservation by which at every turn Kant ascribes subjectivity, in a sense excluding objectivity, to the unity of opposites which he found in the æsthetic judgment. Schiller's account of æsthetic semblance and the play impulse may be treated under this head, as the positive form under which he envisages the objective nature of beauty.

And to this we must add, 2, as a corollary the first recognition, based on definite conceptions, of a difference between modern principles of art — whether to be called principles of beauty or by some other name—and those which had currently been assigned to the art of antiquity. The link between the objectivity of the beautiful and the latitude of the perception or principle which constitutes it, depends upon the dynamical nature of an objective principle, demanding as it does a relevancy to the movements and phases of the human mind, instead of acquiescence in the first indolent impressions of feeling.   Indications of the actual range of Schiller's æsthetic sympathies may fairly be treated in this connection.

Objectivity of   1. At the close of chap. ix. I alluded to the event-
Beauty.   ful decade which followed the publication of the *Kritik d. Urtheilskraft.*   The first of its characteristics which comes before us is that it contains nearly the whole of Schiller's work in theoretical æsthetic.   From 1792 till after 1800 there appeared almost yearly, for the most part in publications such as *Thalia* and the *Horen*,[1] papers or short treatises by Schiller dealing with æsthetic problems. From 1795 onwards, it must be remembered, Goethe and Schiller were in active correspondence, so that in the writings of either the ideas of the other were to some extent represented.   Their "period of genius" lay behind them.   In 1795 Schiller was in his thirty-sixth and Goethe in his forty-sixth year.   *Werther* and *Götz v. Berlichingen* were things of twenty years ago.   The *Räuber* was written at least fourteen years before.   The romantic movement which their stormy youth had inaugurated was now developing in other hands.

The Schlegels, for example, began their activity in this decade, an activity which furnished to profounder thinkers and critics of greater real genius than themselves, a splendid wealth of material and a constant reminder of the historical antithesis between the classical and the romantic.   It should be added that Voss's Homer (the *Iliad* new, the *Odyssey* revised) appeared in 1790, and F. A. Wolf's *Prolegomena* in 1795.   This was the epoch in which Schiller, the descendant of Lessing[2] and Winckelmann no less than of Kant, was brought face to face with the question whether or no the art-impulse and the sense of beauty rested on a true immanent

---

[1] In which Goethe and Schiller co-operated in 1795-6.   Schiller's *Letters on The Æsthetic Education of Humanity* and his paper on "*Naive and Sentimental Poetry*" appeared in it.
[2] Compare the titles of Lessing's *Erziehung d. Menschengeschlechts*, and Schiller's *Briefe über d. Æsthetische Erz. d. Menschheit.*

principle and tendency in the universe, not merely imputed to it by arbitrary reflection.

For Schiller's general position the letters on the Æsthetic Education of Humanity give the most complete results. Going at once to the heart of his ideas, in his relation to Kant, we find that he believes himself in accord with the spirit but not with the letter of the Kantian system. It is natural, he says, for a philosopher, as intellectual, to seem to treat feeling as a mere hindrance to reason, and this is what in the letter Kant appears to do. But in the spirit or inevitable interpretation of his system this is not so, for the sensuous impulse must be taken as co-ordinate with, and not subordinate to, the rational impulse. The idea of reciprocity, drawn from a new work of Fichte,[1] is applied in this account of co-ordination, which is also described as reciprocal subordination.[2] In short, sense and reason are capable of appearing in harmony only because it is their ultimate nature to be in harmony. The subjective conception is dropped as untenable in face of a complete estimate of man. " In the one-sided moral estimate the reason is satisfied when its law has absolute supremacy ; in the complete anthropological estimate, in which content counts as well as form, and feeling has a voice, the distinction [between the suppression and the completion of individuality] is of all the more importance. Reason demands unity, nature variety, and both systems of legislation lay their claims on man."[3]

The "ideal man"[4] is represented by the State, but is not realised in his fulness by any state which remaining in abstraction kills out individuality. The alternative and better way is that the ideal principle of the state should enter into and ennoble the individual till he becomes capable of participating in a spiritual unity without sacrificing the natural variety which is his element. Even the artist must *seem* to respect his material ; the statesman must do so in reality. The point of all this lies in the conception that the " parts," whether conceived as the particulars of nature or of feeling, or as unsocialised individual human beings, are really in

---

[1] *Grundlage der gesammten Wissenschaftslehre*, 1794, another of the remarkable works that influenced this critical time.
[2] *Briefe ü. Aesth. Erziehung*, No. 13, note.
[3] *Ib.*, No. 4.
[4] Again an idea drawn from Fichte, Letter 4, note.

themselves capable of unity and organization. Here we have
implied the central principle of idealism, that nothing can be
made into what it is not capable of being. Therefore when
certain syntheses and developments are actual it is idle to
deny that they are objective or immanent in the nature of the
parts developed.

The central proof and example of these principles, as well
as the most effective influence in raising mankind from the
first nature of savagery to the second of civilization, Schiller
believes to exist in fine art, which he identifies with general
refinement of life and manners in a way that is capable of, but
requires, justification. A single quotation will put his view
completely before us.

" Beauty is therefore indeed an *object* for us, because reflection is the condition under which we have a feeling of it ; but
at the same time it is a state of our *subject*, because feeling is the
condition under which we can have a perception of it. It is
therefore a form, because we contemplate it ; it is life, because
we feel it. In one word, it is at once our state and our act.

" And just because it is both of these at once, it serves as
a triumphant proof that receptivity by no means excludes
activity, nor matter, form, nor limitation, infinity,—that
therefore the necessary physical dependence of man in no way
destroys his moral freedom. It proves this, and, I must add,
nothing else can prove it. For as in the enjoyment of truth
or of logical consistency feeling is not necessarily one with
thought, but follows accidentally upon it, such feeling can
only prove that a sensuous nature may be sequent upon a
rational one, and conversely ; not that both can exist together,
not that they can act reciprocally upon each other, not that
their union is absolute and necessary. Just the opposite inference would be more natural. The exclusion of feeling
while we think, and of thought while we feel, would lead us
to infer the incompatibility of these two natures, as in fact the
analytic reasoners can adduce no better evidence that pure
reason is realisable in humanity than that it is imperative for
it to be so. But as in the enjoyment of beauty or of æsthetic
unity there takes place an actual union and interpenetration
of matter with form and of receptivity with activity, this very
fact demonstrates the compatibility of the two natures, the
realisableness of the infinite in the finite, and therefore the
possibility of the most sublime humanity.

"We ought, therefore, no longer to be in perplexity to find a passage from sensuous dependence to moral freedom, seeing that in beauty a case is given wherein the latter is able perfectly to co-exist with the former, and man is not obliged to escape from matter in order to assert himself as spirit. Now if man is free without ceasing to be sensuous,[1] as the fact of beauty teaches, and if freedom is something absolute and supra-sensuous as its idea necessarily involves, then it can no longer be a question how he succeeds in ascending from the limits [of sense ?] to the absolute, or in opposing himself to sensuousness in his thought and will, as in beauty this is already accomplished. In one word, the question can no longer be how he passes from beauty to truth, seeing that the latter *as a capacity*[2] is already contained in the former, but only how he pioneers his path from common to æsthetic reality, from mere feelings of life to feelings of beauty."[3]

Little need be added to this passage after our prolonged discussion of Kant. We see at once that objectivity is the whole root of the import thus ascribed to beauty ; but further that it must be such an objectivity as is compatible with existence in mind, in perception, in feeling, and in utterance. Only it is worth while to observe the extreme logical clearness, not usually characteristic of him, with which Schiller apprehends the nature of synthesis.[4] The factors which are to be united in the beautiful cannot, he says, be genuinely combined unless they are first unmistakeably distinguished, and then so united that each wholly disappears in the product of their union. Unless they disappear in the product, they cannot be truly united ; for as they appear in severance they are opposed to each other. The term which indicates this disappearance[5] in a higher import is occasionally used by Goethe

---

[1] Schiller to Goethe, *Br. W.*, 3, 262. "Poetry and art have two conditions : they must rise above the actual, and remain within the sensuous."

[2] Cf. Letter 21, the passage which excited Mr. Ruskin's indignation by affirming that beauty *only* changes man's whole nature to a free rational or second nature, but "discovers no *single* truth, helps us to fulfil no *single* duty." Cf. *Mod. Painters*, 2, 134. Mr. Ruskin cannot have had the context before him.

[3] Letter 25.

[4] Letter 18.

[5] "Aufgehoben "=preserved by destruction. Schiller goes too far perhaps in saying that "no trace of the division must remain in the whole product." But it is much easier to understate than to overstate the change effected in parts by incorporation in a new whole.

in a similar sense ; but the peculiar logical context of this passage suggests that its use as a technical term of Hegelian dialectic may be due to the " Æsthetic letters."

Beauty, then, though subjective, as Kant said, is also objective, as he meant.   In what positive character, we naturally ask, does it manifest itself within human perception and activity ?   Schiller's answer to this is furnished in the kindred ideas of æsthetic semblance and of the play-impulse. Preserving the fundamental Kantian features of pleasure in mere form, and of contrast with practical purpose, respectively, Schiller attempts to draw from them important consequences relative to the growth of civilization.   Much that is true and striking is brought forward by him with reference especially to the rigid practicality of primitive life, and the advance implied in such enjoyment as that of seeing for seeing's sake, which is coincident with the awakening of the play-impulse, the impulse to a purely ideal activity.[1]

a. The doctrine of æsthetic semblance (ästhe-

Æsthetic Semblance. tischer Schein) is developed by Schiller out of Kant's account of æsthetic form, which, in speaking of poetry, he also described as a semblance (Schein) that is not deceptive.   Schiller presses home this idea with considerable acuteness and with the full powers of his rhetoric, and has thus made the Kantian distinction between beauty knowledge and practice a common-place of literature, although it can hardly be said that he derives from it any substantive truth which was not included in Kant's four paradoxes. Æsthetic semblance, he insists, is Honest, that is to say, makes no pretence at being more than semblance ; and is Independent, that is to say, is not such as to be capable of enhancement of the pleasure which it gives, through the real existence of the object simulated.   Real objects may indeed be æsthetically contemplated, but only in as far as we distinguish their semblance from their existence.   And this is a harder task than to appreciate the work of art in which this separation is performed ready to our hand.

Thus æsthetic semblance is distinguished at once from deception, whether sensuous or logical, and from the appetitive

---

[1] Letter 26.   " As soon as man begins to receive pleasure through the eye [mit dem Auge zu geniessen], and seeing obtains an independent value for him, he has become æsthetically free, and the play-impulse is awakened."

or practical relation to reality ; and by emphasising from an anthropological standpoint the gradual growth of an interest in the semblance, and the fact that all difficulties, apparently connected with representative beauty, really arise not from the unreality of the semblance, but from insufficient attention to its "honesty,"—its confessed unreality—he paves the way for a truer conception than Kant possessed of the relative value of natural and artistic beauty, and for a definite justification of the place held by the beautiful in civilised life.   His paradox that man is civilised only in proportion as he has learnt to value the semblance above the (common-place practical) reality is a tremendous reversal of the position taken up by Plato, and was influential in the later course of post-Kantian speculation.

There is a difficulty in the psychical distinction which this doctrine of semblance may be held to involve.   How can one kind of sense-perception be set down as semblance, and another as reality ?   Why should visual or auditory sensations be taken to belong to form, while those of taste, smell and touch are set down as giving sheer reality ?   Surely the one group are as " objective " or " subjective " as the other !   Schiller, though successful in the development of doctrines, is not helpful in exactly tracing their roots, and here he falls decidedly behind Kant.   We saw that in Kant's account of the pleasure of simple sensations he at least faces this ultimate difficulty with perfect candour.   He treats æsthetic character as dependent on the presence of " form " in contrast with mere sensory stimulation.   And " form," which is for him the essence of æsthetic semblance, is a property or nature in sensation distinguishable from its mere existence as sense-stimulation.   In ranking sensations according to æsthetic quality he therefore follows a principle which is at least intelligible, and probably contains the true basis of the distinction between the æsthetic and the non-æsthetic elements in sense.   Schiller replaces this principle by a more popular phrase.   " Reality," he says, " is the work of things ; semblance is the work of man."   He may mean by this semblance the structural import of any perception ; but clearly as it stands the antithesis tells us nothing, for every sensation is a reaction of our organism. His rhetoric expresses in striking phrases what we commonly assume, but does not help us to justify it,   " In the eye and ear aggressive matter is already hurled back from the sense,

and the object is set at a distance from us, while in the animal
senses we are directly in contact with it." [1]   Here no attempt
is made to point out in what characteristic of sensations the
"form" resides, and what constitutes their "reality," The
distinction between the æsthetic and the non-æsthetic senses,
which was accepted as a fact by Plato's time, is simply assumed by Schiller.

The Play-
impulse.

b. The idea of the play-impulse is also obtained
through a rhetorical development of suggestions
made by Kant.   It springs from his constant use
of the term "play," to indicate the free action of the faculties
in harmony which constitutes æsthetic judgment, and consequently to denote any mode of succession in time in which
such sensations as those of music or colour present the charm
of art.

In its simplest form, according to the account elaborated by
Schiller, which strikingly anticipates the ideas of Mr. Herbert
Spencer,[2] the play-impulse is the mere discharge of accumulated energy which demands a vent.   " The animal plays
.   .   .   when the superfluity of life pricks itself into activity."
In a higher phase it may be said to arise when man awakes
to the pleasure of seeing for its own sake.[3]   When he has
thus noted the "form" or "semblance," it is only one step
further to confer independence on it by imitation.   No doubt
the anthropological sequence is wrong at this point ; imitation
is much older than conscious enjoyment of form ; but it is
plain that the connection which Schiller insists on is real, and
the only difficulty is the eternally recurrent one of distinguishing degrees of consciousness in a developing activity.   At
every point the play-impulse and the imitative or dramatic
tendency—the tendency to enjoy simulation or semblance—
are closely connected, and it seems true that in all games and
amusements there is involved a certain mimicry of life.[4]

Schiller's further account of the growth of art and the
feeling for beauty, as the play-impulse gradually filling up its
empty sense of freedom with a content of expression, is full of

[1] *Br.*, 26.
[2] *Br.*, 27.   Cf. H. Spencer, *Psychology*, ii. 627.   Was Schiller the "German
author" there mentioned ?
[3] *Br.*, 26.
[4] *Br.*, 15.   Cf. Prof. Brown, *The Fine Arts*, Pt. I.

suggestions which later theory has realised, more particularly as to the aspect which seems most alien to the play-idea pure and simple—the nature of the beautifying instinct as applied to objects of use or necessity. " What [1] he (man just passing from sensuous to æsthetic ' play') possesses, what he produces, must no longer bear merely the traces of utility, the over-careful impress of a purpose ; [2] besides the service, for which it exists, it must also reflect the ingenious understanding which contrived it, the loving hand which executed it, the free and cheerful mind which chose and set it up to look at. . . . Even his weapons are no longer to be objects of terror only, but they are to give pleasure also, and the cunningly wrought sword belt claims no less attention than the mortal edge of the sword." [3]

Finally the history of the play-impulse develops into an analysis of the social character of art, resting ultimately upon ideas thrown out by Kant in connection with social interest in beauty,[4] and the essential communicability of æsthetic feeling. " We cannot universalise either our sensuous or our intellectual pleasures, for the former are essentially individual, the latter neglect the deep-seated bases of personality. In beauty alone we are at once the individual and the race ; it can make the whole world happy, and every being forgets its limitations while under the spell of the beautiful. [5]

The defect of a play-theory of the beautiful is its tendency to cut life in two between work and play. " Ernst ist das Leben, heiter ist die Kunst " is a jarring sentiment, unless we interpret it so largely that the natural associations of the words are gone. Towards such a theory Schiller seems at times to be drifting [6] under stress of the metaphor which he adopts. The two real links between beauty and the play-impulse are

---

[1] *Br.*, 27.

[2] It is easy to see how in every phrase Schiller's rhetoric rests upon Kant's logic.

[3] See Mr. W. G. Collingwood's *Philosophy of Ornament* for a sketch and appreciative account of the reindeer dagger-haft of the Dordogne.

[4] *Krit d. U.*, sect. 41, where most of Schiller's account of progressive refinement is anticipated.

[5] *Br.*, 27, Cp.
　　　　" Deine Zauber binden wieder
　　　　　Was die Mode streng getheilt."
　　　　　　　　—From Schiller's *Hymn to Gladness.*

[6] E.g. *Br.*, 15, end

their common freedom from practical ends, and their common
tendency to simulation or, in the very largest sense, the ideal
treatment of reality.   In other respects "play" suggests to
us amusement and the relaxation of our faculties, and seems
not to do justice to the serious need of self-utterance, nor to
the element of expressiveness involved in all work in which
the craftsman has any degree of freedom.   The play-impulse
is in short only æsthetic where its primarily negative freedom is charged with a content which demands imaginative
expression ; and any impulse which takes such a form is
æsthetic, whether or no it chances to remind us of "play."

Thus "the Kantian Schiller,"[1] by his enthusiasm no less
than by his genius, has not only affirmed the objectivity of
the beautiful, but has vindicated its place and value in the
evolution of civilised man.   By so doing he followed and
also stimulated the growing tendency to understand by
objectivity and truth something more than mere fact and
correctness, and to find the truest reality in that which has
a meaning and a causal influence within the sphere of human
life.

Opposition of   2. Having recognised the beautiful as a real
"Antique" and expression of man's being, uniting the extremes
"Modern."   of his mind, and continuous from the first dawn
of civilisation, Schiller could hardly avoid directing his attention to the contrast of the antique and the modern which
seemed to contradict this continuity.   Such a contrast, we
saw in chapter 9, was the historical or actual shape in which
the inherent dualism of man's nature forced itself on the
attention of an age which had become aware of the past.
From the time of Dante downward, some kind of answer had
been demanded to the question, whether the life of antiquity
rested on the same principles as that of the modern world, or
on better, or on worse.   As knowledge was gathered and
free intelligence awoke, the consciousness of this antagonism
became more profound, and the efforts to resolve it more
adequate.   In the chapter referred to, I attempted to give
some picture of the process by which the common humanity
of the ancient world revealed itself to the modern, more
especially through literature to Lessing and through plastic
art to Winckelmann.   I endeavoured to show that each of

---

[1] Hartmann, *Æsth.*, i. 24.

these great interpreters, though in some degree taken captive by the objects of his study, and inclined to ascribe
finality to their temporary conditions, nevertheless found
within these limits enough significance and variety to suggest the relativity of the beautiful to human nature, and the
interpretation of its oneness in accordance with that relativity. The work of scholarship and archæology was tending,
as we saw, in the same direction. But yet on the whole, before Lessing's death, the reaction of the later Renaissance was
hardly spent. The pseudo-Hellenic tradition, though widened
and humanised into a genuine Hellenic enthusiasm, still
imposed upon the age. "Gothic" art was not understood.
Lessing's Aristotelian defence of Shakespeare operated to
reinforce as well as to deepen the principles of classical
taste. It was not till the age of genius against which Lessing so hotly protested, that the full meaning of modern art
came home to the German mind. Goethe, as Bernays says,
"liberated the century."

Besides the definite influences which have been mentioned,
the French revolution was filling the air with electricity.
"Freedom" was a word with a meaning in 1795, and the
work of Kant, Schiller, and their successors, in bringing
down freedom from a metaphysical heaven to terrestrial life,
had an import for their contemporaries which we are apt to
forget.

Did the principles of beauty as hitherto understood, according to the tradition of the Renaissance gradually widening
into a true Hellenic sympathy—did these principles fairly
cover the æsthetic judgments and productions of that tumul-
tuous age? It is interesting to note in the words of Goethe
how this antagonism took form in the intercourse between
Schiller and himself.[1]

"How curious it was [Schiller's relation to Kant] appeared
fully when my connection with Schiller became animated.
Our conversation dealt entirely with our work or with
theory, usually both together ; he preached the gospel of
freedom, I defended the rights of nature from curtailment.
Out of goodwill to me, perhaps, rather than from conviction,
he refrained from treating the good mother (Nature) in the
Æsthetic letters with the unkind expressions which made the

---

[1] "*Einwirkung d. neueren Philosophie*," *Werke*, xxx. 341.

paper 'Anmuth u. Würde'[1] so odious to me. But as I on
my side obstinately and perversely extolled the advantages
of the Greek mode of poetry, and of that founded upon it or
derived from it, and not only so, but asserted that manner to
be the exclusively right and desirable one, he was forced
to more precise reflection, and it was to this very dispute
that we owe the treatise, *Ueber naive u. sentimentale Dichtung.*[2] The two modes of poetry, he concluded. were to be
co-ordinate and acknowledge each other's claims

"By this he laid the first foundation of the whole new
development of Æsthetic ; for ' Hellenic ' and ' Romantic,'
and any other synonyms that may have been invented, are
all derivable from that discussion, in which the original question had concerned the predominance of real, or of ideal
treatment."

Kant in his "Observations" briefly describes the "Naive"[3]
as "the noble and beautiful simplicity which bears the impress of Nature, and not of Art."   This rather than the fuller
account in the *Critique of the Power of Judgment*, was adopted
by Schiller as the point of departure for his distinction.   In
both cases, however, Kant is referring primarily to social
intercourse.   Schiller on the contrary, applying the idea
within the limits of Art, is obliged in some degree to modify
its relation to Nature.   The root of his antithesis is expressed
when he says that the poet either *is* Nature or *seeks* Nature ;
the former is the Naive and the latter the Sentimental poet.[4]
But the sense in which a poet can *be* Nature is doubtful, and
the poles of the contrast tend to approximate.   For if the
Naive means an intentional and conscious self-identification
with Nature—and in Art it must tend to that meaning—it at
once becomes difficult to distinguish from sentimentality, and
the two are at least co-ordinate if not identical.   This is certainly true of the *sense of the Naive* which Schiller traces in
the decadence of art and among the most artificial nations,
e.g. the French.   Such a sense is a species of the sentimental,
and so far we are off the track of the distinction between
ancient and modern.

But in spite of this difficulty Schiller succeeds by a really
brilliant critical enquiry in establishing a difference, within the
region of art, between Nature at first hand and Nature at

---

[1] 1793 (?).   [2] 1795–6.   [3] *W.*, iv. 420.   [4] *W.*, xii. 231.

second hand. There was, he points out, among the Greeks, little sentimental interest in external Nature—the purest case of the natural. Their unity with the world did not admit of reflection. Even in dealing with man they show an analogous freshness and directness. Schiller's comparison[1] of the meeting between Glaucus and Diomede in the *Iliad* with that between Ferrau and Rinaldo in Ariosto, is as felicitous as any example in Lessing or in Matthew Arnold. The principle of the implied antithesis is obvious, and forms the basis of all later dealing with the history of art. We shall have to dwell upon it in treating of Schelling and Hegel, and need not therefore discuss it here.

That however there are modern "naive" poets Schiller himself points out, having Goethe among others in his mind ; and he adds that they are exceedingly inconvenient to criticism by confounding all its distinctions. They do in fact point to a higher unity, of which Schiller gives no sufficient account, beyond the schism of merely romantic art. But his primary idea could not be better illustrated than by his confession of his own early difficulties in appreciating Shakespeare. "When[2] at a very early age I first became acquainted with him, I was indignant at his coldness, his insensibility, which permitted him to jest in the moments of highest emotion, to let the clown break in upon the most heart-rending scenes in Hamlet, Lear, Macbeth. . . . Misled by my acquaintance with recent poetry so as in every work to look first for *the poet*, to meet him heart to heart, and to reflect with him upon his object, in short to look at the object only as it is reflected in the subject, I found it intolerable that here the poet never showed himself and would never let me question him. . . . *I was not yet capable of understanding Nature at first hand.* I could only endure the picture of it as reflected through the understanding, and to that end the French sentimental poets and the Germans from 1750–1780 were the right people for me." Here we trace the connection of Naive and Realistic, Sentimental and Idealistic treatment, which is emphasised elsewhere in the treatise, and which Goethe, as we saw, considered to have been its starting-point. We may add, to show that the principles affecting poetry and other art were closely connected in Schiller's mind,

---

[1] *W.*, xii. 226.   [2] *Ib.*, 226.   Schasler, 1. 635.

that in a criticism on an exhibition of pictures upon set subjects which Goethe had initiated he writes as to "The other German attribute, of sentimentality," "A tearful Hector and a melting Andromache were to be feared, and they are not absent." [1]

The ancients, he concludes, were great by limitation, the moderns by infinity, a distinction verbally reproduced by Schelling and possessing the same importance for later philosophy as the contrast of "naive" and "sentimental" itself, which it simply reiterates in a generalized technical form. The advance made by Schiller consisted in placing the antique and modern principles on an equality, as stages in a natural evolution.   His predecessors had not fairly and fully admitted the difference between them, but even when they recognised the greatness of the moderns, had endeavoured to force them into the mould of the ancients.   It was Schiller who inaugurated the idea that it is not necessary to reduce differences to a vanishing point in order to assert continuity of principle.

Schlegel on   3. The treatise on naive and sentimental poetry
Schiller.   soon produced its effect.   In 1797 there appeared Fr. v. Schlegel's Essays on the Study of Greek Poetry,[2] with a preface, which, referring to Schiller's treatise, declared that the principles of objective beauty could not be held to apply to modern poetic art.   For, in defiance of the maxim that beauty must give a disinterested pleasure, the poet now relies on subjective fascination, poetic "effect," and an interest in the existence of the ideal ; these are his essentially "sentimental" characters.   It will at once be seen that Kant's abstraction from positive content, by which he set down a relation to the ideal as impurity in æsthetic judgment, here recoils on the theory of the beautiful with destructive effect.   Schlegel further points out that the sentimental mood becomes poetry only through the characteristic, that is, through the representation of what is individual.   Otherwise, I presume he must mean, it can have no plastic or structural form adequate to the depth of individual emotion which is its material. Thus Greek Tragedy, he thinks, might claim the title of objective, as conforming to the accepted canons of a beautiful whole ; while Shakespearian tragedy, "which organises

---

[1] *W.*, xii. 388.   [2] *W.*, 5.

out of sentimental and characteristic elements a self-complete and perfectly self-dependent interesting whole," should go by the name of "interesting tragedy." This name is therefore intended by Schlegel to take the art to which it applies out of the category of beauty as determined by Kant and by the lovers of antiquity. Whether such an exclusion was substantially justified by Kant's theory is another question. It is not certain that Shakespearian tragedy implies even an interest in the reality of an ideal in the sense which Kant considered extra-æsthetic. It may be doubtful whether Schlegel clearly appreciated the distinction between pleasure in æsthetic semblance and pleasure in the reality of objects or ideals, the latter of which alone is to be considered an unæsthetic interest. Rightly or wrongly, however, Schlegel, in handling this distinction borrowed from Schiller, ranks Shakespeare, not like Schiller, with the ancients, but as the very centre and standard-bearer of the moderns. It seems plain, as hinted above, that both critics are right. Shakespeare points to a modern art which shall transcend romantic dualism and again be classical.

In this same volume, for the first time in the history of æsthetic, mention is made of the "Theory of Ugliness."[1] Beauty is defined as "the pleasant manifestation of the good"; ugliness as "the unpleasant manifestation of the bad." We must suppose that an unpleasant manifestation of the good and a pleasant manifestation of the bad are taken to be impossible. The attempt is thus made to regard ugliness as wholly outside beauty and corresponding to it as its embodied negation. But Schlegel soon finds that the positive embodiment of a negation is a troublesome conception to handle,[2] and that in as far as it is positive the intensest ugliness will need the very greatest powers to represent it, and will always contain elements of the beautiful. The distinction which might meet this obvious difficulty does not seem to occur to him. The positive negation will be, so we should say, in some degree a confusion—a parody or perversion of the type of beauty to which it is correlative.

Schiller on Schlegel. 4. The very inconsistency however of Schlegel's suggestions makes them an indication of a rapid revolution, both in taste and in theory. A remarkable

---

[1] *W.*, 5, p. 147.   [2] P. 151.

letter from Schiller to Goethe[1] shows the effect, probably of
this very work of Schlegel, on the further history of the problem.   Schiller will not put up with the dualism which
(exaggerating his own antithesis) modern writers are labour-
ing to introduce ; but yet he is so far impressed by their
contention that he is inclined to abandon the term beauty
altogether, and choose another word of less narrow associations.   I quote the entire passage.

" I fancy that this would be the right moment to pass in
review the works of Greek art, in the light of the idea of the
characteristic ; for Winckelmann's and Lessing's conception is
still generally prevalent, and our most recent writers on
æsthetic, dealing with poetry as well as with sculpture, take
endless pains to liberate Greek beauty from all traces of the
characteristic, and to make this latter the distinctive mark of
modern art.   I think the recent æsthetic writers, in their
struggles to separate the idea of beauty and present it in a
certain purity, have pretty nearly hollowed it out, and turned
it into an empty sound.   The opposition between the beautiful and the correct or true ['Treffende'] has been pushed
much too far, and a demarcation which only the philosopher
is in the habit of making (and which is only justifiable in one
aspect), has been accepted far too coarsely.

" Many, again, make another kind of mistake, in referring
the idea of beauty far too much to the content of the work of
art instead of to the treatment of it ; and then of course they
must be puzzled when they have to comprehend under the
same idea of beauty the Apollo of the Vatican and other
figures like it, of which the content is enough to make them
beautiful, with the Laocoon, or a Faun, or other painful or
ignoble representations.

" As you know, the same is the case with poetry.   How
people have toiled and are still toiling to justify the crude and
frequently low and ugly realism [' Natur,' the natural facts,
whether of man's behaviour, or of other kinds] of Homer and
the tragedians, in consonance with the idea they have formed
of Greek beauty.   I wish some one would at last venture to
dismiss from circulation this idea and the word beauty itself,
to which all those false notions are, in fact, inseparably

---

[1] *Br.-wechsel*, 3. 158.   July, 1797.

attached, and, as is reasonable, to set up in its place *truth* in the completest sense of the word."

Truth, of course, is not here to be taken in an intellectual sense. The "Kantian" Schiller knows better than that. What the passage means is, first, that he is quite sure that the pseudo-classical idea of beauty cannot be stretched so as to cover romantic art; and secondly, looking back upon Greek art in the light of romanticism, he is inclined to believe that even for it the current idea of the beautiful is much too narrow. Therefore he thinks a new term must be chosen, which merely indicates the need of expression and of a matter to be expressed, and he sees that this characteristic matter will be found among the Greeks as in modern art. Now that the valuable quality of art, whether we call it "beauty" or by some other name, is understood to be a necessary and objective expression of human life and the unity of nature, there is no reason for trying to narrow the scope of its manifestations. And therefore the thinker who was the first to proclaim its concrete objectivity was also the first who in set terms discarded all formal and traditional limitations to the compass of its unity.

In the realm of formative art and of music Schiller had no special powers of appreciation. He made no positive contribution to the theory of specific arts[1] or of their relations with each other. His sympathy for landscape seems not to have been wider than that of his generation.[2] He treats a thunderstorm,[3] with its gloom abruptly broken by lightning, as a case of the ugly whose effect is sublime or rather exalting (" Erhebend"). He restricts the conception of grace to movements of the human form.[4] He does not give important aid even in the discrimination of particular forms of poetry. He pronounces the plot of Corneille's *Cid* undoubtedly the best in literature because it demands no wickedness.[5] His real achievement lay in the sphere of the general principles of poetic fancy which are the foundation of all the individual arts and are profoundly connected with the springs of life and thought.

---

[1] See Schasler, 1. 626.
[2] See however the Review of Mattheson's poems, *W.*, xii. 343. Cf. Schasler, 1. 648.
[3] *W.*, xi. 570, 1.   [4] See Schasler, 1. 603.   [5] *W.*, xi. 543.

Goethe.   II. To the student of Goethe there will appear to be something like profanity in the attempt to confine his magnificent profusion of ideas within the limits of æsthetic formula. And it must clearly be understood that in the following pages there is no pretence of gathering the full harvest of his immense activity, but only an effort to insist upon some dominant convictions the importance of which is avouched by the whole course of his ideas concerning art and beauty. The English reader who turns hopefully, for an appreciation of Goethe's æsthetic position, to the most recent and able historians among his countrymen, will experience a sharp disappointment. By common agreement he is treated as a popular writer of the school of Winckelmann, and thus finds no place at all in Hartmann's post-Kantian history,[1] while in Schasler[2] and Zimmermann[3] alike he is divorced from Schiller and annexed to Mengs and Winckelmann as a pre-Kantian æsthetician. Such a view, though superficially favoured by the order of treatment which Hegel has adopted for a special purpose,[4] is absolutely at variance with chronology, with Goethe's fundamental ideas and his recorded judgment of his own relation to Kant,[5] and with his place as the central figure of that creative time, the last decade[6] of the eighteenth century, when the ideas of a new philosophy were forged by co-workers whose individual contributions can hardly be distinguished to-day.

The ground of these contradictory estimates is very simple, and forms a convenient introduction to the study of Goethe's conceptions. Winckelmann, of course, detected the inevitable impact of expression upon beauty. By insisting upon all that we now understand as "expression" it is verbally possible to find in him a doctrine of the significant or characteristic, which in reality he did but apprehend darkly and remotely. Now there is no doubt at all that Goethe's reflections upon beauty and especially upon art are centrally determined by the anti thesis of beauty in the narrower sense and significance or

---

[1] v. Hartmann, *Æsth.*, i. Einl. vii.
[2] *Krit. G. d. A.*, i. 494.
[3] *Aesth.*, i. 355.
[4] *Ib.*, i. 24.
[5] *Einwirkung d. neueren Philosophie, W.*, 30. 340.
[6] *Ib.*, " Diese für mich so bedeutende Epoche, das letzte Zehnt des vergangenen Jahrhunderts."

character.   It is therefore possible to speak of him as dealing with Winckelmann's problem and nothing more.

But such a view neglects the whole essence of the matter. Winckelmann started from abstract beauty, but was compelled, by his historical knowledge and sympathy, to supplement it by a graded intrusion of the expressive, which though necessary to the beautiful, increases as true beauty diminishes. He remained almost wholly within the domain of plastic art, having just a word to say on painting, but not a word on music or poetry.   But Goethe, if he dealt with similar elements, *approached them in the reverse order*.   His point of departure was the idea of the characteristic as the excellent in art, that is to say, as the beautiful in the wider sense of the word which we have determined to adhere to.   This principle he supplemented at a later time by the limiting postulate of formal beauty, beauty in the narrower sense, chiefly as a safeguard against misunderstandings and eccentricities.   This reversal of Winckelmann's position is essential, not accidental. It was the outcome of the new organ of æsthetic perception which Winckelmann had helped to create, and the germ of a wider and deeper sense of beauty.   It originated in the defence of Gothic architecture against the effete pseudo-classical tradition, and was supported by the widest appreciation of painting, music, and poetry.   In technical philosophy its significance is quite unmistakable.   Beauty—the excellence revealed in art and æsthetic appreciation generally—is the datum to be analysed.   To assume the unanalysed datum, or its most formal analysis, as a principle, while confessing that another and a thoroughly concrete principle is perplexingly active within and outside it, is candid and suggestive, but logically impotent.   To identify the datum with a concrete principle which leads to a profound analysis, while admitting that there is still a border line at which a formal residue of the datum fails to be adequately explained, is a new step in scientific comprehension.   We will now consider Goethe's æsthetic convictions in the latter aspect.

Gothic
Architecture.   1. In 1773, twenty-four years before Hirt's famous article in *Horen* upon the Beautiful of Art as the Characteristic, there appeared a small, badly-printed, anonymous book,[1] *von Deutscher Art u. Kunst*, " On German

---

[1] Scherer, ii. 82

X

style and art." The authors were Möser, Herder, and Goethe. The contribution of the latter was the short paper, " Deutsche Baukunst," "German architecture," which in spite of an excess in youthful rhetoric—Goethe was only twenty-four when it was published—is perhaps the profoundest æsthetic utterance of the eighteenth century. For in it we have the germ of those ideas which were to find their full expression eighty years after in the chapter, " On the Nature of Gothic," in Mr. Ruskin's *Stones of Venice.* I fear that the indifference of our philosophic historians to the former utterance is but too well explained by their unfamiliarity with the latter, and all that it implies. The relation of all work to the life of the individual workman is not indeed insisted on by Goethe, but the point of view which he adopted was one in which this relation was necessarily involved. I will make a few extracts from this short paper, which does not, so far as I am aware, exist in an English translation. The points to be noted for our theoretical purpose are :—

i. The writer's attitude towards the pseudo-classicism of the late Renaissance.

ii. The sympathy for "Gothic" architecture, and criticism of the kind of disparagement which the name implies.[1]

iii. The indication of a theory of characteristic art.

I will arrange the quotations under these three heads. The subject of the paper is Strasburg cathedral.

Attitude to the Renaissance Tradition. i. " ' It is in petty taste,' says the Italian, and passes by. ' Quite childish,' lisps the Frenchman, and triumphantly taps his snuff-box à la Grecque. What have you both done, that you should despise it ?

Has not the genius of the ancients, arising from their grave, cast yours into captivity? You crawled under the mighty ruins to steal their proportions, you built your patchwork palaces with the sacred fragments, and deem yourself custodian of the arcana of art, because you can give account of colossal buildings by inch and line. If you had felt more than measured, if you had caught the spirit of the masses which astounded you, you would not simply have copied, because they did it, and it is beautiful ; you would have made your designs necessary and true, and living beauty would have sprung from them with creative power.

---

[1] Cf. *Stones of Venice*, vol. ii " On Nature of Gothic."

" So you have painted your wants with a show of truth and beauty. The splendid effect of the columns impressed you; you wanted to have columns too, and you built them into walls; you wanted to have colonnades, and you surrounded the forecourt of St. Peter's Church with marble passages which lead nowhere, so that mother Nature, who detests and despises the useless and unnecessary, impelled your populace to prostitute them to public cloacæ, till you avert your eyes and hold your nose before the wonder of the world.

" All this goes on its way; the artist's whim serves the rich man's caprice; the tourist stares, and our *beaux esprits*, called philosophers, elaborate their art-principles and art-histories out of protoplastic fables, while true men are murdered by the evil genius in the forecourt of the mysteries." [1] . . .

" . . . The column [2] is in no sense an element of our dwellings; it contradicts the essence of all our buildings. Our houses do not arise out of four columns at four corners; they arise out of four walls on four sides, which serve instead of columns, exclude columns, and, where you add them, make them a burdensome superfluity." " Beware of dishonouring the name of your noblest artist, and hasten to contemplate his excellent work. If it gives you an unpleasing impression, or none at all, why then fare you well; harness your horses and away to Paris!" We trace in all this the same coincidence of genuine racial art-feeling and regrettable national antagonism which so strongly influenced Lessing. It was inevitable that the modern spirit should grow fierce as it turned against the tradition which fettered it in every movement. We saw before that St. Peter's has always been a touchstone of Renaissance feeling. Goethe cannot have been the first hostile critic, for at this time he had not seen Rome, and his information must have been drawn from other writers. But his readiness to blaspheme is a striking sign of the times.

"Gothic" as a disparaging term. ii. " When I first went to see the cathedral, my head was full of general conceptions of good taste. I reverenced, from hearsay, harmony of masses and purity of form, and was a sworn foe to the confused caprices of Gothic decoration. Under the rubric 'Gothic,' like an article in a dictionary, I had collected all the mistaken

---

Winckelmann was murdered 1768.
Directed against the Abbé Laugier, Scherer, vol. ii., " Goethe."

synonyms that had ever come into my head, 'undefined, disordered, unnatural, a heap of odds and ends, patchwork, overloaded.' No wiser than a people that called the whole world 'barbarians' I called everything Gothic that did not fit my system, from the elaborate doll and image work with which our bourgeois aristocracy decorate their houses, to the grave remains of old German architecture, which in view of a few bizarre curves, I censured to the old tune as 'Quite overloaded with ornament'; and so, on my way, I shuddered at what I expected to see, a misformed, curly-bristled monster.

"How unexpected was the feeling with which the sight amazed me, when I stood before the building. My soul was filled by a great and complete impression, which because it was composed of a thousand harmonious details, I was able to taste and enjoy, but in no way to understand and explain. How constantly I returned to enjoy this half-heavenly pleasure, to comprehend in their work the giant-spirit of our elder brothers! . . . How often has the evening twilight interrupted with friendly rest the eye fatigued by its exploring gaze, when the countless parts melted into complete masses, which, simple and great, stood before my soul, and my powers arose gladly at once to enjoy and to understand. . . . How freshly it greeted me in the morning brilliance, how gladly I observed the great harmonious masses, vitalised in their numberless minute parts, as in the works of eternal nature, down to the smallest fibre, all of it form, and all bearing upon the whole; how lightly the enormous firm-based building rises into the air; how broken it is, and yet how eternal! . . . And so do I not well to be angry when the German art-scholar, giving ear to envious neighbours, mistakes his own advantage, and disparages this work with the unintelligible term 'Gothic,' when he should be thanking God that he is able to proclaim aloud, 'This is German building, *our* building, of which the Italians have none, still less the French.' And if you will not concede yourself this privilege, prove that the Goths really built like this, in which proof you will find some difficulty." . . . "But you, dear youth, shall be my companion, you who stand there in emotion, unable to reconcile the contradictions which conflict in your soul; who now feel the irresistible power of the great totality, and now chide me for a dreamer, that I see beauty, where you see only strength and roughness."

The continuation of the same passage suggests a general theory to justify this "perception of beauty" where others see only strength and roughness. The force of customary language takes Goethe back into the antithesis which he has just transcended. But we must bear in mind throughout that beauty in the largest sense always tends to coincide, as Goethe has just employed the term, with the whole excellence which belongs to fine art, *quâ* fine art, and is appreciated by æsthetic perception, *quâ* æsthetic. Even in Winckelmann we saw that "true" beauty falls outside that which is especially and distinctively called by the name of beauty, just as Goethe is about to oppose "true" and "great" art to "beautiful" art in the narrower sense.

"Characteristic" Art. iii. (Continued after "roughness" above.) "Do not let a misconception come between us ; do not let the effeminate doctrine of the modern beautymonger make you too tender to enjoy significant roughness, lest in the end your enfeebled feeling should be able to endure nothing but unmeaning smoothness. They try to make you believe that the fine arts arose from our supposed inclination to beautify the world around us. That is not true! For in the only sense in which it could be true it may be asserted by a citizen or artisan, but not by a philosopher." (The art-impulse, as Goethe is about to describe it, would be called an impulse to *beautify* things, only by those who include all formative work under beauty, as a citizen may the laying out of a new street, or an artisan the construction of a machine. Goethe's mood as here expressed is very complex ; he sympathises in substance with the "citizen," but yet feels that he can only make his point clear through the distinction, in itself objectionable, which the philosopher draws. Such, at least, appears to me the true meaning of the passage.)

"Art (he continues) is formative long before it is beautiful (fine), and yet is then true and great art, very often truer and greater than beautiful art itself. For man has in him a formative nature, which displays itself in activity as soon as his existence is secure ; so soon as he is free from care and from fear, the demi-god, active in repose, gropes round him for matter into which to breathe his spirit. And so the savage remodels with bizarre traits, horrible forms, and coarse colours, his "cocos," his feathers, and his own body. And though this imagery consists of the most capricious forms

yet, without relations of shape, its parts will agree together;
for a single feeling has created them into a characteristic
whole.

Now this characteristic art is the only true art.   When it
acts on what lies round it from inward, single, individual,
independent feeling, careless and even ignorant of all that is
alien to it, then whether born of rude savagery or of cultivated sensibility, it is whole and living.   Of this you see
numberless degrees among nations and individuals.   The
more that the soul rises to the feeling of those relations which
alone are beautiful and eternal, whose main chords can be
demonstrated, whose secrets can only be felt, relations in
which alone the life of the godlike genius rushes forth into
happy melodies ; the more that this beauty penetrates the
being of a mind, seeming to be of one origin with it, so that
the mind can tolerate nothing else, and produce nothing else ;
so much the happier is the artist. . . . Here stands his work ;
approach, and recognise the deepest feeling of truth and
beauty in relations issuing from a strong rough German soul,
on the narrow and gloomy sacerdotal arena of the middle
age."   And below, after attacking the affected and feeble
painting of his own days, "masculine Albert Dürer, whom
the moderns mock at, the most wooden of your forms please
me better."

Now it is true that this early love for Gothic buildings was
driven into the background in Goethe's mind by his inclination to "a more developed art" (that of the Greeks), as he
tells us in his autobiography[1] (1811).   This mention of the
subject, however, shows how near it was to his heart, for it
was in this particularly that his later life seemed to him to
link itself to the impulses of his early years.   The proverb,
"What we wish for in youth is given us abundantly in age,"
is verified for him by this connection.   Again, the order of
development in Faust must strike every one as analogous to
the poet's own history, the devotion to Helena being super-
imposed upon the basis of northern life, and leaving its influence behind when the contact ceases.

The approximation between art and science, by which, for
good and evil, Goethe was so greatly fascinated, consisted for
him in their common relation to the typical and the charac-

[1] *W.*, 17. 348.

teristic. The *Critique of the Power of Judgment*, with which alone of Kant's writings he really sympathised, confirmed his conviction of this affinity, and justified in his eyes the " restless impulse" which had always led him to search for the typical or the fundamental.[1] In all this his thought is close to the " characteristic," as understood by science as well as in art. Some genera of flowers, for example, seem to him full of character, others vaguely defined and characterless. His researches into the metamorphoses of plants were guided of course by ideas of an underlying type. It is quite plain that the import, character or significance, was always for Goethe the central point in any work which appealed to man, and even, though subject to a Kantian reservation, in any product of nature.

Definitions of Hirt and Meyer. 2. But it is quite in accordance with Goethe's dislike of the abstract and incomplete that we find the idea of the " characteristic," as a substantive principle of art, entering into æsthetic not through him, but through his friends Hirt, a critic, and Meyer, an artist, both travellers and learned in the facts of art, and both contributors to *Horen* [2] (1795–8).

Their opinions are adduced and criticised by Hegel in the Introduction to the *Æsthetic*.[3] Meyer who followed Goethe in a relative antagonism to Hirt, fancied that the view which he and Goethe shared was fundamentally different from that which Hirt maintained. But there is really no profound distinction between them, beyond the limitation retained by Goethe which we have already noticed, the super-addition of beauty to significance as a condition under which the latter must appear in art. Hirt, echoing Baumgarten, identified the beautiful with the perfect for eye or ear ; but he developed the idea of perfection into that of the intention of nature as expressed in generic or specific characters. Meyer, following Goethe, laid down that the principle of (ancient [4]) art was the significant, but the result of successful treatment was the

---

[1] " *Einw. d. n. Philos.*" and " *Anschauende Urtheilskr.*," *W.*, 30. 342 and 351.

[2] *Die Horen*, a review in which Schiller and Goethe co-operated. It was above the reading public at that time, and lived only three years.

[3] *Æsth.*, i. 23, E. Tr. 32 ff.

[4] See Schiller's letter above. Hirt's aggressive attitude had forced the question of the characteristic to be raised even about ancient art.

beautiful. Both of these formulæ, as Hegel points out, depend essentially on the relation of content to form and affirm to begin with that the excellence of art consists in expression adequate to a meaning. In describing the nature of this meaning there is, we find, a tendency of the extremes to meet, for characterisation which is merely generic or specific and not individual leans to the side of abstraction and classicism as against individualism and romanticism, and points back to Reynolds' arguments in favour of his grand style. And the postulate of "beauty in treatment" may indicate either that the individual is to be conventionalised, or that beauty can be found in individuality by those who have eyes to see. We shall find the antithesis more fully stated by Goethe himself, and need only note with regard to these minor writers that by contributing to *Horen*, and constantly supplying Goethe with material through private correspondence, they helped to animate the movement which during these years was communicating itself to the future leaders of philosophy.

Goethe's Analysis of the Excellent in Art. 3. The general results of this active epoch were summarised by Goethe in the dialogue, "The Collector and his Friends"[1] (1798), which exhibits his ideas in a form as nearly systematic as any that he cared to give them, and is the first attempt in the history of æsthetic to represent[2] the excellent in art as a concrete into which there enter many degrees and phases of expressiveness.

Hirt makes a mistake, Goethe writes[3] to Schiller in 1797, by not recognising that it would take his explanation as well as Winckelmann's *and* Lessing's, and many others, to define Art. But, so far, he is quite right, Goethe continues, in insisting on the characteristic and pathetic even in formative art. "The Collector and his Friends" is practically a dramatisation of the view taken in that letter, and consequently forms a discussion of opinions which I presume to be those of Hirt's paper in *Horen*,[4] and turns on a specific and a general question. The specific question arises out of Hirt's assertion that even in Greek art the characteristic is the dominant principle,

---

[1] "*Der Sammler u. die Seinigen*," *W.*, 24. 235.
[2] For Winckelmann hardly intends to attempt this, though he makes contribution to such a view.
    Br., *W.*, 3. 152.
[4] See p. 194 above on Hirt's later work.

and that no extreme of pain or horror is avoided in it; and refers to the conciliation of this account, which is not absolutely denied, with the views of Winckelmann and Lessing. The "character," it is urged on behalf of the Niobe group, appears "only in the most general lines which permeate the work like a spiritual skeleton." This metaphor of the skeleton or framework as the correlative of the characteristic is often in Goethe's mind, and points to an intolerable dualism between the characteristic and the beautiful. But it is not his only view. The general question dealt with in the treatise, starting from the relation of character and beauty, refers to the total synthesis of qualities demanded by the excellence of art. "Let an artist have wrought a bronze eagle which fully expresses the generic conception of the eagle (this is Hirt's narrow idea of the characteristic), and let him now desire to place it on the sceptre of a Zeus. Will it be suitable? No, it must have in addition what the artist imparted to the Zeus to make him a god.—I see, interrupts the "Characteristiker" (supposed, with reason, to represent Hirt); you are referring to the grand style of Greek art; but I only value it in as far as it is characteristic." In the remarkable passage which follows, Greek art is not, as the common view of Goethe would lead us to expect, treated as the highest possible. "It satisfies," he says, "a high demand; but not the highest." "The generic conception leaves us cold [this is the ordinary attitude towards Hirt's "characteristic," which shows how remote it was understood to be from the individual characterisation which we identify with romance and naturalism], the ideal [of the Greek grand style] raises us above ourselves; but we want more; we want to return to a full enjoyment of the individual, without letting go either the significant or the sublime. This enigma can be solved only by beauty; it gives life and warmth to the scientific [still thought of as distinguishing the 'characteristic']; and softens the significant and lofty; so that a beautiful work of art has gone through the whole cycle, and is again a sort of individual, which we are able to make our own."

Thus the characteristic and the ideal become individual through the fusing power of beauty. Goethe is here, as almost always, wavering between the conception of beauty as abstraction or omission, which at the bidding of some principle not clearly understood, softens or, too probably, enfeebles the harsh outlines of definite individuality, and a conception of it as depending on the insight which discovers in the strongest details of individual portraiture a forcible grace of their own. Goethe never wholly threw off the dualism implied in the former view.

At the close of the dialogue, those qualities of artists and art-judges, *i.e.* of æsthetic percipients, which have been noticed in the course of discussion, are finally reviewed one by one as essential elements in the excellence of art, and are then thrown into a tabular form, constructed so as to present an elaborate analysis of beauty in this its wider sense.[1]

In this scheme, each of three essential elements in the excellence of art—Art-truth, Beauty, and Finish,—is presented as the synthesis of two opposite qualities or tendencies, one of which is " serious," and the other " playful," while both are mere onesided *mannerism* as contrasted with their synthesis which alone can be called *style*. Thus Art-truth is the union of the purely imitative and the fanciful tendency, Beauty of the characteristic and the inclination to mere decorative curvilinear form (after Hogarth's theory), and Finish of "minute accuracy" and "expressive sketchiness." And further, Art-truth, Beauty, and Finish, must themselves be united in order to make up the excellence of art.

Here, it will be observed, we do not escape from the dualism involved in the appearance of beauty as contributory to that peculiar excellence of fine art, which must be set down as coincident with the beautiful in the widest sense. But yet the spell of a beauty that is devoid of content or defies analysis is now broken for ever. For the beauty constituted

---

[1] I transcribe the table with a translation in brackets.

Ernst allein (Serious only).	Ernst und Spiel verbunden (Serious and playful combined).	Spiel allein (Playful only).
Individuelle Neigung (Individual tendency).	Ausbildung in's Allgemeine (Formation of a quality having general value).	Individuelle Neigung (Individual tendency).
Manier (Mannerism).	Styl (Style).	Manier (Mannerism).
Nachahmer (Copyists).	Kunstwahrheit (Artistic truth).	Phantomisten (Capricious fancy).
Characteristiker (Artists who seize the essential characters).	Schönheit (Beauty).	Undulisten (Decorative grace; curvature).
Kleinkünstler (Minute pedants).	Vollendung (Finish, completion).	Skizzisten (Expression without completion.—Impressionist ?)

by Goethe's synthesis is not a limit that enfeebles expression, but the combination of two kinds of expressiveness, that is, of characterisation by essential attributes, and formal or decorative symbolism.

From such a construction of the idea of beauty it is only a step to regarding the other syntheses as subordinate to it no less than the factors of its own synthesis. In a theory of expression, taking account of its successive gradations, the general decorative principles or "curves of beauty," would rank lowest and condition all else; the "capricious fancy" devoid of substance and significance, would be considered as a mere failure to seize the import of things, and as possessing less content than the conscientious "copying" of nature, in which "pedantic minuteness" would be an aspect or element. And at a higher stage, as the first achievement of the penetrative imagination, the "impressionist sketch" would be considered to herald and precede the full grasp of "characteristic" reality in all its detail and with all its import. By some such modified presentation, which would not involve any considerable change of principle, we should obtain an anticipation in all essentials of the most recent analyses which deal with beauty according to its grades of symbolic or expressive power. The unimportant position assigned by Goethe to capricious fancy is especially noteworthy, as a criticism on the constantly recurring fallacies which confuse the imaginative with the fictitious.

The restriction of this dialogue to the arts of sculpture and painting enhances its value, because it was precisely in these arts that the principles of Lessing and Winckelmann, to which Goethe's letter referred, had their strongest hold, and if "the characteristic and pathetic" could be vindicated in this region, their recognition in the other arts would follow *a fortiori*. From this time forward beauty was necessarily considered in respect of its content, and formalistic theory, the acceptance of data of æsthetic enjoyment as ultimate, was, strictly speaking, an anachronism. Even the study of Winckelmann (1805) which Goethe began to prepare soon [1] after writing this dialogue, was mainly directed [2] to insisting on the organic evolution of art as an epoch-making discovery.

---

[1] 1799, *Br.*, *W.*, 5. 162.
[2] See p. 242 above.

Conclusion.   4. It was through the life-work of Goethe and
Schiller, and their many friends and contemporaries
—through the development of the Kantian æsthetic judgment, limited by abstraction and subjectivity, into an objective
concrete content which grows with the life and mind of man,
that the data of modern æsthetic were finally prepared for
incorporation in the answer to its problem.   Their revival
of the German theatre, as a form of art, gave the world little
of permanent value beyond the two parts of Faust; but their
reflective synthesis of the Greek and the Briton,[1] by which
they continued the work of Lessing, typifies the revolution
which I have attempted to trace in the principal spheres of
æsthetic appreciation.   If no new art crowned this revolution
—for music was not *directly* affected by it—yet a new philosophy did ; and it was amid the fermentation of this last ten
years, whose tendencies I have been attempting to sketch,
that the first great organic thinkers of the nineteenth century
gathered the convictions of their early manhood.

---

[1] Schiller's verses on the representation of Voltaire's Mahomet at Weimar.
See p. 238 *supra.*

CHAPTER XII.

OBJECTIVE IDEALISM.   SCHELLING AND HEGEL

Schelling.   I. "SCIENCE attained its absolute standpoint in Schelling's philosophy, and although art had previously begun to assert its peculiar nature and dignity in relation to the highest interests of humanity, yet it was now that the actual notion of art and its place in scientific theory were discovered."[1]

In Hegel's opinion, expressed in this passage, the true line of philosophical succession ran from Schiller to Schelling. Hegel himself was born in 1770, Schelling in 1775; but the younger of the two friends for some time took the lead, and was a professor lecturing to crowded audiences before Hegel's name began to be known.   From Hegel's correspondence with Schelling in 1795 we can see something of the intellectual excitement which the two friends shared under the influence of Kant, Fichte, and Schiller, whose Æsthetic letters in *Horen* for that year Hegel mentions as a masterpiece that had greatly delighted him.[2]   Taken in connection with these early letters, and with his own first essays in philosophy [3] wholly on the lines of Fichte, Schelling's important works of 1800 and 1802–3, the *System of the Transcendental Idealism* and the *Philosophy of Art*,[4] show conclusively how his mind was carried forward under Schiller's influence.   For Schelling continually refers to Schiller and Winckelmann, who furnished him with the objective material by which he enlarged into a historical and metaphysical theory the Kantian ideas respecting art as related to nature and to genius. which form at this time the framework of his thought.   The term "absolute,"

---

[1] Hegel's *Æsth.*, i. ; E. Tr., p. 120, and see ch. xi. above, p. 286.
[2] H.'s *Briefe*, 1. 16.
[3] 1794–5, *e.g. Vom Ich als Princip d. Philosophie.*
[4] The *Philosophy of Art* was delivered in lectures, but was not published till after Schelling's death.   Parts of it appeared in other lectures about 1802. See preface to vol. v. of the *Werke*.

and the idea of construing the objective unity, to which Kant
pointed, and which Schiller helped to substantiate, in terms
of an Ego, a principle somehow analogous with the "self"
as shown in will and knowledge, were drawn from Fichte.
Hegel, in one of the letters already alluded to, referring to
Schelling's earliest Fichtean tract, writes to him as follows,
"From Kant's system and its ultimate completion I expect a
revolution in Germany, which will start from principles already present and only needing to be worked out in general
bearings, and applied to all existing knowledge.   But there
will always be a kind of esoteric philosophy, and the idea of
God as the absolute Ego will belong to it."[1]   This is a fore-
boding of the identification which constitutes the stumbling-
block and the attraction of objective idealism, the identification
of the Deity with an immanent unity of things, not possessing
separate existence or personal self-consciousness.   For Fichte
this absolute unity was a phrase only ; its substance was to
be given by his successors.   Schelling, in attempting this
adventure, assigns to art and beauty as an objective synthesis
a position in the scheme of reality even higher than that
which subsequent theory concedes to them.

We shall sufficiently understand Schelling's place in the
general history of æsthetic if we briefly consider—

i. The objectivity which he ascribes to art and beauty in
its connection with his absolute standpoint.

ii. The dynamical and historical treatment of the antithesis
between ancient and modern life and art.

iii. His contributions to the estimate and classification of
the particular arts.

I purposely spoke of Schelling's place in the "general"
history of æsthetic.   His criticisms and appreciations of individual works of art, and of particular periods and tendencies,
are of too great mass to be at all thoroughly treated here.   It
is hard to say how much Hegel owes to him, or how far they
are both drawing from common sources among the data of
æsthetic.   The great treatise on the Philosophy of Art was
not published before Hegel's death, but he may have heard it
and would certainly hear about it, or meet with it in MS.,
when delivered as lectures in 1802 and after.   And many of
its ideas were made known in published papers and addresses.

---

[1] *Br.*, 1. 15 (1795).

There is very little in Hegel's *Æsthetic* which might not have been suggested, in however bizarre or negative a mode, by observation and theories that are to be found in Schelling.

Objectivity of Art and Beauty. i. If we bear in mind the essential ideas of Kant and Schiller, a few quotations from Schelling's *System of Transcendental Idealism* (1800) will show us how he took up their suggestions into an audacious theory.

"The whole system," he writes in the conclusion of this work, "falls between two extremes, of which one is denoted by the intellectual intuition [which Kant aims at], the other by the æsthetic intuition [the substance of Schiller's system]. What the intellectual intuition is for the philosopher, the æsthetic intuition is for his object. The former as merely necessary to the philosopher's peculiar tendency of mind, does not occur in the ordinary consciousness as such ; the latter, which is nothing but the intellectual intuition made universal or objective, at least *may* occur in every consciousness. From this it may be seen *that* and *why* philosophy as philosophy can never have universal validity.[1] The one thing to which absolute objectivity is given, is Art. Take away, it may be said, the objectivity of art, and it ceases to be what it is, and becomes philosophy ; give philosophy objectivity, and it ceases to be philosophy, and becomes Art. Philosophy, attains the highest, but it brings to that point, so to speak, only a fraction of the man. Art brings the whole man as he is to the cognition of the highest, and this is the eternal distinction and the marvel of art."[2]

"Every æsthetic production starts from an essentially infinite separation of the two activities [the conscious one of freedom, and the unconscious one of nature—drawn from Kant's treatment of Art in relation to Genius] which are separated in all free productions. But as these two activities are to be represented in the product as *in union*, this product represents an infinite in finite form. Now the infinite represented in finite form is Beauty. The fundamental character of every work of art, which comprehends in it the two former characters [infinite meaning and infinite reconciliation or satis-

---

[1] Plainly a reminiscence of Schiller's *Æsth. Br.*, 27 near the end on art as addressing the *whole* man. The superiority here assigned to art over philosophy is the distinctive point in which Hegel and Schelling differ. Cf. *Æsth.*, *Br.*, 15, and p. 295 *sup.*

[2] *Werke*, 3. 630.

faction—taken as = repose, a reference to Winckelmann] is therefore Beauty, and without beauty there is no work of art."[1] The subsequent passage, which Schasler[2] professes himself unable to understand, is a simple explanation, following Kant, of the sublime as a more purely subjective reconciliation than that embodied in beauty, depending on an effort of mind less directly prescribed by the object of perception[3] than is the case with the beautiful *par excellence*.

"The product of art," he says in another place, "is distinguished from the organic product chiefly in this, (*a*) that the organic being represents previous to separation what æsthetic production represents subsequently to separation but reunited; (*b*) that organic production does not issue from consciousness, and therefore not from the infinite contradiction[4] which is the condition of æsthetic production. The organic product of nature is therefore not necessarily beautiful."[5]— The last clause states a point of view distinctive of the time, which we are now tending to abandon. "But this unknown, which in this case (in art) brings into unexpected harmony the objective[6] and the conscious[6] activity, is nothing other than that Absolute [Schelling's footnote calls it "Das Urselbst," the fundamental self or unconscious but immanent principle of the world; the absolute ego of Hegel's letter above] which contains the universal ground of the pre-established harmony between the conscious and the unconscious."[7] He then connects the operation of the unconscious in art-production with Kant's doctrine of genius. The absolute has no existence apart from its expressions.

The place of art in Schelling's philosophy is sufficiently

---

[1] *W.*, 3. 620-1.

[2] *G. d. A.*, 2. 834.

[3] Kant, *K. d. U.*, p. 100.

[4] This recurring phrase "infinite contradiction" and "infinite reconciliation" or solution may be best understood by thinking of an attempt to bring disparate ideas and processes into terms of each other. The failure to do this is the "infinite contradiction," as *e.g.* moral action never quite satisfies the moral will. The "infinite reconciliation" is the discovery of an idea or process or product in which the disparates cease to diverge and are both of them "satisfied."

[5] *W.*, 3. 621.

[6] Kant's "Nature" and "Freedom," as before. This passage shows with striking clearness how his *postulate* of an underlying unity was developed by Schelling.

[7] *W.*, 3. 615.

indicated by these quotations, but one more may be added which sums up the whole matter in the most striking way.

" The system of knowledge is to be regarded as complete when it returns to its first principle, Transcendental Philosophy, therefore, is only complete when it can show the identity (*viz.* the principle that *the same* activity which is productive in action *with* consciousness, is productive in the world *without* consciousness)—the highest solution of its whole problem, *in its principle* (the Ego).

It is therefore postulated that this activity, conscious and unconscious at once, shall be shown in the subjective, *in consciousness itself.* Such an activity is the æsthetic activity alone, and every work of art can only be understood as the product of such a one. The ideal world of art and the real one of objects are therefore products of one and the same activity ; the coincidence of the two (the conscious and the unconscious) without consciousness[1] gives the real world, with consciousness the æsthetic world.

The objective world is only the primitive and still unconscious poetry of mind ; the universal organon of philosophy, and the keystone of its entire arch, is the philosophy of art." [2]

We have here before us in the plainest language both the " absolute standpoint " in philosophy and the new conception of art, to which Hegel points in his account of Schelling. His close relation to Kant and Schiller is evinced by every line of the passages from which my quotations are taken. We hear nothing as yet of the supra-sensuous and theosophic world of beauty, into which pseudo-Platonic abstractions Schelling fell in later years. We have nothing but the answer, in terms of Fichte and Schiller, to the Kantian demand for an underlying unity between nature and freedom. More especially we are to observe that the Absolute does not exist in the form of consciousness, except in the human race, and that the ideas or archetypes[3] are the particular forms in which it is revealed to æsthetic perception. Often we

---

[1] Coincidence of the conscious and unconscious activity without consciousness seems to mean that organic beings which end by being conscious, are built up causally without the operation of consciousness. In art, he says, the reverse is the case ; an unconscious product is consciously built up.

[2] *W.*, 3. 349.

[3] Urbilder.

might think that we are reading Schopenhauer.[1] The "Absolute" standpoint is what we more popularly call the modern standpoint. It negatives the idea of irrational conditions in causation—for rational conditions are merely the definite attributes of a systematic universe—of idle reservations in knowledge, or dualistic separation between the orders of things. It rests on the conviction of human freedom, not as alien to nature, but as rooted in the system to which nature belongs; not as supernatural therefore, but as natural. If Nature and Freedom are hostile or disconnected, the one is conditioned by the other. If they are expressions of the same principle, then their apparent contradictions are modes of co-operation, and each, as expressing the absolute whole which includes all conditions (*not*, which is abstract, undefined, and devoid of conditions) is itself absolute, or free from any interference other than that ultimately rooted in its own nature.

The free faith, courage, and enterprise, implied in such a standpoint are, historically speaking, characteristic of the modern spirit, and reach the extreme of audacity in many thinkers to whose views the philosophy of the Absolute, as they understand it, is in diametrical antagonism. But whatever may have been its follies and its extravagances, no misunderstanding is possible of the main tendency of objective Idealism, as we have watched it developing from Kant's tentative solution of the antithesis of the age. It simply consists in the vindication of concrete unity or rational system as the nature of the world in which we live. Inner and outer,[2] natural and supernatural, spiritual and material, are henceforward terms that have lost their meaning, except in reference to the higher and lower purposes of man. And the principal instrument in this revolution has been the growing belief in the objectivity of the æsthetic judgment, as a union of sense and reason.

Historical Treatment of "Ancient and Modern." ii. It has been said that the fundamental difference between ancient and modern philosophy lies in the fact that the one came before the other.

---

[1] *E.g. W.*, 3. 371. "Music is the archetypal rhythm of Nature and the Universe, which by means of this art breaks through into the world of secondary existence" (*der abgebildeten Welt*).

[2] Cf. Goethe's lines, "Ins Innere der Natur," especially the end,—
    "Vor allem doch zu prüfen ist
    Ob Kern du oder Schale bist."

The same is true of the general contrast between the antique and the modern. Thus the modern is never simple ; it is always, so to speak, on the top of something else ; always charged with a contradiction, with a reminiscence, in one word, with a history.

Schiller's analysis of the reflective spirit in the sphere of poetry[1] had done something to focus the growing sense of this peculiarity in a distinct conception of development. For Schelling, with his pronounced idea of an underlying unity, such a conception became a central problem of philosophy ; and with Schiller constantly before his mind, he persistently refers a whole nest of antitheses concerning the "ancient and modern" to a principle which he endeavours to expound in a highly abstract form.

In this abstract form the principle in question turns on the opposition between "Finite" and "Infinite." The demand, it is said, which was fulfilled by Greek mythology, was directed to the representation of the Infinite within the Finite, while that involved in Christianity is rather to subordinate the Finite to the Infinite.[2] Obviously, in giving a meaning to these highly formal antitheses, the application of which is in one writing actually reversed,[3] the whole question is, which are to be taken as the defining terms. And there is no doubt that however the expressions are arranged, the defining term is Finite for ancient mythology, and Infinite for Christianity. The intended contrast may be fairly paraphrased thus : that in the ancient world the intellectual or ideal import of objects or mythological persons was measured by the carrying capacity, so to speak, that is, by the power of adequate representation, inherent in such objects or persons as given to fancy or perception. The god, for example, meant no more than could fairly be taken as exhibited in the form attributed to him. The symbolism of spiritual things in sensuous forms was therefore adequate, but only by sacrificing range and depth in the spiritual things themselves. In the modern or Christian world, on the other hand, the intellectual or spiritual import is dominant, and refuses to be measured by the carrying capacity of any object or person presented to fancy

---

[1] Principally in the tract on *Naïve and Sentimental Poetry*, which Schelling quotes largely in the "Philosophy of Art."

[2] *W.*, 5. 430 ("The Philosophy of Art ").

[3] *W.*, 5., Preface.

or perception. The Christ, for example, or the Virgin Mary, suggests an inexhaustible wealth of spiritual ideas. Instead of an adequate symbolism there is, therefore, only an inadequate or suggestive symbolism, in other words, an allegory. This recurrent formula of finite and infinite, wherever it is used in Schelling with reference to the imaginative basis of art, seems to mean that in the one case the infinite (ideal) is narrowed down to the finite (sensuous), and in the other the finite (sensuous) is racked and stretched and brought to an expressiveness more like that of feeling and thought, to admit the import of the infinite (ideal). It is indeed painful to us, and we hold it false, when we are told that modern art is essentially allegory, which is the conclusion that Schelling draws from the entire subordination of symbol to import in the modern imagination. But we must recall what was said in the earlier chapters of this work respecting the power exerted by a profound import in exhausting the significance of the sensuous object on which it is imposed. In fact, art which is *in this strict technical sense* allegorical, by suggesting more than it can adequately convey, is not mechanical, arbitrary or conventional, which are the faults of common allegory, but is likely to strain every resource of natural expressiveness to the furthest limit, although, when all is done, more remains behind in the shape of mere suggestion.

In a lecture of the year 1802 (published 1803) "*On the historical construction of Christianity,*"[1] the same antithesis is stated in another form. Christianity is here contrasted with the Greek religion as the *historical* with the *natural* view of the universe. The conception is ultimately the same as that just examined. The modern man, it is maintained, has been taught to regard the universe as a moral kingdom,[2] a world of change and movement in which a power and unity is revealed, greater and more durable than any isolated manifestation of it. The divine itself is made known to him not as a permanent figure, but as a vanishing historical personage, whose abiding with the world is not sensuous but ideal. For the Greek, the gods were permanent objective parts of nature, and the world was a fixed system without essential movement or progression. Those who are familiar with the politico-ethical

---

[1] *W.*, 5. 286 ff.
[2] All this seems suggested by Kant's *Religion innerhalb der Grenzen d. R. V.*

standpoint of Plato and Aristotle will feel the profound justice of these ideas.[1]   The notion of a world-evolution was wholly alien to the Greeks.   We on the contrary, it is urged by Schelling, are in our whole life founded on history.   And history belongs to the world of mind, not to the world of nature.   The entire medium and texture of modern life is thus ideal in the sense that it is charged with traditions, and principles, and conceptions of a moral or providential order, interwoven in human history, in which we recognise that man has his being.   Obviously this contrast has only a relative truth. We deny to the Greek a historical consciousness because his historical consciousness is lost to us.   Yet after all it remains true that he lived by sight and we live by faith.   The mere fact that his life lies at the root of ours is enough to produce this result.   The medium of our life is succession, that of his life was coexistence.   And succession can be a medium of life only through ideas.   For the Christian, history is the symbol of God.[2]   The effect of such a conception on the theory of art is to exhibit modern beauty as charged with a burden of ideal meaning which is hostile to the simpler forms of sensuous expression, and taxes to the utmost the capacities of the most varied and flexible media.

And more strictly within the field of art we find the same principle applied by Schelling in the remarkable paper "On Dante in a philosophical aspect."[3]   This paper was the basis of my treatment of Dante in ch. vii., and it is now only necessary to point its reference to Schelling's view of modern art.   The contrast of finite and infinite or of nature and history becomes, in its application to the particular work of art, the contrast of genus and individual.   The "subjectivity" forced upon the modern mind by its reflective and historical basis asserts itself in art as individuality, whereas in the Greek world expression was abstract, "exemplary" or typical, and the utterance rather of the racial than of the individual genius.   This conception is no doubt suggested or reinforced by Wolf's treatment of the Homeric poems as a racial rather than an individual achievement.

The law of modern poetry, till the great modern epic shall

[1] See Newman's *Introduction to Ar. Politics*, conclusion.
[2] Cf. the Erdgeist's song in *Faust*.
[3] 1802-3, *W.*, 5. 152.

be written, [1] is, Schelling writes, [2] in the paper on Dante, "that
the individual shall form into a whole that portion of the world
which is revealed to him, and shall create his mythology for
himself out of the material of his time, its history and its
science.   For as the ancient world was universally the world
of genera, so is the modern world that of individuals ; in the
former the universal is really the particular, the race acts
as an individual (Wolf's theory of the Epos) ; in the latter,
on the contrary, the starting point is the particular, which
necessarily *becomes* universal.   In the former, for this very
reason, everything is permanent, imperishable ; number has,
so to speak, no power, as the universal idea coincides with
that of the individual ; in the latter, change and movement
are the abiding law ; no closed circle, but only one extensible
to infinity by means of individuality can contain its principles.
And because universality belongs to the essence of poetry,
it is a necessary requirement that through the height of
peculiarity the individual should again become of universal
import, and through the completeness of particularity should
again become absolute.   It is through this character of absolute individuality, of utter incomparability with everything
else, which his poem possesses, that Dante is the creator of
modern art, which cannot be conceived apart from this arbitrary necessity and necessary arbitrariness."

The individual, it will be observed, has in the modern world
to create his own mythology.   The belief expressed elsewhere[3]
that "Natur-philosophie" is the first adumbration of the future
world-mythology, may be taken as an anticipation of the
Modern Painters, in as far as the essence of the latter work
is to disclose the rational and symbolic content of natural
phenomena.   In affirming, therefore, that mythology is necessary to Art, Schelling is only demanding a certain range of
fancy, organised in terms relevant to the expressive powers of
particular arts, and possessed of a certain universal recognition
or validity   Shakespeare, for example, he regards as having
created his own mythology.[4]   Mythology which is *used*, as

---

[1] *I.e.* a poem that shall summarise the modern world and be its single work,
as Homer was that of the early Greek world.   The idea that we are now in
the "rhapsode" stage, the stage of utterance which will one day make up a
whole, is plainly a bizarre application of Wolf's ideas.

[2] *W.*, 5. 154.   [3] *Ib.*, 443–5 ("Philosophy of Art").   [4] *Ib.*, 445.

the antique mythology in modern poetry, he sets down as
sheer frigid formalism.[1]

The qualities of modern sentiment and imagination, which
all these antitheses are intended to embody, stand in essential
relation to the comparative importance and elaboration of
different species of art in ancient and in modern times. The
sensuous vehicles of artistic expression have different capacities and are appropriate to different modes of feeling and
utterance. Therefore the classification of the several arts is
in immediate dependence on the view adopted as to the line
of progress which is to be ascribed to æsthetic imagination
and sensibility. It is very remarkable that Schelling's general
definition of beauty[2] coincides with the formula which he
applies to ancient imagination in contrast with modern—"the
presentation of the infinite within the finite." It is clear, from
what has been said, that this formula must be interpreted so
as to include both sides of the antithesis, with one side of
which it is at first sight identical. Modern beauty is still the
presentation of the infinite in the finite, but in it the finite, as I
endeavoured to explain, is both degraded into an inadequate
symbol, and is also racked and burdened to the uttermost, so
that it may take on something of the character of the infinite
which it has to express. It agrees with the whole course of
our inquiry to find that, in a natural and unsophisticated sense,
antique beauty and beauty proper coincide, while in order to
bring modern beauty under the head of beauty proper the
defining term needs a good deal of interpretation.

The Particular   iii. In the discourse "on the relation of For-
Arts.   mative Art to Nature,"[3] Schelling brings together
the conception of the imitation of nature in a new and profound sense with the conception of characteristic beauty.
Having liberated the latter from the contradiction which
Goethe suffered to remain in it, he applies the joint result to
the distinction between sculpture as the peculiarly antique,
and painting as the peculiarly modern art.

The fault of the old view that art aims at the imitation of
nature, which gave no explanation how the beautiful which
was to be imitated differed from the ugly which was not, lay,
as he points out, in regarding Nature as a lifeless aggregate of
objects. The moment that Nature is recognised as a living

---

[1] *W.*, 5. 443.   [2] See above, p. 319.   [3] *W.*, 7. 287 (1807).

whole, the expression of reasonable powers, the rule of "imitation," and the aim of "idealisation" becomes clear.   "We
must transcend the given form in order to restore it as in
telligible, vital, and genuinely felt."[1]   Even Winckelmann
who had a true feeling for nature, did not, so Schelling con
tinues, explain that form is beautiful purely because and in as
far as it reveals the idea.   The common demand[2] for "idealisation" implies that beauty is negatively related to reality.
But this is not the case ; on the contrary, the value of true
idealisation is to reveal the vital and essential in nature   Thus
the negative notion of the ideal, or of characterisation as opposed to the ideal, is defective.   Form is not a limit imposed
ab extra on body ; it is spontaneous and positive, the expression of a creative force.   "When the artist seizes the look
and essence of the idea which works in the individual, and
makes it emphatic, he forms the individual into a self-existent
world, a genus, an eternal type."[3]   "Nature is characteristic
from its first beginnings," up to the human form ; and the
characteristic persists throughout as the operative foundation
of the beautiful.[4]

Goethe's comparison[5] of the characteristic in art to the skeleton of a body is here admirably criticised and supplemented.
The skeleton is not separable from, or prior to, or more real
than the soft expressive parts which it supports.   The true
characteristic corresponds to the expression of the whole
figure, flesh and bones, active and passive.   The framework
can never be justly contrasted with the completed form and
its beauty.

Here, then, in the full task laid upon the artist we have
the point of the difference between sculpture and painting.
Sculpture, the essentially ancient art, cannot cope with the
"characteristic variety" of nature; it does not represent space,
but has its space in it [is in real space] and is therefore obliged
to reduce its world almost to a point.   Thus it can only represent such beauty as remains beautiful when treated as a single
and simple whole.   The painter, who belongs distinctly to
the modern world, has all creation before him, and can use
all grades of the characteristic and apparently less beautiful
as contributory to the wider totality of his work.   It must be

---

[1] *W.*, 7. 299.   [2] *Ib.*, 302.   [3] *Ib.*, 304.
[4] *Ib.*, 307.   [5] In *Der Sammler u. die S.*

granted, however, that in conformity with the very natural inconsistency which pursues us throughout, Schelling is constantly tempted to treat the simplest and most uniform beauty as the highest and truest, following the tradition which at the same time he breaks down.

The distinction between sculpture and painting is further examined on its merits and with a true feeling of their relation, but is expressed in language that bears traces of superstition. Sculpture[1] presents its ideas by means of bodily things; painting by an almost spiritual medium. Such phrases suggest but do not clearly explain the difference of expressive capacity between carved material of a uniform colour, and pigments laid upon a flat surface. The conclusion, however, is just ; sculpture, he says in effect, is fettered by its material and cannot express more of the mind than is very definitely revealed in permanent and tangible relations of form ; it fails seriously *if* overcome by the matter with which it deals, and in any case cannot carry spiritual expression beyond a point at which the powers of the material are fairly balanced by the expressiveness imposed upon them. Painting, on the other hand, is ideal throughout (*in comparison* with sculpture, that is) : its "pictures *are* pictures, and not things ; " it is less fettered by its medium than sculpture, and therefore, though its fall is greater *if*[2] it sets matter above spirit (on the principle *corruptio optimi pessima*), yet it has a far higher capacity of subordinating its medium to a spiritual import.[3]

Schelling's æsthetic sensibility begins here to show its limitations. He is, by personal preference, chiefly concerned to prove that soft or rapturous expression is consistent with characteristic beauty ; and this predilection happens to do good service, because the characteristic had always been regarded as primarily hard and rigid. But when he comes to treat Guido Reni as the genuine painter of "soul," we

[1] *Ib.*, 7. 316.
[2] *N.B.* this "if" in view of following note.
[3] See Pater, *Renaissance*, p. 63. "Colour is no mere delightful quality of natural things, but a spirit upon them by which they become expressive to the spirit." I cannot pass unnoticed Schasler's strangely curious misreading (*Krit. G. d. A.*, p 854) of this passage in Schelling, which he spends half a page in satirising as self-contradictory, because, from neglect of the context, he has construed a hypothetical expression as categorical. The reader of his 1200 pages is forced to wonder whether much of his time might not have been saved if the author had been more lavish of his own.

recognise that he is on the downgrade of sentimentalism, and that the superstitions of his later life are casting their shadows before.

Schelling's systematic classification of the arts is of value rather as the first thorough-going attempt at such a classification, and as giving occasion, by the way, for a good deal of analysis of their respective powers and peculiarities, than for any permanent importance in the leading distinction on which it is based. It plainly follows Kant's division, to which, it will be remembered, Kant himself attached but little importance, into arts of speech and of form, adding to the latter category the art of music, which Kant placed apart under the head of the beautiful play of sensations.

But Schelling connects this main division of the arts with the same abstract principle which represents to him the difference between the modern and the antique. The arts of the Real series are embodiments of the Infinite in the Finite—the principle, as we saw,[1] of beauty in general, and more especially of antique beauty, Those of the Ideal series are cases of the subordination of the Finite to the Infinite.[2] It is here more plain than ever that the terms of the two antitheses do not occupy strictly contrasted places. In both of them the Infinite, that is, ideas, is the matter represented, and the relatively Finite, the form, is in both the medium of representation. But in the one the Finite retains its sensuous or material limitations to the full, in the other it is tyrannised over by the meaning and assumes in some degree an infinite or ideal character. Language is a case of this principle. The word loses its individual material being—its look, shape and sound[3] become a matter of indifference—and we go straight to the idea which it suggests. The two antitheses would express their intention more intelligibly if they spoke of Representation of the Infinite in Finite form, and Representation of the Infinite in Infinite form, it being understood that form can only be infinite relatively and through an extension of its natural functions.

Now as the second formula, that of modern art and of the ideal series, falls outside the definition of beauty proper, which

---

[1] P. 327 *supra.*
[2] *W.*, 5. 630.
[3] I do not admit that *in art* its sound is indifferent.

is one with the formula of ancient art and of the real series, we might have expected to find a view of historical succession underlying the distinction between the two series. Traces of such a view, but traces only, are to be found in the remark[1] that the ancients were plastic in their poetry, while modern poetry is (as in Dante) far more arbitrary and capricious and all but impossible to reduce to typical species. We observed that the contrast between sculpture as typically antique and painting as typically modern was rightly drawn elsewhere.

The other and very remarkable feature of the construction of these two series, is the involution of "powers," or phases within phases, by the repeated application of an identical formula to elements previously obtained by that same formula. This process prevails indeed throughout Schelling's philosophy. Thus in the realm of mind (itself an Ideal unity) Art and Philosophy were respectively unities in which the Real and the Ideal predominated; in Art, again, the two series in question are unities of the Finite and Infinite, in each of which one of these principles prevails over the others. And, moreover, within each series there is a predominant real, a predominant ideal, and their "indifference" or equally-balanced unity. Thus in Poetry, whose forms constitute the ideal series, the relatively real is the Lyric, the ideal *par excellence* is the Epic, and the synthesis of the two is the Dramatic. In the real series the real *par excellence* is music, the relatively ideal is painting (I cannot think why), and the synthesis of the two is sculpture. Within sculpture again Architecture appears as a sub-form distinct from the bas-relief and from sculpture in the round, as real *par excellence* and corresponding to music—a frozen music, as Schelling calls it.

I do not adduce all this as of any value in its substantive application as handled by Schelling, but for two historical reasons. In the first place, any thread of systematic connection, however quaint or unreal, which causes a complete and impartial survey to be made for the first time of the whole range of a subject, is of immense historical importance and stimulating effect. Schelling's elaborate discussion of music, for example, is a new thing in æsthetic theory; and however much we may regret the parallel drawn between it and architecture, yet the conception of it as representing[2] pure

---

[1] *W.*, 5. 632. [2] *Ib.*, 5. 502.

movement abstracted from objects, and the real form of things
and events, has much in common with Schopenhauer and with
later conceptions.

But secondly, whether or no Hegel's dialectic may have
originated in these ideas of Schelling, the triplicity in synthesis (suggested of course by Kant) and involution by re-
application of identical formulæ, are important principles in all
philosophical construction, though readily lending themselves
to a futile ingenuity.   It is incontestably true that analogous
phases repeat themselves, and repeat themselves cumulatively,
in mind and nature. The world moves forward not merely
from one condition to another, but as a whole of conditions,
each of which reproduces itself according to its law of differentiation within the general phase which the whole has assumed
according to this same law.[1]   Thus the general idea that the
entire system of the arts recurs on different planes and with a
different centre, as the whole of life is pushed forward into
special conformity with one type of expression, by the results
of its own activity, is thoroughly just, and is a principle which
might be the foundation of a synthesis between a linear
classification of the arts and their history in time.   Not the
mere progression from art to art, but the movement of the
characteristic centre of artistic utterance would be the point
in which history would justify classification.

Schelling's own serial arrangement is, however, merely a
piece of arbitrary formalism.   If we ask what it substantially
means, there is no answer.   In what sense are lyric, epic and
dramatic poetry a second series corresponding to music, painting and sculpture?   We are not told that the order of the
series is an ascending order either in evolution or in power of
presentation, and however we read them we cannot make it
such. The logical framework of the arrangement seems not to
correspond to any progression in the qualities of art as art,
and we should give it the best effect by reading the real series
backwards from sculpture to music, and the ideal forwards
from lyric to dramatic poetry, which would destroy the correlation of the terms and therefore cannot be intended.   Though
a rough idea of progress from perception to fancy may have

---

[1] Thus we might say, in the Christian world there is the heathen Christian
the Greek Christian, and the Christian Christian.

decided Schelling to do his best with Kant's suggestion, the double series really cuts the development in two ; the triplets of the separate syntheses are independent of each other, and their cross analogies are futile. Any pair of arts can be thus regarded as analogous, and there is hardly any pair that has not been so regarded. What just estimate of the value of the arts is formed by Schelling, as in the case of music, is in spite of the serial arrangement and not derived from it. Such parallel series have been the foundation of many subsequent classifications of the arts, even of that proposed by Schasler. But unless it is thoroughly explained why there are two series, and how the beginning of the one is related to the close of the other, and, if cross correspondences are alleged, why they are really essential to the notion of the arts supposed to correspond, I see no meaning in arrangements of this kind. The problem of classification is to illustrate the affinity between individuals either in origin or in function or in both. I cannot see that the superficial resemblance between sculpture and the drama, or between epic poetry (some prefer to say lyric) and painting, throws any light on any question of the kind. Hartmann's distinction, coincident with that of Schelling's series, between arts of perceptive semblance and arts of imaginative semblance, will be discussed in its place.

With Schelling we are fairly launched on nineteenth century æsthetic. The objectivity and necessary historical continuity of the sense of beauty as a supreme expression—Schelling will have it to be *the* supreme expression—of the absolute or divine reality as uttering itself through man, has become an axiom of philosophy. The negative notions of the beautiful and of the characteristic are shown to be imperfect, and their opposition to be unreal. The principle of progressive and cumulative synthesis, according to a law which is constantly re-applied to its own results, is exhibited, though incoherently and inconsistently, in a classification of the fine arts.

All this was really achieved, but how far it entered into history by affecting his successors is a different question. The "Philosophy of Art" was given in lectures and circulated in MS., but probably had only a partial effect. I cannot say for certain whether it was known to Hegel. But the published lectures and papers and the *System of Transcendental Idealism*, contain all that is of importance, except the detailed treatment of the arts, and there can be no doubt that Hegel, while largely drawing from common sources, was also, as is shown by the lectures on Æsthetic, immensely influenced by Schelling's views of art and of æsthetic philosophy.

The genius and character of the two men were extraordinarily different, and extraordinarily suitable the one to go before and the other to follow. Schelling at his best has a profusion of thought and brilliancy of suggestion with which Hegel cannot compare. But soon the reader finds that he is an untrustworthy guide; impatient, incoherent, credulous, with no sterling judgment of art, and with a constant bias to the sentimental and the superstitious. Hegel is persevering, laborious, consistent, remarkable for his healthy and masculine judgment of art, while sympathetic and even passionate below the surface. He detests rhetoric, to which Schelling was prone, and the reader feels that fail as he may, he is always making a genuine effort to grasp the essence and get to the heart of his subject. Considering the close early connection between the two great thinkers, and the immense range of recent material of which they shared the inheritance, it may be said that while we prefer Hegel to Schelling, this is partly because Schelling is best represented in Hegel.

Hegel.
Dialectic in the Æsthetic.
II. i. Hegel's æsthetic system, as represented with substantial fidelity in the lectures on æsthetic,[1] makes no parade of the dialectic method which constitutes the essential difficulty of his other philosophical works. Questions as to the degree in which the Dialectic controls the construction of the Æsthetic, must be argued not with reference to the structure of the latter, which is tolerably plain, but with reference to the nature of the former, which will never perhaps be thoroughly agreed upon. Therefore the Dialectic as such does not concern us here, and I propose to spare my readers almost all enquiry into it, only saying enough to explain my own conviction that in the æsthetic we possess a specimen of the reasonable connection which the

---

[1] This work on *Æsthetic* was published in 1835, having been put into shape after Hegel's death out of materials consisting of Hegel's MSS. of the lectures, in which the introductions were for the most part fully written out, and of the notes taken by pupils, several sets of which were collected for the purpose. The work is substantively reliable, but must not be regarded as a literary production from Hegel's hand.

dialectic was intended to emphasise, without the constant parade of unfamiliar terms which have been thought to be mere lurking-places of fallacy. The evolution of beauty, as Hegel describes it, depends on a principle analogous to that which Schelling appealed to in a far more artificial form. In every process of change construed according to the postulate of causation, that which ceases to exist must be supposed so to cease because its nature is no longer adequate to the claim made upon it by the connected system within which it has its being. In a formal and technical sense, therefore, it may be contended that in every causal process, any element which ceases to be, must necessarily be replaced by something more adequate than itself to the requirements of the process as a whole. But such a deduction would be purely formal, because it is possible that the elements of the causal connection might be of a limiting or destructive character, and the reason for the better adaptation of the succeeding element to these demands might lie in its possessing not a larger but a scantier content. To conditions which forbid life, a corpse is better adapted than a living man. But within any evolution which has in fact a progressive character the formal principle just indicated will have a real bearing. Any vanishing element, in being replaced by something which better harmonises with the systematic and causal process as a whole, is giving way before necessities which in part its own activity has modified into a form in which it can no longer meet them. Thus, for instance, physical decay is not the only reason why a man's life-work ends when he is old. Plato's successor must be not Plato but Aristotle, and granting that adaptability is a matter of degree, still, considering life as a system of phases which determine each other, it seems clear that Plato could not become Aristotle by a mere prolongation of his days. The succeeding factor, which meets the new necessities that mould it, is by the very condition of its existence carrying on the life-work of its predecessor in a more complex form, weighted alike with what it achieved, and with what it died in failing to achieve. If we are pleased to express these relations by saying that every positive existence, in a progressive evolution, passes over into its negation, which then necessarily makes way for a further positive result, including both the earlier positive and its negative, the phraseology is technical but not I think altogether unintelligible. And if we are asked how a bare negation can enter into the determination of any positive result, we might point to the possibility that Hegel may have been aware that within a concrete and causal process there is no such thing as a bare negation. However this may be, we have only to master the conception of a necessary progressive movement so far as will enable us to follow the structure of the Æsthetic. For this purpose one more point is necessary to be noted. The successor inherits a task modified by his predecessor, but yet the same, in the sense of bearing the same relation to the causal system which surrounds them both. And therefore there is a certain truth in the quaint terminology of Schelling, which treats the successive phases of evolution in any particular direction as "powers," or specialised intensifications, produced by the reiterated application of an identical process to results generated by itself.

I will now attempt a brief account of the most interesting features of Hegel's æsthetic system, relying on the abstract, in great part probably from his own hand, which is printed in the Appendix, for a complete conspectus of it, which would otherwise have occupied the whole of my space in the text as essential to understanding the relation of the parts to each other.

The Conception of Beauty. ii. Beauty is the Idea as it shows itself to sense.[1] The Idea, we must remember, does not imply consciousness, although both life and consciousness are reckoned among the forms of its manifestation. But the Idea as such is the concrete world-process considered as a systematic unity. As its "show" or "semblance" (Schein) the beautiful is at once distinguished from the true,[2] which is the Idea as it is for thought, and therefore has an identical substance with that of beauty but a different form. It is also, as by Kant, distinguished from the good, useful, and pleasant, all of which have to do with will or desire.

As belonging neither to theory nor to Desire, the Beautiful is said to be "infinite," that is to say, free from relativity, whether according to the law of sufficient reason, or according to the alien purposes imposed by desire on its object. The infinite in this peculiar sense is the self-contained or the self-complete ; that which satisfies the perception and does not refer it away through a series of causes or purposes lying outside itself. If endless infinity may be compared to an

----

[1] *Æsth.*, I. 141.   [2] *Ib.*

infinite straight line, Hegel's true infinity, of which the beautiful is a leading example, may be compared to a circle or a sphere,

There is thus nothing "abstract" in Hegel's "idea," which is the very concrete itself, nor any unreality in his "ideal," which is, as we shall see, the idea as manifested in the chief historical types or phases of art.

The Beauty of Nature.   *a.* But the "first" (simplest or lowest) existence of the Idea is in Nature, and the "first" beauty is the beauty of nature.[1] The beauty of nature, of course, exists only *for* the perceiving consciousness,[2] but Hegel devotes to it a brief separate treatment as differing from the beauty of art in not having been consciously produced with a view to æsthetic effect. He is partly influenced by the idea of nature as contrasted with man, and only includes man in his account of natural beauty as an afterthought,[3] and in some degree as a contrast to the beauty of animals. The difficulty, however, in the separate treatment of natural and artistic beauty, at once makes itself felt in the fact that landscape scenery, which is dealt with in a few words under this former head, is more fully spoken of when the *art* of painting comes to be discussed.

The beauty of nature, as distinguished from man, which Hegel begins by considering, was something that he did not fully feel. He understood that inanimate nature may be in apparent sympathy with human moods, but he had no detailed justification to offer for their coincidence, nor any sense of character and import in mountain form or cloud formation or water movement. His gaze is concentrated on the individual organism and its progressive manifestation of life, in which for the first time the idea seems to him to attain a partially adequate self-revelation, and he devotes more attention to the plant than to the rocks, more to the animal than to the plant, and subsequently more to the human being than to the animal.

We do not feel, I believe, this exact progression of æsthetic value in the ratio of organic development. The landscape, and plant life as the vesture of the earth, seem to us more yielding and sympathetic to our moods than the concentrated life of the individual animal; and great as is the beauty of the

---

[1] *Æsthetic,* i. 148.   [2] *Ib.,* 157.   [3] Cf. pp. 167 and 184.

horse or the tiger, they do not appear readily or continuously
in our higher enjoyment of the beautiful. They are not, like
man, spiritual in themselves; but yet they are sufficiently
individual to resist subordination to our general æsthetic sentiments. But in exalting the beauty of the human form as
the sole adequate incarnation of the idea, Hegel is in harmony
with the best feeling and criticism of to-day, in spite of the
immense recent extension of our sympathy with inanimate
nature.

His discussion of beauty and ugliness in the forms of
animals,[1] is half-hearted, and seems to admit that ugliness
may be relative. Creatures seem ugly to us, he says, whose
forms are typical of qualities opposed to vitality in general, or
to what we have learnt to regard as their own special or
typical form of animate existence. Thus the sloth as wanting in vitality, and the platypus as seeming to combine irreconcilable types, and crocodiles and many kinds of insects,
simply, it would appear, because we are not accustomed to
consider their forms as adequate expressions of life, are all
regarded as ugly. This implies that below the level of man
and art there is no absolute ugliness, a view to which I shall
have to recur.

Beauty of Abstract Form. But further, as the vitality of nature even in
animals falls short of characteristic individuality,
the expression of the idea must also be looked for in
formal and abstract attributes,[2] pervading all nature, and
representing to sense a unity that does not amount to the
unity of soul life. This external beauty shows itself as the
beauty of abstract form and as the abstract unity of sensuous
matter. Under the former head it includes those geometrical
embodiments of unity which I have especially drawn attention to in antique theory. Hegel enumerates them as regularity (of mere repetition), symmetry (of repetition with a
difference), lawfulness (a far-reaching conception, applying to
all totalities in which a number of differences are bound together by a common law, and not merely as repetitions of
one another: parabolic curves, Hogarth's line of beauty, the
different lines of the human arm in two opposite contours, are
given as examples); and harmony (the same relation between
chiefly qualitative attributes as lawfulness between chiefly

[1] P. 166.   [2] 169 ff

quantitative attributes, quantity and quality passing into one another at this point, The relations of colour are given as an example. The beauty still consists in the principle of totality, presented through the suggestion of an agreement in qualities that differ).

Beauty in Unity of Sense-Material. And in addition to this scale of principles he emphasises as the abstract unity of sensuous matter what appeared by their side in Plato, the effect of purity or simplicity in the sensuous medium, such as colour, tone, or even shape. Here, in passing, he refers to sympathy with landscape scenery as explicable in some cases by this principle, as when we are pleased at the clear sky, or the bright sea. But as a rule, even in the account of abstract beauty, his eye has been on individual formations, on crystals, plants, and animals. As regards this sensuous purity, which we discussed in connection with Plato and with Kant, we have only to note that Hegel attempts to distinguish, as is right, between purity for sense-perception (freedom from sheer disturbance, as from dirt in colour, and from noise in tone) and simplicity of physical origin. This latter he mistakenly believes also to condition a peculiar kind of sense-impression, and he unluckily instances violet as a colour which is not in itself simple or one of the essential species of colour![1]

Now since natural beauty, no less than that of art, admittedly exists only for perception, we may regard the whole region of the beautiful as forming for Hegel, in spite of the contrast between nature and art, a continuous and ascending scale ; so that this abstract beauty becomes, as we have throughout considered it to be, a set of general conditions imposed by the formal principle of unity in variety on all sensuous expression *quâ* expressive, but not exhausting the content even of a curve or colour, much less of any more individual presentation.

But purely natural beauty—the beauty of things as common perception sees them—is essentially defective,[2] owing to its incapacity, even granting that the actual human form belongs to it, for representing the unity of a spiritual being at every point of the sensuous shape. In a striking passage Hegel explains how nearly the human form, in contrast to

---

[1] Violet is a primary colour.   [2] i. 180.

that of animals, fulfils this requirement,[1] by the hue and
sensitiveness of the skin, its peculiar appearance of life, and
so on.   But even the human body is overlaid with the mark-
ings of nature and accident, and in modern times by a dress
which resists expression ; and all this hinders the spiritual life
from perfectly shining through its form.

Beauty of Art;   β. It is therefore necessary that the idea, which
the Ideal   has found the fullest non-sensuous expression of
itself in the human intelligence, should proceed as it were to
repeat consciously the process by which it was unconsciously
embodied in nature, and construct for itself a more adequate
representation equally actual for sense in the second nature
of art.   Now the entire subjective aspect of this process,
the matter which is imagined in forms capable of representation, constitutes, according to Hegel, the Ideal, that is to
say, the Idea so translated into the terms or tendencies of
imagination as to be capable of direct or indirect presentation to sense.   Concreteness is the bridge to artistic realisation.[2]

Nature and the   (1) The relation of the Ideal to Nature, with
Ideal.   reference to imitation and so-called idealisation is
simply and sufficiently stated by Hegel.

Imitation.   Simple imitation he does not wholly despise,
but, following the track of Aristotle, refers our pleasure in it
to our " satisfaction in mental production."   This satisfaction
he is inclined to defend, as the just pride of the mind in being
able to do with a simple material of its own choice,[3] the
essence of what nature can only do with enormous and varied
real resources.   It may be regarded either as an exaltation
of the thing imitated into the medium of mind, or even as an
irony directed against mere sensuous reality.   Objects thus
imitated delight us, he says, not because they *are* so natural,
but because they *are made* so natural.[4]   This is a profound
judgment, indulgent with the indulgence of a great mind ; for
to a philosopher enthusiastic for the highest conceptions of
art, nothing could be more repulsive than the reduction of it
to sleight-of-hand in imitation.[5]   The ultimate defect of pure
imitation is, then, that it is *formal*, regardless of the individual matter or meaning of what it represents.

P. 184.   [2] See Appendix I.   [3] See p. 12, supra.
   [4] Cf. Introd. E. Tr., p. 82,   [5] *Ibid.*

Idealisation.   In seizing this matter or meaning, and impressing a universal character on the perceptible imagery of representation, we have the second stage and true essence of fine art ;[1] *poetry* as opposed to *making*.   However concrete and particular may be the forms of art, they must be different for having passed through the mind, which is the faculty of universals.   If the artist imitates nature, it is not because she has done this or that, but because she has done it *right*.[2] Nature, in short, "is an empty indefinite phrase.[3]   Poetry [as the general spirit of art] will always be obliged to insist upon the energetic, essential, distinctive, and the ideal is this expressive essence, not the *merely* actual, to represent whose details in any scene *e.g.* in a scene of every-day life, would be languid, spiritless, wearisome, and intolerable."

It is plain to an observer of to-day that the two opposite senses of idealisation, in respect of which Hegel's masculine feeling sympathised strongly with Herr v. Rumohr's attack on the so-called followers of Winckelmann in his cultus of the ideal,[4] are ultimately bound up with the two opposite senses of the universal in logic.   If the universal is the empty abstract, and its symbol is width of area, idealisation means superficiality and loss of individual content.   If the universal is the full concrete, and its symbol is a centre with radii, idealisation means profound insight and wealth of individual characterisation.   Hegel uses the latter notion in æsthetic, as he introduced it into logic.   The two modes have in common, however, the physical limitations of art and its appeal to perception under definite conditions ; in both, therefore, there is a certain selection and omission, which facilitates the too ready confusion between them.

Idealisation: Absolute or Relative.   Behind this view of imitation and idealisation as stages of the penetration of nature by the mind, there may be raised a further and more speculative question, namely, " Is the superiority of art to nature absolute or relative ?" *i.e.* is the idealisation necessary

---

[1] i. 206.   [2] *Ibid.*   [3] i. 210.

[4] " Out of this recognition (of the Greek ideal by Winckelmann) there arose a yearning for idealistic representation, in which people thought they had found beauty, but really fell into insipidity, unvitality, and characterless superficiality."—*Æsth.*, i. 202.   How Schasler could say (i. 386) that Hegel's *Æsthetic* contained only one short remark on Winckelmann passes my comprehension.

merely for the limitedness of our perception and the physical
conditions of representation, or does it put into nature more
than the greatest artist could see to be really there if his
knowledge were unlimited, and the picture frame unnecessary?
Hegel is more neutral on this point in the *Æsthetic* than
might be expected from his philosophy of nature, in which he
seems to treat the natural as contingent. In the *Æsthetic*
he speaks of the uniform, direct and solidly coherent sequences
of nature as a corrective of arbitrary conventionalism in art,[1]
and treats the question whether art or nature is the more
beautiful in mere form as empirical, and not to be settled by
theory.[2] I do not believe that he ever thought of Nature
as contingent in the sense of being uncaused or outside the
reign of law. Its contingency probably meant for him its
apparent indifference to human purposes. He undoubtedly
thought, however, that the Ideal (=the beauty of art) had
undergone an *actual* change by passing through the human
mind, and was charged with something more than the deepest
insight could find in nature, including man as he is in the
prose life of every day. We probably still assent to this judgment, but with considerable deductions arising from our new
sympathy with the reason displayed in the inanimate world.
The art of music, it must be remembered, at once breaks down
any attempt to say in general theory that the real world of art
in no way transcends that of external existence.

Subject to the reservation which has been indicated, and
which is practically represented by the life-work of Ruskin,
Hegel's treatment of the Ideal is the greatest single step
that has ever been made in æsthetic. Winckelmann had
portrayed the Ideal as in its perfection one and abstract.
Kant, while recognising it as an embodiment of life, had on
this very ground excluded it from æsthetic, because relative
to the will. It was Hegel who while maintaining its æsthetic
nobility in the sense of Winckelmann, and crediting it with
the full æsthetic purity demanded but denied to it by Kant,
at the same time accepted the extension and differentiations of
it so as to constitute the principle and matter of art in all its
phases and limits. As an illustration of the mode in which
even the commonest nature may enter into the Ideal or the
beauty of art, Hegel in this discussion of its relation to

---

[1] Introd. E. Tr., 87.   [2] i. 217.

nature[1] briefly anticipates the eloquent defence of Dutch and German paintings, which forms the conclusion of the special section on painting in the third volume.

The Ideal in Life and Action. (2) It was natural considering the novelty of the attempt to break down the wall of abstraction round the Ideal, that Hegel should devote nearly one-eighth

---

[1] I subjoin this defence in its shorter form given in the discussion of the Ideal, because it is an excellent illustration of Hegel's critico-historical treatment, and of the range and depth of the ideal as he conceived it. Serious objections are now taken against the Dutch school in particular both on general grounds and with reference to their colouring. (Ruskin, *A. F.*, 5. 24.) I have not the special knowledge which would entitle me to offer an opinion on this latter head, and Hegel's apology only deals with their range of subject, and with the spirit in which they approached it.

"[The Dutch genre-paintings] ought not simply to be thrown aside under the title of common (mean) nature. If we look close at the real content of these pictures it is not so 'common' as is generally thought.

"The Dutch chose the content of their representations from the present of their own life, and they are not to be censured for having realised this present over again in the medium of art. What is brought before the eyes and heart of the living world must be something that belongs to it, if it is to claim its interest to the full. To know what interested the Dutch at that time we must ask their history. The Dutchman had to a great extent created the very soil on which he lived and worked, and was compelled continually to defend and preserve it against the onset of the sea; townsmen and peasants alike, by spirit, endurance, and bravery had cast off the Spanish dominion under Philip II., son of Charles V., that mighty prince of this world, and along with political liberty had conquered for themselves freedom of religion, and that in the religion of the free. It is this civic spirit and enterprise in small things as in great, in their own country and on the high seas, their frugal, yet neat and cleanly housewifery, and the pride and pleasure of the self-consciousness that they owe it all to their own activity—it is all this that constitutes the general substance of their pictures. This is not a low matter and argument, to be regarded with the patrician insolence of "good society" from the vantage-ground of courts and their manners. It is this intelligent cheerfulness in a well-earned enjoyment, which pervades even the animal pieces, and shows itself as pleasure and physical satisfaction, and it is this fresh and wakeful freedom and vitality of mind in apprehension and presentation that forms the highest aspect of these pictures." After comparing with them as of the same general species, some beggar children of Murillo, as "contented and happy almost like the Olympian gods . . . human beings harmoniously created, with no vexation or discontent in them," he ends by observing that such genre pictures ought to be of small size, so as to pass for something trivial. They would be intolerable if they made the claim upon us of being represented in life size. "This," he concludes, referring to the whole passage, "is how 'common' Nature must be felt, in order to be fit for art."—*Æsth.*, i. 212.

of his entire set of lectures [1] to the perfectly general question, not, *what* shapes it must assume in entering into concrete life, *but*, how it can enter into life at all. It is in this discussion that he points to a heroic past as the best ground for the art of individual character, being evidently impressed by the conflict of individual courage with orderly civilisation depicted in different relations in *Götz v. Berlichingen, Don Quixote* and the *Räuber*. In a civilised social order, for example, the punishment [2] of crime no longer depends on individual heroism ; it is not even a single action, but is broken up into parts played by separate agents—police, judge and jury, gaoler or executioner. Thus the great moral powers of society no longer reside in the breast of particular persons but in the co-operation of millions, and the latter relation is more difficult of portrayal than the former.

This view coheres with the whole conception of art as, in its evolution, tending to pass out of the most strictly artistic region, and as not possessing in modern civilisation the same sole supremacy that it claimed in the Periclean age, or in the first flush of the Renascence. Whatever we may think of the future of fine art, the facts which favour such a conception are patent and undeniable ; and, if disputed, it must be so disputed as to allow these facts their due weight. [3]

The whole of this part of the work, constituting as it were a complete analysis of action in general into the elements of its necessary context—the spirit of the age, the situation, the collision of duties, the motive, the character—is directed to showing how " ideality " can be maintained in the treatment of the most detailed complications and serious aspects of life ; while the false " ideal," the fancy of a golden age or idyllic existence, [4] fails of true ideality by the very withdrawal from vigorous concreteness which was meant to constitute its beauty. In *Hermann and Dorothea*, it is pointed out, Goethe avoids this weakness with marvellous skill, by setting

---

[1] i. 193–365.　　　　[2] i. 232.

[3] *Ib.* "However excellent we think the statues of the Greek gods, however nobly and perfectly God the Father and Christ and Mary may be portrayed, it makes no difference, our knees no longer bend." He has just said that we may hope for the continual progress of art, only its form has ceased to meet the supreme need of our age. It is untrue that he thinks art to be " played out."

[4] i. 325. He is speaking primarily of Gessner.

the domestic story against the dark background of the revolutionary war. Before leaving this part of the system it is well to notice that the section on Abstract Externality [1] as an element in the expression of the Ideal is almost a reproduction of the section on " the external beauty of abstract Form " [2] as an element in the expressiveness of nature. The editors are probably responsible for the repetition, but Hegel must have treated the subject in both places on different occasions. The untenableness of a working distinction between the beauty of Nature and that of Art could not be more strikingly illustrated.

Evolution of the Ideal. (3) After this general discussion about the relation of the Ideal to particulars, the actual self-particularisation of the Ideal is represented as a process, according to the simple dialectic indicated above; [3] and this process is the framework of the entire system.

It will be seen from the extract printed in the Appendix that in *the first place* the whole world of imagined beauty or concrete fancy, which is called the "ideal," is conceived as passing through phases determined by the progression of intelligence and also by the cumulative result of the sequence itself. And in *the second place*, the human mind being at all times a many-sided whole, the same needs of expression which thus separate themselves each into its own successive phase in time, also appear, as a co-existing group of modes of fancy, relative to different media of expression, within each of the great historical forms or stages of the "ideal" or art-consciousness.

The former set of successive phases are what Hegel calls the three forms of art, symbolic, classical, and romantic, and taken together make up the main outline of the historical evolution of the ideal.

The latter group of co-existing modes of expression, a group which repeats itself within each of the historical art-forms, is the system of the several arts, primarily differentiated from each other by the sensuous vehicles which they respectively employ.

Therefore the whole set of particular arts, Architecture, Sculpture, Painting, Music, and Poetry, recurs within each of the three progressive Art-Forms, the Symbolic, the Classical,

[1] i. 325.   [2] i. 169.   [3] P. 335.

and the Romantic.   And the same needs of expression being at the root of both differentiations of the ideal, the successive and the simultaneous, it follows that though all the arts recur in each epoch, yet in each recurrence one or more of them have a prerogative rank, depending on the coincidence of their special tendency with the spirit of the age within which they then are.

Thus for the symbolic art-form architecture is central or characteristic—for the classical art-form, sculpture—and for the romantic art-form, in conformity with its greater mobility and variety, the three remaining arts, painting, music, and poetry, are characteristic, but music above all is the central romantic art.[1]

The dialectic continuity which underlies the progression of these historical forms of art may be simply expressed as follows. We start with man's universal need to set the seal of his inner being on the world without, in order to recognise himself therein.[2]

The Symbolic Art-form.   The first gropings of the mind after sensuous expression are like dreams, often like nightmares; the spirit of man is not yet fully awake, and lays its half-formed fancies arbitrarily in the objects of sense.[3]   This is in Hegel's language symbolic art, not in the wide sense in which all art appeals to natural symbolism,[4] but in the narrow sense in which a symbol is opposed to an embodiment or representation. Here all is arbitrary and irrational, a search for adequate expression, because nothing is yet formed which is adequate to be expressed.

The Classical Art-form.   But the half-formed is on the way to the fully formed. The awakening mind reacts against its nightmares[5] by realising its own nature as a compact and definite self in a compact and definite world of relations, and seizes for the representation of its definite reasonable unity

---

[1] See extract in Appendix, on Music.
[2] See Introd. to *Æsth.*, E. Tr., 59.
[3] See Ruskin on Indian Art. *Aratra Pentelici*, 226, and *Two Paths*, 11.
[4] See Kant on the Symbol, above.
[5] How profound is this view we are now learning more thoroughly year by year, as we trace the long preparation in which the Greek spirit learned what it needed from Oriental sources, only to put all monstrosity under its feet, and rise up like Ethert Brand, in the fairest human form.

the natural and adequate symbol furnished by the human figure.

The Romantic Art-form. In the world-movement, however, the compact and definite self is no enduring phase. The little Greek sphere of fixed natural relations is torn asunder by the great historical forces operative both within and without it, and the idea, assuming the form of a progressive antithesis, in which the Greek past is itself a factor, can no longer be adequately represented in a compact and simple shape, but demands embodiment, if not actually in thought, then in some medium of sense as nearly as possible approximating to thought.

At this point we may recall the sources of the conception before us. The combination of these three stages with the three sets of particular fine arts suggests a connection with Schelling's "powers"; that is to say, the process which generated the three successive forms of art is again represented within each one of them by the division into particular fine arts. The distinction again between "classical" and "romantic," which is essentially that between the simple or fixed and the divided or moving, is drawn in material from the historical contrast with which we dealt at length in the "Data of modern æsthetic," and in form from Schelling's antithesis of "Natural" and "Historical," itself derived from Schiller's Naive and Sentimental. The whole notion of a concrete idea as the reality, is referred, we must bear in mind throughout, by Hegel to Schiller. The direction assigned to the movement from classical to romantic makes explicit, as Schelling himself does not, the notion latent in his "real" and "ideal" series of arts. The addition of the symbolic art-form as a pre-classical stage is a reflex, materially, of the interest excited by the Schlegels and other Romanticists in Oriental poetry and antiquities, and thus the parallel drawn by Hegel between the Symbolic and the Romantic tendency corresponds to the fact that the same anti-classical contrast and rebellion brought the data of both into notice. The technical term Symbolic appears to be a special application of the idea of symbol or allegory, the former being extended to the whole of art by Solger, and the latter by Fr. v. Schlegel.[1] It is needless to say that the notion of the "classical" which

---

[1] i. 392, cf. Zimm., *A.*, i. 698.

forms the centre of the whole evolution is in the spirit of
Winckelmann and draws its sterling soundness from Hegel's
intense sympathy with him and with his subject.   And finally,
the exceedingly suggestive treatment of the Ideal, not as an
exclusive phase of Art, but as the whole range of fancy that
is reacted on and specialised into concreteness by the general
demands of expression in each age, and further by the particular sensuous vehicles which determine the powers of the
several fine arts, is probably, I submit, due to Schelling's idea
of mythology as a *sine qua non* for art.   For this mythology
essentially meant the organised province of imagination applicable to a particular range of artistic production.   The modern,
as we know, had, according to Schelling, to make his mythology for himself out of the material given to the intelligence
of his age.   This concrete aspect of the imagination in itself
and apart from the actual work of production, has never, so
far as I am aware, been duly noted by professional art-philoso-
phers except in a degree by Schelling and Hegel, and in one
particular region by writers on music.   That not only the
musician imagines in tones, and the poet in ideas, but the
sculptor in marble,[1] the ironworker in iron, the wood-carver
in wood, and the painter in colour—this is the vital principle
which lies at the root of the due classification of the arts, and
is thoroughly comprehended in Hegel's "ideal."

"This highly trained skill in the thoroughly perfect mani-
pulation of the material is involved in the notion of the Ideal,
as it has for its principle the total incorporation in the sensuous
and the fusion of the inward spirit with the outward being."[2]
The demands of execution are subsequently and separately
treated, so that we must clearly grasp that Hegel is here
speaking of the artistic imagination *quâ* imagination only, and
requires even so that it should be moulded, so to speak, by
habitual intercourse with its material.   Thus the differentiation of the ideal leads up to the classification of the arts.

---

[1] That is, of course, in ideas of form, but in ideas of form suggested,
moulded, and modified by the habitual feeling of what it is to express oneself
in marble. The modern sculptor, it would seem, thinks in clay ! See Collingwood, Ruskin's *Art Teaching*, 281, and Hegel quoting Winckelmann, *A.*,
ii. 442.

[2] Hegel, *ib.* The strictures on working in clay only, for marble statues,
follow this passage.

Classification of the Arts. (4) Hegel's classification of the arts is briefly explained by himself in the abstract printed in the Appendix. It is only necessary here to comment on three distinctive points concerning it.

The Double Basis of Classification. *a.* If the combination on which it rests was thoroughly carried out, each separate art would be treated in three forms, symbolic, classical, and romantic, just as each of these three art-forms would be pursued through the peculiarities of the five different arts. Thus the classification is founded upon a combined historical and analytic principle, which is supposed by Hegel to represent the same differentiation, both in succession, and in co-existences repeated within phases of the succession. The culminating point of the group of particular fine arts at any period is thus to be found in that branch of art which corresponds within the co-existent system to the then dominant phase of the succession. Architecture, the art of incomplete symbolism, is the climax of preclassical or merely symbolic art; sculpture, the art of complete and compact though limited expressiveness, is the climax of classical or self-complete and balanced artistic production of the Greek age, and so on.

The recent historians of æsthetic agree in condemning this double principle of classification. Schasler[1] thinks that it contradicts itself in treating a single art under more than one form, although he sees that the empirical facts give some support to such a method. Hartmann[2] considers that the confusion between the division of forms of style (!) and the division of the particular arts is fatal to Hegel's whole system, and especially he complains that the "confusion" recurs within the treatment of each separate branch of art. Zimmermann[3] makes similar criticisims on the intermixture of historical and philosophical principles, and on the feature of recurrence, and, in addition, can find no distinction between the symbolic and the romantic, and infers that both of these, being inadequate in form to their import, must fall outside beauty.

From Zimmermann, an able writer of the Herbartian school, and a pure formalist in æsthetic, no other criticism could be expected. He thinks that history should be severed from philosophy as absolutely as the story of Newton's apple from astronomical theory. " The conception of symbolism would

---

[1] 982.   [2] i. 536.   [3] i. 709 ff.

exist if there had never been a work of art bearing that character, nor a period, nor a people devoted to it."[1] This is indeed the high *priori* road. The conception of linguistic or algebraical symbolism would no doubt have existed if only language and algebra had existed and fine art had never been heard of. But whether out of these essentially different species of the genus the conception of æsthetic symbolism would have been generated, if no æsthetic sensibility had ever been observed, I must take leave to doubt. The whole nature of the philosophical sciences is here at issue.

When on the other hand Schasler and Hartmann, both of them in name objective idealists, take a similar view of a German thinker, a foreigner hesitates to express an opposite opinion. It will be simplest to attach the observations which appear necessary to a short recapitulation of the empirical facts which suggested and support the treatment in question.

Facts that support the Double Basis. β. None of the philosophical sciences are as independent of history as the exact sciences. Philosophy is essentially concrete ; and though its principles are bound to be clear, its logical sequences coherent, and its distinctions objective, yet even in Logic, the abstraction of abstractions, it is wholly impossible to motive and correlate the phenomena without referring to their empirical context in the more and less developed language and intelligence of peoples. Yet in Logic we are dealing on the whole with a system of which the parts, the individual sciences, are able to co-exist in their highest form and vitality. In æsthetic this is not so, and in spite of the unity of art all evidence points to the conclusion that it cannot possibly be so.

Architecture was the most important art of the pre-classical period and extra-classical world, though in this world and period we do not find the culmination of architecture. This is all that the theory absolutely requires ; but the other arts comply with it less grudgingly. Sculpture was the pride of Greek art, and in Greek art we find the greatest achievements of pure sculpture. For us, Greek painting and music hardly exist ; and though this, if a sheer accident, ought not to influence our theories (as it probably has influenced them) yet we know enough to conjecture with likelihood that acquaintance with these productions would not, when brought into compar-

[1] Zimmermann, i. 711.

ison with their modern correlatives, have profoundly modified our ideas of the history of art. Greek poetry is, beyond any doubt, romantic in comparison to Greek sculpture, and plastic or narrowly classical in comparison to modern poetic art. Painting and music, as we know them, practically begin with the modern world, and music in particular attains greatness after the impulse of formative art, if not wholly exhausted, had lost its centrality and certainty of achievement. Not only are these arts romantic *par excellence* as compared with the sculpture and architecture even of modern times, but they attained their culmination, so far as history has yet gone, within the romantic development, and as a whole,[1] in separate and distinct epochs. With reference to poetry, the universal art, it would indeed be unbecoming to speak of a modern superiority so far as excellence is concerned ; but in that which separates poetry from the other arts, its profoundness, its freedom, and its spirituality, it cannot be denied that modern poetry is more poetic and less " plastic " than that of Greece.

Now in every classification it is well to begin by exactly framing or limiting the matter which we propose to classify, and in view of these facts which show the disparateness of much of our material, this framing is automatically effected with singular felicity by subordinating the analytic distinction of the arts to the historical distinction of the art-forms. Thus when Hegel treats at length of symbolic classical and romantic[2] architecture, we understand that these three forms are essential distinctions in architecture, and that architecture again is the " symbolic " species *par excellence* in each of these art-forms. It is idle to treat of architecture or sculpture, as Hartmann does, by *mere* general analysis, avoiding all reference to their characteristic periods ; the natural peculiarities of the object-matter are neglected, and nine-tenths of the important phenomena are omitted. The relation, for example, of fine architecture to building or engineering on the one hand and to sculpture on the other is thus discussed, wholly

---

[1] Turner was contemporary with Beethoven, but this can hardly break down the statement in the text. For all we yet know, Turner was an isolated genius. At least he is not connected with the first prime of modern art.

[2] Hegel's treatment of this is much influenced by Goethe's *Deutsche Baukunst.* See *A.*, ii. 332.

without reference to the actual development of architectural decoration in the greatest periods, and to the position of the artist-workman in regard to Greek, and again in regard to romantic, ornament. The most important issues are consequently either unmentioned or just baldly alluded to.[1] The wholly unfree character imputed by Hartmann to architecture and all the minor arts and crafts cuts a troublesome knot conveniently at first sight, but leave the far worse perplexity behind, that on this view some beautiful art *quâ* beautiful is unfree. Nothing but a more appreciative treatment, such as even in a short abstract[2] that of Hegel is seen to be, can combine the truth of Hartmann's idea with that of Ruskin's equally extreme doctrine that architecture is throughout subordinate to sculpture.

Principle of Analytic Classification. γ. But when, leaving the successive art-forms, we come to consider the co-existing system of the arts, a definite ground of classification is unquestionably necessary. Here, as often happens, the wealth of Hegel's knowledge and industry has disconcerted his critics and even his followers.

At the close of the chapter printed in the Appendix, Hegel mentions two possible abstract principles of classification ; the sensuous medium, and the relation to space and time. The former might be treated either with reference to the actual material employed, or, as in a fuller passage,[3] with reference to the effect on the spectator's perception. Schasler[4] is unable to see why, having mentioned this basis of division, in the latter passage, he at once lets it fall (and we might add, that of space and time also), and recurs to the principle of symbolic classical and romantic as the only one which is really concrete.

These others, it should be noted, may be taken as exhausting the principles in vogue both before and after Hegel. Kant and Schelling had divided the arts of form from the art which makes use of speech, and Hegel observes that this results

---

[1] Let any reader compare Hartmann's treatment of architecture in vols. i. and ii. of the *Æsthetic* with the chapter on the "Nature of Gothic" in Ruskin's *Stones of Venice*; or with the passages quoted from Wm. Morris, above pp. 95 and 124, or with the chapter "Architecture" in Mr. Collingwood's vol. on *Ruskin's Art Teaching*, or with the discussion in Prof. Baldwin Brown's *Fine Arts*, and then turn to Hegel on "Romantic Architecture," *Æsth.*, ii. 332.
[2] See App. I.   [3] *A.*, ii. 253.   [4] 1003.

from the division according to organs of sense, except that
music, which Schelling threw in with the arts of form, must be
separated as by Kant *qua* art of sound, while the speaking
art is more truly to be reckoned as one whose medium is
imagination. Thus modified, the division is practically that of
Hartmann (Arts of the eye, Arts of the ear, Art of the fancy).
Lessing, on the other hand, had, we remember, distinguished
formative art from poetry (music was not within his horizon)
by their relations to space and time, which in the form of rest
and motion are the principles of Schasler's division. Now
why does Hegel let fall, after mentioning them, both these
principles, and recur to the threefold division of art-forms ?
Simply because, in motiving this latter division he is able to
exhaust the content of both these abstract principles, while,
even taken together, they are not sufficient to found a division
upon.

We should observe that he employs[1] the first, before dropping it, to clear the ground by excluding the non-æsthetic
senses of touch, taste, and smell ; the two latter as dealing with
matter in process of dissolution and therefore as destructive
if not appetitive in their relation to the object, and the former
as in contact only with the pure particular as such, and consequently unable to apprehend a systematic unity in sensuous
form. This is probably the true differentia of non-æsthetic
senses, and all other non-æsthetic characteristics in them are
only of importance as conditions or results of this.

The point then of Hegel's concrete principle of division, by
which he simply enquires into the powers and conditions of the
several arts as human activities producing a certain effect by
more or less material means, is this, that by not tying himself
down to any abstract principle he is able to let each art stand
out free in its full individuality, instead of ranking painting with
sculpture against music with poetry, or the like. If, for example
we approach the question simply as one of sensuous appear
ance to the observer, then we lose all touch of the material
which sets his task to the artist ; but this is the essential
difference *e.g.* between sculpture and painting ; moreover, all
formative arts at least are essentially athletic,[2] and through
their relation to the artist we obtain an invaluable insight into
the nature of expressive self-utterance which later criticism

---

[1] *A.*, ii. 253.   [2] Collingwood, p. 242.

in England has independently developed. The character of each individual art is thus scrutinised by Hegel with a view to the coincidence between its expressive capacity as a whole and any content or import which it appears especially fitted to embody. For it is on the balance and reaction between expression and import that the distinction of the art-forms hinges. No parallel series are established. The analogy between architecture and music is simply noted, by the side of other analogies which music presents, as is a somewhat un-promising resemblance between sculpture and epic poetry.

The result on the whole is a linear classification, represent-ing the increasing ideality of the arts in terms of all the bases of division which I have mentioned, more gradually and more justly than the real and ideal series of Schelling and many others, and allowing, by the method that has been described, for the enormous difference between the " ideal " art of poetry in Greek and in modern times. The intervals between the arts may be imagined as equal, for the three romantic arts are allowed full and free individuality within their class-heading, and music in particular is for the first time put in its true place as the art in which pure feeling and necessary structural form—the two extremes of the mental world—are brought into absolute oneness, so that without any recognisable object or idea the movement of things [1] in as far it interests our feel-ing is built up into an organic and necessary fabric.

It has been said that Hegel's classification is a descending series.[2] This is not so ; the romantic arts are the culmination of art as such, though it is mere truth to say that they are not the culmination of beauty in the narrower sense. Whether art, in attaining its culmination, does not tend to pass beyond itself,[3] just as in architecture it has not wholly attained its idea, is another question ; and whatever the future may have in store (which is no subject for philosophy) there is no doubt that the whole ground and content of life, being thoroughly reflective and intellectual, is quite otherwise related to the beautiful to-day than it was in Greece or in the Middle Ages.[4] In saying that the art-spirit is essentially in evolution we do not deny that the evolution may be renewed on a higher level than before.

---

[1] *Æsth.*, iii. 145.   [2] Hartmann, i. 12ʸ.
[3] *A.*, ii. 234 ff.   [4] See esp. *Æsth.*, ii. 232.

Four Leading Conceptions defined.   iii. It is undoubtedly difficult to get a net result out of Hegel. Being aware of this quality, whether as I think, a merit, or as the reader may think, a defect, I will attempt before passing on to put together his views on four cardinal points of æsthetic, which, taken in combination, limit, begin, and end his account of the beautiful. Beauty itself, we may hope, has been sufficiently defined ; in its narrower sense by the classical ideal, in its wider sense by the whole evolution of the art-forms.

Ugliness.   (1) No systematic treatment is devoted to ugliness. We gather from a passage on carica-ture [1] that ugliness always involves distortion. This I take to mean the suggestion of a type by a presentation which, in suggesting, parodies it. The reference [2] to natural ugliness confirms this; it appears to be there treated as relative to our habitual judgment of typical character, though this does not exclude the possibility that our judgment may be ob-jective. False characterisation seems then to be the essence of ugliness.

There is a curious and instructive problem as to whether ugliness proper is present in the imperfect or symbolic phase of the ideal. Here the vicious and uncouth presentation of, say, an Indian idol, has its viciousness duly grounded in that of the content, the conception of Deity, which is to be ex-pressed. For this reason, I presume, Hegel seems to shrink from applying to such forms as these the technical word " ugly " (hässlich), though he describes them as vicious, distorted, deformed. They are, he says, not beautiful,[3] but as attempting to express the absolute in plainly inadequate form they have a certain analogy to the sublime. The fact is that Hegel's notion of beauty is so positive throughout, that he is not led to devote any special treatment to what, as its negation, falls outside his track of enquiry. If we can exhaust the positive, we can easily infer the place of the different kinds of negative. So far his method is far more instructive than many which are purely schematic. Opposite, contrary, counter-part, negation, are all of them mere formal terms, and tell us nothing at all unless we know the context and mode of genesis of the opposition or negation in question. But if we know the latter points, the technical terms can be

---

[1] Introd., E. Tr., 43.   [2] *Supra*, p. 338.   [3] i. 427.

readily supplied.   In Hegel the ugly is, it would seem, the
positive negation of a typical content, given as the portrayal
of that content, *i.e.* the analogue of falsehood or confusion
of relations.   The character of Molière's miser is called an
ugly (hässlich) abstraction ; I imagine because it is a partial
character alleged as a portrait of a concrete man.   Rudeness,
austerity, and the grotesque are not ugliness ; the romantic
ideal intentionally turns its back on classical beauty without
leaving the realm of beauty as such.   Common life *qua*
common, in which no great character [1] is perceptible, is the
world of prose as contrasted with the general poetic sphere of
art, but is not spoken of as ugly.

The Sublime.   (2) The sublime in the strict sense [2] lies at the
threshold of beauty, and belongs to the "sym-
bolic" art-form.   As the basis of his treatment of it Hegel
quotes from Kant : [3] "The strictly sublime can be contained
in no sensuous form, but attaches to ideas of reason, which
although no adequate representation is possible for them, are
yet stirred up and evoked in the mind by this very inadequacy,
which can be represented in sensuous form."   The sublime in
general, Hegel continues, is the attempt to express the infinite
without finding in the realm of phenomena any object which
proves itself fitting for this representation.
     As a case of inadequate expression it is akin to the ugly or
at least to the deformed and monstrous of the symbolic (its
own) phase of art.   We remember that to Schiller the same
appearance might be both ugly and sublime.   But yet these
montrosities have only "an echo of the sublime," because they
half satisfy, or are taken to satisfy, the need of expression by
the very distortion, or magnitude, barbaric splendour and the
like (false or endless infinity), which makes them monstrous ;
whereas, in the true sublime, a sharp consciousness of inadequacy is required.
     The purest type of this consciousness is found in Jewish
religious poetry, which contrasts all created things as perishable being,[4] with the one abstract God, in the sense that no
creature can be supposed in any way to represent Him ; so
that this true sublime cannot take the shape of formative art,
but only of poetry.   This ascription of sublimity to the relation
between the Jewish God and the created world is as old

---

[1] i. 190.   [2] i. 455.   [3] *K. d. U.*, p. 99.   [4] i. 466.

as Longinus, as Hegel points out[1] with reference to the example: "Let there be light, and there was light." Burke takes an instance from Job; and Kant, in a noble passage,[2] finds the highest type of the sublime in the very prohibition of the Decalogue, "Thou shalt not make to thyself any graven image," comparing it in spirit with the non-sensuous character which he ascribes to the moral law. The Psalms, Hegel continues, give for all time classical specimens of true sublimity, in the exaltation of the feelings which passes over everything else to worship the power of God only.[3] Nothing in the universe, they insist, can claim independence, for everything exists simply by His power and as subservient to Him.

It is instructive to compare this estimate of the Psalms in the work of a great systematic philosopher, with the continual reference to them in Ruskin, who while feeling their sublimity to the full, does not appreciate the entire hostility to the spirit of formative art, nor the temper of separation between God and man, in which they are conceived.

"Sublimity," Hegel says at this point, "involves on the side of man the feeling of his own finiteness and his insuperable remoteness from God." The conception of immortality, therefore, cannot exist at this stage. The consciousness of God as law is the germ of a more affirmative relation to him.

The sublime, though entering into the symbolic phase of the ideal, is specifically distinct from beauty and the ideal in the narrower or classical sense.[4] Still more is it incompatible with the romantic art-form in which the absolute is received into the individual subject in the form of love, "the ideal of romantic art";[5] and man himself, at one with God, becomes the expression of the infinite. The depths of import in romantic art, which "turns its back on classical beauty,"[6] make it possible, indeed, to extend the idea of sublimity as other writers have done, through all the more serious expressions of the relation between the individual man and the universe, as for example, through the sphere of religious and tragic feeling. Here, however, the question becomes verbal.

---

[1] i. 468.   [2] *K. d. U.*, 134–5.
[3] i. 471. The 104th and 90th Psalms are those which he quotes, laying stress on such verses as civ. 29 : "Thou hidest Thy face, they are troubled ; Thou takest away their breath, they die," etc., and xc. 5, 6, 7 : "Thou carriest them away as with a flood," etc.
[4] i. 466.   [5] ii. 150.   [6] ii. 124, 133.

I need only point out that Hegel's usage is limited by a clear logical and historical differentia — the sense of inadequate expression ; while any modern phenomena in which this sense appears to revive, as for the individual in his weakness and particularity it plainly may, are most simply treated as sublime by analogy. The individual, in any stage of culture, includes and may reproduce at times any past phase of human feeling.

The Tragic.   (3) The tragic is therefore, in Hegel's eyes, outside the sublime. As a poetic form it is the greatest achievement both of classical and of romantic art. It depends, primarily, on the collision of real spiritual forces, such as the family and the state, in individuals whose action has therefore an aspect both of rightness and of wrongness. And these forces, especially in ancient tragedy, forming the substance of the individual personality, cannot be detached therefrom, and involve, in the issue by which the conflict re-stores unity to the spiritual world, the destruction of the persons who represent them. This identification of the entire personalities with their substantive aims or rights, is the secret of the unhappy ending which Aristotle thought the better in ancient tragedy. His underlying reason plainly was that the happy ending, which he contemptuously assigns to comedy, involves the abandonment of essential purpose by the persons of the drama. Hegel's short account of the Antigone explains his conception better than any comment.[1]

"The completest species of this development is possible, when the persons in conflict appear, in respect of their concrete being [individuality, birth, position, etc.], each as including the whole of the sphere concerned. They then, in their own nature, are in the power of that against which they do battle, and injure that, which by the law of their own existence they ought to honour. So, for example, Antigone lives within Kreon's civil authority ; she herself is a king's daughter, and the betrothed of Hæmon, so that she was bound to pay obedience to the sovereign's command. Yet Kreon, too, who on his side is father and husband, was bound to respect the sanctity of blood-relationship, and not to command what violated that piety. Thus each of them has immanent in him or herself that against which they respectively rebel, and they are seized and broken by that very principle which belongs to the sphere of their own being. Antigone suffers death unwed, but Kreon too is punished in his son and in his wife, who seek their own death, the one because of Antigone's end, and the other because of Hæmon's. Of all that is noble in the ancient and modern world—I know pretty nearly all of it, and it is right and possible to know it—the Antigone appears to me, from this point of view, the most excellent, the most satisfying, work of art."

In the more subjective solution of the *Œdipus* at Colonus, Hegel finds a beginning of modernism, though no anticipation of the Christian consciousness, which is not, like the Greek, restored or reconciled within the intelligence, but rather disowns altogether its earthly being. In modern tragedy, then, the depth and interest of individuality and the formal maintenance of its consistency, in some degree take the place of the single moral right and duty constituting the whole personality. The surrounding circumstances are admitted in all their variety and contingency, and there is therefore a difficulty in keeping the necessary connection between the character and the issues of the plot. In the Shakespearian drama the character is made to work itself out inevitably, exhibiting and accepting in itself the consequences of its action. But if the connection between character and issues is lost, and the story becomes one of pure innocence oppressed by the chances of a hostile world, then the tragic element is destroyed, and the effect is no longer tragic, but an idle or futile melancholy or horror.[1]

When on the other hand the conflict of aims or interests reacts on the character, in virtue of its subjectivity, so as to produce a harmonious whole without sacrifice of individual lives, as is the case in a few ancient dramas, *e.g.* the Philoctetes, then the law of tragedy, which consists in the sacrifice of individuals to principles or aims inseparable from them, is abandoned, and we have the modern "drama of real life,"[2] which may arise, as Lessing explained, either out of tragedy or out of comedy. Shakespeare seems purposely to distinguish certain plays as tragic by the sacrifice of individual life, but a comedy like *Measure for Measure* touches all depths of *mental* suffering. There is a risk in the modern drama of

---

[1] 573.   [2] 539.

the whole development being thrown into the mere character, without a substantive aim to give it continuity, so that the
knave is converted, and forgiven, but we are not satisfied, for
we are sure that this development is unreal, and that he remains a knave in spite of all.[1]   A subjectivity which sets itself
free from every particular import is in its cycle and degree
the dissolution of the beautiful, which lies in the concrete
unity of subject and object.

The Comic.   (4) As this complete triumph of subjectivity[2]
the comedy of Aristophanes marks the close of one
period, and the comedy of Shakespeare[3] perhaps that of another.   The comic in this pre-eminent sense must be sharply
distinguished from the laughable.   Only that is truly comic,
in which the persons of the play are comic for themselves as
well as for the spectator, and so escape all seriousness, bitter-
ness or disappointment when their futile purposes are destroyed by the means they take to realise them.   Comedy
starts from the absolute reconciliation which is the close of
tragedy,[4] the absolute self-certainty and cheerfulness which
nothing can disturb.   This is the attribute as of the Aristophanic persons so of Shakespeare's comic characters, among
whom Falstaff is "the absolute hero";[5] a sort of greatness
runs through them, a freedom and strength of individuality
and superiority to external failure.   Serious modern comedy,
such as Molière's Avare, has not this ideal characteristic, and
therefore tends finally to pass into the prosaic world of the
ordinary drama, the mere ingenious representation of com
monplace intrigue.

Conclusion.   iv. I may conclude in Hegel's words,[6] from the
last two pages of the Æsthetic lectures :—
" With the development of comedy we have arrived at the
close of our scientific discussion.   We began with symbolic
art, in which subjectivity is struggling to find itself a content
and form, and to become objective ; we advanced to classical
art, which sets before itself in living individual shape the sub-

---

[1] 576.   Cf. e.g. The Two Gentlemen of Verona.
[2] iii. 533.   "Whereas in Tragedy the externally valid comes out victorious,
stripping off the one-sidedness of the individual . . . in Comedy, conversely,
it is subjectivity which in its infinite security keeps the upper hand."   This
form is drawn from Schelling, who defines Comedy as the converse of Tragedy
having "necessity in the subject and not in the object."
[3] iii. 579.   [4] iii. 557.   [5] iii. 207.   [6] iii. 579-80.

stantive content which has become distinct ; and we ended in
the romantic art of the heart and the feelings with the absolute
subjectivity moving freely in itself in the form of mind, which,
satisfied in itself, no longer unites with the objective and
particular, but brings into consciousness for itself the negative
character of this dissolution in the humour of comedy. Yet
in this culmination comedy is leading straight to the dissolution of art in general. The aim of all art is the identity,
produced by the mind, in which the eternal and divine, the
substantively true, is revealed in real appearance and shape
to our external perception, our feelings and our imagination.
But if comedy displays this unity only in its self-dissolution,
inasmuch as the Absolute, endeavouring to produce itself into
reality, sees this realisation destroyed by interests which have
obtained freedom in the real world, and are directed only to
the subjective and accidental, then the presence and activity
of the Absolute no longer appears in positive union with the
character and aims of real existence, but exclusively asserts itself
in the negative form, that it destroys everything which does not
correspond to it ; and only subjectivity as such displays itself
in this dissolution as self-confident and self-secure.[1]

" In this way we have now, down to the close, arranged every
essential principle of beauty and phase of art into a garland of
philosophy, the binding of which is among the noblest achievements that science has in its power to fulfil. For in art we
have to do with no mere toy of pleasure or of utility, but with
the liberation of the mind from the content and forms of the
finite, with the presence and union of the Absolute within the
sensuous and phenomenal, and with an unfolding of truth
which is not exhausted in the evolution of nature, but reveals
itself in the world-history, of which it constitutes the most
beautiful aspect and the best reward for the hard toil of reality
and the tedious labours of knowledge. And therefore it was
impossible that our study should consist in any mere criticism
of works of art, or suggestions for their production, but it had

---

[1] See above, p. 354 for a discussion of the idea that Hegel believes art to
be *finally* ended, on which the close of the Introduction is a sufficient com-
mentary. But we must claim extraordinary insight for him, who, still under
the spell of Schiller and Goethe, described the present exhaustion of the art-
impulse and the conditions hostile to it in language approaching that of Ruskin or William Morris.

no other aim than to pursue the fundamental idea of the beautiful and of art through all the stages which it traverses in its realisation, and by means of thought to make them certain and intelligible."

CHAPTER XIII.

"EXACT" ÆSTHETIC IN GERMANY.   SCHOPENHAUER TO STUMPF

Need of Exact Æsthetic. 1. It is difficult, I said in the last chapter, to get a net result out of Hegel; and strictly speaking, in science as science there can be no net result, no conclusion detachable from the inferential process. But yet the historico-philosophical method, which insists on giving us the whole whenever we ask for the minutest part, seems to some minds, and in some hands really is, an evasion of direct issues. The desire for a plain answer to a plain question found representatives in post-Kantian philosophy, whose importance, overshadowed at the time by the very bulk of the Hegelian writers, has effectually asserted itself in the period of reaction.

Schopenhauer. 2. The inaugurators of this movement were Herbart (1776–1841) and Schopenhauer (1788–1860). I shall treat of Schopenhauer first, in order to avoid interposing an account of him between Herbart and the Herbartians. It may seem strange to class with "exact" philosophers a writer who is *prima facie* a mystic; but it must be remembered that the root of mysticism is a love of directness amounting to impatience, and a repugnance to the circuitous approaches of systematic thought. This same characteristic may be a defence for the brevity which our treatment will display from this point onwards; for the exact or formal thinkers, to whom on the whole Schopenhauer belongs, being indifferent to content and caring chiefly about given form, are able to state their conceptions almost in axiomatic shape, instead of developing them historically. In the following chapter, it may also be remarked, it will be possible to deal as briefly with Hegel's principal successors, because in dealing with them the mass of his ideas may be presupposed.

Schopenhauer a kind of post-Kantian. i. Schopenhauer is a true post-Kantian both in his data and in his theory. In addition to the Greek and English culture of the time, he was profoundly influenced by the ancient Indian philosophy, which we remember the Romantic teacher, Fr. von Schlegel, did much to bring into prominence.[1] The fashionable pessimism and mysticism of cultivated Europe owes its origin in a great measure to Schopenhauer.[2]

As a theorist, Schopenhauer starts from Kant, whose demarcation of æsthetic he accepts in essentials, and whose conception of the thing-in-itself he identified, here following suggestions of Fichte and Schelling,[3] with an underlying will, as opposed to the "idea" of Hegelianism, which is the unity of the world interpreted on the analogy of the intellect. This will, as the ultimate reality, is incapable of being the object of knowledge ; and becomes such an object, not in itself, but only in its "objectifications," which are the external types of specific existence, forming a system of grades in the completeness with which they represent the will, and identified by Schopenhauer with the " Platonic ideas." These ultimate typical individualities, for such they are in opposition to the concepts of science, are only known as divined by artistic perception, being self-contained, and satisfactory to the contemplative sense. They are wholly distinct from such notions as consist in relations under the law of sufficient reason, which, forming an endless chain, forbid the mind to rest in them.

For our immediate purpose the main interest of Schopenhauer's position is its abstractness, which is complementary to the vast historical complexity of Hegelianism. History, for him, is unessential to the idea ;[4] only the eternal types which are framed within it are able to represent, for example, the idea of man. For knowledge of phenomena, the true method is that of the "understanding" with its clear relations according to the law of sufficient reason ; for knowledge of reality, the visions of art. The moving concrete of "reason" seems nonsense to him ; his "ideas" correspond to the fixity of species ; in everything he prefers the definite and the permanent. The

---

[1] By his work, *On the Language and Wisdom of the Ancient Hindus*, 1813, Schopenhauer was personally acquainted with the Orientalist Mayer, and constantly refers to Duperron's Latin translation of the *Upanishads*, 1801. See art. "Schopenhauer," *Encycl. Brit.*, by W. Wallace.

[2] See *e.g. Amiel's Diary*, with its constant reference to Mâyâ.

[3] "Will is the ultimate being." Schelling, quoted by Wallace, art. "Schopenhauer," *Encycl. Brit.*

[4] *Will and Idea*, vol. i. 236, E. Tr.

movement and evolution of things as we know them is part of
the illusion belonging to our mode of knowledge ; "velle non
discitur " ; the real underlying character of the universe and of
each individual is one and unchangeable.   He delights in the
simple rationality of the Greek temple,[1] and cannot appreciate
Gothic buildings, approval of which, as he very naively says,
would upset all his theories of the æsthetic purpose of architecture.   Their interest depends, he thinks, on associated
ideas ; but these have no place in strict æsthetic judgment.[2]
The distinction between classical and romantic poetry means
to him that the former deals with natural motives, and the
latter with artificial ones,[3] specially those of the Christian
myth, chivalry, and the ridiculous Christo-Germanic woman
worship.[4]

We shall find this preference for the classical predominate
among the " exact " thinkers ; naturally, as their view is, in
sum, a recurrence to classical æsthetic, armed with the
methods of modern science.

His account of
the Beautiful
and its Modifi-
cations.
ii. The beauty of the beautiful, for Schopenhauer, has two sides ; it frees us from the will,
and therefore from the whole apparatus that
attends our greatest vice and misfortune, the will to live,—from
explanation, causation, means and ends, purpose, desire ;[5] and
on the other hand it fills our minds with an " idea," an objectification of the will at a certain grade which we see in, and as
the essence of, the merely particular object presented to our
æsthetic perception.   As everything is in some degree an
objectification of the will, everything is in some degree characteristic, and in some degree beautiful.[6]   There is no further
difference between art and nature than that in art the artist
lends us his eyes to look through ; but then his genius can

---

[1] *Werke*, iii. 473 ff. (German).
[2] This view, which Herbart apparently shares (*W.*, viii. 12), reveals a tremendous chasm between these early " exact philosophers " and Mr. Ward, who
thinks associated ideas one of the most important elements of æsthetic.
Article " Psychology," *Encycl. Brit.* Fechner is with Mr. Ward on this point.
See p. 384 below.
[3] *Werke*, iv. 92.
[4] Hegel considers Schiller's reverence for woman a distinct proof of his
insight into the synthesis of sense and reason (*Æsth.*, Introd., E Tr. p. 119).
This contrast of views is typical
[5] *Will*, etc., i. 270, E. Tr.
[6] *Ib.*, 271.

understand the half-uttered speech of nature,[1] and so produce what she desired to produce, but failed.   This understanding is possible because of the unity between the will which we are, and the will which Nature embodies.   Such an under-standing or anticipation is the Ideal.

Ugliness appears to be merely defective manifestation [2] or partial objectification of the will, and so, in agreement with what was said of beauty, would be merely relative.   The sub-lime is the same as the beautiful, except that it presupposes a hostile relation between the objects contemplated and the individual will, which hostility, being overcome by an effort, gives rise to a spiritual exaltation of the subject in attaining, by this special effort, the pure contemplation of the idea in the hostile object.[3]

The arts are arranged rather according to their object-matter than according to their medium,[4] but with regard to the determination of the former by the latter, and so very much in the order in which Hegel placed them.   The fault of the latter in looking too exclusively to grades of life as a key to the value of the art representing them is paralleled by Schopenhauer.   The peculiar position of architecture and music, however, as not representing any individual objects, gives him occasion for a remarkable treatment of both.   The aim of architecture, which has no characteristic *individual* idea to present, must be, he infers, to put before perception the simplest qualities of matter, gravity, cohesion, rigidity, and the like.[5]   This is why the Gothic concealment of the rela-tion between burden and support, which the Greek beam-architecture is supposed to display in its nakedness, is incom-patible with the aim which he ascribes to the art.   Apart from its peculiar application, this principle of bringing out the quali-ties of a material is one of great importance, and conspicuous

---

[1] *Will.*, etc., i. 287, E. Tr.

[2] *Ib.*, 289.

[3] *Ib.*, 260–1.

[4] Schopenhauer's ingenious modification and defence of Goethe's colour-theory appears to be in harmony with modern physiological ideas.   He inter-prets Goethe's account of colour as light mixed with darkness, to mean that colour involves a partial activity of the retina (light), and a partial inactivity (dark), and lays down the principle that the retina always tends to a complete activity, the parts of which, if not simultaneous, as in white light, are successive, as in complementary images.   See *Ueber das Sehen u. d. Farben*. Werke, i.

[5] i. 277, E. Tr.

by its absence in almost all other æsthetic philosophers except Hegel.

Music, the analogy of which to architecture is very reasonably treated, the enormous difference between the two arts being duly emphasised,[1] is placed by itself, outside and above the series of the other arts. It is not like them, "the copy of the ideas, but the copy of the will itself, whose objectivity they are."[2] The expression is mystical, as in Schopenhauer's whole conception of the will in the universe ; but if we treat it as an analogy much may be said in its favour. We saw how strongly both Aristotle and Plato insisted that music was the most adequate or only adequate "imitation of life and character," or "of moral temperament." We may partly justify the extension of the comparison to the will *in the universe*, by Schopenhauer's clear recognition following Leibnitz, of the broad basis of modern music in the necessary numerical relations which underlie the region of musical sound,[3] but the sense of which acts on the musical consciousness as the sign only, and not as the thing signified ; and thus we may fairly bring together Schopenhauer's conception of music as "the quintessence of life and events,[4] without any *likeness* to any of them," with the theory of Hanslick as modified by Lotze,[5] according to which music embodies "the general figures and dynamic element of occurrences," considered as carrying our feelings with them. This notion has a just and important bearing on imitative music in the strict sense, which is criticised, in terms of the theory, as addressing itself to the intermediate conception of things, the phenomenon of the will, and not to the will or underlying reality, or, as we might say, to the *spirit* of life and occurrence itself. " Such (imitative) music is entirely to be rejected."[6] This judgment

---

[1] Schopenhauer comments on the phrase, "frozen music," ascribing it to Goethe and not to Schelling. I do not know how the priority stands as between them.

[2] i. 353, E. Tr. Readers of Browning will be reminded of *Abt Vogler*, both by the comparison between music and architecture, and by the direct assimilation to the will.

[3] Schopenhauer quotes with approval, " Musica est exercitium arithmeticæ occultum nescientis se numerare animi," which Schelling had quoted before him, from Leibnitz. Schop., *W*, i. 331, E. Tr.

[4] i. 339, E. Tr. See App. II. below.

[5] *G. d. A.*, 487.

[6] *World as Will and Idea*, 341, E. Tr.

repeats that of Plato. The general theory is closely analogous to that of Schelling. " Music, as representing pure movement, is above all others the art which strips off the bodily." [1]

Criticism of Schopenhauer. iii. Schopenhauer's attitude to concrete Idealism must not be judged by his attacks upon Hegel and Schelling. His whole doctrine in æsthetic is essentially a form of the theory of the characteristic, though always with a leaning to the distinct and plainly rational as against the suggestive and profoundly emotional. Though sense, as he knows quite well, is the organ to which beauty is relative, yet he always speaks of æsthetic perception as a form of knowledge distinguished only by being free from will. This defect reacts on his system by a certain want of sympathy in the treatment of architecture [2] and tragedy,[3] the highest function of the latter being necessarily for him negative, to produce resignation. Except for this, and an insertion of landscape gardening after architecture in the series of arts, Schopenhauer is in the substance of his views a very fair representative of post-Kantian æsthetic, while in literary form he is *facile princeps* among German philosophers. Such a doctrine as Hegel's opposition between true and false infinity is far more easily approached by the non-philosophical reader through Schopenhauer's contrast between the æsthetic object and the object of theoretical knowledge.

But if the main element in his account of music was after all a mystical conception, for a blind will is perhaps even harder to bring together with the unity of the world than an active unconscious idea, he nevertheless justified at least the place which Hegel assigned to music as the central romantic art, and impressed upon the philosophical and the musical world, in telling language, the problem of its mysterious powers.

Herbart. 3. It will be remembered that the object of æsthetic judgment first presented itself to Kant as " form," and that the symbolic or significant nature of this " form" only pressed itself upon him as his inquiries continued, and subject to some doubt whether " significance" as such was not extra-æsthetic.

---

[1] Schelling, *W.*, v. 501.   [2] See above, p. 365.
[3] The motives of the Antigone and Philoctetes are " Widerwärtige oder gar ekelhafte." *W.*, iii. 43 (German).

His Formalism and its Consequences. i. In attachment to the idea of pure form, and agreeing with Schopenhauer in a strong antagonism to the historico-philosophic school, HERBART took his own way of vindicating the objective validity of the æsthetic judgment.[1] Like Kant, he considers this judgment essentially individual, on the ground that abstract universality is incompatible with the complete presentation of the form submitted to judgment. And again like Kant, in fact though not in words, he ascribes to this judgment objective validity because of its permanent truth about the same object[2] under the same conditions. For modern logic such an "individual" judgment is plainly universal.[3]

The pure form, then, with reference to which objective individual judgments are made, consists, in his view, of relations and nothing but relations, simply as presented, and wholly dissociated from context. These are the "æsthetic elementary relations," and the enumeration of these is the task of æsthetic science. We are startled to find that among such relations those of will to will are included, so that ethics becomes a branch of æsthetic. This does not, however, involve confusing the act of will with the æsthetic judgment. The good implies both these conditions; the beautiful, only one of them. [4]

The first immediate consequence of this view is a protest against the generalising predicates such as " pathetic, noble, pretty, solemn," and the like, drawn from species of subjective emotion, which find a place in common æsthetic. They have not only the fault of subjectivity, but also that of abstractness. They tell us nothing of the special beauty and ugliness in particular arts ; nothing in music, where the question is of tone ; nothing in sculpture, where the question is of contours.[5] And so Herbart is with some justice hard upon writers like Schelling, who find in every art the excellence of some other, and not its own. The real type of the relations which he desires to discover and enumerate is in the relations of harmony between musical notes. These, he said in a foot-note

---

[1] Zimmermann, *A.*, i. 773. Herbart, *W.*, viii. 27.
[2] Logically "subject"; Herbart is contrasting it with the subject as percipient.
[3] See p. 341 *supra*, on Idealisation.
[4] *W.*, ii. 74.
[5] *W.*, i. 130.

which was afterwards modified, perhaps as too rashly candid,
were the only æsthetic elements which had for centuries been
determined and recognised with almost complete certainty.[1]
He only aims at simple forms, "elements;" no clear and
unambiguous judgment can be passed upon a highly complex
work of art or nature.   The combination of the elements
belongs to the doctrine of art.

The second immediate consequence of his view is that the
simple has no æsthetic quality,[2] and according to Zimmermann[3] he even pushes this conclusion against the beauty of
tones and colours perceived in isolation.   It is so obvious that
no presentation is really simple (extension in space or time
sufficing to render it complex) that to decide this vexed question, which has already been touched upon more than once,[4]
on such a ground, seems extraordinarily naive.   And there are
deeper reasons for questioning the rightness of the conclusion,
even if we take tone and colour as approaching simplicity.

Herbart did not carry out systematic researches in æsthetic.
It is worth while, however, to take note of some of his most
suggestive remarks.

His Division   ii. His primary division of æsthetic elementary
of   relations is that between the simultaneous and
Æsthetic Relations. the successive ; but all the arts, he finds, par-
ticipate in both.   The effect of the predominance of succession
on poetry is worked out in a way that reminds us of the
Laocoon.[5]   But in poetry the simple relations are difficult to
state owing to the lapse of time between their terms.   In
tones and colours it is easier, and there should be a science of
colour harmony like that of harmony in music.[6]   An exceedingly instructive example of Herbart's views is given at this
point in an answer to the objection, "the importance of which
is derived only from its audacity," that the numerical relations
which underlie the relation of harmonising tones are not the
elements of positive beauty in music, and but for the composer's genius, which gives them soul and significance, might

---

[1] *W.*, i., 150, note, withdrawn after 3rd edition.   General-bass (Thorough-
bass) he considers a part of æsthetic.   *Z.*, i. 770.

[2] *W.*, i. 137.

[3] i. 797.

[4] In treating of Plato, Kant, and Hegel.

[5] *W.*, i. 149–50.

[6] *Ib.* This natural idea cannot be pressed.   **See below on Zimmermann.**

produce mere monotony. "This soul and significance," he replies, "may be great with great artists, and little with little ones ; in any case we must abstract from it *here*, for we are speaking of the elements, and of the degree of accuracy with which they are determined. The mind of the artist can make no change in this." In an earlier edition he had written, "Then harmony would have to be banished from æsthetic."[1] This conception of æsthetic seems to give up the game, so far as a complete explanation of concrete beauty is concerned.

The harmonious in tones and colours depends on "blending before inhibition"[2] which must mean much the same as the capacity of forming parts in a whole. The account of symmetry gives no special importance to the curves of varying curvature, and even appears to say that the circle[3] is a predominant form in flower-contours, which shows very defective æsthetic observation. Yet there is a profound suggestion in the same passage as to the deeper equilibrium which replaces symmetry in the forms of plants and in landscapes, as depending on the balance demanded by perception, at present, Herbart says, inadequately understood. The limited conception of curve-beauty[4] is characteristic of Herbart's view, which prefers in everything the finite and complete. But yet he is led to the suggestive remark that if there is a general formula of beauty, it is "to lose something of regularity, in order at once to regain it,"[5] *i.e.* apparently to suggest the rule by deviations from it—an elementary case of progress accompanied by negation.

Classification of the Arts. iii. Herbart's classification of the arts does not rest upon the above principles of the simultaneous and successive, but on a distinction which is intended to correspond to that between classical and romantic art, or as Zimmermann subsequently called it, art of complete and of incomplete presentation. The arrangement[6] is as follows :—

| Architecture. | Landscape Gardening. |
| Sculpture. | Painting. |

[1] *W.*, i. 151 and footnote.
[2] "Verschmelzung vor der Hemmung." *Ib.*
[3] Can "die Kreisform" be a general term for "curves"?
[4] It may be objected to my criticism that the higher curve-beauty would not belong to Symmetry. But I do not find it treated elsewhere in Herbart.
[5] *W.*, i. 155
[6] *Ib.*, 171.

Church Music.   "Entertaining" Music.
Classical Poetry.   Romantic Poetry.

The one group is supposed to consist of arts that "can be looked at on all sides" (like sculpture), the others keeping in a soft twilight and admitting of no complete critical exploration. The distinction as applied to music has of course met with adverse criticism, appearing to omit, for example, the orchestral symphony. The root of it is probably to be found in the passage on harmony above alluded to, where the footnote goes on to argue that the beauty of "chorales" depends almost entirely on harmony, and therefore, it would follow, is readily deducible from the æsthetic elementary relations constituted by the laws of harmony. In commenting on the classification, Herbart seems to imply that only those who wish art to *express* something will care for the arts of the second group, and that their charm really rests on extra-æsthetic attractions.

Criticism and   iv. It is no objection to Herbart's theory that
Estimate.   it proposes to deal at first only with simple cases of beauty. To analyse what lends itself to analysis is the first rule of science, and the importance which he attaches to the numerical and physical basis of harmony is not exaggerated. A real objection might arise if it were seriously maintained that the beauty of more complex shapes in nature and art could be dealt with as a mere combination of the beauties of elementary forms. This would be, for instance, to treat the human figure as a decorative element. The crux of true æsthetic is to show how the combination of decorative forms in characteristic presentations, by an intensification of the essential character immanent in them from the beginning, subjects them to a central significance which stands to their complex combination as their abstract significance stood to them in isolation. But this objection comes later. Every one must welcome the plain statement of simple problems which concern the point where meaning passes into shape, and the attempt to deal with the pleasantness of perceptive states *qua* perceptive, as consisting of reactions and combinations having their own psychical effects *qua* reactions and combinations. Therefore the theory of formalism was practically opportune.

On the theory of the theory, so to speak, there is more to be said.

Prima facie, if we are to start from the given in æsthetic perception, it would seem that we cannot start from relations. Beauty as perceived lies rather in qualities than in relations, and a relation as such can only exist for discursive thought, which is not compatible with æsthetic perception. The point, then, of the very relations into which the formalist analyses the simpler cases of beauty seems to lie not in their satisfactoriness to perception, but in their satisfactoriness to the intellectual craving for explanation. As numerical or geometrical relations, apart from sense-presentation, one is in no way preferable to another. Considered, therefore, as an analysis of the actual perception of beauty, the reduction to relations *is* the assignment of a very simple import or significance to such perceptions, and there is no reason on the same principle for not going the whole length and finding in them the symbols of character or of moral law, just as much as symbols of numerical or symmetrical relation And in fact, conformably to what was said of the limitations of classical æsthetic, the recognition of a deeper import makes the actual analysis of expressive elements far more subtle, and therefore more complete within the bounds of formalism, than that which only looks for formal relations. Let any reader compare with Herbart or Zimmermann on symmetry, repetition and curvature, either Hegel's treatment of the same subjects in the section on the beauty of nature, or Ruskin's in the last chapter of *Elements of Drawing*, and he will see the difference between formalism within idealism, which has plenty of room for it, and formalism which pretends to exclude all idealism. Yet Ruskin himself finds elements in beauty which he can make no attempt to explain,[1] and it is well that there should be exact analysts who urge us to state or describe these given ultimate elements, and in every case to begin research by definitely enumerating the most direct and tangible cases of the phenomenon to be explored.

4. Zimmermann,[2] a professor at the university
Zimmermann. of Prague, who with the Austrian professors went over to the school of Herbart,[3] has been criticised at a great length and with extreme severity by Hartmann,[4] and also by

---

[1] *Elements of Drawing*, p. 322, and *Mod. P.*, vol. i. p. 25, and iii. 160 ff
[2] Author of *Geschichte d. Æsthetic.* 1858. *Allgemeine Æsth.*, 1865.
[3] Erdmann, *Hist. of Phil.*, iii. 33, E. Tr.
[4] *Æsth.*, i. 269 ff.

Vischer [1] in a rejoinder to Zimmermann's attack on Vischer's great work.

It would not be diffcult, following the line taken by these critics and indicated in my observations on Herbart, to convict Zimmermann's formalism of abstractness where it is pure, and of inconsistency where it appeals to content. But we shall find it more profitable to consider what fruitful ideas are represented in æsthetic by this movement (in which Zimmermann attaches himself so closely to Herbart that, while greatly developed, his thoughts cannot be readily distinguished from those of the latter), which though giving an impression of perversity and eccentricity, may yet be seen to rest on a definite conception that has a solid foundation.

The Distinctive Nature of Formal Æsthetic.   i. It cannot indeed be reasonably maintained, in view of the elaborate treatment devoted by such a thinker as Hegel to mathematical, chromatic and musical beauty, that idealism as such neglects the plain fact that all beauty exists in and for sense-perception or fancy.   But yet it might be urged with truth that there has been, as was admitted in the first chapter of the present work, a solution of continuity at one point of the objective analysis.   By what mechanism, or under what *particular* necessity, do sensuous forms which are highly and harmoniously expressive, give pleasure to the percipient owing to that expressiveness?   The idealist relies mainly on a concrete analysis of what is recognised as beautiful.   He does not aspire to legislate, but only to explain.   He can show that where, and in as far as, the trained perception is pleased, the presentation which pleases is one that has, as we say, "something in it."   He may in proportion to his knowledge and his critical acuteness, pursue his researches into every detail of the sensuous semblance, as for instance into its geometrical properties, and prove that, in comparison with a less beautiful perception, it either reveals a deeper idea, or exhibits its idea more adequately to sense. If, however, we ask how to demonstrate that beauty must be pleasant, his answer will be less ready, for the great idealists have dealt but little with the exact psychology [2] of ideas in interaction.

---

[1] *Kritische Gänge*, no. 6.

[2] I must not be understood to admit that they have not dealt with psychology at all.   I should doubt whether any other writer has approached Hegel's Philosophy of Mind, as a study of the phases of subjectivity.

The idealist will reply, and rightly, that all self-manifestation, with its weaker phase self-recognition, is naturally pleasant. But he might hardly be able to show by what mechanism pleasure is annexed to the contemplation of a symmetrical pattern, or a harmonious arrangement of colour, or to the hearing of a musical chord. And in popular criticism this difficulty sometimes amounts to a formidable contradiction. " The drawing is incorrect, but full of feeling." " The performance (musical) was inaccurate, but full of fire." In each of these judgments the two predicates are not *in pari materia*. The first predicate refers to form, the second to content. But the quality indicated by the second must be conveyed to eye or ear through positive form—through a definite operation of mechanical means—no less than the first. Through what form is it conveyed? The popular mind drops the analysis as soon as it presents some difficulty, and consequently commits itself to an absolutely fatal antithesis. I do not say that formalistic æsthetic has very much better success in practice, its cruces arising, as Herbart admitted [1] and as the critics insist, just where the deeper qualities begin. But it is something that we should be kept in mind of the problem.

Now this the formalist, and especially the Herbartian formalist, will do for us. He begins by pointing out that in the current of our ideas there are excited certain pleasures and pains by the mere operation of ideas upon one another in respect of their identity or opposition, and their consequent tendency to reinforce or depress one another. If these relations of pleasure and the reverse can be worked out in any degree of detail so as to coincide with the phenomena of æsthetic pleasantness, the result would be a definition of æsthetic pleasure, not merely *de facto* as the pleasure of expressive presentations, but *de jure* as the pleasure produced by certain tensions, depressions and excitations arising in the course of ideas, definable without going beyond the course of ideas itself.

Zimmermann's attempt to discover the fundamental forms which, in the coexistence of ideas, give rise to pleasure and the reverse, and to apply them to the determination of beauty in nature and in art, is admittedly not as successful as its

---

[1] P. 371 *supra*.

conception was opportune.   But it is desirable to make ourselves acquainted with its general nature.

Meaning of the   ii. All turns on the " Together," the " Zusam-
"Together."   men " in Herbart's phrase which is adopted by
Zimmermann. Simple images carry with them an addition
(Zusatz) of feeling, but this fuses itself with them and is in its
nature unæsthetic, because it hinders the distinct perception
of that which rouses the feeling.[1]   The addition which arises
when two or more images [2] are brought " together " is different in this respect.   It is distinguishable from the relation
perceived, without being removable from it, and consists in a
feeling of pleasure or otherwise which simply *is* the tension [3]
between the parts of the compound image.   It, the tension
felt as pleasure or otherwise, *is* therefore the æsthetic judgment, which is thus identical and self-evident.

The complex image is not a sum of lifeless parts.   It is a
psychical group of ideas, whose parts are ideas which are
living forces, and their " Together " is vital and active, producing tension and relaxation of them against and among
each other. [4]   These inter-relations are therefore essentially
active and actual ; they are not mere mathematical relations
and cannot be concentrated into an exponent. [5]

Now, of course, *what* sounds or colours are harmonious or
not, is decided by the ear and eye.   But for what reason in
general anything pleases or displeases, that is, as only forms
please or displease, by *what kind of forms* anything, whatever it be, pleases or displeases, this can be decided neither
by the eye, nor by the ear, nor at all by experience, but only
by thought.   For, for this purpose we need the question,
what forms, that is, what kind of " together " between the
perceptions (whatever they may be perceptions of) are, generally, *possible ;* and this question we can decide without first
considering the specific nature of the content, of the per-

---

[1] *A.,* 25.
[2] I desire to avoid interrupting this account with comment, so I simply
draw the reader's attention to this absolute opposition of simple and compound.   Where the simple is to be found, and how a presentation is to be
broken up into definite related parts, seems an ultimate difficulty of the view
before us.
[3] *A.,* 24.
[4] *Ib.,* 26.
[5] *Ib.,* 27.

ceptions (or "ideas") which are in the "together," as given in sound to the ear, and in colour-sensation to the eye. "*The conception of psychical ideas which possess a content (Quality) and a definite energy (Quantity) is sufficient for this purpose.*"[1]

"Æsthetic, as it has to do with those forms only by which every matter pleases or displeases, if only it is homogeneous, *i.e.* capable of entering into forms at all, is therefore not an empirical but an *a priori* science."[2]

Elementary and Simple Forms. iii. Thus the science is built up deductively, beginning with the elementary or simple forms of "Together"—those which involve two terms only—and proceeding to the derivative or complex forms, which involve more terms than two, and can always be analysed into the simple forms.[3]

Beginning with two terms only, and regarding them according to quantity and quality only (disparate terms being incapable of entering into æsthetic form), he finds that in quantity they can be compared only as more or less intense, and formulates the "pure form of Quantity." "The stronger idea is pleasing compared with the weaker; the weaker is unpleasing compared with the stronger."[4] In Quality the only cases which do not reduce the two terms to one are those of predominant identity and predominant discrepancy. These give rise to the harmonious and the unharmonious forms of Quality.[5]

These original forms are further subdivided into their several cases or applications, and these are then made the basis of the derivative forms, being the same principles in application to a number of terms greater than two in each case.

The original principle of Quantity (I take this case as an illustration) divides *genuinely* into the forms of the *great*, which rests on comparison of definite large and definite small, and the *perfect*, in which the greater is considered as the purpose of the less.[6] This is a category of Herbart's æsthetical ethic, which Zimmermann introduces into æsthetic proper. *Spuriously*, further, the form of Quantity gives rise to the sublime, when the aspiration after an infinite quantity, which cannot really be presented in idea, is compared with a definite

---

[1] *A.*, 37.   [2] *Ib.*, 42–3.   [3] *Ib.*, 41.
[4] *Ib.*, 31.   [5] *Ib.*   [6] *Ib.*, p. 35.

quantity. The qualitative difference between an aspiration and a quantity is thus taken account of, and the sublime falls outside pure quantity and complete conception, and becomes one of the twilight or romantic conceptions.

In the "harmonious form of Quality," [1] the pleasure which harmony produces is ascribed to the predominant identity of the qualities of the terms, and confirmation is claimed for the view on the ground of Helmholtz's researches. My reason for mentioning this particular instance, in which probably the theory is seen at its best, is that the good fortune which has attended the explanation of musical consonance by the ratio between periods of oscillation, has made Zimmermann very eager to extend a similar proceeding to the explanation of colour harmony. But there is no real correspondence between the two cases. It is very doubtful whether complementary colours are to a cultivated sense those that naturally harmonise.[2] If they were so, then the explanation by blending of the identical would be false, for true complementary colours share absolutely no element of light [3] with each other. And the eye is absolutely incapable of detecting the elements of a compound colour, and being pleased or the reverse in consequence of their ratios of oscillation.[4] No one knew, before it was experimentally determined, that yellow was a combination of red and green. Every one believed that green was a combination of blue and yellow. Thus it is fairly certain that no form of the numerical analysis which accounts for musical harmony will also account for colour harmony. Æsthetic judgment appears, in the above case of red and blue, to be distorted by the desire to find demonstrable " relations " in the colour scale. If such relations exist, they are not parallel to those of sound.

The general theory as applied to these cases is expressed as follows. "The identical element in the content of the two terms of the form, will seek to produce blending; the opposed

---

[1] *A.*, 42.

[2] Cf. *Z. A.*, 250, on "red and blue," which he condemns as " peasant's fashion," because not complementary, with Ward in *Encycl. Brit.*, art. "Psychology," p. 69, where this combination is explained as belonging to a more refined taste than that which enjoys red and green.

[3] Disregarding the mere impurity of ordinary coloured light, on which Zimmermann is ultimately driven to base his theory. *A.*, 43, note.

[4] Helmholtz's *Lectures*, First Series, E. Tr., p. 92.

elements to produce inhibition. The former, which would naturally take place in consequence of the partial identity of the qualities, is hindered by the latter, which keeps the members of the form apart. The opposition sets up tension between the terms which the identity is attempting to unite. Through this there arises a state like that of the *question*. If then the identity of the members prevails, this tension is relaxed ; the opposition that causes it is overcome without being abolished ; blending takes place, and with it a feeling of pleasure." [1]

One more very simple example in which Zimmermann applies his views ought in justice to be mentioned, for it has, I think, considerable interest. Building up the work of art from its simplest elements, Zimmermann starts with the Imagination of abstract Synthesis. [2] A point in space, he here explains, is simple, and so without æsthetic quality. Two points, even, have no æsthetic relation, being strictly undistinguishable. And because they are without æsthetic relation, so is the distance between them. (I should have thought, that on Zimmermann's principles, this was because *qua* distance it is simple.) If two such distances (systems of two points) are presented, an æsthetic relation arises. Assuming them to be unequal, then according to the form of quantity the greater is pleasing, the lesser unpleasing. Hartmann objects to this form that it makes the æsthetic judgment, upon the presentation as a whole, self-contradictory. But the fact is, I think, well observed, and the contradiction, as I understand, is Zimmermann's postulate. For he continues by pointing out that if there is a common measure (I presume " to perception" should be added), the discord is reconciled and the case of agreement sets in, accompanied with pleasure. If the distances are incommensurable, the percipient is stimulated to supply a distance that will harmonise them ; and in the " metrical " beauty—beauty of pure measurement—so arising, there is the semblance of disproportion overcome by the ultimate perception of proportion. Thus there is, he would, I imagine, desire us to infer, a sense of economy or simplifica-

---

[1] *A.*, 43–4.
[2] P. 188. I take this to be the meaning of his " Zusammenfassendes Vorstellen," which is a first stage followed by " Empfindendes Vorstellen " and " Gedanken Vorstellen."

tion against waste and destruction, that is to say, combined
with enlargement of the field of consciousness.

Psychological
Meaning of the
Theory, and
its Value.

iv. In the end, all these principles of pure form
within the course of ideas appear to be cases of
a sort of ratio between attention, which is a
quantity that has a limit, and the field of consciousness. Ideas or images accompanied by adequate attention are, it is suggested,[1] always pleasant. Enlargement of
the field of consciousness, therefore, is as such accompanied
with pleasure, so long as it is compatible with adequate attention. Economy of attention is pleasant as instrumental to
adequacy. Interruption or baffling of attention is relatively a
narrowing of the field of consciousness, and is felt as tending
to inadequacy of attention. Such waste of attention by interruption and baffling is felt for example in dissonance. The
confusion of a discord is compared to " trying to reckon up a
sum in one's head, and failing because the numbers are too
high."[2] All mere interruption is painful in itself. Flickering
lights, meaningless noises, false rhythms,[3] intermittent irrita-
tions of the skin, are analogous examples.[4] Clearness, truth in
rhythm, in short, simplification, are economical of attention
and so pleasant in themselves.

It is obvious that in this doctrine of pleasantness, which as
determined by the pure inter-relation of images is, as far as it
goes, æsthetic pleasantness, we have a counterpart to the
principle of unity in variety as applied by objective analysis
to nature and art. Could the formalistic doctrine be elaborated in detail for the other departments of æsthetic, as it has
been in the prerogative example of musical consonance and
dissonance, we should obtain as a result a complete translation
of objective æsthetic into terms of the course of ideas with its
pleasantness and unpleasantness, just as we have, in recent
psychology, important rudiments of such a translation for
logic and for ethics in the theory of apperceptive masses
guiding both the unpractical and the practical course of the
mind. It seems natural, however, that this very abstract

---

[1] By J. Ward, " Psychology," in *Encycl. Brit.* I have attempted to throw
together the explanation of pleasantness due to intensity and to quality.
[2] Preyer, quoted by Ward, l.c.
[3] " I would rather go to the treadmill for an hour than walk a mile between
two asynchronous bipeds."—Henniker's *Trifles for Travellers.*
[4] Ward, l.c., and Helmholtz, *Lectures,* Series i. p. 88.

kind of explanation (abstract, because dealing merely with identity and contrast as such) should continue to be most effective within the limits which Herbart assigned it,[1] and should give way to more worldly language when we come to analyse the individual shapes in which æsthetic unity embodies itself. Zimmermann manages to deduce a "form of the characteristic" from his abstract principles, but being a relation of identity between *archetype* and *copy*, it is not convincing as applied within the course of ideas.

But it is very much to have a clear explanation of simple extreme cases ; in such explanation almost every science finds its strictest demonstrative support, and to feel the whole value of a really definite formal æsthetic it is only necessary to read Plato's statement[2] of the true problem of harmonic theory in connection with the discoveries of the " *Tonempfind-ungen.*"

Fechner.   5. If we are to be in earnest with formal æsthetic, it is plainly necessary to take steps for testing the actual agreeableness of various isolated forms to unbiassed taste. To have attempted this task by systematic experiment is the merit of Fechner,[3] whose researches, although including valuable enquiries into the beauty of association, display on the whole a decidedly formalistic bent.

Criticism of Previous Inquiries.   i. He prefaces the account[4] of his own experiments with geometrical form by referring to the ideas of previous enquirers, upon which he passes two noticeable criticisms. First, he observes, nearly all of them aim at establishing some one normal form or relation as *par excellence* that of beauty, whereas in fact each of these has value only within certain limits, and there is no such thing as a normal line or shape of beauty. Secondly, it has been the rule by way of obtaining the pure form to omit all reference to association, which is really a much more important element of the

---

[1] See p. 371 *supra*.

[2] *Rep.* 531 C. " To consider what numbers are harmonious, and what are not so, and for what reason in each case." Plato is demanding the real reason, as opposed to the empirical observation of consonance. He is fully in the spirit of modern science, although of course he did not know where to look for his reason.

[3] The well-known writer on " Psychophysics." His principal work bearing on Æsthetic is *Vorschule d. Æsthetik,* 1876.

[4] *Vorsch. d. A.,* i. 184.

beautiful than the *pure* form itself. Among the forms of beauty
suggested by previous enquirers, he enumerates the circle
as handed down from antiquity, the ellipse as advocated by
Winckelmann, the undulating and spiral lines and the pyramidal shape insisted on by Hogarth; the square, and in
general the relation 1 to 1, preferred by recent German
writers as the most readily comprehensible and therefore the
most æsthetically advantageous relation ; the simple rational
relations generally (1 to 1, 1 to 2, etc.) on the same ground ;
and finally Zeising's golden section, propounded by him, not
merely as a normal æsthetic relation, but as a proportion predominant throughout the whole of nature and art.[1]

Experiments with   ii. One set of Fechner's experiments may be
Rectangles, etc. briefly described to show the kind of observations
made and results attained. He asked[2] for judgments of distinct preference and rejection from a large number of different
persons upon the satisfactoriness, elegance, or beauty of ten
rectangles of equal area, cut out in white card and laid unsorted
on a black surface. They varied in shape from a square to
a figure with sides as 2 : 5, the golden-section rectangle with
its sides as 21 : 34 being seventh in order of length, counting from the square. Generally speaking, the judgments
of preference increased and the judgments of rejection diminished from the two extremes (square[3] and longest rectangle)
to the golden-section rectangle, which had 35 per cent.
of the preferences, and absolutely no rejections. It would
have been interesting to try a differently framed series. I
should suggest a tendency to prefer a form that was not
extreme in the given series.

Most of the persons began by saying that it all depended
on the application to be made of the figure, and on being told
to disregard this, showed much hesitation in choosing.

Fechner's general results with regard to these figures and
to the division of straight lines into segments, are that the
square[4] and the rectangle nearest to it on the one hand, and

---

[1] Cf. p. 41 above. The proportion in question, it will be remembered, is
that in which the lesser is to the greater as the greater to the sum of the two.
It is applied by Zeising to any two principal dimensions in a figure.

[2] *V. d. A.*, i. 192 and 195.

[3] The square, however, had a few more preferences than the rectangle next
to it. The longest rectangle had no such preference over its neighbour.

[4] See note [3].

the longest rectangle on the other hand, are the least pleasing. The simple rational relations (corresponding, it has been suggested, to musical consonance) show absolutely no superior pleasantness to those which can only be expressed by ratios of much larger numbers (corresponding to dissonance). The golden-section rectangle, and its immediate neighbours have a real superiority in pleasantness to the other rectangles. The least deviation from symmetry has a far more decided unpleasantness than a proportionally much greater deviation from the golden section.

In dividing a horizontal line, the golden section is decidedly less pleasant than bisection.[1] In dividing a vertical figure, say in determining the point of insertion of the arm of a cross, the golden section is less pleasant than the ratio of 1 : 2.

These results, together with the uncertainty of judgment shown by those who contributed to them, support the general view which I have taken of formal beauty. Doubtless some slight but definite reason exists for the preference thus displayed as between certain figures, but conformably to the slightness of the content which such bare forms can symbolise, it is readily overcome by any concrete application of them. Thus in the measurements of picture frames, there is customarily a wide deviation from the golden section, and the customary ratio between height and breadth is different according as the height exceeds the breadth, or the breadth exceeds the height.[2] This shows the overpowering influence of the concrete upon the abstract. For sheer abstract figures, height and breadth have no meaning.

The slight exceptional rise of preference for the square seems quite intelligible, owing to the unique character impressed upon this figure by the total absence of difference between its sides. Mere uniqueness, incapability of being confused with anything else, is attractive *per se*. Simplicity, stability, and many such properties naturally connect themselves, and have always been felt to do so, with this same absence of difference in the dimensions of this figure.[3] At

---

[1] See on Zimmermann, p. 379 above.

[2] *V. d. A.*, ii. 292. If height is greater, it is to breadth as 5 : 4; if breadth, it is to height as 4 : 3; *i.e.* there is a feeling against excess of height, probably not hard to explain.

[3] τετράγωνος ἄνευ ψόγου. "Foursquare without blame," of the good man in **Ar.** *Ethics*, i. 10, 11.

the same time difference has its attractions ; but plainly must
go far enough to escape confusion with the square, and attain
some sort of balance (the grounds of which I do not profess
myself able to suggest) before it can surpass the pleasantness
of the simple unity of the square.

Æsthetic Laws.   iii. Fechner's æsthetic laws, with the exception of the law of association and perhaps of the
law of economy, are very much the laws of Greek æsthetic.
Such are the law of unity in variety, of congruousness, of
clearness.

But newer ground is opened up by his treatment of the
principle of association [1] and of the law of economy.

In speaking of Herbart, we saw reason to suspect that in
ascribing the pleasantness of presented qualities to their
dependence on abstract relations, the narrow paths of strict
formalism had already been abandoned. For if we once go
behind the sensuous presentation, are we not in fact looking
for a reason ? What indeed is a ratio, for the perception of
beauty, if it is not a reason? Granted that smoothness of
the course of our ideas, and its reverse, may attach to such
relations, may not other less abstract and more controlling
properties attach to them as well ? If we assume that this
criticism is just, it follows that even in exact enquiry the
candid course is to admit that we are looking not only for an
actual cause of pleasure, but for a reason in the cause, while
we retain the spirit of " formalism " so far as to insist that no
reason shall be relevant but one which is inherent in, and not
casually annexed to, the sense-presentation.[2] Schopenhauer
and Herbart were right in being suspicious of association ; for
association may be taken to mean arbitrary or chance connection. Mr. Ruskin's treatment of the pathetic fallacy [3] is an
invaluable analysis of the dangers of ungrounded association.

But yet, those who do not admit that any elements of the
universe are " cut off with an axe " from the rest, may fairly
approve of an enquiry into the inherent æsthetic associations
of given forms ; and if the phrase which I have used is held
to be a contradiction in terms, then the part of it which we

---

[1] *A.*, i. 93.
[2] This is in the main Herbart's attitude to association ; see Fechner's Criticism, *A.*, i. 119.
[3] *M. P.*, iii. 157, 173.

must retain is the limitation " inherent," and the term " association " must be replaced by " significance " or " symbolism."
It is *prima facie* a reasonable extension of formalism to ask
what sort of content this or the other form is by its essential
constitution adapted to express.

Fechner has boldly attacked the most difficult because least
analysable of all æsthetic problems, that of the import or
"associations" of the isolated colours.[1] His execution of the
attempt does not seem equal to his conception of it. He relies
almost wholly on the distribution of colours in nature. But
plausible as it may seem to associate our feeling for red with the
ideas of blood and fire, or our feeling for blue with the idea of
the sky, I have serious doubts whether their association ought
really to be treated as essential. It must be clearly understood that in any decoration *which definitely recalls the forms
of plants* there is more to be considered than the association
of colours as such. I do not say that we should not be
shocked if a plant were presented in decoration with red
leaves and green petals; but yet the colours even of plants
are very freely treated for decorative purposes, and we have
not the least dislike to a plant form depicted entirely in shades
of red. *A fortiori* the colour in itself, when no natural form
is portrayed, and the colour harmonies, certainly seem to be
independent of naturalistic association ; and probably some
investigations on the older lines, referring to purity or other
actual properties of the hue as affecting the eye, not neglecting its implied harmonious or inharmonious relation to our
ordinary surroundings, would have better success than the
mere reference to natural associations. It may be pointed out
as supporting this view, that a very slight difference of shade
and of gradation throws association wholly off the track. The
colour of a very hot fire has nothing that reminds us of blood-
red, and I do not believe that a house door painted with the
green of the first spring leaves would have any kind of association with the beauty of spring.

In analysing the inherent associations of the concave and
convex[2] Fechner seems more successful, plainly owing to the
greater facility for analysis afforded by their complex forms
He has no difficulty in showing that the concave appears as
a rule receptive, and the convex exclusive or repellent, except

---

[1] *M.P.*, iii. 100. [2] *Ib.*, 105

in the case of surfaces such as those of cushions, which are convex in order to become concave.

In this region of essential association Fechner does not obtain any great results. But, if detailed analysis, such as exact æsthetic pursues, is to have any value at all, I think that his method points in the right direction.

As a case closely analogous to the results of such analysis, we may treat the phenomena of the law of economy, which Fechner ranks, after his eclectic manner, as "a principle of æsthetic." In reality, this principle is merely a deduction from the law of unity in variety, and as directed against superfluity in the parts of an æsthetic structure coincides almost verbally with Aristotle's warning, that a part which is not necessary is no part of the whole.[1]

"In their treatise on the organs of locomotion," writes Professor Vierordt,[2] "the brothers Weber[3] have demonstrated, in several passages and by striking examples, that the æsthetically beautiful is also on the whole the physiologically correct; that the two coincide, that the impression of beauty (ease, unconstrainedness, freedom) is always produced by results attained at the least possible expense of muscular force."

This principle, as Fechner observes, may be treated either with reference to the content of our presentations, in which it is pleasant to us, through sympathy, to see the economical employment of force, or with reference to the course of our presentations, there being an economy of attention in the observation of movements that are economical in the expenditure of force. Both of these aspects of the law of economy were insisted on by Mr. Herbert Spencer,[4] as early as the years 1852 and 1854 respectively. The second is capable of being treated as a law of pure formalistic psychology, and Fechner is led by it to raise the whole question of the psychical nature and conditions of pleasure, without, however, arriving at a positive conclusion. Only he decides that it is impossible to set up the law of economy as

---

[1] P. 32 above.
[2] Quoted by Fechner, *V. d. A.*, ii. 263.
[3] See reference to their work in Ward, "Psychology," *Encycl. Brit.*
[4] Essay on "The Philosophy of Style" and on "Gracefulness," republished in *Essays Scientific, Political, and Speculative,* vol. ii.

the fundamental principle of æsthetic psychology. It is, indeed, as we have seen, a plainly derivative law.

It is worth while, in order to remove a seeming contradiction with the deepest æsthetic criticism, to point out that this principle, being simply a consequence of the relation of parts within a whole, can have no claim to determine what the nature of the whole, its essence or purpose, shall be. Thus we find room for the apparently antagonistic principle of lavishness or sacrifice.

A good engineer does not adjust his supporting forces with absolute exactness to the greatest estimated burden. He leaves a margin of safety against unforeseen hazards which has, even in works of pure utility, a sort of æsthetic effect in the mental security of all who are concerned with the structure. And so, we are told to-day, with apparent truth, a certain lavishness of force is a noble quality not merely in the ornament, but in the very substantiality and strength of domestic buildings. Security of mind, the sense of permanence, the absence of any suggestion that the building is meanly calculated to the immediate owner's interest, appear to be æsthetic properties which demand a certain bounty and largeness in the provision of strength and solidity.

In a more intense degree these same properties take the form of " sacrifice ";[1] but neither a margin of safety, nor lavishness, nor sacrifice, is identical with waste or incompatible with economy. A large conception of purpose and effect is one thing ; the most effective adjustment of forces to it when conceived is another.

From Fechner we have gained but little in positive principle, but something in method and tangible elucidation, which latter is very necessary to æsthetic science if it is not to hang in midair. And our judgment of formal æsthetic, that it is the theory of antiquity armed with the methods of modern science, has in him received a striking confirmation.

Stumpf. Scope of his Analysis. 6. So far, finally, as I am able to form an opinion on the development of psychological theory respecting music in the hands of Professor Stumpf,[2] it appears

---

[1] See " Lamp of Sacrifice " in *Seven Lamps of Architecture*, where the distinction between bounty and waste is well insisted on, and Wordsworth's sonnet on King's College Chapel.

[2] Author of *Musikpsychologie in England*, 1885, and *Tonpsychologie*, of which vol. ii. appeared in 1890.

to me that Herbart's original admissions retain their full force.[1]
The completed work of musical art, even in the comparatively
simple form of an entire melody, does not, as I gather, come
strictly within the scope of his analysis.   The facts of consonance produced by the "blending" of tones, an ethical or
emotional import[2] ascribed to single sounds of certain definite
types (soft deep notes, soft high notes, etc.) and to certain
definite intervals, and some very general conditions of musical
pleasure such as dim analogies with verbal utterance, and the
constant renewal of the listener's expectation, appear to be the
only factors which exact psychology is able as yet to discern
by analysis within the musically beautiful.   The difficulty
which Herbart admitted still remains; the elements which
can be readily analysed do not penetrate into the characteristic differences which make one musical whole beautiful and
another trivial or tedious.   And there is in the background
a dark suspicion that these alleged expressive qualities of
isolated factors may be really faint associative suggestions
drawn from the character which they assume in those complex combinations of which they most readily remind us.

Conclusion.   7.   In taking leave at this point of purely
formal or exact æsthetic—for in the English and
German writers who have yet to be considered we shall only
find it in subordination to other ideas—I will attempt in a
few paragraphs to estimate its achievement and its prospects.

How judge of   i. We must not test it by a standard which it is
Formal Æsthetic. a blunder to apply to any æsthetic theory whatever.   No æsthetic theory[3] can give appreciable assistance in
the construction of individual works of art, or can adequately
represent their beauty in another, viz. an intellectual medium.
We should do injustice to Herbart and Zimmermann, if we

[1] Not being qualified to judge independently in musical questions, I here
follow the representations of the late Mr. Edmund Gurney in the paper "The
Psychology of Music," *Tertium Quid*, ii. 251. My only addition to his argument
consists in noting the parallelism between defects which he ascribes to the
views of Prof. Stumpf, and the admissions made by Herbart. See p. 371 above.

[2] This ascription while far too little for objective idealism is far too much
for exact formalism.

[3] What about counterpoint, which Herbart includes in æsthetic? The
answer is, that the artist may embody his experience in rules, though it is
hazardous, especially outside music, to attach great value to them. But these
rules are data of æsthetic, not its content, because they come from the
practice of the art and not from reflection upon its capacities.

were to interpret their conviction of the all-importance of elementary relations, as indicating the belief that works of genius could be constructed by rule and line, or fairly represented in a system of abstract reflections. For exact æsthetic, as for the æsthetic of concrete idealism, the only conceivable problem is the explanation of beauty in the light of general principles aided by the analysis of individual examples given in nature or in art.

Lesson of its History.
ii. If therefore formal æsthetic is pronounced a failure in the presence of concrete individual beauty, this verdict does not refer to the task of prior construction, nor of reproduction in intellectual form, but only to the problem of subsequent analysis for speculative purposes. Allowing for the greater depth and variety of modern exact science as compared with that of antiquity, the work of formal æsthetic in modern times corresponds with the strictly Greek æsthetic of Plato and Aristotle, and is checked, as in the main theirs also was checked, at the point where beauty passes into concrete individual form. Whole and part, unity in variety, simple colours, simple sounds (to which in modern times we must add simple consonances and unsuccessful attempts to deal with colour-harmony), spatial figures, rhythms (and in modern analysis the peculiar case of rhyme) are the object-matter about which exact æsthetic is able to supplement the suggestions of the Greek philosophers from the wealth of modern physics and modern psychology.

That with this achievement it has attained its limit as an independent method appears to be proved both by its divergences and by its concessions.

We cannot but be surprised when we find that the thinkers who set out by holding tight to the beautiful datum in its sensuous peculiarity,[1] are also those who attribute its peculiar effectiveness to the most abstract and isolated underlying relations. It is true that the relation is conceived as a genuine cause operating in an assignable mode, and not reducible to a mere mathematical expression, but this does not alter the fact that the operation, as defined by the relation, is of so general a nature as to be void of relevancy to the individual beautiful effect in a context of art, as distinguished from that which is not beautiful in such a context.

---

[1] Herbart, l.c., p. 369 supra.

And thus, to refer for a moment to an English writer for the sake of illustration, we find that within the exact school the peculiarity of the concrete datum comes at last to be vehemently asserted,[1] against the psychological side of the school, as incompatible with the analysis of it by dissolution, and with the reference of its character in fragments to abstract and isolated relations.

This antagonism seems really to be implicit in Herbart. Intellectual analysis of the datum, when once entered upon, cannot come to rest in abstractions. It must go forward till it recognises[2] on the intellectual side a concreteness adequate to that which the datum of beauty exhibits on the sensuous side.

The concessions of formal æsthetic tell the same tale. In Zimmermann as compared with Herbart we notice, *a*, the inclusion of the " characteristic" in the list of formal relations— an extraordinary *tour de force;* and, *b*, the softening of the opposition between classical and romantic, which in Herbart and Schopenhauer meant a degree of preference for the more narrowly definite forms of art, into a distinction, applicable to all periods of history, between beauty that attaches to complete conception and beauty attached to incomplete conception and dependent for its attractiveness on subjective interests. Room is thus made to include great work of any period under the term " classical."

Further, in Fechner, in Prof. Stumpf, and in the best recent English psychology and exact musical theory,[3] the principle of association is accepted as of paramount importance, in contradiction with Schopenhauer, and essentially with Herbart. Even the term "utterance" has been applied by the very competent analyst[4] above referred to, as indicating by analogy a peculiar impression which beautiful melody conveyed to his mind.

These divergences and concessions exhibit, if I am right, the spectacle, too familiar in philosophy, of the concrete world-spirit freakishly decoying into blind paths the explorer who has refused his guidance, and coming in by the window when he is barred out at the door.

---

[1] By Gurney, *Tertium Quid*, ii. 279, in opposition to Stumpf.
[2] I do not say " constructs."
[3] *E.g.* in Ward and Gurney.
[4] Gurney, *ib.*, 274.

iii. It has been remarked with regard to what used in ethics to be called Utilitarianism, now commonly known as Hedonism, that it takes upon itself the hazard of exclusiveness. Other theories do not profess to exclude it, but it professes to exclude them. The same is true of the relation between formal æsthetic and the æsthetic of concrete idealism. There can be no precise analysis of the psychical operation of beautiful form for which a place is not ready and waiting in the theory of beauty as expressiveness. Enough has been said, I hope, in dealing with the Greek thinkers to make this relation absolutely clear. Only it may be well to supply out of the present chapter a single link which there remained in a great measure hypothetical. We then supposed that the simple forms which please, derive their satisfactoriness from some latent affinity, other than sensuous stimulation, between them and the feeling of intelligent beings. In the principle of economy as applied to the pleasure of watching graceful movements, by Fechner and his authorities, we appear to follow the actual operation of such a latent harmony. In the first place, movement economical of force embodies the principle of organic unity, negatively requiring the absence of superfluous elements. Ultimately indeed the principle develops into that of the characteristic. This absence of superfluity we realise in terms of feeling by inherent association with our own muscular adjustments. And in the second place it is suggested that in the apprehension of such movements our attention is so economised that as a psychical occurrence the apprehension is easy and pleasant *per se*, so that we have at once our satisfactory content and an agreeable perception of it. And as adequacy of expression to content is not an accident, but the very essence of beauty, it is not improbable that this thoroughgoing connection between the working of our attention and the properties of a beautiful content may turn out to be normal. It is plain, of course, that in concrete cases of beauty the psychical occurrences must be required to take on very complex shapes, which may or may not in individual minds undo their own agreeableness by fatigue owing to their sheer quantity, or by contradictions beyond the reconciling power of the individual mind in question.

The reader should remember that for the reason alleged

above, the principle of lavishness is not opposed to that of economy. The most graceful movements are often those which are superfluous when judged by definite purposes of life; but their course will possess a harmonious unity which will be distinguishable from the inharmonious and wasteful abruptness of similar movements ungracefully performed.

Finally, it may be laid down that idealism without detail is idle speculation; and formal or exact æsthetic, in its various shapes as the observation of universally beautiful structure, as its analysis into abstract relations, and as the causal explanation of their agreeableness in terms of the psychical movement, is an indispensable instrument in the hand of idealism.

But in the analysis of the great individual creations of art or the more complex effects of nature, it is not probable that all the links of formal explanation will ever be supplied. In these cases the delight of self-utterance and self-recognition overrides, though it cannot dispense with, the elements of abstract satisfaction, and the appreciation of character and passion and the moods of Nature, though at every turn sustained and elucidated, will not be exhaustively analysed by exhibiting the rationale of composition in all its minutiæ, and of harmonious effect upon sense-perception. And moreover we shall find that in the employment of such analysis, conformably to a principle on which I have more than once insisted, the interpreter who is on the alert for refinements of import—that is, the idealist with a grasp of reality—will distance all competitors.

CHAPTER XIV.

THE METHODICAL COMPLETION OF OBJECTIVE IDEALISM.

Type of the
Later Objective
Idealism.

1. WHILE the votaries of exact æsthetic were attempting to explain the pleasantness of beauty in terms of psychological analysis, the heirs of objective Idealism were striving to attain a corresponding precision in the method of their content- or expression-theory. In the course of this attempt they called attention to a neglected question of supreme æsthetic importance in the problem of ugliness, and also in some degree included the formalistic point of view in their own by appropriating from modern science its best warranted analyses of æsthetic phenomena.

On the other hand, with the increased accentuation of method, and the attempt to summarise results in accurate abstractions, their work has unavoidably assumed a certain tinge of scholasticism. By this term I designate the divorce between content and formulation ; nor can I altogether conceal my conviction that the appreciation of actual beauty among the German æsthetic philosophers of the last half century is less vital, though infinitely more learned, than that shown by the giant race whom they succeeded.

One characteristic of the most distinguished of the recent æsthetic writers in Germany demands our special attention, although in criticising it the present writer is also by implication criticising himself. It is easy to say that the substantive strength of the idealist school resides throughout in its historical research, and in illustration of this to compare the historical method of Schelling and Hegel, or of Winckelmann and Schiller, with the historical treatises of Schasler, Zimmermann,[1] Carriere, Lotze, and Hartmann. But when we look closer at the two types of thought which are thus compared,

---

[1] Taking Zimmermann, who is a formalist, as representing by his historical treatment the *rapprochement* between formalists and idealists alluded to above.

we observe an essential difference between them.   In the earlier type, the historical factor depends upon the conception that the evolution of beauty in all its phases and stages is the object-matter of æsthetic science.   The "dialectic" is conceived as "immanent"—as consisting, that is to say, in the operation of historical forces and in the cumulative influence of the human mind upon itself.   The opinions of philosophers do not appear in æsthetic, but are more completely correlated with the world and with each other in the full context of the history of philosophy.

In the later type, the science has become definitory and formal, and the history, no longer directly included in the object-matter of the science, has turned into a chronicle of philosophic opinion.   In this way the science and the history have fallen apart ; and we have passed from the scientific history of the actual beautiful, to its formal, though would-be concrete, analysis on the one hand, and to the history of æsthetic philosophy as such upon the other.   Now it is true that the latter may be utilised as the clarified expression of the former ; and it is true that Schasler, and more fully the learned and enthusiastic Carriere, have understood the historical problem in this way.   The present writer however, while aware that he is to a great extent following in their track, has attempted to bend back the line of historical enquiry towards the evolution of beauty as an objective though mental phenomenon, and away from the mere affiliation of philosophical opinions.

Transition to the Later Objective Idealism.   2. But before proceeding to deal with the critical and methodical views of such writers as those just mentioned, it is necessary to trace the antecedents of their position in the admission within æsthetic philosophy of the theory of ugliness, which had been knocking at the door ever since the beginning of romantic art, if not ever since Plotinus.

Solger.   a. We saw that Lessing admitted the ugly into poetry as a means to the comic and the terrible,[1] while denying it a place in formative art ; and that Schlegel[2] definitely proposed it as an object of theoretical inquiry, intending to keep it wholly outside the beautiful, but finding how inevitably it forced its way in.   In Goethe and

---

[1] P. 226 *supra.*   [2] P. 301 *supra.*

Schiller, Kant and Hegel, we found no elaborate treatment of this subject. In Goethe and Hegel, however, this was partly due to the very amplitude and robustness of their conception of beauty. For the fact of real æsthetic moment on this side is the extension and deepening of the beautiful by the inclusion of apparent ugliness, and when this, the ugly that can enter into the beautiful, is provided for, the detailed analysis of the ugly, if any, that can never be taken up into beauty, is less essential to æsthetic science. We observed upon Goethe's sympathy for the strong and the significant or characteristic, and we noted that for Hegel ugliness is a relative conception, depending on a contradiction with true individuality, and only rising to absoluteness if and in as far as such a contradiction assumes the form of irreconcilable perversity. In this point, the existence of apparent or merely relative ugliness, he is more truly represented by the thoroughly concrete theorists such as Schasler and Hartmann, than by those who, with Rosenkranz—though even they not wholly—consider ugliness as essentially falling outside the beautiful.

This latter view, which was necessary to pave the way for an explicit recognition of the place of apparent ugliness within concrete characterization, is briefly and pregnantly formulated in Solger's lectures on Æsthetic.[1] I quote a leading passage, from which Solger's relation to Schlegel and also to later theorists on the subject of ugliness, may be clearly seen :—

The Comic and the Tragic, Solger is maintaining,[2] both lie within the conception of the beautiful. Beauty as such is the perfect unity of idea and phenomenon ("*Erscheinung*"), and is opposed both to the pure idea, and to the commonplace phenomenon or manifestation ("*Erscheinung*") of reality. Tragedy is the "idea" as emphasized by annihilation of it (in the phenomenon[3]). Comedy is the idea recognised as asserting itself throughout even the most commonplace existence. But if, instead of asserting itself, it ceases to be

---

[1] Delivered 1819, prepared for publication by Heyse, and published in 1829 (before the appearance of Hegel's *Æsthetic*). The lectures are more direct and scientific in style than Solger's dialogue *Erwin* (1815) appears to be. For an estimate of Solger, see Hegel's *Æsth.*, Introd., E. Tr. p. 131.

[2] *Vorlesungen über Aesthetik.* pp 100–102.

[3] P. 102.

recognised in the sphere of common life and phenomena, then either we have the prosaic view of the world, which fails to be ugly only because it is wholly apart from æsthetic feeling, or we have ugliness, which arises "when [1] the human mind finds in the commonplace phenomenon (' *in der gemeinen Erscheinung* ') something essential, wherein the phenomenon, divorced from the idea, has independent reality. This element," he continues, " becomes as an independent principle the opposite of beauty, and so the commonplace phenomenon becomes the exact opposite of the idea.[2] In this consists the principle of the ugly, the basis of which is not in mere defectiveness by the standard of natural laws. And, again, the ugly does not consist in the serious (prosaic) consideration of things ; this belongs rather to moral judgment, being wholly removed from the conception of the beautiful.

" If anything is to be recognised as the opposite of the beautiful, *the same thing must be looked for in it that is looked for in the beautiful, and the opposite found.* If the idea is really lacking, and the mere phenomenon gives itself out for the essence, then the ugly makes its appearance. The ugly is a rebellion against the beautiful, as the evil against the good. It is always a pretended principle, in which the different tendencies of existence converge [as they do truly in the beautiful]. Natural imperfections are not ugly, except in so far as in this complication of external forces something is taken to reveal itself which aims at concentrating these mere forces as essential in themselves.[3] Bodily ugliness only arises through a false principle of mere existence [*e.g.* of animal as against spiritual existence, or mere cell-growth against healthy animal life] being foisted upon the human organism. Just so, a disposition which opposes itself to the beautiful by concentrating the commonplace into a single point,[4] and acquiescing therein, is an ugly disposition. Mere contingency and maladaptation, therefore, are not enough to constitute ugliness ; it is necessary in addition

---

[1] *Vorlesungen über Aesthetik,* p. 101.

[2] The derivation of Vischer's view from this is very plain ; see *K. G.,* vi., 113, on the war between the idea and and the image ("Bild," or " Erscheinung ").

[3] *i.e.* no doubt, as forming an individual existence antagonistic to that in which they appear—like parasites, etc.

[4] In the sense, I imagine, of making it a purpose.

that in the things which are thus self-contradictory there shall be a unity, which [really] could only be the idea, but is sought for in purely phenomenal existence.

" The ugly is the first form in which commonplace existence opposes itself to the beautiful, Like evil, it displays itself only as the negation of the idea, but as a negation that assumes positive shape, inasmuch as it aspires to set itself in the place of the latter."—" The ugly is therefore positively opposed to the beautiful, and we can only regard them as absolutely exclusive of each other."

The noteworthy results of this conception are two.

First, real ugliness is thus treated as a positive negation or falsehood aspiring to the place of beauty, and therefore absolutely exclusive of the latter and excluded by it. This, in so far as we are able at all to recognise real or invincible ugliness as a fact, we shall find to be the true explanation of that fact.

But secondly, as ugliness is thus identified with a certain positive relation of the same factors that enter into beauty, as something in which we look for beauty though we do not find it, an affinity between the two is admitted. There thus arises a tendency to bring the ugly closer and closer to the frontier of the beautiful, as bearing special relation to one or other of the species generated within the phases of beauty by the changing correlation of its elements. Thus, as I understand Solger in the *Lectures on Æsthetic*, though he does not think that the ugly *quâ* ugly can come within the borders of art (and in this, with Weisse and against Rosenkranz, he is surely right), yet it is essential to his view that beauty in passing through its phases from the sublime to the comic comes very close to the ugly, from which it is only saved by the self-assertion of the strong and cheerful idea or ideal within the most wretched phenomenal details, giving rise to the spirit of true comedy.

Here we have the germ of a theory dealing not only with ugliness outside the beautiful, but with the appearance of a necessary movement within the realm of beauty towards something akin to ugliness.

Reference to Weisse and Vischer. β. I do not propose to attempt an adequate account of Weisse[1] or of Vischer.[2]

Weisse appears to have had the substantial

---

[1] Weisse's *Aesthetik*, 1830.
[2] Vischer's *Aesthetik*, 1846–57, comprises two vols. of general theory re-

merit of insisting on the position of ugliness in æsthetic
theory, and especially of insisting on Solger's point that positive or actual ugliness (as distinct from mere defectiveness of
beauty) is something that claims the place and simulates the
powers of the beautiful—a morbid but fascinating presentation. He does not contemplate the entrance of what is really
ugly into the region of art except through entire subordination, which in his view can only take place by means of the
comic or the romantic spirit. Thus, as Hartmann observes,
the characteristic is omitted, excepting, we must add, in as far
as it takes comic or romantic form. As a consequence of this
omission it would seem that little light can be thrown on the
enlargement or deepening of beauty in the strict sense. We
want to know how beauty itself is found to be modified and
graduated, as in Winckelmann's account of it, by the claims
of expression and of the characteristic with their introduction of apparent ugliness, and the addition of the comic and
romantic to the forms of beauty does not thoroughly facet his
problem. The defective synthesis betrays itself in defective
æsthetic judgment. Thus, we are told, Weisse can see no
beauty in waste and desert places. It seems to him that in
them the inorganic elements refuse their function of acting
as a basis for organic life. This notion is descended from
Hegel's exaggerated estimate of the æsthetic importance
attaching to the ascending scale of organic life. It is wholly
discrepant with our present feeling for the beautiful.[1]

Moreover Weisse, as also Vischer and Rosenkranz, attempted a dialectic construction of the phases of beauty, somewhat on Solger's lines, bringing the ugly into special connection with the progressive movement from the sublime to the
comic. There is no doubt that some connection may be
traced between the phases of beauty and its progressive
power of mastering and subordinating to itself the sterner and
stranger elements of presentation. We have seen in Hegel
an attempt to exhibit such a movement, with full explanation
of the immanent causes and cumulative influences by which
the successive stages were brought to pass It would be
foolish to imply that Hegel's analysis is final, and I only refer

---

specting beauty, continued in four vols. entitled *Die Künste*, dealing
copiously with the several arts.
[1] For Weisse's view of ugliness see Hartmann, *Aesth.*, ii. 364 ff.

to it in order to emphasise the distinction between a dialectic which assigns its own definite import, and one which seems simply to ring the changes upon technical terms of æsthetic, and logical designations for forms of negative relation, which, apart from a very explicit context, convey no import at all.[1] The self-conflicts of the beautiful lead, it is said, from the sublime through the ugly to the comic (Weisse), or the evolution passes from the sublime through the comic to the beautiful [2] (Vischer), or the beautiful denies itself in the ugly and is restored to itself in the comic (Rosenkranz).

The underlying perception throughout all these expressions is probably that embodied in the passage quoted above from Solger and also involved in Hegel's view of the comic, that any conflict or meanness can be reconciled with beauty, if the strong and genial spirit of the ideal pervades it with a sense of victorious security. But in all this, though much truth is implied, there is no thorough-going reconstruction of the idea of beauty ; beauty remains a phase of the excellent in art, among other phases, or else is stretched into an unmeaning title, and the actual affinity that permeates the whole world of characteristic expression, which Goethe and Hegel had grasped, is in danger of being lost to view.

In the case of Vischer, the enterprise of coping with his immense array of volumes is rendered especially disheartening by the fact that the author himself in his later years has criticised [3] his great work with severe candour. Two points are noteworthy. In the second part of the *Æsthetic*, following upon the metaphysic of the beautiful which occupies the first volume, and treating of " The beautiful in its one-sided existence," he had dealt with beauty (i.) in its "objective" existence as the beauty of nature, and (ii.) in its " subjective " existence as imagination. This distinction, in virtue of which his treatment of natural beauty extended into an immense range of detail, surveying inorganic and organic nature, the types of humanity and the course of history, his later criticism rightly condemns. " The section on natural beauty must go." [4] All beauty is in perception, and in fact whenever art and imagination are dealt with it is essential to recur to the

---

[1] See below on Rosenkranz.
[2] See Schasler, *A.*, 959.
[3] Vischer, *Kritische Gänge*, No. 5, 1863 ; No. 6, 1873.
[4] *Krit. G.*, v. 11.

material afforded them by nature. The views of chap. i. of the present work could not be more strikingly confirmed. We see a genuine treatment of natural beauty in its true relation to art in the whole range of Mr. Ruskin's critical labours.

Again, Vischer's later criticism condemns as inadequate the position given to ugliness in his great work.[1] He now admits that Weisse and Schasler have estimated more truly than himself the necessity of ugliness as an element without which the concrete modifications of the beautiful cannot arise.

It must be added that in his treatment of poetry he remains wholly on the old ground of the distinction into Epic, Lyric, and Dramatic, and therefore fails to appreciate the problem presented by the cessation of some types and the substitution of others for them. Thus he attempts to force the *Divina Commedia* into the form of an Epic, and as this is plainly impossible, pronounces the form of Dante's poem to be in contradiction with the essence of poetic art.[2] How far more profound is Schelling's estimate![3]

On the other hand it should be noted that Vischer has some conception of the relation between art and workmanship,[4] of the difficulties raised for the latter by modern mechanical production for the world-market,[5] and of the problems affecting the future of art[6] in their whole perplexing intensity. There is much, therefore, in his works that would be of interest to the reader to-day, could it be disengaged from his formal dialectic and from the huge bulk of his volumes. But there is not much, I should imagine, which cannot now be obtained from other sources, and I therefore cannot help fearing that this colossal monument of real knowledge, capacity, and industry will have little effect on the future course of æsthetic science.

Rosenkranz. γ. I now pass to Rosenkranz, who while belonging to the earlier post-Hegelians by his attachment to the ideas of Solger, yet treated the question of ugliness with a detail and insight which made his work a point of transition to the later and more thoroughly concrete conceptions. The connection is well marked by the fact that

---

[1] *Krit. G.*, vi. 115.
[2] *Die Künste*, Bk. iv., p. 1300.
[3] See p. 325 *supra*.
[4] *Die Künste*, i. 87.
[5] *Ib.*, 337.
[6] *Aesth.*, ii. 298.

Schasler dedicates his *Kritische Geschichte der Aesthetik* to Rosenkranz.

Ugliness as such. i. The title of Rosenkranz's work, *The Æsthetic of Ugliness*,[1] indicates his point of view. The editor of Kant, and biographer of Hegel, he desired to complete the fabric of æsthetic theory on the side of it which appeared to him, not unjustly, to be defective. He accordingly conceives of Ugliness as a distinct object-matter, outside the beautiful, and thus demanding separate treatment, but determined throughout by relativity to the beautiful, and thus belonging to æsthetic theory.

The ugly as such[2] is the negation of the beautiful, inasmuch as the same factors which give rise to beauty are capable of being perverted into their opposites—I should have preferred to say, "perverted, by a change of relation, into *its* opposite." Ugliness and beauty are genuinely distinct, and the former does not enter into the latter as a constituent part ; but yet, as both contain the same factors, it is possible for the ugly to be subordinated to the beautiful in a further and more complex phase of æsthetic appearance, viz. the comic. As I understand Rosenkranz, therefore, the comic, though akin to the beautiful, does not form a species of it, but is rather a continuation of its principle in a new shape, after the rebellion of the ugly has been overcome.

There is an obvious analogy between these ideas and those of Solger. The philosopher's chief interest is still concentrated on the ugly as given in natural opposition to the beautiful, and not on the qualities within the acknowledged beautiful which exhibit an affinity between it and what is commonly taken to be ugly. Our principal concern, therefore, is with the mode in which positive negation is here conceived, as tending to limit the sphere of the most genuine ugliness ; with the very remarkable ground on which ugliness is after all admitted within the frontiers of fine art ; and with the use made throughout of the notions of negation and contrariety, which is typical for the whole range of post-Hegelian dialectic.

The Æsthetic of ugliness follows a course analogous to the Æsthetic of beauty. Ugliness,[3] as the negation of beauty,

---

[1] *Aesthetik des Hässlichen*, 1853.
[2] *A. d. H.*, p. 7.
[3] *A. d. H.*, p. 167, cf. p. 63.

D D

must be the positive perversion of the sublime (into the mean
or commonplace, "*gemein*"), of the pleasing ("*gefällig*," into
the repugnant, "*widrig*"), or of the simply beautiful (into
caricature). And thus, although defective form and want of
natural or historical truth ("Formlessness" and "Incorrectness") are lower grades in which the tendency to ugliness
reveals itself, yet true or real ugliness is not attained until in
a being capable of freedom we find the attribute of un-freedom
positively manifested in the place which freedom should hold.[1]
The tendency of this view, although allowance is made for the
application of such ideas by analogy to unconscious objects, is
of course to restrict the range of real ugliness to man and
art.[2]

It is remarkable how little the *de facto* kinship of so-called
ugliness and familiar beauty has down to this time struck the
perception of æsthetic theorists with the exception of Hegel
and Goethe. The sublime has indeed at last come to be
ranked as a species of the beautiful,[3] which is a great advance
on the theory of Kant. But on the whole Rosenkranz con-
templates the task before him as a descent into "the hell of
the world of beauty,"[4] a desolate and miserable region, and
seems to have no feeling for the pervading elements of force,
depth, splendour and grace, within the strange, the tragic,
and the terrible, which unmistakably and beyond dispute carry
some qualities of the simplest beauty, often in the highest perfection, through much of the sphere in which ugliness reigns
for the commonplace observer. We do not feel, with him,
that it is a painful and almost perilous adventure to enter into
the infernal world of Dante [and of Milton ?], of Orcagna and
Michael Angelo, of Spohr [and of Berlioz ?]. I throw the
blame of his attitude in these respects partly on the æsthetic
conditions of the early nineteenth century, partly on the tradition of Winckelmann's "ideal," which, like every tradition,

---

[1] P. 167.
[2] P. 4. "The ugliest ugliness is not that which disgusts us in objects of
nature, in the swamp, the distorted tree, in toads and reptiles, goggle-eyed
fish monsters, and massive pachyderms, in rats and monkeys [I do not admit
the view of real ugliness implied in this enumeration]; it is the egoism which
reveals its madness in malicious and frivolous gesture, in the furrows drawn by
passion, in the shifty look of the eye, and in crime." Cf. p. 53, on the morbid
delight of a corrupt age in depraved art.
[3] P. 167.
[4] P. 3.

rapidly lost the depth and vitality of its founder's ideas. It seemed necessary to indicate this deep-seated quality of the author's feeling, although I am about to show that he makes an important step towards the recognition of this very affinity against which he was so strongly biassed.

Ugliness Ld Art. ii. The "ugliest ugliness," of which I spoke above, includes the ugliness *of* art, *i.e.* ugly or bad art. But especially to a thinker for whom the ugly is so prominent a fact as it is for Rosenkranz, there is also an inevitable question concerning the ugly *in* art. This question he meets with candour and insight, though in doing so he raises a contradiction fatal to the unity of his own doctrine.

Starting from the assumption, which in the sense implied is more than doubtful, that art arises from the yearning after pure unmixed beauty,[1] he asks the obvious question : " Is it not, then, the sharpest contradiction when we see art reproducing the ugly as well as the beautiful ? " And if we reply that it reproduces the ugly only *as* beautiful, has this any result except to pile up a second contradiction on the top of the first ?[2]

The first answer which presents itself, that the ugly is admitted into art only as a foil that heightens the beautiful, and therefore for the sake of beauty and not in its own right, Rosenkranz rejects, justly, though not perhaps on the true ground. For he regards beauty as something distinct, positive, and independent, and therefore refuses to consider it as in need of any foil or dark background. No doubt this view has a relative truth in so far as beauty is positive and *real* ugliness is negative. But it rests too much on a supposed separateness and purity of the beautiful, treating it always as something obvious and given, incapable of strangeness and difficulty, and not demanding any special effort or capacity to penetrate its depths and disguises. The truer reason, that what commonplace perception views as ugly is often far too prominent in the noblest art, and too deeply imbued with undeniable qualities of beauty, to be explained as a mere foil for beautiful elements distinct from itself, seems hardly to have been within the scope of Rosenkranz's æsthetic judgment or analysis But it was something gained to be rid of the "foil" theory, for any reason whatever.

[1] P. 35.   [2] P. 36.

The second answer which he suggests is of great significance. " If[1] art is not to represent the idea in a merely one-
sided way, it cannot dispense with the ugly. The pure ideals
exhibit to us no doubt the most important, that is, the positive
element of the beautiful ; but if mind and nature are to be
admitted to presentation in their full dramatic depth, then the
ugly of nature, and the evil and diabolic, must not be omitted.
The Greeks, however much they lived in the ideal,[2] had
nevertheless their Hekatoncheires, Cyclopes, Satyrs, Graiæ,
Empusæ, Harpies, Chimæras ; they had a lame god, and
represented in their tragedies the most horrible crimes (*e.g.*
in the Œdipus and the Oresteia), madness (in the Ajax),
nauseating diseases (in the Philoctetes), and in their comedy,
vices and infamies of all kinds. *Moreover, along with the
Christian religion, as that which teaches men to know evil in
its root and overcome it fundamentally, the ugly is finally and
in principle introduced into the world of art. For this reason
therefore, in order to depict the concrete manifestation of the
idea in its totality, art cannot omit the portrayal of the ugly.
Its apprehension of the idea would be superficial if it tried to
limit itself to simple beauty."*

Does the so-called ugly, we then naturally ask, undergo any
modification when it presents itself in art ?

Rosenkranz gives a twofold answer.   In the first place
what is ugly cannot have independent existence in art.
Though it is false that beauty needs a foil, it is true that
ugliness does.   The ugly old woman whom painters place
beside Danae could not be the subject of a separate picture,
except either in genre-painting, when the situation gives the
æsthetic interest, or as a portrait, which is primarily concerned
with historical correctness.[3]   I take it that these exceptions,
in their context, are startling to our judgment. Of course
the example is the author's, and if we are to understand it as
ex hypothesi a case of ugliness insuperable by art, the question falls to the ground.   But a few pager before[4] he has
referred to the same figure as a " wrinkled, sharp-chinned "
old woman   Does he mean that every figure with marked
signs of extreme old age is incapable of beauty, and that *good*
genre and portrait-painting fall outside beautiful art except
in as far as they happen to deal with youthful and graceful

---

[1] P. 38.   [2] See p. 14 *supra*.   [3] P. 40.   [4] P. 36.

subjects? I believe that he does mean something of this kind in the main, and so far shows himself to be on a low level of æsthetic insight. But there are cases in which real ugliness—the perversion of characteristic function—has been introduced into art by great masters, and of these the author's theory is true. He gives well-known examples from Paul Veronese's Marriage in Cana. And he also instances the phenomena of dissonance, which, as dissonance presupposes musical sound (a true dissonance can hardly be recognised in natural noises), may be taken as having an element of artificial or intentional perversion which causes them to verge upon real ugliness. Such actual perversions, or contradictions usurping the place of characterization, do seem to demand a quantitative subordination, or submergence in a mass of beauty, and cannot be made independent objects of art by any force or depth of presentation. I take it that music could not be made with nothing but discord, nor could the nauseating details introduced by Veronese in the Marriage in Cana be the subjects of independent pictures. So far Rosenkranz seems on firm ground. Our complaint of him is not that he denies independent æsthetic value to the extreme perversions in art, but that he does not appear to distinguish them with certainty from the incomparably greater range of the quaintly, rudely, grotesquely, terribly or intricately characteristic, all of which passes in common parlance as ugly.

His second answer has deeper import. The ugly, he says, when it appears in art, must not indeed be *beautified*, for this would be to intensify its hideousness by adding fraud to rebellion; but yet it must be "idealized" by subjection to the general laws of beauty, for example to the laws of symmetry, harmony, proportion, and force of individual expression.[1] The result of such idealization is not to soften or disguise its ugliness, but just the reverse, namely to accent its characteristic and essential lineaments.[2] But yet in doing so there must arise a certain negative consequence. Unessential matters of painful or sickening detail are crushed out, just as in the representation of commonplace beauty unessential fascinations are crushed out. It is not the desire for fraudulent palliation, but the despotism of the fundamental meaning, that operates with this effect.

---

[1] P. 44.　　[2] P. 43.

It is plain that we have here a strange intermediate position assigned to the ugly in art. Three suggestions force
themselves upon us in consequence.

a. If, as we have maintained throughout, the æsthetic perception of nature differs only in degree from the æsthetic perception which is art, must not the same reservations be read
back into the doctrine of ugliness in nature, which are here
applied to the ugly as it appears in art ?

b. The province of apparent ugliness or of what we might
call the *difficult* in beauty, which hardly fulfils the author's
definition of ugliness but appears to be excluded by him from
the beautiful, is thus nearly reconciled with the beautiful in
substance though not in name ; for when idealized in the
sense required it would simply resolve itself into cases of the
characteristic beautiful subject to the laws of abstract or formal
expression, in virtue of which latter, through assuming strong
and significant form and structure, it becomes pleasing even
to the decorative sense.

c. It must even be doubted whether ugliness according to
the author's definition, the positive negation of beauty, can
submit to the idealization he describes without being undone
as ugliness and presented as beauty. A contradiction, confessed and explained, is no longer a contradiction ; and the
perversion of character or individuality revealed and stig-
matised in its true light and relations, ceases to be a positive
perversion. The essential distinction is that which Rosenkranz seems to have firmly grasped, between idealization
as intensifying the lineaments of perversion and emphasizing
their core and essence in vigorous presentation, and idealization as fraudulently softening and disguising their character
by causing them to approximate to a type of beauty, in which,
whether in another sense beautiful or no, they cannot possibly
have any share. This all-important distinction will occupy
us again.

The Forms of   iii. A word remains to be said upon the forms
Opposition.   of opposition by which the entire discussion is
determined.

Ugliness, we saw, is the negation [1] of beauty, or, as negation *per se* can take no sensuous form, we prefer to call it the
perversion of beauty, whose constituent elements are perverted

---

[1] " *Negation* " or " *Negativ-Schönes*," pp. 7, 10, 61.

(*verkehrte*) in it   Now the term " opposite " (" *Gegensatz* " or
" *Gegentheil* ") by which he often describes the relation
between the qualities forming an antithetical pair, is a very
appropriate term for positive negations or perversions in their
relation to one another, but it is not a term which explains
itself apart from a complete exposition of the nature of the
series or classification in which it is employed.   And accordingly we find an almost ludicrous confusion in the usage
of these terms by the æsthetic writers with whom Rosenkranz
deals.   Thus " the true opposite (" *Gegensatz* ") of the sublime
is not the ugly as Ruge and K. Fischer say, nor the comic,
as Vischer thinks, but the pleasing (" *gefällige* ")." [1]
The first thing then that Rosenkranz has in his mind is
that the negative opposition in which each form of the ugly
stands to its corresponding form of the beautiful must be
distinguished from the " positive opposition " in which each
species [2] of the beautiful stands to one or more of the others.
This is a step towards clearness, but needs further elucidation.   *All* definite opposition is between positives negatively
related, and these epithets, " positive " and " negative," mark
no distinction *prima facie* between kinds of opposition.
Strictly speaking, opposition can only arise between judgments, for any two given contents are simply different, and
only become opposed in as far as they may be considered to
be candidates for the same place.   Moreover, it must be noted
that all common logical opposition is interchangeable ; that is
to say, when B is the opposite or negation of A, then A is
also and in the same sense the opposite or negation of B.   If
the one is, then the other is not ; but we are not informed, by
the mere fact of opposition, which is to stand and which is to
fall.   We must beware of confusing falsehood and negation.
No ordinary logical symbols or technical terms will represent
falsehood or confusion of relations.   We must therefore state
the whole matter more distinctly.
In the first place the beautiful and the ugly seem to be
regarded as two co-ordinate *genera* under the conception
æsthetic, which *genera* are so related that to every species of
the one there corresponds a species of the other formed by
a false attribution of elements present in the former species.
But if so, while no doubt it is the case that logically speaking

[1] P. 61.   [2] P. 63, see above p. 402 for these species.

the beautiful is a positive opposite of the ugly, just as the ugly is of the beautiful, yet this purely logical relation, being inter- changeable, does not adequately describe their connection. We must therefore understand that the one genus is repre- sented by some such symbol as "A is x y," the other by a symbol involving self-contradiction such as "A is $x_1 y_1$," which really belong to A_1, and not to A. Granting this explanation, we then have two sets of "oppositions"; the opposition between each form of the true series and the corresponding form of the false series, and the oppositions between the different terms of the true series (disregarding those between the different terms of the false series). Now in the former case, the terms being given in pairs, it is possible to speak of "the opposite" of any given term, although it may not be self- evident where this opposite is to be found, that is, how the pairs of terms are to be arranged, and it is also possible that one term may have two or more opposites, even though its peculiar counterpart is its opposite *par excellence.* In fact, Rosenkranz opposes the sublime to the petty, mean or frivo- lous, whereas I should have primarily opposed it to the false sublime—the portentous, monstrous, or exaggerated. No doubt in different senses it may be "opposite" to either of these species of the ugly,—to the latter, I should have said, in the stricter sense, as that which arises by mistake out of the sublime itself, to the former no doubt as to something very far removed from the nature of the sublime, being in fact as I think *the true opposite of the pleasing or pretty, which is for Rosenkranz the opposite par excellence of the sublime in the beautiful series.*

For we must consider also the opposition between the forms of the beautiful. Now these are *ex hypothesi* a series comprising three or more types, which may be multi- plied at pleasure by refinement of analysis. Therefore there is no meaning in speaking of the "opposite" of any form within the series unless and until we determine what we mean by opposition *par excellence* within such a series. Rosenkranz seems to take it that according to an old definition the oppo- sites are the most divergent species under the same genus, and so opposes the sublime to the pleasing. But plainly the whole thing is a question of degree, and if there is to be a "simple beautiful"—a conception which I view with some suspicion—the sublime must certainly be opposed to *it.* No doubt Rosenkranz is influenced by remoteness in opposing the sublime to the petty in ugliness, just as in opposing it to the pleasing in beauty. But it seems that, as between beauty and ugliness, the only security for any approach to an objective classification is to pair off the genuine form with the form which represents a mistaken feeling for that genuine form, and, as between the forms of beauty, there is little use in speaking of pairs of opposites *par* excellence, the important matter being to establish a fairly representative series, from which the kinds and degrees of opposition can then be read off with genuine significance.

The later Objective Idealism. 3. In including under the term "Objective Idealism" the views of Carriere, Schasler and Hartmann, I am not following the phraseology of these writers themselves. Carriere designates his own standpoint as that of Ideal-Realism,[1] and Schasler[2] accepts this same term, or "the synthesis of Idealism and Realism," as the description of his æsthetic principle. Hartmann includes the views of these two writers with those of Hegel, Vischer, and others under the title of concrete idealism, which he also claims for his own theory. He assigns to Schelling, Schopenhauer, Solger, Weisse, and Lotze, the position of abstract idealists, from their common tendency to speak in a pseudo-Platonic manner (which Hartmann takes to be genuinely Platonic[3]) of a super-sensuous world of ideas or patterns by approximation to which and in no other way the sensuous world possesses beauty. It is an essentially true remark[4] of Hartmann, though not literally correct, when in justifying his distinction between the abstract and the concrete idealists, he urges that the Idea of Beauty ("*Idee der Schönheit*") of which Weisse and Lotze constantly speak, could have absolutely no meaning for Hegel. For according to him "the idea" or concrete world-movement *becomes* beautiful when expressed to sense-perception or fancy, and in this aspect may be called the "ideal" or perhaps for the sake of brevity "the beautiful"; but Hegel could never speak of the idea of beauty in the sense of a beauty which existed as a super-sensuous idea.[5] Of course again the conception or

---

1 *Æsth.*, ii., Preface. 2 *K. G. d. A.*, pp. 1125 and 1132.
3 *A.*, i., Pref. vii. 4 *A.*, i. 93 footnote.
5 Hegel, *A.*, i. 135 and 141, where in fact the term "Idee des Schönen"

notion of beauty employed in æsthetic science is quite different from an abstract idea with which beauty could be identified.

But I have no doubt that Schelling, though he fell into abstract idealism in later years, was next to Schiller and by an advance upon Kant the founder of the view that beauty is the presentation of the inmost law of things to sense and fancy, and for our purpose it will be simplest to omit the degrees of abstract and concrete idealism, and to select a term which indicates the *bonâ fide* endeavour to find beauty in the reasonableness of the world displayed to sense. All who have genuinely attempted this may fairly be called objective idealists in æsthetic. The divergence into abstract monism—which *ex hypothesi* must be dualism—or into abstract idealism, is in some degree a matter of defective philosophical expression or of over-reliance on emphatic metaphor, and is a confusion that partly in appearance and partly in reality has beset the very greatest philosophers, including, as is too well known, even Plato himself.

"Ideal-Realism" on the other hand expresses a history or problem rather than a theory or a solution. It indicates a combination of two views which have respectively no philosophical meaning except as universal and exclusive. As it stands, therefore, it indicates mere eclecticism. But its intention is divined and embodied in the phrase objective idealism.

Carriere.   *a.* Carriere published his *Æsthetic* in 1859. Before the appearance of the third edition in 1886 he had supplemented it by the splendidly conceived work in five volumes (first edition, 1862 ; third edition, 1886), *Art in the Context of the Evolution of Culture, and the Ideals of Humanity,*[1] on which I have already drawn in speaking of Christian art in its first beginnings.

Carriere does not make any notable advance in matters of principle. Three points may be mentioned on which, whether for good or evil, his views are significant.

---

does occur, give an absolute justification of Hartmann's meaning. "We called (l. c., p. 135) the beautiful the *Idea* of the beautiful. This means that the beautiful itself is to be apprehended as Idea, and that as particularised Idea, viz. as Ideal," *i.e.,* " the sensuous show of the Idea," p. 141.

[1] *Die Kunst in Zusammenhange d. Cultur-entwickelung u. d. Ideale d. Menschheit.*

The Ugly.   i. He feels the full importance of Weisse's and Rosenkranz's treatment of the ugly. He himself stands on this question between the old and new, and although never thoroughly precise and scientific in his expression, appears to apprehend the essence of the question more justly than the later thinkers. It might be doubted, however, whether he sees the full reasons for the view which they adopt.

He attacks Weisse's dialectic progression from the sublime through the ugly to the comic,[1] absolutely refusing to conceive of the ugly as a kind of the beautiful. In the latest edition of his work he is able to comment upon Schasler, whose view, shared by Hartmann, that the ugly is an *essential* element in the characteristic and therefore in the beautiful, he no less decidedly rejects. The free[2] and the individual we must have in beauty, but not the ugly, which is the *falsely* free and individual. I shall return later to this doctrine, with which in substance I agree.

On the place of ugliness in art, however, Carriere agrees with Rosenkranz. For the sake of completeness it must be admitted,[3] but only either as idealized or as subordinated. It is to be noted that in these ways the ugly is said to be "overcome," and in its idealization its "repulsiveness" is destroyed. Even the case of a noble expression in features that are normally ugly is counted under this head, and unidealized ugliness—that which cannot stand alone—is yet to submit to the laws of the composition in which it is introduced. In all this there is a degree of vacillation which shows that the limits of "simple beauty" are becoming uncertain, and that the admission of the ugly into art will ultimately resolve itself into an extension of the frontier of beauty.

Division of the Arts.   ii. Carriere arrives[4] at the same general arrangement of the arts which Hegel proposed, and towards which, for different reasons and with many varieties of minor detail, æsthetic theory appears to be gravitating. He starts from the distinction of co-existence in space and succession in time, and their combination in the movement of a life and reality that has co-existence as well as succession. These three principles are taken to correspond to the "three arts" of form, of music, and of poetry. Within each of these "three

---

[1] *A.*, i. 147.   [2] *Ib.*, 148.   [3] *Ib.* 159, cf. 162–3.   [4] *Ib.*, i. 625–6.

arts" there is again a triple distinction. In the "art" of form Architecture corresponds to inorganic matter, Sculpture to organic individual shape, and painting to the combination of the two in individual life. Music is divided as instrumental, vocal, and the combination of the two ; poetry into epic, lyric and dramatic. The distinctions of "inner perception," according as its object is mind in general, personality as a whole; and personality in its particular relations with other persons, have to do duty as the basis of division alike for music and for poetry.

The triads thus established within music and poetry appear in both cases to rest on distinctions which reverse the order of development, and in the case of music also reverse the order of artistic scope and capacity. Hegel, though separated from the date of Carriere's third edition by more than half a century, during which a completely new appreciation of music has grown up, yet rightly places pure instrumental music as the higher or completer development in comparison with "accompanying" music. Wagner is responsible for a tendency towards art-combinations in the later writers, and perhaps also in Carriere.

Attitude to the   iii. The larger work on *Art in its Connection*
Renaissance.   *with Culture*, etc., displays in many ways a more genuine conception of æsthetic science than the abstract systems, including Carriere's own, which I have ventured to characterize as scholastic. A content-theory—and objective idealism is essentially a content-theory—must at least indicate its relations with the evolution of the content to which it refers, and as I have already observed, we do not obtain this content in the recorded opinions of philosophers, but only from the history of art and civilization. It might, however, be possible to indicate these relations without undertaking so colossal a task as that of combining a history of civilization with a history of art, so that after all the critical points of the latter hardly receive the attention which is their due.

It has been said [1] that the historical division of forms of art upon which this work is founded, into oriental, classical, mediæval, renaissance, and modern, is a great advance upon all previous divisions of the kind. I doubt, however, whether there is an essential difference between this and Hegel's

---

[1] By Hartmann, *A.*, i. 247.

division, except in as far as modern art is recognised—this was a necessary supplement—and the renaissance period is distinguished from the mediæval in a way which indicates an antiquated view of the renaissance. But in fact Carriere only makes these subdivisions within a wider framework [1] by which the whole period from the Christian era to the close of the renaissance is thrown into one, under the name of the age of feeling (*Gemüth*) in opposition to the early oriental and classical Greek periods, united within the "age of nature," and to the modern time, from the eighteenth century on-wards, as "the age of mind." Thus the essential unity of Christian art is recognised, though the late development of music is not very appropriate to the distinction between the age of feeling, to which the classical time of music should surely belong, and the "modern" age of mind. The difference between oriental art and that of classical Greece is represented, not altogether falsely, by a distinction of degrees of perfection within the "age of nature."

It might be suggested as a simpler and more natural arrange-ment to start from the distinction of classical, as corresponding to a natural monism, romantic as corresponding to a dualism of sense and spirit, full of tension arising from the effort to bring them together or merge the one in the other, and modern as corresponding to a comparatively monistic attitude at a higher level than that of Greece, the "two worlds" having come together in the concrete import of one. The "symbolic" art of Hegel would then appear as a preface or introduction—as an essay, essentially imperfect, towards the beauty which realized itself in classical Greece. The parallelism, which Hartmann suggests, between the relation [2] of symbolic to classical, and mediæval to renaissance, would falsify the whole construction In any such analogy the second pair of terms would have to be not mediæval and renaissance, but Christian and modern. But the reality of a modern art-period, unless we extend its further limit to include Shakespeare whom no dualism seems to affect, is a question which does not trouble Carriere as much as it ought. Let us grant that the music of the eighteenth and nineteenth centuries is a new and splendid phenomenon in the history of art ; yet in relying upon this we are *ipso facto* admitting a

---

[1] *Die Kunst*, p. 2.　　[2] *A.*, i. 252.

certain discontinuity with the older art-world. And we cannot, with Carriere, take the generation of Goethe and Schiller
as an age of abundant poetic production having permanent
value. Moreover the well-known peculiarities of nineteenth-
century achievement in art, however magnificent it may have
been in isolated instances, are such as to make us think twice
before accepting a "modern" art-age, beginning with the
eighteenth century, as anything more than a problem and a
hope. I suspect that the true line of division will be found
to fall in the sixteenth century, Shakespeare marking a singu-
larly fortunate transition, and Rubens and Rembrandt the
beginning of a new period.

Schasler.   β. Schasler's *Critical History of Æsthetic*, dedi-
cated to Rosenkranz, appeared in 1869. It is an
immense, but very fresh and readable work, filling 1,200 pages.
It was intended to be the basis of an æsthetic system, and is
called "Part I.," but a Part II. commensurate with it has
never appeared, its place being taken by *The System of
the Arts*, 1882, and an "*Æsthetic*," *or outline of the Science
of Beauty and Art* in 1886. These are works of the size and
class of our University Extension manuals, and do not add
much of importance to the views suggested in the *Critical
History*. The object-matter of the science has here come
off second-best in the division of labour that characterizes
the later idealism.

Conceptions   i. And the observations made above upon the
indicated by   later post-Hegelian writers in general, hold espe-
the "History." cially true of this history. Its aim is to furnish the
critical foundation of a theory of æsthetic, and there is no
reason to deny its value for this purpose if we clearly understand of what kind that value must be. The "dialectic," for
example, which is here exhibited in the progress of philosophic thought from Plato to Hegel, is the dialectic of a
branch of the history of philosophy, not the dialectic or cumulative progress of a kind of apperception in the human intelligence. The two are connected, and Schasler uses the former
to elucidate the latter. But we are not here dealing at first
hand with the causes and nature of changes in æsthetic perception, as we are in Winckelmann, Schelling, Schiller, Hegel
and in Carriere's larger work.

This attribute pervades the whole theory. We are to
watch, so Schasler tells us, by means of the critical history,

the intellectual genesis of the æsthetic consciousness.[1] But
granting that he enables us to do this, what is the nature of
the outcome ?   We see, no doubt, how the æsthetic consciousness, as a philosophical analysis of the beautiful, draws nearer
and nearer to completeness.   But we are saddened to find
that as this takes place the æsthetic consciousness, as the
creative and perceptive enjoyment of beauty, becomes doubtful
and disturbed.   "The modern artist,[2] by reason of the inherent need of reflexion, has for ever forfeited the full and
free possession of the artist-paradise."   We are looking at
the genesis of a philosophy, but *pari passu*, we may think, at
the decay of an art-world.   The question is not at present
how far this may be true, but how far the intellectual process
which is thus *primâ facie* separable from the art-process is of
value as an introduction to the study of the latter.   The
change of emphasis from æsthetic to philosophical evolution
may probably indicate some degree of confusion in the author's
view.   If he means that the true aim of art is only coming
into sight as beauty for beauty's sake becomes an explicit
purpose, he commits a very serious blunder, and inverts the
relations of the art-ages of the world.

But so again the " Ideal-Realism " which is for him the
result of the whole evolution, is *not* a principle or property of
art or beauty, *but* a method of æsthetic science.[3]   Realism for
him indicates, historically speaking, what we have called
"exact æsthetic," the æsthetic of Herbart and Schopenhauer.
It has no connection with Realism or Naturalism in art as we
understand it to-day.

In order to strengthen my grounds for differing sharply and
widely from so gifted and eminent a writer as the author of
the critical history, I feel bound to add to some comments
which I have already passed upon a kind of hastiness and
perversity that I find in him, another indication of a careless
or biassed procedure.

He has an æsthetic theory of colour of his own,[4] founded
upon the theories of Goethe, which he maintains, though

[1] *K. G. d. A.*, i. 61.
[2] *Ib.*, i. xxxii.
[3] See Hartmann, i. 248. His criticism here seems perfectly just.   Schasler's
" realism " in fact means Induction.
[4] *Æsth.*, i., 78 ; see *K. G. d. A.* i. 495.

needing some modification, to be thoroughly justified as against the Newtonian analysis. If such ideas were scarcely pardonable in Hegel more than fifty years before, what is to be said of them in a writer for whom not even national bias could any longer be an excuse? I do not complain that he is unacquainted with the work of English physicists, but surely he might have studied Helmholtz.[1]

---

[1] The weak point of his theory on purely æsthetic ground is that the suggestion of *warmth* in colour, on the unequal combination of which with luminosity he lays stress in determining the æsthetic character of colours, cannot be directly obtained as he assumes, from the actual heating powers of the various coloured rays. More complex suggestions than this must be brought in. In any case it is hopeless to suppose that anything more can be done for æsthetic with Goethe's theory than with the accepted analysis. See Helmholtz, *Lectures*, i. 29.

I may insert here two kindred points, which are not of sufficient importance to be treated in the text, though they bear strongly on the question of judgment and accuracy.

He cites quite incorrectly, and without a reference, one or other, I cannot tell which, of the familiar passages in which Hegel alludes, with a passing tinge of irony, to the use of the term "philosophy" in England. The passages are *Gesch. d. Philosophie*, i. 37, and (shorter) *Logic*, p. 13 (E. Tr. Wallace, p. 11), and though too long to extract they are worth turning up in comparison with Schasler, p. 1158, if we want to measure the difference between a great mind and a critic in search of an ill-natured joke. Hegel's interest is in both cases serious. In one he quotes from the practice of German universities a trace of the ancient meaning of "philosophy," the survival of which he is noting in England. And both passages end with an observation, plainly aimed at the public familiar to him, to the effect that in England philosophy is at least a name for something that people value.

More closely bearing on our subject is another extravagance of our author. In quoting Dickens' *Hard Times* for the sake of its attack upon English "common sense," he altogether fails to discern that, just and good as are in many ways the ideas of that delightful story, yet on the specifically æsthetic question of fact and fancy Dickens is attacking his own side and the principles which are the source of all that is greatest in his own and every other art. This phenomenon will surprise no student. The typical scene of *Hard Times* on this point is the school scene which parodies an inspector's attempt to bring home to the children the relation of imagination to reality. In 1856, the year in which the novel appeared, there appeared also the 4th edition of the 2nd vol. of the *Modern Painters*, containing an account of the *Penetrative Imagination*, and the first edition of the 4th vol. containing (p. 331) the words, "Be assured of the great truth—what is impossible in reality is ridiculous in fancy." I hold no brief for the Science and Art Department. We all know its defects. But it is absolutely plain that the movement, going back to 1835, in which it originated, was a form of the movement for a return to nature and life in education, with which Dickens, if he had understood its real scope, would have heartily sympathised.

Ugliness and Modifications of the Beautiful.   ii. Schasler states his theory of ugliness explicitly in the *Æsthetic*,[1] referring, at the same time, to passages in the *History*, to which, in principle, his later exposition adds nothing.

Starting from the researches of Rosenkranz, and agreeing with him so far as concerns the position of ugliness outside the world of art and beauty, and corresponding to it phase for phase, he also acquiesces in the traditional view as to the wide range of the ugly in the works of nature. But he attempts to strike out a new principle in dealing with ugliness where it enters, or is absorbed in, the sphere of art.

The ugliness, indeed, of bad or false art, a case on which Schasler well insists, falls under the first-mentioned head of ugliness outside true art, of which it is the strongest example. In regard to it, therefore, we have no more to say, except to indicate here and there in passing how it is supposed to arise by the derangement of relations within genuine art.

It is with reference to the ugly within the beautiful that Schasler has a new view to propound.

The ugly, he believes, essentially enters into all beauty whatever; and more than this, is the active element or dialectic negation by which æsthetic interest is impelled to the creation of definite or characteristic beauty in its various forms. I find it difficult to explain this view further, without entering upon a criticism of it. This it is more convenient to defer till Hartmann's ideas, which are in principle the same as Schasler's, are also before us. The comparison, however, of the ugly to the negative, reiterated allusions to the lines in *Faust* which attribute creative impulse to the Spirit that denies, and repeated comparisons of the ugly with the false and the wicked as essential manifestations of freedom and therefore not to be held deplorable phenomena, give us some clue to the author's meaning. He distinctly denies the view of Rosenkranz, that in entering into art, as demanded by the "idea" for the sake of completeness, the ugly remains ugly. On the contrary, *quâ* an element in the characteristic, it is absorbed in the special and definite form of beauty which has in each case arisen in consequence of the stimulus that it gave. The contrast of masculine and feminine beauty is always in

---

[1] Pp. 19–24 referring to the *K. G. d. A.*, pp. 795, 763, 1021–4, 1028, 1036–8.

Schasler's mind.   He feels that such sharply opposed forms
of the beautiful contain elements which a little dislocation
would make ugly.   And he is confident, and with justice, that
such sharply antagonistic forms there are and ought to be,
and that for example the ideal of a human type in which
sexual differences should disappear, favoured by some late
Greek art and by Winckelmann, is a wholly false ideal.   He
points out that the characteristic qualities or features of either
sex, if transferred *as primary* characteristics to the other sex,
would at once become ugly.

He is thus obviously relying on the undeniable and important fact that the positive modifications of beauty, such as the
sublime and the graceful, are negatively related to each other.
He also thinks that the works of nature, *as normally perceived*
(this condition may save the truth of his view), are widely and
generally defective in beauty.   He appears then to be infer-
ring that the selection and characterization of definite content
in suitable form by art or æsthetic perception is, to begin with,
stimulated by defect of beauty in that which by immediate
presentation suggests this idealizing process.   And further,
he maintains, if I understand him rightly, that the characteristic creation so produced, is by its exclusive or special characterization (as of sublimity, austerity, or the like), *ipso facto*
forfeiting some elements of the beautiful which are accessible
both to a more simple and also to a co-ordinate type of beauty.
Thus both by "concretion" against the abstract, and by
divergence against the equally concrete, ugliness asserts
itself as a factor, but a latent or absorbed factor, in the degrees
and types of beauty.   The only modifications of beauty which
Schasler recognises are the sublime and the graceful.   These
divisions plainly correspond, as Cicero pointed out, to masculine and feminine beauty.   It may not be worth while to subdivide the content further, but it would be easy to do so, and
Hartmann does it in great detail.

The above theory of ugliness is suggestive, and undoubtedly
opens the way for larger ideas of beauty, by definitely giving
the characteristic its place as the central fact of beautiful expression.   I shall criticise it in treating of Hartmann.

The beauty of art passes over into ugliness either by a
confusion between two phases of beauty such as the sublime
and the graceful,[1] or by the intensification of some characteristic

---

[1] As Schasler says *K. G. d. A.*, 1022 of the father of gods and men represented as dancing in Offenbach's *Orpheus*, "the gracefuller, the uglier."

till it destroys the harmony of the system to which it belongs
and becomes caricature. Thus the monstrous or horrible is
the false sublime, and so on. Such are the points at which the
latent ugliness within art passes into actual and invincible
ugliness outside art.

The Classification   iii. "As regards[1] the principle of division to
of the Arts.   be used in classifying the arts, it need here only
be remarked that the author, in fundamental contrast with all
the above-named writers on æsthetic (Hegel, Weisse, and
Vischer), bases it on the simple antithesis of *rest* and
motion ; an antithesis which of course can also be regarded
as that of ' Matter and Mind,' or ' Material and Form,' or
'Space and Time,' but, more carefully considered, lies at the
root of all these antitheses. Now on this antithesis the author
founds an arrangement of the arts as a strictly articulated
double series, whose corresponding terms form a coherent
parallelism. If Hegel, Weisse, and Vischer found themselves
obliged to assume a triple arrangement, and carried it out, each
of them in a quite different way, but with the greatest show
of consistency, by help of the dialectic method—which herein
displayed a really admirable elasticity—it seems that these
thinkers were chiefly forced to their conclusion by a fatal *gap*
in the parallelism, which with every effort they were unable
to fill. It is obvious, that is to say, that if, like the naive
ancients, we arrange the arts according to their means of presentation and organs of perception, and designate one group
as ' arts of the eye ' (Architecture, Sculpture, Painting), and
the other group as 'arts of the ear' (Music, Poetry), it is
possible to co-ordinate the two series, so that music corresponds
to architecture, and poetry to painting ; but then there seems
to be no kind of art on the other side corresponding to sculpture and comparable with it. This fatal gap was an awkward
blot in the system, the true articulation of which was otherwise plain."

"As will be seen later from the development of the principle of division, the author has adhered to the *double* arrangement as the only rational and natural one ; and what principally urged him to this course—besides the inner necessity
of the notion—was the fact that in the triple division no room
was to be found for a very essential grade in the evolution of

---

[1] *K. G. d. A.*, i. xxv. (Preface).

the notion of beauty, viz. the mimic rhythm of the moving
form.   For if, with Schlegel, we consent to designate architecture as frozen music, we might with far more justice designate
sculpture as the frozen mimicry of form, or the dance (panto-
mimic representation, of course not in a comic sense), as unfrozen sculpture."

This division involves at first sight two principles,[1] one the
principle of simultaneity and succession which distinguishes
the two series from one another, and the other, specifically
stated in the *System d. Künste*, the principle of increasing
difference in weight ("*Gewicht*,"[2] predominance or importance),
of material and idea, which distinguishes the several arts within
each of the series.   These two principles Schasler reduces to
one by a lax argumentation identifying both of them with
the antithesis of rest and motion, which embodies as he thinks
the essence of the whole set of antitheses, " Matter and
Force—Material and Shape—Nature and Mind."[3]   The "reduction" of these profound antitheses to one of their most
external and abstract results is a bad point of departure for
the appreciation of the concrete value of the fine arts.

On this classification and its principle I make three observations.

The Parallelism.   *a.* The whole parallelism[4] appears fantastic.

I see no antecedent desirability in creating two series at all
or in the correspondence of arts which Schasler thinks essen-

---

[1] Discussed in Schasler's *System d. Künste*, p. 236.

[2] In distinguishing sculpture from painting he seriously means *weight*,
("*Schwere*," *System d. K.*, p. 80).   There is therefore an equivocation in the use
of the word " *Gewicht* " all the more objectionable that a certain meaning in
the phrase can be detected, and would have repaid explanation.

[3] *S. d. K.*, p. 256.

[4] I subjoin Schasler's scheme as printed p. 124 of the *System d. Künste*.

I. Hauptgruppe :	II. Hauptgruppe :
Künste der " simultanen " Perception :	Künste der "successiven" Perception : a) Productive : b) Re-productive (Hilfs-) Künste :
1. Architektur	1. Musik—Virtuosenthum.
2. Plastik	2. Mimik—Mimische Darstellung.

| 3. Malerei | Landschaftsmalerei. subj.
Genremalerei. . . obj.
Historienmalerei. . subj.
obj. | 3. Poesie | Lyrik—Deklamation.
Epik—Rhapsodik.
Dramatik —Schauspielkunst. |

tial. The only justification for the plan would be that some definite and essential relations were symbolized by the parallelism. In any case, no doubt there is something of a break between painting and music. But it is a break which must be traversed in a definite direction. No help is got by throwing music wholly out of its historical position, which is also that taken by it on an impartial survey of its powers and tendencies, and beginning with it a new series in which the fact of the fresh beginning remains wholly unexplained in its relation to the close of the other series. The distinction by eye and ear is broken down when mimic dancing is placed in the second group. The distinction by rest and motion is compatible with such an arrangement only in the most superficial sense. Motion is not the medium or element of this so-called art, but merely a modification by gesture of the human figure and inseparably attached to its spatial reality.

The detailed correspondences are not less wild. No doubt the definite though very narrow resemblances between music and architecture were worth noting once for all. Neither of these arts is primarily imitative, and both depend largely on rhythmical intervals which can be numerically represented. But when this is said, all is said. The inseparable combination of time-relation and tone-relation which is, as I understand, the essence of melody, finds little or nothing in architecture to answer to the tone-relations ; while the refinements of harmony and orchestration, which are but faintly foreshadowed in the subtlest colour-combinations known to the painter's art, have nothing at all corresponding to them in architecture. For if its coexistent rhythmical intervals have already been compared to melody, they must not be used over again in a lax comparison with harmony. On the other hand, the organic decorative form to which architecture presses forward finds no genuine analogy in music. Of the mimic dance in comparison with sculpture I will speak separately. The correlation of lyric, epic and dramatic poetry, with landscape, genre and historical painting, can only throw the reader into amazement. Landscape painting, as we know to-day, demands the highest characteristic objectivity of expression, and only through this attains its measure of subjectivity. Lyric poetry does not demand and can hardly, in spite of recent developments, receive a fully-organized characteristic content. Genre-painting, though good in its place, is, for the reason pointed out by Hegel,[1] essentially trifling in scale, and cannot have the large and grand style which is the essential of the epos. While historica' painting, if in genuine art there is such a category at all (implying, as it seems to, a historical, *i.e.* non-æsthetic interest, instead of an æsthetic interest in the presentation of a content which happens to be suggested by history) involves a relation to mere fact wholly alien to the drama. Moreover, the un-criticised inclusion of the three traditional types of poetry as essential forms of art, in a place subsequent to music and correlative with painting, without the smallest indication that two out of the three have apparently ceased to exist, and the third is fundamentally changing its character, displays in a striking form the difficulties that attach to an entire dissocia-tion of æsthetic from the temporal evolution of beauty.

The Mimic Dance.   *b*. About the mimic dance very little need be said, for Schasler all but confesses the absurdity of the position which he assigns it,[2] which is not redeemed by the suggestion that it bears an epic character in contrast to the essentially lyrical character of music.

I only desire to take the opportunity of pointing out a principle which appears to me to determine many questions with reference to the secondary arts, though it does not apply to the true decorative or "minor" arts. A true æsthetic material, in which ideas or emotions are to be freely symbol-ized, is the better indeed for definite and peculiar properties, but must not have in itself any individualized organization. Such an organization cannot but collide with any expression, in producing which it is to be treated as mere material. Organisms and individuals are bad material for the artist to work with. In landscape gardening, as in acting or the mimic dance, there is a collision between the natural indi-vidual and the homogeneous unity demanded by the idea. The work cannot be made in one piece under the dominion of one spirit. In a lesser degree the same applies to objects represented as well as to the material of representation. Flowers, trees, animals are manageable in landscape, but represented for their own sake they impose their individuality on the artist, not having, like man, a complete spirituality of their own, yet refusing to be recast in the spirituality of his

---

[1] In his defence of Dutch painting.   [2] *S. d. K.*, 105.

mood. They remain, therefore, as a rule, more or less in the region of studies.

Thus I hold it absurd in principle to speak of the mimic dance as fluid or unfrozen sculpture. In sculpture the whole form is re-created by a single spirit in a single homogeneous material. In acting or the mimic dance the individual is and remains a given natural form, which is determined first by nature and then by its own intelligence and feeling, and can never in principle, however great its capacities, begin to fulfil the condition of a homogeneous medium cast into a single form as the expression of a single idea. The approximation of the dance to an art is nearest where the lowest place, that of mere decorative combination, is claimed, and where the individual form does little, and is only a unit in a pleasing pattern of motions.[1]

The Material.   *c.* Another refinement has told with disastrous effect on Schasler's appreciation of a fundamental principle of artistic expression. The *material* of art, Schasler insists,[2] is the marble or the paint ; the *means* or *medium* of representation is the perceived form and colour. In music and poetry, of course, material and medium all but coincide. But where they are separable the material tends to be omitted from consideration in favour of the medium ; even Schasler's reference to its weight, in his distinction of the arts, comes to lack justification, and Hartmann, accordingly, objects to it.

Thus the whole range of considerations that attach to the feeling for material, and to the moulding of fancy by the habit of thinking in a certain material, are omitted.[3] No attention is paid to the " minor " arts, in which the differences of treatment spring obviously and directly from the differences of material, and from love and experience, for example, of the " metal,"[4] as it is alive in the workman's

---

[1] See above, p. 208, Hogarth's comparison of the " stick and ribbon ornament" to a country dance.

[2] *S. d. K.*, ch. 2.

[3] *S. d. K.*, 60. " The form which it (the marble) possesses as a natural substance, *i.e.* its external stratification and inner texture, has nothing to do with the form given it by sculpture." If he had compared it with wood and bronze he could never have said this.

[4] *i.e.* In this case the melted glass. W. Morris, " The Lesser Arts of Life " in *Lectures on Art* by Poole, Morris, and others, p. 196. " In the hands of a good workman the metal is positively alive, and is, you may say, coaxing him to make something pretty "

hands ; and thus the only true analogy for the classification of the " higher " arts is hopelessly lost. Yet even through music and poetry the same relation persists. The musician thinks, we are told, in the tones of particular instruments, and writes with the colour and feeling proper to each. Even the poet must have the feeling of a familiarity with his material, and his attempts and achievements cannot be the same in Greek and Latin, in Italian and in German, in French and in English.

I am confident that except through this recognition of the workman's sympathy with his material, a recognition which Hegel in some degree possessed, and which recent English criticism has much more completely expounded, nothing solid and sane can be done in the classification of the arts.

I have unavoidably laid stress on points in which I differ from Schasler. His very clearness and freshness of style make his errors glaring in the eyes of those who think that they are errors. But with all his prejudices and caprices he stands on the true ground of modern æsthetic. He is the first to accept the principle that elements which may readily become difficult and displeasing, are not only permissible but essential in art, and are so essential because of their being involved in that penetrating idealization which is the central attribute of the beautiful, and which is recognised by him in all its depth under the name of the characteristic.

γ. Hartmann, who combines the conclusions o.
Hartmann. Schopenhauer with the substantive views of Hegel, and has attained a European popularity equalled among recent philosophers only by that of Mr. Herbert Spencer, has produced as his fourth principal work, following upon the *Philosophy of the Unconscious*, the *Ethic*, and the *Philosophy of Religion*, a comprehensive treatise on æsthetic (1886). Like Schasler's system as originally projected, it consists of two parts, the first historical and the second purely theoretical. The historical part is confined to "German æsthetic from Kant onwards"; the second portion is entitled "a Philosophy of the Beautiful," and fills 836 pages, as compared with 582 of the first part. This ratio compares significantly with Schasler's 1200 pages of history, followed only by theoretical works on a smaller scale. Moreover, within the first part, Hartmann deals in separate essays, partly historical and partly critical, with detached questions in

æsthetic theory—a very valuable treatment, but one which yet further diminishes the space allotted to pure history.

Significance of i. I begin by noting that Hartmann refuses to the History. deal with the æsthetic of the ancients. Though admitting the historical interest of such studies, he considers that the "Aristotelian principle of imitation" and the "Platonic abstract idealism " are rightly held to be of no further moment for æsthetic theory ; while Aristotle's *Poetic*, owing to Lessing's glorification of it, has still an undeserved reputation, and Plato's obscure indications of æsthetic views are obviously not worth the emphasis that is laid upon them.

This is only part of the author's general opinion that the historical and philological interest prevalent at the Universities leads to an over-estimate of the value of ancient philosophy in general, as of ancient æsthetic in particular.[1]

In presence of this view, which as regards the pure theory of æsthetic has much in its favour, it seems desirable to point out a fundamental distinction. Granting for the sake of argument, what I cannot here discuss, that the work of ancient philosophy is fully absorbed in modern thought, and that for scientific completeness, at least in the theory of beauty, it is sufficient to start from eighteenth- and nineteenth - century researches, there is still a question as to the obligation imposed upon a content-theory by the peculiar nature of the matter with which it deals. Art, like philosophy, is a national and historical product, and cannot be adequately treated with the complete formal detachment with which exact science approaches its objects. Thus I might not so much miss the treatment of Greek æsthetic theory if I found in its place an appreciation of what beauty was for the Greeks. This we get, though at second-hand, in Müller's, Schasler's or Zimmermann's history of æsthetic philosophy, as we get it at first hand in Winckelmann's, Schelling's, Hegel's, or Goethe's treatment of Greek art. But by omitting the æsthetic and not inserting the art, Hartmann has dropped out half the content of the science, being inveigled into doing so through the notion, fostered by histories of æsthetic opinion, that Greek philosophy came into the subject only for the sake of its pure contributions to theory. Now really, the introduction of Greek theory into æsthetic science in a historical form was a

---

[1] Hartmann's *Aesth.*, i., Preface.

survival of the treatment of the Greek sense of beauty as an
integral part of the object-matter, and taken as a clarified
expression of that sense had value at once as theory and as
content.

The facility with which this integral element of content is
let go seems to be in fact accounted for by a purely popular
and naive position assumed by the author in respect of
modern art.[1] He appears to share the confusion which we
trace in Schasler, between the abstract and concrete purposes
of the artist, with the accompanying presumption that because modern reflection understands the mission of art better
than earlier theory, therefore modern art itself is more favourably situated than that of earlier times. " Only modern art,
which has broken with all mythology, can approach the
true aim of art."[2] I have already referred to the problem
thus raised, especially in my treatment of the Renaissance.
In its most acute modern phase it is excellently discussed by
Professor Bryce in his work on *The American Common-
wealth*;[3] much of course must depend on the sense in which
"modern" art, in this usage contrasted with that of the middle
age and early Renaissance, is understood, and the time at
which it is taken to have begun. I have already expressed
my views upon this question.[4]

But if, as is too plainly the case, the author means to
represent the course of art as a progress which has continued
during the last three hundred years[5] in the same sense and

---

[1] i. 126. [2] *Ib.* [3] Vol. iii. p. 554 ff. [4] P. 413 *supra.*
[5] See i. pp. 126-7. " Therefore it is only modern art, which has broken
with all mythology, that can approach the true art-problem, to symbolize for
sense the human spirit, which in its ideal aspiration knows the divine spirit
to be immanent in it, through the totality of its ideal moods and actions.
Against this colossal substantive advance we can make no account of the
formal difficulties which are opposed to art by the abstract changes and ugly
externalities of modern life ; it only results that formal beauty must more and
more give way to characteristic beauty as the ideal content becomes deeper
and more subtle." . . . " All this does not overthrow Hegel's dictum,
that the ideal content attainable by art is limited by its sensuous vehicle, but
it reverses Hegel's estimate of the value of ancient, mediæval [Wm. Morris'
" modern"], and modern art into the *opposite*, viz. from a descending [this is
false as regards Hegel's view of the two first terms] into an ascending series,
not merely in conformity with content in the general progress of culture, but
also from the purely æsthetic standpoint which takes account of content only
in as far as it is adequately symbolized to sense."

degree with the progress of civil freedom, material prosperity, mechanical invention, and the natural and critical sciences, then this fundamental error explains his inability to appreciate the depth of Hegel's insight into the art-forms and art-periods, and his indifference to the historical articulation of content, outside of which the object-matter of the science of æsthetic simply does not exist.

I now turn to a point in which Hartmann's history has done good service. He is the first writer who has distinctly held up to view the difference between abstract and concrete idealism in the history of æsthetic philosophy, and has thus placed the theory of the beautiful on a clear foundation from which I believe it will not be dislodged. He points out with great acuteness how all subsequent tendencies of German æsthetic exist in germ within Kant's *Critique of the Power of Judgment*, and he distinguishes these tendencies as I.: the Æsthetic of Content, including, i. Idealism—*abstract* from Schelling and Schopenhauer to Weisse and Lotze, *concrete* from Hegel to Carriere and Schasler—and ii. the Æsthetic of Feeling as in Kirchmann and Horwicz ; II. the Æsthetic of Formalism in Herbart and Zimmermann ; and III. Eclecticism in Fechner. The distinction which he especially insists on, that between concrete and abstract idealism, depends on grasping or not grasping the essential doctrine of " Æsthetic show" (*Schein*), viz. that beauty, though it *symbolizes* ideas, only *exists* in the concrete forms of sense and fancy, so that in speaking of an idea of beauty we are already on slippery ground, and in speaking of beauty as having existence in an abstract idea we fall into sheer nonsense.[1] And against concrete Idealism, he insists, there is really no opposition. All opposition against Idealism is founded on the conception of it as abstract idealism. In this respect as in others the distinction shares the fortunes of that on which in fact it is founded, the logical distinction between the abstract and concrete universal.

In another matter Hartmann has brought against the older concrete Idealism one of those useful objections, which though they may not be needed to correct the actual thought of a previous philosopher, are certainly needed to correct the popular interpretation of it. Following Schopenhauer, and especially insisting on the views of Trahndorff (a contemporary of Hegel

---

[1] See above, p. 409, on Hegel and Hartmann.

whose works I only know through Hartmann) he accuses Hegel of an icy intellectualism, and desires to supplement his view by that of Trahndorff, who considers beauty as "love apprehending itself"[1]—"love" being extended into the general sense of a demand for union. "Beauty," Hartmann suggests as a definition on the basis of Trahndorff, "is the life of love apprehending its own ground and purpose in the idea."[2] Hegel's first definition is, it will be remembered, that beauty is the presentation of truth to sense and fancy. I believe that the proposed supplementation is fanciful, just as I believe that Schopenhauer's "will" adds nothing to Hegel's "idea." A blind impulse is nothing ; and if the unconscious will is nothing apart from direction by the unconscious idea, then we return after all to the idea as a system of unconscious forces, a paradox which we might as well have faced to begin with. Hartmann, I think, fails to see that the æsthetic show or semblance, just because it is a concrete image reborn of the mind, necessarily embodies feeling as well as perception, because every concrete utterance of mind, every utterance of mind as a whole of sense fused with idea—is stamped into what it is by a certain feeling. This is quite plain throughout Hegel, especially when *love* is explained to be *the ideal, i.e.* the essence of concrete expression, in romantic art. But if any one could doubt this æsthetic truth, it was well to have it made plain. And this service Hartmann has rendered.

In order to set the matter in the clearest light, he has devoted a careful discussion in the systematic treatise[3] to the conception of the æsthetic " Schein," pointing out that this conception includes the projection of feeling into the object, while such a term as " Anschauung " need not suggest this inclusion. In the same connection, moreover, he is anxious to elucidate the nature of the æsthetic " Schein-gefühlen," or actual though ideal and impersonal feelings roused by beauty. This discussion again is clear and helpful, and being so, cannot be pronounced superfluous, although it really does no more than develop in methodic form what Aristotle, as interpreted by Lessing and Bernays, had pointed out with reference to the idealization of "fear" through "pity," and the reference of æsthetic emotion to the self widened into humanity.

---

[1] Hartmann, *Aesth.*, i. 146 ff.   [2] *Ib.*, 148 ff.   [3] *Aesth.*, ii. 22.

The degrees of Beauty and Ugliness. ii. In spite of the criticisms which I felt bound to make upon Hartmann's conception of the course of æsthetic evolution, it is undeniable that he has grasped in intellectual form the general result towards which æsthetic philosophy has been gravitating, and according to the theory which I have adopted must necessarily gravitate.

The orders of Formal Beauty. a. He carries out with methodical completeness the conception of "formal beauty" as only a lower grade of the beauty that depends upon content, and as passing upwards by degrees of concreteness into individual and characteristic expressiveness, which not only modifies the more abstract and formal elements of expression, but also includes and employs them. The "Concretionsstufen," or planes of concreteness, are set out systematically with a far greater scientific knowledge and completeness than that shown by Hegel in his corresponding account of symmetry, repetition, and the like. They comprehend six orders of formal beauty—unconscious formal beauty or the sensuously pleasant ; the mathematically[1] and the dynamically pleasing ; the passively teleological (as shown for example in decorative beauty); the vital, bearing of course a substantial relation to some of the mathematical and dynamical forms ; and last of the "formal" orders, the regular or normal type in any species. All these elements of beauty are counted as formal, though each of course has one grade more of concreteness than that which precedes. Finally there comes the concretely beautiful or microcosmically individual, in which there is realized the true essence of beauty as characteristic expression. It will be obvious to the reader that the definition of beauty laid down in the first chapter of the present work, which has served as our guide through the evolution of the æsthetic consciousness, is presupposed in this arrangement of grades and planes.

Ugliness in Nature. b. The treatment of the problem of ugliness,[2] which Hartmann shares with Schasler, is encumbered by a prior difficulty concerning ugliness in nature, which I will try to clear away in a few words. Not content with bringing relative ugliness into all beauty, Hartmann finds real ugliness widely distributed in nature, and in explaining this conviction betrays a very serious dualism, corresponding to the importance which he falsely attaches to a conscious aim

---

[1] The catenary curves are mentioned, p. 112.   [2] *Aesth.*, ii. 142, 501.

at beauty as such in art. Nature, he says, is often ugly because and in as far as she does not aim at beauty ; often she
aims at beauty, and then she is beautiful. Now the former
notion is doubtful, the latter false. Let us put the distinction
clearly. Art is the better, to our perception at least, for being
consciously adapted and selected, but *not* for consciously
aiming at "beauty for beauty's sake." Beauty is the *result* of
rationality expressed for sense ; art aims not at beauty but at
the best expression of some particular content. So again
beauty in nature, *i.e.* in the external world as normally perceived, is not helped or hindered because natural processes are
simply causal and exclude a conscious purpose directed to
beauty. Thus far all is analogous with art. Beauty and
ugliness are results of the particular modes in which at times
these causal processes harmonize, or seem to us to interfere,
with each other, and consequently with the needs of our perception. The consciousness of art, and the unconsciousness
of nature are alike in being immersed in particular contents
which determine them throughout, and an abstract aim outside
and undetermined by special content is as impossible for the
former as for the latter.

But Hartmann appears to regard it as occasionally possible
for the latter, *i.e.* for nature. This seems a wild idea. For, is
nature ever aiming at beauty when she is beautiful ? Certainly not. Does Hartmann really believe that the colours of
birds and flowers have a decorative purpose [1] independent of
natural selection ? Surely this is an antiquated notion. Their
purpose, if any can by analogy be ascribed to them, is the
survival of the species in which they are displayed ; their
result is beauty, because to our perception they are striking
or harmonious. The whole opening for characteristic beauty
in nature, and the possibility of seeing it in the mechanically
determined forms of water, earth, rock, and vapour is destroyed by this idle dualism. Nature, we must take it,
is absolutely logical, and therefore, *primâ facie*, beautiful
throughout. Individualities and their interference *may* no
doubt produce in nature an analogy to ugliness, though it
is to be remembered that in all development there is some
interference, even interference which may be called hostile.[2]

[1] See p. 242 of Grant Allen's *Colour Sense.*
[2] The peculiar beauty of the Scotch fir is closely bound up with the sense of

But it is at least possible that the advantage of representative art is chiefly in introducing limitations appropriate to our powers and knowledge, and in compensating us for them by an artificial completeness or microcosmic character. In theorizing on the ugly of Nature, as we select it, we must bear in mind the infinite context from which, in perceiving, we dissociate it.

Moreover we do not admit that even in art it is well or possible to make beauty as such the guide and purpose. The abstraction is empty, and kills all content. The artist or the lover of natural beauty must be mastered by something in particular, something that lays upon him the necessity of appreciation or of expression. Though he is conscious, and nature is unconscious, yet with him, as with nature, beauty [1] is not a purpose but a result. In this we see the depth of Goethe's aphorism [2] that the *principle* of art is the *significant*, the *result* of successful treatment is the beautiful. The principle is what guides ; the result is not necessarily the aim. It is very suggestive in connection with this idea of an abstract aim that Hartmann finds it necessary to exclude architecture wholly from the free fine arts.

Ugliness in Beauty. *c.* "The beautiful of the lower grades suffers diminution by reason of the laws of form that prevail in the higher grades." [3] Thus uniform repetition is lost in symmetry, simple bilateral symmetry is lost in the subtle balance of a picture, the highest refinements of form, it is said, are incompatible with devotion to the more recon-

---

resistance and definite strength conveyed by its rugged and broken outline. Those who are familiar with the rare sight, only to be seen in sheltered places, of fine trees of this species retaining all their branches regularly developed, and consequently presenting an unbroken and symmetrical contour, must have felt that, splendid as such individuals are, they hardly show the same character as the scarred veterans of the hillside.

[1] See Introd. to Hegel's *Aesth.*, E. Tr., p. 36.

[2] With all abstract terms there is a difficulty of usage arising from the possibility of taking them as concrete. *A* beauty, *i.e.* a thing which is beautiful, is no doubt what the artist yearns to create. But this means, I presume, that he has in him a content which cries out to him for full and harmonious expression in a certain medium which is suitable to it and has already moulded its idea. But just because it is *a beauty*, it cannot be beauty as such. Abstraction is a sure sign of decadence. Art for art's sake is a silly notion. I am not sure that in its root it is not Abstract Idealism of the supposed Platonic type.

[3] Hartmann, *Aesth.*, ii. 217.

dite harmonies of colour, smooth or simple tone-combina-
tions do not meet the needs of great musicians at their
greatest, and the normal generic regularity of human lineaments (the so-called Greek or statuesque outline) or the
uniformity of respectable character must be departed from in
painting and in the drama in order to reveal fully the beauty
of individual characterization.

"Ugliness," [1] then, "is just so far æsthetically justified as
it is a vehicle of the concretion of the beautiful" (*der Kon-
krescenz des Schönen*). That which is *comparatively beautiful*
as against the relatively more abstract beautiful of the lower
grades, is *characteristic* as against the other concrete beauties
of its own level. "The more [2] characteristic any beauty is
upon its own level, the more serious are the forfeitures which
it imposes on the beauty of lower levels ; that is, within every
grade the formal ugliness which is æsthetically indispensable
is the greater as the beauty is more characteristic."

Technically, therefore, Hartmann appears to maintain : (1)
that there is ugliness in all beauty, but not *quâ* ugliness, only
quâ an element in beauty ; and (2) that all ugliness is only
relative, being "the expression of the illogical in a world which
is essentially logical." [3] The different modes in which, on the
highest or individual plane, it is "overcome," produce such
modifications of the beautiful as the touching, the comic, the
tragic, and the humorous.

No Ugliness in   (1) It seems then that the ugliness which nor-
Beauty.   mally enters into beauty is what we may call
apparent ugliness only, that is to say, a merely relative intricacy or narrowness which at first sight taxes the inexperienced perception. It does not seem that to a just appreciation
it is in fact ever presented *as* ugliness. This doctrine, nomin-
ally in polar antagonism to that of Rosenkranz, but practically
not very different from his, may in general be accepted as a
conclusive testimony to the width and depth of true beauty,
in which the strong and the significant play an increasing part
as the education of the individual and of the race proceeds
from the formally to the characteristically expressive.

Taken more in detail, however, the conception arouses a
certain doubt. Ought the strong and definite to be called
ugly at all, when it does not assume the shape of a disguised

---

[1] Hartmann, *Aesth.*, ii. 219.   [2] *Ib.*, 220.   [3] *Ib.*, 256.

contradiction in which the part fraudulently claims to be the whole? Mr. Ruskin [1] once said that genuine imagination was distinguished by the power of making a right or beautiful whole out of ideas that taken apart were wrong or ugly. But he has since modified the expression of this view. It is plain, indeed, that every definite element readily becomes illogical in an improper context. All features of characteristic beauty are therefore *potentially* ugly, and the more so, the more they are characteristic.

The doctrine of a *necessary* forfeiture as we ascend the grades of concreteness is more doubtful, and may be seriously misleading. There is, it is true, a fascination in spiritual expressiveness superadded to a grave deformity in face or figure. But if the theory means that this is the normal type of the characteristic, then the theory is false. True ugliness, the fraudulent perverse of the beautiful, is not an essential element in the characteristic, though the characteristic has power in the last resort to " overcome " even this. But expression may be the " flower and native growth " of noble body as of noble mind. As in the head of Goethe or of Pericles, it may be the natural intensification of vital meaning rising from a structure nobly planned throughout. The departure from the lines of statuesque regularity, demanded by individualization, may—I do not say that it always does—introduce lines and colours of greater and not less formal beauty than those laid down by the " generic " type.

And so with the whole set of gradations. It is a truism that repetition undergoes a change when it passes into symmetry. It is not so clear that it undergoes a loss. It is a truism that bilateral symmetry undergoes a change when it passes into the balance of a Turner landscape ; but whether it is lost is an arguable question. Without discussing the purely logical problem of the meaning of change and loss in dialectic, which is merely verbal so far as concerns æsthetic, I will merely point out that the theory seems wholly to lose sight of the true clue which is also the *crux* in this question, viz. the complete permeation of apparent ugliness by the tissue and texture of simple beauty. The point which strikes us to-day is not merely how ugliness enters into beauty, but how beauty enters into ugliness, as indeed the doctrine of

---

[1] *Mod. Painters*, ii. 148 ff.

"planes of concretion" requires, when rightly understood. In the great works of great masters, however strange or difficult from their intricacy, originality, or profoundness, the decorative texture is usually more splendid, more harmonious, and more lavish in beautiful detail, than is possible in slighter productions if they are not to be oppressed and overloaded. A special work has been published dealing with the patterns on the robes of the great pictures in our National Gallery, and they well deserve it. What decorator ever painted a velvet gown like Tintoret, or cut in marble such lines and folds as the drapery of the "Fates" in the East pediment of the Parthenon —surely the most beautiful block of marble in the world? What composer of ballet-opera can vie with Beethoven in wealth of melody? Are there any verses in the most graceful poems of Tennyson that for sheer beauty of sound and rhythm can compare with Ugolino's story of the hunger-tower, or with the words of Prometheus in his agony, or of Macbeth in his despair?

The conception of a simple forfeiture of formal beauty by all individualization is incompetent to face such questions as these. It is by recognising that concrete characterization, even though difficult or terrible as a whole, yet gives more and not less play to the absolutely indisputable elements of formal beauty, that we are first led to conjecture its true place in the beautiful world. While the painting of the English "pre-Raphaelite" artists still appeared ugly to the common taste in England, it happened that among other points, so Mr. Ruskin tells us, the critics attacked their perspective in particular drawings. Here at last was a plain issue; Mr. Ruskin took his stand upon it, and was able as he conceives to show conclusively that on the pure question of correctness the critics were mistaken. Such a proof, only affecting relations low down among the elements of formal beauty, paves the way for the idea that the art, which is so far correct, may have some beauty in it after all.

What we really have to do with in the whole of this problem is an extension of the sense of beauty by which its familiar and formal basis is not narrowed but on the contrary is both enlarged and fortified. If Hartmann only means that the painter can achieve what the sculptor would be mad to attempt, that we knew before. If he means that the painter, in his more intricate works, loses the balance and harmony of sculpture,[1] we say, No, it does not follow. We have not merely to suggest that a forfeiture of sculptural beauty is incurred by passing on to painting and music, but something deeper and wider than this, viz. that all true characterization is capable of entering into beauty *without* essential forfeiture of the qualities which have always been known as beautiful.

Real Ugliness. (2) Whether there is or is not insuperable ugliness, *i.e.* whether some ugliness is absolute and some merely relative, or all merely relative, seems to be one of those problems in which a difference of degree passes at length into a difference of kind. But the important point to fix upon is this, that *not* mere contradiction is *the* illogicality which corresponds to ugliness, but only such contradiction as is disguised by fraud or confusion. Exposed contradiction is reconciled contradiction ; confusion, the contradiction given as a positive existence, is the only genuine falsehood. Therefore what we have to dread as ugliness insuperable either by healthy perception or by the " characteristic " of art, is not the narrow, the rude, the terrible, the grotesque, or even the vicious when frankly and forcibly revealed for what it is ; as plainly represented in their apparent ugliness, these elements become modifications of the beautiful. We must look for insuperable ugliness in its highest degree in the falsely beautiful produced by the confusion of aims and feelings in conscious representation, *i.e.* in art. We shall find it in the sentimental presented as touching, the effeminate as tender, in the feeble taken to be delicate, the tawdry taken to be brilliant, and the monstrous taken to be strong. Its lower degrees we shall find in the utilitarian works of man, not always as ugly in themselves, except when they present a simulated show of ornament devoid of interest or vitality, or as in discords of sound and colour introduce an artificial definiteness that has no æsthetic relations, but creating by their simple abstract shapes and un-

---

[1] An objection occurs here. Why, if painting has all that sculpture had, and more, do we still care for sculpture after painting has been developed, or for painting when music has been developed? I suppose the answer is that the "something more " is something more than for all purposes we want and so is, in one sense, something less. This " lessness " does not depend on the loss of an element, but on the inseparable fusion of two elements, one of which we may justifiably desire to have by itself. It may also be noted that sculpture and painting have never held *quite* the same position, since painting and music respectively reached their highest development, as they had before.

graded colours an element of interference with the subtle and variously graduated content of external nature. In external nature itself it is hard by this standard to pronounce anything insuperably ugly except perhaps those disfigurements of individuality which indicate an alien life asserting itself victoriously within a higher form of existence. Speaking generally, is it not true that vegetable decay is beautiful or tolerable, and animal decay is ugly? It must be noted that in man the spirit may overcome disfigurement. A wounded animal is apt to be ugly; the dying Nelson is heroic.

I do not think that Hartmann has given weight to this distinction between the negative and the false, or the contradictory and the confused. And therefore, though he has done good service by his robust insistence on the characteristic, I cannot think that he has wholly mastered the nature of the extension which that insistence demands from the sense of formal beauty. The whole in great art, I repeat, is frequently shocking to the untrained perception; the parts are what we first see to be endowed with formal beauty.

To conclude this subject, I may add that Hartmann does well by laying down clearly that ugliness and evil have absolutely no connection except as reflexes in different worlds of the same apparent irrationality within an ultimate rationality. Beauty, as we have seen, is symbolic, not imitative, and therefore goes behind the form of morality, which is co-ordinate with it, to that soul of things which art and morality render, each in its own way.

The division of the Arts.   iii. "We base the division of the arts[1] on that of æsthetic semblance (*Schein*), so that we draw it from the nature of the case. The division of the æsthetic 'Schein' places in the foreground a division into arts of perception and arts of fantasy, which is then crossed by a secondary division into threes; accordingly we shall first have to separate the free arts [the unfree arts including architecture and the 'lesser' arts are placed in a wholly separate classification] into two divisions as arts of perceptive 'Schein' and of imaginative 'Schein' (Phantasie-Schein), and subsequently to subdivide each of these groups into threes. Thus we obtain to begin with as a primary antithesis the contrast of arts of perception and poetic art, by which poetry is

---

[1] Hartmann, *Aesth.*, ii. 625.

assigned its due ideal rank as an art of higher phase (Potenz);
but further, we obtain the parallelism of the arts of perception
with the species of poetry, corresponding to one another as
formative art to Epic poetry, Music to Lyric poetry, and
'Mimik' (acting and the mimic dance) to the Drama.

"The lover of abstract designations will be glad to find
in the primary dichotomy of arts of perception and arts of
fancy, the truth of Schelling's division into a real and an ideal
series, and the friends of dialectic triads will recognise to their
satisfaction, in the secondary triple division of the two groups,
the triad of objective, subjective, and subjective-objective.
The secondary triple division represents in addition, among
the arts of perception the contrast of Rest, Change, and
Motion, or Spatiality, Temporality, and Spatio-temporality, or
eye-semblance, ear-semblance and the two together ; while in
the arts of the reproductive imagination (reproduktiven Phan-
tasieschein) it represents at least the predominance or equilibrium of the elements in question. In both groups or series,
finally, the secondary triple division represents the predominance of perception, of feeling, and the equilibrium of the
two. It is obvious at first sight that the epos, intended for
recitation, is in its plastic and coloured (plastisch-koloristischen)
vividness just as analogous to formative art, as the song, which
is meant to be sung, to music, and the drama, which is meant
to be played, to 'Mimik' ; and these analogies and parallelisms
have so often been noted and insisted on in detail, that it is
absolutely incomprehensible how it has been left for me finally
to combine them."

"Finally [1] we have to answer the question how the compound arts are related in æsthetic value to the simple arts.
Here there are two extreme views ; one rejects the compound
arts altogether, because each of their elements is hindered by
its relation to the others in the freedom and independence
of its development; the other view treats of the simple arts
only as steps on the ladder to the achievement of the total
work of art, and sees the true realization of the work of
art according to its idea exclusively in the latter. As usual
the truth lies between them. The simple arts can no more
replace the complex ones than the latter can make the former
superfluous. As surely as 'Mimik' [2] judged by its abstract

[1] P. 824. [2] See above, p. 422, On the principle of conflict.

æsthetic value, stands higher in the system of arts than the one-sided arts of rest and change [*i.e.* formative art and music!] which it synthetically transcends and absorbs, but yet the practice of the latter is not replaced or made super-fluous by this fact [How kind!], as surely as poetry stands higher in æsthetic value than the arts of perception which it synthetically transcends and absorbs, without thereby annihilat-ing the *raison d'être* of formative art, music, and 'Mimik,' as surely as the quaternary complex arts stand higher in abstract æsthetic than the ternary, without thereby requiring that the song, the oratorio, the ballet, or the stage play, should wholly give place to the opera, just so surely the simple arts are bound to maintain their place in general besides the complex ones, although the latter occupy in the system a higher posi-tion in abstract æsthetic value."

This, I must observe at once, is really method run mad. Assuming that the phrase "transcending and absorbing" has, as it may have when reasonably interpreted, a meaning in comparing the powers of music with those of painting, or the powers of painting with those of sculpture, is it not quite clear that no analogy holds from this fusion of powers or qualities in the nature of a single medium or type of fancy, like sound compared with paint, to the mechanical combination of them by the association of different media in separable aspects of a compound work? The whole passage, which I quoted because it puts Hartmann's view conveniently to-gether, and shows the outrageous results of the extreme Wagnerian influence (I do not say of Wagner's own theo-retical writings, with which I am not acquainted), could hardly have been written by any man with a true feeling for any branch of art.

The principle of division with its results is of the same general kind with that of Schasler, and is subject to the same criticisms in respect of the double series, the neglect of the material and its inspiration,[1] and of the decorative or "lesser" arts (to which neglect we may add in Hartmann's case the low position assigned to architecture), the insertion of "Mimik" at a high point in the scale, and the parallelism between the traditional species of poetry and the other forms of art. There is, however, an attempt to deal with more modern forms of

---

[1] Just referred to, p. 552, but not further employed.

poetic art, as for example the dramatic lyric,[1] the nature of which is fairly explained, but is set down with the usual formula as a transition to the drama, from which it is really quite alien, being essentially an individual characterization, and, so far as we yet see, incompatible with the tendency to combine characters in a drama that will really work. The culmination of the whole system in the "quaternary combination" has already been criticised. The problem of these combinations is closely akin to one of translation, the question being how far the same idea can have its aspects adequately and harmoniously rendered in different media. Now translation from the language of one art into that of another is a hopeless thing except in a few happy or very easy cases. Sometimes the same content which has moulded itself in one medium will by suggestion but without compulsion mould itself correspondingly in another, and then a great combination will arise.[2] But the arc for which two great minds will follow the same orbit, or for which the same mind, however great, can control two disparate media, is necessarily small, and its limit is the inevitable limit of great work in complex art. The true complex art, indeed, has been banished from the genuine arts by the author. In architecture, so organic yet simple is its growth, so vast its extension, and so intimate yet unambitious its inter-relation with the joys and needs of life, not only very many workmen but very many kinds of workmanship can be brought together with spontaneity and success. Architecture is the true type of a complex art.

We have seen the inheritance of the great idealists being methodically completed in the hands of able and learned men, who thought it well, and justly, to borrow the apparatus of accurate science and formal definition from the "exact" enquirers who were opposed to the earlier concrete idealism Issues are more plainly stated, the theory of formal beauty is exhibited with more method and detail; on any branch of æsthetic production some sensible observations may be found by using the elaborate tables of contents of the later systematic writers.

But with methodic completion and the general acceptance of fairly enlightened views scholasticism has set in. The touch of life is lost; the passion for novelty passes into

---

[1] P. 740 ff.   [2] As in Beethoven's use of the Hymn to Gladness.

bizarre suggestions, and the desire to make discoveries, incompatible with the philosophic temper, displays itself in idle
rearrangements and refinements of classification.

Clearness of methodic arrangement and the habit of telling
one's story plainly, together with a full recognition of the
place and import of beauty as apart from edification, from
amusement or sensuous satisfaction, from imitation, and from
mere formal decoration, have been won by the idealist
methodisers with the help of the exact æstheticians, and
will not again be lost. But from the theory of content and
expression which has thus been perfected, the content has
itself in some degree oozed away. It may be mere national
prejudice, but I believe it to be a well-grounded conviction,
which causes me to turn to England for a re-animation of the
bond between content and expression. As the true value
of German idealism in general philosophy was never understood, till the genius of English naturalists had revolutionised
our conception of the organic world, so the spirit of German
æsthetic will not be appreciated until the work of its founders
shall have been renewed by the direct appreciative sense of
English art and criticism. With a very brief account of this
in the ensuing chapter I propose to conclude the present
work.

CHAPTER XV.

BEGINNINGS OF A THEORETICAL REUNION BETWEEN CONTENT AND EXPRESSION.

Philosophic Conditions of recent English Æsthetic. 1. ÆSTHETIC theory in Germany, we saw reason to think, was the operative ferment from which German Idealism sprang, and was immediately reacted upon by that Idealism. The English mind travelled by a different road and arrived at a corresponding æsthetic position from complementary but different data.

Between the two movements there was little direct contact. From Alison in 1790 to Mill, Spencer, and Bain in the middle of the nineteenth century, British psychological philosophy maintains its course, attributing æsthetic effect mainly to association, and advancing the real problem, viz. what is accidental in association and what is not, little beyond the point at which Burke had left it. True English æsthetic has not sprung from philosophy or philosophers, except through the negative contact of Mr. Ruskin with Alison and Burke. Only Herbert Spencer, as has been noticed above,[1] made a real contribution to the ideas of spontaneity and economy in the beautiful, in the latter case certainly anticipating Fechner, and independently confirming the results of the brothers Weber.[2] On the other hand Spencer's theory of the vocal origin of music is not even directed to a serious problem. Granting for the sake of argument that musical beauty was first apprehended through the voice, we gain from this no sort of explanation as to the conditions which underlie the musical expressiveness of the voice itself. The fragmentary and partial, although prior in time, must be explained by the systematic, and not the systematic by the partial. In so far as voice-modulation has musical expressiveness, its beauty depends upon musical relations, which in a vastly wider range of effect than that of vocal cadences are the matter to be explained.

---

[1] P. 386 *supra*.   [2] See p. 386 *supra*.

With German philosophy, previously to the development
of the English æsthetic of which I am about to treat, and
during its course, there has been I believe but a very slight
and negative connection. How far the pregnant ideas filtered
through Coleridge and Carlyle may have influenced Mr.
Ruskin is a question which I cannot answer.[1] But no such
influence seems to me to be needed as an explanation of his
life work. Other conditions, not proceeding either from
philosophers or from the universities, were more effectually
brought to bear.

General Influ-   2. The French Revolution, to which, as Car-
ence of the   lyle suggested, the intellectual work of Goethe's
Time.   generation bore a strange analogy, marked rather
than created an immense disquieting force in many directions.
Our islands, thrown back on their insularity by the Peninsular
War, nevertheless felt the electricity of the general atmosphere. I will enumerate rather than attempt to analyse the
conditions which constituted the "data" of our "modern
æsthetic."

Antiquities.   a. Winckelmann had grumbled, we remember
that valuable antiquities were constantly being
carried off and shut up in English country houses, and England like other countries was eager for the spoil, under the influence of a revived Renaissance connoisseurship. Before 1815
no Greek works of the fifth century B.C. were in the British
Museum. In that year, after a discussion that is now amusing
to read,[2] showing once more how taste worked back from the
lesser and later to the greater and earlier antiquities, the

---

[1] I should have thought that Mr. Collingwood exaggerated the probability
of connection ; see Ruskin's *Art Teaching*, p. 16.

[2] I extract an account of this matter from a lecture by Miss Sellers, printed
in the *U. E. Journal*, March, 1892.

"The Government, to whom Lord Elgin had repeatedly offered the Marbles
for sale, had been as often dissuaded from the purchase by the judgment of
artists, and in particular of the 'connoisseur,' Mr. Payne Knight, whose
prejudiced action in this matter may, however, be forgiven, when we remember the beautiful bronzes and other objects which he afterwards bequeathed to the Museum. In 1815 the Government was roused by the
admiration which the Italian sculptor, Canova, had evinced for the Marbles,
to appoint a Committee to reconsider the matter of the purchase. The
account of the last battle is worth reading from Haydon's own biography :—

"'The Committee opened its proceedings. West, President of the Royal
Academy, Lawrence, Nollekens, Flaxman, and Westmacott were summoned

Elgin marbles and about the same time the Phigaleian frieze were acquired for the Museum. Since that date the lacunæ in the periods represented have been filled up by works of the sixth, fourth, and third centuries B.C., and the eyes of students have been familiarized with the real value and sequence of phases of beauty which Winckelmann had so marvellously divined.

on the side ot English art ; on the side of the connoisseurs, Mr. Payne Knight, Lord Aberdeen, Sir Charles Long, Lord Farnborough, and seven others. Lord Elgin's chief witnesses were W. Hamilton and Haydon.

" ' Lord Elgin and Haydon were both favourably impressed with the Committee at opening, but it soon began to show the cloven foot. The favourable witnesses were hurried over, but to the opposite side was paid the greatest attention and respect. Of the professional witnesses, Nollekens called them "fine things," Westmacott called them "good things." Flaxman said they were " the most excellent things of the kind he had seen, though he preferred the Apollo Belvedere to the Theseus " (the gods forgive him !). Chantry said " they were according to Nature in the grand style." West feebly praised them, but Lawrence spoke out for them manfully. He said he considered them " examples of the highest style of art, of essential importance to art, and particularly to historical painting." Mr. Payne Knight was equally decided. He said Lord Lansdowne's Venus or Mercury was " each worth any two " of the " articles " in Lord Elgin's collection, that the Theseus was "spurious," and the rest of the "articles very poor." Lord Aberdeen and his friends followed in much the same strain. And then came the turn for the examination of Lord Elgin's professional witness, Haydon. For three days, on one plea or another, Haydon was put off by the Committee. At length, on the afternoon of the third, they commissioned Mr. Banks, M.P., one of their number, to inform Lord Elgin that " Mr. Haydon would not be examined out of delicacy to Mr. Payne Knight." '

"After this rebuff, Haydon stung not only by his personal defeat, but by the fear that the Marbles might be lost to the nation after all, wrote that celebrated pamphlet entitled, *On the Judgment of Connoisseurs being preferred to that of Professional Men*, in which, after mercilessly showing up the falsity of the taste of the time (particularly that of Mr. Payne Knight), he passes to his immortal defence of the Marbles. ' To these divine things,' he concluded, with an enthusiasm which all the bombastic style of the time cannot dim—' to these divine things I owe every principle of art I may possess. I never enter among them without bowing to the great Spirit of Art that reigns within them. I thank God daily that I was in existence on their arrival, and will continue to do so to the end of my life. Such a blast will Fame blow of their grandeur, that its roaring will swell out as time advances, and nations now sunk in barbarism, and ages yet unborn, will in succession be roused by its thunder, and be refined by its harmony. Pilgrims from the remotest corners of the earth will visit their shrine and be pacified by their beauty.'

" The outburst silenced the opponents, the Marbles were purchased for the Museum, but Haydon, poor man, paid dearly for his victory, by bringing down upon himself the undying hatred and persecution of the men whose ignorance and false judgment he had exposed."

Science.   *b.* It is a striking fact[1] that the first volume of *Modern Painters* was published in the same year as Stuart Mill's *Logic* (1843).   It is needless to recite the history, familiar, I hope, in its outlines "to every schoolboy," of the achievements of the scientific spirit during the present century.   Its result, for our purpose, may be stated in general language as the recognition of rational system throughout the universe accessible to man.   More particularly, on the side facing æsthetic theory, we may signalize two tendencies within this movement.   First, it brought nature nearer to man, and showed him his own intelligence both mirrored in its causation and rooted in its evolution ; and secondly, it revealed in all phenomena, inorganic, organic, and belonging to humanity, the definite distinctive characteristics which on the one hand had stamped them for what they individually were, and on the other displayed them in their microcosmic relations as meeting-points of the complex influences that permeate the universe.   In this latter connection the life work of Sir Charles Bell,[2] directed against the abstract ideal in art and towards a causal theory of expressiveness in the human face and figure, paved the way for Darwin's researches upon that subject.   The whole result of geology, and of the organic sciences guided by the principle of natural selection,[3] has been to the same effect, and even the phenomena of colour in plants and animals have been shown to play their part in the causal system.[4]   In this last relation the conception forces itself on the mind that the import of colour distinctions might perhaps be approached not only by assuming the connection of wave-length and hue, and asking how on this hypothesis organisms

---

[1] Collingwood, op. cit. 20 and 76.

[2] *E.g. Lectures on the Anatomy and Philosophy of Expression,* 1st ed. 1806, re-written 1840 (Geo. Bell & Son, 1880).   It is remarkable that in this work he gives the same explanation of Laocoon's alleged silence as that of Goethe (did Goethe get it from him ?) viz. that from his physical attitude Laocoon *could* not cry out.   Payne Knight's ideas, which he is combating, show entire ignorance of Lessing.   Knight actually says that no tragedian could let a hero cry out at his death-wound without making the audience laugh.   I must own that the representation of Agamemnon's death-cry, which Knight seems not to know of, did once in my recollection cause a smile.

[3] Of course this principle was not made known till long after Mr. Ruskin's work had begun.   The *Naturalist's Voyage* must have appeared about the same year with the *Modern Painters* and Mill's *Logic.*   Its second edition bears date 1845.

[4] See Grant Allen on the *Colour-Sense.*

are benefited by the possession of this or that reflecting surface, but also by examining this connection itself, as a relation that must have been causally determined in the course of evolution.   It is conceivable that some advantage was to be found in the wave-length[1] commonest on the earth's surface being seen as green rather than as red.   Only the ethereal undulation was given ; the corresponding sensation, for all we know, was modifiable.

Romantic Natur-   *c.*   As a complementary counterpart to the
alism.   scientific revelation of the world as responsive to reason, there developed with amazing rapidity the conviction —sentimental in Schiller's sense—that the world had also a response for feeling.   The mere history of the tour and the guide-book, from Rousseau, Goethe, and De Saussure, through Wordsworth [2] to Ruskin, and thence to the modern sentimental tourist of the worse or better type, would well repay the writing.   With the tourist come the field geologist and the field botanist, and with these come the landscape painter.   It was rather through Wordsworth, Turner, Lyell, and Darwin, than through a Winckelmann, a Lessing, or a Schiller, that the new renaissance dawned in England.   The insularity of our country had to do with this detachment.   No one can read Goethe's story of his childhood without seeing how his imagination was affected by the pageants of the Empire at Frankfort—the visible organic continuity into which he was born.   The sense of history and the spirit that is sympathetically critical of the religions and philosophies of past times were wanting to the leaders of our thought.   Those who were sympathetic were not critical ; those who were critical were not sympathetic.   Yet from the time of Walter Scott our sentimentalism became capable of a historical colouring ; a new feeling for Gothic architecture and the "lesser arts " arose ; attempts, however ill-directed in some respects, were made to familiarize our people with the art and workmanship of other times and countries ; and when the " pre-Raphaelite brotherhood " had begun its enterprise and the voice of Carlyle had made itself heard, the same spirit of thoroughness, audacity, and penetrative insight that was con-

---

[1] See Grant Allen, op. cit. on the prevalence of green on the earth's surface in early times of evolution.

[2] Author, it must be remembered, of a *Guide to the English Lakes !*

quering the intellectual world under the banner of science, began to reorganize the world of feeling under that of romantic naturalism in art. For I must repeat that normally and on the large scale romance and naturalism are the same. The modern yearning for external nature has the same root as the modern love of symbolism, of character, and of passion. It is only a would-be scientific naturalism,[1] at once prurient and moralistic, that is opposed to romance, and a conventional romantic sentiment, remote from the feeling for genuine passion, that is opposed to naturalism.

The Democratic Spirit. *d.* It ought not to be supposed that I am wandering from my subject if I point out in the briefest words that behind and within all these phenomena there was operative the rising spirit of democratic solidarity. In England we did not derive this spirit by way of philosophical inspiration from the Hellenes ; it sprang up from complex causes, including the destructive aspect of science, but also more deeply rooted in the European and national circumstances of the time, and it carried our interest to Hellas,[2] not Hellas to it. The "watchword of Reason and Freedom "[3] and the ideal of a human and beautiful life for every man were not popularized here, as in Germany, through professorial and scholarly persons in association with classical culture, and historical continuity, and the dominant philosophy of the universities. On the contrary, they were wrought out in various detail by political and social reformers, by abstract sceptical philosophers, by poets and men of letters, by artists and by special students of art and history. Therefore the connection of social life with beauty was long un-

---

[1] It is not my business to attempt the work of the art-critic. The philosopher's task begins when he has the best critical opinion before him. But I may appeal to my readers to judge whether it is not true that the three antiæsthetic tendencies of art, the "scientific," the moralistic, and the impure, are constantly found in union. Of course, an artist may have great genius and yet be hampered in his art by a theory which has these results.

[2] I mean to genuine Hellenic thought and politics and beauty. The phil-Hellene enthusiasm of Byron, Shelley, and Keats forms no doubt an important link through European politics with the spirit of the time, but had, I believe, little effect in the way of spreading a real feeling for Hellenic antiquity. The fact that Keats knew the Greeks only through the classical dictionary is most instructive with regard to the connection between art-stimulus and learning. Grote's *History* is plainly a *result* of political sympathy. He believed that Athens progressed by Reform Bills.

[3] Hegel, *Briefe.*

apparent. The reformers thought first of the industrial system and of the franchise, the poets and philosophers of sentiment and of knowledge, while the artists lived exclusively for their art. The spirit of humanity was in all of them alike, but was not aware of its own identity; and thus the connection of life and art, of content and expression, was reached, so to speak, underground by a *de facto* induction, and was perhaps more vitally grasped, though far less clearly and systematically expounded, than where as in Germany it had to be attained by the concurrent intellectual labours of many men endowed with philosophical genius and reviewing an immense field of ordered material.

Synthesis of Content and Expression. 3. The strength and weakness of the best English æsthetic of the last half-century—the work principally of Mr. Ruskin and Mr. William Morris—lies in its restriction to the field of formative art. Never before, so far as I can form a judgment, has such critical and literary genius been combined with such definite skill in the object-matter of research; but on the other hand —I make this quite obvious reservation once for all, and I need not recur to it—no one whose interest is directed to art as a whole could be satisfied with a theoretical treatment which seems not merely to ignore the arts of music and poetry, but even at times to imply their non-existence. In this criticism I am alluding to the reiterated doctrine of the unity of art understood as equivalent to the assertion that if one art dies then all are dead. I do not doubt that this idea points to a profound truth, or that a diseased social condition reacts upon the sense of beauty in all its manifestations. But here, as everywhere, we must distinguish the partial from the perverse. It is simple matter of history that all the various arts have never flourished in their perfection—nay not even in a fair degree of forwardness—in the same period and in the same country. We know well that the several arts touch their culminations not simultaneously but in succession, and while I fully admit that the prosperity of art in general falls within the great Art-age that closed with the Renaissance, yet we must not shut our eyes to the fact that music finds its only complete and independent development (and of landscape painting almost as much may be said) full two centuries after the unity of the art-tradition, as our critics understand it, had perished. But in spite of all this, at least within the theory of formative art a new vitality of connection is supplied by the work of our great writers, which precisely justifies, by an undesigned coincidence, the conception of the early concrete Idealists of Germany, and supplements what is defective in the arid formalism of their successors.

The Characteristic. i. Mr. Ruskin's theoretical treatment of ugliness [1] does not seem to be bold enough for truth. Technically speaking, he seems to hold the position of Rosenkranz, that ugliness can never become beautiful, but yet is essential to art for the sake of completeness. To live wholly in beauty, he is said to teach,[2] is unhealthy—a monstrous position, if beauty is comprehensively understood.

But this is not a matter of first-rate importance. As we have insisted throughout, the true question is in the first instance as to the range and vigour of beauty itself. Now in one aspect of this question we owe something like a revolution to the English art and criticism of this century. This aspect is our appreciation of external nature in the form of landscape scenery. Schasler, we may remember, thought landscape so wholly a matter of subjective mood that he made it in his classification the corresponding term to lyric poetry. Now in an ultimate sense it must be true that when we feel the beauty of Nature we read our moods into her phenomena. But we may do this profoundly or superficially, conceitedly or humbly, ignorantly or with insight. If we have eyes for what Hegel calls the "uniform, direct, and solidly coherent sequences of nature," we enter into it as though for its own sake, and only by so doing can we recognise in it our deeper selves. It is this point of view that we owe to Mr. Ruskin's unwearied justification of the art of Turner, and it is not too much to say that he like Winckelmann has given the mind a new organ for the appreciation of beauty. "The characteristic" in nature as a whole, though a point of view imperatively demanded by the theory of Goethe, Hegel, and Schelling, was a region in which we found them weak.[3] They thought more of the individual formation, the crystal, the plant, the animal, while

---

[1] See Collingwood, *Ruskin's Art Teaching.*
[2] *Ib.*
[3] Goethe's morphology had more to do with the specific than with the individual characteristic.

the co-operating laws and larger combinations of phenomena were scarcely within the range of the characteristic as they understood it. But fully in the spirit of science—though guarding himself, as I think, far too timidly from urging scientific study upon the artist—Mr. Ruskin has pointed out with loving appreciation the value and import of variable curves, graduated colours, and the nature and stratification of earth and rock, so that to the nature-lover versed in this expressiveness, the hills and plains, the cliffs and river-courses are able to tell their story like a human face. Without intellectual analysis, through the mere habit of sympathy, they are construed as determined by movements continuously varying, and showing themselves in growth, decay, and resistance, that is in lawfulness and individuality. It seems needless to dwell at length on ideas so familiar to all students of natural beauty, but to discharge my duty as a historian, who must not leave his readers to do his work wholly for him, I will extract two passages that illustrate the beauty of characteristic expression in matters in which if we can find it we may find it anywhere.

" A steep [1] bank of loose earth of any kind that has been at all exposed to the weather contains in it, though it may not be three feet high, features capable of giving high gratification to a careful observer. It is almost a fac-simile of a mountain slope of soft and decomposing rock ; it possesses nearly as much variety of character, and is governed by laws of organization no less rigid. It is furrowed in the first place by undulating lines, caused by the descent of the rain ; little ravines, which are cut precisely at the same slope as those of the mountain, and leave ridges scarcely less graceful in their contour, and beautifully sharp in their chiselling. When a harder knot of ground or a stone occurs, the earth is washed from beneath it, and accumulated above it, and there we have a little precipice connected by a sweeping curve at its summit with the great slope, and casting a sharp dark shadow ; where the soil has been soft, it will probably be washed away underneath until it gives way, and leaves a jagged hanging irregular line of fracture ; and all these circumstances are explained to the eye in sunshine with the most delicious clearness; every touch of shadow being expressive of some particular truth of structure, and bearing witness to the symmetry into which the

---

[1] *Modern Painters*, i. 307.

whole mass has been reduced. Where this operation has gone on long, and vegetation has assisted in softening the outlines, we have our ground brought into graceful and irregular curves, of infinite variety, but yet always so connected with each other, and guiding to each other, that the eye never feels them as *separate* things, nor feels inclined to count them, nor perceives a likeness in one to the other ; they are not repetitions of each other but are different parts of the same system. Each would be imperfect without the one next to it." " The truths of form in common ground are quite as valuable (let me anticipate myself for a moment) quite as beautiful, as any others which nature presents." " A really great artist dwells on every inch of exposed soil with care and delight, and renders it one of the most essential, speaking, and pleasurable parts of his composition."

Or take an example in which the central character of a whole complex of natural scenery is summed up in a single architectural product, which therefore, if brought before the eye in art, prescribes the law for the whole region that is perceived.

" All rivers,[1] small or large, agree in one character, they like to lean a little on one side ; they cannot bear to have their channels deepest in the middle but will always, if they can, have one bank to sun themselves upon, and another to get cool under ; one shingly shore to play over, where they may be shallow and foolish and childlike,[2] and another steep shore under which they can pause and purify themselves, and get their strength of waves fully together for due occasion. . . . Two arches over the same span of river, supposing the butments are at the same depth, are cheaper than one, and that by a great deal ; so that, where the current is shallow, the village mason makes his arches many and low : as the water gets deeper and it becomes troublesome to build his piers up from the bottom, he throws his arches wider ; at last he comes to the deep stream, and as he cannot build at the bottom of that, he throws the largest arch over it with a leap,

---

[1] *Elements of Drawing*, p. 263 ff.
[2] I cannot but regret the playful expressions of this passage, for my present purpose, as liable to misunderstanding, though no one who has read Mr. Ruskin on the *Pathetic Fallacy* will misunderstand them. The *fact* about river-courses is familiar to all.

and with another little one or so gains the opposite shore.
Of course as arches are wider they must be higher, or they
will not stand ; so the roadway must rise as the arches widen.
And thus we have the general type of bridge, with its highest
and widest arch towards one side, and a train of minor arches
running over the flat shore on the other ; usually a steep bank
at the river-side next the large arch ; always of course a flat
shore on the side of the small ones ; and the bend of the river
assuredly concave towards this flat, cutting round, with a
sweep into the steep bank ; or, if there is no steep bank, still
assuredly cutting into the shore at the steep end of the
bridge.

"Now this kind of bridge, sympathizing, as it does, with the
spirit of the river, and marking the nature of the thing it has
to deal with, is the ideal of a bridge."

The characteristic, thus apprehended, including in its expression signs of the feeling with which the sympathetic or
idealised self enters into the world-life thus symbolised, is
fully in the sense of Hegel, but possesses a wealth and vigour
which in the beauty of landscape scenery his eye was never
trained to appreciate. And here, in its simplest form, if we
bear in mind the nature of the curves and graduated surfaces
demanded according to the above exposition, is the vital bond
between content and expression.

The Life of the Workman. ii. In speaking of Goethe's *German Building*[1]
I alluded to the chapter "On the nature of Gothic"
in *The Stones of Venice*. In this chapter and in those
essays on the same theme, enriched with the knowledge and
feeling of the practical designer, which we owe to Mr. Wm.
Morris, the unity of content and expression is stated on a
higher level, or as Schelling would have said, in a higher
"power." Here the root of identity is not a causal process of
nature assigned a meaning by analogy, but it is the life of a
self-conscious being. The reason why this identity had to be
specially and forcibly dragged to light in the case of the workman in architecture is that in this art only (including in it "the
lesser arts of life") could it ever be attempted to divorce
them. No one would maintain as a general doctrine that a
dramatist might confine himself to constructing his scenario,
and leave his secretary to write the dialogue, or that a painter

---

[1] P. 306 *supra.*

might be satisfied[1] with furnishing the cartoons for a picture, and leave it to a journeyman to execute. But just because in these higher arts the inseparability of content and expression is pre-supposed, owing to the high degree of individual talent demanded even for tolerable performance, the connection of the two aspects within these arts is assumed rather than scrutinised, and is apt to drop out of its true place in the theory. Architecture at once challenges an answer. It is determined by utility of some kind ; it is not primarily a representative art ; the work set to the individual workman appears simple, partial, and definite. Why need he be thought of as an artist, or the determination of his mind freely by a content instead of mechanically by a gauge be insisted on at all ? We have here a limiting case. I answer in Mr. Ruskin's words.[2]

" It is, perhaps, the principal admirableness of Gothic schools of architecture, that they thus receive the results of the labour of inferior minds ; and out of fragments full of imperfection, and betraying that imperfection in every touch, indulgently raise up an unaccusable whole." " For the best that is in them (the workmen) cannot manifest itself unless in company with much error. Understand this clearly. You can teach a man to draw a straight line, and to cut one, or to strike a curved line and to carve it, and to copy or carve any number of given lines or forms, with admirable speed and perfect precision,[3] and you find his work perfect of its kind ; but if you ask him to think about any of those forms, to consider if he cannot find any better in his own head, he stops; his execution becomes hesitating ; he thinks, and ten to one he thinks wrong ; ten to one he makes a mistake in the first touch he gives to his work as a thinking being. But you have made a man of him for all that. He was only a machine before, an animated tool." "On the other hand, if you will make a man of him, you cannot make a tool.

---

[1] Approximations to such practices on the part of fresco painters and of sculptors who work only in clay raise the same problems as architecture.

[2] *Stones of Venice*, ii. 161–2.

[3] In so far as true Greek work is classed with the " servile " work, there seems to be here a certain neglect of the extreme difference between Greek and Roman ornaments. Greek moulding-curves, we are told, cannot be struck with compasses, and if they are copied such copying as this surely requires some free qualities in the workman. I regret that my technical ignorance disqualifies me from entering further into this subject. See p. 35 *supra.*

Let him but begin to imagine, to think, to try to do anything
worth doing, and the engine-turned precision is lost at once.
Out come all his roughness, all his dulness, all his incapability ;
but out comes the whole majesty of him also ; and we know
the height of it only when we see the clouds settling upon
him." "And on the other hand go forth again to gaze upon
the old cathedral front where you have smiled so often at the
fantastic ignorance of the old sculptors ; examine once more
those ugly goblins and formless monsters, and stern statues,
anatomiless and rigid, but do not mock at them, for they are
the signs of the life and liberty of every workman who struck
the stone ; a freedom of thought and rank in the scale of being,
such as no laws, no charters, no charities can secure ; but which
it must be the first aim of all Europe at this day to regain for
her children."

It is probable that some readers may not recognise that we
have here in essence the same problem with that which, following Kant, nearly all German writers discuss under the title of
" Genius " ; that is to say, the peculiar endowment by which
the rational content is given in a state of active and productive
feeling, and by which all production of beauty is distinguished
toto cælo from everything in the nature of scientific apprehension. " In artistic production, the spiritual and sensuous side
must be as one." [1]   The bond of union is this, in short, that as
in a natural process the form expresses the law, so in the work
of a man, as long as no machine intervenes, his operative
ideas *quâ* operative, together with their results in the way
of automatic activity, are expressed in the production of his
hands.   The work reveals the man, and the man is the incarnation (in sense and feeling) of ideas.   This is in conscious
production the link between content and expression.   I do
not substantially assent to the criticism passed by popular
writers upon Mr. Ruskin, that he turns æsthetic into ethic.
We are dealing, of course, with a thinker who cares no jot for
system or formula ; but if we try to interpret, we must interpret fairly by the whole drift of his doctrine.   I may here
refer [2] to what I said in dealing with Plato as to the essential

---

[1] Hegel's *Æsth.*, Introd., E. Tr. p. 74.   Hegel says in another place of the
gem-cutter that he must have his ideas in the form of [muscular and tactile]
feeling, for he cannot so much as see his minuter work.   Plainly this, in some
sense, is true of all art.
[2] On the moralistic principle in Plato, p. 18 *supra*.

connection between the content of ethic and that of æsthetic, which it is a worse error to neglect, than to state with technical incorrectness. I do not think that in the main Mr. Ruskin is chargeable with anything but a technical defect in philosophic formulation. I will admit, however, that there are occasional sermons which I cannot altogether defend, and which are chiefly to be regretted because they give a passing interest to malicious platitudes which no one would otherwise attend to.[1]

It is necessary to observe that in this feeling for content we recognise the social spirit and the spirit of true history, which has in all provinces of research gained ground during the present century. In Germany, we observed, the historical led up to the æsthetic synthesis;[2] in England æsthetic insight has had a remarkable influence both on historical research and on economic theory.

Content and Expression in the "Lesser Arts." iii. Less ambitious than the immense literary activity of Mr. Ruskin, but of the very highest critical quality, are the contributions of Mr. Wm. Morris to the theory of expression on the basis of the lesser arts. The neglect of these arts has been throughout the weak point of the intellectual æsthetic of Germany (Plato knew better) ; but it was only in the later methodisers of idealism that, as we saw, the feeling for material fell wholly away, and was replaced in the classification of the arts by all sorts of mere abstract corollaries from the nature of their media. I do not believe that the question of the classification of the "higher" arts can be properly approached except from the point of view supplied by the simple experience of the distinctions which arise automatically and react on the fancy and the design in the use of such materials as clay, glass, wood, metal, and stone. I quote enough to show in what way this vital feeling of the material operates upon the connection of content and expression, and upon the general definition of beauty.

---

[1] No one would turn his head to listen to the remark that "All art is useless," which is as old as Aristotle in matter, and claims attention merely by a certain malice of expression, if Mr. Ruskin had not challenged it by maintaining in a vein of paradox easily intelligible, that all art is useful.

[2] Although the latter again affected the former ; Ranke seems to have been first interested in his subject by Walter Scott's novels, though adversely to their representations. It was the historic interest in the form it took for the romantic school that preceded philosophical æsthetic.

"No doubt[1] many of you have wandered through the galleries of the admirable museum of South Kensington, and like me, have been filled with wonder and gratitude at the beauty which has been born from the brain of man. Now consider, I pray you, what these wonderful works are, and how they were made ; and indeed it is neither in extravagance nor without due meaning that I use the word wonderful in speaking of them. Well, these things are just the common household goods of those past days, and that is one reason why they are so few and so carefully treasured. They were common things in their own day, used without fear of breaking or spoiling— no rarities then—and yet we have called them ' wonderful.'

" And how were they made ? Did a great artist draw the designs for them—a man of cultivation, highly paid, daintily fed, carefully housed, wrapped up in cotton wool, in short, when he was not at work ? By no means. Wonderful as these works are, they were made by 'common fellows,' as the phrase goes, in the common course of their daily labour. Such were the men we honour in honouring those works. And their labour—do you think it was irksome to them ? Those of you who are artists know very well that it was not ; that it could not be. Many a grin of pleasure, I will be bound—and you will not contradict me—went to the carrying through of those mazes of mysterious beauty, to the invention of those strange beasts and birds and flowers that we ourselves have chuckled over at South Kensington. While they were at work, at least, these men were not unhappy, and I suppose they worked most days, and most part of the day, as we do."

" That[2] thing which I understand by real art is expression by man of his pleasure in labour."

" Now[3] as to the kindred art of making glass vessels. It is on much the same footing as the potter's craft. Never till our own day has an ugly or stupid glass vessel been made ;[4] and no wonder, considering the capabilities of the art. In the hands of a good workman the metal is positively alive,

---

[1] Morris's *Lectures on Art*, p. 55.

[2] *Ib.*, p. 58.

[3] *Lectures on Art*, by Morris and others, p. 195.

[4] There is much that sounds like this in Hartmann's *Aesth.*, ii. 136 ff., but it will be observed that his reprobation of fraudulent ornament starts from the postulate of simple utility, and does not allude in any degree to the connection of shape etc. with the pleasure of the craftsman.

and is, you may say, coaxing him to make something pretty. Nothing but commercial enterprise capturing an unlucky man and setting him down in the glassmaker's chair with his pattern beside him (which I should think must generally have been designed by a landscape gardener)—nothing but this kind of thing will turn out ugly glasses. This stupidity will never be set right till we give up demanding accurately gauged glasses made by the gross. I am fully in earnest when I say that if I were setting about getting good glasses made, I would get some good workmen together, tell them the height and capacity of the vessels I wanted, and perhaps some general idea as to the kind of shape, and then let them do their best. Then I would sort them out as they came from the annealing arches, (what a pleasure that would be!) and I would put a good price on the best, for they would be worth it, and I do not believe that the worst would be bad."

"For [1] all that, it is true that these non-architectural races (let the Chinese stand as a type of them) have no general mastery over the arts, and seem to play with them rather than to try to put their souls into them. Clumsy-handed as the European or Aryan workman is (of a good period, I mean) compared with his Turanian fellow, there is a seriousness and meaning about his work that raises it as a piece of art far above the deftness of China and Japan ; and it is this very seriousness, and a depth of feeling which brought to bear upon the matters of daily life is in fact the soul of Architecture, whatever the body may be ; so that I shall still say that among ourselves the men of modern Europe, the existence of the other arts is bound up with that of Architecture. . . . For this art of building is the true democratic art, the child of the man-inhabited earth, the expression of the life of man thereon."

The views thus eloquently but quite definitely expressed are not a matter below the consideration of philosophy, although they would need development and explanation in order to hold true of the individual and highly imaginative forms of art. They supply an essential factor in æsthetic theory which neither the bare doctrine of characteristic expression nor even the closer analysis attempted by formalist æsthetic have the power to furnish. As I said above, the true correlative to these conceptions is Kant's doctrine of

---

[1] *Lectures*, by Morris and others, p. 184.

genius,[1] and, I may add, Schiller's doctrine of play, and Hegel's of the ideal. The theoretical question is this : Granted that art and beauty have a content, the revelation of which to sense is their distinctive mark, yet how, by what mechanism, so to speak, is the content got into the form of utterance in a definite object appealing to sense ? The answer is given on a small scale, but justly and profoundly, by the lesser arts of life. The content gets into the product through being in the man, and through being in the man in such a way that in as far as he is free in his producing activity, the content will, by means of disciplined habit together with overmastering impulse, modify his production with satisfaction to himself. Psychologists tell us that pleasure appears to indicate both harmony and expansion of the self. The content which appears in art seems then to operate through that expansion of the self which comes in utterance, and which from the nature of the content claims to be a harmonious expansion. I suppose, in fact, that every expansion *quâ* expansion must be harmonious. Contradiction baffles and exhausts attention, and so counteracts expansion.

Thus the simple genuine experience which this artist-writer puts before us, corroborates and completes the theories both of the great idealists and of the "exact" æstheticians. The man, as he is when his nature is at one with itself, or, as Schiller says, when he is at play, is the needed middle term between content and expression ; and the characteristic utter-ance that genuinely issues from the fulness of a man's heart may be savage, clumsy, or grotesque, but will not be ugly.[2] How different all this is from " the piece of slang[3] that does not mean the harmless thing it seems to mean — art for art's sake," and from the false accuracy[4] of the doctrine that banishes architecture out of the province of the free arts, while allowing that it is beautiful.

---

[1] Cf. Morris and others, p. 217. " Some beautiful piece of nature must [if we are to make good wall-paper designs] have impressed itself on our notice so forcibly that we are quite full of it, and can, by submitting ourselves to the rules of art [the formal principles of expressiveness] express our pleasure to others."

[2] Cf. Goethe's *Deutsche Baukunst*, p. 309–10, *supra*.

[3] Morris's *Lectures on Art*, p. 54.

[4] See Hartmann on Architecture, and on the merits of the question, cf. Prof. Brown, *Fine Arts*.

iv. The synthesis of content and expression in
that "characteristic" which overmasters the mind
and feeling receives a splendid development in
Mr. Ruskin's analysis of "The penetrative Ima-
gination."[1]   I am sorry to learn[2] that in later years Mr. Ruskin
abandoned the fruitful distinction here drawn between Imagination and Fancy.   The name of Imagination, he applied, when
this chapter was written, to the insight which seizes the heart
of a matter, and works from within outwards, while Fancy he
identified with the spirit that luxuriates in detail without ever
piercing to the core.   And the deepest truth is touched when
he reminds us that thus understood Imagination is charged
with love and fire, while Fancy is indifferent and frigid, "one
of the hardest-hearted of the intellectual faculties."   I observed, in reproducing Goethe's scheme of æsthetic qualities,
upon the subordinate position which it assigns to the "Phan-
tomisten,"[3] or votaries of capricious fancy.   The fact is, that
from Aristotle's account of tragedy as representation of life
and action to Shakespeare's "holding the mirror up to
nature,"[4] we do not find capricious or unreal fancy in the
work or theories of the greatest men.   But I do not know
that the consequences of this truth had been drawn out with
the requisite audacity before the *Modern Painters* was written.
I need not point out how such a view of imagination must
crown the growing recognition of the characteristic in beauty.

"It may seem[5] to the reader that I am incorrect in calling
this penetrating possession-taking faculty Imagination.   Be it
so ; the name is of little consequence ; the faculty itself, called
by what name we will, I insist upon as the highest intellectual
power of man."   "Every great conception of poet or painter
is held and treated by this faculty.   Every character that is
so much as touched by men like Æschylus, Homer, Dante,
or Shakespeare, is by them held by the heart ; and every
circumstance or sentence of their being speaking or seeming is

[1] *Modern Painters*, vol. ii. sect. II. c. 3.
[2] Collingwood, *Ruskin's Art-teaching*, p. 138.
[3] P. 314, *supra*.
[4] On the other hand, Shakespeare's account of imagination as a faculty of
the unreal is put in the mouth of Theseus, the half-contemptuous, though wise
and liberal sovereign.   The account of it as deceptive is given to Touchstone.
[5] *Modern Painters*, vol. ii., chap. " of Imagination Penetrative."

seized by process from within and is referred to that inner
secret spring of which the hold is never lost for an instant ;
so that every sentence, as it has been thought out from the
heart, opens for us a way down to the heart, leads us to the
centre, and then leaves us to gather what more we may."

How far the synthesis of beauty and essential expressiveness which we should expect to accompany such an idea of
the imagination has really been attained by Mr. Ruskin is a
point on which it would be rash to pronounce. Between the
first and the second volume of the *Modern Painters* there was
an interval of at least three years, and in forming a final
opinion it would not be just to confine ourselves to these two
volumes, nor even to the *Modern Painters* as a whole.

At first sight, and judging by those two first and more
purely theoretical volumes, a natural and laudable inconsistency
would seem to have overtaken him, the inconsistency which
we have so often noted as arising from the self-assertion of
the wider, as against the narrower and more familiar meaning
of the term " beauty." The first volume, in laying out the
gigantic scheme of the work, enumerates as distinct subjects
of treatment within the excellence of Art, ideas of Power,
Imitation, Truth, Beauty, and Relation. Here Beauty ranks.
as in name it did for Goethe, and as in fact it did for Rosenkranz, as one among other excellences of art as art. In the
further course of the same volume ideas of Power (*i.e.* exe-
cutive skill) are discussed with comparative brevity, and a
very prolonged discussion of ideas of Truth absorbs the re-
mainder of the volume. It is plain from the whole course
of the treatment that Truth of the genuine kind, though pro-
fessedly distinguished from beauty, is here treated as an
element of excellence in art. Now in the second volume
the scheme is formally pursued by the discussion of Ideas of
Beauty as a co-ordinate element in the excellence of art ; but
the plan seems to develop in the author's hands, and it may
be a question whether in the very fairly systematic account—
beginning with typical (*i.e.* pretty much what we have called
formal) beauty, and proceeding to the various grades of
" vital " beauty in an order that practically corresponds to the
arrangement of Hegel or Hartmann—the "idea of beauty"
has not re-expanded so as to include the elements which were
referred to in the previous volume as outside the region of
the beautiful. Formally then, we have not escaped from the

dualism which appears in Goethe, according to which beauty is only one among other excellences of art as art.   Yet if we absorb the account of "Truth" in the first volume into the doctrine of the degrees of typical and vital beauty—all characteristic—laid down in the second, and complete the whole conception by the analysis of the penetrative imagination, there will be little left to desire in the range ascribed to the beautiful.   The immense predominance of instances in which ugliness is predicated of art, and the opinion of its extreme rarity in Nature, harmonise with the idea of its essence suggested in the present work.   And even if it is wrong in theory to consider Nature as all but perfectly beautiful, and if we are to admit that by conflict and mutilation she produces ugliness as insuperable as any to be found in art or the works of man (which I do not believe), still the general idea that, as she is typical of reason, her fundamental principle is to be beautiful[1] is far nearer to the truth than the *borné* perception which sees ugliness in the desolate, the quaint, the sombre, or the chaotic, and in all uncommon or transitional animal forms.   The fact is, as Professor Baldwin Brown[2] has well pointed out, that the northern artist was the first to be in thorough sympathy with the wilder and more mysterious aspects of our globe.

Classification of Material applied to Poetry.   v. It may be asked in what sense the classification by sensuous material is to apply to poetry.   *What* is the material of poetry ?   I think that in replying we must take a distinction.

It is best in all philosophy to start from the simple facts of denotation as prescribed by well-established connotation ; from the application, that is, of the term we are discussing, as determined by usage duly grounded in habit and experience. If we ask, then, whether poetry is a matter of fancy or imagination, and independent of a particular kind of sensuous material, namely sonorous and rhythmical language, let us begin by putting the question whether there are any poems which are not in verse.   Considering the English version of the Old Testament poetical books, and I suppose the originals of these books also, which are rather rhythmical than metrical, or other translations into prose from more distinctly metrical originals, we must accede to the opinion that only rhythm and not metre is essential to poetry.   But even this is an indulgent

---

[1] Vol. ii. p. 63.   [2] *The Fine Arts.* Part III.

construction. In the full development of its nature what we call poetry unquestionably demands metre. Without quantity, or systematically recurring accent, or rhyme, we have not the definite signature by which the poet in versification stamps his imaginative expression with a form and harmony of its own and of his own.

In this, then, the proper and accepted sense, poetry is an art distinguished from the other arts and characterised in itself by its material, which is metrical or rhythmical language, and always a particular language, demanding a particular treatment no more the same with that of any other language than the treatment of wood can be the same with that of marble.[1] It is essential to poetry as such to have beautiful and characteristic sound. I do not therefore agree with those who set down the imagination as the true material of poetry. Of course there is a difference in degree. While no art can use wholly meaningless form, yet the pure formal beauty of sensuous material can be employed in formative art—I will venture no opinion about music—with a freedom from definite significance which would shock us in the use of language. As a limiting case, where language is used for purposes which are all but purely decorative, we may think of the "refrain," which is most effective in my judgment when it fills a place in the meaning and grammatical structure at each recurrence. Yet in some forms of verse it is not expected to do this, but merely to bring a certain sound and a certain element of fancy before the mind at intervals, like the repeat of a pattern. On the whole, however, meaning is required from the forms of every art, and in abstaining from "nonsense verses," poetry is merely complying with the fundamental law of beauty.

But though we hardly ever speak of a poet who is not an artist in language, nor of a poem which is not in words, it is true that in a sense poetry is the universal art; or, to adhere more closely to usage, all art has the quality which we call "poetical." This is no doubt an attribute of imagination acting in a certain way, best described as the penetrative imagination of which we spoke above. All sensuous and

---

[1] Let anyone think for a moment of the difference between the Greek, the Latin and the German or English Hexameter, or the Greek and Latin Sapphic or Alcaic.

concrete ideas, even abstract thought-sequences as embodied
in a whole of individual and typical import, can be the material
of this imagination, and therefore it enters into and is operative in all recognition and production of the beautiful.   But
like most analogical usage, this employment of the term
" poetical " is hazardous.   There is always a risk of confusing the special with the general import, and of meaning
by a "painted" or a "musical" poem, not merely that the
picture or piece of music shows a high degree of penetrative
imagination and ideal feeling, but that it trenches on the
province of poetry proper by telling a story or describing a
character, which is rather a vice than a merit.

To speak of poetical moods or ideas as occurring in the
mind, without reference to art, is again a different usage from
either of the above ; it only refers to moods and ideas fit for
poetry, but not in fact thrown into poetic shape, just as a
pictorial or musical idea may come into the mind which for
any of various possible reasons we do not proceed to complete
as a work of painting or music.

It is by far the truest as well as the simplest view to take
poetry proper according to its connotation in common speech,
as confined to words in metrical or at least in peculiarly
rhythmical arrangement, and to treat all other usages of the
term as merely analogous in different degrees.   I may fortify
this position by the remark that while I do not deny the
poetical quality of the Psalms, of certain passages in Carlyle,
and of occasional brief portions in many prose authors, yet
what is usually called poetical prose appears to me to be not
poetry but rhetoric, a thing scarcely compatible with poetical
quality, although in certain cases of passionate pleading they
have a point of contact.   I have not, of course, said that all
verse is poetry ; I am only discussing how far poetry can
extend into what is commonly called prose, not how far
prose can extend into what is commonly called poetry.   I
presume that here again the penetrative imagination, with
its attendant depth of ideal feeling, would be the difference
required in addition to metrical language.   This is the root of
the Aristotelian " universality " of poetry.

Conclusion.   4.   I have now to the best of my power fulfilled the promises of the first chapter.   I have
attempted to present the fundamental theory of beauty
entertained by the ancients as the basis of the most pregnant

conceptions reached by the moderns,[1] and have shown how æsthetic reflection passed from the formal to the characteristic, from the beauty of the picture-frame to the beauty of the picture,[2] following slowly upon the growth in width and penetration of the actual æsthetic consciousness or sense of the beautiful. We have seen how in this progression the sense of beauty has been almost infinitely extended, not by superficial generalisation but by the acquisition of a deeper sympathy. The predicate "ugly" has been in the main expelled from the region of inanimate nature and almost from the non-human organic world and has been banished to the morbid or fraudulent productions of the human consciousness in the search for beauty. As specific doctrinal systems of the supernatural in contrast with the natural, and with them the theory of antecedent intellectual design in creation, have faded away, the vision of man has been sharpened for the direct appreciation of unity and immanent reason both in the world and in his own life. And it is possible now to understand how the unresting dualism of the romantic consciousness was an essential moment in the evolution of the spiritual monism of to-day from the naturalistic monism of classical Greece. Of this spiritual monism, in its formulated philosophical shape, we have traced the genesis in immediate connection with the speculative apprehension of the æsthetic synthesis.

On the other hand, if we turn from the critical and reflective appreciation of beauty to the realm of beautiful production, it is idle to deny that we find ourselves faced by a solution of continuity such as in recorded history has had no precedent. The practice of art "for the people and by the people, a joy to the maker and the user,"[3] no longer exists in the more civilised nations of the world, and *pari passu* with the spread of civilisation is ceasing to exist where it has hitherto survived. A few words on the present demands of Æsthetic science and on the outlook and future of the concrete sense of beauty may fitly conclude this work.

Requirements of Æsthetic Science to-day.   i. The divorce from history which is so marked in recent methodising æsthetic ought not to continue. It is quite within the powers of a thorough

---

[1] See p. 4 *supra.*   [2] See pp. 41-2 *supra.*
[3] Mr. William Morris *passim.*

philosophical treatment to combine the achievements of formal analysis with a due regard for the joint evolution of content and expression, and for the possible non-permanence of æsthetic species.   The spirit of Mr. Ruskin, Mr. Morris, and Mr. Pater,[1] with something of the historical system of Hegel, and the precise lucidity of Herbart and Helmholtz, might find their place in a philosophical science, employing the same variety of intellectual *organa* with modern psychology, or with biology in its most comprehensive signification. Of one side, and that the chief side, of such a treatment Carriere has furnished a splendid example in his *Art in its Connection with the Development of Culture* ; but in order rightly to indicate this connection it cannot be necessary to compile a complete history of civilisation and place it by the side of a complete history of art.   More division of labour than this must surely be possible, and an over-estimate of the magnitude of the enterprise leads by a natural reaction to the abundance of commonplace and second-hand work from which Carriere is not free.

    For the purpose which I have indicated the first necessity is to open our eyes to the present condition of the arts, and to ascertain what in them is living, and what species, under present conditions, are dead or in suspended animation.   I know nothing more wearisome than the purely generalised and systematic discussion of the epic and the drama,[2] without allusion to the times of their greatness and the conditions of their genesis.   Taking the drama, for our purpose, to mean genuine stage-plays that have permanent literary value, we see at once that tragedy at all events has flourished but twice in the world's history, and that only for brief periods, namely, for three-quarters of a century at Athens, and for a century and a half in England and France together.   The comic and bourgeois drama no doubt has a wider range, but also the total quantity of comedy which to-day survives in literature belongs, I imagine, to quite definite and not very protracted periods.

---

    [1] I am aware that the work of the philosopher must be inferior in tact and original feeling for art to that of the skilled art-critic.   But unless he can gather *something* of genuine sympathy and insight, his actual work *quâ* philosophy will be spoilt by his simply not knowing what beauty means.
    [2] Hegel has the excuse of having lived when the Greek renaissance was in its first flush of splendour, and when the Goethe-Schiller drama seemed to herald a revival of the theatre.

As for epics, the name is taken from the Iliad and Odyssey *par excellence*, and every subsequent epic has in fact been a new species, differing from these and from all the rest in significance, in national import, and in conditions of genesis.

What are our forms of poetry to-day? In what relation do they and the conditions from which they spring stand to the great works of the past and the conditions from which they sprang? To whom do they appeal? Do Lessing, Goethe, and Schiller hold the popular stage in Germany to-day? Do Racine, Corneille, and Molière hold the stage in France? If not, then, in each case, why not, and what has taken their place, or has anything done so? Do the people care for drama that has literary value? Would they care for it if they could get it? These are not questions of otiose curiosity. The answers depend on simple fact, but their import is the material for philosophy. It is the pervading and fundamental problem of content and expression.

The same kind of investigation might be applied to other kinds of art, not of course with purely statistical[1] methods and results, but in order to ascertain in what impulse it originates and to what need it corresponds, and to correlate the feeling of the beautiful, and the connection of content and expression, thus revealed, with the evolution of the æsthetic consciousness down to the present time. The novel, or bourgeois epic, would have to be considered in its peculiar adaptation to the conditions of modern life, which are in many ways so hostile to the formative arts. "How should any man," it may be said, "desire to-day to address his fellows otherwise than through the printed book, by which his thoughts are carried at once, exactly as he sets them down, all over the civilized world? Had Leonardo lived in this century, he would have been a great writer of criticism."

More might be done, I feel confident, for the analysis of musical expression than has yet been attempted. The subject has fallen to the ground between rival theorists. Musicians have rightly and naturally refused to believe that the tone-structure can be rendered into common language, but in practice, though not perhaps in theory, have tried to endow it

---

[1] Though statistics would be interesting and valuable. For whom and by whom are the thousands of canvases painted that are sent in to the Academy year by year?

with imitative powers ; formalists have attempted to assimilate all musical expression to the single relation of consonance and dissonance ; associationists have approached the problem from the still more trivial and abstract observation of cadences resembling those of emotional speech.   And thus it is left to the unmusical philosopher to protest that there must be more in it than all this put together ; that the consideration should be initiated positively, not negatively (*i.e.* by mere transference from, and comparison with this or that which is not music) ; that in music we have a material or medium with certain perfectly definite properties, different from those of any other sensuous vehicle, and obviously lending itself to particular kinds of combinations, transitions, idealised motions with a character impressed on them which is more than that of bare motion, more even than bare rhythmical motion ; and pervading the whole, both in co-existence and in succession, an audible lawfulness and necessary precision of structure, as clear and as mysterious as that of nature herself.   Surely it must be possible, following upon the track of Plato, Schopenhauer and Hanslick, to steer between the hazards of denying, with Mr. Gurney, that any explanation or analysis can at all unveil the mystery of melody and harmony, and of asserting with the formalist or the associationist that it is all a question of smooth intervals or of suggested cadences of voice.   Surely the character, the typical spirit and mode of combination, transition, repetition and so forth, within important musical works, could so far be detected by a subtle but impartial criticism as to throw light on the connection of expression and content within the region of musical beauty.[1]

In the æsthetic of the future Psychology has, as I have already indicated, a leading part to play.   Though I do not believe in æsthetic as the analysis of expression apart from the analysis of content, it appears that to analyse the pleasurable nature of utterance or expression will be a necessary pendant to analysing the kind of content which, in the course of evolution, comes to demand embodiment or appreciation.   We spoke of the law of economy in attention, as connected with the principle of economy in graceful movement, and ultimately

---

[1] The notes which I print as Appendix II. are to my mind examples of the sort of analysis required.   Of course there may be much criticism of this kind in specialist works on music with which I am not acquainted.

with the Platonic and Aristotelian conception of the necessary relation between whole and part. Can this or similar translations into the psychical movement be applied to other and more complex contents? Is it not by more than mere reproductive memory, is it not rather by a true sense of indwelling properties, that the hand of the free workman is guided to the springing curve whose peculiar law of formation causes it to be felt at once as expressing the very joy of vitality? What is the nature of the delight in simple colours, and is it an illusion to suppose that we perceive them as simple? What of tones in the same way, and of combinations both of colour and of tone? Can anything be done with them analogous to what has been done in the comparison of circular and catenary curves? What is the connection between sense and sound in verse? Does not the sense, by suggested emotion, affect the sound? Is the relation of splendid versification to the expression of profound ideal feeling rooted in the nature of mind? How is it distinguished in regard to artistic truth from the case in which the passion wholly lames the utterance? Under what conditions does emotion disable, and under what conditions does it stimulate the expressive power? Again, what are the effects of scientific training upon æsthetic capacity? Is the deficient visualisation of ideas, said to be observed among men of abstract intellectual pursuits, an indication of deep-seated hostility between the two modes of mind, or only a plea for more vital and concrete training in intellectual things? How does the general theory of pleasure and pain connect with the æsthetic theory of beauty and ugliness? In short, what is the psychical connection between content and expression, or between the nature of either of these and its pleasurableness?

The Future of Art. ii. It is impossible to believe that just as the sense of beauty has become deeper and stronger [1] than ever before, the productive capacity of art has received

---

[1] I quote an excellent statement of the gain which has come to the modern sense of beauty by a deeper and wider sympathy. I refuse to believe, with the gifted author, that it involves a corresponding loss. " Haggard Egdon appealed to a subtler and scarcer instinct, to a more recently learnt emotion, than that which responds to the sort of beauty called charming and fair.

" Indeed, it is a question if the exclusive reign of this orthodox beauty is not approaching its last quarter. The new Vale of Tempe may be a gaunt waste in Thule : human souls may find themselves in closer and closer harmony

its deathblow.   But it is idle to look back, or to deny that if, of the present hostile conditions, there are many that may and must be removed, yet many again are, and must be permanent. The basis of life will always henceforward be intellectual and historical, not naive and natural, except in the sense of a second nature.   No single tradition can ever again enthrall the world from father to son in a mere routine of faith, and bind the artist-workman securely to his one good custom as the only rule he knows.   The soul has won its intellectual liberty, and with it an infinite capacity for making mistakes, and this it will never surrender.   We shall increasingly employ the printing press and the machine.   Formative art can never again be the chief instructor of peoples.   It is idle to rail against conditions demonstrably inherent in a life that has behind it two thousand active years of art, science, religion, and philosophy.

Yet even from an æsthetic standpoint these losses are not without their gain.   Even machinery has its good tidings for us, if rightly used.   Many of the reforming æstheticians seem to me to forget that it is worse to do by hand what can be done well by machinery, than to do by machinery what can only be done by hand.   In the latter case you try to make a machine do a man's work, which is impossible.   In the former you make a man do a machine's work, which is immoral. " Whatever can be done (that is properly done) by machinery, ought to be done by machinery."[1]   The present system combines both evils.   But what is needed is not to join the ranks of the machine-breakers, but to draw the line rightly between mechanical and non-mechanical production.   Some critics are fond of saying that we make nothing well now but the instruments of war.   They omit one class of appliances, the instruments of science.   A compound microscope of the present day is one of the greatest triumphs of intellect in workmanship that the world has ever seen.   We must not forget these things, for they mean a new power in the human beings who

---

with external things wearing a sombreness distasteful to our race when it was young.   The time seems near, if it has not actually arrived, when the chastened sublimity of a moor, a sea, or a mountain will be all of nature that is absolutely in keeping with the moods of the more thinking among mankind."   Hardy's *Return of the Native.*

[1] Henniker's *Trifles for Travellers.*

make them.   Exaggeration is always harmful, besides being false.

And if we are surrounded by ugliness of our own making, we have a larger and keener sense of beauty.   If the habit of reading threatens the position of formative art, the world of literature is open to all men, as never before, while music is a comparatively recent gift to humanity.   A comparison with the great epochs of the past may give us hope.   Our finest spirits feel to-day much what Aristophanes felt when he attacked Euripides, and when it seemed to him that poetic art in its noblest sense had departed to the world below.   So a Renaissance critic might have felt, with greater justice, after the death of Michael Angelo.   It is true that in the last hundred years, although certain reservations are to be made such as I have pointed out, with reference to music, landscape, portrait painting, and poetic art, yet the discord has cut deeper than ever before, and the popular art-tradition is interrupted.   But the mind is stronger to-day, and the self is fuller, and we know that it lives by movement and not by fixity.   The deeper discord can therefore be borne, and is a testimony to the strength of the life which it does not fatally maim. Naturally, it will take a longer time to resolve, and we cannot anticipate in what shape the resolution may come.   But in spite of all hostile conditions, man is more human now than ever he was before, and he will find out the way to satisfy his imperious need for beauty.

APPENDIX I.

DIVISION OF THE SUBJECT.

In order that the reader may have fully before him the structure of Hegel's partly analytical classification of art-forms,[1] I reproduce here *in extenso* the closing section of the Introduction to his *Æsthetik*, Vol. i. pp. 89–114, from the translation with notes, which I published some years ago.[2]

1. It has already been said that the content of art is the Idea, and that its form lies in the plastic use of images accessible to sense. These two sides art has to reconcile into a full and united totality. The *first* attribution which this involves is the requirement that the content, which is to be offered to artistic representation, shall show itself to be in its nature worthy of such representation. Otherwise we only obtain a bad combination, whereby a content that will not submit to plasticity and to external presentation, is forced into that form, and a matter which is in its nature prosaic is expected to find an appropriate mode of manifestation in the form antagonistic to its nature.

The *second* requirement, which is derivable from this first, demands of the content of art that it should not be anything abstract in itself. This does not mean that it must be concrete as the sensuous is concrete in contrast to everything spiritual and intellectual, these being taken as in themselves simple and abstract. For everything that has genuine truth in the mind as well as in nature is concrete in itself, and has, in spite of its universality, nevertheless, both subjectivity and particularity within it. If we say, *e.g.* of God that he is simply *One*, the supreme Being as such, we have only enunciated a lifeless abstraction of the irrational understanding. Such a God, as he himself is not apprehended in his concrete truth, can afford no material for art, least of all for plastic art. Hence the Jews and the Turks have not been able to represent their God, who does not even amount to such an abstraction of the understanding, in the positive way in which Christians have done so. For God in Christianity is conceived in His truth and therefore, as in Himself thoroughly concrete, as a person, as a subject,[3] and more closely determined, as mind or spirit. What He is as spirit unfolds itself to the religious apprehension as the Trinity of Persons, which at the same time in relation with

---

[1] Compare p. 352 *supra*.

[2] *The Introduction to Hegel's "Philosophy of Fine Art,"* translated into English. Kegan Paul, Trench & Co., 1886.

[3] It is natural for a reader to ask in *what* person or subject God is conceived to have reality. It appears certain to me that Hegel, when he writes thus, is referring to the self-consciousness of individual human beings as constituting, and reflecting on, an ideal unity between them. This may seem to put a non-natural meaning on the term "person" or "subject," as if the common element of a number of intelligences could be a single person. It is obvious that the question hinges on the degree in which a unity that is not sensuous but ideal can be effective and actual. I can only say here, that the more we consider the nature of ideal unity the higher we shall rate its capabilities.

itself is *One*. Here is essentiality, universality, and particularity, together with their reconciled unity; and it is only such unity that constitutes the concrete. Now, as a content in order to possess truth at all must be of this concrete nature, art demands the same concreteness, because a mere abstract universal has not in itself the vocation to advance to particularity and phenomenal manifestation and to unity with itself therein.

If a true and therefore concrete content is to have corresponding to it a sensuous form and modelling, this sensuous form must, in the third place, be no less emphatically something individual, wholly concrete in itself, and one. The character of concreteness as belonging to both elements of art, to the content as to the representation, is precisely the point in which both may coincide and correspond to one another; as, for instance, the natural shape of the human body is such a sensuous concrete as is capable of representing spirit, which is concrete in itself, and of displaying itself in conformity therewith. Therefore we ought to abandon the idea that it is a mere matter of accident that an actual phenomenon of the external world is chosen to furnish a shape thus conformable to truth. Art does not appropriate this form either because it simply finds it existing or because there is none other. The concrete content itself involves the element of external and actual, we may say indeed of sensible manifestation. But in compensation this sensuous concrete, in which a content essentially belonging to mind expresses itself, is in its own nature addressed to the inward being; its external element of shape, whereby the content is made perceptible and imaginable, has the aim of existing purely for the heart and mind. This is the only reason for which content and artistic shape are fashioned in conformity with each other. The *mere* sensuous concrete, external nature as such, has not this purpose for its exclusive ground of origin. The birds' variegated plumage shines unseen, and their song dies away unheard, the *Cereus* [1] which blossoms only for a night withers without having been admired in the wilds of southern forests, and these forests, jungles of the most beautiful and luxuriant vegetation, with the most odorous and aromatic perfumes, perish and decay no less unenjoyed. The work of art has not such a naïve self-centred being, but is essentially a question, an address to the responsive heart, an appeal to affections and to minds.

Although the artistic bestowal of sensuous form is in this respect not accidental, yet on the other hand it is not the highest mode of apprehending the spiritually concrete. Thought is a higher mode than representation by means of the sensuous concrete. But although in a relative sense abstract, yet it must not be one-sided but concrete thinking, in order to be true and rational. Whether a given content has sensuous artistic representation for its adequate form, or in virtue of its nature essentially demands a higher and more spiritual embodiment, is a distinction that displays itself at once, if, for instance, we compare the Greek gods with God as conceived according to Christian ideas. The Greek god is not abstract but individual, and is closely akin to the natural human shape; the Christian God is equally a concrete personality, but in the mode of pure spiritual existence, and is to be known as *mind* [2] and in mind. His medium of existence is therefore essentially inward knowledge and not external natural form, by means of which He can only be represented imperfectly, and not in the whole depth of His idea.

But inasmuch as the task of art is to represent the idea to direct perception

[1] *Fackeldistel* = "Torch thistle," a plant of the genus *Cereus*, Nat. Order *Cactaceæ*.
[2] Or "as spirit and in spirit."

in sensuous shape, and not in the form of thought or of pure spirituality as such, and seeing that this work of representation has its value and dignity in the correspondence and the unity of the two sides, *i.e.* of the Idea and its plastic embodiment, it follows that the level and excellency of art in attaining a realization adequate to its ideal,[1] must depend upon the grade of inwardness and unity with which Idea and Shape display themselves as fused into one.

Thus the higher truth is spiritual being that has attained a shape adequate to the conception of spirit. This is what furnishes the principle of division for the science of art. For before the mind can attain the true notion of its absolute essence, it has to traverse a course of stages whose ground is in this idea itself; and to this evolution of the content with which it supplies itself, there corresponds an evolution, immediately connected therewith, of the plastic forms of art, under the shape of which the mind as artist presents to itself the consciousness of itself.

This evolution within the art-spirit has again in its own nature two sides. In the *first* place the development itself is a spiritual [2] and universal one, in so far as the graduated series of definite *conceptions of the world* as the definite but comprehensive consciousness of nature, man and God, gives itself artistic shape; and, in the *second* place, this *universal* development of art is obliged to provide itself with external existence and sensuous form, and the definite modes of the sensuous art-existence are themselves a totality of necessary distinctions in the realm of art—which are *the several arts*. It is true, indeed, that the necessary kinds of artistic representation are on the one hand *qua* spiritual of a very general nature, and not restricted to any one material; [3] while sensuous existence contains manifold varieties of matter. But as this latter, like the mind, has the Idea potentially for its inner soul, it follows from this that particular sensuous materials have a close affinity and secret accord with the spiritual distinctions and types of art presentation.

In its completeness, however, our science divides itself into three principal portions.

First, we obtain a *general part*. It has for its content and object the universal Idea of artistic beauty—this beauty being conceived as the Ideal—together with the nearer relation of the latter both to nature and to subjective artistic production.

Secondly, there develops itself out of the idea of artistic beauty a *particular* part, in as far as the essential differences which this idea contains in itself evolve themselves into a scale of *particular* plastic [4] forms.

In the *third* place there results a *final* part, which has for its subject the individualization of artistic beauty, that consists in the advance of art to the

---

[1] The idea of art.

[2] The two evolutions are, speaking roughly, (i.) that of the subject-matter; (ii.) that of the particular mode of art: (i.) *e.g.* you have Egyptian, Greek, Christian religion, etc., with the corresponding views and sentiments, each in its own relation to art; (ii.) you have, as a cross division to the former, the several arts—sculpture, music, poetry, etc., each having its special ground and warrant.

[3] He is asking himself why sound or paint, etc., should correspond to one type of art as theoretically defined—this being intellectual, not sensuous, at root—and answers that these media *qua* natural objects have, though more latent than in works of art, an import and purpose of their own, which reveals itself in their suitability to particular forms of art.

[4] "*Gestaltungsformen.*" I use "plastic" all through in a pregnant sense, as one speaks of plastic fancy, etc.: meaning ideally determinate, and fit for translating into pictures, poetry, etc. These "plastic forms" are varying modifications of the subject-matter of art.

sensuous realization of its shapes and its self-completion as a system of the several arts and their genera and species.

2. With respect to the first part, we must begin by recalling to mind, in order to make the sequel intelligible, that the Idea *qua* the beautiful in art is not the Idea as such, in the mode in which a metaphysical logic apprehends it as the absolute, but the Idea as developed into concrete form fit for reality, and as having entered into immediate and adequate unity with this reality. For the *Idea as such*, although it is the essentially and actually true, is yet the truth only in its generality which has not yet taken objective shape ; but the *Idea* as the *beautiful in art* is at once the Idea when specially determined as in its essence individual reality, and also an individual shape of reality essentially destined to embody and reveal the Idea. This amounts to enunciating the requirement that the Idea, and its plastic mould as concrete reality, are to be made completely adequate to one another. When reduced to such form the Idea, as a reality moulded in conformity with the conception of the Idea, is the *Ideal*. The problem of this conformity might, to begin with, be understood in the sense that any Idea would serve, so long as the actual shape, it did not matter what shape, represented this particular Idea and no other. But if so, the required truth of the Ideal is confounded with mere correctness, which consists in the expression of any meaning whatever in appropriate fashion so that its import may be readily recognised in the shape created. The Ideal is not to be thus understood. Any content whatever may attain to being represented quite adequately, judged by the standard of its own nature, but it does not therefore gain the right to claim the artistic beauty of the Ideal. Compared indeed with ideal beauty, even the presentation will in such a case appear defective. From this point of view we must remark to begin with, what cannot be proved till later, that the defects of a work of art are not to be regarded simply as always due, for instance, to individual unskilfulness. *Defectiveness of form* arises from *defectiveness of content*. So, for example, the Chinese, Indians, and Egyptians in their artistic shapes, their forms of deities, and their idols, never got beyond a formless phase, or one of a vicious and false definiteness of form, and were unable to attain genuine beauty ; because their mythological ideas, the content and thought of their works of art, were as yet indeterminate in themselves, or of a vicious determinateness, and did not consist in the content that is absolute in itself. The more that works of art excel in true beauty of presentation, the more profound is the inner truth of their content and thought. And in dealing with this point, we have not to think merely perhaps of the greater or lesser skill with which the natural forms as given in external reality are apprehended and imitated. For in certain stages of art-consciousness and of representation, the distortion and disfigurement of natural structures is not unintentional technical inexpertness and want of skill, but intentional alteration, which emanates from the content that is in consciousness, and is required thereby. Thus, from this point of view, there is such a thing as imperfect art, which may be quite perfect, both technically and in other respects, *in its determinate* sphere, yet reveals itself to be defective when compared with the conception of art as such, and with the Ideal   Only in the highest art are the Idea and the representation genuinely adequate to one another, in the sense that the outward shape given to the Idea is in itself essentially and actually the true shape, because the content of the Idea, which that shape expresses, is itself the true and real content. It is a corollary from this, as we indicated above, that the Idea must be defined in and through itself as con-

crete totality, and thereby possess in itself the principle and standard of its particularization and determination in external appearance. For example, the Christian imagination will be able to represent God only in human form and with man's intellectual expression, because it is herein that God Himself is completely known in Himself as mind. Determinateness is, as it were, the bridge to phenomenal existence. Where this determinateness is not totality derived from the Idea itself, where the Idea is not conceived as self-determining and self-particularizing, the Idea remains abstract and has its determinateness, and therefore the principle that dictates its particular and exclusively appropriate mode of presentation, not in itself but external to it. Therefore, the Idea when still abstract has even its shape external, and not dictated by itself. The Idea, however, which is concrete in itself bears the principle of its mode of manifestation within itself, and is by that means the free process of giving shape to itself. Thus it is only the truly concrete Idea that can generate the true shape, and this correspondence of the two is the Ideal.

3. Now because the Idea is in this fashion concrete unity, it follows that this unity can enter into the art-consciousness only by the expansion and re-conciliation of the particularities of the Idea, and it is through this evolution that artistic beauty comes to possess a *totality of particular stages and forms*. Therefore, after we have studied the beauty of art in itself and on its own merits, we must see how beauty as a whole breaks up into its particular determinations. This gives, as our *second part, the doctrine of the types of art*. These forms find their genesis in the different modes of grasping the Idea as artistic content, whereby is conditioned a difference of the form in which it manifests itself. Hence the types of art are nothing but the different relations of content and shape, relations which emanate from the Idea itself, and furnish thereby the true basis of division for this sphere. For the principle of division must always be contained in *that* conception whose particularization and division is in question.

We have here to consider *three* relations of the Idea to its outward shaping.[1]

(a) First, the Idea gives rise to the beginning of Art when, being itself still in its indistinctness and obscurity, or in vicious untrue determinateness, it is made the import of artistic creations. As indeterminate it does not yet possess in itself that individuality which the Ideal demands; its abstractness and one-sidedness leave its shape to be outwardly bizarre and defective. The first form of art is therefore rather a mere search after plastic portrayal than a capacity of genuine representation. The Idea has not yet found the true form even within itself, and therefore continues to be merely the struggle and aspiration thereafter. In general terms we may call this form the *Symbolic* form of art.[2] In it the abstract Idea has its outward shape external to itself in natural sensuous matter, with which the process of shaping begins, and from which, *qua* outward expression, it is inseparable.

Natural objects are thus primarily left unaltered, and yet at the same time invested with the substantial Idea as their significance, so that they receive the

---

[1] "*Gestaltung*." I do not think this means the process of shaping, but the shapes taken collectively.
[2] *I.e.* not in a separate ideal shape devoted to it. He means that man takes a stock or stone as representation or symbol of the divine, and as there is no real connection between divinity and the stone, it may either be left untouched and unshaped, or be hewn into any bizarre or arbitrary shape that comes to hand : see next paragraph.

vocation of expressing it, and claim to be interpreted as though the Idea itself were present in them. At the root of this is the fact that natural objects have in them an aspect in which they are capable of representing a universal meaning. But as an adequate correspondence is not yet possible, this reference can only concern *an abstract attribute*, as when a lion is used to mean strength.

On the other hand, this abstractness of the relation brings to consciousness no less strongly the foreignness of the Idea to natural phenomena ; and the Idea, having no other reality to express it, expatiates in all these shapes, seeks itself in them in all their unrest and proportion, but nevertheless does not find them adequate to itself. Then it proceeds to exaggerate the natural shapes and the phenomena of reality into indefiniteness and disproportion, to intoxicate itself in them, to seethe and ferment in them, to do violence to them, to distort and explode them into unnatural shapes, and strives by the variety, hugeness, and splendour of the forms employed [1] to exalt the phenomenon to the level of the Idea. For the Idea is here still more or less indeterminate and non-plastic, but the natural objects are in their shape thoroughly determinate.

Hence, in view of the unsuitablity of the two elements to each other, the relation of the Idea to objective reality becomes a *negative* one, for the former, as in its nature inward,[2] is unsatisfied with such an externality, and as being its inner universal substance [3] perists in exaltation or *Sublimity* beyond and above all this inadequate abundance of shapes. In virtue of this sublimity the natural phenomena and the human shapes and incidents are accepted, and left as they were, though at the same time understood to be inadequate to their significance, which is exalted far above every earthly content.

These aspects may be pronounced in general terms to constitute the character of the primitive artistic pantheism of the East, which either charges even the meanest objects with the absolute import, or again coerces nature with violence into the expression of its view. By this means it becomes bizarre, grotesque, and tasteless, or turns the infinite but abstract freedom of the substantive Idea disdainfully against all phenomenal being as dull and evanescent. By such means the import cannot be completely embodied in the expression, and in spite of all aspiration and endeavour the reciprocal inadequacy of shape and Idea remains insuperable. This may be taken as the first form of art,—Symbolic art with its aspiration, its disquiet,[4] its mystery and its sublimity.

(β) In the second form of art, which we propose to call " *Classical*," the double defect of symbolic art is cancelled. The plastic shape of symbolic art is imperfect, because, in the first place, the Idea in it only enters into consciousness in *abstract* determinateness or indeterminateness, and, in the second place, this must always make the conformity of shape to import defective, and in its turn merely abstract. The classical form of art is the solution of this double difficulty ; it is the free and adequate embodiment

---

[1] This description is probably directed, in the first place, to the Indian representation of deities, and would apply to those of many barbaric religions. But its truth may be very simply verified in daily observation of the first attempts of the uneducated at plastic presentation of their ideas, where costliness, ingenuity, labour, or size take the place of beauty.
[2] " *Sie als Inneres.*"
[3] *I.e.* an idea or purpose which gives these partial and defective representations all the meaning they have, although they are incapable of really expressing it.
[4] " *Gährung*," lit. " fermentation."

of the Idea in the shape that, according to its conception, is peculiarly appropriate to the Idea itself. With it, therefore, the Idea is capable of entering into free and complete accord. Hence, the classical type of art is the first to afford the production and intuition of the completed Ideal, and to establish it as a realized fact.

The conformity, however, of notion and reality in classical art must not be taken in the purely *formal* sense of the agreement of a content with the external shape given to it, any more than this could be the case with the Ideal itself. Otherwise every copy from nature, and every type of countenance, every landscape, flower, or scene, etc., which forms the purport of any representation, would be at once made classical by the agreement which it displays between form and content. On the contrary, in classical art the peculiarity of the content consists in being itself concrete, and, as such, the concrete spiritual; for only the spiritual is the truly inner self. To suit such a content, then, we must search out that in Nature which on its own merits belongs to the essence and actuality of the mind. It must be the absolute [1] notion that *invented* the shape appropriate to concrete mind, so that the *subjective* notion —in this case the spirit of art—has merely *found* it, and brought it, as an existence possessing natural shape, into accord with free individual spirituality.[2] This shape, with which the Idea as spiritual—as individually determinate spirituality—invests itself when manifested as a temporal phenomenon, is *the human form.* Personification and anthropomorphism have often been decried as a degradation of the spiritual ; but art, in as far as its end is to bring before perception the spiritual in sensuous form, must advance to such anthropomorphism, as it is only in its proper body that mind is adequately revealed to sense. The migration of souls is in this respect a false abstraction,[3] and physiology ought to have made it one of its axioms that life had necessarily in its evolution to attain to the human shape, as the sole sensuous phenomenon that is appropriate to mind. The human form is employed in the classical type of art not as mere sensuous existence, but exclusively as the existence and physical form corresponding to mind, and is therefore exempt from all the deficiencies of what is merely sensuous, and from the contingent finiteness of phenomenal existence. The outer shape must be thus purified in order to express in itself a content adequate to itself ; and again, if the conformity of import and content is to be complete, the spiritual meaning which is the content must be of a particular kind. It must, that is to say, be qualified to express itself completely in the physical form of man, without projecting into another world beyond the scope of such an expression in sensuous and bodily terms   This condition has the effect that Mind is by it at once specified as a particular case of mind, as human mind, and not as simply absolute and eternal, inasmuch as mind in this latter sense is incapable of proclaiming and expressing itself otherwise than as intellectual being.[4]

Out of this latter point arises, in its turn, the defect which brings about

---

[1] " *Der ursprüngliche Begriff*," lit. " the original notion."

[2] *I.e.* God or the Universe *invented* man to be the expression of mind ; art *finds* him, and adapts his shape to the artistic embodiment of mind as concentrated in individual instances.

[3] Because it represents the soul as independent of an appropriate body—the human soul as capable of existing in a beast's body.

[4] " *Geistigkeit.*" " The nature of thought, mind, or spirit." It cannot be here rendered by mind or spirit, because these words make us think of an isolated individual, *a* mind or soul, and neglect the common spiritual or intellectual nature, which is referred to by the author.

the dissolution of classical art, and demands a transition into a third and higher form, viz. into the *romantic* form of art.

(γ) The romantic form of art destroys the completed union of the Idea and its reality, and recurs, though in a higher phase, to that difference and antagonism of two aspects which was left unvanquished by symbolic art. The classical type attained the highest excellence, of which the sensuous embodiment of art is capable ; and if it is in any way defective, the defect is in art as a whole, *i.e.* in the limitation of its sphere. This limitation consists in the fact that art as such takes for its object Mind—the conception of which is *infinite* concrete universality—in the shape of *sensuous* concreteness, and in the classical phase sets up the perfect amalgamation of spiritual and sensuous existence as a Conformity of the two. Now, as a matter of fact, in such an amalgamation Mind cannot be represented according to its true notion. For mind is the infinite subjectivity of the Idea, which, as absolute inwardness,[1] is not capable of finding free expansion in its true nature on condition o. remaining transposed into a bodily medium as the existence appropriate to it.

As *an escape from such a condition* the romantic form of art in its turn dissolves the inseparable unity of the classical phase, because it has won a significance which goes beyond the classical form of art and its mode of expression.[2] This significance—if we may recall familiar ideas—coincides with what Christianity declares to be true of God as Spirit, in contradistinction to the Greek faith in gods which forms the essential and appropriate content for classical art. In Greek art the concrete import is potentially, but not explicitly, the unity of the human and divine nature ; a unity which, just because it is purely *immediate*[3] and *not explicit*, is capable of adequate manifestation in an immediate and sensuous mode. The Greek god is the object of naive intuition and sensuous imagination. His shape is, therefore, the bodily shape of man. The circle of his power and of his being is individual and individually limited. In relation with the subject,[4] he is, therefore, an essence and a power with which the subject's inner being is merely in latent unity, not itself possessing this unity as inward subjective knowledge. Now the higher stage is the *knowledge* of this *latent* unity, which as latent is the import of the classical form of art, and capable of perfect representation in bodily shape. The elevation of the latent or potential into self-conscious knowledge produces an enormous difference. It is the infinite difference which, *e.g.*, separates man as such from the animals. Man is animal, but even in his animal functions he is not confined within the latent and potential as the animal is, but becomes conscious of them, learns to know them, and raises them—as, for instance, the process of digestion—into self-conscious science. By this means Man breaks the boundary of merely potential and immediate consciousness, so that just for the reason that he knows himself to be animal, he ceases to be animal and, as *mind*, attains to self-knowledge.

If in the above fashion the unity of the human and divine nature, which in the former phase was potential, is raised from an *immediate* to a *conscious* unity, it follows that the true medium for the reality of this content is no

---

[1] It is the essence of mind or thought not to have its parts outside one another. The so-called terms of a judgment are a good instance of parts in thought which are inward to each other.

[2] Compare Browning's *Old Pictures in Florence.*

[3] *I.e.* in the form of feeling and imagination—not reflected upon.

[4] Subject, *i.e.* conscious individual person.

longer the sensuous immediate existence of the spiritual, the human bodily shape, but *self-conscious inward intelligence*.[1] Now, Christianity brings God before our intelligence *as spirit*, or mind—not as particularized individual spirit, but as absolute, in *spirit* and in truth. And for this reason Christianity retires from the sensuousness of imagination into intellectual inwardness, and makes this, not bodily shape, the medium and actual existence of its significance. So, too, the unity of the human and divine nature is a conscious unity, only to be realized by *spiritual* knowledge and in *spirit*. Thus the new content, won by this unity, is not inseparable from sensuous representation, as if that were adequate to it, but is freed from this immediate existence, which has to be posited[2] as negative, absorbed, and reflected into the spiritual unity. In this way, romantic art must be considered as art transcending itself, while remaining within the artistic sphere and in artistic form.

Therefore, in short, we may abide by the statement that in this third stage the object (of art) is *free*, concrete intellectual being, which has the function of revealing itself as spiritual existence for the inward[3] world of spirit. In conformity with such an object-matter, art cannot work for sensuous perception. It must address itself to the inward mind, which coalesces with its object simply and as though this were itself,[4] to the subjective inwardness, to the heart, the feeling, which, being spiritual, aspires to freedom within itself, and seeks and finds its reconciliation only in the spirit within. It is this *inner* world that forms the content of the romantic, and must therefore find its representation as such inward feeling, and in the show or presentation of such feeling. The world of inwardness celebrates its triumph over the outer world, and actually in the sphere of the outer and in its medium manifests this its victory, owing to which the sensuous appearance sinks into worthlessness.

But, on the other hand, this type of Art,[5] like every other, needs an external vehicle of expression. Now the spiritual has withdrawn into itself out of the external and its immediate oneness therewith. For this reason, the sensuous externality of concrete form is accepted and represented, as in Symbolic art, as something transient and fugitive. And the same measure is dealt to the subjective finite mind and will, even including the peculiarity or caprice of the individual, of character, action, etc., or of incident and plot. The aspect of external existence is committed to contingency, and left at the mercy of freaks of imagination, whose caprice is no more likely to mirror what is given *as* it is given, than to throw the shapes of the outer world into chance medley, or distort them into grotesqueness. For this external element no longer has its notion and significance, as in classical art, in its own sphere, and in its own medium. It has come to find them in the feelings, the display of which is *in themselves* instead of being in the external and *its* form of reality, and which have the power to preserve or to regain their state of reconciliation with themselves, in every accident, in every unessential circum-

---

[1] "*Innerlichkeit*," lit. "inwardness."

[2] Taken, considered as or determined to be negative.

[3] "Inward," again, does not mean merely inside our heads, but having the character of spirit in that its parts are not external to one another. A judgment is thus "inward."

[4] *I.e.* does not keep up a distinction between percipient and object, as between things in space. Goodness, nobleness, etc., are not felt to be other than or outside the mind.

[5] The romantic.

stance that takes independent shape, in all misfortune and grief, and even in crime.

Owing to this, the characteristics of symbolic art, in difference, discrepancy, and severance of Idea and plastic shape, are here reproduced, but with an essential difference. In the sphere of the romantic, the Idea, whose defectiveness in the case of the symbol produced the defect of external shape, has to reveal itself in the medium of spirit and feelings as perfected in itself. And it is because of this higher perfection that it withdraws itself from any adequate union with the external element, inasmuch as it can seek and achieve its true reality and revelation nowhere but in itself.

This we may take as in the abstract the character of the symbolic, classical, and romantic forms of art, which represent the three relations of the Idea to its embodiment in the sphere of art. They consist in the aspiration after, and the attainment and transcendence of the Ideal as the true Idea of beauty.

4. The third part of our subject, in contradistinction to the two just described, presupposes the conception of the Ideal, and the general types of art, inasmuch as it simply consists of their realization in particular sensuous media. Hence we have no longer to do with the inner development of artistic beauty in conformity with its general fundamental principles. What we have to study is how these principles pass into actual existence, how they distinguish themselves in their external aspect, and how they give actuality to every element contained in the idea of beauty, separately and by itself *as a work of art*, and not merely as a general type. Now, what art transfers into external existence are the differences [1] proper to the idea of beauty and immanent therein. Therefore, the general types of art must reveal themselves in this third part, as before, in the character of the fundamental principle that determines the arrangement and definition of the *several arts ;* in other words, the species of art contain in themselves the same essential modifications as those with which we become acquainted as the general types of art. External objectivity, however, to which these forms are introduced through the medium of a sensuous and therefore *particular* material, affects these types in the way of making them *separate* into independent and so particular forms embodying their realization. For each type finds its definite character in some one definite external material, and its adequate actuality in the mode of portrayal which that prescribes. But, moreover, these types of art, being for all their determinateness, its *universal* forms, break the bounds of *particular* realization by a determinate form of art, and achieve existence in other arts as well, although in subordinate fashion. Therefore, the particular arts belong each of them specifically to *one* of the general types of art, and constitute *its adequate* external actuality ; and also they represent, each of them after its own mode of external plasticity, the totality of the types of art.[2]

Then, speaking generally, we are dealing in this third principal division with the beautiful of art, as it unfolds itself in the several arts and in their creations into a *world* of actualized beauty. The content of this world is the beautiful, and the true beautiful, as we saw, is spiritual being in concrete shape, the Ideal ; or, more closely looked at, the absolute mind, and the

---

[1] *I.e.* species, modifications naturally arising out of a principle.
[2] Thus *e.g.* Sculpture is *the* art which corresponds *par excellence* to the general type called Classical Art ; but there is *a* Symbolic kind of sculpture, and I suppose *a* Romantic or modern kind of sculpture, although neither of these types are exactly fitted to the capabilities of Sculpture

truth itself. This region, that of divine truth artistically represented to perception and to feelings, forms the centre of the whole world of art. It is the independent, free, and divine plasticity, which has thoroughly mastered the external elements of form and of medium, and wears them simply as a means to manifestation of itself. Still, as the beautiful unfolds itself in this region in the character of *objective* reality, and in so doing distinguishes within itself its individual aspects and elements, permitting them independent particularity, it follows that this centre erects its extremes, realized in their peculiar actuality, into its own antitheses. Thus one of these extremes comes to consist in an objectivity as yet devoid of mind, in the merely natural vesture of God. At this point the external element takes plastic shape as something that has its spiritual aim and content, not in itself, but in another.[1]

The other extreme is the divine as inward, as something known, as the variously particularized *subjective* existence of the Deity ; it is the truth as operative and vital in sense, heart, and mind of individual subjects, not persisting in the mould of its external shapes, but as having returned into subjective, individual inwardness. In such a mode, the Divine is at the same time distinguished from its first manifestation as Deity, and passes thereby into the diversity of particulars which belongs to all subjective knowledge—emotion, perception, and feeling. In the analogous province of religion, with which art at its highest stage is immediately connected, we conceive this same difference as follows. *First*, we think of the earthly natural life in its finiteness as standing on one side ; but, then, *secondly*, consciousness makes God its object, in which the distinction of objectivity and subjectivity is done away. And at last, *thirdly*, we advance from God as such to the devotion of the community, that is, to God as living and present in the subjective consciousness. Just so these three chief modifications present themselves in the world of art in independent development.

(α) The *first* of the particular arts with which, according to their fundamental principle, we have to begin, is architecture considered as a fine art. Its task lies in so manipulating external inorganic nature that it become[2] cognate to mind, as an artistic outer world. The material of architecture is matter itself in its immediate externality as a heavy mass subject to mechanical laws, and its forms do not depart from the forms of inorganic nature, but are merely set in order in conformity with relations of the abstract understanding, *i.e.* with relations of symmetry. In this material and in such forms, the ideal as concrete spirituality does not admit of being realized. Hence the reality which is represented in them remains contrasted with the Idea, as something external which it has not penetrated, or has penetrated only to establish an abstract relation. For these reasons, the fundamental type of the fine art of building is the *symbolical* form of art. It is architecture that pioneers the way for the adequate realization of the God, and in this its service bestows hard toil upon existing nature, in order to disentangle it from the jungle of finitude and the abortiveness of chance. By this means it levels a space for the God, gives form to his external surroundings, and builds him his temple as a fit place for concentration of spirit, and for its direction to the mind's absolute objects. It raises an enclosure round the assembly of those gathered together, as a defence against the threatening of the storm, against rain, the hurricane, and wild beasts, and reveals the will to assemble, although ex-

---

[1] Architecture as relative to the purposes of life and of religion.
Die schöne Architectur.

ternally, yet in conformity with principles of art. With such import as this it has power to inspire its material and its forms more or less effectively, as the determinate character of the content on behalf of which it sets to work is more or less significant, more concrete or more abstract, more profound in sounding its own depths, or more dim and more superficial. So much, indeed, may architecture attempt in this respect as even to create an adequate artistic existence for such an import in its shapes and in its material. But in such a case it has already overstepped its own boundary, and is leaning to sculpture, the phase above it. For the limit of architecture lies precisely in this point, that it retains the spiritual as an inward existence over against the external forms of the art, and consequently must refer to what has soul only as to something other than its own creations.

(β) Architecture, however, as we have seen, has purified the external world, and endowed it with symmetrical order and with affinity to mind ; and the temple of the God, the house of his community, stands ready. Into this temple, then, in the *second* place, the God enters in the lightning-flash of individuality, which strikes and permeates the inert mass, while the infinite[1] and no longer merely symmetrical form belonging to mind itself concentrates and gives shape to the corresponding bodily existence. This is the task of *Sculpture*. In as far as in this art the spiritual inward being which architecture can but indicate makes itself at home in the sensuous shape and its external matter, and in as far as these two sides are so adapted to one another that neither is predominant, sculpture must be assigned the *classical form of art* as its fundamental type. For this reason the sensuous element itself has here no expression which could not be that of the spiritual element, just as, conversely, sculpture can represent no spiritual content which does not admit throughout of being adequately presented to perception in bodily form. Sculpture should place the spirit before us in its bodily form and in immediate unity therewith at rest and in peace ; and the form should be animated by the content of spiritual individuality. And so the external sensuous matter is here no longer manipulated, either in conformity with its mechanical quality alone, as a mass possessing weight, nor in shapes belonging to the inorganic world, nor as indifferent to colour, etc. ; but it is wrought in ideal forms of the human figure, and, it must be remarked, in all three spatial dimensions.

In this last respect we must claim for sculpture, that it is in it that the inward and spiritual are first revealed in their eternal repose and essential self-completeness. To such repose and unity with itself there can correspond only that external shape which itself maintains its unity and repose. And this is fulfilled by shape in its abstract spatiality.[2] The spirit which sculpture represents is that which is solid in itself, not broken up in the play of trivialities and of passions ; and hence its external form too is not abandoned to any manifold phases of appearance, but appears under this one aspect only, as the abstraction of space in the whole of its dimensions.

(γ) Now, after architecture has erected the temple, and the hand of sculpture has supplied it with the statue of the God, then, in the third place, this god present to sense is confronted in the spacious halls of his house by the *community*. The community is the spiritual reflection into itself of such

---

[1] In the sense "self-complete," "not primarily regarded as explained by anything outside," like a machine or an animal contrasted with a wheel or a limb, which latter are finite, because they demand explanation and supplementation from without, *i.e.* necessarily draw attention to their own limit.

[2] *I.e.* shape taken simply as an object filling space.

sensuous existence, and is the animating subjectivity and inner life which brings about the result that the determining principle for the content of art, as well as for the medium which represents it in outward form, comes to be particularization [dispersion into various shapes, attributes, incidents, etc.], individualization, and the subjectivity which they require.[1] The solid unity which the God has in sculpture breaks up into the multitudinous inner lives of individuals, whose unity is not sensuous, but purely ideal.[2]

It is only in this stage that God Himself comes to be really and truly spirit—the spirit in His (God's) community ; for He here begins to be a to-and-fro, an alternation between His unity within Himself and His realization in the individual's knowledge and in its separate being, as also in the common nature and union of the multitude. In the community, God is released from the abstractness of unexpanded self-identity, as well as from the simple absorption in a bodily medium, by which sculpture represents Him. And He is thus exalted into spiritual existence and into knowledge, into the reflected[3] appearance which essentially displays itself as inward and as subjectivity. Therefore the higher content is now the spiritual nature, and that in its absolute shape. But the dispersion of which we have spoken reveals this at the same time as particular spiritual being, and as individual character. Now, what manifests itself in this phase as the main thing is not the serene quiescence of the God in Himself, but appearance as such, being which is *for* another, self-manifestation. And hence, in the phase we have reached, all the most manifold subjectivity in its living movement and operation—as human passion, action, and incident, and, in general, the wide realm of human feeling, will, and its negation,—is for its own sake the object of artistic representation. In conformity with this content, the sensuous element of art has at once to show itself as made particular in itself and as adapted to subjective inwardness. Media that fulfil this requirement we have in colour, in musical sound, and finally in sound as the mere indication of inward perceptions and ideas ; and as modes of realizing the import in question by help of these media we obtain painting, music, and poetry. In this region the sensuous medium displays itself as subdivided in its own being and universally set down as ideal.[4] Thus it has the highest degree of conformity with the content of art, which, as such, is spiritual, and the connection of intelligible import and sensuous medium develops into closer intimacy than was possible in the case of architecture and sculpture. The unity attained,

---

[1] The terms used in the text explain themselves if we compare, *e.g.* a Teniers with a Greek statue, or again, say, a Turner with the same. "Subjectivity" means that the work of art appeals to our ordinary feelings, experiences, etc. Music and poetry are still stronger cases than painting, according to the theory. Poetry especially can deal with *everything*.

[2] The unity of the individuals forming a church or nation is not visible, but exists in common sentiments, purposes, etc., and in the recognition of their community.

[3] An expression constantly applied to consciousness, because it can look at itself. *Cf.* :—

> "'Tell me, good Brutus, can you see your face?'
> 'No, Cassius ; for the eye sees not itself
> But by reflection, by some other things.'"
> *Julius Cæsar.*

[4] Posited or laid down to be ideal ; almost = pronounced or made *to be* in the sense of *not being; e.g.* musical sound is "ideal" as existing, *qua* work of art, in memory only, the moment in which it is actually heard being fugitive ; a picture, in respect of the third dimension, which has to be read into it ; and poetry is almost wholly ideal, *i.e.* uses hardly any sensuous element, but appeals almost entirely to what exists *in the mind.* "Subdivided," "*besondert,*" like "*particularisirt*" above ; because of the variety and diversity present in the mere material of colours, musical sounds, and ideas.

however, is a more inward unity, the weight of which is thrown wholly on the subjective side, and which, in as far as form and content are compelled to particularize themselves and give themselves merely ideal existence, can only come to pass at the expense of the objective universality of the content and also of its amalgamation with the immediately sensuous element.[1]

The arts, then, of which form and content exalt themselves to ideality, abandon the character of symbolic architecture and the classical ideal of sculpture, and therefore borrow their type from the romantic form of art, whose mode of plasticity they are most adequately adapted to express. And they constitute a *totality* of arts, because the romantic type is the most concrete in itself.[2]

i. The articulation of this *third sphere* of the individual arts may be determined as follows. The *first* art in it, which comes next to sculpture, is painting. It employs as a medium for its content and for the plastic embodiment of that content visibility as such in as far as it is specialized in its own nature, *i.e.* as developed into colour. It is true that the material employed in architecture and sculpture is also visible and coloured; but it is not, as in painting, visibility as such, not the single light which, differentiating itself in virtue of its contrast with darkness, and in combination with the latter, gives rise to colour.[3] This quality of visibility, made subjective in itself and treated as ideal, needs neither, like architecture, the abstractly mechanical attribute of mass as operative in the properties of heavy matter, nor, like sculpture, the complete sensuous attributes of space, even though concentrated into organic shapes. The visibility and the rendering visible which belong to painting have their differences in a more ideal form, in the several kinds of colour, and they liberate art from the sensuous completeness in space which attaches to material things, by restricting themselves to a plane surface.

On the other hand, the content also attains the most comprehensive specification. Whatever can find room in the human heart, as feeling, idea, and purpose ; whatever it is capable of shaping into act—all this diversity of material is capable of entering into the varied content of painting. The whole realm of particular existence, from the highest embodiment of mind down to the most isolated object of nature, finds a place here. For it is possible even for finite nature,[4] in its particular scenes and phenomena, to make its appearance in the realm of art, if only some allusion to an element of mind endows it with affinity to thought and feeling.

ii. The *second* art in which the romantic type realizes itself is contrasted with painting, and is music. Its medium, though still sensuous, yet develops into still more thorough subjectivity and particularization. Music, too, treats the sensuous as ideal, and does so by negating,[5] and idealizing into the indi-

---

[1] Again, the subject of a Turner or Teniers is not objectively universal, in the simplest sense ; not something that is actually and literally the same everywhere and for every one. And both painting and music (immediately sensuous elements) are less completely amalgamated with the ideal, represent it more solidly and thoroughly than the statue, so far as the ideal is itself external or plastic.

[2] The greater affinity of romantic art with the movement and variety of the modern spirit displays itself not only in the greater flexibility of painting, music, or poetry, as compared with architecture and sculpture, but in the fact that the Romantic type contains these three arts at least, while the Symbolic and Classical types had only one art each.

[3] This is drawn from Goethe's doctrine of colour, which Hegel unfortunately adopted in opposition to Newton's theory.

[4] He means landscape, principally.

[5] "*Aufheben*," used pregnantly by Hegel to mean *both* "cancel," "annul," *and*, "pre-

vidual isolation of a single point, the indifferent externality [1] of space, whose complete semblance is accepted and imitated by painting. The single point, *qua* such a negativity (excluding space) is in itself a concrete and active process of negation [2] within the attributes of matter, in the shape of a motion and tremor of the material body within itself and in its relation to itself. Such an inchoate ideality of matter,[3] which appears no longer as under the form of space, but as temporal ideality,[4] is sound, the sensuous set down as negated, with its abstract visibility converted into audibility, inasmuch as sound, so to speak, liberates the ideal content from its immersion in matter. This earliest inwardness of matter and inspiration of soul into it furnishes the medium for the mental inwardness—itself as yet indefinite,—and for the soul [5] into which mind concentrates itself; and finds utterance in its tones for the heart with its whole gamut of feelings and passions. Thus music forms the centre of the romantic arts, just as sculpture represents the central point between architecture and the arts of romantic subjectivity. Thus, too, it forms the point of transition between abstract spatial sensuousness, such as painting employs, and the abstract spirituality of poetry. Music has within itself, like architecture, a relation of quantity conformable to the understanding, as the antithesis to emotion and inwardness ; and has also as its basis a solid conformity to law on the part of the tones, of their conjunction, and of their succession.

iii. As regards the *third* and most spiritual mode of representation of the romantic art-type, we must look for it in *poetry*. Its characteristic peculiarity lies in the power with which it subjects to the mind and to its ideas the sensuous element from which music and painting in their degree began to liberate art. For sound, the only external matter which poetry retains, is in it no longer the feeling of the sonorous itself, but it is a *sign*, which by itself is void of import. And it is a sign of the idea which has become concrete in itself, and not merely of indefinite feeling and of its *nuances* and grades. This is how sound develops into the *Word*, as voice articulates in itself, whose import it is to indicate ideas and notions. The merely negative point up to which music had developed now makes its appearance as the completely concrete point, the point which is mind, the self-conscious individual, which, producing out of itself the infinite space of its ideas, unites it with the temporal character of sound. Yet this sensuous element, which in music was still immediately one with inward feeling, is in poetry separated from the content of consciousness. In poetry the mind determines this content for its own sake, and apart from all else, into the shape of ideas, and though it employs sound

---

serve," " fix in mind," " idealize." The use of this word is a cardinal point of his dialectic. See *Wiss. der Logik*, i. 104. I know of no equivalent but " put by," provincial Scotch " put past." The negation of space is an attribute of music. The parts of a chord are no more in space than are the parts of a judgment. Hegel expresses this by saying that music idealizes space and concentrates it into a point.

[1] The parts of space, though external to each other, are not distinguished by qualitative peculiarities.

[2] " *Aufheben*."

[3] " Ideality of matter : " the distinctively material attribute of a sonorous body, its extension, only appears in its sound indirectly, or inferentially, by modifying the nature of the sound. It is, therefore, " idealized."

[4] Succession in time is a degree more " ideal " than co-existence in space, because it exists solely in the medium of memory.

[5] " *Seele* : " mind on its individual side, as a particular feeling subject. " *Geist* " is rather mind as the common nature of intelligence. Thus in feeling and self-feeling, mind is said to concentrate itself into a soul.

to express them, yet treats its solely as a symbol without value or import. Thus considered, sound may just as well be reduced to a mere letter, for the audible, like the visible, is thus depressed into a mere indication of mind.[1] For this reason the proper medium of poetical representation is the poetical imagination and intellectual portrayal itself. And as this element is common to all types of art, it follows that poetry runs through them all and develops itself independently in each. Poetry is the universal art of the mind which has become free in its own nature, and which is not tied to find its realization in external sensuous matter, but expatiates exclusively in the inner space and inner time of the ideas and feelings. Yet just in this its highest phase art ends by transcending itself, inasmuch as it abandons the medium of a harmonious embodiment of mind in sensuous form, and passes from the poetry of imagination into the prose of thought.

5. Such we may take to be the articulated totality of the particular arts, viz. the external art of architecture, the objective art of sculpture, and the subjective art of painting music and poetry. Many other classifications have been attempted, for a work of art presents so many aspects, that, as has often been the case, first one and then another is made the basis of classification. For instance, one might take the sensuous medium. Thus architecture is treated as crystallization; sculpture, as the organic modelling of the material in its sensuous and spatial totality; painting, as the coloured surface and line; while in music, space, as such, passes into the point of time possessed of content within itself, until finally the external medium is in poetry depressed into complete insignificance. Or, again, these differences have been considered with reference to their purely abstract attributes of space and time. Such abstract peculiarities of works of art may, like their material medium, be consistently explored in their characteristic traits; but they cannot be worked out as the ultimate and fundamental law, because any such aspect itself derives its origin from a higher principle, and must therefore be subordinate thereto.

This higher principle we have found in the types of art—symbolic, classical and romantic—which are the universal stages or elements[2] of the Idea of beauty itself. For *symbolic art* attains its most adequate reality and most complete application in *architecture*, in which it holds sway in the full import of its notion, and is not yet degraded to be, as it were, the inorganic nature dealt with by another art. The *classical* type of art, on the other hand, finds adequate realization in sculpture, while it treats architecture only as furnishing an enclosure in which it is to operate, and has not acquired the power of developing painting and music as absolute[3] forms for its content. The *romantic* type of art, finally takes possession of painting and music, and in like manner of poetic

Hegel seems to accept this view. Was he insensible to sound in poetry? Some very grotesque verses of his, preserved in his biography, go to show that his ear was not sensitive. Yet his critical estimate of poetry is usually just. Shakespeare and Sophocles were probably his favourites. And, as a matter of proportion, what he here says is true. It must be remembered that the beauty of sound in poetry is to a great extent indirect, being supplied by the passion or emotion which the ideas symbolized by the sounds arouse. The beauty of poetical sound in itself is very likely less than often supposed. It must have the capacity for receiving passionate expression; but that is not the same as the sensuous beauty of a note or colour. If the words used in a noble poem were divested of all meaning, they would lose much, though not all, of the beauty of their sound.

[2] "Stages or elements." "*Momente*," Hegel's technical phrase for the stages which form the essential parts or factors of any idea. They make their appearance successively, but the earlier are implied and retained in the latter.

[3] Adequate, and so of permanent value.

representation, as substantive and unconditionally adequate modes of utterance. Poetry, however, is conformable to all types of the beautiful, and extends over them all, because the artistic imagination is its proper medium, and imagination is essential to every product that belongs to the beautiful, whatever its type may be.

And, therefore, what the particular arts realize in individual works of art, are according to their abstract conception simply the universal types which constitute the self-unfolding Idea of beauty. It is as the external realization of this Idea that the wide Pantheon of art is being erected, whose architect and builder is the spirit of beauty as it awakens to self-knowledge, and to complete which the history of the world will need its evolution of ages.

APPENDIX II.

THE following notes on specific examples of musical expression have been furnished me by Mr. J. D. Rogers, as mentioned in the preface. They appear admirably to illustrate the conception of music, as the spirit of actions and events, suggested by Plato and Aristotle, and in modern times popularised by Schopenhauer.

1. Schumann's *In der Nacht* used to summon up before my imagination the picture of the moon struggling through the clouds on a windy night—emerging and disappearing by turns; then for a while reigning "apparent queen" amid white fleecy clouds, which are not sufficient to intercept its light. During two moments even this silken veil is withdrawn, only to be succeeded by a bank of black clouds, for a long time impenetrable, at last penetrated at intervals a little more irregular and with a brightness a little wilder and more meteoric than before; finally—the light is put out and quenched by the storm.

I learnt some years afterwards that Schumann also associated this piece with a picture, the idea of which occurred to him after he had written the entire set of *Fantasiestücke* to which it belongs. It was a picture portraying the story of Hero and Leander; his picture is not incompatible with mine. In his the clouds correspond to the waves, the moon to a swimmer, buried and stifled in their troughs or flashing and calling out from their crests. Where the moon triumphs in my story, in his there is a love scene on the shore, accompanied by the distant rippling of the waves; it seems almost as though

> "The billows of cloud that around thee roll
> Shall sleep in the light of a wondrous day."

But, no; there comes the plunge back into waves blacker than before—tossings to and fro—cries from the swimmer and from the shore—and, finally, "night wraps up everything."[1] The music can be rendered after the manner of Max Müller either into a Lunar myth, or into a Greek legend. What the moon does, and what the Greek hero did in the story, are to a great extent the same; and music interprets that important element or attribute which is common to both.

2. If music seizes hold of the spirit or soul of any event or series of events, has—it may be asked—any composer attempted to represent God? God in the sense in which the word is used in the common phrase, "God in history," or in which God is described in Tennyson's *Higher Pantheism*, or Wordsworth's *Tintern Abbey*. I reply by an instance. Brahms' German requiem has often been praised for the rich elaboration of its detail, its blending of the antique

---

[1] Schumann's *Jugendbriefe*, 21 April, 1838. "Von Krägen habe ich eben einen Brief —er schreibt mir viel Schönes über die Phantasiestücke und schwärmt ordentlich nach seiner Art darin—'die Nacht' wäre 'gross u. schön' schrieb er, u. sein liebstes, mir beinah' auch. Später, als ich fertig war, habe ich zu meiner Freude die Geschichte von Hero und Leander darin gefunden. Du kennst sie wohl. Leander schwimmt alle Nächte durch das Meer zu seiner Geliebte die auf dem Leuchtthurm wartet, mit brennender Fackel ihm den Weg zeigt. Es ist eine schöne, romantische Sage. Spiel' ich 'die Nacht,' so kann ich das Bild nicht vergessen—erst, wie er sich ins Meer stürzt—sie ruft—er antwortet—er durch die Wellen glücklich an's Land—dann die Cantilena, wo sie sich in den Armen haben—dann wie er wieder fort muss, sich nicht trennen kann—bis die Nacht wieder alles in Dunkel einhüllt. Sage mir doch ob auch dir dies Bild zur Musik passt."

and modern, its contrapuntal devices fused in the crucible of romanticism. But it has yet finer and deeper merits. The solemn opening, " Blessed are they that mourn," is set to the same music as the solemn close, " Blessed are the dead." In the middle of the piece the name of God is introduced for the first, and almost the last time, [1] to the words, "The souls of the righteous are in God's hand." That name is translated into music by the pedal note, which is held down from beginning to end of the fugue to which these words are set. The pedal note persists, makes its presence felt throughout ; is all-enduring, all-pervading ; the fugue starts from it, and finally, after many intricate wanderings, returns to it ; it is the fundamental note—the foundation of the first and last chords, and, although many different, and apparently incompatible, harmonies are found in the course of the fugue, these harmonies are all finally resolved into the initial harmony, of which that pedal note is at once the characteristic note and the epitome. Everything proceeds from it and returns to it ; it alone is permanent, and steadily, continuously, irresistibly self-asserting. Neither poetry nor painting nor architecture can express mysteries such as these with such searching force and directness.

3. Mozart's *Requiem*,[2] like Brahms', ends with the same music as it began with, and in both instances the words to which the music is set are quite different in the first and last number. The first number of Mozart's work represents death ; the last number represents immortality. The same agitation, the same solemnity, and, we must add, the same uncertainty clothes both ideas. There is a wonderful touch in Mozart's closing number, which seems to have escaped most writers. It can scarcely be understood without a passing reference to what precedes it. Compared with most of Mozart's works, this work stands alone for its restlessness—its quick changes from mood to mood. "Confutatis Maledictis" begins with cursing—then a prayer for blessing intervenes—finally, it ends in a sigh of despair. "Lachrymosa" begins sentimentally, then comes the stern march of inevitable fate, and suddenly there is a glimpse of almost voluptuous pleasure. In each of these two cases the three moods are not blended ; they succeed one another, and with a rapidity which is amazing in a writer who is usually diffuse and does not delight in contrasts. The optimistic vein is separated and viewed apart ; it is unmistakable, and its prevailing characteristic is, that it is always in the major, not in the minor mode, and is usually a cadence. But there is another means of identifying the major mode with a happy ending, and the minor mode with an unhappy ending—as those modes are used in this particular work. The "Sanctus" is a transposition of the "Dies Irae" from minor into major. Wrath is the minor of beatification in Mozart's *Requiem*. It is, therefore with intense, almost painful, interest that we look forward to the last cadence of all. Will it be minor or major? Most of Mozart's devices in this work are referable to older writers—Handel, Haydn, and every composer is represented by turns. His last cadence of all is one which we search for in vain in the immediately preceding centuries, although in the middle ages it was the most usual conclusion of all. There is no "third" in the last chord. Mozart's last chord is neither major nor minor ; it might be either ;

---

[1] It comes in the next number, whose main themes are echoed from the number which we are discussing.

[2] Some parts of the Requiem are (it is believed) not by Mozart ; this æsthetic criticism is based on the assumption that the main parts were written and the idea of the whole conceived by one author.

it deliberately shirks answering the momentous question by quietly omitting its most important constituent part. He dare not answer the terrible question, which he seems to have carefully provided himself in the preceding sections of the work with definite musical means for answering. The work is anxious, fitful, and moody throughout ; as was once said of it, " it seems to blush"; it is pale and rosy by turns ; it ends with a final culminating uncertainty.

4. There is no better instance than that afforded by Wagner's *Meistersinger*, of music entering as an element of living interest into an idea or a story. Here are a few typical instances of music supplying the sense which the text or the situation only hint at in a far-off inconclusive way, or else leave absolutely unexplained.

(a) In the first place, it adds to our knowledge of Hans Sachs' character. At the beginning of the Second—as at the beginning of the Third Act—Hans Sachs is seen musing. The subject of his meditation is Walter's Spring song, " So new and yet so old." It was a love song, couched in the spirit—as Hans Sachs says, in Act iii.—which leads to elopement, not to marriage ;[1] it was fiery, impetuous, and reckless. The stormiest phrase in the song, " Es schwillt und schwallt," is the very phrase which made most impression upon the other Meistersinger, and also upon Hans Sachs. But the former, when they quote it—or rather when the orchestra tells us it is running in their heads—exaggerate its restlessness, and the pedal " G," which they interpolate, makes it undignified and unharmonious.[2] Hans Sachs' memory purifies and refines it; to him it presents itself as gentle, melancholy, and subdued (p. 170).[3] The harmonies are richer, the rhythm graver, the love portrayed is of that sort which is longsuffering and kind ; still it is the same love, the same melody, in spite of its transformation. So, too, with the other snatches from Walter's melodies ; they are all quoted accurately, but are toned down and ennobled in the quotation. Nothing brings home to one more forcibly than this, the distinction, the maturity, and the quiet grasp of Hans Sachs' artistic genius. The highest critical gift is that which enables its possessor to select wisely, and to exalt what it selects. And we hear that Hans Sachs possesses this gift in a perfect form.

(β) Again there is one point in which the music, while developing Hans Sachs' character, contains the secret upon which a leading incident in the play turns. Look at the music appropriated to Hans Sachs in his interview with Eva in the second act. It is obviously built upon a ground-bass taken from the four rising semi-tones, which play so large a part in Walter's first song, " Am stillen Herd." If the music is to be trusted, Walter's invisible (but audible) presence casts its shadow across the relations between Hans Sachs and Eva. But there is no suggestion of this explanation in the text. Let us follow the musical hint a little further. This series of semi-tones constitutes a nucleus which branches out into many different directions ; for instance, it is often accompanied by a " counter-subject," or presented in a rhythmical cadence—the spirit of which is happily caught by David (p. 39), when he sets it to the words, " Sorg' und Acht." Hans Sachs is presented to

---

[1] " Mit solchem Dicht und Liebesfeuer
    Verführt man wohl Töchter zum Abenteuer :
    Doch für liebseligen Ehestand
    Man andre Wort' und Weisen fand."

[2] See p. 123 of the piano score.
[3] Of the piano score.

us as the true workman—one who learns by taking trouble.   Or it is linked
with the kindly, easy-going phrase (see pp. 124, 314), in which Hans Sachs
conveys his friendship to Walter (comp. p. 409).   Or else the counter-subject
contains in embryo those notes—a falling 6th and rising 5th, both minor—
which afterwards impart such grave sadness and resigned conviction to the
monologue of " Wahn ! Wahn ! " in which Hans Sachs assumes the prophetic
mantle, and answers the pessimistic question—" Why do the people imagine
a vain thing ? " by the optimistic reply—" Nothing happens without it."   The
spirit of the monologue is not querulous, or rhetorical, or noisily impotent,
like that of false prophets ; but more like that of the Miltonic Manoa :

> " Nothing is here for tears, nothing to wail
> Or knock the breast ; no weakness, no contempt,
> Dispraise, or blame ; nothing but well and fair " ;

   The content of the monologue is—if we may quote Goethe with a change
—" Illusion ceases to be an evil because it is universal."   But here the music
only reveals Hans Sachs' manner and attitude towards speculative problems ; towards Art and Work, or in *his* ordinary intercourse with friends ; it
throws no light on the problem, why should a recollection of Walter haunt
Hans Sachs when he is with Eva ?   A fourth counter-subject of semi-tones
creeping in an opposite direction sometimes attends the primal phrase ; and
it is here that the secret is told.   A tiny gradual transformation in this phrase
makes it pass into the theme which pervades Tristan and Isolde,[1] while Hans
Sachs is saying to Eva, " If I did win your hand, you and Walter would make
a King Mark of me."   The words came suddenly, almost abruptly ; but the
music has from the first foreshadowed and unfolded this explanation.   The
music and the music alone has seized and interpreted what is the key of the
whole situation.
   (γ) There is a phrase consisting of a sequence of descending 4ths and
ascending 3rds, which at one time or another applies to every personage of
the play, or even forms a part of what they sing.   There is a glimpse of it
when Eva says to Magdalene, " Mir ist als wär' ich gar wie im Traum " (20).
Hans Sachs, who has a happy knack of wedding voice to verse, sings to it the
words, " Mein Freund in holder Jugendzeit " (310).   It is the prelude to
Walter's song, " Am stillen Herd," in which he describes himself as having
a vision of spring in winter time.   The very Lehrbuben (p. 32) reproduced
it in the first hurrying staccato notes of the 2nd scene.   It is faintly echoed
in Walter's allusion to " Singkunst " (p. 40) ; and a sequence of descending
4ths dominates the love scene of Hans Sachs and Eva in the 2nd Act (cf.
p. 352).   It is the common bond which connects the Preislied, Beckmesser's
Serenade, and the gay Motive which recurs wherever the Masters allude to
the preparations for celebrating the Johannis Fest.   The intimate alliance between these two last motives is vividly illustrated by Hans Sachs, who in
" Wahn ! Wahn ! " shows the Johannis Fest Motive insensibly melting into the
twitterings and chirrupings of Beckmesser ; and if only those who play
Beckmesser's part acted with as much intelligence as fun, the audience would
easily perceive the near kinship of his with Walter's prize song.   Put all these
attributes together and the phrase may be fairly named " the Spirit of the
time and place "—the Zeitgeist and Genius loci in one—which breathes on
all alike, just and unjust, but which only the worthiest partake worthily ;

---

[1] 2 series of four *rising* semi-tones, accompanied by a counter-subject, first of two then of
three descending semi-tones.

which was young and (like Watts' picture of the Zeitgeist), looking straight
forward; which loved graceful forms, and worshipped Art; which anticipated
the birth of spring; and was, so to speak, the dream of young Germany, for
it dreamt of "what the world would be when the years have died away."

(δ) Again here is a matter in which Wagner's music takes us into the very
heart of mediæval history   People do not sufficiently realise the way in which
Wagner's *Meistersinger* music drives home into the hearer, not only the intimate
association but the absolute identification of Art, Industry, and Religion,[1] which
the mediæval guilds effected.   Take the first four bars of the overture; they
are bars so stately and pompous, that even when the Lehrbuben reproduce
them on the occasion of the Johannis Fest (p. 416, 417) in quick bustling
time, the hearer feels that they have added a cubit to their moral stature
since the time when they regarded the Johannis Fest as a kind of jolly,
rollicking Bank holiday (Act ii., init.).   They are first used in the play to
denote "the tribunal which awards the prize to the Meistersinger" (p. 22),
and the impartiality which should characterise that tribunal (p. 127).   On
pp. 74 and 75 Pogner emphasises the high worth of Art, and the honour which
Germany does to Art—and on p. 108 Kothner expounds the principles on
which the Meisterlied must be constructed—to this phrase.   The words to
which it is set convey a high ideal of artistic appreciation; an ideal which
the guild of Meistersinger always aspired to and in the last scene of the play
attained.   The heraldic trapping and all the pomp and pageantry (pp. 24-294);
the formalities and procedure (*e.g.* p. 421), the external lip-worship (see
p. 408) of the guild are represented by a different phrase; the phrase which
we are discussing is appropriated to the spiritual objects and deeper meanings
of its existence.   And—says the music—these objects and deeper meanings
are to the guild as a religion.   They had a religious origin, and they are still
religious in their character.   For these four bars—omitting the second only
—are the subject of the chorale with which the play opens; and Hans Sachs
baptizes the mastersong of Walter to the same theme.   It is this union of Art
and Religion in the guild—emphasised as it is by their employing the same
themes—which makes the laying of the scene of the first Act in the ante-chapel
of the Katharinen-kirche natural and appropriate.   Peace flowed from this
union.   The heavy scales going in these bars in opposite directions occur several
times in the play, once (p. 72) to typify the people of Nürnberg, once (p. 189)
to the words "lasst uns in Ruh' verschnaufen," once to "Liebes Nürnberg
so friedsam" (p. 299).   Nürnberg attained rest and peace in the trades-unions
whose members pursued art with religious fervour.   Carlyle, after visiting Dr.
Arnold at Rugby, described what he saw as "the rarest sight in the world," "a
temple of industrious peace."   So to the Nürnbergers their industrial guild of
the Meistersinger was just this; a temple of peace: and the music does more
than merely describe it as such; it impresses upon us, and illustrates and
justifies for us this description.   It takes and treats this description as the
kernel and centre of the whole drama of Nürnberger life.

(ε) Of course Wagner uses his "Leit Motif," or "Independent Episodes,"
or "Phrases," in very different ways, in different plays.   The peculiar characteristic of the Meistersinger is that in it the phrases are used to add or
develop ideas.   Just as the action starts a new train of ideas in the intermezzo

---

[1] "The notes of English feeling are few, but they are deep; Industry, Art, Religion,
so runs the solemn scale" Disraeli.   In Wagner they are not a scale, but a chord; they do
not follow, but unite with one another.

of the Probelied,[1] and, in the song, " Eva aus dem Paradies,"—so the music lends a new sense to the character of the chief persons in the play, and the moral and intellectual atmosphere which they breathe. In the Götterdämmerung, for instance, the main use to which the music is put is to suggest absent images, to denote objects, or imitate a picturesque effect. It is brilliantly done ; for instance, the glow of the magic fire which surrounds Brünnhilde has a sudden periodic expansion and crescendo at the end of every bar, as though some one were blowing on the furnace ; again, the Rhine daughters swim and laugh (unmässig) to the same consecutive fifths so orchestrated as to be a musical illustration of the metaphor " Floods of laughter ; " again, the hero is dubbed Knight in one phrase, Hunter in another, Gold-seeker in another, and so on—Wagner christens his attributes, not his mere body, by some musical phrase ; again, there is singular appropriateness in the galloping horses (compare Berlioz' Damnation de Faust), and the horn behind the stage (compare Beethoven's Leonora), and the creeping worm (compare Haydn's Creation) ; but we feel that all this is what is more properly called programme music ; music is specialised to the suggestion of certain images and objects, just like the language of everyday life ; and however brilliant the enhanced effect which it produces in the opera, we feel that it could be dispensed with. Language already does that duty well enough ; why bring in music to improve upon what is good, to illustrate what is clear ? Either music has a distinct duty to do, or it has no business there. This criticism only applies to the employment of " Leitmotif " in the Nibelungen Lied. It does not apply to the barbaric rhythms, the rude force, the abrupt changes, and the gorgeous harmonies which seem to me to take the hearer right back into the heart of the early Icelandic world.

(ζ) Nor must we for one moment think that Wagner even in the *Meistersinger* is a perfect artist. Here are two instances of mortal frailty. On p. 189 Hans Sachs sarcastically alluded to Walter's " Hochmuth " in a phrase usually appropriated to the officious Beckmesser *(e.g.* p. 125). Wagner can hardly mean to insinuate that some portion of Beckmesser's spirit is passing over into Hans Sachs. Again, the sequence of descending 4ths and ascending 3rds alluded to in the above is an exact description of the horn-motive in the Nibelungen Lied. It might seem hypercritical to criticise the phrases of one play by the light of the phrases of another play ; but Wagner has challenged this criticism by his allusion to Tristan and Isolde. And, of course, the orchestration is different ; but would a great musician attach so much importance to a detail of orchestration ? Brahms, like Beethoven and Schubert, loves to sound out a phrase on every instrument of his orchestra in succession,[2] and we feel that this is the real musical tradition handed down

---

[1] " In einer Dornen-hecken
    Von Neid und Gram verzehrt,
    Musst' er sich da verstecken
    Der Winter Grimm-bewehrt,

    Von dürrem Laub umrauscht,
    Er lauert und lauscht
    Wie er das frohe Singen
    Zu Schaden könnte bringen."

[2] *e.g.* From the treble piano to the bass drum in the pianoforte concerto in D **minor.**

to us by the great masters, and conformed to by Wagner when at his best—
that the identity of the phrase must be admitted, on whatever instrument or
instruments it is played.   And Wagner was at his best not in the *Nibelungen
Lied*, but in the *Meistersinger ;* and even in the *Meistersinger* he was not a
perfect artist.   Perhaps it is that music cannot quite do what he wanted it
to do.

BIBLIOGRAPHY.

A fairly complete Bibliography of the subject is given in *A Guide to the Literature of Æsthetics*, by C. M. Gayley and F. N. Scott, Berkeley, U.S.A., 1891. Prof. Knight's *Philosophy of the Beautiful* also refers to an immense number of works, especially in recent English and American literature. The undermentioned books, except where the contrary is stated, are such as I have actually employed in preparing the present work, and are without exception such as have some genuine interest for the student, who can, I hope, ascertain from the body of my treatise for what purpose each of them is serviceable.

1. Historical and auxiliary to history.

a. Complete Histories of Æsthetic theory both ancient and modern:—

Schasler's *Kritische Geschichte der Aesthetik*, 1872. 2 vols. 1218 pp. (continuously paged).

Zimmermann: *Aesthetik, erster, historisch-kritischer Theil,* 1858. 1 vol. 800 pp.

Cf. also Erdmann's *History of Philosophy.* 3 vols. (E. Tr., 1890).

Carriere : *Die Kunst im Zusammenhang der Culturentwickelung u. die Ideale der Menschheit.* 5 vols. Werke 4–9, 1886.

Sully's article " Æsthetic," in *Encycl. Britannica.*

Knight's *Philosophy of the Beautiful.* Part I. History, 1889.

b. Partial histories of æsthetic or art-consciousness, and auxiliary works :—

i. Ancient.

Eduard Müller's *Geschichte der Theorie d. Kunst bei den Alten.* 2 vols. 1834.
[A most thorough and valuable work, on which Schasler's is largely founded].

Winckelmann's *Geschichte der Kunst des Alterthums.* Werke, 3–6. First published about 1765.

Hirt : *Geschichte der bildenden Künste bei den Alten.* 1833.

Ritter and Preller's *History of Philosophy in extracts from the original sources.*

Overbeck's *Die Antiken Schrift-quellen zur Geschichte d. bildenden Künste bei den Griechen.* 1868.

Overbeck's *Geschichte d. griechischen Plastik.* 2 vols.

A. S. Murray's *History of Greek Sculpture.* 2 vols.

Miss J. E. Harrison's *Mythology and Monuments of Ancient Athens.*

R. L. Nettleship : *Essay on the Theory of Education in the Republic of Plato,* in Abbott's *Hellenica.* 1880.

Prof. H. Nettleship on " Latin Criticism," *Journal of Philology,* xviii.

Mackail's *Greek Anthology, with Introduction.* 1890.

Prof. W. Wallace's *Epicureanism.*

Prof. S. H. Butcher's *Some Aspects of the Greek Genius.* 1891.

Bernays : *Zwei Abhandlungen über die Aristotelische Theorie des Drama.* 1857.

Article " Archæology," by A. S. Murray, in *Encyclopædia Britannica,* with many other articles treating of ancient writers and schools of philosophy.

It is to be borne in mind that no English student ought to be content with a mere literary knowledge of the ancient art-consciousness, which he has un-rivalled opportunities of studying in its products in the British Museum.

ii. Modern.

Lotze's *Geschichte der Aesthetik in Deutschland.* 1868, pp. 672 [beginning with Baumgarten].

Hartmann : *Aesthetik. Erster historisch-kritischer Theil.* 1886, pp. 580 [Kant to Schasler].

Lessing's *Leben u. Werke, Danzel u. Guhrauer,* with additions by Maltzahn and Norberger. 2 vols. 1200 pp. in all. 1880. [A very full account of the literary conditions of the German 18th century].

Mark Pattison's *Essays,* on Wolf and Scaliger.

Pater's *Marius the Epicurean,* and *Studies in the History of the Renaissance.*

Scherer's *History of German Literature.* [E.Tr.].

Articles in the *Encyclopædia Britannica* :—

   Scholasticism, Prof. A. Seth.
   Image-worship, Rev. J. S. Black.
   Neo-Platonism, Prof. Harnack.
   The Catacombs, Rev. Canon Venables.
   Mosaic,
   Schools of Painting, } Prof. Middleton.
   Sculpture,
   Wood-carving,
   Mural Decoration, Prof Middleton and Mr. Wm. Morris.

And many articles on particular philosophers and schoolmen.

2. Systematic works, *i.e.,* direct contributions, partial or complete, to the theory of beauty.

The ancient and mediæval writers, referred to in the text, need not be enumerated. Many important extracts from the less accessible works will be found in Ritter and Preller, and in Overbeck's *Schriftquellen*; in the latter especially under the head of Pheidias, *e.g.* the famous passage of Philostratus on imagination (No. 801): also Lucian's account of the Calumnia of Apelles (No. 1874).

Longinus : Havell's translation with introduction by A. Lang. 1890.

Corneille's Works : vol. i., containing the life by Fontenelle ; vol. x., containing the three "discourses" on the drama ; Voltaire's notes throughout.

Lessing : *Laocoon, Hamburgische Dramaturgie,* and *Wie die Alten den Tod gebildet* (see too the plays *Miss Sara Sampson, Minna v. Barnhelm,* and *Emilia Galotti*).

Shaftesbury : "*Characteristics,*" 5th ed. 1732.

Burke's *Inquiry into the Origin of our Ideas of the Sublime and Beautiful* Works, vol. i. 1761.

Kaimes' (Home's) *Elements of Criticism.* 9th ed. 1817.

Hogarth's *Analysis of Beauty* [I have not seen]. 1753.

Reynolds in *Idler,* Nos. 76, 79, 82. 1758-9.

Schiller : Werke 11 and 12, containing *Briefe über die Aesthetische Erziehung d. Menschheit* (also published separately in a small pamphlet), *Anmuth u. Würde, Ueber naive u. sentimentale Dichtung, Review of Matheson's poems.*

Schiller and Goethe : *Briefwechsel.*

Goethe : *Deutsche Baukunst.* 1773. *W.* 25.

Der Sammler u. die Seinigen. 1797. *W.* 24.

Winckelmann u. sein Jahrhundert. 1805. *W.* 24.

Einwirkung der neueren Philosophie. Undated. *W.* **30.**

Wahrheit u. Dichtung. 1811 ff. *W.* 17.

Friedrich von Schlegel: *Essays on the Study of Greek Poetry. Werke* 5. 1797.

On the Language and Wisdom of the Ancient Hindus. 1813 [I have not seen this].

Kant : *Werke* (Rosenkranz' edition). Vol. iv. containing
    Beobachtungen über das Gefühl des Schönen u. des Erhabenen, 1764 ; and *Kritik der Urtheilskraft.* 1790.

Schelling : *System des transcendentalen Idealismus. W.* 3.

Philosophie der Kunst. W. 5.

Ueber Dante in philosophischer Beziehung, ib.

Ueber das Verhältniss der bildenden Künste zu der Natur. W. **7.**

Hegel's *Briefe,* Nos. 1–16. 1887.

Aesthetik. 3 vols.

Geschichte der Philosophie (and E. Tr.) on Kant and Schelling.

Introd. to the Aesthetic, translated by Hastie and by B. Bosanquet.

Schopenhauer : *Werke* (German) vol. ii. *Die Welt als Wille u. Vorstellung. Buch* 3, *Das Objekt der Kunst* (E. Tr. Trübner, vol. i.). Lives of Schopenhauer by Prof. W. Wallace (see also his article in *Encycl. Brit.*) and by Mr. Belfort Bax.

Herbart : *Werke,* 1, 2 and 8.

Zimmermann : *Aesthetik,* vol. ii. *Zweiter Theil. Allegemeine Aesthetik als Formwissenschaft.*

Fechner : *Vorschule d. Aesthetik.*

Edmund Gurney : "*Power of Sound*" [this I do not know well] and essays entitled *Tertium Quid.* 1887.

Helmholtz : *Popular Lectures* [E. Tr. 1880].

J. Ward : Articles "Psychology" and "Herbart" in *Encycl. Brit.*

Solger's *Vorlesungen über Aesthetik,* publ. 1829 [given 1819].

Solger's *Erwin* (Dialogue) I have not seen.

Vischer: *Aesthetik,* 2 vols. 1846–7.

Die Kunst. 4 vols. 1851–7.

Kritische Gänge, Nos. 5 and 6, including the *Selbstkritik.* 1866 and 1873.

Rosenkranz: *Aesthetik des Hässlichen,* pp. 451. 1853.

Lotze : *Grundzüge d. Aesthetik* (Diktate). 1884.

Schasler: *System d. Künste* (a manual). 1885.

Grundzüge der Wissenschaft d. Schönen u. der Kunst (a small 2 vol. work) 1886.

Carriere : *Aesthetik,* 2 vols. 1859.

Hartmann : *Zweiter systematischer Theil der Aesthetik.* 1887. 800 pp.

J. Sully : " Aesthetic," in *Encycl. Brit.*

Ward : " Psychology," *Ib.*

H. Spencer : *Essays, Scientific, Political and Speculative* (republished in 3 vols. 1891).

Bain's *Mental and Moral Science.*

Grant Allen : *The Colour-sense.* 1890.

Collingwood's *Philosophy of Ornament.* 1884.

Ruskin's works : for list and estimate see Collingwood, *Ruskin's Art-Teaching,* 1892 ; note especially chapter *On Nature of Gothic,* in *Stones of Venice* and chapter *On Penetrative Imagination* in *Modern Painters,* vol. 2.

Prof. Baldwin Brown : *The Fine Arts* (Murray's University Extension Series).

Wm. Morris : *Lectures on Art*, 3rd edition, 1883 ; also the two lectures, v. and vi. *On the History of Pattern-designing*, and *On the Lesser Arts*, in the joint vol. of lectures by W. B. Richmond, Morris and others (Macmillan, 1882), entitled "*Lectures on Art*, delivered in support of the Society for the Protection of Ancient Buildings." See too the essays prefatory to the *Catalogues of the Arts and Crafts Exhibitions*.

Edward Caird : *Essays on Literature and Philosophy*. 1892. [Papers on Rousseau, Dante, Goethe and Wordsworth especially valuable. I regret that I had not the advantage of seeing these in time to profit by them.]

INDEX TO HISTORY OF ÆSTHETIC.

GEORGE ALLEN & UNWIN LTD
London: 40 Museum Street, WC1

Auckland: P.O. Box 36013, Northcote Central, Auckland N.4
Bombay: 15 Graham Road, Ballard Estate, Bombay 1
Barbados: P.O. Box 222, Bridgetown
Buenos Aires: Escritorio 454–459, Florida 165
Calcutta: 17 Chittaranjan Avenue, Calcutta 13
Cape Town: 68 Shortmarket Street
Hong Kong: 105 Wing On Mansions, 26 Hancow Road Kowloon
Ibadan: P.O. Box 62
Karachi: Karachi Chambers, McLeod Road
Madras: Mohan Mansions, 38c Mount Road, Madras 6
Mexico: Villalongin 32–10, Piso, Mexico 5, D.F.
Nairobi: P.O. Box 4536
New Delhi: 13–14 Asaf Ali Road, New Delhi 1
Ontario: 81 Curlew Drive, Don Mills
Rio de Janeiro: Caixa Postal 2537–Zc–00
São Paulo: Caixa Postal 8675
Singapore: 36c Prinsep Street, Singapore 7
Sydney, N.S.W.: Bradbury House, 55 York Street
Tokyo: P.O. Box 26, Kamata

MUIRHEAD LIBRARY OF PHILOSOPHY
THE DISCIPLINE OF THE CAVE
J. N. FINDLAY

The lectures make use of the Platonic image of the Cave to emphasize the fact that men feel their familiar experience to be full of many and strange restrictions, and to involve puzzles and discrepancies which they do not even see the possibility of solving and removing. Deep-set philosophical perplexities of this sort can be seen as arising out of the misunderstanding and meaningless abuse of ordinary ways of thinking and speaking. But they can equally be seen, in the Platonic phrase, as 'drawing us towards being', providing an apagogical proof of the 'absurdity' of ordinary thought, speech and experience except as modified and supplemented in ways which may point altogether beyond it. What may be called a mystical and otherworldly element, and a graded series of experiences in which it is enjoyed, may therefore need to be introduced into or rendered explicit in all our experience, action and diction, not as some gratuitous modification or addition, but in order to give a viable sense to the most commonplace human utterances and activities. The presuppositions of such a manner of reasoning of course involve much fundamental criticism and revision of contemporary conceptions of language, logic and meaning and of their relation to experience and to the teaching of the use of words.

Demy 8vo. 32s. net

MEMORY
BRIAN SMITH

In this book Dr. Smith tries to bring together two lines of enquiry about memory: under what circumstances we are entitled to say we remember, and what is actually going on in us when we are remembering.

His aim is to discover how and why it is that we simply do have the same kind of certainty about many things in the past as we have about what is happening around us in the present; in short to discover the basis of the authority our memories have over us.

Dr. Smith draws a distinction between memory-claims—the beliefs we assert about the past—and remembering—the experience which leads us and entitles us to make those claims. He then attempts to discover what kind of present experience is necessary for the making of what kind of claim about the past.

This involves a detailed consideration of the differences, and similarities, between remembering events, remembering how to do things and remembering our own past perceptual experiences, and leads to a full investigation of the nature and imagery and the relationship of imaging to remembering.

Whilst rejecting standard behaviorist accounts of memory as inadequate, he quite cheerfully embraces a mechanistic view of human thought and his theory of memory as it finally emerges is strongly reminiscent of Locke's 'storehouse of ideas'—but without the dualism.

Demy 8vo. 40s. net

GEORGE ALLEN & UNWIN LTD